Why Do You Need This New Edition?

If you're wondering why you should buy this new edition of *The Fourth Genre*, here are a few great reasons!

1. Twenty-four new readings explore the Gulf oil spill, the "slow book" movement, the Virginia Tech shooting, role-playing games, and more, keeping the topics for discussion and response engaging and relevant.

2. New selections introduce emerging forms such as the video essay and contemporary forms such as the digital essay and blog to expand the range of compositions you might consider authoring.

3. The revised introduction overviews changes in the genre, including its adaptation of new media, to provide you with context for understanding the new readings in the anthology.

4. New selections that demonstrate multiple strategies for combining images and words in effective contemporary compositions include a visual essay and graphic memoir.

5. New readings in Part 3 pair texts by emerging writers with the writers' commentary on the works, making composing processes visible.

PEARSON

The Fourth Genre

Contemporary Writers of/on Creative Nonfiction

SIXTH EDITION

Robert L. Root, Jr.
Central Michigan University

Michael Steinberg
Michigan State University

Pearson

Boston   Columbus   Indianapolis   New York   San Francisco   Upper Saddle River
Amsterdam   Cape Town   Dubai   London   Madrid   Milan   Munich   Paris   Montreal   Toronto
Delhi   Mexico City   São Paulo   Sydney   Hong Kong   Seoul   Singapore   Taipei   Tokyo

Acquisitions Editor: Lauren A. Finn
Marketing Manager: Sandra McGuire
Senior Supplements Editor: Donna Campion
Production Manager: Jennifer Bossert
Project Coordination, Text Design, and Electronic Page Makeup: S4Carlisle Publishing Services
Cover Design Manager: Wendy Ann Fredericks
Cover Designer: Kay Petronio
Cover Photos: clockwise from top left: © Fotalia; © amana images inc./Alamy; © Fotalia;
   and © iStockphoto
Visual Researcher: Rona Tuccillo
Senior Manufacturing Buyer: Roy L. Pickering, Jr.
Printer and Binder and Cover Printer: R. R. Donnelley and Sons Company, Harrisonburg

Credits and acknowledgments borrowed from other sources and reproduced, with permission, in this textbook appear on the appropriate page within text or on pages 419–422.

Library of Congress Cataloging-in-Publication Data
   The fourth genre : contemporary writers of/on creative nonfiction/Robert L. Root, Jr.,
Michael Steinberg.—6th ed.
      p. cm.
Includes bibliographical references and index.
   ISBN-13: 978-0-205-17277-1
   ISBN-10: 0-205-17277-6
 1. Essays. 2. Essay—Authorship. 3. Reportage literature. 4. Reportage literature—Authorship.
5. Creative nonfiction. I. Root, Robert L. II. Steinberg, Michael, 1940– III. Title.
   PN6142.F68 2012

   808.4—dc22   2011006708

10 9 8 7 6 5 4 3 2 1—DOH—15 14 13 12 11

www.pearsonhighered.com

ISBN 10: 0-205-17277-6
ISBN 13: 978-0-205-17277-1

The essay is a notoriously flexible and adaptable form. It possesses the freedom to move anywhere, in all directions. It acts as if all objects were equally near the center and as if "all subjects are linked to one another" (Montaigne) by free association. This freedom can be daunting, not only for the novice essayist confronting such latitude but for the critic attempting to pin down its formal properties.

—*Phillip Lopate*

Admirers of nailed-down definitions and tidy categories may not like to hear it, but all writers and readers are full-time imaginers, all prose is imaginative, and fiction and nonfiction are just two anarchic shades of ink swirling around the same mysterious well. Those of us who would tell a story can only dip in our pens. We can never claim full certainty as to which shade of ink we're using.

—*David James Duncan*

The boundaries of creative nonfiction will always be as fluid as water.

—*Mary Clearman Blew*

Don't spread it around, but it's a sweet time to be an essayist.

—*Joseph Epstein*

Contents

PART 2 *Talking About Creative Nonfiction*   241

PART 3 *Composing Creative Nonfiction* 345

Alternative Contents

Forms and Processes of Creative Nonfiction

PARTS 1 AND 3 *Forms of Creative Nonfiction*

Essays

Memoirs

Personal Reportage

Personal Cultural Criticism

Alternative Nonfictions

Brief Nonfiction—

Blogs—

Graphic Memoir—

PARTS 2 AND 3 *Processes and Criticism of Creative Nonfiction*

Preface

What's New to the Sixth Edition

To keep current with the field of creative nonfiction the sixth edition provides

- A revised introduction which includes an overview of changes in the genre, its promising new directions and its adaptation of new media;
- Inclusion of twenty-four new readings, including examples of the visual essay, the video essays, the graphic memoir, the digital essay, and the blog to expand models of contemporary creative nonfiction for students;
- Replacement of older texts with newer readings from current print and online publications, still maintaining a balance among essays, memoirs, personal reportage, and personal cultural criticism;
- Additional pairings in Part 3 of an essay or memoir by an emerging writer with a commentary on the composition of the text, to further illustrate the composing processes of writers in the fourth genre;
- Additional voices providing further generational and ethnic diversity among the writers, to broaden the range of subjects and experiences represented.

Beginning the Conversation

Rationale and Overview

The Fourth Genre, Sixth Edition, is an anthology devoted to contemporary works of creative nonfiction. The readings in all three sections encompass the genre's full spectrum: personal essays, memoirs, literary journalism, and personal cultural criticism. Creative nonfiction regularly appears in small magazines, reviews, literary journals, and trade magazines; in print and online journals focused exclusively on creative nonfiction (e.g., *Fourth Genre, River Teeth, Creative Nonfiction, Brevity)*; and in book-length memoirs and essay collections. The boundaries between subgenres are highly flexible. Its writers often braid narrative telling with fictional and poetic techniques and combine portraiture and self-reflection with reportage and critical analysis. In that regard, *The Fourth Genre* highlights the elasticity and versatility of this still-evolving genre.

Creative nonfiction binds together three disparate strands notable in most English departments: literature, creative writing, and composition/rhetoric. Traditionally, the study of literature centered on analysis and interpretation in three genres—poetry, fiction, and drama; the study of creative writing also focused on those genres; and composition was the domain of nonfiction. But in the past several decades this unnatural separation has been bridged by the prominence of creative nonfiction as the fourth genre. We now think of creative nonfiction simultaneously as a form of literature, as a goal of creative writing, and as the aesthetic impulse in composition.

This book, then, attempts to present creative nonfiction in a framework that emphasizes its versatility and flexibility.

- It is a reader for writers of creative nonfiction, providing a range of samples of the forms and strategies practiced by many contemporary writers.
- It is an anthology for students of nonfiction literature, providing not only examples of its variety but also theoretical and critical responses to the form by critics, teachers, and the writers themselves.
- It is a collection for students of composing practices, providing reflections on the forms and strategies used by the essayists, memoirists, literary journalists, cultural critics, poets, and novelists who write creative nonfiction.

These specifications make *The Fourth Genre* most suitable for courses in composition, creative writing, and genre literature.

The emergence of the fourth genre in recent years has led to not only the proliferation of creative nonfiction courses and programs around the country and abroad but also to an abundance of anthologies and collections of personal essays, nature writing, literary journalism, cultural criticism, travel writing, and memoirs, as well as the increasing inclusion of creative nonfiction in literary magazines. Workshops in creative nonfiction are now regularly included at writer's conferences and writer's workshops, and some conferences are devoted solely to the subject. *The Fourth Genre,* therefore, represents our attempt to compile a contemporary anthology/reader that approaches creative nonfiction from a number of perspectives, trying not to let our efforts prescribe its boundaries or place limits on its possibilities.

Creative nonfiction encompasses a variety of styles, sensibilities, and forms. Its writers share a common desire to speak in a singular voice as active participants in their own experience. This impulse often overlaps with the writer's need to mediate that experience by serving as a witness/correspondent, thus creating a unique synergy. As a result, creative nonfictionists may write to establish or define an identity, to explore and chronicle personal discoveries and changes, to examine personal conflicts, to interrogate their opinions, and to connect themselves to a larger heritage and community. Given this context, the style, focus, and structure of each work may vary. Any given piece can be lyrical, expository, meditative, informational, reflective, self-interrogative, exploratory, analytical, and/or whimsical. Moreover, a work's structure might be a traditional "linear" narrative or it may create its own disjunctive and segmented form. And as media and technology change, writers of creative nonfiction have found expression in electronic and interdisciplinary hybrid forms such as the graphic memoir, the video essay, and the documentary.

To take advantage of the genre's flexibility, as well as of its emphasis on the writer's presence and voice, we have chosen readings that are representative, accessible, and challenging to students in advanced composition and undergraduate/graduate creative writing workshops, as well as to students in genre-specific literature courses. We assume that student readers will be asked to write their own creative nonfiction, and that, at the same time, they will be developing a personal/critical theory that reflects the genre's possibilities.

Perhaps our most vital concern is to initiate a writer-to-reader conversation on and about creative nonfiction. Therefore, we've designed the book to be interactive by dividing it into three separate yet interconnected sections: a representative anthology of personal essays, memoirs, works of literary journalism, and personal/cultural criticism as currently practiced by recognized and emerging writers; a gathering of essays and articles that centers on more general matters of craft, definition, and theory; and a section in which several emergent writers discuss how their accompanying works of creative nonfiction were composed.

This organization encourages student writers to learn their craft the way most successful writers have learned theirs: by reading what other writers have written, by picking up tips and ideas from writers about the way they write, and by applying to their own writing specific craft strategies culled from the readings.

Selections and Organization

The Fourth Genre's most distinctive features are the range and scope of the readings and the interconnectedness of the three sections. In selecting these particular works, we have tried to maintain a balance between writing that is serious and informal, rigorous and pleasurable. In all instances, our criteria were that the writings be stimulating and that they have literary worth; that they be wide ranging in subject and form, familiar at times and challenging at others; and that they be strong examples of the kind of thought-provoking and authentic writing that is being done in the genre today.

In addition, several other considerations have guided our choices. Discussions of creative nonfiction often overemphasize its grounding in actuality and place too little emphasis on the personal, autobiographical, and "literary" impulses (discovery, exploration, reflection) that generate much of this writing. We feel that creative nonfiction's identity is more closely connected to the spirit of Montaigne's work than it is to matters of subject, reportage, and research. That is to say, Montaigne's essays were first and foremost intimate and *personal,* and he actively cultivated self-exploration and self-discovery. As such, his writings express the digressions, meanderings, meditations, ruminations, and speculations that characterize a singular, idiosyncratic mind at work. As Montaigne himself says, "It is myself I portray."

This point of view is not meant to duck the issue of self-examination as it extends to larger connections and broader subjects. Quite the contrary. In fact, we believe that, whatever the subject, the writing that we do about it grows out of individual interest, curiosity, and often passion about that subject. It is this kind of curiosity and self-exploration that marks the majority of pieces in this book—be they personal essays, memoirs, reportage, or academic criticism—or a commingling of more than one of those subgenres.

Other concerns that guided our choices were:

- to interest aspiring writers and curious readers who come to this genre from an assortment of academic disciplines;
- to spotlight representative, accessible writers from a variety of fields— literature, science, nature writing, women's studies, journalism, rhetoric and composition, and cultural studies among them;
- to offer readings that remind us of the breadth and possibilities of this continually evolving genre.

To these ends, we present the reader with a broad range of writings, as well as essays and articles by writers and teachers about the forms in which they work. Along with pieces by established writers, we've tried to select works that are less frequently taught and anthologized—provocative writing that we think will stimulate fresh and enthusiastic responses from students and teachers. In choosing these particular readings, we're hoping that *The Fourth Genre* will generate numerous alternatives for using creative nonfiction in the classroom.

Part 1, Writing Creative Nonfiction, is an anthology/sampler of contemporary creative nonfiction. It is intended to showcase the variety of voices and personas, the flexibility and expansiveness, and the range of subject matter and structures that creative nonfiction is able to embrace. Part 1 is also a representative mix of thematic explorations, self-portraitures, investigations into subject matter and ideas, and intimate personal discoveries and disclosures. Not only do the specific subjects change as they are taken up by different writers, but the techniques each writer uses to explore his/her subject can vary widely. Some writers use straightforward narrative and reportage, others blend narrative telling with fictional techniques such as scenes, characters, and dialogue. Still others explore their subjects in more lyrical, discursive, or poetic ways.

However diverse these approaches might be, the individual pieces are marked by the distinctiveness of the author's presence, no matter whether he or she is the center of the piece or an observer-reporter. Therefore, in all the writings in this section we're privy to the thinking mind and imagination of the writer as he/she attempts to explore what Marianna Torgovnick describes as "some strongly felt experience, deeply held conviction, long term interest, or problem that has irritated the mind."

In Part 2, Talking About Creative Nonfiction, we have chosen essays by working writers and teachers who are as passionate about discussing matters of craft as they are articulate in explaining their theories about the nature of creative nonfiction. Because several of these authors have also written pieces that appear in Part 1, we invite the reader to pair self-selected works to see what kinds of strategies, theories, and perspectives the writers have developed. In addition, we also suggest that both teachers and students examine how the essays in Part 1 can serve as examples of the kinds of theoretical stances that the writers and teachers in Part 2 advocate.

Another way to approach the writing in Part 2 is to view it as a writer's conversation about the possibilities and limits of the genre. Consider, for example, the differing views on literal and imagined truth in memoir as proposed by Mary Clearman Blew and Patricia Hampl; or compare Carl Klaus's notion that the persona in a personal essay is a complex construct, "a fabricated thing, a character of sorts," with Steven Harvey's contention that "Choice—not invention or reportage—gives direction and purpose" to a personal essay; or examine Marianna Torgovnick's passionate approach to using the personal voice in academic writing with Vivian Gornick's distinction about the memoirist's use of materials familiar to journalists. You can also use this section of the book to probe more deeply into the assortment of composing strategies (i.e., the use of differing narrative stances and personas; the employment of disjunctive and segmented mosaics; and the pointedly fictional and poetical techniques that memoirists, personal essayists, literary journalists, and cultural critics adopt in their writings).

All of these perspectives, then, anchor the genre in the notions, theories, and designs of working writers, many of whom are also writing teachers. As such, they give the reader an "inside" and personal look at the various ways the genre is evolving, and at the same time offer a broader, more inclusive view of how contemporary creative nonfiction is being written and defined.

In Part 3, Composing Creative Nonfiction, several writers add their voices to the conversation by discussing their composing processes, sharing decisions on the drafts and revisions that their works-in-progress have undergone. As a result, they focus our attention on the writing process itself.

We created this section not only to give aspiring student writers an inside look at how these pieces evolved, but also to demonstrate the many possibilities that characterize this genre. We also think that student writers will benefit greatly from paying attention to the disclosures from emerging writers, especially as these writers supplement and reinforce the readings in Parts 1 and 2. In addition, the cross-references between all three sections open up the conversation further by revealing additional aspects of its texts and authors.

Essentially then, Part 1 is an anthology *of* creative nonfiction, Part 2 an anthology *on* creative nonfiction, and Part 3 a shorter collection *of and about* the writing of creative nonfiction.

The readings in all three sections, and the book's interactive organization, therefore, express why we think that creative nonfiction is the most accessible and personal of all four literary genres, and why we believe in extending this dialogue to curious and interested students.

Apparatus

In keeping with the spirit of the genre's flexibility, we have provided a minimum of editorial apparatus. We assume that teachers will mix and match whatever readings suit their inclinations and teaching designs. And rather than impose a thematic, historical, or sub-generic interpretation on its users, or lock the book into a pattern based on our course designs, we prefer to emphasize the genre's multiple dimensions and possibilities. Moreover, in keeping with our intent to acquaint students (and teachers) with the rich body of work that's being produced in creative nonfiction today, we've tried to make this anthology as flexible and user-friendly as possible. We want to give students permission to think of themselves as apprentice/fellow writers, to urge them to experience their writing as an inside/out activity, and finally to guide them in learning to read in more "writerly" ways.

That said, along with this Preface we have provided some guidelines and rationales for using the book. The Introduction offers an expanded discussion of creative nonfiction as the fourth genre, explaining in detail what we believe to be the five main elements of creative nonfiction. In the section on Writers, Readers, and the Fourth Genre, we talk about personal connections between writer and reader; we also give examples of why we think creative nonfiction is both a literary and a transactional genre, a genre that pushes at boundaries as well as a genre whose practitioners write primarily to connect themselves in more intimate, expressive, and personal ways with their readers. In the section entitled Joining the Conversation, we discuss the notion of why we designed *The Fourth Genre* as an evolving conversation on the art and craft of writing creative nonfiction. Moreover, in the introductions to all three sections, we offer overviews of each section, as well as suggestions for using the book interactively.

Another apparatus is contained in the book's Tables of Contents. The first Table of Contents is organized alphabetically to give teachers and students the option of deciding what readings to match up or pair with one another. The Alternative Table of Contents cross-references the readings from Parts 1 and 3 according to Forms of Creative Nonfiction, and categorizes the Part 2 and Part 3 readings under the heading of Processes and Criticism of Creative Nonfiction, providing alternative ways to subcategorize the readings. They are meant to be suggestive rather than prescriptive; any number of these readings could fit into multiple categories and we hope readers will not simply follow our suggestions but also pair and compare readings on their own.

Supplements from the Publisher

Instructor's Manual

In addition to the guidelines within the text, the authors have written a comprehensive and detailed instructor's manual. It gives specific teaching suggestions and explanations for using the book in three different classroom settings. Moreover, it offers an assortment of options for organizing the materials in composition, creative writing, and literary genre courses. In all instances it includes brief discussions of the readings as creative nonfiction, as well as suggestions for pairing or clustering selections according to subgenres, compatible themes, and issues of craft. It also provides questions that offer different perspectives on the readings and that address matters of composing. Finally, it offers a variety of writing prompts and suggestions for dealing with students' writing in all three classroom settings.

Please Note: The instructor's manual is available online at www .pearsonhighered.com.

The only online application to integrate a writing environment with proven resources for grammar, writing, and research, MyCompLab gives students help at their fingertips as they draft and revise. Instructors have access to a variety of assessment tools including commenting capabilities, diagnostics and study plans, and an e-portfolio. Created after years of extensive research and in partnership with faculty and students across the country, MyCompLab offers a seamless and flexible teaching and learning environment built specifically for writers.

Acknowledgments

The authors are grateful for the recommendations and advice of reviewers of previous editions of the anthology as well as to teachers, students, and readers who have informally shared their responses to readings with them at conferences and workshops and in classrooms and hallways. They and the publishers especially thank the reviewers who provided recommendations and advice for this sixth editon: Kevin Ball, Youngstown State University; John Bradley, Northern Illinois University; Amy Hodges Hamilton, Belmont University; Judith Szerdahelyi, Western Kentucky University; and Jeffrey White, Bellevue College.

Introduction

Creative Nonfiction, The Fourth Genre

A Note on Where We Are

With each new edition of *The Fourth Genre,* we've had occasion to review the field of creative nonfiction and to observe its evolution into an increasingly substantial and imaginatively energetic presence on the literary stage. To keep pace with that evolution, we have included fresh approaches to the genre in each edition, adding to traditional and long-established forms—linear or conjunctive or narrative forms of the personal essay, the memoir, literary journalism, and expressive academic discourse—experiments in voice, persona, structure, and language, and highlighting the role imagination plays as a means for exploration and discovery. As innovation continues to march in step with tradition, we've needed to continually rethink our notions and preconceptions about nonfiction. It's the work of the genre's writers and teachers that elucidates and informs those innovations and developments; it's that work that has helped us keep in step with the genre.

Over the past decade, we've traced the emergence of a more eclectic body of creative nonfiction, that consists of more experimental, riskier manifestations of its forms: essays that make the kinds of imaginative and linguistic leaps that the best lyric poetry does; memoirs that combine personal narrative with analysis, research, and reportage; literary journalism and personal/critical essays whose narrators have become more present and, in some instances, more personal in their works; ventures out into electronic, digital, and visual forms made possible by ever-changing technology; and writing that launches itself off from the scaffolding of the body of nonfiction that came before it.

Fourth genrists seem ever more willing to dance across the borders of other genres and, in a sense, to hybridize their own nonfiction with the strategies and attitudes of those other fields. From fiction they draw on narrative elements of plot, character development, and scene; from drama, the creation of conflict through the use of dialogue and scene construction; from poetry, a freedom of imagination, an innate sense of rhythm and language, an eye for imagery, and a comfort and ease with metaphor; from journalism and scholarship, skills of research and reportage and ways of grounding personal presence in reliable representations of actuality. Moreover, in terms of texture and tone, the most powerful and most exciting work is sometimes graceful and dignified, sometimes flip and playful—sometimes factual, sometimes truth seeking.

It stands to reason that the more tools and resources a writer has at hand, the more far-reaching and compelling the writing is likely to be. Consequently, the contemporary essay/memoir looks to us more tentative and complex, still developing, and, as such, hard to pin down and explain. And as the genre grows, it will, as Diane Ackerman says of the natural world, continue to evolve "as variously possible."

To Begin With—

Creative nonfiction is the fourth genre. When we first made this declaration, in the first edition of this book, we were reminding readers that literary genres are not limited to three but that creative or literary nonfiction merited equal status with fiction, poetry, and drama. Our use of the term "fourth genre" was not intended to indicate ranking but rather to acknowledge parity. We also hoped to get around some of the confusion surrounding the term "creative nonfiction" and the idea that all nonfiction must be, by definition, non-literature. Happily, in the period since that first edition, the acceptance of creative nonfiction as a literary genre has become widespread and the term—along with the tag "fourth genre"—has become almost commonplace. Though the terms "creative nonfiction" or "literary nonfiction" may be only decades old, writers have been composing literary forms of nonfiction for centuries. After all, whether creative or imaginative or literary, it is being nonfiction that distinguishes it from the other literary genres.

As Mary Clearman Blew has observed, "The boundaries of creative nonfiction will always be as fluid as water." We picture its mercurial existence as locations on a series of intersecting lines connecting the poles of the personal and the public, the diary and the report, the informal and the formal, the marginalia and the academic article, the imaginative and the expository. Creative nonfiction essays are located on these lines somewhere within the boundaries set by neighboring genres, not only "the three creative genres" of fiction, poetry, and drama but also the "expressive" genres of diary, journal, and autobiography and the "objective" genres of traditional (as opposed to literary) journalism, criticism, polemic, and technical writing. It may be fair to say that creative nonfiction centers in the essay but continually strains against the boundaries of other genres, endeavoring to push them back and to expand its own space without altering its own identity. With the advent of electronic and digital technology, the potential in Internet and video communication, the versatility of the word processing software writers have access to, and the imagination and creativity of writers drawn to the genre, those fluid boundaries are continually expanding and proving to be more flexible.

The Elements of Creative Nonfiction

Yet despite all the elusiveness and malleability of the genre and the variety of its shapes, structures, and attitudes, works of creative nonfiction share a number of common elements, although they may not all be present all the time in uniform proportions. The most pronounced common elements of creative nonfiction are *personal presence, self-discovery and self-exploration, flexibility of form, literary approaches to language*, and *veracity*.

Personal Presence

[handwritten margin note: same food different spices]

Writers of creative nonfiction tend to make their personal presence felt in the writing. Whatever the subject matter may be—and it can be almost anything—most creative nonfiction writing (as Rosellen Brown says of the essay) "presents itself, if not as precisely true, then as an emanation of an identifiable speaking voice making statements for which it takes responsibility" (5). In such writing the reader encounters "a persona through whose unique vision experience or information will be filtered, perhaps distorted, perhaps questioned"; the writer's voice creates an identity which "will cast a shadow as dense and ambiguous as that of an imaginary protagonist. The self is surely a created character" (5).

[handwritten margin note: objective - o personal pinions objective - dds personal]

Throughout the various forms of creative nonfiction, whether the subject is the writer's self (as perhaps in personal essays and memoirs) or an objective, observed reality outside the self (as perhaps in nature essays and personal cultural criticism), the reader is taken on a journey into the mind and personality of the writer. Some writers directly engage in interrogations of the self by unequivocally examining and confronting their own memories, prejudices, fears, even weaknesses. Others are more meditative and speculative, using the occasion of remembered or observed experience to connect to issues that extend beyond the self and to confirm or question those connections. Still others establish greater distance from their subjects, take more of an observer's role than a participant's role, yet even as they stand along the sidelines we are aware of their presence, because their voice is personal, individual, not omniscient.

This sense of the author's presence is a familiar element of essays and memoirs, of course. These center on the author's private reflections and experiences. As essayist Phillip Lopate writes,

> The hallmark of the personal essay is its intimacy. The writer seems to be speaking directly into your ear, confiding everything from gossip to wisdom. Through sharing thoughts, memories, desires, complaints, and whimsies, the personal essayist sets up a relationship with the reader, a dialogue—a friendship, if you will, based on identification, understanding, testiness, and companionship. (xxiii)

But personal presence can also pull subject-oriented writing (principally journalistic and academic writing) into the realm of creative nonfiction. Arguing a need for "writerly models for writing about culture," Marianna Torgovnick insists, "Writing about culture is personal. Writers find their material in experience as well as books, and they leave a personal imprint on their subjects. They must feel free to explore the autobiographical motivation for their work, for often this motivation is precisely what generates writers' interests in their topics" (3). Including this personal voice in cultural criticism surrenders some of the authority—or the pretense of authority—generally found in academic writing, but substitutes for it the authority of apparent candor or personal honesty. What Rosellen Brown writes of the personal essayist is applicable to all creative nonfiction writers: "the complex delight of the essayist's voice is that it can admit to bewilderment without losing its authority" (7). This sense of personal presence is one of the most forceful elements of creative nonfiction.

Self-Discovery and Self-Exploration

As many writers in this book suggest—either directly or indirectly—this genre encourages self-discovery, self-exploration, and surprise. Often, the writer "is on a journey of discovery, often unasked for and unplanned," Rosellen Brown writes. "The essayist is an explorer, whereas the fiction writer is a landed inhabitant" (7). Phillip Lopate speaks of self-discovery that takes place in essays as writing that "not only monitors the self but helps it gel. The essay is an enactment of the creation of the self" (xliv). This genre grants writers permission to explore without knowing where they'll end up, to be tentative, speculative, reflective. Because writing creative nonfiction so often reveals and expresses the writer's mind at work and play, the genre permits us to chart the more whimsical, nonrational twists and turns of our own imaginations and psyches. Writers who seem most at home with this genre are those who like to delve and to inquire, to question, to explore, probe, meditate, analyze, turn things over, brood, worry—all of which creative nonfiction allows, even encourages.

Such interests may seem at first glance appropriate only to a narrow range of "confessional writing," but in much of the best creative nonfiction, writers use self-disclosure as a way of opening their writing to a more expansive exploration. This genre, then, is a good choice for writers who like to reach for connections that extend beyond the purely personal. As W. Scott Olson writes, "As the world becomes more problematic, it is in the little excursions and small observations that we can discover ourselves, that we can make an honest connection with others, that we can remind ourselves of what it means to belong to one another" (viii).

Flexibility of Form

One of the most exciting developments of creative nonfiction is the way in which contemporary writers "stretch the limits of the form" and "are developing a [nonfiction] prose that lives along the borders of fiction and poetry" (Atwan, 1988, x). Contemporary creative nonfiction uses the full range of style and structure available to other literary and nonliterary forms. Most often, readers have noticed the use of fictional devices in creative nonfiction, particularly in what is termed "the nonfiction novel" or in certain examples of literary journalism, which Mark Kramer has defined as "extended digressive narrative nonfiction" (21). Rosellen Brown, who refers to the personal essay as a "nonfiction narrative," believes it is "every bit as much an imaginative construction as a short story" and that "it must use some, if not all, of the techniques of fiction: plot, characterization, physical atmosphere, thematic complexity, stylistic appropriateness, psychological open-endedness" (5).

And yet, while narrative elements may frequently play a part in creative nonfiction, the genre often works with lyrical, dramatic, meditative, expository, and argumentative elements as well. As Annie Dillard says, "The essay can do everything a poem can do, and everything a short story can do—everything but fake it" (xvii). It can also do everything a diary, a journal, a critical article, an editorial, a feature, and a report can do. As we're learning, it can also do everything a blog, a hyperlinked article, a documentary film, a graphic novel, and a personal video can do.

Moreover, perhaps more frequently than in other genres, creative nonfiction writers are likely to innovate and experiment with structure. They draw not only on narrative chronology and linear presentation but also on nonlinear, "disjunctive," or associative strategies. They use different angles and perspectives to illuminate a point or explore an idea, drawing on visual and cinematic techniques such as collages, mosaics, montages, and jump cuts. They can leap backward and forward in time, ignoring chronology of event to emphasize nonsequential connections and parallels; they can structure the essay around rooms in a house or cards in a Tarot deck; they can interrupt exposition or narrative with passages from journals and letters or scenes from home movies. Part of the excitement of the genre is its openness to creative forms as well as to creative contents, its invitation to experiment and push at boundaries between genres, and its ability to draw upon an unlimited range of literary techniques.

Literary Approaches to Language

The language of creative nonfiction is as literary, as imaginative, as that of other literary genres and is similarly used for lyrical, narrative, and dramatic effects. What separates creative nonfiction from "noncreative nonfiction" (if we can be forgiven the use of that term for a moment to categorize all nonfiction outside this genre) is not only "the unique and subjective focus, concept, context and point of view in which the information is presented and defined" (Gutkind v–vi) but also the ways in which language serves the subject. This is partly what Chris Anderson is alluding to when he writes that certain essays and journalism are not literary (x), and what Barbara Lounsbery means by claiming that, no matter how well the other elements of a nonfiction work are achieved, "it may still fail the standards of literary nonfiction if its language is dull or diffuse" (xv). When Annie Dillard turned from writing poetry to writing literary nonfiction, she

> was delighted to find that nonfiction prose can also carry meaning in its structures and, like poetry, can tolerate all sorts of figurative language, as well as alliteration and even rhyme. The range of rhythms in prose is larger and grander than it is in poetry, and it can handle discursive ideas and plain information as well as character and story. It can do everything. I felt as though I had switched from a single reed instrument to a full orchestra. ("To Fashion" 74–75)

When the writer of poetry or fiction turns to creative nonfiction, as novelist Kim Barnes does in her memoir, *Into the Wilderness,* or poet Garrett Hongo does in his memoir, *Volcano,* they bring with them the literary language possible in those other genres and are able to use it.

But poets and novelists aren't the only ones drawing on literary techniques in nonfiction. Some journalists have taken so literary an approach to their reportage that they have created a writing form that straddles literature and journalism, and often can be identified as a form of creative nonfiction. In addition, a number of primarily academic writers have sought a more personal perspective in the cultural criticism they write. They have made the language of their academic discourse more expansive, more intimate, more literary, allowing the reader to share their subjective reactions to the ideas and experiences they discuss. Like Thoreau, they retain rather than omit "the *I,* or first person," acknowledging, as he did, that we "commonly do not remember that it is, after all, always the first person that is speaking" (3). By doing so they do not simply present their information or opinions but also extend *themselves* toward the reader and draw the reader closer. In essence, they move the written work beyond presentation into conversation.

The writer in creative nonfiction is often the reader's guide, pointing out the sights along the way, the places of interest where special attention is required. In such writing the reader is treated like a spectator or an audience. But often the writer is the reader's surrogate, inviting her to share the author's space in imagination and to respond to the experience as if she is living it. In such writing the reader is treated like a participant. In creative nonfiction, then, in addition to exploring the information being presented—the ways various ideas, events, or scenes connect to one another and relate to some overarching theme or concept or premise—the reader also has to examine the role the writer takes in the work. The writer's role and the structure of the writing are not as predictable in creative nonfiction as they are in other forms, such as the news article or the academic research paper, the sermon or the lecture. As in poetry or fiction, the structure of the essay or article may be experimental or unexpected, an attempt to generate literary form out of subject matter instead of trying to wedge subject matter into an all-purpose literary form. When it departs from linear, tightly unified forms to achieve its purpose, contemporary creative nonfiction doesn't simply meander or ramble like the traditional essay ("My Style and my mind alike go roaming," Montaigne said); instead, it moves in jump cuts, flashbacks, flash-forwards, concentric or parallel or tangential strands. Readers sometimes have to let the works themselves tell them how they should be read.

Veracity

Because it sometimes draws on the material of autobiography, history, journalism, biology, ecology, travel writing, medicine, and any number of other subjects, creative nonfiction is reliably factual, firmly anchored in real experience, whether the author has lived it or observed and recorded it. As essayist and memoirist Annie Dillard writes, "The elements in any nonfiction should be true not only artistically—the connects must hold at base and must be veracious, for that is the convention and the covenant between the nonfiction writer and his reader" ("Introduction" xvii). Like the rest of us, the nonfiction writer, she says, "thinks about actual things. He can make sense of them analytically or artistically. In either case he renders the real world coherent and meaningful, even if only bits of it, and even if that coherence and meaning reside only inside small texts" (xvii).

But factuality or veracity is a trickier element than it seems. As David James Duncan observes,

> We see into our memories in much the way that we see across the floor of a sunbaked desert: everything we conjure, every object, creature, or event we perceive in there, is distorted, before it reaches us, by mirages created by subjectivity, time, and distance. . . . The best that a would-be nonfiction writer can do is use imperfect language to invoke imperfectly remembered events based on imperfect perceptions. (55)

Artistry needs some latitude; self-disclosure may be too risky to be total, particularly where it involves disclosure of others. Creative nonfiction writers sometimes alter the accuracy of events in order to achieve the accuracy of interpretation. Some of this is inadvertent—the great challenge of memoir writing is knowing how much we remember is reliable and accepting the likelihood that we are "inventing the truth." "You can't put together a memoir without cannibalizing your own life for parts," Annie Dillard writes in "To Fashion a Text." "The work battens on your memories. And it replaces them" (70). Memories blur over time and edit themselves into different forms that others who had the same experience might not recognize. Finding the language to describe experience sometimes alters it, and your description of the experience becomes the memory, the way a photograph does. At the least, we may feel a need to omit the irrelevant detail or protect the privacy of others not as committed to our self-disclosure as we are. The truth may not necessarily be veracious enough to take into court or into a laboratory; it need only be veracious enough to satisfy the writer's purpose and the art of the writing.

Digression: The Contentious Issue of "Truth"

Partly due to occasional revelations of dishonesty, prevarication, and outright fraud in some works of nonfiction and partly due to varied interpretations of what "creative nonfiction" really is, the issue of "truth" is discussed and debated more often in regard to the fourth genre than in regard to other genres. The first issue is easily addressed: no one defines "creative" as "dishonest" or "fraudulent" and no one encourages nonfictionists to be dishonest or fraudulent. The second issue is more problematic: If you approach creative nonfiction as if it were a scholarly, journalistic, scientific, or historical genre, then you likely emphasize verifiable factuality—that is, the use of evidence that can be independently corroborated or confirmed by anyone investigating the accuracy of the assertions or reportage. In regard to those subgenres or branches of nonfiction, there is no argument; the difficulty only emerges when applied to "creative nonfiction," the branch of non-fiction which includes memoirs, essays, literary journalism, and personal cultural criticism. Creative nonfiction need not be academic or journalistic and, more to the point, need not rely on verifiable factuality—that is, it usually draws on experiences, emotions, memories, and interpretations which are, by their very nature, impossible to corroborate or confirm by an independent investigator.

For example, how can you verify whether Annie Dillard ever locked gazes with a weasel as she declares she did in "Living Like Weasels"? You can look up her reference to Ernest Thompson Seton and track down his eagle story, perhaps, but other than interrogating Dillard herself or finding an inadvertent videotape of her and the weasel, as in an episode of *CSI*, you simply have to take her word for it that the event happened. The same thing is true of Dagoberto Gilb's story of seeing a man reading his novel in a train car where a weak battery on Gilb's computer made him sit near the only electrical outlet in the car. Think of the difficulty of tracking all those little facts down, including the train schedule, the date of the experience, the text Gilb typed on the computer. As Robert Atwan observes in his Foreword to *The Best American Essays 2006*, "the unverifiable world is vast and accommodating." He encourages readers to ask themselves: "If a report of something is wholly unverifiable, should we even concern ourselves with the issue of truth?" It's a rhetorical question: The answer is "No."

That said, we should also consider a further aspect of the fourth genre. Because another approach to it is from the direction of literature, with its emphasis on narrative, dialogue, character, and lyricism—in other words, drawing on aspects of fiction, drama, and poetry—the issue of truth is often raised in regard to how much liberty the writer has taken with the "facts." All nonfiction writers have to decide the pertinence or relevance of particular evidence to the kind of work they hope to write; they have to be selective about what they include and what they exclude. Something is always left out of every piece of writing, and the writer always has to make choices about what difference those acts of omission will make. Some information merely distracts or, even worse, disengages the reader from the primary focus of the writing; it is better left out. For example, since so much of literary nonfiction is about personal experience rather than about public events, rigorous identification of all participants, including the most tangential bystander, may divert attention from the purpose of relating the experience in the first place.

All writing also performs acts of commission—deliberately altering experiences and events to narrow focus on those elements the writer most wants the reader to attend to, to remember, to see as significant. The acts of omission are inevitable and less problematic than the acts of commission, since they may involve altering facts or inventing information. Some of these are minor and, by now, routine: Memoir, reportage, and ethnographic research frequently disguise the identity of witnesses and participants on ethical grounds, as well as grounds of relevance. Readers may not need to identify real-life individuals and authors have to decide whether to expose private lives to public scrutiny. Name changes are common acts of commission.

More troublesome, to some readers, are an author's conflation of time—by representing something that took place over several days as taking place in one or two—and the use of composite characters—characters composed of two or more other characters to create a third, who never actually existed. These would surely be unacceptable in noncreative nonfiction, but in more literary forms, and within certain limits in those forms, they are not. Memoirists often see memoir as a form of literature rather than a form of history or journalism. As Vivian Gornick explained about her having "made a composite out of the elements of two or more incidents" and "played loose with time [by] relating incidents that were chronologically out of order," she did these things "for the purpose of moving the narrative forward. . . . for the sake of narrative development." She emphasizes that "none [of the incidents] . . . had been fabricated." Gornick's distinction—that she has fashioned her material, not fabricated it—is an important one.

Though they usually stay within traditional boundaries of factuality, very often writers in the fourth genre are deliberately exploring the ground between truth and imagination. The lines of demarcation between truth and fact, or between fashion and fabrication, are difficult to locate absolutely. Writers of the fourth genre walk those lines more delicately than those in other forms but in the end they endeavor to represent the unverifiable world in which we all live as truthfully as they can.

Writers, Readers, and the Fourth Genre

The interaction between the writer and the genre the writer works in influences the outcome of the work. Writers of other nonfiction forms such as criticism, journalism, scholarship, or technical and professional writing tend to leave themselves out of the work and to view the work as a means to an end; they want to explain, report, inform, or propose. For them the text they produce is a vehicle, a container or a package, to transport information and ideas to someone else, the intended readers. Some people have referred to these forms as *transactional writing*. Writers of other literary forms such as poetry, fiction, and drama tend to put themselves in the work and to view the work as an end in itself; they want to reflect, explore, speculate, imagine, and discover, and the text they create is a structure—an anchored shape like a sculpture or a monument or a building—to which interested readers are drawn. The result is often called *poetic* or *creative writing*. Writers of creative nonfiction by definition share the qualities of both groups of writers, and the work they create reflects varying measures of both kinds of writing.

Many creative nonfiction writers in this book joined this conversation from the direction of their writing in other literary genres. Experienced poets or fictionists, they came to the fourth genre by way of personal essays and memoirs, nonfiction forms compatible with the desire for lyric and narrative expression, the desire to give voice to memory and meditation and acts of emotional and intellectual discovery. They came to it not only because of a need to write nonfiction but also because of a desire for creative expression. Similarly, creative nonfiction is also written by critics, journalists, and scholars who approach their writing the way essayists and memoirists do—that is, by inhabiting the work and by approaching it from a literary perspective more than (or as much as) from a critical, reportorial, or scholarly perspective.

We don't necessarily see sharply definable boundaries here, whose coordinates we can map precisely—neighboring nonfiction forms often share the same terrain for a long distance on either side of their common border. Yet, just as when you're traveling you don't need precise knowledge of geography or topography to sense that you're not in Kansas (or Vermont or California) anymore, so in reading you can also sense when a text is a work of "literary" nonfiction and not the "transactional" forms usual to journalism, scholarship, or criticism.

Because nonfiction in general has sometimes, mistakenly, been regarded as if it were an arid, barren wasteland of non-literature surrounding lush, fertile oases of literature, it is important to make this clear: a great deal of nonfiction has always been literary, and it is the contemporary writers of literary or creative forms of nonfiction who are the focus of this book. Although the non-literary forms of nonfiction are not our focus, in some of those forms it is frequently difficult to notice when a writer slips over the border into the literary form. To make it easier to talk about creative nonfiction, then, we urge you to see it centered in the approaches taken by the essayist and memoirist and spiraling outward toward aesthetically oriented critics and literary journalists.

Working Definitions

Readers frequently ask us to be more specific about the definition we'd apply to creative nonfiction and the distinctions we'd make among the various forms. In spite of our insistence that it's impossible, even counterproductive, to try to pin down subgenres and that definitions are better intuited from examining texts *[handwritten in left margin: creative nonfic. reader + writer should have a direct connection*

fiction- connect w/ characters and plot]

than delineating characteristics, for the purposes of discussion about the genre we do have some working definitions in mind. As long as readers remember that we're not attempting to make absolute distinctions among forms, and that we can argue for placing most texts in multiple categories, we'll offer here some provisional descriptions that might help clarify distinctions.

First of all, we think of nonfiction as *the written expression of, reflection upon, and/or interpretation of observed, perceived, or recollected experience*. As a genre of literature made up of such writing, it includes such subgenres as the personal essay, the memoir, narrative reportage, and expressive critical writing; its borders with other reality-based genres and forms (such as journalism, criticism, history, etc.) are fluid and malleable. We would place nonfiction works on a line stretching from the most informative to the most literary. Works of creative nonfiction tend to concentrate more heavily, but not exclusively, on the literary end of that line. As a result, we might think in terms of four major categories:

- *Essay*—an author's engagement in prose with a subject or an experience; it becomes a personal essay when the author's own individual, idiosyncratic self, worldview, or experience is essential to the writing. The "plot" of the personal essay is the arc of the writer's thinking—that is, his or her reflections, reactions, speculations, associations, confusions—all of which are being employed in the service of trying to make sense of a topic, an experience, or a situation that perplexes and preoccupies the writer (e.g., Sherry Simpson's "Natural History, or What Happens When We're Not Looking" or Dagoberto Gilb's "Northeast Direct").
- *Memoir*—a record of and reflection upon past events which the author experienced or witnessed. It is generally more concentrated or focused in time or circumstances than an autobiography would be. Literary memoir, in particular, tends to express how the writer's past history has helped shape his or her present self (e.g., Judith Ortiz Cofer's "Silent Dancing" or Mimi Schwartz's "My Father Always Said").
- *Cultural criticism*—an investigation of or reaction to or interpretation of specific artifacts or aspects of the culture—artistic, social, historic, political, etc. It becomes personal (and becomes creative nonfiction, though it may also be called "narrative scholarship" or "personal academic discourse") when the investigator is up front about his or her individual involvement with or experience of the topic (e.g., Chet Raymo's "Celebrating Creation" or Marianna Torgovnick's "Experimental Critical Writing").
- *Journalism*—a report on public events or current affairs or occurrences of general public interest; it becomes literary journalism when the author includes his or her own perspective or behavior as part of the reportage or elects to use the techniques of literature (those of fiction, poetry, drama, film, memoir) as a means of presenting the reportage (e.g., Jennifer Kahn's "Stripped for Parts" or John McPhee's "The Search for Marvin Gardens").

In practice, as many of the works in this anthology illustrate, any of these categories can spill over into any or all of the others, fuse together, blend, dance back and forth across boundaries.

Reading Creative Nonfiction

readers want to be involved

Readers come to creative nonfiction with different expectations from those they bring to the other genres. At the core of those expectations may be, in a sense, the hope of becoming engaged in a conversation. Much fiction, drama, poetry, and film is presented as performance, as entertainment essentially enclosed within itself—we are usually expected to appreciate or admire its creators' artistry whether or not we are encouraged to acknowledge their intensity or insight. Much non-literary nonfiction (various forms of journalism and academic writing, for example) is presented as a transaction delivering information, sometimes objective, sometimes argumentative—we are usually expected to receive or accept their creators' knowledge or data the way we would a lecture or a news broadcast. Creative nonfiction, which is simultaneously literary and transactional, integrates these discourse aims: it brings artistry to information and actuality to imagination, and it draws upon the expressive aim that lies below the surface in all writing. Expressive writing breaks the surface, most notably in personal writing like journals, diaries, and letters, but it has connected with the reader most prominently in the personal or familiar essay. Other forms of writing have at center the personal impulse, the need for expression, but the essay has traditionally been the outlet by which that impulse finds public voice.

Readers turn to creative nonfiction to find a place to connect to the personal voice, to connect not to art or knowledge alone but to another mind. This means that writers too have a place to connect, a genre that gives them permission to speak in the first person singular, not only about their knowledge and their beliefs but also about their uncertainties and their passions, not only about where they stand but also about the ways they arrived there, not only about the worlds they have either imagined or documented but also about the worlds they have experienced or inhabit now. Creative nonfiction may be the genre in which both reader and writer feel most connected to one another.

Joining the Conversation

We think of *The Fourth Genre* as an inclusive, ongoing conversation about the art and craft of writing creative nonfiction. We want to exemplify and describe this evolving genre, allow it to define itself and preserve its vital elasticity, and avoid arbitrary and imprecise subcategorizing and classifying. Unlike conversations in real life, a conversation in an anthology allows only one speaker at a time to speak and no one is interrupted by anyone else. The reader is the one who has to make the individual speakers connect. We've tried to make the conversation a little easier to follow by putting the speakers in different rooms. The people who simply share their own examples of creative nonfiction have the largest room, at the front of the anthology, where the writing more or less speaks for itself. The people who have ideas and opinions about the nature of this genre, the kinds of writing it contains and the kinds of writers who produce it, have another room, where both those who write creative nonfiction and those who study or examine it have their opportunities to speak. In the final room are those who attempt to explain how they wrote their own specific examples of creative nonfiction—the circumstances of composition, the tribulations of drafting and revising—where the conversation focuses on the composing processes of working writers.

In real life you wouldn't be able to hear all the speakers in this conversation, but in an anthology you can, because the speakers wait until you get to them before they speak. In spite of the layout of the place, you should feel free to wander back and forth among the rooms, following someone else's recommendations or your own inclinations and intuitions. Naturally, we encourage you to join the conversation; provide your own examples; discuss your own ideas of genre, theory, and technique; and share your own composing processes.

Read selections in Part 1, Writing Creative Nonfiction, to get a sense of the range of contemporary creative nonfiction. The writers here reveal the variety of voices and personas, the flexibility and expansiveness, and the breadth of subject matter and structures creative nonfiction may adopt. It is a representative blend that includes examples of the personal essay, the memoir, the travel essay, the nature essay, the lyric essay, literary journalism, and personal cultural criticism. (See the Alternative Table of Contents for further subdivisions and categories.) These selections also present a range of forms and structures, from the narrative and the lyrical to the discursive and the reportorial, from the traditional (chronology or argument) to the individual and unconventional (unique arrangements of segments or organization around a pattern).

Many of these works demonstrate the futility of labels, qualifying easily under the genre heading of creative nonfiction for personal presence, literary language, and other defining elements but straddling the boundaries of two or more subgenres, perhaps simultaneously literary journalism and personal essay, travel narrative and environmental reporting, or memoir and cultural criticism. Instead they model the intimate relationship between form and content in creative nonfiction. Perhaps they will also suggest to you ways to invent forms which serve your own ends as a writer.

Read selections in Part 2, Talking About Creative Nonfiction, to get a sense of what writers, critics, and scholars have to say about the nature of creative nonfiction and its various subgenres. Many of the authors in this section have also written selections in Part 1. They take the form personally, sometimes discussing their own personal motives and composing strategies, sometimes the elements of the form they work in. As some of them point out, the tradition of essayist/critic goes back centuries, to the work of Montaigne, Addison and Steele, and Lamb and Hazlitt, but as this genre reemerges, it is contemporary practitioners, for the most part—the people who write and teach creative nonfiction—who are setting the terms of this conversation. This section mixes thoughts, opinions, speculations, critiques, theories, and assertions by working writers about the art and craft of their genre.

Many of the Part 2 pieces can be paired with essays in Part 1. Writing in Part 1 often serves as examples of the more theoretical positions in Part 2; writing in Part 2 often gives new perspective on writing in Part 1 when you compare memoirs with the memoirists' discussion of the form, essays with the essayists' reflections on being essayists, and cultural criticism with the critics' justifications for personal academic writing.

Other authors also give us insight into the forms and issues of creative nonfiction—the art of the memoir or of literary journalism, the elements of the disjunctive form, or the question of truthfulness in nonfiction texts. Such essays attempt to give a personal perspective to a critical speculation on the forms in which the writers are working. They ground the genre in the behaviors and motives of working writers rather than in disembodied theories of literature or composing. They give the reader the opportunity to step back from the individual readings and take a longer view of process and text.

Read selections in Part 3, Composing Creative Nonfiction, for a sense of the work habits, craft techniques, and serendipity they use to create a work of creative nonfiction. Here, in commentary written especially for this anthology, a group of writers discuss their composing processes for specific works, also reproduced in this section. They share drafts, explain revisions, and map the motives for changes in their works-in-progress. They focus our attention in this conversation on the most fundamental aspect of the work, the composing itself, and bring us to the place where the reader can continue the conversation as a writer. If Part 1 gives us examples of the variety of creative nonfiction and Part 2 gives us a lively discussion of the practices and products of the genre, Part 3 gives us a chance to sit at the shoulders of the writers themselves and follow them through the twists and turns of creation. These writers reflect in their practices the ways writers in other parts of the book created their own selections. By example they suggest ideas and strategies that we can use in our own composing processes.

We think the fourth genre is the most accessible and urgent genre. It may not be necessary to read all three parts of the book or to read all selections in the parts you do read to get a sense of what creative nonfiction is about. We hope the book is flexible enough that readers can get what they want from it by coming at it from a number of different directions. Yet readers who do read in all three parts will get a fuller understanding of the breadth and power of this genre. And because the time is particularly right for other writers to join this conversation, we hope that wide reading in this book will help spur your writing of creative nonfiction and give you a writer's perspective on the art and craft of the fourth genre.

Robert L. Root, Jr. and Michael Steinberg

Works Cited

Anderson, Chris. "Introduction: Literary Nonfiction and Composition." *Literary Nonfiction: Theory, Criticism, Pedagogy*. Ed. Chris Anderson. Carbondale: Southern Illinois University Press, 1989. ix–xxvi.

Atwan, Robert. "Foreword." *The Best American Essays 1988*. Boston: Ticknor & Fields, 1988. ix–xi.

Atwan, Robert. "Foreword," *The Best American Essays 2006*. Boston: Houghton Mifflin, 2006: xii.

Blew, Mary Clearman. "The Art of the Memoir." *Bone Deep in Landscape: Writing, Reading, and Place*. Norman: University of Oklahoma Press, 1999. 3–8.

Brown, Rosellen. "Introduction." *Ploughshares* 20:2/3 (Fall 1994): 5–8.

Dillard, Annie. "Introduction." *The Best American Essays 1988*. Boston: Ticknor & Fields, 1988. xiii–xxii.

———. "To Fashion a Text." *Inventing the Truth: The Art and Craft of Memoir*. Ed. William Zinsser. Boston: Houghton–Mifflin, 1987. 53–76.

Duncan, David James. "Nonfiction=Fiction." *Orion* 15:3 (Summer 1996): 55–57.

Gornick, Vivian. "A Memoirist Defends Her Words," Salon.com http://dir.salon.com/ books/feature/2003/08/12/memoir_writing/index.html

Gutkind, Lee. "From the Editor." *Creative Nonfiction* 1:1 (1993): v–vi.

Hongo, Garrett. *Volcano: A Memoir of Hawai'i*. New York: Knopf, 1995.

Karr, Mary. *The Liar's Club: A Memoir*. New York: Viking Penguin, 1995.

Kramer, Mark. "Breakable Rules for Literary Journalists." *Literary Journalism*. Ed. Norman Sims and Mark Kramer. New York: Ballantine, 1995. 21–34.

Lopate, Phillip. "Introduction." *The Art of the Personal Essay: An Anthology from the Classical Era to the Present*. New York: Anchor/Doubleday, 1994. xxiii–liv.

Lounsbery, Barbara. *The Art of Fact: Contemporary Artists of Nonfiction*. Contributions to the Study of World Literature, No. 35. New York: Greenwood Press, 1990.

Montaigne, Michel de. *The Complete Works*. Trans. Donald M. Frame. Stanford: Stanford UP, 1957. 761.

Olson, W. Scott. "Introduction." *Old Friends, New Neighbors: A Celebration of the American Essay*. Ed. W. Scott Olson. *American Literary Review* 5:2 (Fall 1994): v–viii.

Thoreau, Henry David. *Walden*. Ed. J. Lyndon Shanley. Princeton: Princeton UP, 1973. 3.

Torgovnick, Marianna. "Introduction." *Eloquent Obsessions: Writing Cultural Criticism*. Ed. Marianna Torgovnick. Durham: Duke University Press, 1994.

Part I

Writing Creative Nonfiction

Contemporary creative nonfiction, like any other literary genre, offers a great deal of latitude to writers in terms of what they are able to do in the form. "There are as many kinds of essays as there are human attitudes or poses," the great American essayist E. B. White once observed. "The essayist rises in the morning and, if he has work to do, selects his garb from an unusually extensive wardrobe: he can pull on any sort of shirt, be any sort of person, according to his mood or his subject matter—philosopher, scold, jester, raconteur, confidant, devil's advocate, enthusiast" (vii). In general, the observation is appropriate for the whole range of creative nonfiction.

This section of the book samples widely from the range of contemporary creative nonfiction. Its selections reveal the variety of voices and personas, the flexibility and expansiveness, and the range of subject matter and structures creative nonfiction may adopt. It is a representative blend, demonstrating the malleability of the genre. In recent years, creative nonfiction has become ever more malleable.

All of the readings may be said to represent four major strands in contemporary nonfiction: essay, memoir, literary journalism, and expressive cultural criticism, but the boundaries between these strands are highly permeable. Much of what is collected here might be classified in more than one strand. Jo Ann Beard's chilling narrative of a highway encounter is both memoir and essay; Jonathan Lethem's account of his multiple viewings of *Star Wars* could be considered as essay, memoir, and/or cultural criticism. The author's presence, so vital to the memoir and, to a greater or lesser degree, to the essay, is clearly vital as well to writing that might be considered personal reportage, such as David Gessner's observations on-site about the Gulf oil spill or Shari Caudron's lighter immersion among Barbie collectors.

These readings suggest that the writer's feeling about the subject has more to do with the way the final version reads than any arbitrary set of generic guidelines. Even as we hint at the variety of the pieces in this part of the book, we have to acknowledge the futility of labels. It is not a uniform structure or organization that links these selections but the common thread of the writer's personal presence, some times at considerable remove in essays not obviously about personal experience yet nevertheless there, examining subject matter in the light of personal inquiry. Often the shapes they create draw on other genres—like the lyric essays of Lia Purpura, Joni Tevis, and Kathryn Winograd, so strongly infused with a poetic sensibility—or on hybrid forms—like Maggie McKnight's graphic memoir, Shelley Salamensky's reliance on photographs, or the video essays of Eula Biss and John Bresland—or on online formats—like Tracy Seeley's and David Gessner's blogs.

Writers use creative nonfiction not as a vessel to be filled with meaning but rather as a way of constructing a shape appropriate to the meaning they create by writing. The various patterns and structures let us see how intimately form and content are connected in creative nonfiction, and how they can be invented to serve the ends of the author. They extend our understanding of the range of writing creative nonfictionists do.

"What happened to the writer is not what matters; what matters is the large sense that the writer is able to *make* of what happened," Vivian Gornick once observed, writing about the author's presence in memoirs. "The narrator in a memoir is an instrument of illumination, but it's the writing itself that provides revelation" (5). These selections suggest to us the possibilities of form, structure, voice, persona, approach, presentation, ways of describing what happened, ways of making sense of what happened. Reading widely in Part 1 will not only give you a solid sense of what we write when we write creative nonfiction but also open up your own possibilities for subject matter and design. Reading other writers triggers our own memories and our own speculations. We don't so much imitate others' subjects and structures as use them as a bridge to our resources and inventions.

This mini-anthology, Part 1, is complemented by the other two parts of the book, in which writers talk about the forms and processes of creative nonfiction. We invite you to explore those other sections in connection with your reading here. Writers always find it helpful to see what other writers are doing, to hear them talk about how they are doing it, and to free-associate with their own memories and reflections from the ideas and stories that others share. Those who read these selections with a writer's eye will discover insights and perspectives that will serve their own writing well.

Note: Sources for online versions of writing by Eula Biss, John Bresland, David Gessner, and Tracy Seeley are found at the end of their articles.

Works Cited

Gornick, Vivian. "The Memoir Boom." *Women's Review of Books* 13:10–11 (July 1996): 5.
White, E. B. "Foreword." *Essays of E. B. White.* New York: HarperCollins, 1997.

Out There

Jo Ann Beard

It isn't even eight A.M. and I'm hot. My rear end is welded to the seat just like it was yesterday. I'm fifty miles from the motel and about a thousand and a half from home, in a little white Mazda with 140,000 miles on it and no rust. I'm all alone in Alabama, with only a cooler and a tape deck for company. It's already in the high 80s. Yesterday, coming up from the keys through Florida, I had a day-long anxiety attack that I decided last night was really heat prostration. I was a cinder with a brain; I was actually whimpering. I kept thinking I saw alligators at the edge of the highway.

There were about four hundred exploded armadillos, too, but I got used to them. They were real, and real dead. The alligators weren't real or dead, but they may have been after me. I'm running away from running away from home.

I bolted four weeks ago, leaving my husband to tend the dogs and tool around town on his bicycle. He doesn't love me anymore, it's both trite and true. He does love himself, though. He's begun wearing cologne and staring into the mirror for long minutes, trying out smiles. He's become a politician. After thirteen years he came to realize that the more successful he got, the less he loved me. That's how he put it, late one night. He won that screaming match. He said, gently and sadly, "I feel sort of embarrassed of you."

I said, "Of what? The way I look? The way I act?"

And he said, softly, "Everything, sort of."

And it was true. Well, I decided to take a trip to Florida. I sat on my haunches in Key West for four weeks, writing and seething and striking up conversations with strangers. I had my thirty-fifth birthday there, weeping into a basket of shrimp. I drank beer and had long involved dreams about cigarettes, I wrote nearly fifty pages on my novel. It's in my trunk at this very moment, dead and decomposing. Boy, do I need a cup of coffee.

There's not much happening this early in the morning. The highway looks interminable again. So far, no alligators. I have a box of seashells in my back seat and I reach back and get a fluted one, pale gray with a pearly interior, to put on the dashboard. I can do everything while I'm driving. At the end of this trip I will have driven 3,999 miles all alone, me and the windshield, me and the radio, me and the creepy alligators. Don't ask me why I didn't get that last mile in, driving around the block a few times or getting a tiny bit lost once. I didn't though, and there you have it. Four thousand sounds like a lot more than 3,999 does; I feel sort of embarrassed for myself.

My window is broken, the crank fell off in Tallahassee on the way down. In order to roll it up or down I have to put the crank back on and turn it slowly and carefully, using one hand to push up the glass. So, mostly I leave it down. I baked like a biscuit yesterday, my left arm is so brown it looks like a branch. Today I'm wearing a long-sleeved white shirt to protect myself. I compromised on wearing long sleeves by going naked underneath it. It's actually cooler this way, compared to yesterday when I drove in my swimming suit top with my hair stuck up like a fountain on top of my head. Plus, I'm having a nervous breakdown. I've got that wild-eyed look.

A little four-lane blacktop running through the Alabama countryside, that's what I'm on. It's pretty, too, better than Florida, which was billboards and condos built on old dump sites. This is like driving between rolling emerald carpets. You can't see the two lanes going in the opposite direction because there's a screen of trees. I'm starting to get in a good mood again. The best was Georgia, coming down. Willow trees and red dirt and snakes stretched out alongside the road. I kept thinking, That looks like a *rope*, and then it would be a huge snake. A few miles later I would think, That looks like a *snake*, and it would be some snarl of something dropped off a truck.

Little convenience store, stuck out in the middle of nothing, a stain on the carpet. I'm gassing it up, getting some coffee. My white shirt is gaping open and I have nothing on underneath it, but who cares, I'll never see these people again. What do I care what Alabama thinks about me. This is a new and unusual attitude for me. I'm practicing being snotty, in anticipation of being dumped by my husband when I get back to Iowa.

I swagger from the gas pump to the store, I don't even care if my boobs are roaming around inside my shirt, if my hair is a freaky snarl, if I look defiant and uppity. There's nothing to be embarrassed of. I bring my coffee cup along and fill it at the counter. Various men, oldish and grungy, sit at tables eating eggs with wadded-up toast. They stare at me carefully while they chew. I ignore them and pay the woman at the counter. She's smoking a cigarette so I envy her.

"Great day, huh?" I ask her. She counts out my change.

"It is, honey," she says. She reaches for her cigarette and takes a puff, blows it up above my head. "Wish I wudn't in *here*."

"Well, it's getting hotter by the minute," I tell her. I've adopted an accent in just four weeks, an intermittent drawl that makes me think I'm not who everyone thinks I am.

"Y'all think this's hot?" she says idly. "*This* ain't hot."

When I leave, the men are still staring at me in a sullen way. I get in, rear-range all my junk so I have everything handy that I need, choose a Neil Young tape and pop it in the deck, fasten the belt, and then move back out on the highway. Back to the emerald carpet and the road home. Iowa is creeping toward me like a panther.

All I do is sing when I drive. Sing and drink: coffee, Coke, water, juice, coffee. And think. I sing and drink and think. On the way down I would sing, drink, think, and weep uncontrollably, but I'm past that now. Now I suffer bouts of free-floating hostility, which is much better. I plan to use it when I get home.

A car swings up alongside me so I pause in my singing until it goes past. People who sing in their cars always cheer me up, but I'd rather not be caught doing it. On the road, we're all singing, picking our noses, embarrassing our-selves wildly; it gets tiresome. I pause and hum, but the car sticks alongside me so I glance over. It's a guy. He grins and makes a lewd gesture with his mouth. I don't even want to say what it is, it's that disgusting. Tongue darting in and out, quickly. A python testing its food.

I hate this kind of thing. Who do they think they are, these men? I've had my fill of it. I give him the finger, slowly and deliberately. He picked the wrong day to mess with me, I think to myself. I take a sip of coffee.

He's still there.

I glance over briefly and he's making the gesture with his tongue again. I can't believe this. He's from the convenience store, I realize. He has on a fishing hat with lures stuck in it. I saw him back there, but I can't remember if he was sitting with the other men or by himself. He's big, overweight, and dirty, wearing a thin unbuttoned shirt and the terrible fishing hat. His passenger-side window is down. He begins screaming at me.

He followed me from that convenience store. The road is endless, in front there is nothing, no cars, no anything, behind is the same. Just road and grass and trees. The other two lanes are still invisible behind their screen of trees. I'm all alone out here. With him. He's screaming and screaming at me, reaching out his right arm like he's throttling me. I speed up. He speeds up, too, next to me. We're only a few feet apart, my window won't roll up.

He's got slobber on his face and there's no one in either direction. I slam on my brakes and for an instant he's ahead of me, I can breathe, then he slams on his brakes and we're next to each other again. I can't even repeat what he's screaming at me. He's telling me, amid the hot wind and poor Neil Young, what he wants to do to me. He wants to kill me. He's screaming and screaming, I can't look over.

I stare straight ahead through the windshield, hands at ten and two. The front end of his car is moving into my lane. He's saying he'll cut me with a knife, how he'll do it, all that. I can't listen. The front end of his Impala is about four inches from my white Mazda, my little car. This is really my husband's car, my beloved's. My Volkswagen died a lingering death a few months ago. There is no husband, there is no Volkswagen, there is nothing. There isn't even a

Jo Ann right now. Whatever I am is sitting here clenched, hands on the wheel, I've stopped being her, now I'm something else. I'm absolutely terrified. He won't stop screaming it, over and over, what he's going to do.

I refuse to give him an inch. I will not move one inch over. If I do he'll have me off the road in an instant. I will not move. I speed up, he speeds up, I slow down, he slows down, I can see him out of the corner of my eye, driving with one hand, reaching like he's grabbing me with the other. "You whore," he screams at me. "I'll *kill* you, I'll *kill* you, I'll *kill* you . . ."

He'll kill me.

If I give him an inch, he'll shove me off the road and get his hands on me, then the end will begin in some unimaginable, unspeakable style that will be all his. I'll be an actor in his drama. We're going too fast, I've got the pedal pressed up to 80 and it's wobbling, his old Impala can probably go 140 on a straightaway like this. There will be blood, he won't want me to die quickly.

I will not lose control. I will ride it out. I cannot let him push me over onto the gravel. His car noses less than two inches from mine; I'm getting rattled. My God, he can almost reach me through his window, he's moved over in his seat, driving just with the left hand, the right is grabbing the hot air. I move over to the edge of my seat, toward the center of the car, carefully, without swerving.

In the rearview mirror a speck appears. Don't look, watch your front end. I glance up again; it's a truck. He can't get me. It's a trucker. Without looking at him I jerk my thumb backward to show him. He screams and screams and screams. He's not leaving. Suddenly a road appears on the right, a dirty and rutted thing leading off into the trees. He hits the brakes, drops behind, and takes it. In my rearview mirror I see that the license plate on the front of his car is buried in dried mud. That road is where he was hoping to push me. He wanted to push my car off the highway and get me on that road. He was hoping to kill me. He was hoping to do what maniacs, furious men, do to women alongside roads, in woods. I can't stop pressing too hard on the gas pedal. I'm at 85 now, and my leg is shaking uncontrollably, coffee is spilled all over the passenger seat, the atlas is wet, Neil Young is still howling on the tape deck. By force of will, I slow down to 65, eject the tape, and wait for the truck to overtake me. When it does, when it comes up alongside me. I don't look over at all, I keep my eyes straight ahead. As it moves in front of me I speed up enough to stay two car lengths behind it. It says *England* on the back, ornate red letters outlined in black. England.

That guy chased me on purpose, he *hated* me, with more passion than anyone has ever felt for me. Ever. Out there are all those decomposing bodies, all those disappeared daughters, discovered by joggers and hunters, their bodies long abandoned, the memory of final desperate moments lingering on the leaves, the trees, the mindless stumps and mushrooms. Images taped to tollbooth windows, faces pressed into the dirt alongside a path somewhere.

I want out of Alabama, I want to be in England. The air is still a blast furnace. I want to roll my window up, but I'd have to stop and get the crank out and lift it by hand. I'm too scared. He's out there still, waiting behind the screen of trees. I have to follow England until I'm out of Alabama. Green car, old Impala, unreadable license plate, lots of rust. Seat covers made out of that spongy stuff, something standing on the dashboard, a coffee cup or a sad Jesus. The fishing hat with a sweat ring around it right above the brim. Lures with feathers and barbs. I've never been so close to so much hatred in my whole life. *He wanted to kill me.* Think of England, with its white cows and broken-toothed farmers and dark green pastures. Think of the Beatles. I'm hugging the truck so closely now I'm almost under it. Me, of all people, he wanted to kill. Me. Everywhere I go I'm finding out new things about myself. Each way I turn, there it is. It's Jo Ann he wanted to kill.

By noon I want to kill him. I took a right somewhere and got onto the interstate, had the nerve to pee in a rest area, adrenaline running like an engine inside me, my keys threaded through my fingers in case anyone tried anything. I didn't do anything to earn it, I realize. His anger. I didn't do anything. Unless you count giving him the finger, which I don't. *He* earned that.

As it turned out, my husband couldn't bring himself to leave me when I got back to Iowa, so I waited awhile, and watched, then disentangled myself. History: We each got ten photo albums and six trays of slides. We took a lot of pictures in thirteen years. In the early years he looks stoned and contented, distant; in the later years he looks straight and slightly worried. In that last year he only appears by chance, near the edges, a blur of suffering, almost out of frame.

Just before we split, when we were driving somewhere, I told him about the guy in the green car. "Wow," he said. Then he turned up the radio, checked his image in the rearview mirror, and smiled sincerely at the passing landscape.

Ode to Every Thing

Eula Biss / John Bresland

Apple, cup, car, dog, doll, glove. . . .

The books I read to my infant son have no plot. They aren't stories. They are just pages and pages of things.

Leaves, melon, monkey, owl, river, socks. . . .

We didn't own many things before he was born, but now we have all the furniture of life, all the plastic of parenthood. We have so many things I never wanted, and I'm surprised now by my love for these things. I love the blue cup, the orange ball, the yellow duckie, the white blanket, the brown bear. . . .

Before he was born I was already moved by the sight of things that would be his. It was a premature nostalgia. I spent my pregnant days finding, buying, cleaning, sorting his things. It didn't bother me that all these things belonged to someone who didn't even yet belong to himself. Part of me believed that his soft little clothes, washed and folded but not yet filled, would call him here. Part of me suspected that it was not the boy who made the velveteen rabbit real, but the rabbit that made the boy real.

In the weeks after he was born we watched the planes coming in, hanging over the lake in holding patterns while we rocked him and walked him at midnight, at 2, at 4, at dawn, sleepless, aching, the planes still hanging over the lake, the baby's eyes still open, and I remember a moment of fear as I looked down at his mouth and through it saw only darkness. He had just arrived from nowhere and his mouth was like a portal back to that empty place. He needed nothing here, only rocking and walking and the milk that passed between us invisibly.

His things, the duckies, the trucks, the teddy bears, were for us. They were the anchor we threw down. They were the language we offered, blunt and limited but bright.

I saw, just after laying him in his crib for the first time, a bomb, a small bomb carried by one of the airplanes we had hung above him. When I saw the bomb

I knew that this body I was bathing and rocking and feeding would be taken from me, that these sleepless nights and bloodless days would come, in the end, to nothing. And all these things would be left behind—the duckies and trucks would outlast us.

But the bomb was not a bomb. It was a fuel tank. And so we continued rocking and walking, singing and talking, reading him the names of things.

Big rig, dump truck, tractor, delivery truck, digger, scraper, bulldozer, tow truck, fire engine, garbage truck . . .

There are too many things. We keep losing them and throwing them out and putting them away and we still can't even name them all. But it may be these things, these three trains, these six balls, these two lions, these eight apples that keep us tethered here, keep us physical, keep us from slipping back into whatever dust or dark or light we came from. . . .

Source: Biss, Eula, and John Bresland, "Ode to Every Thing," *Requited* http://www .requitedjournal.com/index.php?/form/eula-biss-and-john-bresland/.

The Answer That Increasingly Appeals

Robin Black

A phenomenon that fascinates me:
   Patina.

A fragment of something I wrote on that subject:
   "Are we taking the patina approach?"
   "Yes."
   It was the only way.
   I lived in fear of every scrape, of every drop of water on our new, much too expensive leather chair—until he asked and I answered and we took the patina approach. We held our eyes screwed shut for just about one year, the official period of mourning in many religions (mine to name but one), until each individual scratch and every stain just disappeared, merging into something wonderful.
   A short period of endurance. In retrospect. For something so lovely.
   (Forgiveness itself, as I now understand.)
   It takes your breath away.

A funny question:
   What exactly is my religion?

9:34 a.m. Nov. 7, voice mail message left by me:
   "Rabbi, hi. My name is Robin Black, Robin Black Goldberg. My husband, Richard, and I are members of the synagogue, yours, and our daughter Elizabeth is having a bat mitzvah this coming April. Becoming a bat mitzvah this April.

I guess that I'm calling because I am feeling some conflict about this due in part, maybe entirely, to the fact that my father, who is dying right now, isn't Jewish. My mother is.

"Anyway, we were wondering if we could come in to talk to you about this. Just us. Not Elizabeth. I am really not looking to dump my ambivalence on her. To burden her. Our phone number is 555-1429, and if we could come in, maybe just to sort some of this through, I would really appreciate that."

9:42 a.m. Nov. 7, overstatement to my husband made by me:
"Sometimes I feel that I am the bravest person I have ever met."

9:47 a.m. Nov. 7, deceptively complex thing my brother says to me on the phone:
"There's actually a new book out called *The Half-Jewish Book* that I was going to buy you for Christmas, but it costs twenty-five dollars. In fact, I was wondering if maybe this Christmas we could just skip grown-up gifts altogether."

9:47 a.m. Nov. 7, my immediate response:
"Actually, I could really use some presents this year."

My most prized possession:
The handsewn Christmas stocking my grandmother made for me. It's velvet, a deep red that I have never been able to match. Edged in green satin ribbon and covered with miniature toys. A half-inch frying pan with quarter-inch fried eggs. An impossibly small pair of scissors, which actually do cut. And jingle bells. There's a little baby doll girl attached to the center of the front, and when you lay the stocking flat her eyes fall shut. But when the stocking is hung, her eyes open wide. They're blue, just like mine. I liked knowing as a child that the doll was hanging there to watch Santa Claus when he arrived. I named her Robin, after myself.

6:03 p.m. Nov. 7, snippet of conversation between my husband and me:
"The rabbi didn't return my call, by the way. I guess my spiritual crisis can just wait."
"Well, I'm not trying to excuse the guy, but generally Monday is their day off. They work weekends, you know."
"Oh. No. I didn't know."

10:12 a.m. Nov. 8, snippet of my telephone conversation with the rabbi:
"So, I don't know, I assume, Rabbi, that this isn't uncommon. People who are mixed. Having mixed feelings. You've dealt with this kind of thing before, I assume?"
"Well, yes. Though usually it's been resolved by now."
"Oh."
"But why don't you and Richard come in and we'll see where we go from here."
"Thank you. That would be great."

Reason my father is concerned about authorizing anyone to pull the plug:
  Fear of eternal damnation as a result of assisting in his own suicide, which is a mortal sin.

Helpful hint from me to you:
  The proportions on the Manischewitz Matzo Meal box are wrong. In their matzo ball recipe. You want to put in a lot more liquid than they say. Twice as much. And you want to let the mixture get back up to room temperature after you have refrigerated it. And you want to refrigerate it for longer than they say. And sometimes, for reasons I will never understand, you may have to let them cook for up to three times as long as you think. Even if you have done absolutely everything else right.

4:32 p.m. Nov. 8, statement made by me to Elizabeth that documents my ambivalence about not burdening Elizabeth with my ambivalence:
  "We're going to meet with the rabbi on Friday to discuss my feelings about your bat mitzvah."

Something about Elizabeth that started when she was ten, the meaning of which I do not understand:
  She won't eat pork.

Way she handled this when we were in Italy, where just about every sauce contains pork:
  Asked her parents loudly at every meal: "Is this pig?"

Something that I like about myself:
  Despite enormous temptation, born of tremendous inconvenience (not to mention irritation) I have never misled Elizabeth about whether something we were eating was or was not pig. And never will.

Precise cost, tax excluded, of The Half-Jewish Book: A Celebration:
  USA $22.95
  CANADA $32.95

A request for advice:
  To Whom It May Concern,
  I have a question. I am in need of some advice.
  I am meeting with my rabbi this coming Friday to discuss with him the ambivalence I feel as a half-Jew/half-Southern Methodist in having my daughter bat mitzvahed this coming spring. In having her become a bat mitzvah, that is. My husband will also be at this meeting. I do not know the rabbi at all, but he is about our age, either side of forty. I assume that he is a spiritual person, at least I hope that he is, and I hope that he is an intelligent person as well. Because I think that the problem I am struggling with is a complex one, quicksilver, a matter of balance and of shades of identity.

I have chosen to raise my daughter as a Jew for two reasons. The first is that it is important to my husband that she be raised that way—though to be fair, he would be fair. He's not a bully on matters like this. Or anything, in fact. Not at all. But I like giving him this. The second reason is that I want her to have somewhere to turn in times of loss. I want her to have a spiritual home to come home to. When life hurts her. If she chooses to. I don't have a home like that, and when I have been hit hard, hit with grief, I have longed for that. I have felt at sea.

I think that it's too late for me, but this is a gift of sorts that I want to give to her.

So my question is, on Friday, for this meeting, what should I wear? Seriously. This isn't the punch line. I don't know what the right thing is to wear. I've never met with a rabbi before.

Question Elizabeth will ask when my father dies:
    "Am I allowed to say kaddish for Grandfather even though he wasn't Jewish?"

Authority with which I will say, "Of course":

Circa 1975, my mother on the subject of organized religion:
    "It's all horseshit."

Throughout my childhood, my father on the subject of organized religion:
    "If I really wanted to be rich, filthy rich, wealthy beyond all dreams of avarice, and did not believe in the Lord, Jesus Christ, which I most certainly do, I would make up a religion and just watch the money come pouring in."

After her heart attack, my mother, again, on the subject of religion:
    "I know it's all horseshit, but are you comfortable promising me that someone will say kaddish for me when I am gone?"

Principle by which my cabinets are organized:
    One cabinet is for food and one for ingredients. Some things, like dried beans and like sugar, are hard to categorize, but there are only two cabinets to look in. So nothing that we store is truly lost.

11:57 a.m. Nov. 10, driving to see the rabbi, nicest thing my husband has ever said:
    "I love you, you know."

Rhetorical question I must never ask Elizabeth again:
    "Do you have any idea what this is costing us?"

11:59 a.m. Nov 10, emotion that overwhelms me as we enter the synagogue hand in hand:
    Sadness.

What I am wearing:
    A black skirt and a black turtleneck. My earrings are made of miniature compasses that actually work, and my brooch is a teeny, tiny triptych of an Italian

landscape. They all sort of go together because both the triptych and the compasses are framed in gold.

Number of minutes late the rabbi is for our meeting:
    Twelve.

Noon to 12:12 p.m. Nov. 10, thing I try to do for twelve minutes:
    Not to think the rabbi is keeping us waiting because he thinks that I am a bad Jew.

Letter I will never send:
    To the Authors of *The Half-Jewish Book: A Celebration:*
    First I would like to thank you. For celebrating me. Because I think that you're correct and it isn't done nearly enough. In my opinion. And thank you as well for making a few other points. Like that half-Jews are also half–something else. That the other half isn't just a blank. That's a very important observation and one that I agree does get lost in the shuffle all too often.
    But now I have a terrible confession to make: I hated your book. First of all, there's no index, which is a pain in the ass, but that isn't my main issue here. I only mention the index problem because after I read it, something struck me as odd and I went to look up "religion" in the index. And there wasn't one. "Religion" or "religious observance" or "practices of mourning." Anything like that. But there was no index, and I'm pretty sure, having flipped through the pages again and read the chapter headings, absolutely no discussion of how half-Jews might comfortably handle issues of loss and of mourning. What the role of ritual is. No real examination of the pain that might be inherent for some of us in having nowhere obvious to turn. Because, while I do leave room here for individual choice, there does appear to be, judging from history and all, a pretty strong and common human pull toward wanting to believe. And toward wanting to know what it is that you believe. And what you don't.
    And even toward belonging to a community that shares at least some of your beliefs. And that can help you, I don't know, perform rituals without thinking them through. Without having to make decisions about it all the time.
    Is that a crime?
    I personally find that an impossible thing to have.
    Because every step toward one half is a step away from the other.
    So I do agree with your basic premise, that there's a need to stop treating us all like the problem children of the Judeo-Christian era, but who's kidding whom here?
    Simple, it is not.

Reason I will never send that letter:
    I really haven't figured out why I hated their book so much. And it was kind of nice of them to celebrate me. And, as it turns out, I'm not particularly articulate on the subject of their book. Not yet.

Occasions for the grief that left me feeling at sea:
I lost two pregnancies, two babies I very much wanted to have.

12:25 p.m. Nov. 10, thing my husband accuses me of being, in front of the rabbi, that I deny:
Angry.

12:42 p.m. Nov. 10, statement I hear coming out of my own mouth:
"I feel like I am betraying my father. At a particularly inopportune time."

12:47 p.m. Nov. 10, thing the rabbi accuses me of being, in front of my husband, that I deny:
Angry.

How I feel at being accused of being angry:
Well, angry. Of course.

Snippet of conversation I have had with Elizabeth, time and time again:
Her: Why do I have to go to Hebrew School?
Me: Because nobody made me go.
Her: That doesn't make any sense.
Me: (sigh) I don't care what you do when you grow up. Honestly. I just want
   you to make whatever decisions you make from the inside. The inside
   of something.
Her: You make it sound so simple. Do you know even what we actually do?
Me: Humor me. I'm a mother. I'm allowed to make mistakes. Maybe this is
   another one.
Her: I don't think it's a mistake.
Me: So what's the problem?
Her: It's just boring, that's all.

What I have written so far of the speech I hoped to give at Elizabeth's bat mitzvah:
Just about thirteen years ago, when I was new to mothering, and was very
close to drowning in the joy of having you, somebody, a friend, watching how
I reveled in your every moment, said this to me. She said: Enjoy these days,
because you know, the very first step that your child takes is taken away from you.

At the time, I thought that she was very wise, and maybe she was. And her
wisdom wounded me, because all that I could feel was the completeness I knew in
pressing you to my skin. So this image of your leaving me was painful for me, because it did ring true. And as it turns out, as I now see, it is true that with each day,
with every new challenge you take on and meet so well, you do take steps away
from being the baby I nestled against myself. You have likes and dislikes that differ
from mine. You shed with every passing second another need you have for me. As
you gain competence, strength, independence, tastes of your own. These qualities
you have so beautifully acquired, and that you carry with you so gracefully.

But now I also know that even in her wisdom, my advisor left out the other
side. The other view that I have gained, not from wisdom but through experience.
The salve, the balm, the reason why every mother is not inevitably doomed to

grief. For with each step that my baby girl takes away from me, a woman takes a step in my direction. A beautiful, competent, strong, brilliant, complex, compelling young woman who is my own. You are no further from me now, my love, than you were when you were first born. No further from me now than you were the moment before you were born. You are as close to me now when you stand beside me as you were pressed onto me, an infant, soft and sleeping, sprawled across my chest.

The number of pieces into which my heart breaks when I learn that there is no time allotted for the mother to speak:
    How many pieces are there?

12:41 p.m. Nov. 10, what my husband says as my eyes begin to fill:
    "Are you sure, Rabbi? It would be a really great way for her to feel involved."

One of many reasons I love my husband:
    Moments like that.

12:41 p.m. Nov. 10, the rabbi's response:
    "I'm afraid that isn't possible."

12:43 p.m. Nov. 10, obvious thing that suddenly occurs to me for the first time:
    This bat mitzvah isn't about me.

Reason my mother stopped lighting Shabbos candles when I was eight years old:
    She realized that she was just going through the motions, just reduplicating the customs of her home, and that she didn't believe in the ritual itself.

Two things Elizabeth invariably does at take-off in a plane:
    Prays in Hebrew.
    Holds tight onto her mother's hand.

12:56 p.m. Nov. 10, the one thing I know for sure:
    I want to go home.

Letter I may actually send someday:
    Dear Rabbi,
    It may not have looked like it to you at the time, but meeting with you when we did was actually a tremendous help to me. I actually had to eat some fairly good-size crow with my husband afterward. He had said seeing you might be helpful. I, well to be frank, I scoffed.
    I think that what you said to me that helped the most was . . .

Reason that that sentence never ends:
    I don't really understand why it helped. And to the extent that I think it did, it had nothing to do with him. And I just don't think you can say that in a letter of that kind. A thank-you note to your rabbi.
    In fact I think this is just another letter I will never send.

What I will do while my husband recites the parental blessings in Hebrew:
Stand next to him. Hold his hand. And keep my lips sealed.

Question to ponder:
If the rabbi had told me I'm a bad Jew, why would I care?

Fact that also needs to be pondered:
I would care. I would care a great deal.

Question that persists:
But why?

Odds that someday I will talk to a Christian minister about settling this sense of dislocation in myself:
Fifty-fifty.

The most likely reason that my father will not be attending Elizabeth's bat mitzvah:
He will be dead.

What it looks like when someone draws their dying breath:
I can only tell you what my mother's mother looked like. I went to the door of her room, to check on her, because we knew that she wasn't going to last much longer. I loved her very much. She taught me how to cook. And when I saw her chest move up and then move down I thought to myself, Well, she's okay; and I stood there, in her doorway, relieved and safe because it hadn't happened yet. She lay buried deep in blankets, nothing much left of her, her long hair splayed out gray across a pink pillow case. And as I leaned against the doorjamb, the side with the mezuzah fastened there, watching her I slowly realized that her chest had never risen after that, and that what I had just witnessed was her death.

What my daughter eats when I have scrambled eggs and bacon:
Scrambled eggs.

Where I am left to turn when I am in pain:
Here. There.
And everywhere.

A funny question, repeated one more time:
What exactly is my religion?

Answer that increasingly appeals:
The Patina Approach:
A short period of endurance
For something that is so lovely
It takes your breath away.

Fiction

Michelle Bliss

Virginia Tech Shooting Leaves 33 Dead

The New York Times

April 16, 2007—Thirty-three people were killed today on the campus of Virginia Tech in what appears to be the deadliest shooting rampage in American history, according to federal law-enforcement officials. Many of the victims were students shot in a dorm and a classroom building. . . . The killings occurred in two separate attacks on the campus in Blacksburg, Va. The first at around 7:15 a.m., when two people were shot and killed at a dormitory. More than two and a half hours later, 31 others, including the gunman, were shot and killed across campus in a classroom building, where some of the doors had been chained. Victims were found in different locations around the building.

Lisa called him Seung back then, before all the news reports identified him as Cho.

"Seung, would you like to comment on this story?" she would ask, after the rest of us had discussed at length whatever short story we had read the night before for class, Advanced Fiction Writing, English 4704.

"Anything?" Lisa would tuck her straw-straight blonde hair behind her ears, recross her runner's legs, and wait for something to shatter the silence that kept hovering in the middle of our workshop circle. I usually spent those moments shuffling my papers, taking an inventory of what stories I had placed in my gray Virginia Tech folder and which ones I had pulled out for the remainder of class. A girl across from me would pick at her pencil eraser, carving it with her thumbnails. Others stared at the dusty tile floor in the center of our ring of desks or pulled their sleeves back to peer at their watches, tracing the second hand's path with their eyes. We tried to ignore what was happening, as if our teacher was just calling roll and had already called our names—a pesky administrative task that had to be done, and we had to be patient and sit through it each day.

After maybe five silent seconds, Seung would shake his head back and forth, such a slight gesture it could easily be missed. Then he would lower his face so that the bill of his maroon-and-orange Virginia Tech baseball cap was perpendicular to the top of his desk. Since he usually sat at about the two o'clock mark of our workshop circle, directly across from my spot at around eight or nine o'clock, I rarely saw more than an inch and a half, maybe two, of his pale, narrow chin and drooping, half-moon mouth. After another five seconds of fidgeting and staring, the rest of us would turn to our neighbors and finally to the teacher, hoping the tension would pass over us like a cloud, never imagining that in six months Seung would fire 174 bullets, killing twenty-seven students and five teachers before himself and injuring another twenty-six students in the deadliest school shooting in U.S. history.

"Ok." Soft and forgiving, Lisa's response offered us a bridge back to the discussions and banter we were used to in other classrooms. The moment had passed and we were on to something like "Good Country People" by Flannery O'Connor or maybe a draft of a story by one of us.

Effective beginnings, discussed in a book we read for class called *Fiction Writer's Workshop* by Josip Novakovich, hook the reader instead of punching him. They invite the reader into the story by introducing character, theme, and style, as well as a crisis. The reader feels invested in the story from the beginning. Except you, Seung, never let any of your family members, counselors, roommates, teachers, or classmates invest themselves. Without the news coverage of your death, all I knew was that you were detached, disconcerting, that boy who was barely even physically present. I had no idea that you were a part of my Bible as Literature class, where I was and where you were scheduled to be the morning you died. Now, I can picture where you sat each week, about one o'clock to my seven o'clock. But if our teacher had never told me you were in our class, I would not remember your ghostly presence at all.

Your suitemates described you as a fragile guy, someone they were careful with because they didn't want to send you into some "shut-down, lock-out mode." They said you were a sullen loner, creepily quiet, someone who avoided eye contact and offered only one-word answers—if any. They stopped inviting you out to dinner or to parties when you pulled out a knife and stabbed at their friend's carpet.

One of your psychiatrists said that your severe social anxiety disorder was "painful to see," and your childhood art therapist remembers your depictions of tunnels and caves, which, although not alarming on their own, were indicators of suicidal and homicidal thoughts when coupled with your symptoms of depression. There were also the houses you modeled out of clay, "houses that had no windows or doors."

Your classmates said that you were what you wanted to be—the question mark you scrawled defiantly on the attendance sheet for your British Literature class. Your writings were "like something out of a nightmare," so much so that in the fall of 2005 our English department chair, Lucinda Roy, was forced to pull you from a class in which Professor Nikki Giovanni threatened to resign if you were not removed. Lucinda spent the rest of that semester working with you in a one-on-one poetry workshop.

During her twenty-two-year career, you were one of the most troubled students she ever came across. After the shootings, she appeared on the news, saying, "He was so distant and lonely, it was almost like talking to a hole, as though he wasn't really there most of the time." Back in the fall semester of 2005, during a meeting to discuss your behavior in Giovanni's class, a transcript was written by one of Lucinda's colleagues. It reads: "Lucinda asked if he would remove his sunglasses. It is a very distressing sight, since his face seems very naked and blank without them. It's a great relief to be able to read his face, though there isn't much there."

And your family, they seemed to know you least of all. Your sister said that you were someone she "grew up with and loved." She went on, acknowledging, "Now I feel like I didn't know this person." All along your mother urged you to speak, to make friends, to share anything. She grew so frustrated with you as a child that sometimes she shook you, as though maybe your unhappiness might spill out; maybe your words might emerge.

"We are humbled by this darkness. We feel hopeless, helpless, and lost," your sister confessed. "He has made the world weep."

Lisa's class had intimidated me at first. It was *advanced* fiction, labeled advanced because we were required to hand in three stories of at least fifteen pages throughout the course of the semester, sixteen weeks in the fall of 2006. My previous creative-writing teachers had allowed me to squirm by with just seven or eight pages of introduction—of triggering conflicts and birthing characters that I never intended on contextualizing. And those slap-dash jobs simply wouldn't do in an advanced course. On the first day of class, tight-lipped and attempting to maintain a veneer of seriousness that would soon fade, Lisa handed out a list of the criteria she used to evaluate stories. Among the thirteen items listed, including *well-evoked settings, excellent prose rhythms,* and *clear and interesting themes,* number eleven terrified me most: *evidence of genius.*

A core group of us, eight of the original thirteen, did well under these pressures. We met each of our deadlines with fifteen pages of writing or more and turned in workshop critiques in letter format to our peers and to Lisa, each brimming with compliments and gentle suggestions for improvement.

Members of the "rebel group" usually turned in much shorter drafts, days after their deadlines had lapsed. They rarely wrote critiques for the rest of us and tended to skip class when their material wasn't up for workshop. Occasionally they missed their own workshops as well, the ultimate creative writing taboo. Seung was the only exception to both groups, attending every class but never sharing his work or participating in our discussions.

Without most of the rebels, most of the time, we usually scooted extra desks out of the way to tighten our workshop circle. The classroom was big enough to hold about forty students and always seemed bare—the eight of us and Lisa, scrunched in the middle of four cinder-block walls and a maze of desks, with a chalk board and overhead projector we rarely used.

In class, we discussed how setting conveys a certain place at a certain time so that the place, the people, and the action are integrated. You could not have picked a more serene, undeserving setting to destroy. You killed the very people who were talented enough, brave enough, smart enough, and caring enough to actually help you. And you did it in my home. You were a trespasser in the soft, green hills of my town; the safe, stone walls of my school; the strong, unsuspecting patters of my heart. And you slipped out the back door before I could claim what was mine.

In my notes on Novakovich's text, I marked that, in fiction, "whatever happens psychologically can be expressed in the environment." And it's true. Trees are no longer bare in Blacksburg. Instead, I see their trunks adorned with the strips of orange and maroon fabric that were tied around them in the days after. The post office is no longer a welcoming downtown fixture where I send care packages to my friends or premiums to the local radio station's loyal donors. Instead, it's another stop along your dark path, where you mailed your letters and pictures and videos mere minutes before chaining the doors of Norris Hall.

I started wondering how you got to the post office when I saw a picture of you pointing the barrel of your gun at me through my computer screen. Did you take Washington to Main? Or did you run behind my stadium, using the shade of my trees to avoid being seen? Did you cut through the parking lot of my apartment complex? We may have missed each other by only two or three minutes that morning.

And that radio station, WUVT 90.7 FM, where I served as general manager, is no longer my refuge from classes and papers and bad music. It's where I couldn't stand to be, with all of the reporters' nosy, insensitive questions; with the choked voices of my DJs and friends; without Kevin, who was in room 207 of Norris Hall, the German class where you murdered his teacher and four students and wounded Kevin and six more students.

After I was released from Bible as Literature class that day, I called everyone from the station and no one could find our chief engineer, Kevin. I called my friend Kim again and again, hoping to hear that Kevin's cell phone had run out of battery power or that our attempts to reach him had all been lost in the swarm of phone calls in Blacksburg. "I'm ok," she said. "But we can't get a hold of Kevin." "He still isn't picking up." "We just checked his schedule and he had class in Norris." "We're driving to the hospital in Radford." "We're driving to the hospital in Christiansburg." "They can't tell us if he's here." "I just called his mom; she's leaving Pittsburgh right now. I don't know what to tell her—we don't know where he is."

A group of probably twenty of us sat in the waiting room of the ICU at Montgomery Regional Hospital, waiting for Kevin to get out of surgery. We watched press conferences and CNN until a nurse rolled his bed by us, and despite how pale he was, how naked he appeared under his white cotton gown, the blood cleaned from his legs, stomach, chest, and hands, a bullet still lodged inside of him, we knew he would recover. In that brief interaction, Kevin made us all laugh loudly, our nerves pouring out as we crowded around him. He asked what the grand total of our spring fundraiser had been—it was a weeklong pledge-a-thon that had ended at midnight on April 16, less than ten hours before you hurt Kevin. He would eventually request that donations to his recovery be made to WUVT. Some time later that night, his mom thanked us for being there for her son. She had driven several hours that day, not knowing whether Kevin was alive or dead.

You shot Kevin twice in his right leg, one bullet tearing an inchlong gash in his femoral artery. His doctor later said that Kevin knew he was bleeding to death, so he made a tourniquet out of electrical wire he found in his classroom, something he had learned as an Eagle Scout. At the station, during a long year plagued with transmitter malfunctions, we always joked that Kevin could fix anything—and he can.

Partway through the semester we read the story "Good Country People." Flannery O'Connor caught me off-guard as always when the Bible-selling gentleman lured Olga to the top of that two-story barn. As he detached her artificial leg, before pulling out a flask of whiskey and a deck of dirty playing cards from a hollowed-out Bible, I hoped, as I had in the past, that he would put her leg back on and help her down the ladder—like the good country people he pretended to be.

Throughout our class, we read and wrote and talked about subjects like prostitution, drug sales, abortions, date-rape drugs, and violent car crashes. More specifically, I remember our stories containing the details of a baby accidentally thrown into an overhead fan and a double suicide involving a professor and student. Everyone, young and old, rich and poor, good and bad, needs a way to rid themselves of their own thoughts. To scream and curse and cry—to speak—and work through their anger. To escape from the Bible-selling gentleman within us all. To cleanse and begin anew.

Even with our cathartic discussions and writings for class, our disgust and surprise and interest at our own words and how they must have found their way onto the page, we still wondered how Olga would ever get down from that ledge, hoping she would eventually recover from such a shock. On the morning of April 17, 2007, I imagine that other people in Blacksburg awoke as I did, stuck up in that old barn, covered in a groggy haze that allowed me to fleetingly forget the shock of the day before—174 bullets fired; thirty-two innocent people killed; twenty-six innocent people injured; the incomprehensible math of our tragedy.

And from Seung, nothing. No words.

Voice, according to my class notes, is a metaphor that's difficult to define. Persona voices "create the illusion of someone speaking to the reader, in the first person." You attempted to create your persona through death. You had twenty-three years to define who you were and, instead, you waited until the very end to rant about injustices trivial, if even real, in comparison to the injustice you caused. Your videos, dubbed "manifestos" by the media you sent them to, do not cover your dead body in a veil of credibility. They are not an excuse.

During the estimated ten to twelve minutes of shooting your 9mm Glock and .22 caliber Walther at point-blank range within rooms 204, 206, 207, and 211 of Norris Hall, you remained silent. "He never uttered a sound during his entire shooting spree—no invectives, no rationale, no comments, nothing," explained the Virginia Tech Review Panel's report released in August 2007. "Even during this extreme situation at the end of his life, he did not speak to anyone."

On April 19, 2007, a friend of mine, Paul, e-mailed me a list of what he called the "torturous ironies at Virginia Tech." He wrote that "after years of being endlessly offered an audience, a dialogue with his fellow students, his teachers, and counselors, he now wants to command an audience, demand a monologue." He added that "after years of being a self-described question mark, he now wants to provide answers." Paul ends this list, declaring, "the most painful irony of all is this: now that he is finally ready to speak, I can't hear him."

But sometimes, I think that I can. Its physicality—your garbled, monotone words recorded and preserved forever in videos displayed as newsworthy—I can struggle to set aside. The echoes of your voice, though—a terrifying continuation of spirit, of which I keep hoping I've seen the final instance—I cannot bear. In this sense, I hear your voice all the time. I heard your voice when Ryan Lambourn, a twenty-one-year-old man in Australia, created a video game called V-Tech Rampage that traces your route from West A.J. to my post office to Norris, allowing players to shoot bystanders who flail their arms and scream. "Shine" by Collective Soul, with the lyrics you wrote on the walls of your suite: "Teach me how to speak / Teach me how to share / Teach me where to go," is played for the course of the game.

I heard your voice on the radio when Neal Boortz, a nationally syndicated talk-radio host, asked why your victims couldn't defend themselves against you, armed with a gun in each hand, rushing into classrooms averaging 24' × 25'. "How far have we advanced in the wussification of America?" Boortz asked, before continuing, "It seems that standing in terror waiting for your turn to be executed was the right thing to do, and any questions as to why twenty-five students didn't try to rush and overpower Cho Seung-Hui are just examples of right-wing maniacal bias. Surrender—comply—adjust."

I heard your voice from Nathan Jones at Penn State University, who dressed up as one of your victims for Halloween. Jones explained why he dressed up in a Virginia Tech T-shirt, complete with fake bullet wounds and blood dripping down his chest. "It's not that it was funny, it's that we are notorious and infamous in State College, so we have to do things that push the envelope just for shock value." He went on to defend his actions: "The thing is, everybody's making a big stink about Virginia Tech. Virginia Tech was thirty-two deaths out of the twenty-six thousand that happen in America every day." He added, "That's the problem with college students. They all live in an ivory tower of privilege. They don't understand, when it all boils down to it, it's someone wearing a costume."

I heard your voice from NBC News President Steve Capus, who aired your tapes mere hours after receiving them, letting the family members and friends of the deceased and injured stumble upon graphic pictures of you, holding your guns, the last image their loved one may have witnessed.

I continue to hear your voice with the barrage of daily headlines:

> 5 Hospitalized After 14-Year-Old Goes on Shooting Rampage at Cleveland High School (Fox News, October 11, 2007)
> Police: Pennsylvania boy planned 'Columbine' event at high school (CNN, October 11, 2007)
> High School Gunman in Finland Kills Self, Eight Others, Warns of Shooting on YouTube (Fox News, November 7, 2007)
> Omaha Mall Massacre: Police Say 20-Year-Old Gunman Killed 8 People, Wounded 5 Others, Before Killing Himself (CBS News, December 6, 2007)
> Terror at Northern Illinois University: Gunman was a former student armed with an arsenal of weapons (WQAD-TV, February 14, 2008)

"There doesn't seem to be much enthusiasm in our class—about anything." Lisa bobbed her head back and forth with each word as she tried to make some sense out of the situation. "Several people have just dropped off. I mean, they're still registered for our class, but they just never come and haven't turned anything in. It's weird."

"Well, yeah," I paused, suddenly aware that what I chose to say could come across as a criticism of Lisa, the last thing I wanted to do to a teacher who inspired me to write. We stood in her office after our first conference that semester to talk about one of my workshop pieces. Her office was cozy, with chocolates and cups of warm tea. The walls were lined with overflowing bookshelves—stacks of poetry here and piles of fiction there—organized chaos. Her door had several posters taped to the front of it, including one to promote her award-winning book *Toy Guns*.

I would return to her office several times to talk about my class work but also to talk about graduate schools. At the start of the spring 2007 semester, after our class had ended, she wrote letters of recommendation for me and critiqued a few of the essays for my writing portfolio. She also loaned me a copy of a book her friend wrote. The book was filled with her notes to the writer, and I relished such a voyeuristic look at two friends communicating right there on the page.

During our meeting that day, Lisa drew a detailed map of my story with circles and arrows and lists of which characters were where and did what to whom and why. I watched her pencil brush the paper, quickly transcribing her thoughts into a visual representation of my words. Then she handed me her copy of my story. It was filled with her notes: plus signs for a strong line or clear idea and prompting questions to help me navigate through the murky themes and skeletal characters I was now determined to improve in following drafts.

"I guess I've noticed that only a certain group of us ever turn anything in or talk in class," I finally responded. "Like Marilyn," I continued, hoping an example would help. "She's a great writer but she never shows up or turns in her work."

"I know. She *is* a great writer," Lisa sighed. "And there are a bunch of students in our class just like her."

"But then we have people like John," I wanted to highlight the positive as well. "He always does his work and gives good feedback for us," I explained. And he did. Although I disagreed with a lot of what he said, I knew that his opinion was worthwhile and that without his loud laugh and inexhaustible voice our classroom discussions would have fallen short of the hour and fifteen minutes we were required to fill. Our reverberations of thought would have slowed and softened even more than they already did, tired from traveling from one side of the workshop circle back to the other, eventually vanishing in the void around which our desks were arranged.

"Oh yes. I've taught him before. He's great."

Lisa paused, glancing out into the hall before asking, "What about Seung?" She was obviously concerned, looking anywhere for an answer that might explain his strange behavior. I didn't know it then, but she had already alerted the associate dean of Liberal Arts and Human Sciences about him in early September, only a few weeks into our semester. The report of the Virginia Tech Review Panel, requested by Governor Tim Kaine, says that at that time, the associate dean found "no mention of mental health issues or police reports," even though Lucinda Roy had already reported Seung's writing to the associate dean and to a web of other university officials—the vice president for Student Affairs, the assistant provost, the Judicial Affairs director, counselors at the Cook Counseling Center, among others. All of Lucinda's warnings to university officials were eventually ignored or discarded, with the reasoning that since his writing didn't "contain a threat to anyone's immediate safety," Seung had the right to free speech.

"Um."

"I mean, have you ever talked to him? Does he talk to anyone in our class?" she asked hopefully. In addition to alerting the dean, Lisa had encouraged Seung to get counseling with her that fall, which he declined.

"Um." I had talked to just about everyone in that class for one reason or another. Betsy and I were both working on our writing portfolios to apply to graduate school. Terry was up on the indie-music scene in Blacksburg and listened to WUVT. I even saw John at a professor's keg party I went to for a research project that my friend was doing, something about watching cars drive by and counting how many people wore their seat belts.

But even when I think back to days when the class before ours let out late and we all had to camp out in the hallway, eating vending-machine snacks and sitting down against the walls, stretching our legs out on the floor and maybe finishing our reading, usually just talking about this and that, I can't hear his voice or see where he sat among us.

I think I finally told Lisa that I wasn't sure if Seung spoke English, or if he was embarrassed by the little English he could speak.

"Well what about the workshop critiques he's given to you?"

In my mind I turned the pages of the stack of critiques I had received so far that semester, never finding his. "I never got any from him."

"Really? He's been turning them in to me."

"I'm pretty sure. I could double-check—"

"No, I'm sure you're right," Lisa breathed in and out. "I've been teaching him outside of class each week because he doesn't ever say anything in class."

"Does he talk to you then?"

"Sometimes he'll go a half-hour without saying anything to me, just working in my office, even when I ask him questions."

"Oh."

You are not entitled to an ending. But more than I want to admit, your cheap, surprise farewell doesn't, won't end. At night, when I check the locks to my house at least twice, along with the back corners of my too-big walk-in closet, the bath-tub behind that opaque curtain, and underneath the bed, you don't end. Around midnight, when my heater's clicks and drums start to murmur, my dog's irregu-lar snores whisper, and my smoke detector's green light floats above me like a target, you don't end. Each week when I survey my graduate classrooms at the University of North Carolina at Wilmington for windows—big, small, *I could fit through that*, easy-to-open, first floor, second floor, *how many steps to get there?*— and exits—nearby doors, flights of stairs, long and bare hallways—and ducking places—desks, tables, cabinets, *where else?*—and barricades—bookshelves, file cabinets, chairs, me—you don't end. In early spring, when it's time for our annual lock-down drill at the elementary school where I work as a teacher assistant and I show my elementary students how to hide under their desks and tables, away from our window and door, within the cabinets under our classroom sink that they eagerly climb into, giggling as though it's just a game of hide-and-seek, I know that you won't end yet.

And every day, when I wonder why you didn't come to our Bible as Literature class that morning with your guns ready; when I draw a map of our classroom, Pamplin 1001, in my head, circling the second seat from the door, mine, and counting the eleven steps you would have taken from the front en-trance and the four steps you would have taken to my desk; when I catch shards of our class discussion you missed that morning—Abner, the commander of Saul's army—carrying our swords—violence begetting violence—history repeat-ing itself; when I peer through those bottom few inches of our classroom window not covered by blinds to see a line of police officers sprinting by, ready to fire; when I turn on that television in Pamplin 1001, the one a small group of us stared at for two hours, hearing the local news anchors say "seven to eight casualties" and "Norris 204 and 205," while teachers told us to stay calm and quiet, to move away from those windows and the door, to keep trying to reach our parents on cell phones; when I replay the phone conversations I had with my family and friends and even acquaintances while I waited for a teacher to tell us all that we could go home now, not realizing that only the worst news could have traveled that fast, that not everyone would get to go home; and when I see those unarmed boys from the Corps of Cadets bravely guarding the front entrance, not knowing that you were already dead—I'm not sure you will ever end.

Lisa e-mailed our whole class a day or so after the shootings, asking us to come by her office and check in with her so that she could see us and talk about anything we wanted. I stopped by a few hours after I got the e-mail and tried to turn around when I saw another student already in her office. She saw me in the hallway and beckoned me to come inside. The other student had not been in our fiction class, and instead, he was in my Bible as Literature class.

He continued talking as I walked in Lisa's office and sat down. He talked about some of his writings, a poem he had written about a chair—some sort of metaphor to provide distance from what had happened—that read long and I knew immediately that I didn't like it, and philosophy. I tried to keep up, nodding and nodding, not understanding anything being said. At one point I apologized, said that they were having a wonderfully intellectual conversation, but that I just couldn't focus, my mind couldn't work that way or that much, right then. After an hour or so—the time felt infinite as I repeatedly tried to enter the conversation, to care at all, beginning to understand the difficult months of polite, confused, unnecessary small talk that follow a tragedy, that we all had ahead of us—I found a way to worm out of Lisa's office when he was leaving and another student was arriving.

Revision. "Don't fear changing your text radically in search of its best possible shape," advises Novakovich. "And certainly don't hesitate to get rid of whatever does not work." You.

Soundtrack

Lisa Groen Braner

1968

He sings a Beatles song, "Hey Jude," when I am just a baby. It plays on the radio. There are four master composers that begin with the letter B, he tells me later: Beethoven, Brahms, Bach, and the Beatles. My dad sings the Beatles.

1974

I listen to Julie Andrews in my bedroom, scratch the needle across the black plastic and turn up the volume. My sister and I dance and sing about spoons of sugar and flying kites. The baby with fuzzy hair bounces and smiles in my mom's arms—our new sister.

1981

On a spring day after school, I walk home with a boy who plays guitar. He's an eighth-grader with Jimi Hendrix hands. When he plays "Fire" I feel it, watching him strum, sing, and stir. Electric.

1984

Whenever you get scared up here, Dad says, just sing James Brown. Point your skis downhill and sing "I Feel Good." So I do. I ski the powder and sing—tips under snow, around the trees and through the clouds—close behind him.

1990

"The Sky Is Crying" in my empty college apartment. In a room of two chairs, a table, my roommate's stereo, and a glass of wine, my first love shatters. The crack in my heart widens with each blue note B. B. breaks open, spilling Merlot all over the white carpet.

1993

In the workaday world of subway stops and newspapers, I lose myself. One morning, a song rises up in the station. A hidden man sings words that fall on me like raindrops in a desert—"Wade in the Water." I leave my job and start writing.

1994

My future husband and I walk together through the Tuileries. A love song plays, Billy Joel, against Paris twilight. It's a cold June and the crepes warm our hands as we walk past Notre Dame, over the Seine, onto a lamplit street.

1997

No heartbeat, says the doctor. No baby. I didn't hear much after that. As I drive home from the hospital, Mary Chapin Carpenter sings about trouble, sorrow, and choosing to fly. I pack her words away somewhere to play them back later when I can listen.

1998

My newborn son likes it when I sing "Rock-a-Bye-Baby." He locks eyes with me at my breast, smiling at the sudden song. Milk spills from his mouth and rolls down his chin, onto the collar of his clean pajamas. He forgets about the milk when I sing.

2000

I stand in an old pew swaying to a hymn I've never heard before while my newborn daughter sleeps on my shoulder. The words stop in my throat. "Precious Lord, take my hand." I sink into the sound and feel buoyant, helped to stand.

2006

I try to sing "Blue Bayou" for my dad, as I do for my children at night. I know the lyrics, the melody, but my voice won't carry today, not for him lying there dying. The song wavers flat. He is too tired and polite to protest. I stop and sit next to him. It's hard to sing when you're crying, I tell him. Without moving he nods his head yes and understands.

Les Cruel Shoes

John Bresland

Introduction

One day, after I'd been living in Paris for several years, an older French couple stopped me outside a *quincaillerie* and asked for directions to Jules Joffrin, a local métro station. Had they known I was American, I doubt they would have asked, but they mistook me for a native and I struggled to contain my delight.

For years I had longed to be taken for one of them. Which longing had nothing to do with politics or history. It was neither a renunciation of my American belief that one man can make a difference, nor an embrace of the European view that it takes a village. Simply, I wanted to be seen as competent. A man of utility rather than a tourist.

"Keep going where you're going," I said. "Two blocks and you're there." That was that. From then on, by a slight but perceptible degree, I felt a little less clumsy, a little less like a fannypack of a man.

This four-minute video essay, "Les Cruel Shoes," shot with a borrowed mini-DV camcorder, shows one way to locate a sense of belonging, a sense of home, amid the most popular tourist destination on Earth.

"Les Cruel Shoes"

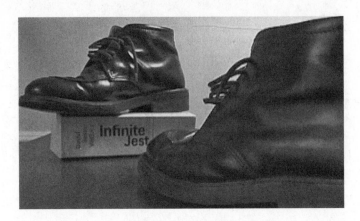

A few years ago, when I first moved here, I found this apartment. I got a local phone number and I got a Paris mailing address. And I got a really great haircut. I bought expensive shoes—beautiful, cruel Italian shoes. And I got a job. That's how I learned to speak French. Getting a job was key because everything fell into place after that. I learned the language—sort of. And I made a couple of friends. This took some time.

I rode the subway to work and, you know, there are these windows all around you. And sometimes I'd check myself out. I'd been living in France for years, checking myself out in subway windows thinking, I still look like a tourist. And that feeling never quite went away.

It was around this time I started running again. You know—jogging. Something I haven't done since high school. And it turned out to be a surprisingly intimate way to see the city. A little spooky sometimes, but intimate. And so different from what I saw during the day.

Take the cobblestone streets. Charming enough by day but, at night? Pretty much just creepy. And those turn of the century buildings, like sculpted works of art during the day, sprout graffiti in the dark.

I think it's fair to say the French are opposed to jogging. Something in their DNA forbidding them to wear sweatpants in public. So they sleep in. And every morning I'm the only runner out there. I'm not exaggerating, either. It's not like I see a lone runner every once in a while. I'm saying I see nobody. Ever.

Running is how I began to feel a little less like a tourist because, even if I look ridiculous, I know the names of these streets, and I know where they lead.

Source: Bresland, John. "Les Cruel Shoes." *Blackbird: An Online Journal of Literature and the Arts*. 4:1 (Spring 2005). http://www.blackbird.vcu.edu/v4n1/gallery/bresland/intro.htm

Befriending Barbie

Shari Caudron

Debbie Baker has extraordinary fingernails. They're long. Very long. And pink. Fantastically pink. So pink that if you weren't completely focused on your conversation with her, you'd be distracted by them. I'm trying not to be. I'm trying to learn why Debbie Baker has more than 3,000 Barbie dolls in her collection.

"So tell me," I ask, "what is it about Barbie that makes you so excited?"

Debbie straightens her right arm and gazes at her spread fingernails. "It's because Barbie is so beauuuutiful," she says. "She's hip. She keeps up with the trends. And she can do anything." Debbie falls silent for a moment as she thinks about all Barbie has accomplished. "I mean she can be a veterinarian. A stewardess. A secretary. *Anything*."

I start to ask about Barbie's other careers when we're interrupted by a stout older woman with dull gray hair. "I need to put up the decorations for tonight's dinner and I can't get into the ballroom," she says. Debbie tells her to use the same entrance that was used for the fashion show. The woman stares at her, mystified.

"I'm with the design company," she says. "I didn't go to the fashion show."

"Oh!" Debbie apologizes. "You looked like a Barbie collector."

The woman widens her eyes and takes a step backward. She looks as if she's just been accused of being a racist, or wearing a thong. "I don't *think* so," she says, and huffs off.

Out of curiosity, I ask Debbie what a Barbie collector looks like.

"Those of us who love Barbie light up whenever we see anything to do with her. We love the dolls. We love the clothes. We love the Barbie '*B.*' And pink," she says, waving her lacquered nails. "We really, really love pink."

I've come to the 22nd annual National Barbie Doll Collectors Convention in an effort to understand the extraordinary attraction to the 11-½-inch plastic doll. A thousand men and women from all over the world have registered and converged on the Adam's Mark Hotel in downtown Denver for four days of doll shopping, workshops and social events.

According to people who study this sort of thing, doll collecting—especially Barbies—is second only to stamp collecting as the most popular collecting hobby in America. As an avowed non-collector, I want to know what the fuss is about. Years ago, I tried collecting antique Roseville pottery and actually managed to acquire five pieces before I lost three of them in a break-up. Of the two I have left, one is chipped and now worth maybe twelve dollars. I'm just not good at this sort of thing. I get bored easily. Plus, I think fanatics are a bit strange. I once attended a slide show given by an avid rock collector who described various pieces in her collection as "droolers" and "show-offs." After advancing to a slide of a rock with sparkling purple crystals, the rock collector slumped in her chair. "Ohhhh," she said. "This one could win a pageant." Afterward, I invited friends to stone me to death if I ever got like that. Because I'm not overly passionate by nature, I'm curious about people who are. A Barbie convention, the kind of place I'd normally not be caught dead at, seems the ideal place to understand where this kind of zeal comes from. Debbie Baker, the convention co-chair, is my first interview and she's giving me a crash course in all things Barbie.

"There are two kinds of collectors," she explains. First there are the people like her who keep their Barbies in the original boxes. To be of any value, the boxes must be clean with no razor cuts or dents. Debbie boasts that all of the 3,000 Barbies arranged around her small apartment are indeed fully boxed. The other group of collectors is known, somewhat disparagingly, as the "de-boxers." These are people who experience no remorse in removing Barbie from her cardboard casing even though the doll's value drops anywhere from forty to eighty percent upon exit. Debbie doesn't get these people.

"I can't watch anyone take Barbie out of her box," she says. "It hurts too much."

When pressed, Debbie confesses that when she first started collecting Barbies at age 18, she too was indiscriminate in her choice of dolls. In the box, out of the box—it didn't much matter. But she soon realized this lack of discipline would overwhelm her.

"If I bought every doll out there, I'd have no place to store them all," she says.

So Debbie decided early on to pursue only the most perfect and pristine specimens. Today, her collection is so valuable she's had to purchase additional insurance on her home.

"Do you collect anything else?" I ask.

"Oh definitely. I collect, let's see, Depression glass, elephants, butterflies, antiques. Oh, and chickens. I love chickens. My whole kitchen is filled with chickens. My convention co-chair also collects chickens and whenever we buy one for ourselves we have to buy one for each other."

"I see," I reply, although of course I don't see at all. I don't understand chickens. I don't understand Barbies. And while Debbie says that she would really like to spend more time with me, she has, you know, a convention to run. She stands and shakes my hand.

"Feel free to walk around," she says. "Barbie people are really friendly."

Debbie walks off to manage some co-chair mini-crisis and I walk into the convention sales area, which won't open for another fifteen minutes. Behind a pink cord, about 150 people wearing psychedelic clothing are standing in line. The theme of this year's conference is "Rocky Mountain Mod," which commemorates the Barbie era from 1968 to 1972, a time when Barbie wore bell-bottoms, hip-huggers and hot pants. To get into the spirit, conventioneers were encouraged to don their own mod-era clothing and every last one of them seems to have complied. In line are people wearing abstract geometric prints, Afro wigs and lime-green fringed vests. Two men at the front of the line are wearing matching striped bell-bottoms, white belts and platform shoes. Any moment now, I expect them to burst into a rendition of "I Got You Babe."

Taking advantage of my privileged position inside the pink cord, I walk around to get a good look at the sales items before the crowd converges. In the sales area, vendors are putting the final finishing touches on display booths and tables that are filled to overflowing with clothing, accessories, books, teeny-tiny jewelry, and more dolls than I've ever seen gathered in one place. The array of dolls is truly mind-boggling. There are I Love Lucy Barbies, Little Bo Peep Barbies, Erika Kane Barbies and Olympic Athlete Barbies. There are Barbies equipped for college, Barbies outfitted as medics in Desert Storm, and a presidential candidate Barbie who ran in both the 1992 and 2000 elections on a platform of animal rights, educational excellence and opportunity for girls. Obviously, Barbie is trying to repair her image. There's even a full military series of Barbies whose costumes, the boxes say, were approved by the Pentagon to ensure realism.

Turning a corner, I spot a boxed doll called the Big Boob Barbie. I stop to stare at it. Her. Whatever. How can there be a doll whose bust is bigger than the original Barbie whose figure, were she a real woman, would measure 39–18–33? I move to get a good look at Big Boob Barbie. She is lying on the sales table in a tight skirt and see-through blouse and appears identical to the standard-issue Barbie except that her breasts cover her entire torso and swell out spectacularly on either side of her body. Plus, she has large brown nipples. Something tells me this may not be an official issue from Mattel.

I stare at the doll with a kind of train-wreck fascination until Mattel's public relations representative, a thin young woman named Katie Caratelli, calls me from across the room.

"There you are!" she says.

I spin around in an effort to shield the well-endowed source of my enchantment. Either Katie hasn't noticed me staring at the doll, or she's too polite to mention it.

Katie grabs my elbow and steers me into an adjoining sales room, stopping along the way to point out the new 30th anniversary Malibu Barbie. "This is the official convention doll," she says, pointing to the dime-sized convention logo embroidered onto Malibu Barbie's tiny yellow beach towel. This particular Barbie has a turquoise one-piece bathing suit, surfboard-straight blond hair, and pink sunglasses just like the original Malibu Barbie thirty years ago. The only difference between that doll and this one is that this one comes equipped with sunscreen.

"See!" Katie says. "It's SPF 30!"

She picks up the box and holds it toward me with two hands as if she's presenting me with a bouquet of roses. I peer inside.

"Nice," I say, although in reality, I fail to come up with anything that resembles a reaction to the doll.

Katie puts the doll back on the shelf and we walk over to a large, well-stocked display booth in the center of the sales room. The booth features dolls from a company named Doll Attic, which is owned by Sandi Holder, a middle-aged woman from California with short reddish-brown hair. I chat with Sandi and learn that she started collecting Barbies when her two daughters were little. Her girls are now in high school and her collection has grown from a part-time family hobby into a 16-hour-a-day Barbie empire that does close to one million dollars in annual sales. She tells me her favorite Barbies are the Bubble Cuts.

"Which ones are those?" I ask.

Sandi leads me to a display table where rows of boxed dolls are stacked five high and arranged chronologically by year of issue. She tells me the Bubble Cuts were produced between 1961 and 1967 and were so named because of the lacquered bouffant-style hairdo. Picture Jackie Kennedy with reddish hair and you have some idea what a Bubble Cut is all about. As I admire the doll, my eyes catch sight of a vintage Barbie with a ponytail and black-and-white striped one-piece bathing suit.

Before I can stop myself, I tell Sandi, "That's the one my sisters played with!" Although I didn't play with Barbie, my older sisters had been fans and their old dolls—including the vintage Barbie on display here—were still around the house when I was a kid. Oddly, I find myself a little thrilled to recognize the doll. I confess this to Sandi.

She laughs. "That's what Barbie is all about," she says. "It's about reliving good memories and helping people get back a bit of their childhood." Sandi, who manages one of the largest Barbie auctions in the country, says the value of those childhood memories is going up each year. At her last auction, an in-the-box original Barbie issued in 1959 went for $15,750—a new auction record. The original price was three dollars. "But for me, money is secondary," she says. "What I like is bringing joy to people's lives."

I ask Sandi if she keeps her own dolls in their boxes. "No way!" she says. "It's like really anal to me to keep them in the box. Of course I respect people who want to do that. I mean, they're my customers. But when I see a Barbie who's been boxed for decades I feel like she's screaming: *Take me out! Take me out!*"

Sandi turns and introduces me to her assistant, George Marmolejo, a veterinarian from the San Francisco Bay Area who started collecting Barbies in the mid 1980s. He's short, wearing a tie-dyed T-shirt and a peace sign around his neck. At last count, he says, George had over 1,000 dolls in his collection, both in the box and out. Unlike other collectors, George swings both ways. But George's affection is not solely reserved for Barbie. He also collects children's books, old toys, vinyl records, and doll accessories.

"Some people collect fishing lures and duck decoys," he says. "That's not my thing, but I can understand why they do it. I mean I'm here, right?" George spreads his arms and looks around the sales room. "Where else can I be surrounded by 1,000 people who understand my passion and don't think I'm nuts when I spend $100 on doll clothes?"

I look around the room at zillions of dolls on display. Where else indeed?

George walks me through Barbie's various incarnations while pointing to dolls on the display table. I learn that Barbie #1 had an exotic face with white irises. Barbie #3 was less exotic, smelled like crayons, and had a tendency to fade. Barbie #5 was a red head with a hollow body. By the time she came around, the fading problem had been worked out.

We come to Sandi's favorite doll and in an effort to show off my new knowledge, I tell George: "Those are the Bubble Heads, right?"

He corrects me. "They're called Bubble *Cuts.*"

George continues his historical tour and I learn about Talker Barbies, the American Girls, Twist 'n Turns—more commonly known as TNTs, and the Living Barbie, who was entirely posable and had flexible hands.

"Are there any other dolls still on your wish list?" I ask.

"Mostly, I'm satisfied with my collection."

"Really? There's nothing else you want?"

"Well," George admits. "I've been looking for a Glimmer Glamour Barbie, which was a Sears exclusive. She goes for between $1,700 and $1,800."

The 22nd Annual National Barbie Doll Collectors Convention is an especially poignant one for collectors because Ruth Handler, the Polish immigrant who created Barbie, recently passed away at the age of 85. After talking with George, I walk into the center of the convention area and see that a memorial to Handler has been set up on a card table. A vase with pink roses sits next to a journal where conference goers can record their thoughts. I scan the entries.

"Without Ruth Handler, all our lives would be emptier."

"Thank you for creating the most beautiful doll in the world that I love so much!!"

"I am 4-ever grateful."

Handler created Barbie, who was named after her daughter Barbara, to be a fashion show doll whose outfits could change with the season, and over the years Barbie's kept up her good fashion sense. According to a fact sheet by Mattel, the company Handler founded, Barbie has had more than a billion pairs of shoes.

She receives over 100 additions to her wardrobe annually, including designs by Givenchy, Versace, Vera Wang and Gucci. Altogether, more than 105 million yards of fabric have gone into producing fashions for Barbie and her friends, making Mattel one of the largest apparel manufacturers in the world.

But to think Barbie is all about clothes would be to sell her short for she is, in fact, quite accomplished, having dabbled in more than 80 careers over the years. She's also an animal lover who's cared for more than 43 pets, including 21 dogs, 14 horses, three ponies, a parrot and a panda. The unquenchable thirst for all things Barbie has swelled the Barbie line into a $2.5 billion-a-year industry. If placed head to toe, the number of Barbie dolls and her family members sold since 1959 would circle the earth more than seven times. That's assuming you could get all those dolls together, which is nigh on impossible. The craze in collecting means that countless Barbies have been taken out of circulation and put on display in the back bedrooms of suburban homes all across America.

All of which begs the question: *why?*

My understanding of Barbie still far from complete, I drive downtown and subject myself to a second day at Rocky Mountain Mod. Upon arriving at the hotel, I look at the convention program and try to decide what activity to attend. Unfortunately, I've already missed the Shagadelic Catwalk fashion show, and the competition room—where conventioneers have entered treasured pieces of their collections for prizes—won't be open until this afternoon. Reading the program, I learn that the rules of the competition are stiff. A doll dressed in "Sparkle Squares," for instance, will not be judged against "Jump Into Lace."

Looking at the schedule, I notice that the Fashion Doll Stole Workshop has just started. Deciding it's time for an up-close Barbie experience, I head to a small windowless conference room and sit down behind a long narrow table covered, naturally, in a pink tablecloth. Around me, about 30 people, mostly women, are hunched over their tables sewing and sticking straight pins into small rounds of fabric. There's a broad range of people here. Two older women in once-a-week beauty-parlor hairdos are reading the directions out loud to one another. A teenager with a black tattoo on her shoulder is breaking a strand of thread in her teeth. Next to me, two women who've just met are swapping stories about their doll clubs back home.

"We made pink, heart-shaped sandwiches at our last meeting."

"How *cute*," her new friend replies. "I'll have to remember that."

They stitch in silence for a few minutes until one asks the other, "Is your husband supportive of Barbie?"

"Oh, definitely. I have our club's Christmas party at my house and he helps me clean and cook and set up tables, and ten minutes before the guests arrive he disappears for the night."

"Sounds like the perfect husband."

As the workshop continues, the participants snip and sew and the room starts to buzz with activity and conversation. In front of me, two women are taking photos of one another holding up their newly made origami stoles. I see smiling teeth and popping flashbulbs and waving Barbies and for the first time since arriving yesterday, I'm feeling left out. Not that I want to sit down and make doll clothes but it would be nice to have a hobby where friends are so easily made and smiles so easy to come by.

After the workshop ends, I ride the hotel escalator upstairs to meet a woman named Judy Stegner, a 43-year-old collector and single mother from Fort Worth, Texas. I've been told that Judy is a devoted collector and ardent advocate for all things Barbie. I notice a woman of medium build with straight-cut blond bangs looking around as if expecting to meet someone. I walk toward her and introduce myself.

"Hi, Shari!" she says, thrusting her hand toward mine. "I'm Judy! It's so nice to meet you! Howsabout we sit right here?"

Judy and I proceed to sit down on a leather bench underneath an enormous stone sculpture of a horse. As we are getting settled, Judy talks nonstop about the convention, and Denver, and the wonderful people she's met in Denver, and the wonderful people she's met at the convention. Her hands and her mouth and her bangs are moving constantly, and her frenetic, fuel-burning activity makes me like her instantly. When at last we are seated across from one another, Judy pushes her glasses, which have slipped down her nose, back into place. She takes a deep breath and begins to tell me, her voice a deep Texas twang, how she met her Barbie friends.

"Well . . . it was Thanksgivin' night in 1998 and my son Justin, who knew I loved Barbie, said to me, 'Mom, there's probably a chat room where you can talk with other Barbie people.' I looked at him like he was crazy. I mean, I didn't know anythin' about the Internet or chat rooms. Justin had to do everything. He found a site, logged me on, even gave me my screen name. I typed in some stupid sentence like 'Hi! I'm Judy. I collect Barbies and I've never done this before.' I was online that night talking to Barbie people until two in the mornin'." Judy laughs and rolls her eyes, as if she still can't *believe* that she of all people was able to figure out the complexities of online communication.

"But you know," she says, "the Barbie collectors I've met on the Internet are great people. I mean, I never could have made it without 'em."

I put down the bottle of water I've been holding. "What do you mean," I ask, "that you couldn't have made it without them?"

Judy exhales. "Well," she says, "maybe you heard about this. In September 1999, there was a shooting at Wedgewood Baptist Church in Fort Worth in which several kids were killed."

I tell her I vaguely recall the story about a man who entered the church during a youth rally and randomly started shooting.

"That's the one," she says. "He murdered seven people that day, including my son Justin." Judy's brown eyes grow pink with tears. "He was my only child."

I look at Judy, stunned by this information. The whir of noise and activity around us comes to an abrupt stop. I smell coffee from a nearby coffee cart. I notice the glossy deep green leaves of a potted plant. Through the window behind Judy, I see silent business people, their bodies bent forward, hurrying to work or meetings or other Very Important Places. How does this woman, how does anybody, go on with the routine of life after something like this?

Judy continues. "Well, my Texas friends gradually dropped out of sight after my son was killed. I mean, I don't blame 'em. They didn't know what to say. This kind of thing is hard for everybody. But my Barbie friends, you wouldn't believe what they did. They called or wrote to me every day. They sent me money. They sent care packages. They helped raise thousands of dollars for a tuition assistance fund in Justin's name. They also contacted Mattel. Can you believe that? They contacted Mattel and the company sent me a special collectible Barbie and a handwritten note the first Christmas after Justin died. My Barbie friends even had a special Angel doll made for me." Judy pauses to raise her glasses and wipe away tears. "I'm so blessed. This is the closest circle of friends I've ever had."

I swallow hard in an effort to hold back my own tears. I can't think of a single, comforting thing to say to Judy and feel deeply ashamed because of it.

Suddenly, Judy jumps to her feet. "Let me show you somethin'," she says.

I sense Judy Stegner is used to putting other people at ease over her grief. She grabs her convention tote bag, pulls out a quilt and unfolds it on the cushioned bench in front of us. The quilt, made to honor her son's life, features 18 hand-sewn panels created by her Internet Barbie friends in California, Texas, Oklahoma, Michigan, Virginia, New York and Australia. The back of the quilt is covered in a white flannel swath of vintage fabric covered with Barbie silhouettes.

Judy bends over and runs her hand along the soft material. "I can't imagine how much that cost," she says. "That's practically antique." As we stand there, admiring the fabric, two women with convention tote bags walk up to Judy and give her hugs.

"I wondered where you were," one of the women says to Judy. "Are you still meeting us for lunch?"

"Absolutely," she replies. "I'll be there as soon as I can."

The women leave and Judy returns her attention to the quilt. "You know, I used to have this hanging on a wall but then I thought that's silly. Quilts are meant to be used. Now I carry it with me everywhere—even here. At home, I curl up with it while watching television or reading a book. It makes me feel good. Makes me feel closer to Justin."

This finally pushes me over the edge, and my voice breaks. "That is so amazing," I say.

"Isn't it?" Judy asks, smiling. "You know, Barbie people everywhere are really giving. We're involved in lots of charities."

Judy then goes on to detail all the non-profit organizations she's been involved with, including Toys 4 Tots, doll auctions that raise money for children's charities, and an organization called Parents of Murdered Children. "Did you know this convention is also a fundraiser?" she asks. "The beneficiary is Angels

Unaware, an organization that provides support for children living with HIV and AIDS. It was started in 1992 by a Barbie collector in Colorado."

"Why do you think Barbie collectors are so giving?" I ask.

"That's easy," she says. "It's because Barbie is about having fun, and when you're having fun you're not stressed and can naturally be more giving. We all have jobs and spouses and kids and things that make life hard. Anything that allows us to play is a good thing, and I don't know why people are so critical of Barbie sometimes. I mean, I can't believe it when people say Barbie is bad for a girl's self-image. That's ridiculous. It's a *doll*. Kids know that. It's adults that make Barbie a problem. In the 1960s, America was barely in space and there was already an astronaut Barbie. How can that be bad for kids?"

Feeling sheepish about my own past criticism of Barbie, I say nothing. Instead, I ask whether or not she plays with her dolls.

"It's total therapy for me to play," she says. "After my son died, I could lose myself for hours."

Across the lobby, another conventioneer calls to Judy and asks if she's ready for lunch.

Judy calls over to her. "I'll be there soon!"

I've never wanted to make sure someone meets up with her friends more than I want to make sure that Judy Stegner meets up with hers. I stand to thank Judy for her time, and she grabs my hand and shakes it vigorously, both of her hands encircling one of mine. It's the kind of handshake you might expect from someone who's just met you at the door and discovered she's won the Publisher's Clearinghouse Sweepstakes. It's not the handshake of a single mother whose only son was murdered in a church.

I leave Judy and walk back through the lobby to the main convention area. Along the way, I see three women seated at a table talking with similar sweepstakes-like enthusiasm. One of them has a blond Bubble Cut Barbie sticking out of the top of her purse. One of Barbie's arms is raised as if she's eager to answer a question. I look at the doll and its owner with something that feels, oddly enough, like admiration.

On the escalator back down to the convention hall, I think about my meeting with Judy and feel both sad and perplexed. I came here looking for an amusing human interest story, the kind of story I've written countless times before. The kind of story that beams a light on a bizarre little corner of the world and—wink, wink—invites readers to laugh with a sense of superiority. But instead of laughing, I'm filled with a vague yearning. I have friends, sure, but would they get together and craft a quilt for me? And I have interests, but do any of them offer "total therapy"?

The afternoon workshop on limb reattachment is just starting and several conventioneers are waiting at the door to see if they'll be admitted despite the fact they failed to pre-register. A young, slim man with dark hair turns to four women nearby.

"Do you think we'll get in?" he asks.

"I hope so," one of the women replies. "I've got two dolls I want to display but I can't get their legs to stay on."

"That's me too," he says, his eyes silently pleading with the door monitor to take pity.

After an anxious, ten-minute wait, the group is admitted and the workshop begins. There are about 35 people here and they're sporting an amazing array of pink. I see pink T-shirts, pink Barbie ball caps, pink hair bands, pink earrings and pink jeweled pins that spell out the name Barbie in fake gemstones. The attendees have laid out an assortment of naked and limbless Barbies on the pink tablecloths.

An instruction sheet listing a seven-step limb reattachment process is handed out. The first step reads: "Heat limb by dropping it into freshly boiled water for 2–3 minutes." To give people a hands-on reattachment experience, so to speak, there is a portable burner with a pot of boiling water set up at the front of the room. Starting with the first row and working backward, everyone will have a chance to dip their limbs and make their Barbies whole again.

While waiting for her turn, a large woman named Brenda Blanchard from Carson, California, begins speaking to me. Brenda is one of the few black people I've seen in this white-bread Barbie world and I'm curious how her interest began.

"I bought my first Barbie, a Holiday Barbie, for my daughter's high school graduation present," she explains.

Brenda speaks wistfully, like a war refugee describing her first taste of ice cream in the free world. "I liked that Holiday Barbie so much I took it back from my daughter. I now have 523 dolls . . . no wait! Let's see, I've bought 12 dolls at the conference so far, add that to . . ." Brenda looks into her forehead and counts silently. "Yep! I've now got 523 dolls."

"Are you an in-the-box collector or a deboxer?" I ask.

"I do both," she confesses. "I buy duplicates of every doll so that I can play with one."

When I ask Brenda what she likes about Barbie, she has no trouble finding an answer. "I used to be a schoolteacher. I like Barbie because she doesn't talk back." Brenda also grew up in a poor family that couldn't afford toys. "I'm making up for lost time." And like Judy Stegner, one of the things Brenda Blanchard loves most about Barbie is that she can lose herself for hours each night dressing and redressing her dolls. "My kids just moved out and it gets kinda lonely," she says. "Oh! And one other thing. I like making clothes and creating dioramas that show dolls involved in different events. In fact, I won an award for a diorama earlier today. It was of the Black Panther Party."

Prior to coming to this workshop I'd stopped in the competition room and noticed Brenda's diorama. It was a small box with an open front, about the size of a toaster oven. Inside was a miniature kitchen, complete with 70's-era macramé curtains and a gold refrigerator. Three black male dolls stood talking to one another, while two black female dolls sat nearby, one trimming the other's hair. There were small black hair cuttings on the floor around them. The caption read:

"Black Panther Party leaders Eldrige Cleaver, Huey P. Newton and Stokely Carmichael prepare for a rally at Lake Merritt while the girls take a break from cooking to make sure they will look good."

Clearly, Brenda has found a way to creatively transform the white Barbie culture into something more directly meaningful for her own life. Instead of rebelling and rejecting the doll entirely—as I would have—Brenda has made it her own.

I tell Brenda that I saw the diorama and was impressed by its level of detail. She smiles and drops her eyes.

"Thank you," she says.

There's no way to neatly categorize Barbie collectors. When I arrived at the convention yesterday, I had narrowly typecast the group as nothing more than middle-aged Midwestern women. Since then, I've talked to a broad range of people, including Jim Faraone, who grew up in the Bronx and speaks like he's straight off the set of a Mafia movie. "I brought toity-seven dawls wit me," he says.

I've talked to men in flannel shirts who accompanied their wives and confess that they, too, enjoy the thrill of the hunt.

I've also learned that Barbie collectors tend to speak in exclamation points. I just witnessed a group of women in matching pink engineer caps approach one of their friends. "You won!" they squealed.

"I won?!" she squealed back.

"Yes! Your Barbie! She won second place! Isn't that great!"

Originally, cynically, I attributed the happy glaze on the conventioneers' faces to some mysterious narcotic effect resulting from prolonged exposure to molded plastic. Now, I'm smiling like the rest of them. And I'm not entirely sure what this means.

On my way out of the convention, I stop to thank the Mattel representative for her assistance, and she gives me a 30th anniversary Malibu Barbie as a memento. She presents it to me gently, with both hands outstretched.

I leave, place Malibu Barbie on the passenger seat of my car, and drive toward the exit of the parking garage. The cashier sees the doll riding shotgun.

"Oh! You have a Barbie!" she says, standing on her tiptoes to get a better look at the doll. "Which one is it?"

"It's the new Malibu Barbie," I say. And as I pick up the doll to show her, I'm astonished to find that I'm a teeny bit proud of my new acquisition.

"See!" I add. "She even has sunscreen."

I'm Just Getting to the Disturbing Part

Steven Church

At *this point in my story, this much I know for sure:* I'm way too big for a pink plastic Barbie pool. At six foot four and 250 pounds, even if I sit cross-legged and squeeze my knees together with my elbows, I can only manage to get my ankles and rear end wet.

When I sit down, most of the water rises up and spills out, soaking into the brittle grass. I flop around in the pool and realize—vaguely at first, in the way that you realize your fly is open only by the way people are staring at your crotch—that to a passerby I probably look like a hairless wildebeest rolling around in a puddle on the hot savannah, a tanker ship in dry dock, a square peg in a round hole. I look like a jerk just wasting water. But I don't care how I appear, because even a little water can save you in this heat.

Rachel points at me and laughs—one of those big toothy wide-mouth laughs. "Oh my God," she says, "you're hilarious."

It seems cruel. But she has room to laugh. She's tiny, about half my size. She fits in the pool just fine. It's positively luxurious for her. She floats like a water bug on her back, paddling her little legs around and mocking me. "That's just wrong," I say when she shows off by submerging her entire body. She splashes me playfully as she climbs out, and the water feels so cold on my skin that it burns, leaving a smattering of wet fire across my legs and belly.

After a few failed attempts at cooling off, I finally figure out that the only way for me to soak my whole body is to fill the Barbie pool to the brim, squat down beside it, and then fall into the water, letting it splash over me and out onto the grass. My best friend, Rob, has to do the same thing, but he's three inches taller than me and skinny, and he looks like a giant gawky heron, flailing in a backyard birdbath.

We're out here because it's hot. And we need to be saved. This is what's important in the story.

Did I mention this: It's the middle of July, and all along the Front Range of Colorado we're suffering the sort of summer heat that burns when you inhale, singeing nose hair and scalding your sinus cavities; the particular brand of intense, abusive heat where your brain seems to expand inside your skull and you feel a little dumber, slower, and sleepier; the kind of heat that makes you see things funny—watery mirages, floating apparitions, ghosts of the everyday.

We have chosen this day, this hell-hot, broiling weekend, to make our final move down to the Front Range of Colorado from Breckenridge—high up in the Blue Valley at 9,000 feet, where the air is thin and cool, the kind of air they name deodorants after—Mountain Fresh, Cool Breeze, etc.

We loaded up the last loads of household junk and hauled it the 160 miles between apartments. We unpacked last night and sweated our way to sleep on the soft furnished mattress in our new apartment. We have no air conditioning. I tossed and turned all night, positioning and repositioning box fans to get the maximum whirlwind effect—all of it ultimately futile—and I finally rose at dawn, dug our coffee maker out of a box, and made a pot of dark French roast. I drank the whole thing and brewed another.

Rachel and I rented this one-bedroom place in Fort Collins, just half a block from the university where I will be attending graduate school for writing, and a short drive from another university where Rachel will begin her master's and certification in education. Rob, my best friend since high school, and his girlfriend, Jen, rented the apartment right next door to us. He's recovering from a botched hernia operation and volunteering with the Larimer County Wild Land Fire Crew, taking courses at the community college. Jen is clerking for a judge in the county court. We're all sort of in between things or just starting something new, definitely in a period of proverbial flux; and we're still getting used to the changes.

Heat is just one of the new challenges. Our apartments are poorly ventilated and stifling. So this morning, Rob and I drove out to Toys "R" Us and bought a pink plastic Barbie pool, the only model they had left. We brought it home, filled it up using a garden hose, and now we're all sitting around it in the backyard in green vinyl lawn chairs, half naked, our feet dipped in the water, taking turns soaking and refilling the pool.

We try not to think about the fact that it's 75 degrees in Breckenridge—sunny, but with a cool breeze and that mountain-crisp air—where we all recently lived and where we all, on some level, still wish we were living. We don't do the math. We don't think about the difference in comfort level that 30 degrees makes. The radio said it could get up to 110 today on the Front Range, and that's just not right. There's a drought, and Horsetooth Reservoir is drying up. There've been news reports about the retreat of water. The other day, it had receded so far they found a dead dog in the mud with cinder blocks tied to its feet. We told ourselves that someone must have tried to put a sick dog out of its misery. There wasn't much left of it—mostly bones and skin, hair and teeth.

It isn't fair, this oppressive heat. It does bad things to your head. Hot weather makes me grumpy. I feel swollen and bloated, oozing with sweat, like a fat sausage roasting on a grill. We try to distract ourselves with booze and food and small talk, but eventually we hit one of those awkward pauses in the conversation, a heat-induced lull that leaves each of us foul-faced and pissy, all thinking the same thing—we gotta get out of this heat before someone gets hurt.

Suddenly Rob's face brightens. "You guys want to take my kayak out to Horsetooth?"

A collective sigh releases from the group and smiles spread around the pink pool.

"Oh yeah, maybe do some swimming?" Rachel pipes in.

Three heads nod in unison.

But Jen the attorney says, "I'm pretty sure swimming is illegal there."

"No way," I protest. "Why?"

"It's dangerous, I guess," Jen says.

"But it's soooo hot," Rachel says.

"Let's just go," Rob says. "It's gotta be better than this." He gestures at the half-empty Barbie bath, bits of grass and dirt floating around, our feet lurking below the surface like pale fish, and in no time we are loading his fiberglass banana-colored kayak onto the roof of his jeep and emptying the pool water in the yard.

Let me tell you what I don't know at this point in my story: I will be afraid of water. It will happen a few years from now. This will be a new fear that develops unexpectedly, and it will be hard for me even to admit, difficult to reconcile with my childhood love of water. But one day I'll be walking along the Poudre River in Fort Collins with my three-year-old son (a boy who will be born and brought home to a house just two blocks away from this very apartment with the pink Barbie pool), and the water in the river will be moving fast, running as high as I've ever seen it, after two full days of rain rolling down from the mountains.

The boy will be the kind of child who likes to get down close and throw rocks in the water, his toes often dipped in at the edge, soaking his kiddie–Vans up to the Velcro straps. I will look at him down by the rushing river, and then up at the swirling brown force moving past, and I'll be seized with irrational gut-dropping panic. I know this now.

Like a brush fire, my imagination will flare up, burst, leap, and I'll picture him falling into the river, bobbing up a couple of times, and disappearing beneath the churn. I'll hear my own footsteps on the bank, running helplessly, and then watch myself dive into the water after him, swim down, deep, searching. I'll go with him. And before I know it, the fire of my thoughts will smolder, tamp, and I'll be back to the present future, nervously chewing my fingernails down to nothing and gripping his hand tight, pulling him back from the water, up to the path, away from my fears. He'll try to wiggle free from my grasp as he reaches for a rock. He'll always be wiggling away.

"I want to throw a rock in that wave, Daddy," he'll say plaintively, pointing at a cascade of foamy brown water pouring over a partially submerged tree.

"I know, buddy. But you have to hold my hand. It's like crossing the street. You always have to hold Daddy's hand when you're near the river."

"Why, Daddy?"

"Because it's dangerous. See how fast the river is moving? If you fell in, you could die."

This is true, but I should find a better way to say it. I don't want to plant fears in the loamy soil of his consciousness. I don't want him to think about dying.

"Because you could drown," I'll say, and pause, trying to shift the conversation away from this topic. "Because it's dangerous. Just trust me, OK?"

"OK, Daddy," he'll say, and I'll know that he means it.

We'll walk a little further along the river and I'll try to tell him about "eddy" currents and how they move backwards, against the flow of the main current, bits of flotsam and detritus swirling in the spin of story. We'll stop to watch several lines and tails spinning madly off of the main push, catching up twigs and debris, spawning tiny whirlpools; but he'll mostly just want to throw rocks at the surface of this scene, this image, this day. I'll still want him to be amazed and curious about water. I'll still want him to find things about rivers that aren't scary. But the fear will still be there, lurking beneath the surface of these casual interactions.

"Eddy," the boy will say. "That's silly."

"That's your Grandpa's name," I'll say.

"I know that, Daddy," he'll say impatiently, because he already knows how things come back again.

The boy will be naturally curious about the most dangerous things—waterfalls and ripples, noisy whitewater and submerged limbs, all the stuff beneath the surface of these days. I want to let him explore. I want to let go, let him learn to swim and survive and all that—but I will have developed this fear of water like I've never had before. It's just there, taking up space, weighing me down—and I don't want to give this burden to my son.

I think I always believed that as I grew older and matured, I'd shed phobias like old luggage or clothes—and I have lost a few along the way. But I never imagined that I'd get mossy green with new fears as the years progressed.

This one. This new fear of water. I can trace it back.

It starts at Horsetooth Reservoir on this miserable hot day in July.

Here is what should be clear by now: We are not alone in the water. Dozens of like-minded people have come to Horsetooth to escape the heat. But the lake is a place of sacrifice. What you gain in water, you lose in shade. What you gain in depth, you lose in vision.

There are few trees here, so people have set up large shade canopies, and bright blue Igloo coolers surround the perimeters like colorful sandbags. The dusty parking lot is crammed with cars. Boats and jet skis buzz up and down the lake, in and out of Satanka Cove, where the public dock is located, and many people have camped or squatted for the day along the banks of the cove, taking occasional illegal dips into the water. Some openly flout the posted warnings against swimming in the cove. We try to be subtle by sitting close to the edge and slipping in just to cool off. We take turns going out in Rob's boat, paddling out into the larger lake and splashing each other.

It's still hot, but it beats the Barbie pool.

The landscape around Satanka Cove is harsh and terra-cotta red, with slabs of uprooted sandstone rising all around like the plates of a buried stegosaurus. In the water, we paddle past striated shelves of crumbling shale. There is no beach, no sand. Just mud and rocks. But there is water and it is cool. We take a few turns, and Rob and I sit on the bank watching Rachel and Jen paddle back up to the edge. We are waiting our second turn out. They beach the boat and Rob straps on a life jacket. He climbs in and I'm helping Rachel out onto the bank, taking her life jacket, when we hear a voice calling to us, an anguished voice.

"Heeeelllp," she calls.

We turn and see an overweight woman in a tank top and jean shorts running toward us. She is screaming and waving her arms around. "Heelllp," she calls out again. I look behind her, expecting to see something or someone chasing her, but there's nothing.

She runs up to us. Rob sits in the boat. She is panting, trying to catch her breath. "He went under," she barks. "He went under and he's not coming up." She turns and points to a small inlet off the main cove, where I'd seen some boys diving from the rocks earlier. "He's not coming up," she repeats, then doubles over and puts her hands on her knees. We both seem to realize immediately what she is saying.

A boy is drowning. He needs our help.

Rob and I look at each other for a second and then take off in the direction from which she came—he in the boat, me running on the bank. Rob paddles like crazy, stirring up great roils of water. I run hard, my sandals slapping on the rock, and we both reach the inlet about the same time. We are the first ones there besides two other guys standing waist deep, breathing deeply, staring hopelessly at the water. They are dark-haired and deeply tanned, younger than us by a few years, and appear to be the drowning boy's swimming companions. Beer cans drift past in the water, and I get a sense of what they've been doing out here at the lake.

"My brother, man!" one of them says. "He went under."

"What happened?" Rob asks.

"We were swimming across and he started splashing and we thought he was joking," the boy says, staring at the water. "We thought he was joking," he says again.

"Where?" Rob asks, paddling his boat up close. I am standing on the opposite bank.

"Right fucking there, man!" the other boy says, pointing at a spot in the water.

Rob slips out of his life jacket and rolls out of his boat into the water. I climb down the bank and slip in over the edge. We both swim out to the area where the boy pointed. We look at each other, take a deep breath, and then dive. Again and again we dive down into the deep green water, surfacing only long enough to catch our breath.

I try to open my eyes underwater, but can't see a thing. I dive down as far as I can go, feeling pockets of cold water as I get closer to the bottom. I hit the mud and sweep my arms and legs out wildly, trying to feel his body, hoping to touch his slippery, cold flesh or maybe grab an arm. But my lungs will only let me stay down for a second or two before I have to swim hard for the surface. It's deep, 15 or 20 feet or more in spots.

As I break the surface and breach, gasping for air, Rob is quick behind me. We take a moment at the surface and then dive down again. I know how this works. I know that every second, every minute counts, and the quicker we can find him, the better chance he has to survive. We dive down repeatedly, finding and feeling nothing. Not a sign. Not a limb. Not a clump of hair or the brush of a swimsuit. Nothing but deep, cold water and slippery mud on the bottom. But we keep diving, dipping down below. Over and over again. There is nothing else to do but try.

I break the surface once and see Rachel swimming out to me. "Go back," I yell. "Please go back!" I can't bear the thought of losing her. By now there are other people in the water, seven or eight of us now, diving down and searching for him. Boats buzz past. I can hear a helicopter coming, rising up over the foothills. The sky looks wiped, skimmed, ironed like a blue shirt. Steep shale walls shade the cove, so it's cool in here. I dog-paddle, kicking my arms and legs out, knifing through the water, and try to breathe deeply, evenly.

A woman in a blue bikini stands on a fishing boat, screaming, "Does everyone have a buddy? You need to have a buddy!!"

I look at Rob. She means a swim buddy. But he's much more than that now.

We swim to the bank and pull ourselves up on the rocks. We've been diving for almost 20 minutes. We sit there, breathing hard, exhausted and weak. We look out at the crew of divers and a boat drifting slowly. Blue Bikini's husband has a sonar fish finder. Someone said we should use it, so now he's trolling back and forth across the inlet. *It's too late*, I think. The helicopter's blades go *thwop-thwop-thwop*, punctuating the air, echoing off the walls of the cove, and it lands lightly just above the boat ramp, kicking up a cloud of white dust.

Suddenly the guy in the boat stops. "Right there," he says, pointing down at his fish finder and then at the water. "There's something big, and it's not moving."

The gaggle of divers kicks and paddles furiously over to the spot, and one by one, each of them disappears under the water like a cormorant. Rob and I slip back in and swim out to the spot. We take deep breaths and dive under again, only to pop back up moments later without ever reaching the bottom. My dog paddle looks more like tired flailing than anything resembling a swim stroke.

"It's deep," I sputter. "I can't touch."

"Me neither," Rob says.

Just then a thin, wiry boy, maybe 17 or 18, breaches and hollers, "I touched him. I felt him lying down there, but I can't pull him up. It's too deep."

Another swimmer says, "Let's try again," and the two of them disappear.

Rob and I make another effort, but I can't get down that deep. I am exhausted, my lungs aching and my limbs all rubbery. We swim back to the bank. I look up and see Rachel and Jen sitting on the opposite bank. Rachel has her arms crossed over her knees and her head down.

"How long?" I ask, shivering from the cold water.

"I don't know," Rob says. "Must be close to a half hour."

"Too long," I say.

"He's gone," Rob says.

We hear the emergency vehicles approaching, their sirens rising and falling with the surrounding terrain until they come screaming down into Satanka Cove. They slip their rescue boat in the water and are upon us in seconds, plowing into the cove and pushing a wide white wake ahead of them. They order everyone out of the water, and a diver in a full wetsuit drops over the edge of the boat. We all wait on the bank for what seems like hours, but it's only a minute or so before the water bubbles, roils, and the diver pushes the boy up through the surface, breaking the thin skin of water that separates us from the deep.

His body thumps loudly against the fiberglass boat. He is fish-limp and heavy with full lungs. They work furiously on him from the minute he's in the boat, trying to revive him, but by the time they get back to the ramp and we have made our way over to the scene, the boy has been loaded into the helicopter and spirited away. He is dead. Everyone seems to know this, and there isn't much to be said about it.

The boy's brother is there, the one who was standing in the water when we first arrived. He looks dazed, confused. A wet towel drapes over his shoulders. Nobody asks us anything. No questions. No clarifications. I'm not sure what I expect, but I keep thinking that we'll need to give a statement or something.

I approach the brother. "I'm so sorry," I say. "I don't know what to say." And then I reach out and try to give him a hug, but it goes all wrong and we sort of half-embrace, each of us getting one arm up and around the other, then quickly separating. He doesn't speak a word. He doesn't seem to recognize me at all. I just stand there, watching him take the long walk up the grey concrete boat ramp, and I feel a cold chill rattle up and down my spine, knowing it's no comfort in the heat of this day.

Here is what I haven't told you up to this point in my story: My brother died when he was 18—killed in his car, slammed into a tree, head smashed in—a violent, noisy sort of death. Totally unlike a drowning. He was just a kid too.

This is how it all comes around again—moments and words caught up in the eddy current of backstory and memory.

They say that you experience euphoria as you are drowning, at least for a moment; but I've always wondered when this comes. At what point? Is it the euphoria of surrender, or something else that water does to the brain? And how exactly would they know? I suppose they interview people who have been pulled back to the surface and revived, given a chance to tell their story.

My brother never had a chance at euphoria. He couldn't have told any stories if he survived. His brain was too bruised, too battered and crushed. I imagine that he believed right up to the end that he could survive, that he would make it, and it hurts me to think he fought it. It hurts to know that I'm the only one who can tell his story.

When we're near the water—any water now—I'm completely paranoid and overprotective of my son. I'm afraid of the possibility, the subtle menace below the surface of a stream, crick, river, pond, or kiddie pool. He'll be four soon, and he still doesn't know how to swim. It helps me to think people can survive being underwater. They can be pulled back. There is a window there, between life and death, and it can last as long as 45 minutes in cold temperatures. I remind myself of this—those stories of kids being pulled from beneath the ice of a frozen lake and revived—and sometimes it works as a kind of psychological salve. Sometimes it helps tamp down the flare of this new fear.

On the rare occasions when we go swimming in a pool together, my son clings to my neck like a baby monkey and won't let go. When I try to get him to dog paddle on his own, his eyes lock onto me, his face is stricken with fear. I hold him out at arm's length, and he lifts his little chin desperately above the surface, squawking, "DADDY DADDY DADDY!" and it nearly breaks my heart every time. I know that we just need to spend more time in the water for him to get used to it and feel comfortable—but sometimes I wonder if I really want him to get comfortable in water.

I worry that I will pass my new fear on to him, that he will inherit it like a great and heavy piece of furniture that he must lug from house to house for the rest of his life. I don't want him to carry the weight of my fears, or he'll never learn to swim on his own, never shed the heft of my pathologies, and never experience the simple fun of gliding through the aqua-blue, weightless world of a swimming pool, skimming his body along the bottom and breaking the surface like a silver fish.

Here's the disturbing part: When that rescue diver pushed that drowned boy up through the skin of water, I couldn't be sure it wasn't my brother's body thumping on the fiberglass hull of the boat. I know it sounds strange, but I experienced some kind of transference in the water that day at Horsetooth. As the time dragged on and I knew the boy's life was slipping away, I felt as if I was slipping closer to my brother. I couldn't stop thinking about him. Every dive down was a dive closer to him. I felt his presence down there, in the dark and quiet green water, as if *he* was that boy on the bottom, waiting for me to pull him back up again.

Perhaps I felt something close to the other side, the chill of death in that deep green water; and I understood how quickly you can cross over, especially below the surface. I was afraid to open my eyes, afraid of what I might see—a smile, a wave, a tassel of hair, the bright neon of a swimsuit, or my brother's face. I was afraid part of me might want to stay down there, swimming in the euphoria of surrender, that I might just unhinge my jaw, swallow, and embrace it. And that's where this must have started, a big part of the reason I now lug around this new father-fear of water. It's hard to drop that day into the past, to just let it go in the wash of memory and watch it bob and roll and slip beneath the surface.

Silent Dancing

Judith Ortiz Cofer

We have a home movie of this party. Several times my mother and I have watched it together, and I have asked questions about the silent revelers coming in and out of focus. It is grainy and of short duration, but it's a great visual aid to my memory of life at that time. And it is in color—the only complete scene in color I can recall from those years.

We lived in Puerto Rico until my brother was born in 1954. Soon after, because of economic pressures on our growing family, my father joined the United States Navy. He was assigned to duty on a ship in Brooklyn Yard—a place of cement and steel that was to be his home base in the States until his retirement more than twenty years later. He left the Island first, alone, going to New York City and tracking down his uncle who lived with his family across the Hudson River in Paterson, New Jersey. There my father found a tiny apartment in a huge tenement that had once housed Jewish families but was just being taken over and transformed by Puerto Ricans, overflowing from New York City. In 1955 he sent for us. My mother was only twenty years old, I was not quite three, and my brother was a toddler when we arrived at El Building, as the place had been christened by its newest residents.

My memories of life in Paterson during those first few years are all in shades of gray. Maybe I was too young to absorb vivid colors and details, or to discriminate between the slate blue of the winter sky and the darker hues of the snow-bearing clouds, but that single color washes over the whole period. The building we lived in was gray, as were the streets, filled with slush the first few months of my life there. The coat my father had bought for me was similar in color and too big; it sat heavily on my thin frame.

I do remember the way the heater pipes banged and rattled, startling all of us out of sleep until we got so used to the sound that we automatically shut it out or raised our voices above the racket. The hiss from the valve punctuated my sleep (which has always been fitful) like a nonhuman presence in the room—a dragon sleeping at the entrance of my childhood. But the pipes were also a connection to all the other lives being lived around us. Having come from a house designed for a single family back in Puerto Rico—my mother's extended-family home—it was curious to know that strangers lived under our floor and above our heads, and that the heater pipe went through everyone's apartment. (My first spanking in Paterson came as a result of playing tunes on the pipes in my room to see if there would be an answer.) My mother was as new to this concept of beehive life as I was, but she had been given strict orders by my father to keep the doors locked, the noise down, ourselves to ourselves.

It seems that Father had learned some painful lessons about prejudice while searching for an apartment in Paterson. Not until years later did I hear how much resistance he had encountered with landlords who were panicking at the influx of Latinos into a neighborhood that had been Jewish for a couple of generations. It made no difference that it was the American phenomenon of ethnic turnover which was changing the urban core of Paterson, and that the human flood could not be held back with an accusing finger.

"You Cuban?" one man had asked my father, pointing at his name tag on the navy uniform—even though my father had the fair skin and light brown hair of his northern Spanish background, and the name Ortiz is as common in Puerto Rico as Johnson is in the United States.

"No," my father had answered, looking past the finger into his adversary's angry eyes. "I'm Puerto Rican."

"Same shit." And the door closed.

My father could have passed as European, but we couldn't. My brother and I both have our mother's black hair and olive skin, and so we lived in El Building and visited our great-uncle and his fair children on the next block. It was their private joke that they were the German branch of the family. Not many years later that area too would be mainly Puerto Rican. It was as if the heart of the city map were being gradually colored brown—*café con leche* brown. Our color.

The movie opens with a sweep of the living room. It is "typical" immigrant Puerto Rican decor for the time: the sofa and chairs are square and hard-looking, upholstered in bright colors (blue and yellow in this instance) and covered with the transparent plastic that furniture salesmen then were so adept at convincing women to buy. The linoleum on the floor is light blue; where it had been subjected to spike heels, as it was in most places, there were dime-size indentations all over it that cannot be seen in this movie. The room is full of people dressed up: dark suits for the men, red dresses for the women. When I have asked my mother why most of the women are in red that night, she has shrugged and said, "I don't remember. Just a coincidence." She doesn't have my obsession for assigning symbolism to everything.

The three women in red sitting on the couch are my mother, my eighteen-year-old cousin, and her brother's girlfriend. The novia *is just up from the Island, which is apparent in her body language. She sits up formally, her dress pulled over her knees. She is a pretty girl, but her posture makes her look insecure, lost in her full-skirted dress, which she has carefully tucked around her to make room for my gorgeous cousin, her future sister-in-law. My cousin has grown up in Paterson and is in her last year of high school. She doesn't have a trace of what Puerto Ricans call* la mancha *(literally, the stain: the mark of the new immigrant—something about the posture, the voice, or the humble demeanor that makes it obvious to everyone the person has just arrived on the mainland). My cousin is wearing a light, sequined, cocktail dress. Her brown hair has been lightened with peroxide around the bangs, and she is holding a cigarette expertly between her fingers, bringing it up to her mouth in a sensuous arc of her arm as she talks animatedly. My mother, who has come up to sit between the two women, both only a few years younger than herself, is somewhere between the poles they represent in our culture.*

It became my father's obsession to get out of the barrio, and thus we were never permitted to form bonds with the place or with the people who lived there. Yet El Building was a comfort to my mother, who never got over yearning for *la isla*. She felt surrounded by her language: the walls were thin, and voices speaking and arguing in Spanish could be heard all day. *Salsas* blasted out of radios, turned on early in the morning and left on for company. Women seemed to cook rice and beans perpetually—the strong aroma of boiling red kidney beans permeated the hallways.

Though Father preferred that we do our grocery shopping at the supermarket when he came home on weekend leaves, my mother insisted that she could cook only with products whose labels she could read. Consequently, during the week I accompanied her and my little brother to La Bodega—a hole-in-the-wall grocery store across the street from El Building. There we squeezed down three narrow aisles jammed with various products. Goya and Libby's—those were the trademarks that were trusted by her *mamá*, so my mother bought many cans of Goya beans, soups, and condiments, as well as little cans of Libby's fruit juices for us. And she also bought Colgate toothpaste and Palmolive soap. (The final *e* is pronounced in both these products in Spanish, so for many years I believed that they were manufactured on the Island. I remember my surprise at first hearing a commercial on television in which "Colgate" rhymed with "ate.") We always lingered at La Bodega, for it was there that Mother breathed best, taking in the familiar aromas of the foods she knew from Mamá's kitchen. It was also there that she got to speak to the other women of El Building without violating outright Father's dictates against fraternizing with our neighbors.

Yet Father did his best to make our "assimilation" painless. I can still see him carrying a real Christmas tree up several flights of stairs to our apartment, leaving a trail of aromatic pine. He carried it formally, as if it were a flag in a parade. We were the only ones in El Building that I knew of who got presents on both Christmas and *día de Reyes*, the day when the Three Kings brought gifts to Christ and to Hispanic children.

Our supreme luxury in El Building was having our own television set. It must have been a result of Father's guilt feelings over the isolation he had imposed on us, but we were among the first in the barrio to have one. My brother quickly became an avid watcher of Captain Kangaroo and Jungle Jim, while I loved all the series showing families. By the time I started first grade, I could have drawn a map of Middle America as exemplified by the lives of characters in *Father Knows Best, The Donna Reed Show, Leave It to Beaver, My Three Sons,* and (my favorite) *Bachelor Father,* where John Forsythe treated his adopted teenage daughter like a princess because he was rich and had a Chinese houseboy to do everything for him. In truth, compared to our neighbors in El Building, we were rich. My father's navy check provided us with financial security and a standard of living that the factory workers envied. The only thing his money could not buy us was a place to live away from the barrio—his greatest wish, Mother's greatest fear.

In the home movie the men are shown next, sitting around a card table set up in one corner of the living room, playing dominoes. The clack of the ivory pieces was a familiar sound. I heard it in many houses on the Island and in many apartments in Paterson. In Leave It to Beaver, *the Cleavers played bridge in every other episode; in my childhood, the men started every social occasion with a hotly debated round of dominoes. The women would sit around and watch, but they never participated in the games.*

Here and there you can see a small child. Children were always brought to parties and, whenever they got sleepy, were put to bed in the host's bedroom. Babysitting was a concept unrecognized by the Puerto Rican women I knew: a responsible mother did not leave her children with any stranger. And in a culture where children are not considered intrusive, there was no need to leave the children at home. We went where our mother went.

Of my preschool years I have only impressions: the sharp bite of the wind in December as we walked with our parents toward the brightly lit stores downtown; how I felt like a stuffed doll in my heavy coat, boots, and mittens; how good it was to walk into the five-and-dime and sit at the counter drinking hot chocolate. On Saturdays our whole family would walk downtown to shop at the big department stores on Broadway. Mother bought all our clothes at Penney's and Sears, and she liked to buy her dresses at the women's specialty shops like Lerner's and Diana's. At some point we'd go into Woolworth's and sit at the soda fountain to eat.

We never ran into other Latinos at these stores or when eating out, and it became clear to me only years later that the women from El Building shopped mainly in other places—stores owned by other Puerto Ricans or by Jewish merchants who had philosophically accepted our presence in the city and decided to make us their good customers, if not real neighbors and friends. These establishments were located not downtown but in the blocks around our street, and they were referred to generically as La Tienda, El Bazar, La Bodega, La Botánica. Everyone knew what was meant. These were the stores where your face did not turn a clerk to stone, where your money was as green as anyone else's.

One New Year's Eve we were dressed up like child models in the Sears catalogue: my brother in a miniature man's suit and bow tie, and I in black patent-leather shoes and a frilly dress with several layers of crinoline underneath. My mother wore a bright red dress that night, I remember, and spike heels; her long black hair hung to her waist. Father, who usually wore his navy uniform during his short visits home, had put on a dark civilian suit for the occasion: we had been invited to his uncle's house for a big celebration. Everyone was excited because my mother's brother Hernan—a bachelor who could indulge himself with luxuries—had bought a home movie camera, which he would be trying out that night.

Even the home movie cannot fill in the sensory details such a gathering left imprinted in a child's brain. The thick sweetness of women's perfumes mixing with the ever-present smells of food cooking in the kitchen: meat and plantain *pasteles*, as well as the ubiquitous rice dish made special with pigeon peas—*gandules*—and seasoned with precious *sofrito* sent up from the Island by somebody's mother or smuggled in by a recent traveler. *Sofrito* was one of the items that women hoarded, since it was hardly ever in stock at La Bodega. It was the flavor of Puerto Rico.

The men drank Palo Viejo rum, and some of the younger ones got weepy. The first time I saw a grown man cry was at a New Year's Eve party: he had been reminded of his mother by the smells in the kitchen. But what I remember most were the boiled *pasteles*, plantain or yucca rectangles stuffed with corned beef or other meats, olives, and many other savory ingredients, all wrapped in banana leaves. Everybody had to fish one out with a fork. There was always a "trick" *pastel*—one without stuffing—and whoever got that one was the "New Year's Fool."

There was also the music. Long-playing albums were treated like precious china in these homes. Mexican recordings were popular, but the songs that brought tears to my mother's eyes were sung by the melancholy Daniel Santos, whose life as a drug addict was the stuff of legend. Felipe Rodríguez was a particular favorite of couples, since he sang about faithless women and brokenhearted men. There is a snatch of one lyric that has stuck in my mind like a needle on a worn groove: *De piedra ha de ser mi cama, de piedra la cabezera . . . la mujer que a mi me quiera . . . ha de quererme de veras. Ay, Ay, Ay, corazón, porque no amas . . .* I must have heard it a thousand times since the idea of a bed made of stone, and its connection to love, first troubled me with its disturbing images.

The five-minute home movie ends with people dancing in a circle—the creative filmmaker must have set it up, so that all of them could file past him. It is both comical and sad to watch silent dancing. Since there is no justification for the absurd movements that music provides for some of us, people appear frantic, their faces embarrassingly intense. It's as if you were watching sex. Yet for years, I've had dreams in the form of this home movie. In a recurring scene, familiar faces push themselves forward into my mind's eye, plastering their features into distorted close-ups. And I'm asking them: "Who is *she?* Who is the old woman I don't recognize? Is she an aunt? Somebody's wife? Tell me who she is."

"See the beauty mark on her cheek as big as a hill on the lunar landscape of her face—well, that runs in the family. The women on your father's side of the family wrinkle early; it's the price they pay for that fair skin. The young girl with the green stain on her wedding dress is *la novia*—just up from the Island. See, she lowers her eyes when she approaches the camera, as she's supposed to. Decent girls never look at you directly in the face. *Humilde,* humble, a girl should express humility in all her actions. She will make a good wife for your cousin. He should consider himself lucky to have met her only weeks after she arrived here. If he marries her quickly, she will make him a good Puerto Rican–style wife; but if he waits too long, she will be corrupted by the city, just like your cousin there."

"She means me. I do what I want. This is not some primitive island I live on. Do they expect me to wear a black mantilla on my head and go to mass every day? Not me. I'm an American woman, and I will do as I please. I can type faster than anyone in my senior class at Central High, and I'm going to be a secretary to a lawyer when I graduate. I can pass for an American girl anywhere—I've tried it. At least for Italian, anyway—I never speak Spanish in public. I hate these parties, but I wanted the dress. I look better than any of these *humildes* here. *My* life is going to be different. I have an American boyfriend. He is older and has a car. My parents don't know it, but I sneak out of the house late at night sometimes to be with him. If I marry him, even my name will be American. I hate rice and beans—that's what makes these women fat."

"Your *prima* is pregnant by that man she's been sneaking around with. Would I lie to you? I'm your *tía política*, your great-uncle's common-law wife— the one he abandoned on the Island to go marry your cousin's mother. *I* was not invited to this party, of course, but I came anyway. I came to tell you that story about your cousin that you've always wanted to hear. Do you remember the comment your mother made to a neighbor that has always haunted you? The only thing you heard was your cousin's name, and then you saw your mother pick up your doll from the couch and say: 'It was as big as this doll when they flushed it down the toilet.' This image has bothered you for years, hasn't it? You had nightmares about babies being flushed down the toilet, and you wondered why anyone would do such a horrible thing. You didn't dare ask your mother about it. She would only tell you that you had not heard her right, and yell at you for listening to adult conversations. But later, when you were old enough to know about abortions, you suspected.

"I am here to tell you that you were right. Your cousin was growing an *americanito* in her belly when this movie was made. Soon after, she put something long and pointy into her pretty self, thinking maybe she could get rid of the problem before breakfast and still make it to her first class at the high school. Well, *niña,* her screams could be heard downtown. Your aunt, her *mamá,* who had been a midwife on the Island, managed to pull the little thing out. Yes, they probably flushed it down the toilet. What else could they do with it—give it a Christian burial in a little white casket with blue bows and ribbons? Nobody wanted that baby—least of all the father, a teacher at her school with a house in West Paterson that he was filling with real children, and a wife who was a natural blonde.

"Girl, the scandal sent your uncle back to the bottle. And guess where your cousin ended up? Irony of ironies. She was sent to a village in Puerto Rico to live with a relative on her mother's side: a place so far away from civilization that you have to ride a mule to reach it. A real change in scenery. She found a man there—women like that cannot live without male company—but believe me, the men in Puerto Rico know how to put a saddle on a woman like her. *La gringa,* they call her. Ha, ha, ha. *La gringa* is what she always wanted to be. . . ."

The old woman's mouth becomes a cavernous black hole I fall into. And as I fall, I can feel the reverberations of her laughter. I hear the echoes of her last mocking words: *la gringa, la gringa!* And the conga line keeps moving silently past me. There is no music in my dream for the dancers.

When Odysseus visits Hades to see the spirit of his mother, he makes an offering of sacrificial blood, but since all the souls crave an audience with the living, he has to listen to many of them before he can ask questions. I, too, have to hear the dead and the forgotten speak in my dream. Those who are still part of my life remain silent, going around and around in their dance. The others keep pressing their faces forward to say things about the past.

My father's uncle is last in line. He is dying of alcoholism, shrunken and shriveled like a monkey, his face a mass of wrinkles and broken arteries. As he comes closer I realize that in his features I can see my whole family. If you were to stretch that rubbery flesh, you could find my father's face, and deep within *that* face—my own. I don't want to look into those eyes ringed in purple. In a few years he will retreat into silence, and take a long, long time to die. *Move back, Tío, I tell him. I don't want to hear what you have to say. Give the dancers room to move. Soon it will be midnight. Who is the New Year's Fool this time?*

A Little While

Edwidge Danticat

My cousin Maxo has died. The house that I called home during my visits to Haiti collapsed on top of him.

Maxo was born on November 4, 1948, after three days of agonizing labor. "I felt," my Aunt Denise used to say, "as though I spent all three days pushing him out of my eyes." She had a long scar above her right eyebrow, where she had jabbed her nails through her skin during the most painful moments. She never gave birth again.

Maxo often complained about his parents not celebrating his birthday. "Are you kidding me?" I'd say, taking his mother's side. "Who would want to remember such an ordeal?" All jokes aside, it pained him more than it should have, even though few children in Bel Air, the impoverished and now shattered neighborhood where we grew up, ever had a birthday with balloons and cake.

When Maxo was a teen-ager, his favorite author was Jean Genet. He read and reread "Les Nègres." These lines from the play now haunt me: "Your song was very beautiful, and your sadness does me honor. I'm going to start life in a new world. If I ever return, I'll tell you what it's like there. Great black country, I bid thee farewell."

Two days after a 7.0 earthquake struck Haiti, on January 12, 2010, I was still telling my brothers that one night, as we were watching CNN, Maxo would pop up behind Anderson Cooper and take over his job.

Maxo was a hustler. He could get whatever he wanted, whether money or kind words, simply by saying, "You know I love you. I love you. I love you." It always worked with our family members in New York, both when he occasionally showed up to visit and when he called from Haiti to ask them to fund his various projects.

The last time I heard from him was three days before the earthquake. He left a message on my voice mail. He was trying to raise money to rebuild a small school in the mountains of Léogâne, where our family originated. The time before that, someone in the neighborhood had died and money was needed for a coffin. With a voice that blended shouting and laughter, Maxo made each request sound as though it were an investment that the giver would be making in him or herself.

When my eighty-one-year-old Uncle Joseph, a minister, left Haiti, in 2004, after a gang threatened his life, Maxo, his son, was with him. They travelled together to Miami, hoping to be granted political asylum. Instead, they were detained by the Department of Homeland Security and separated while in custody. When Maxo was finally able to see his father, it was to translate for the medical staff, who accused my uncle, as he vomited both from his mouth and from a tracheotomy hole in his neck, of faking his illness. The next day, my uncle was dead and Maxo was released from detention. It was his fifty-sixth birthday. Once the pain of his father's death had eased, he joked, "My parents never wanted me to have a happy birthday."

After unsuccessfully pursuing asylum, Maxo returned to Haiti. He missed his five young children, who were constantly calling to ask when he was coming home. There was also his father's work to continue—small schools and churches to oversee all over Haiti. The return, though, was brutal. During our telephone calls, he talked about the high price of food in Port-au-Prince. "If it's hard for me, imagine for the others," he'd say.

His time in detention in the United States had sensitized him to prison conditions and to the lack of prisoners' rights in Haiti. He often called asking for money to buy food, which he then took to the national penitentiary.

This generosity, along with the Haitian sense of kindness and community, is perhaps why, immediately after four stories collapsed on Maxo on January 12th, family, friends, and even strangers began to dig for him and his wife and their children. They managed to free his wife and all but one of his children, ten-year-old Nozial, from the rubble two days later. Even when there was little hope, they continued to dig for him and for those who had died along with him: some children who were being tutored after school, the tutors, a few parents who had stopped by to discuss their children's schoolwork. We will never know for sure how many.

The day that Maxo's remains were found, the call came with some degree of excitement. At least he would not rest permanently in the rubble. At least he would not go into a mass grave. Somehow, though, I sense that he would not have minded. Everyone is being robbed of rituals, he might have said, why not me?

By the time Maxo's body was uncovered, cell phones were finally working again, bringing a flurry of desperate voices. One cousin had an open gash in her head that was still bleeding. Another had a broken back and had gone to three field hospitals trying to get it X-rayed. Another was sleeping outside her house and was terribly thirsty. One child had been so traumatized that she lost her voice. An in-law had no blood-pressure medicine. Most had not eaten for days. There were friends and family members whose entire towns had been destroyed, and dozens from whom we have had no word at all.

Everyone sounded eerily calm on the phone. No one was screaming. No one was crying. No one said "Why me?" or "We're cursed." Even as the aftershocks kept coming, they'd say, "The ground is shaking again," as though this had become a normal occurrence. They inquired about family members outside Haiti: an elderly relative, a baby, my one-year-old daughter.

I cried and apologized. "I'm sorry I can't be with you," I said. "If not for the baby—"

My nearly six-foot-tall twenty-two-year-old cousin—the beauty queen we nicknamed Naomi Campbell—who says that she is hungry and has been sleeping in bushes with dead bodies nearby, stops me.

"Don't cry," she says. "That's life."

"No, it's not life," I say. "Or it should not be."

"It is," she insists. "That's what it is. And life, like death, lasts only *yon ti moman*." Only a little while.

On the Fringes of the Physical World

Meghan Daum

It started in cold weather; fall was drifting away into an intolerable chill. I was on the tail end of twenty-six, living in New York City, and trying to support myself as a writer. One morning I logged on to my America Online account to find a message under the heading "is this the real meghan daum?" It came from someone with the screen name PFSlider. The body of the message consisted of five sentences, written entirely in lowercase letters, of perfectly turned flattery, something about PFSlider's admiration of some newspaper and magazine articles I had published over the last year and a half, something else about his resulting infatuation with me, and something about his being a sportswriter in California.

I was charmed for a moment or so, engaged for the thirty seconds that it took me to read the message and fashion a reply. Though it felt strange to be in the position of confirming that I was indeed "the real meghan daum," I managed to say, "Yes, it's me. Thank you for writing." I clicked the "Send Now" icon and shot my words into the void, where I forgot about PFSlider until the next day when I received another message, this one entitled "eureka." "wow, it is you," he wrote, still in lowercase. He chronicled the various conditions under which he'd read my few and far between articles: a boardwalk in Laguna Beach, the spring training pressroom for the baseball team he covered for a Los Angeles newspaper. He confessed to having a "crazy crush" on me. He referred to me as "princess daum." He said he wanted to propose marriage or at least have lunch with me during one of his two annual trips to New York. He managed to do all of this without sounding like a schmuck. As I read the note, I smiled the kind of smile one tries to suppress, the kind of smile that arises during a sappy movie one never even admits to seeing. The letter was outrageous and endearingly pathetic, possibly the practical joke of a friend trying to rouse me out of a temporary writer's block. But the kindness pouring forth from my computer screen was unprecedented and bizarrely exhilarating. I logged off and thought about it for a few hours before writing back to express how flattered and touched—this was probably the first time I had ever used the word "touched" in earnest—I was by his message.

I had received e-mail messages from strangers before, most of them kind and friendly and courteous—all of those qualities that generally get checked with the coats at the cocktail parties that comprise what the information age has now forced us to call the "three-dimensional world." I am always warmed by an un-solicited gesture of admiration or encouragement, amazed that anyone would bother, shocked that communication from a stranger could be fueled by anything other than an attempt to get a job or make what the professional world has come to call "a connection."

I am not what most people would call a "computer person." I have utterly no interest in chat rooms, news groups, or most Web sites. I derive a palpable thrill from sticking an actual letter in the U.S. mail. But e-mail, though at that time I generally only sent and received a few messages a week, proves a useful forum for my par-ticular communication anxieties. I have a constant, low-grade fear of the telephone. I often call people with the intention of getting their answering machines. There is something about the live voice that has become startling, unnervingly organic, as volatile as incendiary talk radio. PFSlider and I tossed a few innocuous, smart-assed notes back and forth over the week following his first message. His name was Pete. He was twenty-nine and single. I revealed very little about myself, relying instead on the ironic commentary and forced witticisms that are the conceit of most e-mail messages. But I quickly developed an oblique affection for PFSlider. I was excited when there was a message from him, mildly depressed when there wasn't. After a few weeks, he gave me his phone number. I did not give him mine but he looked me up anyway and called me one Friday night. I was home. I picked up the phone. His voice was jarring yet not unpleasant. He held up more than his end of the con-versation for an hour and when he asked permission to call me again, I accepted as though we were in a previous century.

Pete, as I was forced to call him on the phone—I never could wrap my mind around his actual name, privately referring to him as PFSlider, "e-mail guy," or even "baseball boy"—began calling me two or three times a week. He asked if he could meet me in person and I said that would be okay. Christmas was a few weeks away and he would be returning east to see his family. From there, he would take the short flight to New York and have lunch with me. "It is my off-season mission to meet you," he said. "There will probably be a snowstorm," I said. "I'll take a team of sled dogs," he answered. We talked about our work and our families, about baseball and Bill Clinton and Howard Stern and sex, about his hatred for Los Angeles and how much he wanted a new job. Other times we would find each other logged on to America Online at the same time and type back and forth for hours. For me, this was far superior to the phone. Through typos and mis-spellings, he flirted maniacally. "I have an absurd crush on you," he said. "If I like you in person you must promise to marry me." I was coy and conceited, telling him to get a life, baiting him into complimenting me further, teasing him in a way I would never have dared in the real world or even on the phone. I would stay up until 3 A.M. typing with him, smiling at the screen, getting so giddy that I couldn't fall asleep. I was having difficulty recalling what I used to do at night. My phone was tied up for hours at a time. No one in the real world could reach me, and I didn't really care.

In off moments, I heard echoes of things I'd said just weeks earlier: "The Internet is destroying the world. Human communication will be rendered obsolete. We will all develop carpal tunnel syndrome and die." But curiously, the Internet, at least in the limited form in which I was using it, was having the opposite effect. My interaction with PFSlider was more human than much of what I experienced in the daylight realm of live beings. I was certainly putting more energy into the relationship than I had put into any before, giving him attention that was by definition undivided, relishing the safety of the distance by opting to be truthful rather than doling out the white lies that have become the staple of real life. The outside world—the place where I walked around on the concrete, avoiding people I didn't want to deal with, peppering the ground with half-truths, and applying my motto of "let the machine take it" to almost any scenario—was sliding into the periphery of my mind. I was a better person with PFSlider. I was someone I could live with.

This borrowed identity is, of course, the primary convention of Internet relationships. The false comfort of the cyberspace persona has been identified as one of the maladies of our time, another avenue for the remoteness that so famously plagues contemporary life. But the better person that I was to PFSlider was not a result of being a different person to him. It was simply that I was a desired person, the object of a blind man's gaze. I may not have known my suitor, but for the first time in my life, I knew the deal. I knew when I'd hear from him and how I'd hear from him. I knew he wanted me because he said he wanted me, because the distance and facelessness and lack of gravity of it all allowed him to be sweeter to me than most real-life people had ever managed. For the first time in my life, I was involved in a ritualized courtship. Never before had I realized how much that kind of structure was missing from my everyday life.

And so PFSlider became my everyday life. All the tangible stuff—the trees outside, my friends, the weather—fell away. I could physically feel my brain. My body did not exist. I had no skin, no hair, no bones; all desire had converted itself into a cerebral current that reached nothing but my frontal lobe. Lust was something not felt but thought. My brain was devouring all of my other organs and gaining speed with each swallow. There was no outdoors, the sky and wind were irrelevant. There was only the computer screen and the phone, my chair and maybe a glass of water. Pete started calling every day, sometimes twice, even three times. Most mornings I would wake up to find a message from PFSlider, composed in Pacific time while I slept in the wee hours. "I had a date last night," he wrote, "and I am not ashamed to say it was doomed from the start because

I couldn't stop thinking about you." Then, a few days later, "If you stood before me now, I would plant the warmest kiss on your check that I could muster."

I fired back a message slapping this hand. "We must be careful where we tread," I said. This was true but not sincere. I wanted it, all of it. I wanted the deepest bow down before me. I wanted my ego not merely massaged but kneaded. I wanted unfettered affection, soul mating, true romance. In the weeks that had elapsed since I picked up "is this the real meghan daum?" the real me underwent some kind of meltdown, a systemic rejection of all the savvy and independence I had worn for years like a grown-up Girl Scout badge. Since graduating from college, I had spent three years in a serious relationship and two years in a state of neither looking for a boyfriend nor particularly avoiding one. I had had the requisite number of false starts and five-night stands, dates that I wasn't sure were dates, emphatically casual affairs that buckled under their own inertia even before dawn broke through the iron-guarded windows of stale, one-room city apartments. Even though I was heading into my late twenties, I was still a child, ignorant of dance steps or health insurance, a prisoner of credit-card debt and student loans and the nagging feeling that I didn't want anyone to find me until I had pulled myself into some semblance of an adult. I was a true believer in the urban dream—in years of struggle succumbing to brilliant success, in getting a break, in making it. Like most of my friends, I was selfish by design. To want was more virtuous than to need. I wanted someone to love me but I certainly didn't need it. I didn't want to be alone, but as long as I was, I had no choice but to wear my solitude as though it were haute couture. The worst sin imaginable was not cruelty or bitchiness or even professional failure but vulnerability. To admit to loneliness was to slap the face of progress. It was to betray the times in which we lived.

But PFSlider derailed me. He gave me all of what I'd never realized I wanted. He called not only when he said he would, but unexpectedly, just to say hello. His guard was not merely down but nonexistent. He let his phone bill grow to towering proportions. He thought about me all the time and admitted it. He talked about me with his friends and admitted it. He arranged his holiday schedule around our impending date. He managed to charm me with sports analogies. He courted and wooed and romanced me. He didn't hesitate. He was unblinking and unapologetic, all nerviness and balls to the wall. He wasn't cheap. He went out of his way. I'd never seen anything like it.

Of all the troubling details of this story, the one that bothers me the most is the way I slurped up his attention like some kind of dying animal. My addiction to PFSlider's messages indicated a monstrous narcissism. But it also revealed a subtler desire that I didn't fully understand at the time. My need to experience an old-fashioned kind of courtship was stronger than I had ever imagined. The epistolary quality of our relationship put our communication closer to the eighteenth century than the uncertain millennium. For the first time in my life, I was not involved in a protracted "hang out" that would lead to a quasi-romance. I was involved in a well-defined structure, a neat little space in which we were both safe to express the panic and intrigue of our mutual affection. Our interaction was refreshingly orderly, noble in its vigor, dignified despite its shamelessness. It was far removed from the randomness of real-life relationships. We had an intimacy that seemed custom-made for our strange, lonely times. It seemed custom-made for me.

The day of our date was frigid and sunny. Pete was sitting at the bar of the restaurant when I arrived. We shook hands. For a split second he leaned toward me with his chin as if to kiss me. He was shorter than I had imagined, though he was not short. He registered to me as neither handsome nor un-handsome. He had very nice hands. He wore a very nice shirt. We were seated at a very nice table. I scanned the restaurant for people I knew, saw no one and couldn't decide how I felt about that.

He talked and I heard nothing he said. He talked and talked and talked. I stared at his profile and tried to figure out if I liked him. He seemed to be saying nothing in particular, though it went on forever. Later we went to the Museum of Natural History and watched a science film about the physics of storms. We walked around looking for the dinosaurs and he talked so much that I wanted to cry. Outside, walking along Central Park West at dusk, through the leaves, past the horse-drawn carriages and yellow cabs and splendid lights of Manhattan at Christmas, he grabbed my hand to kiss me and I didn't let him. I felt as if my brain had been stuffed with cotton. Then, for some reason, I invited him back to my apartment, gave him a few beers, and finally let him kiss me on the lumpy futon in my bedroom. The radiator clanked. The phone rang and the machine picked up. A car alarm blared outside. A key turned in the door as one of my roommates came home. I had no sensation at all, only the dull déjà vu of being back in some college dorm room, making out in a generic fashion on an Indian throw rug while Cat Stevens' *Greatest Hits* played on the portable stereo. I wanted Pete out of my apartment. I wanted to hand him his coat, close the door behind him, and fight the ensuing emptiness by turning on the computer and taking comfort in PFSlider.

When Pete finally did leave, I sulked. The ax had fallen. He'd talked way too much. He was hyper. He hadn't let me talk, although I hadn't tried very hard. I berated myself from every angle, for not kissing him on Central Park West, for letting him kiss me at all, for not liking him, for wanting to like him more than I had wanted anything in such a long time. I was horrified by the realization that I had invested so heavily in a made-up character, a character in whose creation I'd had a greater hand than even Pete himself. How could I, a person so self-congratulatingly reasonable, have gotten sucked into a scenario that was more akin to a television talk show than the relatively full and sophisticated life I was so convinced I led? How could I have received a fan letter and allowed it to go this far? Then a huge bouquet of FTD flowers arrived from him. No one had ever sent me flowers before. I was sick with sadness. I hated either the world or myself, and probably both.

No one had ever forced me to forgive them before. But for some reason, I forgave Pete. I cut him more slack than I ever had anyone. I granted him an official pardon, excused his failure for not living up to PFSlider. Instead of blaming him, I blamed the Earth itself, the invasion of tangible things into the immaculate communication PFSlider and I had created. With its roommates and ringing phones and subzero temperatures, the physical world came barreling in with all the obstreperousness of a major weather system, and I ignored it. As human beings with actual flesh and hand gestures and Gap clothing, Pete and I were utterly incompatible, but I pretended otherwise. In the weeks that followed I pictured him and saw the image of a plane lifting off over an overcast city. PFSlider was otherworldly, more a concept than a person. His romance lay in the notion of flight, the physics of gravity defiance. So when he offered to send me a plane ticket to spend the weekend with him in Los Angeles, I took it as an extension of our blissful remoteness, a three-dimensional e-mail message lasting an entire weekend. I pretended it was a good idea.

The temperature on the runway at JFK was seven degrees Fahrenheit. We sat for three hours waiting for de-icing. Finally we took off over the frozen city, the DC-10 hurling itself against the wind. The ground below shrank into a drawing of itself. Laptop computers were plopped onto tray tables. The air recirculated and dried out my contact lenses. I watched movies without the sound and thought to myself that they were probably better that way. Something about the plastic interior of the fuselage and the plastic forks and the din of the air and the engines was soothing and strangely sexy, as fabricated and seductive as PFSlider. I thought about Pete and wondered if I could ever turn him into an actual human being, if I could ever even want to. I knew so many people in real life, people to whom I spoke face-to-face, people who made me laugh or made me frustrated or happy or bored. But I'd never given any of them as much as I'd given PFSlider. I'd never forgiven their spasms and their speeches, never tied up my phone for hours in order to talk to them. I'd never bestowed such senseless tenderness on anyone.

We descended into LAX. We hit the tarmac and the seat belt signs blinked off. I hadn't moved my body in eight hours, and now, I was walking through the tunnel to the gate, my clothes wrinkled, my hair matted, my hands shaking. When I saw Pete in the terminal, his face registered to me as blank and impossible to process as the first time I'd met him. He kissed me chastely. On the way out to the parking lot, he told me that he was being seriously considered for a job in New York. He was flying back there next week. If he got the job he'd be moving within the month. I looked at him in astonishment. Something silent and invisible seemed to fall on us. Outside, the wind was warm and the Avis and Hertz buses ambled alongside the curb of Terminal 5. The palm trees shook and the air seemed as heavy and earthly as Pete's hand, which held mine for a few seconds before dropping it to get his car keys out of his pocket. The leaves on the trees were unmanageably real. He stood before me, all flesh and preoccupation. The physical world had invaded our space. For this I could not forgive him.

Everything now was for the touching. Everything was buildings and bushes, parking meters and screen doors and sofas. Gone was the computer; the erotic darkness of the telephone; the clean, single dimension of Pete's voice at 1 A.M. It was nighttime, yet the combination of sight and sound was blinding. We went to a restaurant and ate outside on the sidewalk. We were strained for conversation. I tried not to care. We drove to his apartment and stood under the ceiling light not really looking at each other. Something was happening that we needed to snap out of. Any moment now, I thought. Any moment and we'll be all right. These moments were crowded with elements, with carpet fibers and direct light and the smells of everything that had a smell. They left marks as they passed. It was all wrong. Gravity was all there was.

For three days, we crawled along the ground and tried to pull ourselves up. We talked about things that I can no longer remember. We read the *Los Angeles Times* over breakfast. We drove north past Santa Barbara to tour the wine country. I stomped around in my clunky shoes and black leather jacket, a killer of ants and earthworms and any hope in our abilities to speak and be understood. Not until studying myself in the bathroom mirror of a highway rest stop did I fully realize the preposterousness of my uniform. I felt like the shot in a human shot put, an object that could not be lifted, something that secretly weighed more than the world itself. We ate an expensive dinner. We checked into a hotel and watched television. Pete talked at me and through me and past me. I tried to listen. I tried to talk. But I bored myself and irritated him. Our conversation was a needle that could not be threaded. Still, we played nice. We tried to care and pretended to keep trying long after we had given up. In the car on the way home, he told me I was cynical, and I didn't have the presence of mind to ask him just how many cynics he had met who would travel three thousand miles to see someone they barely knew. Just for a chance. Just because the depths of my hope exceeded the thickness of my leather jacket and the thickness of my skin. And at that moment, I released myself into the sharp knowledge that communication had once again eliminated itself as a possibility.

Pete drove me to the airport at 7 A.M. so I could make my eight o'clock flight home. He kissed me goodbye, another chaste peck I recognized from countless dinner parties and dud dates from real life. He said he'd call me in a few days when he got to New York for his job interview, which he had discussed only in passing and with no reference to the fact that New York was where I happened to live. I returned home to the frozen January. A few days later, he came to New York and we didn't see each other. He called me from the plane back to Los Angeles to tell me, through the static, that he had gotten the job. He was moving to my city.

PFSlider was dead. Pete had killed him. I had killed him. I'd killed my own persona too, the girl on the phone and online, the character created by some writer who'd captured him one morning long ago as he read the newspaper. There would be no meeting him in distant hotel lobbies during the baseball season. There would be no more phone calls or e-mail messages. In a single moment, Pete had completed his journey out of our mating dance and officially stepped into the regular world, the world that gnawed at me daily, the world that fed those five-night stands, the world where romance could not be sustained because we simply did not know how to do it. Here, we were all chitchat and leather jackets, bold proclaimers of all that we did not need. But what struck me most about this affair was the unpredictable nature of our demise. Unlike most cyber romances, which seem to come fully equipped with the inevitable set of misrepresentations and false expectations, PFSlider and I had played it fairly straight. Neither of us had lied. We'd done the best we could. We were dead from natural causes rather than virtual ones.

Within a two-week period after I returned from Los Angeles, at least seven people confessed to me the vagaries of their own e-mail affairs. This topic arose, unprompted, over the course of normal conversation. Four of these people had gotten on planes and met their correspondents, traveling from New Haven to Baltimore, New York to Montana, Texas to Virginia, and New York to Johannesburg. These were normal people, writers and lawyers and scientists, whom I knew from the real world. They were all smart, attractive, and more than a little sheepish about admitting just how deep they had been sucked in. Very few had met in chat rooms. Instead, the messages had started after chance meetings at parties and on planes; some, like me, had received notes in response to things they'd written online or elsewhere. Two of these people had fallen in love, the others chalked it up to a strange, uniquely postmodern experience. They all did things they would never do in the real world: they sent flowers, they took chances, they forgave. I heard most of these stories in the close confines of smoky bars and crowded restaurants, and we would all shake our heads in bewilderment as we told our tales, our eyes focused on some distant point that could never be reigned in to the surface of the Earth. Mostly it was the courtship ritual that had drawn us in. We had finally wooed and been wooed, given an old-fashioned structure through which to attempt the process of romance. E-mail had become an electronic epistle, a yearned-for rule book. The black and white of the type, the welcome respite from the distractions of smells and weather and other people, had, in effect, allowed us to be vulnerable and passionate enough to actually care about something. It allowed us to do what was necessary to experience love. It was not the Internet that contributed to our remote, fragmented lives. The problem was life itself.

The story of PFSlider still makes me sad. Not so much because we no longer have anything to do with one another, but because it forces me to grapple with all three dimensions of daily life with greater awareness than I used to. After it became clear that our relationship would never transcend the screen and the phone, after the painful realization that our face-to-face knowledge of each other had in fact permanently contaminated the screen and the phone, I hit the pavement again, went through the motions of real life, said "hello" and "goodbye" to people in the regular way. In darker moments, I remain mortified by everything that happened with PFSlider. It terrifies me to admit to a firsthand understanding of the way the heart and the ego are entwined. Like diseased trees that have folded in on one another, our need to worship fuses with our need to be worshipped. Love eventually becomes only about how much mystique can be maintained. It upsets me even more to see how this entanglement is made so much more intense, so unhampered and intoxicating, by way of a remote access like e-mail. But I'm also thankful that I was forced to unpack the raw truth of my need and stare at it for a while. This was a dare I wouldn't have taken in three dimensions.

The last time I saw Pete he was in New York, thousands of miles away from what had been his home and a million miles away from PFSlider. In a final gesture of decency, in what I later realized was the most ordinary kind of closure, he took me out to dinner. We talked about nothing. He paid the bill. He drove me home in his rental car, the smell and sound of which was as arbitrary and impersonal as what we now were to each other. Then he disappeared forever. He became part of the muddy earth, as unmysterious as anything located next door. I stood on my stoop and felt that familiar rush of indifference. Pete had joined the angry and exhausted living. He drifted into my chaos, and joined me down in reality where, even if we met on the street, we'd never see each other again, our faces obscured by the branches and bodies and falling debris that make up the ether of the physical world.

Welcome to Afghanistan

Matt Farwell

It's three in the morning and I am falling hard into a five-foot-deep ditch. Like a cartoon character, legs splaying out in front of me, I land square on my back. The wind is knocked out of my chest. Luckily my body armor and helmet absorb most of the impact, and before the last profanity can even leave my mouth the machine gunner walking fifteen meters next to me is there, pulling me up. Under the weight of sixty-five pounds of weapons, ammunition, body armor, and gear, I stumble awkwardly to my feet and continue walking towards the mountain that we have to climb to look for Taliban activity. It's not even light out yet and I'm sweating my ass off, dirty and tired, hands and legs filled with tiny thorns. This day already sucks. Welcome to Afghanistan. As Drill Sergeant Berg would say, during rainy nights at Ft. Benning, "Welcome to the motherfuckin' infantry."

*

Before I was climbing mountains in full battle rattle and falling in ditches, I shared a dive apartment with a capricious college roommate. Dwayne was touched, slightly. He liked to break plates and scream randomly at passersby out of our second-story window. The apartment, in a rapidly gentrifying locale but still clinging to its shady, ghetto roots, was littered with the detritus of two overeducated children of privilege—books and papers stacked on every flat surface not already occupied with beer bottles; a sink overflowing with dishes; polo shirts and khakis strewn on the floor. Life was fun but filled with a certain amount of melancholy, the material maelstrom inside the apartment acting as a window into my conflicted brain. I'd never been particularly happy in college, and by the middle of my third year things were beginning to reach a boiling point. The apartment and what went on there were just the physical manifestations of that slow boil.

My living conditions are just a little different now. Instead of an apartment shared with just one whacked-out roommate, I now have nine crazy infantrymen all crammed into one room. It is thirty feet by fourteen feet, with dusty concrete floors and furniture roughly constructed out of unfinished plywood and two-by-fours. Spread about the room is the debris of nine men in constant flux and motion—white, cold-weather boots here; dirty socks next to them; a rolled up carpet there; half-drunk bottles of water and partially eaten bags of beef jerky and ramen noodles on the shelves and scattered around the floor. Except for the four sets of body armor, helmets, and front-load equipment carriers containing 210 rounds of 5.56 mm ball ammunition; Israeli tourniquets, canteens, and night vision goggles hung neatly off each bunk; and the assortment of M4 carbines, squad automatic weapons, grenade launchers, and shotguns around each bed, it might be familiar to any of my friends in college who live in similar dumps.

"Dude, I think I want to get a tattoo on my head when I go back to the States on leave . . . think I'd get in trouble for that? I want like a big fucking dagger right on the top or maybe some bullet holes or maybe just cracks, you know, like my head is cracked," Clit says.

Clit and I sit in the guard tower, staring emptily at the night below, panning the horizon to look for any movement. Clit speaks each sentence like it bears the utmost importance, but at least his sentences are always interesting.

"I always had a .38 and a TEK on me. The TEK fit perfectly under the seat. I wore gloves everywhere I went. We did a lot of illegal stuff. We used to go out on overpasses with bags of shit and piss and vinegar—like that's no joke, shit and piss and vinegar—and drop it on shit." He throws his cigarette butt over the sandbag barrier on the guard tower, stands up to stretch. He's one of the best guys in the platoon, a natural soldier and leader, smart and resourceful. He's got some great stories from before he joined the Army.

*

While I was growing up, my dad was in the Air Force. When I lived in Turkey and Germany, practically all my friends were military brats. My brother served as a grunt in Ranger Battalion and the 25th Infantry Division before he became an Army helicopter pilot. As a kid the thought of being in the Army had always been in the back of my mind. When it was time to start looking at colleges, I again thought about the military, applying for ROTC scholarships to cover the cost of Duke or Yale, and considered going to West Point. To figure out if I really wanted to become a cadet, I attended a weeklong recruiting session at the U.S. Military Academy. To put it in the most delicate way possible, it sucked. The potential cadets seemed stiff, wooden, and out of touch. The actual cadets were either bitter because they were stuck at the academy on their summer break, or they just seemed too uptight to hang out with. The only one who seemed to have any sort of sense about him was a prior service infantryman who spoke with a thick West Virginia accent around the thick wad of Copenhagen that was per-petually shoved into his lower lip. Most of my days there were spent with a New Hampshire skater whose mom had tricked him into attending, bugging the hell out of the straight-laced applicants and cadets by claiming to be a socialist or refusing to get out of bed in the morning because we were: "An Army of one. A tired Army of one."

West Point was out.

Then I was rejected by my top two college choices. Not getting into Yale was crushing because my girlfriend at the time was a freshman there and I had visions of happily ever after with an Ivy League degree. Not getting into Deep Springs, a bizarre all-male cattle ranch/college hidden in the middle of the California desert and populated by twenty brilliant misfits, was somewhat less of a disap-pointment, simply because it seemed so far out. So I went to the University of Virginia, or "the University," because it had accepted me into its honors program and I had in-state tuition. I decided to go to college in the first place because I was scared not to, because it seemed like the only thing for a smart kid graduating from an exclusive private boarding school to do. I really had no idea what I'd do once I got there.

Days here, whatever they are, are not filled with the same sort of uncer-tainty that occupied my college era. Between the normal humdrum of trying to survive in the heat, with the flies and bad food, there's the lingering knowledge that at any second one of my sergeants can come into the room and tell us to get our gear the fuck on, we've got to go. Our best time is three minutes—to throw on our body armor, load-carrying vest, and helmet, grab our weapons, and run out the door to our up-armored Humvees to respond to whatever crisis might erupt.

*

I remember sitting in UVA's Alderman Library stacks. I had twenty pages waiting to be filled with fleshed-out material from the couple of hundred note cards filled with citations, quotes, facts, and figures that all sat next to the com-puter. They sat there mockingly, a cluster of white paper bones waiting to be animated into a body. I had put an absurd amount of preparation into that paper—hours and hours in the library, on the phone, cruising databases, on the phone with sources, chewing through dusty old archives. All that work, all that preparation, for nothing. Twenty blank pages, all inconsequential pages. I remember thinking: *Why even bother?* All this preparation for something that will be read, halfheartedly, by a TA and then thrown away—another mean-ingless cluster of words carefully arranged and quickly forgotten. It seemed like a microcosm of my whole college career, a bunch of seemingly pointless preparations from grade school on up to receive a piece of parchment that sig-nified nothing except that I can read, write, and show up to class on time. I was frustrated.

*

"Get your shit on and go to the trucks. Scouts got hit with an IED." The three guys from my platoon that I am eating with and I just look at each other for a second—then get up, leaving our trays, and run for the door. We run back to our barracks, half throw on our gear, and sprint out the front door to the truck still buckling and fastening straps.

"Radios on?" I ask, sliding into the back passenger seat, banging my M4 carbine and M203 grenade launcher against the seat's well.

"Yeah, they're good," our driver, Bautista, says as we pull out, while Burke is hopping into the turret behind the .50 caliber machine gun. "How's the FBCB2? Is it showing the screen?" I look up toward the computer monitor next to our lieutenant's seat, the glowing screen flickers to life and shows our map location as we move.

"Yeah, it's coming on."

"Fuck man."

"Yeah. Fuck."

*

Every Tuesday night on top of the dilapidated frat house was the same. James, Jon, me, and a case of Miller Light. James and Jon were both products of an exclusive Manhattan Jesuit high school, overeducated and neurotic. They half discussed, half debated Nietzsche and Heidegger every time we got together. I sat outside the conversation, gulped at my beer, looked at the stars, contributed comments here and there. I'd read those books, thought about them, written papers taking this position or that, but frankly, rants about the "thing unto itself" and the "übermensch" weren't interesting, not tangible at all.

As we got progressively drunker, the talk of continental philosophy drifted a bit. Jon usually started playing his guitar; James ranted about his father, his girlfriend, the normal bitching. Beer cans accumulated around our feet and were crushed. Then I would stumble down the stairs and begin the long walk back to my apartment.

*

"Who's going to get Rashid?" We pull up in front of the Tactical Operation Center and Burke climbs out of the turret, jumping awkwardly off the hood while we are still moving, then stumbling toward our interpreter's room. Rashid, a twenty-three year old Afghani who picked up English while a refugee in Peshawar, comes running out toward our truck. We pass him his body armor and Soviet-made pistol, and then wait to roll out of the gate. My hands are shaking slightly as I put on my gloves.

"Who's got batteries?" Burke asks. The sun will be going down in a couple of hours, and scouts are about that far from our location, so anything we do in the next twelve hours will have to be through the greenish glow of our night vision goggles.

"Um . . . I've got four, plus two in my camera if we're desperate," I tell him.

*

Sara was the beautiful, smart, vivacious Cuban-American senior I'd had a crush on for the better part of my junior year. One day, half-drunk, I slipped a note through her mail slot. It was a note a week in the making—revised over and over, a perfect profession of love and devotion. I received her reply two days later, two pages of beautiful red lettering. Each perfectly formed consonant and vowel was a knife to the heart, each overly precise sentence ripped chunks out of my ego. It was hard to look at the whole letter, so I read it in disjointed pieces, trying to amuse myself by putting the puzzle together. I already knew what it said in so many words.

I had called James's cell phone and told him, wirelessly tethering my burden to him.

"Fuckin' sucks, dude," he'd groaned. "She's a fuckin' bitch. Forget it. Me and Jon are smoking opium. Come over, it's pretty badass, feels like you're a couple of joints and a few Vicodin deep."

I hung up, drove back to my apartment, and demolished half a case of Heineken while watching overdue videos until I passed out. My pillow was wet when I woke up.

*

I'd been cramming my brain for this one particular exam—up all night, wired on Red Bull and nicotine, shoving public policy readings long neglected into my short-term memory. The exam sat on the desk in front of me, a neatly typed-up sheet next to an open blue book. The first question was easy, I recall knowing that one. But after that my mind went blank. I stared. For an hour I stared like that, while pens scratched on paper all around me. I got up, turned in the empty blue book, and walked straight to my dean's office.

"Sir, I fucked up my exam. I'm not sure I can do this anymore."

Within the day, the paperwork was filed, stamped, and put away. Officially I'd withdrawn for the semester and taken a leave of absence from the university. The hardest part was telling my parents. I was a college dropout.

*

"Dammit, I didn't grab any snivel gear."

In my rush to get out to the trucks I hadn't grabbed any raincoats or fleece, nothing to keep me warm during the cold Afghani night. We sit up at the Tactical Operations Center awaiting permission from the battalion commander to enter the fray. We wait for ten minutes, which seems like an eternity, then twenty, and then an hour. We never actually get permission to go tonight and so we return to our rooms, shedding our dusty gear as the adrenaline seeps from our bodies.

*

Still in Virginia, but no longer in school, I had taken a job at Lowe's, plotting my next move while hawking faucets and showerheads. That got old fast, naturally, but I really wasn't planning on going back to college for a while. The Army had always held a certain romantic appeal, even if I had decided West Point wasn't for me: Lowe's was going nowhere, college was boring, and shit . . . why not?

So one day, coming home from work, I walked into an Army recruiter's office and signed up for three years as an infantryman. It had seemed like a logical decision—I'd get some adventure, get out of my head, and get away from, at least for a little while, my privileged white-boy roots for a life in which I was no more special than the next guy with an identical haircut and identical camouflage clothing.

I couldn't see anything else in the Army I wanted to do but pull a trigger, couldn't see myself repairing helicopters or decoding messages or anything like that. I just had the itch to carry all my gear on my back, strap a weapon to my front, and train to "close with and destroy the enemy." Who knows, maybe that enemy was myself.

Into the Gulf:
A Journal–Day 10:
Beyond the Oiled Pelican

David Gessner

I knew pelicans before they were famous. I started studying them when I first moved to the South, seven years ago now, and after a couple of years here I wrote an essay about the birds, and about my daughter and learning to surf, for *Orion* magazine. As I observed and read about pelicans, I learned how much water their enormous gular pouches can hold (21 pints or 17 and a half pounds), what they sound like (nothing, they are more or less mute), and even got to see a newborn emerge from its shell (disgusting and beautiful at the same time). What I didn't and couldn't know was that some years off in the future, pelicans, particularly the oiled variety, would become the media darlings of one of the worst eco disasters in this country's history. What I didn't know was that, while the egrets and laughing gulls and tricolored herons bristled with resentment, pelicans would claim center stage.

I've got nothing against my old friend, *Pelecanus occidentalis*. It's just that the problem with telling the story of the spill in broad and simple strokes, as the national media has almost laughably done, as a kind of adventure story fit for *Boy's Life*—Will they cap the well? Will they fire the evil BP guy? Look there's lots of oil! Oh, now there's not so much oil—is that once the obvious symbols go away the media can too. They can say "Look there aren't so many oiled pelicans anymore," and then do exactly what the *New York Times* did a few days ago, and announce that it turns out the whole oil thing isn't so bad anymore. Okay, back to business everyone. Maybe a better, if less sexy, symbol than pelicans would be those periwinkles I saw in Grand Bay with Bill Finch. They may not look good on the cover of a magazine but they get at the point of what this whole thing is about, what Finch called "connectivity issues." The latest news on the connectivity front is that oil and dispersant droplets have been found on almost all the blue crab larvae that scientists have studied in the Gulf of Mexico.

*   *   *

From Buras I headed north to New Orleans, which is kind of an oiled pelican in its own right. If I was joking about egrets resenting pelicans, then I am deadly serious when I say that Alabamans and Mississippians resent Louisianans for getting most of the media attention, and therefore most of the money, and that within Louisiana itself the rest of the state resents New Orleans for the same reason. It took me almost two hours of driving north to reach New Orleans, which gets at one of the most common misconceptions about the place. If you are like me you picture the city as a whole lot closer to the Gulf, and the oil, than it really is, and though I don't want to take anything away from a citizenry that has endured more pain than Job, the consideration of the spill seemed somewhat more theoretical than it did down in Buras, despite the obvious impacts on tourism and seafood. I stayed at the first hotel I saw after pulling into the French Quarter, The Maison Dupuy, and soon found myself having a drink at a wonderfully cool (I still wasn't using air conditioning in the car and before I changed my sweat-stained shirt it looked like it had been tie dyed) bar called French 75. There I discovered a delightful drink, white rum and fruit and herbs, that I would order every night of my stay and then sit back and savor it, imagining myself to be a kind of Hemingway figure, masculine and romantic. When I asked what it was they said something like "Pisco," which was actually the name of the rum, and it wasn't until the last night of my trip that I learned the real name of the drink, a name that quickly burst my macho pretensions. My drink was called a "Daisy."

My host at the bar was an outgoing and generous man named Kristian Sonnier, who was a regular and was therefore a pal of French 75's renowned bartender, Chris, a bald man with thick black framed glasses who strutted about the place in a white suit coat and black bow tie. (For those with a UNCW connection, he looked almost exactly like a hairless version of Bryan Sandala.) Chris fed me my Daisies and then my delicious Cornish game hen and these perfect little fries (excuse me, *pomme frites*) that looked like their middles had been inflated with a tiny bicycle pump. I probably weighed about fifty pounds more than Kristian, but I noticed that as we shifted to beer and I started slowing down, he started picking up the drinking pace, something that I noted in every New Orleanian I encountered. We took "walking beers" through the French Quarter and headed down to the river in search of the King of the Oiled Pelicans. Kristian said the King was to be found in his natural spot-lighted habitat by the water, espousing about the spill, which the locals found comical since the oil was nowhere near their city. But the locals also loved the King, and the attention he shone on their city, and that love was apparent as we closed in on the CNN truck. Near the truck a small crowd had gathered to watch the white-haired man in the too-tight black T-shirt as he delivered his newscast.

My host the next night, who was somewhat more cantankerous than Kristian, would call Anderson Cooper "the biggest shit stain on the water." I could see it, the whole phony baloney, superstar, simplistic take on complicated issues. But Kristian was more philosophical: "Of course it's kind of funny that he's broadcasting from the river, a hundred miles from the action. But he gives voice to the people's anger. He has Billy Nungesser on quite a lot for instance." And, to his credit, Cooper, when he finished broadcasting, came over to where our small crowd stood and shook hands with the men and hugged the ladies. If there was an edge of Beatlemania to it, the man did his best to conduct himself with dignity, signing things and getting his picture taken and when asked about a good place to get a drink suggesting a street outside of the Quarter (which, after all, is the oiled pelican of the city's neighborhoods) that Kristian said was a good, insider's call. The only truly embarrassing moment was when some college kids began to slather over the poor man. One particularly enthusiastic (drunken) boy went on and on about how much he loved "Anderson" and how he wanted to be him when/if he grew up, and after he got his picture taken next to his man went skipping off down toward the river, lifted on the wings of celebrity ecstasy. That's when I saw my chance. "I can't profess my love for you," I said. "But how about a picture?" At which point, just like the college boy, I threw my arm around him.

*   *   *

I worry about the disconnect between our stories and our realities. I think of watching TV in the Cajun Lodge in Buras with Ryan, the Ocean Doctor and his brother Alan, and the Cousteau gang. We were kind of embarrassed to be sitting there, after having spent the day out on the water, but there was also a kind of unacknowledged giddiness: would our story of heading out in the boat and sampling oysters and fish for contaminants, a story that had after all just happened, also be the lead story on the nightly news? When the first couple of segments passed, and the focus turned to Chelsea's wedding, there was a palpable deflation in the room. Our story wasn't the story. We hadn't made it. Had the whole day been a waste?

It was the only time since I've been down here that I watched a network news show and I did so with fascination. First of all it was kind of funny, the whole over-the-top primary color thing, as if they were talking to children. But more than that was the fact that what they were saying bore almost no resemblance to any of the stories I was finding as I explored the place. In that way it was truly extraordinary. There is a particular danger right now since the new oiled pelican is that there are no oiled pelicans. It's dumbfounding to watch the media nod and accept BP's magic trick of dispersants, as if oil out of sight means no oil at all.

But now I must end with a confession. It's fine and healthy to mock simplistic thinking and all things cliché, but one danger is in building up calluses and no longer recognizing the authentic. Because, as it turns out, my most authentic moment down in Buras, the moment when I felt the deepest empathy for the animal victims of this tragedy, came when watching none other than oiled pelicans.

It happened on my second to last night in Buras, at the animal hospital not far from where I was staying, an impromptu MASH unit in a large aluminum shed where everything—trash cans, barrels of fish to feed the birds, towels, and the boxes that held the birds themselves—was labeled either "oiled" or "not oiled." The Cousteau crew was there to film their rescue of a tricolored heron, and they had let me join them, though I soon wandered off on my own down the rows of plywood boxes that held the birds. On the first box was a sign that said "Escape artist—be careful," though I couldn't see inside to determine who the avian Houdini was. But it was the second box that stopped me in my tracks. Inside were five or six pelicans, huddled together, obviously stunned with fear, their great sword-like bills pulled into their chests. They had come in just that afternoon, it turned out, and they clearly didn't know where they were, though they knew it was terrifying. Their excrement mixed with oil stains on the white sheet below them and a small tub of fish went untouched. They were too black for pelicans, and when one stretched out its three-foot long wing, it looked more like the wing of an osprey or eagle. I stared into one bird's black eyes. I had always seen pelicans as a kind of symbol of imperturbability, since they seemed so much more stolid than the other birds I spent time watching. But this bird was clearly perturbed. It made a point to keep contact with another of the enormous birds, its fellow prisoner. Its expression seemed to say "What the hell has happened to me?"

I stayed with the birds for a while, until one vet, tired of writers and photographers and camera people, decided it was time for us all to leave. I had been surprised before how accommodating the vets had been when we first arrived, explaining what they were doing and answering questions while cleaning off oiled birds with Q-tips. But now they, or at least this one vet, had had enough. The Cousteau crew had been trying to film the triage being performed on the tricolored heron they had brought in, and they were the most polite and least obtrusive of crews, but they were now being hustled out of there. And while it would have been nice to film the complete journey of the bird that they had rescued, you couldn't help but empathize with the vets. By that point everyone in Buras must have been sick of being filmed or written about. It could be fun at times, energizing, like drinking six cups of coffee and running around in a house of mirrors. But the vet was right: enough was enough. It was time, at least temporarily, to expel those of us who were stalking the oiled pelican, and get back to the real work of tending to actual birds.

Source: Gessner, David. "Into the Gulf: A Journal—Day 10: Beyond the Oiled Pelican." *Bill and Dave's Cocktail Hour*. http://billanddavescocktailhour.com/day-10-beyond-the-oiled-pelcian/#more-951 August 5, 2010.

Northeast Direct

Dagoberto Gilb

I'm on board Amtrak's number 175 to Penn Station. I've traveled by train a couple of times in the past year, but last time I discovered that each car had one electrical outlet. Besides lots of room, besides that comforting, rolling motion, it's what I think about now when I think about the train. My Powerbook has a weak battery, and I can plug in and type as long as I want.

The car is empty. Maybe three of us new passengers, two previously seated. So I do feel a little awkward taking the seat right behind this guy who I saw hustle on several minutes before I did. He'd already reclined his aisle seat, thrown his day bag and warm coat on the one by the window. He was settled. I'm sure he was more than wondering why, with so many empty seats all around, I had to go and sit directly behind him. But I felt something too. Why did *he* have to pick a seat a row in front of the electrical outlet? And if he grumbled when I bumped the back of his seat to get by, I grumbled because I had to squeeze past to get over to the window seat behind him.

I'm over it quickly because I've got my machine on and I'm working. And he seems to be into his world too. He's taken a daily planner out, and he's checking a few things. I see this because, his seat reclined, I'm given a wedge view of his face looking forward and to the side. I see his left eye and the profile of his nose when he turns toward his window. When the conductor comes by for our tickets, he asks if there's a phone, then gets up to use it. I get immersed and barely notice him return.

I pause, and my eyes float up. He's holding a thick new book. I'm sort of looking it over with him. The way the cover feels, the way the chapters are set out. It seems like an attractively produced history book, and I bet he just bought it. He puts it down, then reaches over to the seat in front of me and brings up another.

The other book is the paperback of my novel! I *cannot* believe it! He stares at the cover for a moment, then he opens it. He's reading the acknowledgments page! When he's done he turns back to the title page for a moment, then puts the book down. He gets up and goes to a forward car, where the conductor said he'd find a phone.

How improbable is this? I mean, mine is definitely not a Danielle Steel, not a John Grisham. If it is this much shy of miraculous that I would be on a train with someone who had heard of my books at all, how much more miraculous that, because of an electrical outlet on a train, I'd be sitting inches from a person who just purchased the book and is opening it before my eyes? And look at it this way: of the possible combinations of seating arrangements in the train car, how many could give me this angle? And what if he hadn't put his seat back?

I know what you're thinking. That I should lean over and say, Hey man, you will *never* guess who's sitting behind you! No, that's not me. I don't want to do that. I won't. I want him to be my anonymous reader. How many opportunities does a writer have to learn a truthful reaction, really truthful, to his writing? How absorbed will he be? Will he smile at parts, groan at others? How about his facial expressions? Will his eyes light up or go dull?

As he's walking back, he's staring at me a little too strongly—but he can't know who I am. I'm feeling, naturally enough, self-conscious. He can't possibly know he's in the eyes of the author himself—to think it would be even *more* ridiculous than that it's true. It could be the bright yellow shirt I have on, which is a banner really, a United Farm Workers T-shirt celebrating Cesar Chávez. It reads *Cada trabajador es un organizador*. People are always looking at it and I practically can't wear it because they do. But he's not paying attention to my shirt. It's that I'm the dude sitting behind him, typing into his ear, breathing on his neck while we're on this empty train, with so much room, so many seats, with so much possible spacing. I think he probably doesn't like me. He's probably got names for me.

He sits down. He's picked up the book! He's gone to page one and he's *reading!* Somehow I just can't believe it, and I'm typing frantically about him and this phenomenon. He's a big guy, six-two. Wire glasses, blue, unplayful eyes. Grayish hair, indicating he's most likely not an undergrad, and beneath a Brown University cap, which, because he's wearing the cap, indicates he's probably not a professor. Grad student in English? Or he's into reading about the Southwest? Or maybe the cover has drawn him to the purchase. He's turned to page two! He's going! I have this huge smile as I'm typing. Bottom page two, and yes, his eyes shift to page three!

Suddenly he stops there. He gets up again. The phone is my bet. I'm taking the opportunity. I'm dying to know the name of the bookstore he's gone to, and I kind of arch upwards, over the back of the seat in front of me, to see a glossy store bag, when just as suddenly he's on his way back and he's eyeing me again. I squirm under the psychic weight of these circumstances, though now also from the guilty fact that I'm being so nosy. I pretend I am stretching, looking this way and that, rotating my neck—such uncomfortable seats, wouldn't you say?

He's reading the novel *again*. Page four, page five, page six! A woman walks by and he doesn't even glance up, isn't even curious whether she is attractive or not. He's so engrossed! He's *totally* reading now. No, wait. He stops, eyes to the window where it's New England, beautifully composed and framed by this snowy winter. Those tall, boxy two- and three-story board-and-batten houses painted colonial gray and colonial blue, two windows per floor, hip and gable roof, nubs of chimney poking up. Oh no, he's putting the book down. Closes it, mixes it into his other belongings on the seat next to him. It's because he's moving. He must hear my manic typing and he feels crowded and so he's picking up his stuff and going up an aisle. What an astute, serious, intelligent reader I have to feel so cramped! My reader wants to read in silence, be alone with his book and the thoughts generated by it and his reaction to it and he doesn't like some dude behind him jamming up his reading time and space with this muttering keyboard sound—it just makes me *smile* thinking how keen my reader's psychic synapses are to be responding to what his conscious mind cannot know is occurring. It must be a raging psychic heat, a dizzying psychic pheromone. When he has settled comfortably into his new seat, he pulls the novel back up. He's reading again! Reading and reading! When that young woman passes through on her return, no, again, he does not look up. He's dedicated, fully concentrating. He's really reading, one page after another.

New England: white snow, silver water, leafless branches and limbs. Lumber and boat and junk yards. The bare behind of industry, its dirty underwear, so beautifully disguised by winter.

My reader has fallen asleep. We haven't been on the train an hour and my writing has made him succumb to a nap? Nah, I don't find it a bad thing. Not in the slightest. It's really a compliment. How many books do you fall asleep with? The conductor wakes him up, though. He's sorry but he found that daily planner on the seat behind him and wanted to make sure it belonged to him. But my reader goes right back to sleep. He's dead asleep now. A goner. I pass him on my way to buy myself a drink, and he's got his left thumb locked inside the book, his index finger caressing the spine, pinching. You see, my reader does not want to lose his place.

We both wake up at New Haven. Probably getting a little carried away. I thought he might get off here—walking the book into Yale. He reopens it. He's at the beginning of chapter two. He does read slowly. He's lazy? I say he's thoughtful, a careful, considerate reader, complementing precisely the manner in which I wrote the novel. It's not meant to be read quickly. He's absolutely correct to read it the way he does.

Forty-five minutes outside Penn Station, many passengers have boarded, cutting my reader and me off. He is still up there reading, but with the passage of time, and our physical distance blunted more by a clutter of other minds sitting between and around us, the shock and mystery have lessened in me. I have adjusted, accepted it. By now I am behaving as though it were ordinary that a stranger two aisles above is reading my work. Like every other miracle that happens in life, I am taking the event for granted already, letting it fade into the everyday of people filling trains, going home from work, going. He is reading the novel, and I am certain, by the steady force and duration of his commitment, that he fully intends to read unto the end. He and I both can look around, inside the car and out the window, and then we go back, him to the book, me to the computer keyboard, no longer writing about this.

So when the moment comes, ask what, how? Tap him on the shoulder, say excuse me, but you know I couldn't help but notice that book you're reading, and it's such an amazing coincidence, it *really* is *so* amazing how this can happen, but I was just talking with a friend about that very novel this morning—change that—I was talking to two friends, and one thought it was just great, while the other—change that—and one thought it was just great, and I wondered what you felt about it, and how did you hear of it anyway?

After the conductor announces Penn Station, we stand and get our coats on, and, the train still swaying, move down the aisle and toward the door with our bags. I'm waiting right behind him. Can easily tap him on the shoulder. But nobody else is talking. No one, not a word. So I can't either, especially when I'd be making fake conversation. Train stops, door opens, people in front of him move forward, and a woman in an aisle steps in between me and him with her large, too heavy for her suitcase. He's shot out quickly ahead of me now, up an escalator, several more people between us. When I reach the main floor of the station, get beneath the flapping electronic board that posts trains and times and departure tracks, I have caught up with him. He has stopped to get his bearings. Just as I am at his shoulder, he takes off in the same direction I'm going.

So we're walking briskly side by side in cold Penn Station. You know what? He doesn't want to talk. I am sure he has no desire to speak with me. Would definitely not want to have that conversation I'd planned. No time for me to fumble around and, maybe, eventually, tell him how I am the writer. This is New York City, no less. He's in a hurry. He'd grimace and shake his head, brush me off. He already thinks I am one of those irritating people you encounter on a trip, the one always at the edge of your sight, the one you can never seem to shake. And so as I begin a ride up the escalator toward the taxi lines, I watch him go straight ahead, both of us covered with anonymity like New England snow.

On the Bus

Vivian Gornick

For many years I taught one semester a year in graduate writing programs, nearly all of them far from home. Some time ago I was offered a position at a state university two hundred miles from New York and, calculating quickly that I could easily commute, I accepted the job. Sure enough, things worked out as I had hoped, and I came home every weekend. What I did not expect (or bargain for) was that I would be traveling to the school and back on a Greyhound bus. The university, as it turned out, was in the exact middle of nowhere. Like most New Yorkers, I don't own a car, and getting to it by train or plane was so round-about and expensive a process that a four-and-a-half-hour bus ride proved to be the only realistic means of transportation.

The bus I took left the Port Authority terminal in Manhattan six times a day bound for Cleveland, Chicago, and either San Francisco or Salt Lake City. On Monday I'd board it at 5:00 in the afternoon and be dropped at 9:30 in the evening at a truck stop fifteen miles from the school, where I'd be picked up and driven into town. On Thursday nights, I'd be returned to the truck stop at 8:30, and be back at the Port Authority at 1:00 in the morning.

Often I was the only one to leave the bus at this truck stop. Most of the other passengers were headed for Cleveland or Chicago, although a significant number were setting out for either California or Utah, often looking as exhausted at the start as they undoubtedly would be at the finish. The bus was, in fact, a study in exhaustion—a thing I came to realize only slowly. Most of my traveling companions were working-class blacks or Latinos or Asians who didn't speak a word of English, and many of them were badly, even incoherently, put together. But it wasn't the ragged dress code, as I first thought, that gave the bus its der-elict look. It was the exhaustion. Exhaustion is deracinating.

It began in New York in the bowels of the Port Authority terminal, where people started lining up at the lower-level gate more than an hour before the bus was due to leave, although almost no one was actually standing in line. People slumped against the wall, or sprawled across duffel bags, or sat cross-legged on the floor. As the line grew and began to snake ever farther out and away from the gate itself, the lassitude of the crowd grew apace. A kind of low-grade melancholy began to seep into the atmosphere. The Asians were almost entirely silent, the blacks looked asleep on their feet, the Latinos sad and murmurous. The line soon became a crowd of refugees: people with no rights, only obligations. By the time the driver pushed the door open and started taking tickets, everyone looked beaten.

It was always a surprise to me when I found one of the front seats empty. Although those seats were a special concern of mine—on a long trip it is my invariable hope to dream out the front window—by the time I arrived at the gate, there were always twenty-five people ahead of me in line. There go the front seats, I'd sigh inwardly, but when I climbed the steps of the bus, more often than not I'd find one of the four empty. Almost everyone ahead of me had made for the back. By the time we were loaded and ready to go, three out of five passengers were burrowed down in their seats, eyes closed, shoulders slumped, heads disappearing below the level of the backrests.

Sometimes, however, I would have to settle farther back in the bus, and quite often when I did—again to my surprise—the tired-looking person in the next seat would start talking at me: how long was it gonna take to get this show on the road; never can make these recliners work; the leg room here is pathetic. I did not welcome these harmless openers, since I knew that they almost always meant I'd soon be taken hostage. Because I am compulsively sociable, it is impossible for me to turn a deaf ear or an expressionless face to someone speaking to me. Even though I usually end up wishing the earth would open up and swallow the one inflicting tedium on me, on my face there remains an attentive expression and out of my mouth, every now and then, comes an unavoidable "Really!" or "I know what you mean." I have spent a fair amount of my life trapped by those who are boring me into a rage because once they start talking I am forced to listen. It was always remarkable to me on those Monday-Thursday Greyhound trips that those talking to me never seemed to notice that I hardly said a word.

One Thursday night in the late fall of my second year at this school, I climbed onto the bus at the truck stop and found a seat beside a woman sitting three rows back from the front. She was thin, with long blonde hair framing a narrow face, wearing a teenager's tank top, miniskirt, and high-heeled white boots. Her head was propped against the headrest, her eyes closed, her body limp. She seemed drained to the point of illness. But as I sank down beside her, she opened her eyes, turned, and asked if I lived around here. "No," I said. "I don't." "You from New York?" she asked. "Yes," I said. "Nothing like the city," she said. I smiled. "I'm from Cleveland," she said. I nodded. "Ever been in Cleveland?" I shook my head no. "Don't bother," she said. I smiled again. "I live in New York but my mother's sick, so I'm back and forth between Cleveland and New York these days."

Her name was Jewel. Twenty years ago, right after high school (make that twenty-five, I thought), she'd come to New York to become a stage actress. Things hadn't exactly worked out as she had planned, but she said she was one of the most sought-after extras for nearly every movie made in the city. She also worked as a bartender in midtown. Before we got to the Port Authority, Jewel told me that her mother was dying of cancer, her father was a sweet man who had a hard time making a decision, and her brother, a doctor, was keeping their mother alive by some pretty extraordinary artificial means.

A week later, I climbed onto the bus and there was Jewel again, sitting the same three rows back, with the same empty seat beside her. She waved to me, and I felt obliged to sit down next to her. She looked as worn out as she had the week before but, smiling warmly, she asked how my week had been, waited patiently for me to say okay, then launched herself. "I don't know," she began, "something doesn't feel right to me, it just doesn't feel right." I took a deep breath and said, "What do you mean?" "My brother," she said. "It's like he's *obsessed*." She talked steadily for the next two hours.

They'd been raised on a farm just outside Cleveland, her father had never made a living, her mother had been cold to her and devoted to her brother. The brother was married and a father himself, but he seemed never to have felt for anyone what he felt for their mother. Of course, Jewel was just guessing. Nobody ever *said* anything in that family. But her brother and her mother *did* speak to each other every morning, and clearly each preferred the other's company to that of anyone else. When she got sick, he cheerfully went to work to save her. There was no question of not finding a way. But she had not responded to any of the many treatments that had been tried. Now she was a bag of bones and kept saying she thought it was time for her to go. "No, Ma," Jewel's brother kept saying. "Not yet. I can't let you go yet."

Between late October and Christmas of that year, I sat on the bus every Thursday night listening to Jewel rehearse the latest episode in the family romance of the doomed mother and the entranced son. "You should see the two of them in the hospital room," she'd say. "They've got eyes for no one but each other. My father and I just sit there. We don't even look at each other. It's embarrassing. I keep thinking we've got no business watching them." Chekhov once said that people who travel lose all reserve; he must have had Jewel in mind.

I, meanwhile, said almost nothing. Week after week I sat beside Jewel, my body turned toward her, my elbow on the armrest between us, fingers ridging up into either my right or left temple, eyes trained on her face, nearly silent.

On the last Thursday of the semester, I settled into the seat beside Jewel, and we pulled out into a cold, clear night made magical by the colored lights outlining the vast eighteen-wheelers dancing up or down the highway on either side of the bus. I let myself be mesmerized. Hardly noticing that I wasn't really there, Jewel rattled on—he was pulling her back from the grave, the other doctors thought he'd gone over the edge, his wife was on the verge of divorce.

At one in the morning, the driver steered the bus into its Port Authority berth and turned on the inside lights. Everyone in front stood at once, picking up packages, putting on coats. I stepped into the aisle just behind Jewel. As we approached the door, she turned, flung her arms around my neck, and said, "I don't know what I would have done all these weeks without you talking to me."

"Jewel," I protested. "I didn't do anything. You did it all yourself."

For a few moments she looked startled. Then she put her mouth close to my ear and in a voice of unforgettable dignity said, "You let me talk. That's the same thing as talking to me."

I pulled back and looked at her. Her face seemed full of emotion. It was strained but alert, slightly puzzled but oddly excited. One thing it was not was exhausted.

Red Sky at Morning

Patricia Hampl

Years ago, in another life, I woke to look out the smeared window of a Greyhound bus I had been riding all night, and in the still-dark morning of a small Missouri river town where the driver had made a scheduled stop at a grimy diner, I saw below me a stout middle-aged woman in a flowered house-dress turn and kiss full on the mouth a godlike young man with golden curls. But I've got that wrong: *he* was kissing *her*. Passionately, without regard for the world and its incomprehension. He had abandoned himself to his love, and she, stolid, matronly, received this adoration with simple grandeur, like a socialist-realist statue of a woman taking up sheaves of wheat.

Their ages dictated that he must be her son, but I had just come out of the cramped, ruinous half sleep of a night on a Greyhound and I was clairvoyant: This was that thing called love. The morning light cracked blood red along the river.

Of course, when she lumbered onto the bus a moment later, lurching forward with her two bulging bags, she chose the empty aisle seat next to me as her own. She pitched one bag onto the overhead rack, and then heaved herself into the seat as if she were used to hoisting sacks of potatoes onto the flatbed of a pickup. She held the other bag on her lap, and leaned toward the window. The beautiful boy was blowing kisses. He couldn't see where she was in the dark interior, so he blew kisses up and down the side of the bus, gazing ardently at the blank windows. "Pardon me," the woman said without looking at me, and leaned over, bag and all, to rap the glass. Her beautiful boy ran back to our window and kissed and kissed, and finally hugged himself, shutting his eyes in an ecstatic pantomime of love-sweet-love. She smiled and waved back.

Then the bus was moving. She slumped back in her seat, and I turned to her. I suppose I looked transfixed. As our eyes met she said, "Everybody thinks he's my son. But he's not. He's my husband." She let that sink in. She was a farm woman with hands that could have been a man's; I was a university student, hair

91

down to my waist. It was long ago, as I said, in another life. It was even another life for the country. The Vietnam War was the time we were living through, and I was traveling, as I did every three weeks, to visit my boyfriend who was in a federal prison. "Draft dodger," my brother said. "Draft resister," I piously retorted. I had never been kissed the way this woman had been kissed. I was living in a tattered corner of a romantic idyll, the one where the hero is willing to suffer for his beliefs. I was the girlfriend. I lived on pride, not love.

My neighbor patted her short cap of hair, and settled in for the long haul as we pulled onto the highway along the river, heading south. "We been married five years and we're happy," she said with a penetrating satisfaction, the satisfaction that passeth understanding. "Oh," she let out a profound sigh as if she mined her truths from the bountiful, bulky earth, "Oh, I could tell you stories." She put her arms snugly around her bag, gazed off for a moment, apparently made pensive by her remark. Then she closed her eyes and fell asleep.

I looked out the window smudged by my nose which had been pressed against it at the bus stop to see the face of true love reveal itself. Beyond the bus the sky, instead of becoming paler with the dawn, drew itself out of a black line along the Mississippi into an alarming red flare. It was very beautiful. The old caution—*Red sky in the morning, sailor take warning*—darted through my mind and fell away. Remember this, I remember telling myself, hang on to this. I could feel it all skittering away, whatever conjunction of beauty and improbability I had stumbled upon.

It is hard to describe the indelible bittersweetness of that moment. Which is why, no doubt, it had to be remembered. The very word—*Remember!*—spiraled up like a snake out of a basket, a magic catch in its sound, the doubling of the m—*re mem-memem*—setting up a low murmur full of inchoate associations as if a loved voice were speaking into my ear alone, occultly.

Whether it was the unguarded face of love, or the red gash down the middle of the warring country I was traveling through, or this exhausted farm woman's promise of untold tales that bewitched me, I couldn't say. Over it all rose and remains only the injunction to remember. This, the most impossible command we lay upon ourselves, claimed me and then perversely disappeared, trailing an illusive silken tissue of meaning, without giving a story, refusing to leave me in peace.

Because everyone "has" a memoir, we all have a stake in how such stories are told. For we do not, after all, simply *have* experience; we are entrusted with it. We must do something—make something—with it. A story, we sense, is the only possible habitation for the burden of our witnessing.

The tantalizing formula of my companion on the Greyhound—*oh, I could tell you stories*—is the memoirist's opening line, but it has none of the delicious promise of the storyteller's "Once upon a time. . . ." In fact, it is a perverse statement. The woman on the bus told me nothing—she fell asleep and escaped to her dreams. For the little sentence inaugurates nothing, and leads nowhere after its *dot dot dot* of expectation. Whatever experience lies tangled within its seductive promise remains forever balled up in the woolly impossibility of telling the-truth-the-whole-truth of a life, any life.

Memoirists, unlike fiction writers, do not really want to "tell a story." They want to tell it *all*—the all of personal experience, of consciousness itself. That includes a story, but also the whole expanding universe of sensation and thought that flows beyond the confines of narrative and proves every life to be not only an isolated story line but a bit of the cosmos, spinning and streaming into the great, ungraspable pattern of existence. Memoirists wish to tell their mind, not their story.

The wistfulness implicit in that conditional verb—*I could tell*—conveys an urge more primitive than a storyteller's search for an audience. It betrays not a loneliness for someone who will listen but a hopelessness about language itself and a sad recognition of its limitations. How much reality can subject-verb-object bear on the frail shoulders of the sentence? The sigh within the statement is more like this: I could tell you stories—if only stories could tell what I have in me to tell.

For this reason, autobiographical writing is bedeviled. It is caught in a self which must become a world—and not, please, a narcissistic world. The memoir, once considered a marginal literary form, has emerged in the past decade as the signature genre of the age. "The triumph of memoir is now established fact," James Atlas trumpeted in a cover story on "The Age of the Literary Memoir" in the *New York Times Magazine*. "Fiction," he claimed, "isn't delivering the news. Memoir is."

With its "triumph," the memoir has, of course, not denied the truth and necessity of fiction. In fact, it leans heavily on novelistic assumptions. But the contemporary memoir has reaffirmed the primacy of the first person voice in American imaginative writing established by Whitman's "Song of Myself." Maybe a reader's love of memoir is less an intrusive lust for confession than a hankering for the intimacy of this first-person voice, the deeply satisfying sense of being spoken to privately. More than a story, we want a voice speaking softly, urgently, in our ear. Which is to say, to our heart. That voice carries its implacable command, the ancient murmur that called out to me in the middle of the country in the middle of a war—remember, remember (*I dare you, I tempt you*).

Looking out the Greyhound window that red morning all those years ago, I saw the improbable face of love. But even more puzzling was the cryptic remark of the beloved as she sat next to me. I think of her more often than makes sense. Though he was the beauty, she is the one who comes back. How faint his golden curls have become (he also had a smile, crooked and charming, but I can only remember the idea of it—the image is gone). It is she, stout and unbeautiful, wearing her flowery cotton housedress with a zipper down the middle, who has taken up residence with her canny eye and her acceptance of adoration. To be loved like that, loved improbably: of course, she had stories to tell. She took it for granted in some unapologetic way, like being born to wealth. Take the money and run.

But that moment before she fell asleep, when she looked pensive, the red morning rising over the Mississippi, was a wistful moment. *I could tell you stories—* but she could not. What she had to tell was too big, too much, too something, for her to place in the small shrine that a story is.

When we met—if what happened between us was a meeting—I felt nothing had ever happened to me and nothing ever would. I didn't understand that riding this filthy Greyhound down the middle of bloodied America in the middle of a mutinous war was itself a story and that something *was* happening to me. I thought if something was happening to anybody around me it was happening to people like my boyfriend: They were the heroes, according to the lights that shined for me then. I was just riding shotgun in my own life. I could not have imagined containing, as the farm woman slumped next to me did, the sheer narrative bulk to say, "I could tell you stories," and then drifting off with the secret heaviness of experience into the silence where stories live their real lives, crumbling into the loss we call remembrance.

The boastful little declaration, pathetically conditional (not "I'll tell you a story" but "I could"), wavered wistfully for an instant between us. The stranger's remark, launched in the dark of the Greyhound, floated across the human landscape like the lingering tone of a struck bell from a village church, and joined all the silence that ever was, as I turned my face to the window where the world was rushing by along the slow river.

Stripped for Parts

Jennifer Kahn

The television in the dead man's room stays on all night. Right now the program is *Shipmates*, a reality-dating drama that's barely audible over the hiss of the ventilator. It's 4 A.M., and I've been here for six hours, sitting in the corner while three nurses fuss intermittently over a set of intravenous drips. They're worried about the dead man's health.

To me, he looks fine. His face is slack but flush, he breathes steadily, and his heart beats like a clock, despite the fact that his lungs have recently begun to leak fluid. The nurses roll the body from side to side periodically so that the liquid doesn't pool. At one point, a white plastic vest designed to clear the lungs inflates and begins to vibrate violently—as if some invisible person has seized the dead man by the shoulders and is trying to shake him awake. The rest of the time, the nurses consult monitors and watch for signs of cardiac arrest. When someone scratches the bottom of the dead man's foot, it twitches.

None of this is what I expected from an organ transplant. When I arrived last night at this Northern California hospital I was prepared to see a fast-paced surgery culminating in renewal: the mortally ill patient restored to glorious health. In all my preliminary research on transplants, the dead man was rarely mentioned. Even doctors I spoke with avoided the subject, and popular accounts I came across ducked the matter of provenance altogether. In the movies, for instance, surgeons tended to say it would take time to "find" a heart—as though one had been hidden behind a tree or misplaced along with the car keys. Insofar as corpses came up, it was only in anxious reference to the would-be recipient whose time was running out.

In the dead man's room, a different calculus is unfolding. Here the organ is the patient, and the patient a mere container, the safest place to store body parts until surgeons are ready to use them. It can be more than a day from the time a donor dies until his organs are harvested—the surgery alone takes hours, not to mention the time needed to do blood tests, match tissue, and fly in special surgical teams for the evisceration. And yet, a heart lasts at most six hours outside the body, even after it has been kneaded, flushed with preservatives, and packed in a cooler. Organs left on ice too long tend to perform poorly in their new environment, and doctors are picky about which viscera they're willing to work with. Even an ailing cadaver is a better container than a cooler.

These conditions create a strange medical specialty. Rather than extracting this man's vitals right away, the hospital contacts the California Transplant Donor Network, which dispatches a procurement team to begin "donor maintenance": the process of artificially supporting a dead body until recipients are ready. When the parathyroid gland stops regulating calcium, key to keeping the heart pumping, the team sends the proper amount down an intravenous drip. When blood pressure drops, they add vasoconstrictors, which contract the blood vessels. Normally the brain would compensate for a decrease in blood pressure, but with it out of commission, the three-nurse procurement team must take over.

In this case, the eroding balance will have to be sustained for almost 24 hours. The goal is to fool the body into believing that it's alive and well, even as everything is falling apart. As one crew member concedes, "It's unbelievable that all this stuff is being done to a dead person."

Unbelievable and, to me, somehow barbaric. Sustaining a dead body until its organs can be harvested is a tricky process requiring the latest in medical technology. But it's also a distinct anachronism in an era when medicine is becoming less and less invasive. Fixing blocked coronary arteries, which not long ago required prying a patient's chest open with a saw and spreader, can now be accomplished with a tiny stent delivered to the heart on a slender wire threaded up the leg. Exploratory surgery has given way to robot cameras and high-resolution imaging. Already, we are eyeing the tantalizing summit of gene therapy, where diseases are cured even before they do damage. Compared with such microscale cures, transplants—which consist of salvaging entire organs from a heart-beating cadaver and sewing them into a different body—seem crudely mechanical, even medieval.

"To let an organ reach a state where the only solution is to cut it out is not progress; it's a failure of medicine," says pathologist Neil Theise of NYU. Theise, who was the first researcher to demonstrate that stem cells can become liver cells in humans, argues that the future of transplantation lies in regeneration. Within five years, he estimates, we'll be able to instruct the body to send stem cells to the liver from the store that exists in bone marrow, hopefully countering the effects of a disease like hepatitis A or B and letting the body heal itself. And numerous researchers are forging similar paths. One outspoken surgeon, Richard Satava from the University of Washington, says that medicine is only now catching on to the fundamental lesson of modern industry, which is that when our car alternator breaks, we get a brand new one. Transplantation, he argues, is a dying art.

Few researchers predict that human-harvested organs will become obsolete anytime soon, however; one cardiovascular pathologist, Charles Murry, says we'll still be using them a century from now. But it's reasonable to expect—and hope for—an alternative. "I don't think anybody enjoys recovering organs," Murry says frankly. "You tell yourself it's for a good cause, which it is, a very good cause, but you're still butchering a human."

Intensive care is not a good place to spend the evening. Tonight, the ward has perhaps 12 patients, including a woman who moans constantly and a deathly pale man who reportedly jumped out the window of a moving Greyhound bus. The absence of clocks and the always-on lights create a casino-like timelessness. In the staff lounge, which smells of stale pizza, a lone nurse corners me and describes watching a man bleed to death ("He was conscious. He knew what was happening"), and announces, sotto voce, that she knows of South American organ brokers who charge $60,000 for a heart, then swap it for a baboon's.

Although I don't admit it to the procurement team, I've grown attached to the dead man. There's something vulnerable about his rumpled hair and middle-aged body, naked save a waist-high sheet. Under the hospital lights, everything is exposed: the muscular arms gone flabby above the elbow; the legs, wiry and lean, foreshortened under a powerful torso. It's the body of a man in his fifties, simultaneously bullish and elfin. One foot, the right, peeps out from the sheet, and for a brief moment I want to hold it and rub the toes that must be cold—a hopeless gesture of consolation.

Organ support is about staving off entropy. In the moments after death, a cascade of changes sweeps over the body. Potassium diminishes and salt accumulates, drawing fluid into cells. Sugar builds up in the blood. With the pituitary system offline, the heart fills with lactic acid like the muscles of an exhausted runner. Free radicals circulate unchecked and disrupt other cells, in effect causing the body to rust. The process quickly becomes irreversible. As cell membranes grow porous, a "death gene" is activated and damaged cells begin to self-destruct. All this happens in minutes.

When transplant activists talk about an organ shortage, it's usually to lament how few people are willing to donate. This is a valid worry, but it eclipses an important point, which is that the window for retrieving a viable organ is staggeringly small. Because of how fast the body degrades once the heart stops, there's no way to recover an organ from someone who dies at home, in a car, in an ambulance, or even while on the operating table. In fact, the only situation that really lends itself to harvest is brain death, which means finding an otherwise healthy patient whose brain activity has ceased but whose heart continues to beat—right up until the moment it's taken out. In short, victims of stroke or severe head injury. These cases are so rare (approximately 0.5 percent of all deaths in the US) that even if everybody in America were to become a donor, they wouldn't clear the organ wait lists.

This is partly a scientific problem. Cell death remains poorly understood, and for years now, cadaveric transplants have lingered on a research plateau. While immunosuppressants have improved incrementally, transplants proceed much as they did 20 years ago. Compared with a field like psychopharmacology, the procedure has come to a near-standstill.

But there are cultural factors as well. Medicine has always reserved its glory for the living. Even among transplant surgeons, a hierarchy exists: Those who put organs into living patients have a higher status than those who extract them from the dead. One anesthesiologist confesses that his peers don't like to work on cadaveric organ recoveries. (Even brain-dead bodies require sedation, since spinal reflexes can make a corpse "buck" in surgery.) "You spend all this time monitoring the heartbeat, the blood pressure," the anesthesiologist explains. "To just turn everything off when you're done and walk out. It's bizarre."

Although the procurement team will stay up all night, I break at 4:30 A.M. for a two-hour nap on an empty bed in the ICU. The nurse removes a wrinkled top sheet but leaves the bottom one. Doctors sleep like this all the time, I know, catnapping on gurneys, but I can't shake the feeling of climbing onto my death-bed. The room is identical to the one I've been sitting in for the past eight hours, and I'd prefer to sleep almost anywhere else—in the nurses' lounge or even on the small outside balcony. Instead, I lie down in my clothes and pull the sheet up under my arms.

For a while I read a magazine, then finally close my eyes, hoping I won't dream.

By morning, little seems to have changed, except that the commotion of chest X-rays and ultrasounds has left the dead man's hair more mussed. On both sides of his bed, vital stats scroll across screens: oxygen ratios, pulse, blood volumes.

All of this vigilance is good, of course: After all, transplants save lives. Every year, thousands of people who would otherwise die survive with organs from brain-dead donors; sometimes, doctors say, a patient's color will visibly change on the operating table once a newly attached liver begins to work. Still—and with the possible exception of kidneys—transplants have never quite lived up to their initial promise. In the early 1970s, few who received new organs lasted even a year, and most died within weeks. Even today, 22 percent of heart recipients die in less than four years, and 12 percent reject a new heart within the first few months. Those who survive are usually consigned to a lifetime regime of costly immunosuppressive drugs, some with debilitating side effects. Recipients of arti-ficial hearts traditionally fare the worst, alongside those who receive transplants from animals. Under the circumstances, it took a weird kind of perseverance for doctors operating in 1984 to suggest sewing a walnut-sized baboon heart into a human baby. And there was grief, if not surprise, when the patient died of a mor-bid immune reaction just 21 days later.

By the time we head into surgery, the patient has been dead for more than 24 hours, but he still looks pink and healthy. In the operating room, all the intravenous drips are still flowing, convincing the body that everything's fine even as it's cleaved in half.

Although multiorgan transfer can involve as many as five teams in the OR at once, this time there is only one: a four-man surgical unit from Southern California.

They've flown in to retrieve the liver, but because teams sometimes swap favors, they'll also remove the kidneys for a group of doctors elsewhere—saving them a last-minute, late-night flight. One of the doctors has brought a footstool for me to stand on at the head of the operating table, so that I can see over the sheet that hangs between the patient's head and body. I've been warned that the room will smell bad during the "opening," like flesh and burning bone—an odor that has something in common with a dentist's drill. Behind me, the anesthesiologist checks the dead man's mask and confirms that he's sedated. The surgery will take four hours, and the doctors have arranged for the score of Game Five of the World Series to be phoned in at intervals.

I've heard that transplant doctors are the endurance athletes of medicine, and the longer I stand on the stool, the better I understand the comparison. Below me, the rib cage has been split, and I can see the heart, strangely yellow, beating inside a cave of red muscle. It doesn't beat forward, as I expect, but knocks anxiously back and forth like a small animal trapped in a cage. Farther down, the doctors rummage under the slough of intestines as though through a poorly organized toolbox. When I tell the anesthesiologist that the heart is beautiful, he says that livers are the transplants to watch. "Hearts are slash and burn," he shrugs, adjusting a dial. "No finesse."

Two hours pass, and the surgeons make progress. Despite the procurement team's best efforts, however, most of the organs have already been lost. The pancreas was deemed too old before surgery. One lung was bad at the outset, and the other turned out to be too big for the only matching recipients—a short list given the donor's rare blood type. At 7 this morning, the heart went bust after someone at the receiving hospital suggested a shot of thyroid hormone, shown in some studies to stimulate contractions—but even before then, the surgeon had had second thoughts. A 54-year-old heart can't travel far—and this one was already questionable—but the hospital may have thought this would improve its chances. Instead, the dead man's pulse shot to 140, and his blood began circulating so fast it nearly ruptured his arteries. Now the heart will go to Cryolife, a biosupply company that irradiates and freeze-dries the valves, then packages them for sale to hospitals in screw-top jars. The kidneys have remained healthy enough to be passed on—one to a man who will soon be in line for a pancreas, the other to a 42-year-old woman.

Both kidneys have been packed off in quart-sized plastic jars. Originally, the liver was going to a nearby hospital, but an ultrasound suggested it was hyperechoic, or probably fatty. On the second pass, it was accepted by a doctor in Southern California and ensconced in a bag of icy slurry.

The liver is enormous—it looks like a polished stone, flat and purplish—and with it gone, the body seems eerily empty, although the heart continues to beat. Watching this pumping vessel makes me oddly anxious. It's sped up slightly, as though sensing what will happen next. Below me, the man's face is still flushed. He's the one I wish would survive, I realize, even though there was never any chance of that. Meanwhile, the head surgeon has walked away. He's busy examining the liver and relaying a description over the phone to the doctor who will perform the attachment. Almost unnoticed, an aide clamps the arteries above and below the heart, and cuts. The patient's face doesn't move, but its pinkness drains to a waxy yellow. After 24 hours, the dead man finally looks dead.

Once all the organs are out, the tempo picks up in the operating room. The heart is packed in a cardboard box also loaded with the kidneys, which are traveling by Learjet to a city a few hundred miles away. Someday, I'm convinced, transporting organs in coolers will seem as strange and outdated as putting a patient in an iron lung. In the meantime, transplants will survive: a vehicle, like the dead man, to get us to a better place. As an assistant closes, sewing up the body so that it will be ready for its funeral, I get on the plane with the heart and the kidneys. They've become a strange, unhealthy orange in their little jars. But no one else seems worried. "A kidney almost always perks up," someone tells me, "once we get it in a happier environment."

13, 1977, 21

Jonathan Lethem

1. In the summer of 1977 I saw *Star Wars*—the original, which is all I want to discuss here—twenty-one times. Better to blurt this at the start so I'm less tempted to retreat from what still seems to me a sort of raw, howling confession, one I've long hidden in shame. Again, to pin myself like a Nabokovian butterfly (no high-lit reference is going to bail me out here, I know) to my page in geek history: I watched *Star Wars* twenty-one times in the space of four months. I was that kid alone in the ticket line, slipping past ushers who'd begun to recognize me, muttering in impatience at a urinal before finding my favorite seat. That was me, occult as a porn customer, yes, though I've sometimes denied it. Now, a quarter of a century later, I'm ready for my close-up. Sort of.

2. That year I was thirteen, and likely as ideal an audience member as any mogul could have drooled for. Say every kid in the United States with even the passingest fondness for comic books or adventure fiction, *any kid with a television, even,* had bought a ticket for the same film in a single summer: blah, blah, right, that's what happened. So figure that for every hundred kids who traveled an ordinary path (*Cool movie. Wouldn't mind seeing it again with my friends*) there might be one who'd make himself ill returning to the cookie jar five or six times (*It's really still good the fourth time, I swear!*) before copping to a tummy ache. Next figure that for each *five* hundred, one or two would slip into some brain-warped identificatory obsession (*I am* Star Wars. Star Wars *am me, goo goo ga joob*) and return to the primal site often enough to push into the realm of trance and memorization. That's me, with my gaudy *twenty-one*, like DiMaggio's *fifty-six*. But what actually occurred within the secret brackets of that experience? What emotions lurk within that ludicrous temple of hours? *What the fuck was I thinking?*

3. Every one of those twenty-one viewings took place at the Loew's Astor Plaza on Forty-fourth Street, just off Times Square. I'd never seen a movie there before (and unless you count *The Empire Strikes Back*, I didn't again until 1999—*The Matrix*). And I've still never seen *Star Wars* anywhere else. The Astor Plaza was a low, deep-stretched hall with a massive screen and state-of-the-art sound, and newly enough renovated to be free of too much soda-rotted carpet, a plague among New York theaters those days. Though architecturally undistinguished, it was a superior place to see anything. I suppose. But for me it was a shrine meant for just one purpose—I took it as weirdly significant that "Astor" could be rearranged into "astro"—and in a very *New Yorker*-coverish way I believed it to be the only real and right place to see *Star Wars*, the very ground zero of the phenomenon. I felt a definite but not at all urgent pity for any benighted fools stuck watching it elsewhere. I think I associated the Astor Plaza with the Death Star, in a way. Getting in always felt like an accomplishment, both elevating and slightly dangerous.

4. Along those lines I should say it was vaguely unnerving to be a white kid in spectacles routinely visiting Times Square by subway in the middle of the 1970s. Nobody ever said anything clearly about what was wrong or fascinating about that part of the city we lived in—the information was absorbed in hints and mutterings from a polyphony of sources. In fact, though I was conscious of a certain seamy energy in those acres of sex shows and drug dealers and their furtive sidewalk customers, I was never once hassled (and this was a time when my home neighborhood, in Brooklyn, was a minefield for me personally). But the zone's reputation ensured I'd always plan my visits to fall wholly within summer's long daylight hours.

5. Problem: it doesn't seem at all likely that I went to the movie alone the first time, but I can't remember who I was with. I've polled a few of my likeliest friends from that period, but they're unable to help. In truth I can't recall a "first time" in any real sense, though I do retain a flash memory of the moment the prologue first began to crawl in tilted perspective up the screen, an Alice-in-Wonderland doorway to dream. I'd been so primed, so attuned and ready to love it (I remember mocking my friend Evan for his thinking that the title meant it was going to be some kind of all-star cavalcade of a comedy, like *It's a Mad Mad Mad Mad World* or *Smokey and the Bandit*) that my first time was gulped impatiently, then covered quickly in the memory of return visits. From the first I was "seeing it again." I think this memory glitch is significant. I associate it with my practice of bluffing familiarity with various drug experiences, later (not much later). My refusal to recall or admit to a first time was an assertion of maturity: I was *always already* a *Star Wars* fanatic.

6. I didn't buy twenty-one tickets. My count was amassed by seeing the movie twice in a day over and over again. And one famous day (famous to myself) I sat

through it three times. That practice of seeing a film twice through originated earlier. Somebody—my mother?—had floated the idea that it wasn't important to be on time for a movie, or even to check the screening times before going. Instead, moviegoing in Brooklyn Heights or on Fulton Street with my brother or with friends, we'd pop in at any point in the story, watch to the end, then sit through the break and watch the beginning. Which led naturally, if the film was any good, to staying past the original point of entry to see the end twice. Which itself led to routinely twice-watching a movie we liked, even if we hadn't been late. This was encouraged, partly according to a general *Steal This Book*-ish anti-capitalist imperative for taking freebies in my parents' circle in the seventies. Of course somebody—my mother?—had also figured out a convenient way to get the kids out of the house for long stretches.

7. I hate arriving late for movies now and would never watch one in this broken fashion. (It seems to me, though, that I probably learned something about the construction of narratives from the practice.) The life-long moviegoing habit which does originate for me with *Star Wars* is that of sitting in movie theaters alone. I probably only had company in the Loew's Astor Plaza four or five times. The rest of my visits were solitary, which is certainly central to any guesses I'd make about the emotional meaning of the ritual viewings.

8. I still go to the movies alone, all the time. In the absenting of self which results— so different from the quality of solitude at my writing desk—this seems to me as near as I come in my life to any reverent or worshipful or meditational practice. That's not to say it isn't also indulgent, with a frisson of guilt, of stolen privilege, every time. I'm acutely conscious of this joyous guilt in the fact that when as a solitary moviegoer I take a break to go to the bathroom *I can return to another part of the theater and watch from a different seat.* I first discovered this thrill during my *Star Wars* summer, and it's one which never diminishes. The rupture of the spectator's contract with perspective feels as transgressive as wife-swapping.

9. The function or dysfunction of my *Star Wars* obsession was paradoxical. I was using the movie as a place to hide, sure. That's obvious. At the same time, this activity of hiding inside the Loew's Astor Plaza, and inside my private, *deeper-than-yours, deeper-than-anyone's* communion with the film itself, was something I boasted widely about. By building my lamebrain World Record for screenings (fat chance, I learned later) I was teaching myself to package my own craving for solitude, and my own obsessive tendencies, as something to be admired. *You can't join me inside this box where I hide,* I was saying, *but you sure can praise the box. You're permitted to marvel at me for going inside.*

10. What I was hiding from is easy, though. My parents had separated a couple of years earlier. Then my mother had begun having seizures, been diagnosed with a brain tumor, and had had the first of two surgeries. The summer of *Star Wars* she

was five or six months from the second, unsuccessful surgery, and a year from dying.

11. I took my brother, and he stayed through it twice. We may have done that together more than once—neither of us clearly remembers. I took a girl, on a quasi-date: Alissa, the sister of my best friend, Joel. I took my mother. I tried to take my grandmother.

12. That same summer I once followed Alissa to a ballet class at Carnegie Hall and hung around the studio, expressing a polite curiosity which was cover for another, less polite curiosity. The instructor was misled or chose to misunderstand—a thirteen-year-old boy willing to set foot inside a ballet studio was a commodity, a raw material. I was offered free classes, and the teacher called my house and strong-armed my parents. I remember vividly my mother's pleasure in refusing on my behalf—I was too much of a coward—and how strongly she fastened on the fact that my visit had had nothing to do with any interest in ballet. For years this seemed to me an inexplicable cruelty in my mother toward the ballet teacher. Later I understood that in those first years of adolescence I was giving off a lot of signals to my parents that I might be gay. I was a delicate, obedient, and book-ish kid, a constant teacher's pet. Earlier that year my father had questioned me regarding a series of distended cartoon noses I'd drawn in ballpoint on my loose-leaf binder—they had come out looking a lot like penises. And my proclaimed favorite *Star Wars* character was the tweaking English robot, C-3PO.

13. I did and do find C-3PO sexy. It's as if a strand of DNA from Fritz Lang's fetishized girl robot in *Metropolis* has carried forward to the bland world of *Star Wars*. Also, whereas Carrie Fisher's robes went to her ankles, C-3PO is obviously naked, and ashamed of it.

14. Alissa thought the movie was okay (my overstated claims generally cued a compensating shrug in others) and that was our last date, if it was a date. We're friends now.

15. I don't know how much of an effort it was for my mother to travel by sub-way to a movie theater in Manhattan by the summer of '77, but I do know it was unusual, and that she was certainly doing it to oblige me. It might have been one of our last ventures out together, before it was impossible for her. I remember fussing over rituals inside the theater, showing her my favorite seat, and strain-ing not to watch her watch it throughout, not to hang on her every reaction. Afterward she too found the movie just okay. It wasn't her kind of thing, but she could understand why I liked it so much. Those were pretty close to her exact words. Maybe with her characteristic Queens hard-boiled tone: *I see why you like it, kiddo.* Then, in a turn I find painful to relate, she left me there to watch it a second time, and took the subway home alone. What a heartbreaking rehearsal!

I was saying, in effect: *Come and see my future, post-mom self. Enact with me your parting from it. Here's the world of cinema and stories and obsessive identification I'm using to survive your going—now go.* How generous of her to play in this masquerade, if she knew.

16. I spent a certain amount of time that year trying hopelessly to distract my grandmother from the coming loss of her only child—it would mostly wreck her—by pushing my new enthusiasms at her. For instance she and I had a recurrent argument about rock and roll, one which it now strikes me was probably a faint echo, for her, of struggles over my mother's dropping out of Queens College in favor of a Greenwich Village beatnik-folk lifestyle. I worked to find a hit song she couldn't quibble with, and thought I'd found one in Wings' "Mull of Kintyre," which is really just a strummy faux-Irish folk song. I played it for her at top volume and she grimaced, her displeasure not at the music but at the apparent trump card I'd played. Then, on the fade, Paul McCartney gave out a kind of *whoop-whoop* holler and my grandmother seized on this, with relish: "You hear that? He had to go and scream. It wasn't good enough just to sing, he had to scream like an animal!" Her will was too much for me. So when she resisted being dragged to *Star Wars* I probably didn't mind, being uninterested in having her trample on my secret sand castle. She and I were ultimately in a kind of argument about whether or not our family was a site of tragedy, and I probably sensed I was on the losing end of that one.

17. My father lived in a commune for part of that summer, though my mother's illness sometimes drew him back into the house. There was a man in the commune—call him George Lucas—whose married life, which included two young children, was coming apart. George Lucas was the person I knew who'd seen *Star Wars* the most times, apart from me, and we had a ritualized bond over it. He'd ask me how many times I'd seen the film and I'd report, like an emissary with good news from the front. George Lucas had a copy of the soundtrack and we'd sit in the commune's living room and play it on the stereo, which I seem to remember being somewhat unpopular with the commune's larger membership. George Lucas, who played piano and had some classical training, would always proclaim that the score was *really pretty good symphonic composition*—he'd also play me Gustav Holst's *Planets Suite* as a kind of primer, and to show me how the Death Star theme came from Holst's Jupiter—I would dutifully parrot this for my friends, with great severity: John Williams's score was *really pretty good symphonic composition*.

18. The movie itself, right: of course, I must have enjoyed it immensely the first few times. That's what I least recall. Instead I recall now how as I memorized scenes I fought my impatience, and yet fought not to know I was fighting impatience—all that mattered were the winnowed satisfactions of crucial moments occurring once again, like stations of the cross: "Help me, Obi-Wan Kenobi, you're my only hope," "These aren't the droids you're looking for," "If you strike me down, I'll become more powerful than you can possibly imagine," and the dunk shot of

Luke's missiles entering the Death Star's duct. I hated, absolutely, the scene in the Death Star's sewers. I hated Han Solo and Princess Leia's flirtation, after a while, feeling I was being manipulated, that it was too mannered and rote: of course they're grumbling now, that's how it *always* goes. I hated the triumphalist ceremony at the end, though the spiffing-up of the robots was a consolation, a necessary relief. I think I came to hate a lot of the film, but I couldn't permit myself to know it. I even came, within a year or so, to hate the fact that I'd seen the movie twenty-one times.

19. Why that number? Probably I thought it was safely ridiculous and extreme to get my record into the twenties, yet stopping at only twenty seemed too mechanically round. Adding one more felt plausibly arbitrary, more *realistic*. That was likely all I could stand. Perhaps at twenty-one I'd also attained the symbolic number of adulthood, of maturity. By bringing together *thirteen* and *twenty-one* I'd made *Star Wars* my Bar Mitzvah, a ritual I didn't have and probably could have used that year. Now I was a man.

20. By the time I was fifteen, not only had I long since quit boasting about my love of *Star Wars* but it had become privately crucial to have another favorite movie inscribed in its place. I decided Kubrick's *2001: A Space Odyssey* was a suitably noble and alienated choice, but that in order to make it official I'd have to see it more times than *Star Wars*. An exhausting proposition, but I went right at it. One day at the Thalia on West Ninety-fifth Street I sat alone through *2001* three times in a row in a nearly empty theater, a commitment of some nine hours. That day I brought along a tape recorder in order to whisper notes on this immersion experience to my friend Eliot—I also taped *Also sprach Zarathustra* all six times. If *Star Wars* was my Bar Mitzvah then *2001* was getting laid, an experience requiring a more persuasive maturity, and one which I more honestly enjoyed, especially fifteen or twenty showings in. Oddly enough, though, I never did completely overwrite *Star Wars* with *2001*. Instead I stuck at precisely twenty-one viewings of the second movie as well, leaving the two in a dead heat. Even that number was only attained years later, at the University Theater in Berkeley, California, two days after the 1989 Loma Prieta earthquake. There was a mild aftershock which rumbled the old theater during the Star Gate sequence, a nice touch.

21. I'll never see another film so many times, though I still count. I've seen *The Searchers* twelve times—a cheat, since it was partly research. Otherwise, I usually peak out at six or seven viewings, as with *Bringing Up Baby* and *Three Women* and *Love Streams* and *Vertigo*, all films I believe I love more than either *Star Wars* or *2001*. But that kid who still can't decide which of the two futuristic epics to let win the struggle for his mortal soul, the kid who left the question hanging, the kid who partly invented himself in the vacuum collision of *Star Wars*—and real loss—that kid is me.

Portrait of My Body

Phillip Lopate

I am a man who tilts. When I am sitting, my head slants to the right; when walking, the upper part of my body reaches forward to catch a sneak preview of the street. One way or another, I seem to be off-center—or "uncentered," to use the jargon of holism. My lousy posture, a tendency to slump or put myself into lazy, contorted misalignments, undoubtedly contributes to lower back pain. For a while I correct my bad habits, do morning exercises, sit straight, breathe deeply, but always an inner demon that insists on approaching the world askew resists perpendicularity.

I think if I had broader shoulders I would be more squarely anchored. But my shoulders are narrow, barely wider than my hips. This has always made shopping for suits an embarrassing business. (Françoise Gilot's *Life with Picasso* tells how Picasso was so touchy about his disproportionate body—in his case all shoulders, no legs—that he insisted the tailor fit him at home.)

When I was growing up in Brooklyn, my hero was Sandy Koufax, the Dodgers' Jewish pitcher. In the doldrums of Hebrew choir practice at Feigenbaum's Mansion & Catering Hall, I would fantasize striking out the side, even whiffing twenty-seven batters in a row. Lack of shoulder development put an end to this identification; I became a writer instead of a Koufax.

It occurs to me that the restless angling of my head is an attempt to distract viewers' attention from its paltry base. I want people to look at my head, partly because I live in my head most of the time. My sister, a trained masseuse, often warns me of the penalties, like neck tension, that may arise from failing to integrate body and mind. Once, about ten years ago, she and I were at the beach and she was scrutinizing my body with a sister's critical eye. "You're getting flabby," she said. "You should exercise every day. I do—look at me, not an ounce of fat." She pulled at her midriff, celebrating (as is her wont) her physical attributes with the third-person enthusiasm of a carnival barker.

"But"—she threw me a bone—"you do have a powerful head. There's an intensity. . . ." A graduate student of mine (who was slightly loony) told someone that she regularly saw an aura around my head in class. One reason I like to teach is that it focuses fifteen or so dependent gazes on me with such paranoiac intensity as cannot help but generate an aura in my behalf.

I also have a commanding stare, large sad brown eyes that can be read as either gentle or severe. Once I watched several hours of myself on videotape. I discovered to my horror that my face moved at different rates: sometimes my mouth would be laughing, eyebrows circumflexed in mirth, while my eyes coolly gauged the interviewer to see what effect I was making. I am something of an actor. And, as with many performers, the mood I sense most in myself is that of energy-conserving watchfulness; but this expression is often mistaken (perhaps because of the way brown eyes are read in our culture) for sympathy. I see myself as determined to the point of stubbornness, selfish, even a bit cruel—in any case, I am all too aware of the limits of my compassion, so that it puzzles me when people report a first impression of me as gentle, kind, solicitous. In my youth I felt obliged to come across as dynamic, arrogant, intimidating, the life of the party; now, surer of myself, I hold back some energy, thereby winning time to gather information and make better judgments. This results sometimes in a misimpression of my being mildly depressed. Of course, the simple truth is that I have less energy than I once did, and that accumulated experiences have made me, almost against my will, kinder and sadder.

Sometimes I can feel my mouth arching downward in an ironic smile, which, at its best, reassures others that we need not take everything so seriously—because we are all in the same comedy together—and, at its worst, expresses a superior skepticism. This smile, which can be charming when not supercilious, has elements of the bashful that mesh with the worldly—the shyness, let us say, of a cultivated man who is often embarrassed for others by their willful shallowness or self-deception. Many times, however, my ironic smile is nothing more than a neutral stall among people who do not seem to appreciate my "contribution." I hate that pain-in-the-ass half-smile of mine; I want to jump in, participate, be loud, thoughtless, vulgar.

Often I give off a sort of psychic stench to myself, I do not like myself at all, but out of stubborn pride I act like a man who does. I appear for all the world poised, contented, sanguine when inside I may be feeling self-revulsion bordering on the suicidal. What a wonder to be so misread! Of course, if in the beginning I had thought I was coming across accurately, I never would have bothered to become a writer. And the truth is I am not misread, because another part of me is never less than fully contented with myself.

I am vain about these parts of my body: my eyes, my fingers, my legs. It is true that my legs are long and not unshapely, but my vanity about them has less to do with their comeliness than with their contribution to my height. Montaigne, a man who was himself on the short side, wrote that "the beauty of stature is the only beauty of men." But even if Montaigne had never said it, I would continue to attribute a good deal of my self-worth and benevolent liberalism to being tall. When I go out into the street, I feel well-disposed toward the (mostly shorter) swarms of humanity; crowds not only do not dismay, they enliven me; and I am tempted to think that my passion for urbanism is linked to my height. By no means am I suggesting that only tall people love cities; merely that, in my case, part of the pleasure I derive from walking in crowded streets issues from a confidence that I can see above the heads of others, and cut a fairly impressive, elevated figure as I saunter along the sidewalk.

Some of my best friends have been—short. Brilliant men, brimming with poetic and worldly ideas, they deserved all of my and the world's respect. Yet at times I have had to master an impulse to rumple their heads; and I suspect they have developed manners of a more formal, *noli me tangere* nature, largely in response to this petting impulse of taller others.

The accident of my tallness has inclined me to both a seemingly egalitarian informality and a desire to lead. Had I not been a writer, I would surely have become a politician; I was even headed in that direction in my teens. Ever since I shot up to a little over six feet, I have had at my command what feels like a natural, Gregory Peck authority when addressing an audience. Far from experiencing stage fright, I have actually sought out situations in which I could make speeches, give readings, sit on panel discussions, and generally tower over everyone else onstage. To be tall is to look down on the world and meet its eyes on your terms. But this topic, the noblesse oblige of tall men, is a dangerously provoking one, and so let us say no more about it.

The mental image of one's body changes slower than one's body. Mine was for a long while arrested in my early twenties, when I was tall and thin (165 pounds) and gobbled down whatever I felt like. I ate food that was cheap and filling, cheeseburgers, pizza, without any thought to putting on weight. But a young person's metabolism is more dietetically forgiving. To compound the problem, the older you get, the more cultivated your palate grows—and the more life's setbacks make you inclined to fill the hollowness of disappointment with the pleasures of the table.

Between the age of thirty and forty I put on ten pounds, mostly around the midsection. Since then my gut has suffered another expansion, and I tip the scales at over 180. That I took a while to notice the change may be shown by my continuing to purchase clothes at my primordial adult size (33 waist, 15½ collar), until a girlfriend started pointing out that all my clothes were too tight. I rationalized this circumstance as the result of changing fashions (thinking myself still subconsciously loyal to the sixties' penchant for skintight fits) and laundry shrinkage rather than anything to do with my own body. She began buying me larger replacements for birthdays or holidays, and I found I enjoyed this "baggier" style, which allowed me to button my trousers comfortably, or to wear a tie and, for the first time in years, close my top shirt button. But it took even longer before I was able to enter a clothing store myself and give the salesman realistically enlarged size numbers.

Clothes can disguise the defects of one's body, up to a point. I get dressed with great optimism, adding one color to another, mixing my favorite Japanese and Italian designers, matching the patterns and textures, selecting ties, then proceed to the bathroom mirror to judge the result. There is an ideal in my mind of the effect I am essaying by wearing a particular choice of garments, based, no doubt, on male models in fashion ads—and I fall so far short of this insouciant gigolo handsomeness that I cannot help but be a little disappointed when I turn up so depressingly myself, narrow-shouldered, Talmudic, that grim, set mouth, that long, narrow face, those appraising eyes, the Semitic hooked nose, all of which express both the strain of intellectual overachieving and the tabula rasa of immaturity . . . for it is still, underneath, a boy in the mirror. A boy with a rapidly receding hairline.

How is it that I've remained a boy all this time, into my late forties? I remember, at seventeen, drawing a self-portrait of myself as I looked in the mirror. I was so appalled at the weak chin and pleading eyes that I ended up focusing on the neckline of the cotton T-shirt. Ever since then I have tried to toughen myself up, but I still encounter in the glass that haunted uncertainty—shielded by a bluffing shell of cynicism, perhaps, but untouched by wisdom. So I approach the mirror warily, without lighting up as much as I would for the least of my acquaintances; I go one-on-one with that frowning schmuck.

And yet, it would be insulting to those who labor under the burden of true ugliness to palm myself off as an unattractive man. I'm at times almost handsome, if you squinted your eyes and rounded me off to the nearest *beau idéal*. I lack even a shred of cowboy virility, true, but I believe I fall into a category of adorable nerd or absentminded professor that awakens the amorous curiosity of some women. "Cute" is a word often applied to me by those I've been fortunate enough to attract. Then again, I attract only women of a certain lopsided prettiness: the head-turning, professional beauties never fall for me. They seem to look right through me, in fact. Their utter lack of interest in my appeal has always fascinated me. Can it be so simple an explanation as that beauty calls to beauty, as wealth to wealth?

I think of poor (though not in his writing gifts) Cesare Pavese, who kept chasing after starlets, models, and ballerinas—exquisite lovelies who couldn't appreciate his morose coffeehouse charm. Before he killed himself, he wrote a poem addressed to one of them, "Death Will Come Bearing Your Eyes"—thereby unfairly promoting her from rejecting lover to unwitting executioner. Perhaps he believed that only beautiful women (not literary critics, who kept awarding him prestigious prizes) saw him clearly, with twenty-twenty vision, and had the right to judge him. Had I been more headstrong, if masochistic, I might have followed his path and chased some beauty until she was forced to tell me, like an oracle, what it was about me, physically, that so failed to excite her. Then I might know something crucial about my body, before I passed into my next reincarnation.

Jung says somewhere that we pay dearly over many years to learn about our-selves what a stranger can see at a glance. This is the way I feel about my back. Fitting rooms aside, we none of us know what we look like from the back. It is the area of ourselves whose presentation we can least control, and which therefore may be the most honest part of us.

I divide backs into two kinds: my own and everyone else's. The others' backs are often mysterious, exquisite, and uncannily sympathetic. I have always loved backs. To walk behind a pretty woman in a backless dress and savor how a good pair of shoulder blades, heightened by shadow, has the same power to pierce the heart as chiseled cheekbones! . . . I wonder what it says about me that I worship a part of the body that signals a turning away. Does it mean I'm a glut-ton for being abandoned, or a timid voyeur who prefers a surreptitious gaze that will not be met and challenged? I only know I have often felt the deepest love at just that moment when the beloved turns her back to me to get some sleep.

I have no autoerotic feelings about my own back. I cannot even picture it; visually it is a stranger to me. I know it only as an annoyance, which came into my consciousness twenty years ago, when I started getting lower back pain. Yes, we all know that homo sapiens is constructed incorrectly; our erect posture puts too much pressure on the base of the spine; more workdays are lost because of lower back pain than any other cause. Being a writer, I sit all day, compounding the problem. My back is the enemy of my writing life: if I don't do exercises daily, I immediately ache; and if I do, I am still not spared. I could say more, but there is nothing duller than lower back pain. So common, mundane an ailment brings no credit to the sufferer. One has to dramatize it somehow, as in the phrase "I threw my back out."

Here is a gossip column about my body: My eyebrows grow quite bushy across my forehead, and whenever I get my hair cut, the barber asks me diplomatically if I want them trimmed or not. (I generally say no, associating bushy eyebrows with Balzackian virility, *élan vital*; but sometimes I acquiesce, to soothe his fastidious-ness.) . . . My belly button is a modest, embedded slit, not a jaunty swirl like my father's. Still, I like to sniff the odor that comes from jabbing my finger in it: a very ripe, underground smell, impossible to describe, but let us say a combination of old gym socks and stuffed derma (the Yiddish word for this oniony dish of ground intestines is, fittingly, *kish-kas*). . . . I have a scar on my tongue from childhood, which I can only surmise I received by landing it on a sharp object, somehow. Or perhaps I bit it hard. I have the habit of sticking my tongue out like a dog when exerting myself physically, as though to urge my muscles on; and maybe I acciden-tally chomped into it at such a moment. . . . I gnash my teeth, sleeping or waking. Awake, the sensation makes me feel alert and in contact with the world when I start to drift off in a daydream. Another way of grounding myself is to pinch my cheek—drawing a pocket of flesh downward and squeezing it—as I once saw JFK do in a filmed motorcade. I do this cheek-pinching especially when I am trying to keep mentally focused during teaching or other public situations. I also scratch the nape of my neck under public stress, so much so that I raise welts or sores which then eventually grow scabs; and I take great delight in secretly picking the scabs off. . . . My nose itches whenever I think about it, and I scratch it often, especially lying in bed trying to fall asleep (maybe because I am conscious of my breathing then). I also pick my nose with formidable thoroughness when no one, I hope, is looking. . . . There is a white scar about the size of a quarter on the juicy part of my knee; I got it as a boy running into a car fender, and I can still remember staring with detached calm at the blood that gushed from it like a pretty, half-eaten peach. Otherwise, the sight of my own blood makes me awfully nervous. I used to faint dead away when a blood sample was taken, and now I can control the impulse to do so only by biting the insides of my cheeks while steadfastly looking away from the needle's action. . . . I like to clean out my ear wax as often as possible (the smell is curiously sulfurous; I associate it with the bodies of dead insects). I refuse to listen to warnings that it is dangerous to stick cleaning objects into your ears. I love Q-Tips immoderately; I buy them in huge quantities and store them the way a former refugee will stock canned foodstuffs. . . . My toes are long and apelike; I have very little fellow feeling for them; they are so far away, they may as well belong to someone else. . . . My flattish buttocks are not offensively large, but neither do they have the "dream" configuration one sees in jeans ads. Perhaps for this reason, it disturbed me puritanically when asses started to be treated by Madison Avenue, around the seventies, as crucial sexual equipment, and I began to receive compositions from teenage girl students declaring that they liked some boy because he had "a cute butt." It confused me; I had thought the action was elsewhere.

About my penis there is nothing, I think, unusual. It has a brown stem, and a pink mushroom head where the foreskin is pulled back. Like most heterosexual males, I have little comparative knowledge to go by, so that I always feel like an outsider when I am around women or gay men who talk zestfully about differences in penises. I am afraid that they might judge me harshly, ridicule me like the boys who stripped me of my bathing suit in summer camp when I was ten. But perhaps they would simply declare it an ordinary penis, which changes size with the stimulus or weather or time of day. Actually, my penis does have a peculiarity: it has two peeing holes. They are very close to each other, so that usually only one stream of urine issues, but sometimes a hair gets caught across them, or some such contretemps, and they squirt out in two directions at once.

This part of me, which is so synecdochically identified with the male body (as the term "male member" indicates), has given me both too little, and too much, information about what it means to be a man. It has a personality like a cat's. I have prayed to it to behave better, to be less frisky, or more; I have followed its nose in matters of love, ignoring good sense, and paid the price; but I have also come to appreciate that it has its own specialized form of intelligence which must be listened to, or another price will be extracted.

Even to say the word "impotence" aloud makes me nervous. I used to tremble when I saw it in print, and its close relation, "importance," if hastily scanned, had the same effect, as if they were publishing a secret about me. But why should it be *my* secret, when my penis has regularly given me erections lo these many years—except for about a dozen times, mostly when I was younger? Because, even if it has not been that big a problem for me, it has dominated my thinking as an adult male. I've no sooner to go to bed with a woman than I'm in suspense. The power of the flaccid penis's statement, "I don't want you," is so stark, so cruelly direct, that it continues to exert a fascination out of all proportion to its actual incidence. Those few times when I was unable to function were like a wall forcing me to take another path—just as, after I tried to kill myself at seventeen, I was obliged to give up pessimism for a time. Each had instructed me by its too painful manner that I could not handle the world as I had previously construed it, that my confusion and rage were being found out. I would have to get more wily or else grow up.

Yet for the very reason that I was compelled to leave them behind, these two options of my youth, impotence and suicide, continue to command an underground loyalty, as though they were more "honest" than the devious strategies of potency and survival which I adopted. Put it this way: sometimes we encounter a person who has had a nervous breakdown years before and who seems cemented over sloppily, his vulnerability ruthlessly guarded against as dangerous; we sense he left a crucial part of himself back in the chaos of breakdown, and has since grown rigidly jovial. So suicide and impotence became for me "the roads not taken," the paths I had repressed.

Whenever I hear an anecdote about impotence—a woman who successfully coaxed an ex-priest who had been celibate and unable to make love, first by lying next to him for six months without any touching, then by cuddling for six more months, then by easing him slowly into a sexual embrace—I think they are talking about me. I identify completely: this, in spite of the fact, which I promise not to repeat again, that I have generally been able to do it whenever called upon. Believe it or not, I am not boasting when I say that: a part of me is contemptuous of this virility, as though it were merely a mechanical trick that violated my true nature, that of an impotent man absolutely frightened of women, absolutely secluded, cut off.

I now see the way I have idealized impotence: I've connected it with pushing the world away, as a kind of integrity, as in Molière's *The Misanthrope*—connected it with that part of me which, gregarious socializer that I am, continues to insist that I am a recluse, too good for this life. Of course, it is not true that I am terrified of women. I exaggerate my terror of them for dramatic effect, or for the purposes of a good scare.

My final word about impotence: Once, in a period when I was going out with many women, as though purposely trying to ignore my hypersensitive side and force it to grow callous by thrusting myself into foreign situations (not only sexual) and seeing if I was able to "rise to the occasion," I dated a woman who was attractive, tall and blond, named Susan. She had something to do with the pop music business, was a follower of the visionary religious futurist Teilhard de Chardin, and considered herself a religious pacifist. In fact, she told me her telephone number in the form of the anagram, N-O-T-O-W-A-R. I thought she was joking and laughed aloud, but she gave me a solemn look. In passing, I should say that all the women with whom I was impotent or close to it had solemn natures. The sex act has always seemed to me in many ways ridiculous, and I am most comfortable when a woman who enters the sheets with me shares that sense of the comic pomposity behind such a grandiloquently rhetorical use of the flesh. It is as though the prose of the body were being drastically squeezed into metrical verse. I would not have known how to stop guffawing had I been D.H. Lawrence's lover, and I am sure he would have been pretty annoyed at me. But a smile saying "All this will pass" has an erotic effect on me like nothing else.

They claim that men who have long, long fingers also have lengthy penises. I can tell you with a surety that my fingers are long and sensitive, the most perfect, elegant, handsome part of my anatomy. They are not entirely perfect—the last knuckle of my right middle finger is twisted permanently, broken in a softball game when I was trying to block the plate—but even this slight disfigurement, harbinger of mortality, adds to the pleasure I take in my hands' rugged beauty. My penis does not excite in me nearly the same contemplative delight when I look at it as do my fingers. Pianists' hands, I have been told often; and though I do not play the piano, I derive an aesthetic satisfaction from them that is as pure and Apollonian as any I am capable of. I can stare at my fingers for hours. No wonder I have them so often in my mouth, biting my fingernails to bring them closer. When I write, I almost feel that they, and not my intellect, are the clever progenitors of the text. Whatever narcissism, fetishism, and proud sense of masculinity I possess about my body must begin and end with my fingers.

I Met a Man Who Has Seen the Ivory-billed Woodpecker, and This Is What He Told Me

Nancy Lord

The Woods

The swamp forest is only a corridor between rice fields, but the ancient cypress tower there. Winds the week before had bared the trees, laying a carpet of tupelo golds, sweetgum reds, the rusty cypress needles. It was possible to walk dry-footed among the fluted trunks and spreading knees, the wet-season watermarks waist-high on a man.

Woodpeckers

The usual woodpeckers were all there: their bouncing flight, the sounds of rapping, scrabbling on bark. They called *keer-uck* and *querrr-querrr, pik* and *peek, yucka, yucka yucka*. The downy and the hairy were there, the red-bellied, the yellow-bellied sapsucker. The pileated was there, the largest of them, the red crest, drumming like the pounding of mallets, loud. It was a birdy place: the wildness of trees in every aspect of life and death, with pecked-out cavities, with beetles, with peeling bark.

Woodpecker!

This is the word he let out as he grabbed for his wife's arm. He knew what he was seeing, and he could not believe that he was, in fact, seeing it. If for 60 years something has been missing, it takes more than the sight of a large, utterly distinct flying bird to convince a man of what is possible.

Eight Seconds

One for the bird flying toward him from deep forest. Two for the bird landing 12 feet up a cypress trunk and clinging there in profile. Three for the bird sliding around to the back of the tree, hiding itself. Two for the bird flashing back the way it came, a single whomping wingbeat and all that white.

Color

The colossal male crest, of course—the brilliant flame so inescapably, unignorably red and pointedly tall. The white was more the surprise, down the neck and across the shoulders like a saddle, and the two large wedges shaped by folded wings. And the black, the black that was not charcoal, not ebony, only the absolutest of all blacks, and blacker still beside white.

Sound

He never heard the bird, not the *henk, henk* of its call, not its tooting, staccato song, not the double rap that distinguishes its tree knocking from any other woodpecker's. The early naturalists described ivory-bills as social and raucous, but whatever birds have survived have had to be shy and wary, as quiet as bark. They live by stealth.

What He Missed

Not the bill, not the length, which he showed me, holding his fingers apart—"Three inches." Not the thickness of the bill—this time, making a fat circle of forefinger and thumb. What he forgot to notice was the pale color of the bill, the look of ivory. In the blitz of recognition, he missed that, as he missed the very yellow eye.

The Quote

No puny pileated but a whacking big bird, he said, quoting Roger Tory Peterson, who witnessed the ivory-bill in 1941 and called that occasion the greatest birding moment of his long birding career. Peterson kept a page for the bird in his guidebooks, hope against hope, for years after others had shifted it to the extinct category. But a decade ago, even Peterson concluded that the bird had reached its end, like the woodlands it had inhabited, and no longer existed except in memory.

After

For a long time, he had to sit on a log and not say anything. He played the image of the bird over and over and over in his mind. It was too great a thing to comprehend—that he was there, and the bird was there, and he and the bird were breathing the same air. After the descriptions and illustrations by Catesby, Audubon, and Wilson; and after the photos and films from the Louisiana swamps in the 1940s; and after the late but extensive Tanner scholarship about life history and habitat; and after Peterson's passion and despair; and after the fleeting white of new video and all the talk about the ghost bird and the grail bird and the Lord God bird; and after his dead father's lifetime of desire and his own matching but far-fetched desire and all the desire of the world; after all that, the ivory-billed woodpecker was still more than a person could imagine. It was as beautiful and as perfect as only it itself, its living being, could be.

Some Things About That Day

Debra Marquart

The placards I walked through. The wet raincoat on a hook. The questionnaire on a clipboard placed before me. Couples sat around me in the waiting room. They were young. What am I saying? I was only thirty-two.

But I remember, the men seemed the more bereft. Facing forward, their elbows resting on knees, their faces covered with hands. Or pushed back hard in the seats, gazing at a spot on the floor, legs stretched out in the aisles.

Difficult to remember the order in which things happened. The clipboard taken away, my name was called—our names were all called, the waiting room emptying and filling. Small orange pill in a tiny plastic cup. Water for washing it down. I was led to another room.

The gown that tied at the back, the bright fluorescent light, the posters with diagrams on the walls. Plenty of time to look around. The sound of vacuuming in another room.

The doctor arrives, hurried and unfriendly. Her one day in this clinic, she's flown in from another state. Death threats follow her. She asks me if I want to proceed. I tell her, yes. I lie back in the stirrups. The apparatus arrives—a silver canister on wheels with gauges and hoses attached to a long, cylindrical tube, thin like a spout. The sound of vacuuming close now. The nurse by my side, holding my shoulder. The doctor working away behind the thin film of my gown.

A blank space surrounds this moment. Sleepy from the sedative, yes, and numb. But let me not gloss over it. A feeling of tugging, mild discomfort. When the vacuum stops, the doctor asks if I want to know the sex. I tell her, *no*.

When I informed my husband I was pregnant, he said, *Is it mine?* Not the best beginning. We'd been married for a month. Married on Leap Day. Who else's could it be? He had an important meeting at work that day, some critical task. I had driven myself.

Sleep, after the procedure. (My friend tried to soften it for me afterwards. *Just say you had a procedure, dear.*) Nothing about it was procedural. I woke in a room of sleeping beauties. Afterwards, cramping, nausea. Faint, when I woke up, dizzy.

Orange juice and back down for twenty minutes. And then the odd assemblage of street clothes smoothed onto my limbs, the parting advice from the nurse, the script for a prescription pushed into my hand. Strange to walk out the door. The protesters gone. My car started just fine, slipped right into gear. I backed out, went forward. Drove light-headed to the drug store.

At the pharmacy, the man in the white coat looked at me when I handed him the script. Could he see from the prescription where I'd been? A softness dawned on his face. *Go home,* he said. They would deliver it.

Only then, in the car, did I start to cry. So stupid. Over the kindness of the pharmacist. When I got home, my husband was on the couch, watching the NBA playoffs. Even before the drugs arrived—even after—he couldn't stop telling me what a brave girl I had been.

MOTHER'S DAY by Maggie McKnight

In early May of 2004, I experienced my first Iowa hailstorm.

The hailstones were nearly the size of ping-pong balls.

That same week I discovered a mother duck sitting on a nest by the river.

She sat so still and un-blinking. I imagined her to possess a love so fierce that any predator who stalked her would be instantly turned to dust.

I named her Sarah.

That Sunday, I asked a friend to join me in a Mother's Day ritual.

First we visited Sarah, who was sleeping.

Then we sat by the river snacking. I didn't want to get too New-Agey or dreamy but I wanted some way to honor my intention to parent.

Uh... I'm not exactly sure what to do—I haven't done many rituals....

Hm...me neither.

A few weeks earlier, at my annual exam, I had told my nurse practitioner about my parenting plans.

I'm going to start trying to get pregnant this summer. Also I'm single, and gay.

Okay, we'll get you a preconception packet. And you should start taking folic acid now.

She seemed unfazed, as if she heard this kind of thing all the time.

But after the exam, when she went to get some brochures, she came back with bad news.

Unfortunately we can't help you get pregnant because you're single.

Oh.

We only help couples—whether lesbian or straight...

I see.

... so we don't discriminate in that way.

It wasn't until later—after the appointment and the subsequent stop at the drugstore—that I started to feel angry at the clinic's refusal to serve single women.

itch relief

vitamins

What gave them the right to decide who gets to have a baby and who doesn't?

That night, I sat in the rocker in the living room and opened the prenatal vitamins.

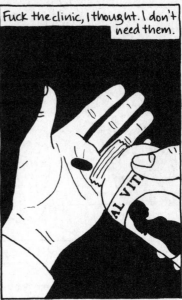

Fuck the clinic, I thought. I don't need them.

If they thought they were helping protect the world against the scourge of single motherhood, they were wrong.

I swallowed my horse-sized vitamin with a big swig of water, sending it forth into the darkness of my body.

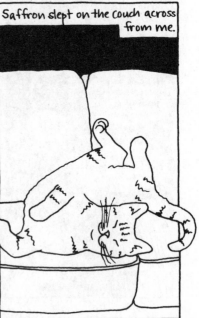

Saffron slept on the couch across from me.

I knew it would be an uphill battle convincing people a young single lesbian had as much a right to be a parent as anyone.

Even before my annual exam, it had already been a struggle.

I had started mentioning my desire to parent to my family some years earlier. My mom was initially very dismissive.

I don't know if she thought I wasn't serious or just hoped I wasn't — but it was clear her main concern was that I have a good (lucrative) career.

I knew it was her way of wanting my life to be better than hers had been. I just thought I should get to choose what "better" looked like.

Finally I had to call her out on it.

the year before I moved

I really don't want to end up supporting this kid....

If that's your attitude, believe me, you'll be the last person I ask if I ever need help.

Once she realized I was serious—and would make my choice regard-less of her support—she started to ease up.

It's just so hard to be broke, Maggie.

I know— but do you regret having us?

And finally I got her.

Of course not.

And do you think we turned out badly because you guys were "broke"?

Sigh. No.

No one ever used the word "feminist" in my family, but I knew that for me, the revolutionary thing to do would be to choose family over work.

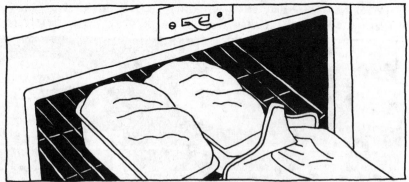

Though obviously as a single parent I'd be doing both.

Now, as I celebrated Mother's Day by the Iowa River, I was trying to do just that. I got out a few things I'd brought along:

A small Buddha statue.

A toy mouse to represent Saffron, my current "child."

And, because it was a sunny day, some sunscreen.

Nothing screams 'mom' like a bottle of sunscreen.

We told stories about our own births. My friend's involved a lot of false alarm trips to the hospital.

hi!

Mine is short: whenever someone asked my parents how they'd named me, they always said I just popped right out and said, "Hi, I'm Maggie!"

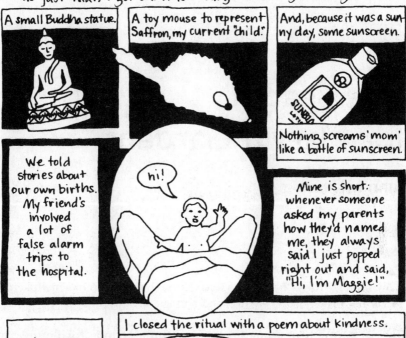

I closed the ritual with a poem about kindness.

My mom always told me I was independent from the day I was born.

...even as a mother protects with her life her child, her only child, so too with a boundless heart should we cherish all beings...

Some weeks later when I returned to visit Sarah, she was gone.

All that remained were some scattered eggshells and the round depression in the ground where she'd kept her vigil.

The Search for Marvin Gardens

John McPhee

Go. I roll the dice—a six and a two. Through the air I move my token, the flatiron, to Vermont Avenue, where dog packs range.

The dogs are moving (some are limping) through ruins, rubble, fire damage, open garbage. Doorways are gone. Lath is visible in the crumbling walls of the buildings. The street sparkles with shattered glass. I have never seen, anywhere, so many broken windows. A sign—"Slow, Children at Play"—has been bent backward by an automobile. At the lighthouse, the dogs turn up Pacific and disappear. George Meade, Army engineer, built the lighthouse—brick upon brick, six hundred thousand bricks, to reach up high enough to throw a beam twenty miles over the sea. Meade, seven years later, saved the Union at Gettysburg.

I buy Vermont Avenue for $100. My opponent is a tall, shadowy figure, across from me, but I know him well, and I know his game like a favorite tune. If he can, he will always go for the quick kill. And when it is foolish to go for the quick kill he will be foolish. On the whole, though, he is a master assessor of percentages. It is a mistake to underestimate him. His eleven carries his top hat to St. Charles Place, which he buys for $140.

The sidewalks of St. Charles Place have been cracked to shards by through-growing weeds. There are no buildings. Mansions, hotels once stood here. A few street lamps now drop cones of light on broken glass and vacant space behind a chain-link fence that some great machine has in places bent to the ground. Five plane trees—in full summer leaf, flecking the light—are all that live on St. Charles Place.

Block upon block, gradually, we are cancelling each other out—in the blues, the lavenders, the oranges, the greens. My opponent follows a plan of his own devising. I use the Hornblower & Weeks opening and the Zuricher defense. The first game draws tight, will soon finish. In 1971, a group of people in Racine, Wisconsin, played for seven hundred and sixty-eight hours. A game begun a month later in Danville, California, lasted eight hundred and twenty hours. These are official records, and they stun us. We have been playing for eight minutes. It amazes us that Monopoly is thought of as a long game. It is possible to play to a complete, absolute, and final conclusion in less than fifteen minutes, all within the rules as written. My opponent and I have done so thousands of times. No wonder we are sitting across from each other now in this best-of-seven series for the international singles championship of the world.

On Illinois Avenue, three men lean out from second-story windows. A girl is coming down the street. She wears dungarees and a bright-red shirt, has ample breasts and a Hadendoan Afro, a black halo, two feet in diameter. Ice rattles in the glasses in the hands of the men.

"Hey, sister!"

"Come on up!"

She looks up, looks from one to another to the other, looks them flat in the eye.

"What for?" she says, and she walks on.

I buy Illinois for $240. It solidifies my chances, for I already own Kentucky and Indiana. My opponent pales. If he had landed first on Illinois, the game would have been over then and there, for he has houses built on Boardwalk and Park Place, we share the railroads equally, and we have cancelled each other everywhere else. We never trade.

In 1852, R. B. Osborne, an immigrant Englishman, civil engineer, surveyed the route of a railroad line that would run from Camden to Absecon Island, in New Jersey, traversing the state from the Delaware River to the barrier beaches of the sea. He then sketched in the plan of a "bathing village" that would surround the eastern terminus of the line. His pen flew glibly, framing and naming spacious avenues parallel to the shore—Mediterranean, Baltic, Oriental, Ventnor—and narrower transsecting avenues: North Carolina, Pennsylvania, Vermont, Connecticut, States, Virginia, Tennessee, New York, Kentucky, Indiana, Illinois. The place as a whole had no name, so when he had completed the plan Osborne wrote in large letters over the ocean, "Atlantic City." No one ever challenged the name, or the names of Osborne's streets. Monopoly was invented in the early nineteen-thirties by Charles B. Darrow, but Darrow was only transliterating what Osborne had created. The railroads, crucial to any player, were the making of Atlantic City. After the rails were down, houses and hotels burgeoned from Mediterranean and Baltic to New York and Kentucky. Properties—building lots—sold for as little as six dollars apiece and as much as a thousand dollars. The original investors in the railroads and the real estate called themselves the Camden & Atlantic Land Company. Reverently, I repeat their names: Dwight Bell, William Coffin, John DaCosta, Daniel Deal, William Fleming, Andrew Hay, Joseph Porter, Jonathan Pitney, Samuel Richards—founders, fathers, forerunners, archetypical masters of the quick kill.

My opponent and I are now in a deep situation of classical Monopoly. The torsion is almost perfect—Boardwalk and Park Place versus the brilliant reds. His cash position is weak, though, and if I escape him now he may fade. I land on Luxury Tax, contiguous to but in sanctuary from his power. I have four houses on Indiana. He lands there. He concedes.

Indiana Avenue was the address of the Brighton Hotel, gone now. The Brighton was exclusive—a word that no longer has retail value in the city. If you arrived by automobile and tried to register at the Brighton, you were sent away. Brighton-class people came in private railroad cars. Brighton-class people had other private railroad cars for their horses—dawn rides on the firm sand at water's edge, skirts flying. Colonel Anthony J. Drexel Biddle—the sort of name that would constrict throats in Philadelphia—lived, much of the year, in the Brighton.

Colonel Sanders' fried chicken is on Kentucky Avenue. So is Clifton's Club Harlem, with the Sepia Revue and the Sepia Follies, featuring the Honey Bees, the Fashions, and the Lords.

My opponent and I, many years ago, played 2,428 games of Monopoly in a single season. He was then a recent graduate of the Harvard Law School, and he was working for a downtown firm, looking up law. Two people we knew—one from Chase Manhattan, the other from Morgan Stanley—tried to get into the game, but after a few rounds we found that they were not in the conversation and we sent them home. Monopoly should always be *mano a mano* anyway. My opponent won 1,199 games, and so did I. Thirty were ties. He was called into the Army, and we stopped just there. Now, in Game 2 of the series, I go immediately to jail, and again to jail while my opponent seines property. He is dumbfoundingly lucky. He wins in twelve minutes.

Visiting hours are daily, eleven to two; Sunday, eleven to one; evenings, six to nine. "NO MINORS, NO FOOD, Immediate Family Only Allowed in Jail." All this above a blue steel door in a blue cement wall in the windowless interior of the basement of the city hall. The desk sergeant sits opposite the door to the jail. In a cigar box in front of him are pills in every color, a banquet of fruit salad an inch and a half deep—leapers, co-pilots, footballs, truck drivers, peanuts, blue angels, yellow jackets, redbirds, rainbows. Near the desk are two soldiers, waiting to go through the blue door. They are about eighteen years old. One of them is trying hard to light a cigarette. His wrists are in steel cuffs. A military policeman waits, too. He is a year or so older than the soldiers, taller, studious in appearance, gentle, fat. On a bench against a wall sits a good-looking girl in slacks. The blue door rattles, swings heavily open. A turnkey stands in the doorway. "Don't you guys kill yourselves back there now," says the sergeant to the soldiers.

"One kid, he overdosed himself about ten and a half hours ago," says the M.P.

The M.P., the soldiers, the turnkey, and the girl on the bench are white. The sergeant is black. "If you take off the handcuffs, take off the belts," says the sergeant to the M.P. "I don't want them hanging themselves back there." The door shuts and its tumblers move. When it opens again, five minutes later, a young white man in sandals and dungarees and a blue polo shirt emerges. His hair is in a ponytail. He has no beard. He grins at the good-looking girl. She rises, joins him. The sergeant hands him a manila envelope. From it he removes his belt and a small notebook. He borrows a pencil, makes an entry in the notebook. He is out of jail, free. What did he do? He offended Atlantic City in some way. He spent a night in the jail. In the nineteen-thirties, men visiting Atlantic City went to jail, directly to jail, did not pass Go, for appearing in topless bathing suits on the beach. A city statute requiring all men to wear full-length bathing suits was not seriously challenged until 1937, and the first year in which a man could legally go bare-chested on the beach was 1940.

Game 3. After seventeen minutes, I am ready to begin construction on overpriced and sluggish Pacific, North Carolina, and Pennsylvania. Nothing else being open, opponent concedes.

The physical profile of streets perpendicular to the shore is something like a playground slide. It begins in the high skyline of Boardwalk hotels, plummets into warrens of "side-avenue" motels, crosses Pacific, slopes through church missions, convalescent homes, burlesque houses, rooming houses, and liquor stores, crosses Atlantic, and runs level through the bombed-out ghetto as far—Baltic, Mediterranean—as the eye can see. North Carolina Avenue, for example, is flanked at its beach end by the Chalfonte and the Haddon Hall (908 rooms, air-conditioned), where, according to one biographer, John Philip Sousa (1854–1932) first played when he was twenty-two, insisting, even then, that everyone call him by his entire name. Behind these big hotels, motels—Barbizon, Catalina—crouch. Between Pacific and Atlantic is an occasional house from 1910—wooden porch, wooden mullions, old yellow paint—and two churches, a package store, a strip show, a dealer in fruits and vegetables. Then, beyond Atlantic Avenue, North Carolina moves on into the vast ghetto, the bulk of the city, and it looks like Metz in 1919, Cologne in 1944. Nothing has actually exploded. It is not bomb damage. It is deep and complex decay. Roofs are off. Bricks are scattered in the street. People sit on porches, six deep, at nine on a Monday morning. When they go off to wait in unemployment lines, they wait sometimes two hours. Between Mediterranean and Baltic runs a chain-link fence, enclosing rubble. A patrol car sits idling by the curb. In the back seat is a German shepherd. A sign on the fence says, "Beware of Bad Dogs."

Mediterranean and Baltic are the principal avenues of the ghetto. Dogs are everywhere. A pack of seven passes me. Block after block, there are three-story brick row houses. Whole segments of them are abandoned, a thousand broken windows. Some parts are intact, occupied. A mattress lies in the street, soaking in a pool of water. Wet stuffing is coming out of the mattress. A postman is having a rye and a beer in the Plantation Bar at nine-fifteen in the morning. I ask him idly if he knows where Marvin Gardens is. He does not. "HOOKED AND NEED HELP? CONTACT N.A.R.C.O." "REVIVAL NOW GOING ON, CONDUCTED BY REVEREND H. HENDERSON OF TEXAS." These are signboards on Mediterranean and Baltic. The second one is upside down and leans against a boarded-up window of the Faith Temple Church of God in Christ. There is an old peeling poster on a warehouse wall showing a figure in an electric chair. "The Black Panther Manifesto" is the title of the poster, and its message is, or was, that "the fascists have already decided in advance to murder Chairman Bobby Seale in the electric chair." I pass an old woman who carries a bucket. She wears blue sneakers, worn through. Her feet spill out. She wears red socks, rolled at the knees. A white handkerchief, spread over her head, is knotted at the corners. Does she know where Marvin Gardens is? "I sure don't know," she says, setting down the bucket. "I sure don't know. I've heard of it somewhere, but I just can't say where." I walk on, through a block of shattered glass. The glass crunches underfoot like coarse sand. I remember when I first came here—a long train ride from Trenton, long ago, games of poker in the train—to play basketball against Atlantic City. We were half black, they were all black. We scored forty points, they scored eighty, or something like it. What I remember most is that they had glass backboards—glittering, pendent, expensive glass backboards, a rarity then in high schools, even in colleges, the only ones we played on all year.

I turn on Pennsylvania, and start back toward the sea. The windows of the Hotel Astoria, on Pennsylvania near Baltic, are boarded up. A sheet of unpainted plywood is the door, and in it is a triangular peephole that now frames an eye. The plywood door opens. A man answers my question. Rooms there are six, seven, and ten dollars a week. I thank him for the information and move on, emerging from the ghetto at the Catholic Daughters of America Women's Guest House, between Atlantic and Pacific. Between Pacific and the Boardwalk are the blinking vacancy signs of the Aristocrat and Colton Manor motels. Pennsylvania terminates at the Sheraton-Seaside—thirty-two dollars a day, ocean corner. I take a walk on the Boardwalk and into the Holiday Inn (twenty-three stories). A guest is registering. "You reserved for Wednesday, and this is Monday," the clerk tells him. "But that's all right. We have *plenty* of rooms." The clerk is very young, female, and has soft brown hair that hangs below her waist. Her superior kicks her.

He is a middle-aged man with red spiderwebs in his face. He is jacketed and tied. He takes her aside. "Don't say 'plenty,'" he says. "Say 'You are fortunate, sir. We have rooms available.'"

The face of the young woman turns sour. "We have all the rooms you need," she says to the customer, and, to her superior, "How's that?"

Game 4. My opponent's luck has become abrasive. He has Boardwalk and Park Place, and has sealed the board.

Darrow was a plumber. He was, specifically, a radiator repairman who lived in Germantown, Pennsylvania. His first Monopoly board was a sheet of linoleum. On it he placed houses and hotels that he had carved from blocks of wood. The game he thus invented was brilliantly conceived, for it was an uncannily exact reflection of the business milieu at large. In its depth, range, and subtlety, in its luck-skill ratio, in its sense of infrastructure and socio-economic parameters, in its philosophical characteristics, it reached to the profundity of the financial community. It was as scientific as the stock market. It suggested the manner and means through which an underdeveloped world had been developed. It was chess at Wall Street level. "Advance token to the nearest Railroad and pay owner twice the rental to which he is otherwise entitled. If Railroad is unowned, you may buy it from the Bank. Get out of Jail, free. Advance token to nearest Utility. If unowned, you may buy it from Bank. If owned, throw dice and pay owner a total ten times the amount thrown. You are assessed for street repairs: $40 per house, $115 per hotel. Pay poor tax of $15. Go to Jail. Go directly to Jail. Do not pass Go. Do not collect $200."

The turnkey opens the blue door. The turnkey is known to the inmates as Sidney K. Above his desk are ten closed-circuit-TV screens—assorted viewpoints of the jail. There are three cellblocks—men, women, juvenile boys. Six days is the average stay. Showers twice a week. The steel doors and the equipment that operates them were made in San Antonio. The prisoners sleep on bunks of butcher block. There are no mattresses. There are three prisoners to a cell. In winter, it is cold in here. Prisoners burn newspapers to keep warm. Cell corners are black with smudge. The jail is three years old. The men's block echoes with chatter. The man in the cell nearest Sidney K. is pacing. His shirt is covered with broad stains of blood. The block for juvenile boys is, by contrast, utterly silent—empty corridor, empty cells. There is only one prisoner. He is small and black and appears to be thirteen. He says he is sixteen and that he has been alone in here for three days.

"Why are you here? What did you do?"

"I hit a jitney driver."

The series stands at three all. We have split the fifth and sixth games. We are scrambling for property. Around the board we fairly fly. We move so fast because we do our own banking and search our own deeds. My opponent grows tense.

Ventnor Avenue, a street of delicatessens and doctors' offices, is leafy with plane trees and hydrangeas, the city flower. Water Works is on the mainland. The water comes over in submarine pipes. Electric Company gets power from across the state, on the Delaware River, in Deepwater. States Avenue, now a wasteland like St. Charles, once had gardens running down the middle of the street, a horse-drawn trolley, private homes. States Avenue was as exclusive as the Brighton.

Only an apartment house, a small motel, and the All Wars Memorial Building—monadnocks spaced widely apart—stand along States Avenue now. Pawnshops, convalescent homes, and the Paradise Soul Saving Station are on Virginia Avenue. The soul-saving station is pink, orange, and yellow. In the windows flanking the door of the Virginia Money Loan Office are Nikons, Polaroids, Yashicas, Sony TVs, Underwood typewriters, Singer sewing machines, and pictures of Christ. On the far side of town, beside a single track and locked up most of the time, is the new railroad station, a small hut made of glazed firebrick, all that is left of the lines that built the city. An authentic phrenologist works on New York Avenue close to Frank's Extra Dry Bar and a church where the sermon today is "Death in the Pot." The church is of pink brick, has blue and amber windows and two red doors. St. James Place, narrow and twisting, is lined with boarding houses that have wooden porches on each of three stories, suggesting a New Orleans made of salt-bleached pine. In a vacant lot on Tennessee is a white Ford station wagon stripped to the chassis. The windows are smashed. A plastic Clorox bottle sits on the driver's seat. The wind has pressed newspaper against the chain-link fence around the lot. Atlantic Avenue, the city's principal thoroughfare, could be seventeen American Main Streets placed end to end—discount vitamins and Vienna Corset shops, movie theatres, shoe stores, and funeral homes. The Boardwalk is made of yellow pine and Douglas fir, soaked in pentachlorophenol. Downbeach, it reaches far beyond the city. Signs everywhere—on windows, lampposts, trash baskets—proclaim "Bienvenue Canadiens!" The salt air is full of Canadian French. In the Claridge Hotel, on Park Place, I ask a clerk if she knows where Marvin Gardens is. She says, "Is it a floral shop?" I ask a cabdriver, parked outside. He says, "Never heard of it." Park Place is one block long, Pacific to Boardwalk. On the roof of the Claridge is the Solarium, the highest point in town—panoramic view of the ocean, the bay, the salt-water ghetto. I look down at the rooftops of the side-avenue motels and into swimming pools. There are hundreds of people around the rooftop pools, sunbathing, reading—many more people than are on the beach. Walls, windows, and a block of sky are all that is visible from these pools—no sand, no sea. The pools are craters, and with the people around them they are counter-sunk into the motels.

The seventh, and final, game is ten minutes old and I have hotels on Oriental, Vermont, and Connecticut. I have Tennessee and St. James. I have North Carolina and Pacific. I have Boardwalk, Atlantic, Ventnor, Illinois, Indiana. My fingers are forming a "V." I have mortgaged most of these properties in order to pay for others, and I have mortgaged the others to pay for the hotels. I have seven dollars. I will pay off the mortgages and build my reserves with income from the three hotels. My cash position may be low, but I feel like a rocket in an underground silo. Meanwhile, if I could just go to jail for a time I could pause there, wait there, until my opponent, in his inescapable rounds, pays the rates of my hotels. Jail, at times, is the strategic place to be. I roll boxcars from the Reading and move the flatiron to Community Chest. "Go to Jail. Go directly to Jail."

The prisoners, of course, have no pens and no pencils. They take paper napkins, roll them tight as crayons, char the ends with matches, and write on the walls. The things they write are not entirely idiomatic; for example, "In God We Trust." All is in carbon. Time is required in the writing. "Only humanity could know of such pain." "God So Loved the World." "There is no greater pain than life itself." In the women's block now, there are six blacks, giggling, and a white asleep in red shoes. She is drunk. The others are pushers, prostitutes, an auto thief, a burglar caught with pistol in purse. A sixteen-year-old accused of murder was in here last week. These words are written on the wall of a now empty cell: "Laying here I see two bunks about six inches thick, not counting the one I'm laying on, which is hard as brick. No cushion for my back. No pillow for my head. Just a couple scratchy blankets which is best to use it's said. I wake up in the morning so shivery and cold, waiting and waiting till I am told the food is coming. It's on its way. It's not worth waiting for, but I eat it anyway. I know one thing when they set me free I'm gonna be good if it kills me."

How many years must a game be played to produce an Anthony J. Drexel Biddle and chestnut geldings on the beach? About half a century was the original answer, from the first railroad to Biddle at his peak. Biddle, at his peak, hit an Atlantic City streetcar conductor with his fist, laid him out with one punch. This increased Biddle's legend. He did not go to jail. While John Philip Sousa led his band along the Boardwalk playing "The Stars and Stripes Forever" and Jack Dempsey ran up and down in training for his fight with Gene Tunney, the city crossed the high curve of its parabola. Al Capone held conventions here—upstairs with his sleeves rolled, apportioning among his lieutenant governors the states of the Eastern seaboard. The natural history of an American resort proceeds from Indians to French Canadians via Biddles and Capones. French Canadians, whatever they may be at home, are Visigoths here. Bienvenue Visigoths!

My opponent plods along incredibly well. He has got his fourth railroad, and patiently, unbelievably, he has picked up my potential winners until he has blocked me everywhere but Marvin Gardens. He has avoided, in the fifty-dollar zoning, my increasingly petty hotels. His cash flow swells. His railroads are costing me two hundred dollars a minute. He is building hotels on States, Virginia, and St. Charles. He has temporarily reversed the current. With the yellow monopolies and my blue monopolies, I could probably defeat his lavenders and his railroads. I have Atlantic and Ventnor. I need Marvin Gardens. My only hope is Marvin Gardens.

There is a plaque at Boardwalk and Park Place, and on it in relief is the leonine profile of a man who looks like an officer in a metropolitan bank—"Charles B. Darrow, 1889–1967, inventor of the game of Monopoly." "Darrow," I address him, aloud. "Where is Marvin Gardens?" There is, of course, no answer. Bronze, impassive, Darrow looks south down the Boardwalk. "Mr. Darrow, please, where is Marvin Gardens?" Nothing. Not a sign. He just looks south down the Boardwalk.

My opponent accepts the trophy with his natural ease, and I make, from notes, remarks that are even less graceful than his.

Marvin Gardens is the one color-block Monopoly property that is not in Atlantic City. It is a suburb within a suburb, secluded. It is a planned compound of seventy-two handsome houses set on curvilinear private streets under yews and cedars, poplars and willows. The compound was built around 1920, in Margate, New Jersey, and consists of solid buildings of stucco, brick, and wood, with slate roofs, tile roofs, multimullioned porches, Giraldic towers, and Spanish grilles. Marvin Gardens, the ultimate outwash of Monopoly, is a citadel and sanctuary of the middle class. "We're heavily patrolled by police here. We don't take no chances. Me? I'm living here nine years. I paid seventeen thousand dollars and I've been offered thirty. Number one, I don't want to move. Number two, I don't need the money. I have four bedrooms, two and a half baths, front den, back den. No basement. The Atlantic is down there. Six feet down and you float. A lot of people have a hard time finding this place. People that lived in Atlantic City all their life don't know how to find it. They don't know where the hell they're going. They just know it's south, down the Boardwalk."

Geas

Ander Monson

Gary Gygax is dead. Sorry. Really sorry for your loss. He has left the building. There will be, at the risk of sounding flip, no resurrection. The founder of Dungeons & Dragons, and in fact the whole idea of role-playing games, often blamed for our increasingly many social ills—from the destruction and desecration of our youths and their drugged-out, sexed-up escapades in high school or in the steam tunnels beneath our colleges to the difficulty we increasingly have in separating game, or fiction, or film, or dream, from reality, just to name a few—Gygax found religion in the years before his death. He increasingly believed in the spirit exceeding the body, a corollary to Dungeons & Dragons, really, which allows the body to be resurrected, resuscitated, raised from the dead. While the theology of D&D has undergone a number of overhauls (from dalliances with demons and devils, immortals, the Ethereal and Astral planes, and some really whacked out and interesting stuff to a more traditional pantheon of deities and demigods and dragons that live forever), it has always been based on the idea that the character extends beyond the body into the nothingness, or whatever you want to fill it with, thereafter. When your character died in D&D, you could either make up a new one or else undertake a quest to try to get your character resurrected.

He died a week ago, nearly, and the fact that I didn't hear about it until now depresses me further. To think I am so disconnected from this gaming, fantasy hinterland from whence I emanated in my teenage years is near crushing to the body. I do claim the moniker of *gamer*, as a descended D&D player, descended as in testicles, as in no longer playing, as in having abandoned that imaginative and physical life (or lack thereof, as some suggest) in college, having given it up after a decade, easily, of playing and entering into that story space after my mother's death—maybe that being a factor, maybe that opened me up for it—and living in my dad's duplex, dice clattering across the downstairs kitchen table, the light luminous and fluorescent above us, with my brother and my friends, Chris, Matt,

Jerry (whose brief dwarf character was named "Cooler"), occasionally Jody (now murdered, and by putting her into the essay at all, by iterating her name, almost obliges me to address that welt, that hurt, to do something with it—she who has left her body some years ago—though I did so at length in another text that will go unmentioned here), and a host of others, who joined us for a game, or for the better part of a decade.

This fact, the fact of his departure from this mortal whatever, feels like punctuation. It closes a door on my life, a door that closed a while ago, in truth, though recently I had been reintroduced to RPGs on my Playstation 2, with *Final Fantasy XII*, a game certainly descended from D&D.

On the day I am trying to reckon with the loss of Gygax, the news is made public that I am leaving this, my current job, a good job with good people, for another job, which will also presumably have good people. The body is already quavering, contemplating giving up my house, this city, this skyline, this weather, and this, my native state, for something else with scorpions and desert. As I work on generating this bit of prose, faculty stop by my office to mock-accuse me for leaving, and to congratulate me. It is a mix. Their emotions, mine. I have loved this office, with its ravine view, and humming fan amid the silence, and green technology. This borders on an elegy for this job, this former iteration of Monson, which will be left behind and vacated like this space, like my parents' former houses, one after another, as we moved from place to place (to Saudi Arabia and away)—and an elegy for my students, whom I have loved also in my way. But elegy is grandiose. I am becoming maudlin. It is too much. I move close and I push away.

I don't even know if this is true emotion, or if it's a role I am expected to play, and am so playing, or how to tell the difference, if there is any at all. If my colleagues and friends here will be sad, exactly, to see me go, or if it is a social obligation, self-pity, envy, or what. I feel I am of this place, that it has acted on me, like other formative places, settings in my life. In D&D we might call this place a continuity of character and action, the overarching scope of the novel, an arc, a *campaign*. Sometimes when the Dungeon Master loses his players, as when they no longer want to play, or are dissatisfied, or bored, or have had their outside lives interfere with the shared ongoing fantasy, or in a case where the plot has become too Byzantine, too dumb, or the players too spoiled, you have to scrap it, the whole world you've created, and start another.

You can also buy another, buy into one of the ongoing campaign-worlds that published D&D "modules" (usually these take the form of a dungeon with a goal, side quests, and lists of dramatis personae) come with. Greyhawk was one. Forgotten Realms, another. Krynn, home of the *Dragonlance* books, another. There are dozens of published worlds with their own continuities, clashing races and clans and what have you. With the Internet and the rise of online gaming, there are surely thousands of collective, published imaginations for you to choose from.

For me it comes down to not wanting to let inertia, the fact of this job and this role, this office, these classes, these students, direct my life. To not get too comfortable, if this isn't a story I am telling myself to enable motion. I haven't signed the new contract yet. I'm still hedging, just a little, until it arrives. I am apologetic for my departure, and there's no reason to be, not really. But the fact of it remains.

Perhaps it is the province of those who are self-involved, or sensitive, or inward-directed, or neurotic, or solipsistic, to overly analyze at length, to ramble on and circle the fact in prose. It allows me to contain two roles at least: both excited at new prospects and sad to be leaving, and aware of these things, both existing. I can play both sides. I can feel torn. I can generate enough emotion to want to line up sentences on a page. Equivocation is one of my character flaws. I like to have it both ways, always, even. It's not quite duplicity, but it's on the road towards it. Equal and opposite reactions. The mind casts itself as passive, as watcher of the action, not as actor. I want to talk about it, and to do it, but to hold the imaginative possibility of action and inaction.

In D&D your character has an *alignment*. This describes his moral compass, his approach to good and evil, law and lawlessness. It can range from Lawful Good to Chaotic Evil. The alignment defines your character perhaps more than anything else. It circumscribes the way you can play your role: whether you are a thoughtful type or a man of action, whether you subscribe to the life of the mind or the body heaving the axe at a troll, and whether you are a force for good in this or another world.

And even as I am always reckoning, always analyzing, equivocating, I move.

So I have to admit that the idea of reckoning with the loss of Gygax is a reductive one: it's naive, a lack of specificity, of deep engagement with the subject. I don't think of him that often, and I'm not even sure how to pronounce his name, which g gets the soft and which the hard, and so I vary (ending up on soft-g *gy* and hard-g *gax*, but if you use both hard g's it's more warriorish, something your paladin could shout on the battlefield as he charges towards a swarming force of orcs). For me he was as myth already, even as living man. I'm sure he got that a lot, being the honored guest at thousands of RPG conferences, having his myth tended to and honored publicly, even as, like many men-made-myth, the public thinks about his past and not his present, not his finding Jesus, not his new game systems. (He left D&D to his former publishing company, TSR [the company that owned D&D until it was sold to Wizards of the Coast in the late '90s; originally it stood for Tactical Studies Rules, demonstrating D&D's origin in tactical war games, and eventually the company jettisoned this moniker so it no longer stands for anything] in 1985 and hadn't looked back.) So the Gygax I know (or conceive of) is at least 20 years old, like light from a closer star, and just a name, almost, a reputation, a signifier that points to the emanation of this game-world in my and others' lives. I know him not at all except by reputation, as what he means, or meant, or, well, means, still: let's be honest, his name will be yoked to D&D and this particular variety (if not all varieties) of nerdery for decades to come, as we see how far the effects of D&D and RPG and gaming culture have permeated our media, our stories.

At the same time, in the last few years D&D has become acceptable to talk about publicly again. The actor slash action star Vin Diesel cops to it, even writing an introduction to a recent retrospective (and really terrible, actually) book about the history of D&D. Television satirist Stephen Colbert talks D&D, or, failing that, the work of J. R. R. Tolkien, about every week or two on his show. The musician Final Fantasy has a whole album centered around the concept of the various schools of magic in third-edition Advanced Dungeons & Dragons. A brilliant essay in *The Believer* by Paul LaFarge interviews and describes and talks about Gygax, and plays a game with him, and comes to its own terms with his history of playing as a player-character.

All these sightings of D&D in the public and now slightly-less-shameful world, and reading LaFarge's essay in particular, mean a lot to me because they enable me to come out, to admit and talk on and worry my history with D&D, which is a way of saying a history with collaborative story or storytelling, which is a subgenre of *interactive fiction* as the current academic term applies to what we formerly called "text adventures" like *Zork* and so on in the world.

Fuck. There's so much here, embedded, impacted in the subject. Like anything suitably primal, it resists being teased apart.

Outside, a dude in a black trench coat and ponytail walks by the window. His tote bag features a bunch of unidentifiable pins. Though I don't know him, his look tells me he is a fellow traveler, that he knows what dodecahedron means, that he could bust out some adjustments to saving throw statistics, that he might, as I did once, subscribe to *Dragon* magazine. I just took a box of back issues of *Dragon* back from my parents' garage, where they were facing certain destruction or donation to Salvation Army.

About once a year I am called to rescue or condemn a box of artifacts of my past life from their position moldering in the basement or the garage. This entails reliving, or reconceiving of, this past life, this former Monson, or stage thereof, and looking at it closely, reentering that space, and deciding what to do with it. The things I used to do are bizarre to me now, biologically so foreign (yet I still contain traces). I can't imagine sitting in the basement of a house with a bunch of other boys, surrounded by a tripartite Dungeon Master's screen filled with statistics and probably a picture of a wizard, exploring some imaginary dungeon. Instead I have no problem with sitting in some dude's rec room (or mine if I had a rec room) playing video games, exploring an imagined, virtual space. This causes me no trouble at all. I cannot comprehend my former tooth-killing interest in eating powdered sugar with a spoon directly out of the bag, occasionally inhaling some by accident and shredding my mucous membranes, quaffing liters of Mountain Dew and rubbing my little belly. (I know the word *quaffing* only as a result of the computer game *Larn*, a version of another popular computer game called *Rogue*, both of which involved wandering through dungeons rudimentarily represented as black space on the black monochrome computer screen and lit up in accordance with your character [itself represented by a character, an ASCII glyph, like a dollar sign or the letter *x* or something, I don't quite remember] as it meandered through the darkness, and turned black space into a white dot against that space. The monsters in the game were all represented by an alphanumeric character, like a *t* for a troll and a *g* for a goblin, and your commands were entered via one-key commands from the keyboard. *Q*, then, was for *quaff*, as in quaffing a healing potion or a poison remedy. Both *Larn* and *Rogue* were solo versions of D&D, albeit with almost no graphics and no social engagement with anything beyond the screen. But they were, in their way, beautiful and immersive.)

All these selves—my Atari 2600 self, recently adopted from said garage; my PC virus writing self, also recently recalled from the dustbin; my teenage criminal self; my computer-gaming self; or my one-time GEN CON (role-playing conference) attending self—they are like characters within the larger campaign of the person, the player—being me, probably (I assume). The distance, psychologically, biologically, between there and now, between those cells, those synapse configurations and these, is almost too great to comprehend. Which should give me hope. That we can grow through obsessions like these suggests a life of disposable stages, something new ahead, a new job, a new place, new levels of dorkiness.

I'm going to head home from this office life and sit down in my sleepy hollow chair, pop a couple Mountain Dews, order Domino's (sausage, green pepper, and onion), and bury my head for a while in video games. That would be a fitting tribute.

▼   ▼   ▼

Q: How many times per day can a hellhound breathe fire?
A: There is no limit on the total number of times that a hellhound can breathe fire, but it may only breathe when the dice roll given in the 1983 *Expert Rulebook*, page 51, says it can breathe fire. (Skip Wiliams, "Sage Advice," *Dragon* #124).
Q: *Geas* and *quest* spells are much abused. For example, couldn't an evil magicuser *geas* a character to never attack him? Couldn't an evil cleric do a similar thing with *quest*?
A: A *quest* must be a specific and finite task; the victim must be able to take actions that will bring about the end of the quest, or the spell has no effect. A *geas* is similar to a *quest* in that it must be specific. (Skip Wiliams, "Sage Advice," *Dragon* #124)

Geas is one of these words that I try to deploy periodically in conversation, or, worse, in *Scrabble*, where I am destined to lose by virtue of my reliance on knowledge gleaned from fantasy books, mythology, or Dungeons & Dragons. This happens way more often than it should because I usually can't differentiate actual knowledge from fantasy knowledge. The wall between the two is glass, and flimsy, clear. In one of my Ancient Greek classes I used some bit of knowledge from the (old, crappy, fantasy) movie *Krull* to underscore a point I was making about the Cyclops, that he had traded one of his eyes to one god or another for the ability to see the future, but that he was tricked: the only future he could see was the day of his own death (or possibly the day of anyone's death, which would be a little more useful). This tidbit was met by the laughter of Stephen Fineberg, my Greek professor, who asked me where I got that from. I confessed. More laughter. Embarrassment. Silence.

A *geas* comes from *geis* in Celtic, Scottish, or Welsh mythologies, which vary a bit. It is essentially a specific curse/quest that a character must live up to or undergo. It is a spell (interchangeable with *quest*) used by magic-users (wizards/sorcerers), or by clerics (religious magic-users) in D&D. D&D is an exceptionally complex and expansive system, covering, I'm sure, thousands on thousands of pages worth of mythology and backstory, game mechanics, sexy weapons. The attraction of the geas spell is one of control—one of the attractions of role-playing games at all, of attaining power over others, of commanding them.

The above quotes are from *Dragon* magazine, a monthly tome devoted to role-playing games, primarily one of the iterations of Dungeons & Dragons. My parents' basement contains issues 75–130 of the magazine. Many pages are dog-eared or show obvious signs of my devotion. My favorite sections in the magazine are the ones where serious players write in and passionately query or debate obscurities, such as the sections above.

▼   ▼   ▼

Version 4.0 of the Advanced Dungeons & Dragons rules comes out in six days, on July 8, 2008. The version I played mostly was 2.0 (the version after D&D—the simpler version—was split into two, the simpler D&D and a more complex AD&D). I haven't paid any attention to the state of all things D&D since I stopped playing shortly before I went to college. I did not have a falling-out with the game, but it just became less fun to me, like it occurred to me that there were, at last, at least, other things to do. I played one role-playing game (or tried to; we got bored and then drunk and then it was over) in grad school, and I played one session of *Vampire*, which came out when I was in college, with two guys who wanted to be called in real life (not in game) "Pasha" and "Ghost," their given names too banal to bother with. They played with some goth girls (*Vampire* attracted the goth girls like nothing else), which was sexy in theory, but there were no capes or bodices, and the experience was, on the whole, a bore.

Really, I don't know if I was ever a very good player of D&D or any role-playing game. I was always the Dungeon Master (DM, or as they say, GM, in other games—and in the new version of D&D), responsible for the creation of the fictional world and for refereeing the play of the game. The storytelling aspect must have appealed to me (and still does), but I've only played a character a handful of times, and I was not good at playing the role, which is a huge part of what makes

RPGs fun, or so I am told. My brother and I both played, and we attended the yearly Gen-Con convention (the big convention for RPGs in America), which took place in Milwaukee, Wisconsin, close to the birthplace of TSR. My brother and I played at the convention, but I remember being too young, among a bunch of college kids and older people, and not really getting it. It was fun, and my father surely deserves an award for indulging the quality of our dorkiness to bring us to the convention, but the game I saw wasn't the same as the game we played. Mostly I remember the fries at one of the Milwaukee malls as I stuffed them into my mouth. They were thick cut, natural, with bits of potato skin, covered in salt. And they came from a mall, not a chickenshit little mall like our hometown Copper Country Mall, where the biggest store for four hours was a JCPenney with their cool, cool cardigans.

Maybe it's more about control. The Dungeon Master makes the rules, knows all—or as much as is possible to know. It was hard for me to be just a player, with a more limited knowledge base, trying to inhabit a character. Maybe it was teenage solipsism, an inability or reluctance to inhabit anyone else. But reading gives the lie to this—that is the function of books, to allow us to inhabit another mind.

The penultimate version of the game was 3.5, presumably preceded by a 3.0, where the company dropped the *Advanced* from the game's title and collapsed the advanced version back to Dungeons & Dragons. You can go to their website to learn all about D&D. Watching their online demo for how D&D is played is a very weird experience for this former player. For one, a girl is involved. That happened rarely. A couple girls played with us a couple times, including one who was later murdered (sad to think of her only in these terms—as murdered girl), but for the most part we were male, juvenile (we were juveniles who were especially juvenile). Various rape fantasies were probably deployed. My memory tastefully omits this. There was looting. Battles. You know. That's what you get with a duplex kitchen full of 13-year-olds eating powdered sugar out of the bag.

Version 4.0 incorporates a board-game element (the dungeons through which the players canter and saunter and creep are 2-D, visual, and the players are represented by pieces, miniatures), as well as having the rules revamped to be significantly less technical. So the way D&D is played is now once again visual, with pieces on a board. This is a huge disappointment. Even looking at it, moving the dorky miniature representations of characters, feels reductive; it gives the lie to the imaginative qualities of the game. Are we getting more stupid? Does this make it an easier sell to parents, less transgressive with media fantasies of deranged kids running through steam tunnels under Michigan State University, taking drugs and fucking, and fighting each other with homemade foils fashioned from cut-off golf clubs? Or maybe "game" has become increasingly visual, requiring more consumption, more procuring and painting of miniatures, as if to better compete with the immersive quality of video role-playing games?

The way it used to be played (or the way we played it, anyhow) involved almost no physical props or presence. It was oral, with collaborative storytelling.

▼   ▼   ▼

Controversy over the athcoid [more commonly known as the gelatinous cube] has long raged among the wise—quite heatedly so in the corridors of the Hall of Beast-Tamers and in the offices of the Imperial Zoo of Amn, the keepers of which have managed to keep a cube alive in captivity for some 12 winters. Over and over, the questions are asked: How intelligent are the cubes? How amorphous are their forms? Of what is their digestive fluid composed, and can it be used as a weapon or in alchemy (or, for that matter, in medicine or in the handling of beasts)? How do athcoids mate—indeed, do athcoids mate?

Ed Greenwood, "The Ecology of the Gelatinous Cube: Unseeing, Unthinking, Unstoppable," *Dragon* #124

▼   ▼   ▼

Many of my friends have mated. I have mated. D&D types mate consistently, often with other gamers. They have Renaissance Faire weddings. My wife dressed up as a wench for her friend's wedding in college. The marriage lasted less than a year.

Chivalry Sports is what appears to be a sporting-goods store in central Tucson. It specializes in reproduction or semi-period regalia for Renaissance Faires and live-action role playing (LARP), and probably everything in between or on the spectrum of this culture, including meeting up with the "girl" you've been chatting with on *World of Warcraft* or on one of the more hardcore, old-school, geek-chic MUDs (multi-user dungeons, all text, a precursor of *Everquest* and *WoW* and other MMORPGs [massively multiplayer online role-playing games], which you likely know because you wonder about your friend, the addict to this game, this representation of reality, this particular version of life).

I pick up a poorly printed flier for the "Empire of Chivalry and Steel," a live-action medieval-recreation society that holds a number of medieval tournaments in which you can fight, craft, sing, and so on. From the website: "The Kingdom of Galandor is the first recognized Sovereign Territory of The Empire of Chivalry and Steel (ECS), Inc., founded on April 10, 1990. Our Kingdom encompasses all of Arizona, with an outlying territory in Illinois. We currently have three territories in our Kingdom: the Marquisate of Altiora (Tucson, AZ), the Marquisate of Solaris (Phoenix, AZ), and the Province of Northwatch (Chicago, IL)." You can find out more about them at Galandor.org.

Don't get me wrong—this is by no means Dungeons & Dragons. We didn't dress up . . . much . . . and if we did, and we held battles in friends' backyards with homemade wooden swords, then that wasn't D&D either but a natural, perfectly healthy, aerobic, enjoyable, undorky, unembarrassing off shoot of our interests. At Chivalry Sports you can certainly buy swords ("Practical Katana and Wazikashi,"

Scramasax, Main Gauche and Cup Hilt Rapier, Viking Swords, etc.), but it's mostly about the period outfits. You can buy a variety of T-shirts sporting logos of dragons ("Night Dragon," "Golden Dragon," "Breakthrough Dragon," "Black Dragon," "Dragon Whisperer," "Draco Basilica," "Whitby Worm," and "Wyverex Cipher," among others), pirate skulls, fairies ("Forest Meadow Fairy," "Purple Fairy"), along with corsets, breeches for little boys, a "Children's Commoner's Vest," a "Knightly Fighting Surcoat," "Druid Robe," and more. The models tend to be a little larger, with longer hair, especially the dudes. There are a lot of goatees. You can outfit your teddy bears with a variety of "Mini-Helms," and of course there are the books on medieval weddings.

This collective devotion to recreating the esoterica of this former culture is admirable. Glorious, even. Anyone could walk into our lame but better-smelling version of the Middle Ages just by coming through the door. I don't pretend that this is entirely due to Dungeons & Dragons, or due to Gygax, since after all, fantasy literature has been around since time immemorial, and even the Society for Creative Anachronism (you know, those kids you see dressed up and battling in armor on college campuses) has been around since 1966, when it originated reportedly (and questionably) as "a protest against the twentieth century." Perhaps all these spawned game worlds are a reaction against the undramatic life of so many (look who's talking, writer, reader, bore) today. The documentary film *Darkon* focuses on the related Darkon Wargaming Club, and specifically the lives of those engaged in a form of live-action D&D, the aforementioned LARP, contrasting the "regular" office, married, Wal-Mart lives of the players with those of their rather more spectacular characters. It's beautiful and hilarious and also more than a little moving to watch them go at it, in the way that watching anyone completely lost in a world—whether fantasy, online, computer gaming, sporting, or whatever—can be. You have to admire the complex and complete lack of self-consciousness, the commitment to the rules and procedures and limits of the world. It's as if they exceed, transcend themselves each minute they play as someone else, as if they become deities, so far beyond the rest of self-conscious us that they barely matter to us, or us to them.

Backing out of Chivalry Sports onto the road, I realize there is a huge grasshopper in the center of my windshield. It's obscene, so splayed, so *there*, such a fact. I have a great view of its petticoat as I accelerate to traffic speed. It seems almost happy as I push out of the city proper and towards the foothills, my speed increasing towards 60 mph. It remains, a gargoyle, a bastion, a bulkhead, uncaring. Usually insects on the windshield are sheared off pretty quickly, but this one is stalwart. When I hit 64 mph, the grasshopper slowly starts to rotate so it faces forward, like a figurehead, Leonardo DiCaprio in *Titanic*, a dog with its face in the wind, wild, eating air. I have no capacity for comprehending the grasshopper brain, or what passes for a brain in a grasshopper (ganglia, loose groups of nerve cells, appear in each section of the grasshopper, though there is a brainlike cluster in the head), but it is still somehow awesome to watch. It is exceeding its natural capacity for speed (they can fly 8 mph) by eight times via the context of my car. At any moment I expect it to be blown off, confused, forced to go aloft, and to return to whatever grasshoppers do for fun or sustenance, if there is a difference. I drive four miles north to the coffee shop where I am planning on working on this essay, and once I pull into the parking spot gently, so as not to dislodge it, having carried it so far with me, it straightens, turns with what appears to be dignity. It slowly climbs to the top of my car, beyond my vision, beyond anyone's vision or capacity for understanding, and disappears.

In Plain Sight

Tom Montgomery-Fate

> *No method or discipline can supersede the necessity of being forever on the alert. What is a course of history or philosophy, or poetry, no matter how well selected, or the best society, or the most admirable routine of life, compared with the discipline of looking always at what is to be seen? Will you be a reader, a student merely, or a seer?*
>
> Henry David Thoreau, *Walden*

A great blue heron pumps slowly across the empty sky. It is headed toward the small river that is the eastern boundary of our land. Last month, five pairs of herons flapped back to our farm, as they have for the last four years, to repair their great prickly bowls of sticks and lay their eggs. The nests are about three feet across and set 90 feet off the ground near the top of a huge sycamore tree. The tree drapes over the Galien River—which is 25 miles long and sprouts tiny branches all over southwest Michigan before draining into the lake. Thirty years ago, the Galien was loaded with fish and was a favorite swimming hole for those who didn't live on the lake. But today it is very sick. Last year the Department of Environmental Equality declared it unsafe for even partial bodily contact. A sample taken at a bridge just down the road contained 40 times the acceptable level of *E. coli* bacteria.

Though herons are not endangered, and rookeries with dozens of nests and hundreds of birds are common, the return of these birds to this 50-acre patch of woods and meadow gives me hope. And the hope is deeper this year, as there are seven new nests in an even taller sycamore tree on the other side of the river. These birds may be the offspring of the first year's hatching, as they often return to their parents' nesting site two or three years later. I'm not sure if the herons' thriving here is due to a new conservation program to clean up the river and control soil erosion, or simply their own adaptation. Either way, if they can find enough fish and frogs to feed themselves and their offspring, it is a good sign.

Our land, like much of the central Midwest, has been wrecked by agriculture, unfettered industry, and new development (half-million-dollar vacation homes have started popping up just down the road). Thus, the animals that live here are the tough kind—raccoons and possums and coyotes; starlings and grackles and turkey vultures—species that could quickly adapt to the ravaged habitat, to erosion and fertilizers and pesticides and herbicides, and to a river that has absorbed them. Their abundance, and the rapid extinction of a myriad of other species, is primarily due to my—to the human's—inability to belong to the ecosystem, to imagine *enough* of anything.

The *E. coli* level in our river exemplifies this human "never-enoughness." Feeding cattle people food (corn) rather than cow food (grass) plays havoc with their digestive tracts (too much starch) and creates the dangerous strain of bacteria. The justification for grain-feeding is economic: grain-fed cattle reach slaughter weight in a little over a year, rather than the four to five years required for grass-fed cattle. The process is also accelerated with growth hormones. And antibiotics are needed to offset the traumatic effects of corn on the cows' intestines. All of this finds its way back into the woodland stream and the human bloodstream.

This afternoon I walk along the river carrying both the reality of the human role in its slow destruction, and the hope of the returning herons. I don't think a writer can ever resolve such conflicts, though it is worth considering *how* one writes about nature. Broadly speaking, it seems some writers seek to discover the unspoiled, the exotic and wild, which they fly to in jets and bush planes. Other writers may seek to recover the spoiled, the non-wilderness. They observe and analyze and reflect on their own towns and cities and suburbs and backyards. Certainly there is value in both approaches, and they sometimes blur or overlap, but I most identify with those writers who stay put, who know their own ground. And it's worth mentioning here that I don't really have a choice. No magazine has offered to fly me to the highlands of Guatemala to count *quetzales*, or to the Philippines to describe the last "healthy" coral reef, or to the Aleutian Islands to observe whale migration.

Yet, clearly the reason the "untouched" wilderness has become increasingly less wild is because it has been touched too many times. Exploration—of the Arctic, of coral reefs, of rain forests—has invariably led to exploitation. Thus, our children and their children will one day understand all that touching and exploring as a kind of violence, as rape. Instead of attempting to get to some new or "pure" bit of the natural world, they will need to learn to find the wild in the recovery of the ravaged, in the return of fish and fowl and wildflowers to the decimated woodlands and rivers of the Midwest.

That is what I seek here—not the marvel of the untouched, but of learning how to be touched by the commonplace. The miracle here is "revision"—learning to see again. I am looking less and less for a pure subject, and more and more for moments of pure sight, for a glimpse of the wild in the mundane, of rapture in the ordinary. Wildness, after all—as Thoreau and others have written—is not an undiscovered insect or island, but a quality of awareness, a way of seeing. And seeing the world always precedes saving it.

Last week I read a little piece of this article to my 12-year-old daughter, Tessa. I was preparing an excerpt for a radio essay about the herons and wanted to see what she thought. She stopped me when I said the word "polluted," because it didn't align with what she had seen. "The river's polluted?" she asked. "But I think it's pretty." "I do too," I said. "It's just that there's a lot we can't see: chemical runoff and livestock excrement, leaking septic tanks, small factories dumping sewage. That kills a lot of plants and fish." "Oh," she said, in a tone that means, "That's enough of an answer for now."

Like Tessa, my eyes are not scientifically trained to see very far past the Galien's façade of health. But on my frequent walks, I notice that minnows and pan fish are very rare. I've seen no crawdads backing out of their muddy holes along the riverbank, and no turtles sunning themselves on deadfalls. Tadpoles and frogs should still be more abundant. And I know all the algae growth diminishes oxygen levels. Yet, a recent paper by the Department of Natural Resources reports the presence of trout and walleye in a part of the river that is less polluted and closer to the lake. As I watch the slow-moving water, I wonder if those fish will ever live here, in this neck of the Galien. I would be happy just to see a sucker or a carp—the bottom feeders that I loved to catch as a kid.

It hasn't rained for a week, so the river is only three feet deep and quite clear. When I reach the next bend and look south, I see the beauty Tessa does: the gurgling riffles around rocks and deadfalls and an abandoned tractor tire. A timeless current runs over the yellow sandy bottom, making a sad music that the wind carries to the blooming wildflowers. These delicate yellow wheels and purple cups and white-petaled tubes—spring beauties, phlox, trillium, jack-in-the-pulpit—dot the green explosion of returning foliage. The trees have already turned the sunlight into a half-formed canopy, which will keep closing for a couple of more weeks until it blocks most of the light and wind from the woods. By then the herons will no longer be visible, and the mosquitoes will be breeding and rising in swarms off the river into the humming, blood-seeking clouds that drift through the stillness and shadow, looking for me.

The other blood seekers I know best—the deer and dog ticks—are already out, though not in full force. They sit waiting for our warm mammalian blood—in trees and on vines, on the tips of thistles and goldenrod and tall grasses, always ready to attack, or I mean to *attach*, to whatever deer or dog or raccoon or person they can find. This behavior, this perching on the leaves and stems with forelegs extended, is called "questing." When something brushes them, they climb on and plunge a beak-like projection into the warm flesh, drawing in a quantity of blood that is a hundred times their "empty" weight. It is mostly the dog ticks that find me—the bigger ones. They crawl out of my socks, or I feel them creeping on my ankles or down my back. I end their quest as quickly as I can, not wanting to find an embedded blood bloat in the morning.

I keep walking along the river. Fifty yards ahead of me, a four-foot-high gray-feathered bird is a statue in the river's swampy oxbow. The curve of its thin neck, head, and beak, and the straight of its body form a ruffled question mark. Presuming he is fishing, I also freeze. This is only the second time I've seen a heron on the ground and not scared it away. Because of the sentinel warning system they use around the rookery, it is hard to get close. I watch him for several minutes, but he soon lifts off in a wild *thwapping*, unfolding eight feet of wing.

Though I've never seen a heron catch a fish on the Galien, I have watched them eat small sunfish at a nearby lake, tilting back their heads to gurgle-swallow them whole. Sometimes they spear perch, to wound or kill them before eating them. Audubon once wrote about watching a heron try to spear a fish in Florida that was so big that the heron got stuck. The fish pulled the impaled heron out and under the water, and nearly drowned it before the bird could unhook itself and escape from its "prey."

I keep tramping along the river, through the wild-rose brambles and reeds. Soon I can hear the herons' funny low grumbling in their nests in the distance. They sound like my Uncle Carl—rough, low voices—like they're trying to both clear their throat and tease me with a question. "*Whaht, Whaht, Whaht, Whaht* are you doing here?" is what I hear. I only visit the birds every three or four weeks, as I don't want to disturb them. Sometimes heron fledglings become so flustered by predators or other distractions that they fall out of the nest to their deaths only days before learning to fly.

When I arrive at the old sycamore tree, I lie flat on my back underneath it with my binoculars aimed at the nests. I watch for perhaps a half hour—until I feel a warm, sticky dripping on my arm, and then on my neck. Could it be . . . ? Yes, guano rain. The birds are crapping on me. I take the hint. But just before I leave, one bird gets anxious. She peers over the rim of the nest at me with a haunting yellow-ringed eye, makes her decision, nervously stumbles around in the sticks for a second, unfolds that great prehistoric *S* of a body, and tumbles into the air with an awkward beauty—quickly drop-gliding to the river bank. Surprised she has flown down rather than up, I remain still and watch the odd stalk of bone and feather and beak take three slow, methodical steps along the sandy bank before swiveling her head to look at me. Then a chemical charge fires: "danger" surges from brain to wings. She is harried, but not a sparrow or wren, so not equipped for quick, fluid movements. The gawky lifting of her body out of the river reminds me of one of the Wright Brothers' early flying machines, which you were never quite sure would make it through takeoff. But unlike those early planes, the heron becomes more graceful as she rises. Once aloft, she is easy in the air. She flies across the canvas of the day as herons have for thousands of years, stroking the empty sky with the wild brush of her gray-blue body. I watch her circle our land and wonder what she sees, what she knows of the quivering strands of life that still connect us.

Grammar Lessons:
The Subjunctive Mood

Michele Morano

Think of it this way: Learning to use the subjunctive mood is like learning to drive a stick shift. It's like falling in love with a car that isn't new or sporty but has a tilt steering wheel and a price you can afford. It's like being so in love with the possibilities, with the places you might go and the experiences you might have, that you pick up your new used car without quite knowing how to drive it, sputtering and stalling and rolling backward at every light. Then you drive the car each day for months, until the stalling stops and you figure out how to downshift, until you can hear the engine's registers and move through them with grace. And later, after you've gained control over the driving and lost control over so much else, you sell the car and most of your possessions and move yourself to Spain, to a place where language and circumstance will help you understand the subjunctive.

Remember that the subjunctive is a mood, not a tense. Verb tenses tell *when* something happens; moods tell *how true*. It's easy to skim over moods in a new language, to translate the words and think you've understood, which is why your first months in Spain will lack nuance. But eventually, after enough conversations have passed, enough hours of talking with your students at the University of Oviedo and your housemate, Lola, and the friends you make when you wander the streets looking like a foreigner, you'll discover that you need the subjunctive in order to finish a question, or an answer, or a thought you couldn't have had without it.

In language, as in life, moods are complicated, but at least in language there are only two. The indicative mood is for knowledge, facts, absolutes, for describing what's real or definite. You'd use the indicative to say, for example:

> *I was in love.*
> Or, *The man I loved tried to kill himself.*
> Or, *I moved to Spain because the man I loved, the man who tried to kill himself, was driving me insane.*

The indicative helps you tell what happened or is happening or will happen in the future (when you believe you know for sure what the future will bring).

The subjunctive mood, on the other hand, is uncertain. It helps you tell what could have been or might be or what you want but may not get. You'd use the subjunctive to say:

> *I thought he'd improve without me.*
> Or, *I left so that he'd begin to take care of himself.*

Or later, after your perspective has been altered, by time and distance and a couple of *cervezas* in a brightly lit bar, you might say:

> *I deserted him* (indicative).
> *I left him alone with his crazy self for a year* (indicative).
> *Because I hoped* (after which begins the subjunctive) *that being apart might allow us to come together again.*

English is losing the subjunctive mood. It lingers in some constructions ("If he *were* dead," for example), but it's no longer pervasive. That's the beauty and also the danger of English—that the definite and the might-be often look so much alike. And it's the reason why, during a period in your life when everything feels hypothetical, Spain will be a very seductive place to live.

In Spanish, verbs change to accommodate the subjunctive in every tense, and the rules, which are many and varied, have exceptions. In the beginning you may feel defeated by this, even hopeless and angry sometimes. But eventually, in spite of your frustration with trying to explain, you'll know in the part of your mind that holds your stories, the part where grammar is felt before it's understood, that the uses of the subjunctive matter.

1. with *Ojalá*

Ojalá means I hope or, more literally, "that Allah is willing!" It's one of the many words left over from the Moorish occupation of Spain, one that's followed by the subjunctive mood because, of course, you never know for sure what Allah has in mind.

During the first months in Spain, you'll use the word by itself, a kind of dangling wish. "It's supposed to rain," Lola will say, and you'll respond "*Ojalá.*" You'll know you're confusing her, leaving her to figure out whether you want the rain or not, but sometimes the mistakes are too hard to bear. "That Allah is willing it wouldn't have raining," you might accidentally say. And besides, so early into this year of living freely, you're not quite sure what to hope for.

Each time you say *Ojalá*, it will feel like a prayer, the "ja" and "la" like breaths, like faith woven right into the language. It will remind you of La Mezquita, the enormous, graceful mosque in Córdoba. Of being eighteen years old and visiting Spain for the first time, how you stood in the courtyard filled with orange trees, trying to admire the building before you. You had a fever then, a summer virus you hadn't yet recognized because it was so hot outside. Too hot to lift a hand to fan your face. Too hot to wonder why your head throbbed and the world spun slowly around you.

Inside, the darkness felt like cool water covering your eyes, such contrast, such relief. And then the pillars began to emerge, rows and rows of pillars supporting red and white brick arches, a massive stone ceiling balanced above them like a thought. You swam behind the guide, not even trying to understand his words but soothed by the vastness, by the shadows. Each time you felt dizzy you looked up toward the arches, the floating stone. Toward something that felt, you realized uncomfortably, like God. Or Allah. Or whatever force inspired people to defy gravity this way.

Later, after ten years have passed, after you've moved to Oviedo and become fascinated with the contours of language, the man you left behind in New York will come to visit. You'll travel south with him, returning to La Mezquita on a January afternoon when the air is mild and the orange trees wave tiny green fruit. He'll carry the guidebook, checking it periodically to get the history straight, while you try to reconcile the place before you with the place in your memory, comparing the shadows of this low sun with the light of another season.

You'll be here because you want this man to see La Mezquita. You want him to feel the mystery of a darkness that amazes and consoles, that makes you feel the presence in empty spaces of something you can't explain. Approaching the shadow of the door, you'll each untie the sweaters from around your waists, slipping your arms into them and then into each other's. He will squint and you will hold your breath. *Ojalá*, you'll think, glimpsing in the shadows the subjunctive mood at work.

2. after words of suasion and negation

In Oviedo, you'll become a swimmer. Can you imagine? Two or three times a week you'll pack a bag and walk for thirty-five minutes to the university pool, where you'll place clothes and contact lenses in a locker, then sink into a crowded lane. The pool is a mass of blurry heads and arms, some of which know what they're doing and most of which, like you, are flailing. You keep bumping into people as you make your way from one end of the pool to the other, but no one gets upset, and you reason that any form of motion equals exercise.

Then one day a miracle happens. You notice the guy in the next lane swimming like a pro, his long arms cutting ahead as he glides, rhythmically, stroke-stroke-breath. You see and hear and feel the rhythm, and before long you're following him, stroking when he strokes, breathing when he breathes. He keeps getting away, swimming three laps to your one, so you wait at the edge of the pool for him to come back, then follow again, practicing. At the end of an hour, you realize that this man you don't know, a man you wouldn't recognize clothed, has taught you to swim. To breathe. To use the water instead of fighting against it. For this alone, you'll later say, it was worth moving to Spain.

Stroke-stroke-breath becomes the rhythm of your days, the rhythm of your life in Oviedo. All through the fall months, missing him the way you'd miss a limb, your muscles strain to create distance. Shallow end to deep end and back, you're swimming away. From memories of abrupt mood shifts. From the way a question, a comment, a person walking past a restaurant window could transform him into a hunched-over man wearing anger like a shawl. From the echo of your own voice trying to be patient and calm, saying, *Listen to me. I want you to call the doctor.* In English you said *listen* and *call*, and they were the same words you'd use to relate a fact instead of make a plea. But in Spanish, in the language that fills your mind as you swim continually away, the moment you try to persuade someone, or dissuade, you enter the realm of the subjunctive. The verb ends differently so there can be no mistake: requesting is not at all the same as getting.

3. with "*si*" or "*como si*"

Si means *if*. *Como si* means *as if*. A clause that begins with *si* or *como si* is followed by the subjunctive when the meaning is hypothetical or contrary to fact. For example:

> *If I'd known he would harm himself, I wouldn't have left him alone.*

But here we have to think about whether the if-clause really is contrary to fact. Two days before, you'd asked him what he felt like doing that night and he'd responded, "I feel like jumping off the Mid-Hudson Bridge." He'd looked serious when he said it, and even so you'd replied, "Really? Would you like me to drive you there?" *As if* it were a joke.

If you knew he were serious, that he were thinking of taking his life, would you have replied with such sarcasm? In retrospect it seems impossible not to have known—the classic signs were there. For weeks he'd been sad, self-pitying. He'd been sleeping too much, getting up to teach his Freshman Composition class in the morning, then going home some days and staying in bed until evening. His sense of humor had waned. He'd begun asking the people around him to cheer him up, make him feel better, please.

And yet he'd been funny. Ironic, self-deprecating, hyperbolic. So no one's saying you should have known, just that maybe you felt a hint of threat in his statement about the river. And maybe that angered you because it meant you were failing to be enough for him. Maybe you were tired, too, in need of cheering up yourself because suddenly your perfect guy had turned inside out. Or maybe that realization came later, after you'd had the time and space to develop theories.

The truth is, only you know what you know. And what you know takes the indicative, remember?

For example: You knew he was hurting himself. The moment you saw the note on his office door, in the campus building where you were supposed to meet him on a Sunday afternoon, you knew. The note said, "I'm not feeling well. I'm going home. I guess I'll see you tomorrow." He didn't use your name.

You tried calling him several times but there was no answer, so you drove to the apartment he shared with another graduate student. The front door was unlocked, but his bedroom door wouldn't budge. You knocked steadily but not too loud, because his housemate's bedroom door was also closed, and you assumed he was inside taking a nap. *If* you'd known that his housemate was not actually home, you would have broken down the door. That scenario is hypothetical, so it takes the subjunctive—even though you're quite sure.

The human mind can reason its way around anything. On the drive to your own apartment, you told yourself, he's angry with me. That's why the door was locked, why he wouldn't answer the phone. You thought: If he weren't so close to his family, I'd really be worried. If today weren't Mother's Day. If he didn't talk so affectionately about his parents. About his brother and sisters. About our future. If, if, if.

When the phone rang and there was silence on the other end, you began to shout, "What have you done?"

In Spain, late at night over *chupitos* of bourbon or brandy, you and Lola will trade stories. Early on you won't understand a lot of what she says, and she'll understand what you say but not what you mean. You won't know how to say what you mean in Spanish; sometimes you won't even know how to say it in English. But as time goes on, the stories you tell will become more complicated. More subtle. More grammatically daring. You'll begin to feel more at ease in the unreal.

For example: *If* you hadn't gone straight home from his apartment. *If* you hadn't answered the phone. *If* you hadn't jumped back into your car to drive nine miles in record time, hoping the whole way to be stopped by the police. *If* you hadn't met him on the porch where he had staggered in blood-soaked clothes. *If* you hadn't rushed upstairs for a towel and discovered a flooded bedroom floor, the blood separating into water and rust-colored clumps. *If* you hadn't been available for this emergency.

As the months pass in Spain, you'll begin to risk the *then*. His house-mate would have come home and found him the way you found him: deep gashes in his arm, but the wounds clotting enough to keep him alive, enough to narrowly avoid a transfusion. His housemate would have called the para-medics, ridden to the hospital in the ambulance, notified his parents from the emergency room, greeted them after their three-hour drive. His housemate would have done all the things you did, and he would have cleaned the mess by himself instead of with your help, the two of you borrowing a neighbor's wet-vac and working diligently until you—or he—or both of you—burst into hysterical laughter. Later this housemate would have moved to a new apart-ment, just as he has done, and would probably be no worse off than he is right now.

You, on the other hand, would have felt ashamed, guilty, remiss for not being available in a time of crisis. But you wouldn't have found yourself lean-ing over a stretcher in the emergency room, a promise slipping from your mouth before you could think it through: "I won't leave you. Don't worry, I won't leave you." *As if* it were true.

4. after impersonal expressions

Such as *it is possible, it is a shame, it is absurd.*

"*It's possible* that I'm making things worse in some ways," you told the coun-selor you saw on Thursday afternoons. He'd been out of the hospital for a few months by then and had a habit of missing his therapy appointments, to which you could only respond by signing up for your own.

She asked how you were making things worse, and you explained that when you told him you needed to be alone for a night and he showed up any-way at 11:00 PM, pleading to stay over, you couldn't turn him away. She said, "*It's a shame* he won't honor your request," and you pressed your fingernails into the flesh of your palm to keep your eyes from filling. She asked why you didn't want him to stay over, and you said that sometimes you just wanted to sleep, without waking up when he went to the bathroom and listening to make sure he came back to bed instead of taking all the Tylenol in the medicine cabi-net. Or sticking his head in the gas oven. Or diving from the balcony onto the hillside three stories below. There is nothing, you told her, nothing I haven't thought of.

She said, "Do you think he's manipulating you?" and you answered in the mood of certainty, "Yes. Absolutely." Then you asked, "*Isn't it absurd* that I let him manipulate me?" and what you wanted, of course, was some reassurance that it wasn't absurd. That you were a normal person, reacting in a normal way, to a crazy situation.

Instead she said, "Let's talk about why you let him. Let's talk about what's in this for you."

5. after verbs of doubt or emotion

You didn't think he was much of a prospect at first. Because he seemed arrogant. Because in the initial meetings for new instructors, he talked as if he were doing it the right way and the rest of you were pushovers. Because he looked at you with one eye squinted, as if he couldn't quite decide.

You liked that he was funny, a little theatrical and a great fan of supermarkets. At 10:00 PM, after evening classes ended, he'd say, "Are you going home?" Sometimes you'd offer to drop him off at his place. Sometimes you'd agree to go out for a beer. And sometimes you'd say, "Yeah, but I have to go to the store first," and his eyes would light up. In the supermarket he'd push the cart and you'd pick items off the shelf. Maybe you'd turn around and there would be a whole rack of frozen ribs in your cart, or after you put them back, three boxes of Lucky Charms. Maybe he'd be holding a package of pfeffernusse and telling a story about his German grandmother. Maybe it would take two hours to run your errand because he was courting you in ShopRite.

You doubted that you'd sleep with him a second time. After the first time, you both lay very still for a while, flat on your backs, not touching. He seemed to be asleep. You watched the digital clock hit 2:30 AM and thought about finding your turtleneck and sweater and wool socks, lacing up your boots, and heading out into the snow. And then out of the blue he rolled toward you, pulled the blanket up around your shoulders, and said, "Is there anything I can get you? A cup of tea? A sandwich?"

You were thrilled at the breaks in his depression, breaks that felt like new beginnings, every time. Days, sometimes even weeks, when he seemed more like himself than ever before. Friends would ask how he was doing, and he'd offer a genuine smile. "Much better," he'd say, putting his arm around you, "She's pulling me through the death-wish phase." Everyone would laugh with relief, and at those moments you'd feel luckier than ever before, because of the contrast.

Do you see the pattern?

6. to express good wishes

Que tengas muy bien viaje, Lola will say, kissing each of your cheeks before leaving you off at the bus station. *May you have a good trip.* A hope, a wish, a prayer of sorts, even without the *Ojalá.*

The bus ride from Oviedo to Madrid is nearly six hours, so you have a lot of time for imagining. It's two days after Christmas, and you know he spent the holiday at his parents' house, that he's there right now, maybe eating breakfast, maybe packing. Tonight his father will drive him to Kennedy Airport, and tomorrow morning, very early, you'll meet him at Barajas in Madrid. You try to envision what he'll look like, the expression on his face when he sees you, but you're having trouble recalling what it's like to be in his presence.

You try not to hope too much, although now, four months into your life in Spain, you want to move toward, instead of away. Toward long drives on winding, mountain roads, toward the cathedral of Toledo, the mosque at Córdoba, the Alhambra in Granada. Toward romantic dinners along the Mediterranean. Toward a new place from which to view the increasingly distant past. You want this trip to create a separation, in your mind and in his, between your first relationship and your real relationship, the one that will be so wonderful, so stable, you'll never leave him again.

Once you've reached Madrid and found the *pensión* where you've reserved a room, you'll get the innkeeper to help you make an international call. His father will say, "My God, he can't sit still today," and then there will be his voice, asking how your bus ride was, where you are, how far from the airport. You'll say, "I'll see you in the morning." He'll reply, "In seventeen hours."

The next morning, the taxi driver is chatty. He wants to know why you're going to the airport without luggage, and your voice is happy and excited when you explain. He asks whether this boyfriend writes you letters, and you smile and nod at the reflection in the rearview mirror. "Many letters?" he continues, "Do you enjoy receiving the letters?" In Spain you're always having odd conversations with strangers, so you hesitate only a moment, wondering why he cares, and then you say, "Yes. Very much." He nods emphatically. *"Muy bien."* At the terminal he drops you off with a broad smile. *"Que lo pases bien con tu novio,"* he says. *Have a good time with your boyfriend.* In his words you hear the requisite subjunctive mood.

7. in adverbial clauses denoting purpose, provision, exception

How different to walk down the street in Madrid, Toledo, Córdoba, to notice an elaborate fountain or a tiny car parked half on the sidewalk, and comment aloud. You've loved being alone in Spain and now, even more, you love being paired.

On the fifth day you reach Granada, find lodging in someone's home. Down the hallway you can hear the family watching TV, cooking, preparing to celebrate New Year's Eve. In the afternoon you climb the long, slow hill leading to the Alhambra and spend hours touring the complex. You marvel at the elaborate irrigation system, the indoor baths with running water, the stunning mosaic tiles and views of the Sierra Nevada. Here is the room where Boabdil signed the city's surrender to Ferdinand and Isabella; here is where Washington Irving lived while writing *Tales of the Alhambra*. Occasionally you separate, as he inspects a mural and you follow a hallway into a lush courtyard, each of your imaginations working to restore this place to its original splendor. When you come together again, every time, there's a thrill.

He looks rested, relaxed, strolling through the gardens with his hands tucked into the front pockets of his pants. When you enter the Patio of the Lions—the famous courtyard where a circle of marble lions project water into a reflecting pool—he turns to you, wide-eyed, his face as open as a boy's.

"Isn't it pretty?" you keep asking, feeling shy because what you mean is: "Are you glad to be here?"

"*So* pretty," he responds, taking hold of your arm, touching his lips to your hair. The day is perfect, you think. The trip is perfect. You allow yourself a moment of triumph: I left him *so that* he would get better without me, and he did. I worked hard and saved money and invited him on this trip *in case* there's still hope for us. And there is.

Unless. In language, as in experience, we have purpose, provision, exception. None of which necessarily matches reality, and all of which take the subjunctive.

On the long walk back down the hill toward your room, he turns quiet. You find yourself talking more than usual, trying to fill the empty space with cheerful commentary, but it doesn't help. The shape of his face begins to change until there it is again, that landscape of furrows and crags. The jaw thrusts slightly, lips pucker, eyebrows arch as if to say, "I don't care. About anything."

Back in the room, you ask him what's wrong, plead with him to tell you. You can talk about anything, you assure him, anything at all. And yet you're stunned when his brooding turns accusatory. He says it isn't fair. You don't understand how difficult it is to be him. Your life is easy, so easy that even moving to a new country, taking up a new language, is effortless. While every day is a struggle for him. Don't you see that? Every day is a struggle.

He lowers the window shade and gets into bed, his back turned toward you.

What to do? You want to go back outside into the mild air and sunshine, walk until you remember what it feels like to be completely alone. But you're afraid to leave him. For the duration of his ninety-minute nap, you sit paralyzed. Everything feels unreal, the darkened room, the squeals of children in another part of the house, the burning sensation in your stomach. You tremble, first with sadness and fear, then with anger. Part of you wants to wake him, tell him to collect his things, then drive him back to the airport in Madrid. You want to send him home again, away from your new country, the place where you live unencumbered—but with a good deal of effort, thank you. The other part of you wants to wail, to beat your fists against the wall and howl, *Give him back to me.*

Remember: purpose, provision, exception. The subjunctive runs parallel to reality.

8. after certain indications of time, if the action has not occurred

While is a subjunctive state of mind. So are *until, as soon as, before,* and *after.* By now you understand why, right? Because until something *has happened*, you can't be sure.

In Tarifa, the wind blows and blows. You learn this even before arriving, as you drive down Route 15 past Gibraltar. You're heading toward the southernmost point in Spain, toward warm sea breezes and a small town off the beaten path. You drive confidently, shifting quickly through the gears to keep pace with the traffic around you. He reclines in the passenger's seat, one foot propped against the dashboard, reading from the *Real Guide* open against his thigh. "Spreading out beyond its Moorish walls, Tarifa is known in Spain for its abnormally high suicide rate—a result of the unremitting winds that blow across the town and its environs."

You say, "Tell me you're joking." He says, "How's that for luck?"

Three days before, you'd stood in Granada's crowded city square at midnight, each eating a grape for every stroke of the New Year. If you eat all twelve grapes in time, tradition says, you'll have plenty of luck in the coming year. It sounds wonderful—such an easy way to secure good fortune—until you start eating and time gets ahead, so far ahead that no matter how fast you chew and swallow, midnight sounds with three grapes left.

In Tarifa, you come down with the flu. It hits hard and fast—one minute you're strolling through a white-washed coastal town, and the next you're huddled in bed in a stupor. He goes to the pharmacy and, with a handful of Spanish words and many gestures, procures the right medicine. You sleep all day, through the midday meal, through the time of siesta, past sundown, and into the evening. When you wake the room is fuzzy and you're alone, with a vague memory of him rubbing your back, saying something about a movie.

Carefully you rise and make your way to the bathroom—holding onto the bed, the doorway, the sink—then stand on your toes and look out the window into the blackness. By day there's a thin line of blue mountains across the strait, and you imagine catching the ferry at dawn and watching that sliver of Morocco rise up from the shadows to become a whole continent. You imagine standing on the other side and looking back toward the tip of Spain, this tiny town where the winds blow and blow. That's how easy it is to keep traveling once you start, putting distance between the various parts of your life, imagining yourself over and over again into entirely new places.

Chilly and sweating, you make your way back to bed, your stomach fluttering nervously. You think back to Granada, how he'd woken from a nap on that dark afternoon and apologized. "I don't know what got into me today," he'd said. "This hasn't been happening." You believe it's true, it hasn't been happening. But you don't know *how true*.

You think: He's fine now. There's no need to worry. He's been fine for days, happy and calm. I'm overreacting. But overreaction is a slippery slope. With the wind howling continuously outside, the room feels small and isolated. You don't know that he's happy and calm right now, do you? You don't know how he is today at all, because you've slept and slept and barely talked to him.

You think: If the movie started on time—but movies never start on time in Spain, so you add, subtract, try to play it safe, and determine that by 10:45 PM your fretting will be justified. At 11:00 PM you'll get dressed and go looking, and if you can't find him, what will you do? Wait until midnight for extra measure? And then call the police? And tell them what, that he isn't back yet, and you're afraid because you're sick and he's alone and the wind here blows and blows, enough to make people crazy, the book says, make them suicidal?

This is the *when*, the *while*, the *until*. The *before* and *after*. The real and the unreal in precarious balance. This is what you moved to Spain to escape from, and here it is again, following you.

The next time you wake, the room seems brighter, more familiar. You sit up and squint against the light. His cheeks are flushed, hair mussed from the wind. His eyes are clear as a morning sky. "Hi, sweetie," he says, putting a hand on your forehead. "You still have a fever. How do you feel?" He smells a little musty, like the inside of a community theater where not many people go on a Sunday night in early January. He says, "The movie was hilarious." You ask whether he understood it and he shrugs. Then he acts out a scene using random Spanish words as a voice-over, and you laugh and cough until he flops down on his stomach beside you.

Here it comes again, the contrast between what was, just a little while ago, and what is now. After all this time and all these miles, you're both here, in a Spanish town with a view of Africa. You feel amazed, dizzy, as if swimming outside yourself. You're talking with him, but you're also watching yourself talk with him. And then you're sleeping and watching yourself sleep, dreaming and thinking about the dreams. Throughout the night you move back and forth, here and there, between what is and what might be, tossed by language and possibility and the constantly shifting wind.

9. in certain independent clauses

There's something extraordinary—isn't there?—about learning to speak Spanish as an adult, about coming to see grammar as a set of guidelines not just for saying what you mean but for understanding the way you live. There's something extraordinary about thinking in a language that insists on marking the limited power of desire.

For example: At Barajas Airport in Madrid, you walk him to the boarding gate. He turns to face you, hands on your arms, eyes green as the sea. He says, "Only a few more months and we'll be together for good, right sweetie?" He watches your face, waiting for a response, but you know this isn't a decision, something you can say yes to. So you smile, eyes burning, and give a slight nod. What you mean is, *I hope so*. What you think is, *Ojalá*. And what you know is this: The subjunctive is the mood of mystery. Of luck. Of faith interwoven with doubt. It's a held breath, a hand reaching out, carefully touching wood. It's humility, deference, the opposite of hubris. And it's going to take a long time to master.

But at least the final rule of usage is simple, self-contained, one you can commit to memory: Certain independent clauses exist only in the subjunctive mood, lacing optimism with resignation, hope with heartache. *Be that as it may*, for example. Or the phrase one says at parting, eyes closed as if in prayer, *May all go well with you*.

Glaciology

Lia Purpura

*P*lan

When the snow began to melt, the drifts left behind a surprising collection of junk—paper cups, socks, Matchbox trucks, a snarl of CAUTION–POLICE–CAUTION tape, pinkly wrapped tampons, oil-rag-T-shirts, banana peels: intimacies of toy box, bathroom, and garage amid the lumps of sand and salt we threw down for traction. It was as if after the big event of snowfall we'd forgotten there was more, still, to be said. A cache of loose details below to attend. A trove poised. A stealth gathering.

Deposition below the singular-seeming white cover.

I shall make my own study of snow and time. I will learn from that which has built the very ground I'm now slipping around on: glaciers. Their formative act: deposition, for example: *fine-grained rock debris, rock flour, and coarse rock fragments picked up or entrained within the base of a glacier and then transported and deposited from either active or stagnant ice. This product of glacial deposition, known as till, consists of particles that follow complicated routes, being deposited on the top or along the sides of the glacier bed, entrained again, and finally dropped. As a sediment, till has certain distinctive features: it exhibits poor sorting, is usually massive, and consists of large stones in a fine matrix of minerals and rock types.*

Poor sorting: I like that: that it all gets dropped, the big stuff enmeshed with the grainy soft stuff. The indiscriminate mess. That it forms a long train, so that seeing it all, one can trail events back. Guess at them. View time. And by way of the whole scattered and shifting pattern, by the gathering eye, make something of these loose details, collecting.

Deposition on Thaw

I will note, though its impetus was warmth, the sharpness of the thaw. During the thaw we were given to see the way snow melted into vertebrae, whole bodies of bone inclined toward one another. Bones stacked and bent in the attitude of prayer, the edges honed and precarious. Forms arced over the sewer grates and curbs as the gutter streamed with bubbly melt. What remained were not yet remains. It was clear how the warmth would eat everything down, but where some parts were colder than the rest, that core kept the figure upright. The shapes were knife-edged, hunched, easing a pain; they grayed and were everywhere pocked with dirt, and unlikely in their strength.

A few days later, just sheering, frayed patches covered the ground, and the elbows of everything poked through. White remained where the ground must have been colder, or wind blew and packed the snow hard.

How to read a land?

There were thicknesses, white places layered in smears that others were trained to read. *Densities* amid the rivulets of veins. *Occlusions. Artifacts.*

I remember, about the X-ray, thinking *Artifacts? That sounds harmless.* Evidence of some action past—a little shard, small bit taken out of my body and sent off for further study. Vase, mirror, tile. Lip of a cup. A thing that remained to be found and told. An image that sings about time.

Deposition on the Shapes of Tasks

Waiting all that long week—for test results, the snow to stop, dough to rise, nightfall—small tasks turned into days. Days unfolded into tasks. The inside-out arms of clothes pulled right, made whole and unwrinkled, took lovely hours. Tasks filled like balloons and rounded with breath; they floated and bumped around the day: some popcorn, some dishes, some mending. And though dressing for sledding, undressing and draping everything wet over radiators was deliberate, a stitch ran through, jagged and taut, cinching the gestures tight with uncertainty. Everything coming down—snow, sleet, threat, delicacy—twined through like a rivulet (the cut water makes in its persistence, its pressure carving) so the bank grows a dangerous, fragile lip. The work of glaciers changes a landscape: old stream valleys are gouged and deepened, filled with till and outwash. *Filled,* of course, over millions of years. In sand-grain, fist-sized increments.

This kind of time illuminated tasks that one would hardly be given to see otherwise. Titled them, even: the scraping of old wax from candlesticks, the tightening of loosened doorknobs. Oil-soaping the piano keys.

Deposition on Fevers and Still Lifes

That week time was ample, broad as a boulevard, a stroll, a meander. Not a tour. Not a map or a path to be found. School was canceled. Scents fully unfolded: coffee, chocolate, and milk marbling together on the stove, thinnest skin across to touch and lift and eat. And like a concentrate of heat itself, my bounded sight burned holes in the things most fixed upon: the ceiling's old butterfly water stain. One rough, gritty chip in the rim of a favorite cup.

It was in this way that joy and severity flared everywhere: along the banks of steep places I went to quickly, glanced, then ran from. They burned together in cornmeal in a pour, the yellow dust that rose and stuck to my hands as I folded in the unbeaten eggs, cold suns to poke and dim with flour—as outside, too, the cold sun dimmed, and the sky sifted and shushed down.

Yes, that week passed with a fever's disheveled clarity. That time, its atmosphere, moved the way fevers by turn dilute and intensify moments, so by evening one cannot reconstitute the day and calls it "lost," calls it "flown," says after a night's sleep "what happened to the day?" Things that week were touched in sweaty uncertainty and weakly released. There were intimacies akin to falling back to a pillow after water, soup, and tea were brought, gratitude unspoken; the night table's terrain, the book, the book's binding, glue at the binding and the word for each sewn section, *folio,* surfacing from far off. The sheet's silk piping to idly slip a finger under for coolness.

In its riotous stillness, that week was a study: Dutch, seventeenth century, with its controlled and ordered high flare and shine. Days held the light and feverish presence of a bowl of lemons in pocked disarray. Always one lemon pared in a spiral of undress, its inner skin gone a flushed, sweet-cream rose. Always the starry, cut sections browning, and the darkness, just beyond the laden table, held almost successfully off. I, with my props—mixing bowl, dough—tilted toward, soaked in late afternoon light, while time raged all around in shadow, the dark stroking cup, quartered fig, plate of brilliant silver sardines left on the counter from lunch.

Deposition on Millennia/Effluvia

To say "a glacier formed this land" sanctifies the blink of an eye.

To see, from the air, glacial streams and think *like a snake* or *ribboning,* and of the land on either side *accordion* or *fan* colludes against awe. Neatens up the work of time. Makes of time a graven thing, handsculpted, carved, and held. Time should seize, should haul us back, then let go, wind-sheared into *now,* breathlessly into the moment's hard strata. Each morning in Rome, my old friend runs in a park along the aqueduct, which breaks and restarts in yellowed fields, its arches sprouting wild grasses, its arches collapsing, the houses, apartments, roads of his neighborhood visible through it, as they have been for nearly 2,000 years. You can sit on rocks in Central Park, soft outcrops undulant as sleeping bodies, formed tens of thousands of years ago, and look up at the city skyline knowing the North American ice sheet flowed exactly that far south. Or hold in your hand a striated stone from Mauritania, abraded at the base of a glacier 650 million years ago, and touch the markings, those simple scratches so easily picked up and put down again on the touch-me table at the museum. Kick any stone beneath your foot, here, in Baltimore, and you're scuffing 300 million, even a billion years of work.

I cast back for any one thing I did on any one day that week: how unencumbered the brushing of my hair, the perfect scrolls of carrot peel I lowered like a proclamation into the hamsters' cage; careless grace of understatement, luxury of simple gesture after gesture (fork to mouth, mouth to glass, fork and glass rinsed in the sink, and—linger here, see the heat pulling fog up the glass, atilt and cooling in the drainboard). I'm calling up the tongue-and-groove gestures, the hook-and-eye moments of the day, so they might again spend themselves freely, mark the layers of events en route, classify the waiting. Cajoled from somewhere back in the morning, the peeling of that tangerine (cut thumb plunged into the yielding core, stinging and wet and red) comes forth.

I am recalling such occasions for attention offered in a day I was free to ignore. And now, am not free at all (for this *is* a deposition): cutting burnt crust away; snagging a sock on a rough stair plank; digging a sliver of dirt from a nail under running water. I am tied to the sight of the world, to things burnished and scoured by use, and by their diminution loved—as I so loved and saved my grandmother's wooden cooking spoon, older than me, smooth as driftwood, when to relieve her boredom, her aide used it to plant and prop a geranium on the balcony. The spoon has folded into its profile, has tucked within it, englaciated, the rim of the aluminum roasting pan (why that of all the nicked sauce pans and ceramic bowls of creamy batters tapped and tapped and tapped against?). I took and washed (as my grandmother no longer can wash) its singed rack burns, its smooth neck, thinned from lifting huge roasts by their taut white lacings.

One idly picks up pinecones, rocks, shells to mark a moment, to commemorate time. One picks them up because they shine out from their mud, or water lapping brightens their veins and shorn faces, or there they are, wedged inexplicably whole in a jetty, and a spiral tip beckons, though the center be partial and broken.

Deposition on Watches

That week my watch broke, so I borrowed my son's digital Monsters, Inc. strap-on. But I missed the clean, white face of my old one, its celestial circular sweep. The digital time that came to replace it dosed its minutes, shifted its numbers too economically one into the next, the angular 2 and angular 5 simple mirror images, a single bar across the middle making the 0 an 8. Then, as the days without schooltime unwound and were lashed together instead by flares of fear, spots of love, solemn noon bell at the cathedral, all the morning's held breath, all the whites piling, like suds, their calm expanse up, it was easy to wear no watch at all. But I have not become a person divested of watches. I miss the circle's perpetuity, dawn and dusk sharing the same space, if only for minutes. The hour pinning itself to the changing light of seasons.

The watch I want now—I saw a picture of it yesterday—posits a looker at the center, who to properly see the numbers would have to turn and face each one: already by 2 the numbers start to tilt so that the 6 is a 9 if you're outside looking in. But a 6 if you're in the middle. I like to think of standing in the center, arms reaching out and brushing all the minutes and hours.

I like the idea of turning to face the hour, having the hours arrayed around me. From a still point, having to face the increments of a day.

Deposition on Failure

Last May, I remember, on this very sidewalk: a fly's soap-bubble, gasoline colors; taut grimace on the face of a baby bird, that hatched and unliving, ancient, pimpled bud on the grass; corms of daylilies, and "corm" itself that most perfect union of "corn" and "worm," meaning exactly the thick, stubborn grub I hacked to separate. I remember the ripe, raw, shivery scents.

But during this thaw, come on so fast now—just for a day, just for caprice, it was 60 degrees.

And when I went out walking and the sun was so soft—an assertion, bravura. Where warmth thawed the planes of bone like a high bank, my face was a running stream again. I took off my mittens and left them in the crook of a tree; it always takes a few days to believe the warmth.

The snow receded, the warmth returned, and I was fine. I was negative. *Negative, negative,* I was thinking, buoyant. The hard winter lifted all at once, the sun came, dewy and beading, the air was sweet and I was fine—oh burgeoning cliché I entertained, cannot believe I entertained: spring bearing its blood-tide and life all abloom, all's well ending well in a spate, a thrall of undulant weather, et cetera. Rising, on cue, such music as dripping icicles conduct, such shine and promise, oh window of light on the nibbled Red Delicious little Sam just dropped. And the neighbors' voices carrying, the out-of-doors voices lofting, reconfiguring again the space between our houses: it was New World Symphony, English horn-solo-fresh. I was a turning season, a spit of land at low tide, a window thrown open. Would you believe it if I told you (told *unto* you, lo! for real) I saw a butterfly—and it was corn-yellow? I resisted the easy convergence—*spring, warmth, I'm fine*—not a bit, and I knew that to be an indulgence, a failure, partial sight. As if I had come to the brightness of that day wholly—wholly—from dark.

But I cannot forget, for this is a deposition, that all that dark week there was this, too: the diamond-blue light at each drift's core. My husband's abundant embrace. Sanctum of my child under quilts. In candlelight, sewing the ghost. Folding a swan. With books, in the folds of a story. Our son, himself, that most beloved unfolding.

And the color of the sky: workshirt-turned-inside-out, and the gray of our house against it, a darker inner seam, revealed. Our house an object that light chose for lavishing, a river stone eddied into calm. The tender crack in a baking loaf, its creamy rift rough at the edges and going gold. Of all the names for snow considered, of all the shifts in tone it made, I found clamshell, bone, and pearl. That week I found lead in the white, mouse in it, and refracted granite. Talc with pepper. Layers of dried mud, zinc, and iron. Blown milkweed and ashy cinder. Silvered cornfield. Uncooked biscuit. Mummy, oatmeal, sand, and linen. Some morning glory. Some roadside aster.

Celebrating Creation

Chet Raymo

> *Even the sparrow finds a home, and the swallow a nest, where she rears her brood beside thy altars.*
>
> Psalm 84:3

Late last summer, in the west of Ireland, I spent a night in the Gallarus Oratory, a tiny seventh-century church of unmortared stone. It is the oldest intact building in Ireland, and one of the oldest in Europe. The oratory is about the size of a one-car garage, in the shape of an overturned boat. It has a narrow entrance at the front and a single tiny window at the rear, both open to the elements. Even during the day one needs a flashlight to explore the interior.

I can't say exactly why I was there, or why I intended to sit up all night, sleeplessly, in that dark space. I had been thinking about skepticism and prayer, and I wanted to experience something of whatever it was that inspired Irish monks to seek out these rough hermitages perched on the edge of Europe, or—as they imagined—the edge of eternity. They were pilgrims of the Absolute, seeking their God in a raw, ecstatic encounter with stone, wind, sea, and sky.

The Gallarus Oratory is something of a tourist mecca, but at night the place is isolated and dark, far from human habitation. From the door of the oratory, one looks down a sloping mile of fields to the twinkling lights of the village of Ballydavid on Smerwick Harbor.

The sun had long set when I arrived, although at that latitude in summer the twilight never quite fades from the northern horizon. It was a moonless night, ablaze with stars, Jupiter brightest of all. Meteors occasionally streaked the sky, and satellites cruised more stately orbits. Inside, I snuggled into a back corner of the oratory, tucked my knees under my chin, and waited. I could see nothing but the starlit outline of the door, not even my hand in front of my face. The silence was broken only by the low swish of my own breath.

As the hours passed, I began to feel a presence, a powerful sensation of something or someone sharing that empty darkness. I am not a mystical person, but I knew that I was not alone, and I could imagine those hermit monks of the seventh century sharing the same intense conviction of "someone in the room." At last, I was spooked to the point that I abandoned my interior corner and went outside.

A night of exceptional clarity! Stars spilling into the sea. And in the north, as if as a reward for my lonely vigil, the aurora borealis danced toward the zenith. How can I describe what I saw? Rays of silver light streaming up from the sea, as if from some enchanted Oz just over the horizon, shimmering columns of fairy radiance. As I watched from the doorway of oratory, I remembered something the nineteenth-century explorer Charles Francis Hall wrote about watching the aurora from the Arctic: "My first thought was, 'Among the gods there is none like unto Thee, O Lord; neither are there any works like unto thy works!' . . . We looked, we SAW, we TREMBLED."

Hall knew he was watching a natural physical phenomenon, not a miracle, but his reaction suggests the power of the aurora even on a mind trained in the methods of science. What then did the monks of Gallarus think of the aurora, 1,300 years ago, at a time when the supernatural was the explanation of choice for exceptional phenomena? Stepping out from the inky darkness of their stone chapel, they must surely have felt that the shimmering columns of light were somehow meant for them alone, a sign or a revelation, an answer to their prayers.

We have left the age of miracles behind, but not, I trust, our sense of wonder. Our quest for encounter with the Absolute goes arm in arm with our search for answers. We are pilgrim scientists, perched on the edge of eternity, curious and attentive. The Gallarus Oratory was built for prayer, at a time when the world was universally thought to be charged with the active spirit of a personal God: Every stone might be moved by incantation, every zephyr blew good or ill; springs flowed or dried up at the deity's whim; lights danced in a predawn sky as a blessing or portent. Today, we know the lights are caused by electrons crashing down from the sun, igniting luminescence. But our response to the lights might still be one of prayerful attention, and they lead us, if we let them, into encounters with the Absolute.

Traditional religious faiths have three components: a shared cosmology (a story of the universe and our place in it), spirituality (personal response to the numinous), and liturgy (public expressions of celebration and gratitude, including rites of passage). The apparent antagonism of science and religion centers almost entirely on cosmology: What is the universe? Where did it come from? How does it work? What is the human self? What is our fate? Humans have always had answers to these questions. The answers have been embodied in stories—tribal myths, scriptures, church traditions. All of these stories derived from a raw experience of the creation, such as my experiences inside and outside of the Gallarus Oratory. All of them contain enduring wisdom. But as a reliable cosmological component of religious faith they have been superseded by what cultural historian and Roman Catholic priest Thomas Berry calls the New Story—the scientific story of the world.

The New Story is the product of thousands of years of human curiosity, observation, experimentation, and creativity. It is an evolving story, not yet finished. Perhaps it will never be finished. It is a story that begins with an explosion from a seed of infinite energy. The seed expands and cools. Particles form, then atoms of hydrogen and helium. Stars and galaxies coalesce from swirling gas. Stars burn and explode, forging heavy elements—carbon, nitrogen, oxygen—and hurl them into space. New stars are born, with planets made of heavy elements. On one planet near a typical star in a typical galaxy life appears in the form of microscopic self-replicating ensembles of atoms. Life evolves, over billions of years, resulting in ever more complex organisms. Continents move. Seas rise and fall. The atmosphere changes. Millions of species of life appear and become extinct. Others adapt, survive, and spill out progeny. At last, human consciousness appears. One species experiences the ineffable and wonders what it means, and makes up stories—of invisible spirits who harbor in darkness, of gods who light up the sky in answer to our prayers—eventually making up the New Story.

The New Story has important advantages over all the stories that have gone before:

It works. It works so well that it has become the irreplaceable basis of technological civilization. We test the New Story in every way we can, in its particulars and in its totality. We build giant particle accelerating machines to see what happened in the first hot moments of the Big Bang. We put telescopes into space to look for the radiation of the primeval explosion. With spectroscopes and radiation detectors we analyze the composition of stars and galaxies and compare them to our theories for the origin of the world. Always and in every way we try to prove the story wrong. When the story fails, we change it.

It is a universal story. Although originally a product of Western culture, it has become the story of all educated peoples throughout the world; scientists of all cultures, religions, and political persuasions exchange ideas freely and apply the same criteria of verification and falsification. Like most children, I was taught that my story—Adam and Eve, angels, miracles, incarnation, heaven, hell, and all the rest—was the "true story," and that all others were false. Sometimes our so-called "true" stories gave us permission to hurt those who lived by other stories. The New Story, by its universality, helps put the old animosities behind us.

It is a story that emphasizes the connectedness of all people and all things. Some of the old stories, such as the one I was taught as a child, placed humankind outside of space and time, gifted us with unworldly spirit, and gave us dominion over the millions of Earth's other creatures. The New Story places us squarely in a cosmic unfolding of space and time, and teaches our biological affinity to all humanity. We are ephemeral beings, inextricably related to all of life, to the planet itself, and even to the lives of stars.

It is a story that asserts our responsibility for our own lives and the future of the planet. In the New Story, no omniscient deity intervenes at will in the creation, answers prayers, or leads all things to a predetermined end. We are on our own, in the immensity of creation, with an awesome responsibility to use our talents wisely.

It is a story that reveals a universe of unanticipated complexity, beauty, and dimension. The God revealed by the New Story is not the paltry personal projection of ourselves who attracted and bedeviled our ancestors. It is, in the words of the Jesuit theologian David Toolan, "the Unnamable One/Ancient of the Days of the mystics, of whom we can only speak negatively (not this, not that), a 'wholly other' hidden God of Glory," or in the felicitous phrase of novelist Nikos Kazantzakis, "the dread essence beyond logic."

We should treasure the ancient stories for the wisdom and values they contain. We should celebrate the creation in whatever poetic languages and rituals our traditional cultures have taught us. But only the New Story has the global authority to help us navigate the future. It is not the "true" story, but it is certainly the truest. Of all the stories that might provide the cosmological basis of contemporary religious feeling, it is the only one that has had its feet held to the fire of exacting experience.

The New Story informed my response to the dancing lights in the night sky at Gallarus. What I saw was not a portent or miracle, but rather nature's exquisite signature of the magnetic and material entanglement of Earth and sun.

As the sun brightened the eastern horizon and the last shreds of aurora faded, I was suddenly startled by a pair of swallows that began to dart in and out of the Gallarus Oratory, hunting insects on the wing. I followed them inside and discovered a nest with three chicks perched on a protruding stone just above the place I had been sitting. The mysterious presence I had felt so strongly in the darkness was not a god, nor spirit, nor succubus, nor demon, but the respirations and featherings of swallows.

Knowing Where You've Been

Robert L. Root, Jr.

The first afternoon. We head for the Blodgett Creek Trail. Our environmental writing workshop at the Teller Refuge takes up the mornings but leaves us the afternoons free, and the three of us are eager to get out into the Montana wilderness. We are midwestern flatlanders, all raised not far inland from the shores of the Great Lakes, though Ron has been a Montanan for nine years now. Waiting after lunch for someone who never shows up, we start out an hour later than we hoped. I drive the Refuge minivan and Linda navigates, directing me from Corvallis across the valley floor to Hamilton and into the foothills of the Bitterroot Mountains. Dirt roads take us gradually up out of pasture land into steep forest. We round a bend, cross Blodgett Creek, and park at the trailhead.

Blodgett Creek is swollen and foaming, a roar and blur of tumbling white water just beyond the trees along the trail. In mid-May western Montana is just beginning its second week of summer-like temperatures, and rapid snow melt generates swift, turbulent run-off. Farmers and ranchers in the Bitterroot Valley worry whether the supply of water will last the growing season.

We strangers, however, eagerly immerse ourselves in new terrain. We set off briskly from the trailhead and, in very little time, see canyon walls, sheer granite facing with jagged rims, emerge above the trees. The trail roughly parallels the creek, passing through narrow bands of ponderosa pine and larch that line its banks. Here the forest is hemmed in by the canyon's narrowness, its inhospitable granite walls, and thick layers of talus piled on the sides of the canyon floor. At a couple of places on the trail we skirt the limits of talus, looking up a forty-five degree angle across a vast slope of dark boulders that ends a third of the way up toward a sheer precipice. The canyon wall here is so solid and impervious that a channel-less white stream of snow melt merely slides down the stone face like hose water down a sidewalk.

-imagery)

We dawdle along the trail. Linda identifies the birds, Ron the flowers, trees, and shrubs; I can only nod appreciatively at each of their pronouncements, finding no rhetorical forms to point out in return. We stroll rather than hike, looking around us as we move. We pause to search for a winter wren or a varied thrush singing in the trees, to examine a ring of blue clematis or some alum root saxifrage rising from the mossy ground, to gaze at a bend in the creek where the overflow has created a calm backwater and the dark shape of a trout drifts through dapples of sunlight. At times we dance up the trail, straddling runoff, leaping from stone to stone, dry spot to damp spot, following the worn path of horses and hikers.

An hour into the walk conversation ebbs and we begin to hike more rapidly. The canyon floor widens and the trail veers away from the creek bed, still tracing the talus wall. Where the forest opens temporarily at a recent burn, Linda drops behind to write in her journal and return more slowly down the slope; Ron and I quicken our pace through the charred trees and flourishing ground cover. The rocky terrain demands more of our attention as we move. Ahead of us, some three miles up from the trailhead, a packbridge crosses the creek, and we set that milestone as our destination. We hike with uncertain urgency, knowing that soon we will have to start back to the workshop for evening events.

Sunday hikers coming down the trail greet us. We overtake a slow-moving family who tell us they have seen a moose three hundred yards back, close to the trail. The pack bridge is still perhaps half a mile ahead, but we turn back, searching the brush for the moose we had overlooked in our rush upward. When we find her, she is lying down behind a log, her long dark head raised just into our view, her large ears scanning the sounds around her. The trail is still on rocky ground, but the moose is twenty yards away amidst a floor of rich green grass spreading among widely-spaced Douglas firs from the slope to the creek. For a few minutes we stand silently, watching her ostentatiously ignore us. Turning back to find her has inadvertently been decisive. By unspoken agreement we hurry back down the trail.

Returning toward the trailhead, I see only the forest ahead of me and occasionally the craggy rim of the canyon emerging on either side. Soon we are in the trees again. I wonder how close we came to the pack bridge, what we might have seen of Blodgett Canyon as we looked back at the Bitterroot Valley crossing the creek, and I find my appetite for the mountains sharpened, not sated, by the hike.

"When you look back at where you have been," Norman Maclean writes, "it often seems as if you have never been there or even as if there were no such place." In his story "USFS 1919: The Logger, the Cook, and the Hole in the Sky," the narrator has paused at the top of a divide, reflecting on where he has been and where he is going. Where he has been is Idaho, at a U.S. Forest Service camp, and more particularly at a lookout tower on Grave Peak; where he is going is Hamilton, in Montana, on the other side of the Bitterroot Mountains, his summer job ended. The distance is thirty-four miles, "fourteen miles up and fourteen miles down with five or six miles still left to go." He intends to walk it in a single day.

istribution of detail

Beginning in a mountain meadow he climbs toward gray cliffs that eventually will place him higher than the mountain goats he spots in the distance; along the way he spooks a bull moose on the trail. On the divide, after marking his own version of the state line in urine, he locates Grave Peak. "From the divide the mountain I had lived on was bronze sculpture. It was all shape with nothing on it, just nothing. It was just color and shape and sky." He muses, "So perhaps at a certain perspective what we leave behind is often wonderland, always different from what it was and generally more beautiful."

From the top of the divide, looking into Blodgett Canyon, he recognizes its glacial orgins. "Coming at me from almost straight below was a Jacob's ladder of switchbacks, rising out of what I later discovered geologists call a cirque but what to me looked like the original nest of a green coiled glacier." He plunges down the Montana side of the divide, cutting straight across the switchbacks, little avalanches following his path. From the bottom of the basin he follows Blodgett Creek to the mouth of the canyon and trudges the remaining five or six miles to Hamilton.

When I told a friend from Montana that I would be spending a week in the Bitterroot Valley, he referred me immediately to Maclean's story and urged me to hike in the canyon. On the flight west I read the story. Disappointed in its lack of detail about the canyon (it really isn't a hiking story, after all) and immediately aware that I wouldn't have time to trek the fourteen miles to Blodgett Pass, I nonetheless checked the trail in a Bitterroots guide and, before the plane had reached Montanan airspace, set myself that goal of reaching the pack bridge.

Now, as I came away from the canyon, pleased with my companions and energized by the experience of the trail, I realized that I was disappointed, and I struggled to figure out why. Perhaps it had to do with not reaching the pack bridge,—with failing to achieve a relatively simple destination—but I wasn't certain why that mattered. Perhaps I hoped to have looked around me and somehow recognized the canyon, discovered the distant switchbacks and the rim of the pass. Perhaps I had hoped that standing on the pack bridge would have placed me so I could see where I had been, where I could be going. While Linda and Ron talked in the van, I tried to remember the words to the children's song about the bear going over the mountain, "to see what he could see." I identified with that bear. As far as I had gone, I still hadn't come away with a sense of knowing where I had been.

The second afternoon. We mill around after the morning workshop, plans shifting, destinations uncertain, finally resolving to go back into the mountains, to another trail. Though eight of us are going, we are all "environmental writers" (by official designation of the Institute) and tend to go to wilderness for solitude, not companionship. At the trailhead, people plan to drop out or stay behind, and the progress up the Mill Creek Trail spreads us out and separates us. Some start out slowly and fall to the rear; others keep on far enough to separate themselves from those behind, then slow down to let those ahead go on without them.

Mill Creek is only a few miles north of Blodgett Creek, descending at the easternmost point of the promontory between Blodgett Canyon and the next canyon north. After a short stretch in open forest, the terrain is often rocky. The forest is dense and broad on either side of the stream, unrestrained by canyon walls. A mile or so along the trail we cross to the north side of the creek on a solid double-log bridge and find ourselves moving parallel to the creek but often away from its banks, intermittently but persistently climbing. Not far beyond the bridge the group is reduced to Ron, Jeff, and me. We begin to push ourselves to reach the falls a couple more miles ahead, making it harder on ourselves by talking about writing most of the way without slackening our pace.

For a little while we parallel sheer canyon walls but soon we are deep into the forest. The walking is easier than in Blodgett Canyon, the terrain more varied, the forest seemingly older, denser. Within a couple miles of the log bridge, past a large boulder and a big wooden sign, we enter the Selway-Bitterroot National Wilderness. Soon the trail steepens and repeatedly winds away from the creek until a final loop brings it closer again. The creek's continuous rumble becomes a roar. Through the trees we can see the foaming waters of the falls and follow the trail up to an opening in the forest near the top.

Beyond the clearing the ground rises sharply again and ahead of us the trail disappears back into forest, but this rounded hump of basalt is covered shallowly with only lichens, wildflowers, and low grasses. Near the creek nothing grows except for a few stunted pines; most of the rock is naked and exposed, shaved clean by plummeting snow melt. Upstream the forest closes in tightly on the creek bed; below the falls the creek is all foamy billows of whitewater slicing through towering forests of ponderosa pine and Douglas fir; across the stream, on the south bank, the trees are thick, impenetrable. Only on the north bank of the falls is the rock swept clean and the surface open to the sun.

We take our time surveying the falls, moving slowly up and down its rock face to consider it from above and below, all the while inundated by the sound of mountain water. As falls go this one is neither majestic nor exceptional, angling down sixty to eighty feet or so rather than plunging vertically from the lip of a precipice. Swollen with snow melt, its foam as white as the snowpack that feeds it, the creek plummets over rugged terraces and outcroppings. We feel its wild power and stand smiling in the spray and the sound, respectful of its reckless turbulence.

The roar makes conversation difficult but Jeff and Ron survey the plant life away from the brink and we each independently declare a desire to camp on the level ground across the clearing. Someone wonders where the trail goes, and I look longingly at the point where it reenters the forest and disappears. The wall of trees prevents us from knowing where we might have gone and, aware that we have overstayed, we turn back toward where we have been to head down the mountainside toward the trailhead and the rest of our party. Our retreat is so swift that I don't notice when I can no longer hear the thunder of the falls and our pace allows me no time to look back.

When I asked my friend from Montana about places to hike in the Bitterroot Valley, he looked thoughtful for a moment, shook his head, and said, "Well, as early as you're going, there'll be too much snow to bag a peak." I laughed and assured him that "bagging a peak" wasn't a priority with me. But the term tended to stay with me on the trip, especially as I trudged along the flat farm roads of the Teller Refuge where the snow-capped peaks of the Bitterroot Range punctuated the horizon. After our return from the Mill Creek Trail, when someone asked me later in the day if I had been "one of the *men* who had gone for distance" on the trail, I thought again about the concept of bagging a peak.

We'd come back to the Mill Creek Trailhead to find the van gone and a note promising that someone would return for us. No doubt we'd delayed people eager to get back to the Refuge, and those who'd stopped along the way had returned to the trailhead with a sense of accomplishment and completion far sooner than we had. If they had been waiting for us, we owed them apologies. But I really couldn't accept the implicit gender explanation for our approach to the hike—after all, I knew from reading their essays that some of the women in the Environmental Writing Institute had had far more arduous adventures than I was ever likely to attempt. The only peaks I've "bagged" not only have not been hard to reach but also were ascended for the view rather than for distance or height.

But the Mill Creek Falls hadn't been a peak, after all, and its distance had only been a few miles. Though I knew what *hadn't* moved me to reach the falls, I wasn't certain what *had*, or why it felt so good to have been there.

The final afternoon. The morning workshop over, the group disperses for various tours and activities. Ron, Valerie, and I meet Janine Benyus and her father, Doug, who both live in the Bitterroot Valley. Janine, whose *Northwoods Wildlife Guide* I value, has volunteered to take workshoppers hiking. Somehow I expect a leisurely excursion and don't bother to change out of sneakers. Although her plan had been to take us to either Blodgett or Mill Creek, when she learns that Ron and I have been to both, she opts for the Bear Creek Overlook Trail instead, a change from creek-bed habitat, a promise of a vista.

Janine drives the minivan to the trailhead, pointing out from the highway the shoulder of the mountain where the Bear Creek Overlook is located. We climb the foothills on back roads threading through pasture lands, then swing onto a twisting, narrow, shoulderless dirt road, an eighty-degree grade sloping away from it. In the front passenger seat my attention is divided between Janine's conversation and the slope we lean toward with every other lurch of the vehicle. Doug Benyus recounts hitting a patch of ice on otherwise dry road a few weeks earlier and plunging over the edge in a Toyota Four-Runner; luckily he had hit a tree a little ways past the edge and was able to back up the slope and continue down the road. Father and daughter tell of other switchback terrors as we ride, but Janine doesn't slow down. I tell myself she knows how to drive these roads better than I, and remind myself to sit in the back on the way down.

The trailhead is an open area on the side of the mountain, with the valley floor a couple thousand feet below, spread out in a gray haze not thick enough to obscure the distant outline of the Sapphire Mountains across the valley. We set out hiking easily through open forest. Lodgepole pines tower above us; the forest floor is carpeted with needles. The wide trail follows a series of switchbacks that take us rapidly up the mountainside with little need for the attentive footing that the creek trails demanded. The day is warm, the mountain breezes refreshing, and our progress consistent. We pause from time to time when Janine draws our attention to some element of the habitat—dwarf mistletoe sprouting from a limb of lodgepole pine, its seeds released by an inner "spring" that fires it fifty feet into the forest, to stick to another tree or be transported on the feathers of the bird that triggered its release; the activity of pitch beetles that bore into pines and, through a symbiotic relationship with bacteria in their mouths and their own excavating, girdle a tree and plug its channels of sap until the tree dies; a blue grouse spooked by Doug Benyus's hound, Barney, fluttering out of reach into a spruce and perching, immobile, waiting for us to lose sight of her. The Benyuses instruct us through a genial symbiosis, feeding each other questions, volunteering each other's information.

Less than halfway up the trail we discover patches of snow across the path. The trees change to spruce and Douglas fir. We look for blazed tree trunks more frequently now, as the trail disappears beneath the snow for longer and longer stretches. Finally, an hour or so into the trail, we reach a turn of a switchback and see an unbroken field of snow stretching through the trees. Janine tells us that it will be mostly snow the rest of the way, and gives us the option of struggling up the slope or turning back and looking for a creekbed. Valerie votes for turning back. Ron and I make noises about not caring either way until the possibility of turning back becomes too real; then we admit to wanting to continue to the overlook. We have seen creek beds, we say, and Valerie urges us to go on while she meanders back.

We are all in tee-shirts, Janine and Ron in shorts, but are kept warm by exertion as we cross the snow. We slip with every step as it gives way beneath us. Often we find ourselves postholing across the snow, sinking in past our ankles, sometimes up to our knees. On separate occasions Janine and I each strike a pocket of air beneath the snow, where it has covered a fallen tree, and plunge in up to our crotches with one leg while the other slips across firmer footing. The icy granules of snow soak through my sneakers and socks and I grumble to myself about my lack of planning until I realize that my hiking boots too would have eventually succumbed to wetness.

It takes us longer than we hoped to reach the crest. The terrain opens up, the trees more stunted and sparse than at lower levels, the snow ranging in ever larger fields. Suddenly we emerge onto the base of a rocky ridge. The timbers of a collapsed line cabin or watch tower poke through a deep covering of empacked snow. Rising above the ridge is a barren crag with contorted shapes of scrub around its base; through the trees on the top of the ridge I look across at a snowy peak dotted with scruffy trees, extending another thousand feet or more above us. The way to the top of the crag is rough and tricky, along precipices and across barren, lichen-free basalt. The west side of our mountain is almost vertical, nearly devoid of plant life except for occasional pioneers jutting from scanty toe-holds in the cliff face. But from that exposed peninsula of rock the three valleys of Bear Creek open out to us.

Directly to the west the South Fork of Bear Creek runs down the center of the valley, lush and green and thickly carpeted with conifers. From where we stand we can see the mountains beyond the valley, the distant sources of Bear Creek's water. To the northwest is another valley, another fork of the creek, that we can trace glinting through the trees until it divides into two more streams, the Middle and North Forks, each descending its own valley. The trees thin out along the slopes of these valleys, turn darker the higher up they go, until they are only random silhouettes against ever-broadening snowfields. All the peaks around us are snow-covered, as must be the peak of the mountain upon whose shoulder we stand.

We are viewing classic glacial terrain. Empty white basins of snow identify cirques, the glacial bowls that will become Bryan Lake and Bear Lake by the end of summer. Above and around them are weathered horns and aretes, the peaks that formed them and the ridges that hold them in place; the valleys extending from the cirques take the wide U-shape of the glaciers that carved them. Directly below us the merged forks of Bear Creek produce a wide foaming cataract rushing snow melt and glacial debris toward the outwash plains that form part of the foothills.

Janine tells us that, when the Pacific plate pushed under the North American plate, it raised the mountains of the Idaho Batholith to a point where the mountaintops became unstable and slid off to the east, creating the broad level plain that would become the Bitterroot Valley (itself later scoured by glaciers) and ending up as the Sapphire Mountains. From this crag we can see beyond the Sapphires to spires of the Garnet Range and the Continental Divide near Anaconda. We can also see a long way toward the beginning of time.

I slowly scan it all with my binoculars. I know that I could sit for hours minutely surveying those valleys and still not feel I had taken them in. Nonetheless I feel myself smiling all the while, feel myself stirred and moved by everything around me. It isn't just the beauty, though it is transcendently beautiful, and it certainly isn't the distance, because everything around us reminds us of how much further we could go. It isn't how far at all but how deep.

That's it. That's the epiphany that dispells my uncertainty about my motives on these hikes. That's what I've been pursuing after all. I simply need to go as deeply into wilderness as it takes before the wilderness comes into me. Sometimes you need to go as deeply as possible where you've never been to reach a place you recognize at once, recognize entirely. That's where I find myself in the Bitterroots.

We stand there a while longer, reveling in arrival. When we finally, reluctantly, turn to descend, I don't need to look back to know where I've been.

self discovery

Postcards from Birobidzhan:

The Life & Death & Life of the Jewish Autonomous Republic

Shelley Salamensky

"On the Eastern Rim of the Habitable Earth"

In the Biblical tale of Enoch, a tzadik, or sage, is flown by an angel to Paradise. A Paradise not in Heaven, but "on the eastern rim of the habitable earth."

My grandmother told the story of an uncle who left Ukraine for "China," on foot, with his children. In each town across the steppe in which he stayed to work, he wrote her family. One by one, the children died. At some point, the letters stopped.

Had it really been China he sought?

The Promised Land

In the 1920s and '30s, Josef Stalin established a "homeland" for Jews in the swamps of what was then called Manchuria, in the far east of the USSR between China and the Arctic Circle.

As throughout the Soviet Union, religion would be banned. But the daily culture of the Jews would be promoted. Communism would be strengthened, Stalin believed, through hybridization with traditional folkways.

Hebrew, likewise, would be discouraged. But Yiddish, the Jewish "workingman's" tongue, would hold a status equal to that of Russian. The JAR (Jewish Autonomous Republic) is, and remains, the only place in history where Yiddish has ever been an official language.

Settler Barracks, Scale Model

While Stalin established other ethnic republics—the Chechen, the Kyrgyz, the Ingush, the Udmurt, and more—these were roughly in these groups' home locations. The JAR would be peopled from the Ukraine, 5000+ miles west. The Jews would be removed from an area in which they were unwelcome and historically tied to mercantile—"petty-capitalist"—pursuits and retrained as proletarian farmers: "peasants," as they joked. And they would serve as a Western bulwark against Japan in this native Inuit and Asian region.

Over time, nearly 40,000 Jews from Ukraine and elsewhere—including the US—lured by ideology or incentives or both, made the treacherous overland journey. Conditions were primitive, the climate deadly, the wetlands near-unfarmable. Over half of the settlers perished or left.

Still, for those who remained, this mock-Zion grew to be a home. Yiddish was taught in the schools and graced all buildings and street signs. Yiddish theater was performed, Yiddish literature written, a Yiddish newspaper published daily. Films were made.

In his later reign of terror, Stalin revoked most of the freedoms he had accorded the oblasts. Nonetheless, far from Hitler's reach, the JAR proved a haven for Jews, and remains, in a sense, the world's only continuous *shtetl* society.

With the fall of the Soviet Union, most Jews of the JAR emigrated to Israel. Yet, recently, some have moved back and others, despite options, have chosen to stay. Today, sixteen percent of the residents of Birobidzhan, the JAR's capital—an admixture of ethnic Russians, Asians, Inuits, and more—are of Jewish extraction.

"Tanya and Tanya," Settler and Native

The writer Michael Chabon describes finding a book of Yiddish "travel phrases"—the way to the train station, how to buy a stamp. For an instant he believes that the phrasebook must correspond to the Yiddishland of his forbears as a living place he can actually travel. When he realizes that, even in 1958, the year the book was published, that Yiddishland was no more, he is devastated. The book—a palpable artifact with no source in reality—strikes him as a cruel prank.

Raised by people grounded in neither the Old World nor the New, and rather lost in life myself, I, like Chabon, longed to "go home." Yet my "homeland" was real. Like Enoch, like the uncle—or like Abraham, impelled by something, or some One, to Go—I went.

Birobidzhan Train Station

Birobidzhan is an historian's nightmare, or dream. A video game arcade and a disco stand steps from the marketplace, where commerce is still conducted by abacus. Vast, near-empty plazas with brutalist monuments and grandiose fountains (one rainbow-lit, blasting Stravinsky and muzaked Lionel Richie 24-7) patchwork between mud streets. Tree-lined mansion boulevards give way to squalid Bloc-Mod ghettos, then rickety pastel huts with outhouses and oft-frozen pumps, and finally the infinite expanse of birch-and-grass taiga plain. Old women sit selling cups of dried beans by deserted roadways.

Even by Russian standards, Birobidzhan is poor. Employment rates and life expectancy are low, alcoholism and child abuse high. The only business booming in town *is* the town. For its seventieth anniversary, grants arrived to reface crumbling mansions and re-cobble the central square. By day, Chinese workers from over the border jackhammer outside the town's sole, stern, Soviet-remnant hotel. The new cheap-alloy statute of the Yiddish writer Sholem Aleichem, who never set foot east of Ukraine, gazes on. By night, the Chinese workers camp and picnic out on its concrete ramparts. I watch them sleep, four floors below my window.

Birobidzhan Coat-of-Arms

The Birobidzhan coat of arms—a stylized rendering of a six-branched menorah bisected by a Soviet-era radio tower and the Bira and Bidzhan rivers, for which the town is named—is emblazoned onto a boggling number of buildings, walls, walkways, and fences. In an inverse "Where's Waldo," I chalk up one hundred, then lose count.

Yiddish, similarly, still shows up on signs: for the post office, the utilities building, streets, cafés. The newspaper includes one Yiddish page per week. Yiddish is still taught in the schools, and still occasionally spoken here. I live out Chabon's dream by purchasing a stamp in Yiddish, the only tongue that a man in line trying to help me and I vaguely share.

Yiddish ATM Sign

And here, unlike elsewhere in Russia, or indeed nearly anywhere else in the world, Jewish "blood" is a point of pride. Everyone I encounter, Jew and non-Jew, speaks of it well. A few members of a would-be Goth gang who call themselves "The Rockers"—though they don't seem to rock as much as to aimlessly shuffle about on the same set of public steps every afternoon—boast of it. The ones who can't appear envious, but nod supportively.

Jewish heritage brings the possibility of repatriation to Israel, viewed in this backwater as the sophisticated "West." And, without its bizarre history, Birobidzhan would be just another dull little town on the tundra.

"Rockers"

I join a tiny coterie of scholars, including two Chasidim and two Yiddishists from Japan, and hobbyists, among them Hirsh, a British-Jewish bird-watcher rumored a billionaire, and Leybl, an itinerant British-Jewish solar-eclipse-viewer salesman. We are feted like celebrities, inevitably—kosher laws long ago having lapsed—with shrimp or ham-and-cheese.

Hirsh and Leybl are introduced to a Leybl and a Hirsh. A student "Jewish dance" recital is assembled in our honor. Some costumes are constructed of chopped-up Jewish prayer shawls; others seem recycled from events commemorating Russia's pagan origins and something to do with medieval Christian clergy. An evocation of a Jewish shtetl wedding features children in chefs' toques bearing trays laden with papier-mâché roast geese, plastic vegetables, and "brick-pack" fruit juice boxes—juice being a luxury in poor parts of Russia today.

While two or three indubitably Jewish kids hora past, few of the students are of Jewish lineage. But all are well drilled, Soviet-style, moving in machinic precision. Their faces glow with zeal and promise. Our group is divided. Can Jewish culture continue without Jews? Does it matter?

Fiddler on the Fountain

Similar dissent arises around which shul the group should attend for Shabbat. Chabad, a worldwide Jewish missionary group of sorts, has erected an enormous stucco synagogue with arched doors and windows limned with red and green neon, oddly suggestive of a Taco Bell. Its education wing is flanked with faux-brick panoramas of the Wailing Wall and stocked with blond mannequins gotten up as Jews.

The young rabbi and his wife, however, are extremely kind, offering much needed support to the community and us. The *rebbetzin* cooks up massive, sumptuous spreads from what sparse kosher provisions she can find. Her dinners demolish any resistance we may have had to the sect. Still, it appears few locals enter.

Across town, in a tumbledown cottage, an elderly lay rabbi and his even more elderly mother-in-law lead services for a small, impoverished cluster of the aged. Gaunt cats leap between pantry shelves and onto the shaky card table that

Model Jews

holds the Torah. Two toothless men borrow the eyeglasses of a third to struggle aloud through the Russian prayer book, line by line. Women in babushka head-scarves take their turns. The lay rabbi, hobbled by a twisted foot, moves painfully about the room, beaming his encouragement.

It is rumored in Birobidzhan that until the *glasnost* period, permitting greater information from abroad, worship here involved Jesus, as well as Moses as a Jesus-like figure. "When you walk in they will hide the icons," I am told. But no apostasy is evident.

Indeed, this seems exactly like *shabbos*, as my grandmother recalled it, in the snug *shtetl* in Ukraine. A beggar woman raps at the back door. The mother-in-law, ready with a bag of bread, steps quickly to the porch, then silently rejoins us.

Cottage Synagogue

Surely this motion, in its simplicity and grace, is one transmitted through the ages wherever the Jews have been: this elder's elders, my own.

We aren't as tough as the settlers, or even as present-day Birobidzhaners. In mere weeks, euphoria turns to exhaustion. Two of our group, contracting salmonella, are locked in infectious diseases wards on the far edge of town. No news in or out, shattered windows—worst, no toilet paper. Their exit papers, when they are finally released, are marked "USSR 1982."

After a bowl of rancid cabbage-meat soup with a big dollop—plop!—not of sour cream, as anticipated, but cheaper, steaming mayonnaise, I stick to cucumbers and tea.

Leybl, the eclipse-viewer salesman, takes a homeless Inuit girl to his room. They share—chastely, he says, and there is no reason not to believe him—the lean plank the hotel calls a bed. She makes tea, watches TV, sings with the commercials. The forbidding Soviet-hangover hall monitor ladies look past it all, as do we.

One night she plies him with beer, combs his thinning hair, attempts to steal his phone, changes her mind, cries, leaves. He's not angry.

Local Minerals

Local Linoleum

He draws a diagram for me of how eclipses work. He's been through England, Turkey, Libya—next stops Siberia, Somalia—to hawk his wares at precise angles of the moon and sun.

We're everywhere and nowhere, sunk in history and lost in space. The petty rules we thought we knew cease to apply.

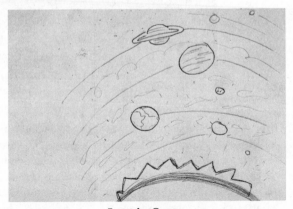

Lost in Space

The fate of the JAR itself is not so sad. The place has held up pretty well, considering.

But me, I am jarred loose by the homey-yet-out-of-context Jewish faces, the landscape, the extremity, the way Leybl's sun and moon seem here to hang too low, too close.

It is as if I have reached the end—of what, I cannot say. The earth? History? In some way, my own life? Though I'll survive, it seems, what will remain will be an afterthought, an afterlife—as with Enoch, flown back just briefly to report on Paradise before the angel whisked him off again.

And I can't shake it.

New Russian-Chinese Friendship Monument

The final leg of my trip, a bumpy cross-taiga ride into achingly bright dawn, is with Menachem, an ultra-Orthodox scholar of sorts from Israel. At fifty-something, he has fifty grandchildren. He has a sly sense of humor and, beneath his long crinkly beard, oddly resembles the actor Gene Hackman.

I doze. He nods his head in time with rock music clearly produced in some Islamic republic, but which he proclaims to be klezmer. We have managed, throughout our stay, to disagree on everything.

My Western ways, I know, are odious to him. His politics and views of women sicken me. Yet in the strangeness of this place we have become something like friends. He is named for the same rabbi my great grandfather was. His family's *shtetl* was not far—not near, but not far—from my family's. We are *landsmen*— less than cousins, yet more than neighbors—from way back. And that's enough for him. And me. We talk about the Old Country as if we'd wandered from it for a week. Even in the Holy Land, he says, he feels as lost, as homeless as I.

Onlookers—less hostile than frightened by his antique, bizarre garb— gather, calling "What are you?" Suddenly protective of him, I shoo them away. When my plane boards, I fear to leave him.

Or fear to allow him to leave me. Tricked out as a ghost from home, Menachem is no more authentic than the JAR itself. But, as with the JAR, he may be as close to where I belong as I'll get, and I have become somewhat attached to him.

My return west is a relief. But before long I come to feel desolate, hollow. Others, back where they live, around the globe, write the same. We promise to meet up in the JAR again. In the moment, we mean it.

The cost is prohibitive, the journey far.

Still, could it be possible that in Stalin's faux-Zion we found a home, illusory and makeshift as it seemed?

Cloud Crossing

Scott Russell Sanders

Clouds are temporary creatures. So is the Milky Way, for that matter, if you take the long entropic view of things. I awake on a Saturday in mid-October with the ache of nightmares in my brain, as if I have strained a muscle in my head. Just a week before I turn thirty-three, just a month before my son turns one, I do not need physics or nightmares to remind me that we also are temporary creatures.

Baby Jesse is changing cloud-fast before my eyes. His perky voice begins pinning labels on dogs and bathtubs and sun. When I say, "Want to go for a walk?" on this morning that began with nightmares of entropy, he does not crawl towards me as he would have done only a few days ago. He tugs himself upright with the help of a chair, then staggers toward me like a refugee crossing the border, arms outstretched, crowing, "Wa! Wa!"

So I pack baby and water and graham crackers into the car, and drive thirty miles southeast of Eugene, Oregon, to a trailhead on Hardesty Mountain. There are several hiking paths to the top, ranging in length from one mile to six. I choose the shortest, because I will be carrying Jesse's twenty-two pounds on my back. I have not come here to labor, to be reminded of my hustling heart. I have come to watch clouds.

Markers on the logging road tell us when we drive up past 2,500 feet, then 2,750 and 3,000. Around 3,250 the Fiat noses through the first vapors, great wrinkled slabs of clouds that thicken on the windshield. In the back seat Jesse strains against his safety harness, his hands fisted on the window, hungry to get out there into that white stuff. I drive the last few hundred yards to the trailhead with lights on, in case we meet a car groping its way down the mountain.

Beside a wooden sign carved to announce HARDESTY MOUNTAIN TRAIL, I park the Fiat with its muzzle downhill, so we can coast back to the highway after our walk in case the weary machine refuses to start. I lean the backpack against the bumper and guide Jesse's excited feet through the leg-holes, one of his calves in each of my hands. "Wa! Wa!" he cries, and almost tips the pack over into the sorrel dust of the logging road. Shouldering the pack requires acrobatic balancing, to keep him from tumbling out while I snake my arms through the straps. Once safely aloft, assured of a ride, he jounces so hard in the seat that I stagger a few paces with the same drunken uncertainty he shows in his own walking.

Clouds embrace us. Far overhead, between the fretted crowns of the Douglas fir, I see hints of blue. Down here among the roots and matted needles, the air is mist. My beard soon grows damp; beads glisten on my eyelashes. A few yards along the trail a Forest Service board, with miniature roof to protect its messages, informs us we are at 3,600 feet and must hike to 4,237 in order to reach the top of Hardesty. Since I came to see the clouds, not to swim in them, I hope we are able to climb above them into that tantalizing blue.

On my back Jesse carries on a fierce indecipherable oration concerning the wonders of this ghostly forest. Giddy with being outside and aloft, he drums on my head, yanks fistfuls of my hair. Every trunk we pass tempts him more strongly than the apple tree could ever have tempted Eve and Adam. He lurches from side to side, outstretched fingers desperate to feel the bark. I pause at a mammoth stump to let him touch. Viewed up close, the bark looks like a contour map of the Badlands, an eroded landscape where you might expect to uncover fossils. While Jesse traces the awesome ridges and fissures, I squint to read another Forest Service sign. No motorized vehicles, it warns, and no pack animals.

I surely qualify as a pack animal. For long spells in my adult life, while moving house or humping rucksacks onto trains or hauling firewood, I have felt more like a donkey than anything else. I have felt most like a beast of burden when hauling my two children, first Eva and now Jesse. My neck and shoulders never forget their weight from one portage to another. And I realize that carrying Jesse up the mountain to see clouds is a penance as well as a pleasure—penance for the hours I have sat glaring at my typewriter while he scrabbled mewing outside my door, penance for the thousands of things my wife has not been able to do on account of my word mania, penance for all the countless times I have told daughter Eva "no, I can't; I am writing." I know the rangers did not have human beasts in mind when they posted their sign, yet I am content to be a pack animal, saddled with my crowing son.

As I resume walking, I feel a tug. Jesse snaps a chunk of bark from the stump and carries it with him, to examine at leisure. Beneath one of the rare cottonwoods I pick up a leathery golden leaf, which I hand over my shoulder to the baby, who clutches it by the stem and turns it slowly around, tickling his nose with the starpoints. The leaf is a wonder to him, and therefore also to me. Everything he notices, every pebble, every layered slab of bark, is renewed for me. Once I carried Eva outside, in the first spring of her life, and a gust of wind caught her full in the face. She blinked, and then gazed at the invisible breath as if it were a flight of angels streaming past. Holding her in the crook of my arm that day, I rediscovered wind.

Fascinated by his leaf, Jesse snuggles down in the pack and rides quietly. My heart begins to dance faster as the trail zigzags up the mountain through a series of switchbacks. Autumn has been dry in Oregon, so the dirt underfoot is powdery. Someone has been along here inspecting mushrooms. The discarded ones litter the trail like blackening pancakes. Except for the path, worn raw by deer and hikers, the floor of the woods is covered with moss. Fallen wood is soon hidden by the creeping emerald carpet, the land burying its own dead. Limegreen moss clings fuzzily to the upright trunks and dangles in fluffy hanks from limbs, like freshly dyed wool hung out to dry. A wad of it caught in the fist squeezes down to nothing.

A lurch from the backpack tells me that Jesse has spied some new temptation in the forest. Craning around, I see his spidery little hands reaching for the sky. Then I also look up, and notice the shafts of light slanting down through the treetops. The light seems substantial, as if made of glass, like the rays of searchlights that carve up the night sky to celebrate a store's opening or a war's end. "Light," I say to Jesse. "Sunlight. We're almost above the clouds." Wherever the beams strike, they turn cobwebs into jeweled diagrams, bracelet limbs with rhinestones of dew. Cloud vapors turn to smoke.

The blue glimpsed between trees gradually thickens, turns solid, and we emerge onto a treeless stony ridge. Clear sky above, flotillas of clouds below, mountains humping their dark green backs as far as I can see. The sight of so many slick backs arching above the clouds reminds me of watching porpoises from a ship in the Gulf of Mexico. Vapors spiral up and down between cloud layers as if on escalators. Entire continents and hemispheres and galaxies of mist drift by. I sit on the trail with backpack propped against a stone ledge, to watch this migration.

No peace for meditation with an eleven-month-old on your back. An ache in my shoulders signals that Jesse, so near the ground, is leaning out of the pack to capture something. A pebble or beetle to swallow? A stick to gnaw? Moss, it turns out, an emerald hunk of it ripped from the rockface. "Moss," I tell him, as he rotates this treasure about three inches in front of his eyes. "Here, feel," and I stroke one of his palms across the velvety clump. He tugs the hand free and resumes his private exploration. This independence grows on him these days faster than his hair.

"Clouds," I tell him, pointing out into the gulf of air. Jesse glances up, sees only vagueness where I see a ballet of shapes, and so he resumes his scrutiny of the moss. "Not to eat," I warn him. When I check on him again half a minute later, the moss is half its former size and his lips are powdered with green. Nothing to do but hoist him out of the pack, dig what I can from his mouth, then plop him back in, meanwhile risking spilling both of us down the mountainside. A glance down the dizzying slope reminds me of my wife's warning, that I have no business climbing this mountain alone with a baby. She's right, of course. But guilt, like the grace of God, works in strange ways, and guilt drives me up here among the skittery rocks to watch clouds with my son.

"Let Daddy have it," I say, teasing the hunk of moss from his hand. "Have a stick, pretty stick." While he imprints the stick with the marks of his teeth, four above and two below, I spit on the underside of the moss and glue it back down to the rock. Grow, I urge it. Looking more closely at the rockface, I see that it is crumbling beneath roots and weather, sloughing away like old skin. The entire mountain is migrating, not so swiftly as the clouds, but just as surely, heading grain by grain to the sea.

Jesse seems to have acquired some of the mountain's mass as I stand upright again and hoist his full weight. With the stick he idly swats me on the ear.

The trail carries us through woods again, then up along a ridge to the clearing at the top of Hardesty Mountain. There is no dramatic feeling of expansiveness, as there is on some peaks, because here the view is divvied up into modest sweeps by Douglas firs, cottonwoods, great gangling heaps of briars. The forest has laid siege to the rocky crest, and will abolish the view altogether before Jesse is old enough to carry his own baby up here. For now, by moving from spot to spot on the summit, I can see in all directions. What I see mostly are a few thousand square miles of humpbacked mountains looming through the clouds. Once in Ohio I lived in a valley which the Army Corps of Engineers thought would make a convenient bed for a reservoir. So the Mahoning River was dammed, and as the waters backed up in that valley, covering everything but the highest ridges, drowning my childhood, they looked very much like these clouds poured among the mountains.

"Ba! Ba!" Jesse suddenly bellows, leaping in his saddle like a bronco rider.

Bath, I wonder? Bed? Bottle? Ball? He has been prolific of B-words lately, and their tail-ends are hard to tell apart. Ball, I finally decide, for there at the end of the arrow made by his arm is the moon, a chalky peachpit hanging down near the horizon. "Moon," I say.

"Ba! Ba!" he insists.

Let it stay a ball for a while, something to play catch with, roll across the linoleum. His sister's first sentence was, "There's the moon." Her second was, "Want it, Daddy." So began her astronomical yearnings, my astronomical failures. She has the itch for space flight in her, my daughter does. Jesse is still too much of a pup for me to say whether he has caught it.

We explore the mountaintop while the ocean of cloud gradually rises. There are charred rings from old campfires. In a sandy patch, red-painted bricks are laid in the shape of a letter A. Not large enough to be visible from airplanes. If Hardesty Mountain were in a story by Hawthorne, of course, I could use the scarlet A to accuse it of some vast geological harlotry. If this were a folklore mountain, I could explain the letter as an alphabetical inscription left by giants. But since this is no literary landscape, I decide that the bricks formed the foundation for some telescope or radio transmitter or other gizmo back in the days when this summit had a lookout tower.

Nearby is another remnant from those days, a square plank cover for a cistern. The boards are weathered to a silvery sheen, with rows of rustblackened nailheads marking the joints. Through a square opening at the center of the planks I catch a glint. Water? Still gathering here after all these years? Leaning over the hole, one boot on the brittle planks, I see that the glint is from a tin can. The cistern is choked with trash.

At the very peak, amid a jumble of rocks, we find nine concrete piers that once supported the fire tower. By squatting down beside one of those piers I can rest Jesse's weight on the concrete, and relieve the throb in my neck. I imagine the effort of hauling enough materials up this mountain to build a tower. Surely they used horses, or mules. Not men with backpacks. So what became of the tower when the Forest Service, graduated to spotter planes, no longer needed it? Did they pry out every nail and carry the boards back down again? A glance at the ground between my feet supplies the answer. Wedged among the rocks, where rains cannot wash them away, are chunks of glass, some of them an inch thick. I pick up one that resembles a tongue, about the size for a cocker spaniel. Another one, a wad of convolutions, might be a crystalline brain. Peering up through it at the sun, I see fracture lines and tiny bubbles. Frozen in the seams where one molten layer lapped onto another there are ashes. Of course they didn't dismantle the tower and lug its skeleton down the mountain. They waited for a windless day after a drenching rain and they burned it.

The spectacle fills me: the mountain peak like a great torch, a volcano, the tower heaving on its nine legs, the windows bursting from the heat, tumbling among the rocks, fusing into molten blobs, the glass taking on whatever shape it cooled against.

There should be nails. Looking closer I find them among the shards of glass, sixteen-penny nails mostly, what we called spikes when I was building houses. Each one is somber with rust, but perfectly straight, never having been pried from wood. I think of the men who drove those nails—the way sweat stung in their eyes, the way their forearms clenched with every stroke of the hammer—and I wonder if any of them were still around when the tower burned. The Geological Survey marker, a round lead disk driven into a rock beside one of the piers, is dated 1916. Most likely the tower already stood atop the mountain in that year. Most likely the builders are all dead by now.

So on its last day the Hardesty fire tower became a fire tower in earnest. Yesterday I read that two American physicists shared the Nobel Prize for discovering the background radiation left over from the Big Bang, which set our universe in motion some fifteen billion years ago. Some things last—not forever, of course, but for a long time—things like radiation, like bits of glass. I gather a few of the nails, some lumps of glass, a screw. Stuffing these shreds of evidence in my pocket, I discover the graham cracker in its wrapping of cellophane, and I realize I have not thought of Jesse for some minutes, have forgotten that he is riding me. That can mean only one thing. Sure enough, he is asleep, head scrunched down into the pack. Even while I peek at him over my shoulder he is changing, neurons hooking up secret connections in his brain, calcium swelling his bones as mud gathers in river deltas.

Smell warns me that the clouds have reached us. Looking out, the only peaks I can see are the Three Sisters, each of them a shade over 10,000 feet. Except for those peaks and the rocks where I stand, everything is cotton. There are no more clouds to watch, only Cloud, unanimous whiteness, an utter absence of shape. A panic seizes me—the same panic I used to feel as a child crossing the street when approaching cars seemed to have my name written on their grills. Suddenly the morning's nightmare comes back to me: everything I know is chalked upon a blackboard, and, while I watch, a hand erases every last mark.

Terror drives me down the Hardesty trail, down through vapors that leach color from the ferns, past trees that are dissolving. Stumps and downed logs lose their shape, merge into the clouds. The last hundred yards of the trail I jog. Yet Jesse never wakes until I haul him out of the pack and wrestle him into the car harness. His bellowing defies the clouds, the creeping emptiness. I bribe him with sips of water, a graham cracker, a song. But nothing comforts him, or comforts me, as we drive down the seven graveled miles of logging road to the highway. There we sink into open space again. The clouds are a featureless gray overhead.

As soon as the wheels are ringing beneath us on the blacktop, Jesse's internal weather shifts, and he begins one of his calm babbling orations, contentedly munching his cracker. The thread of his voice slowly draws me out of the annihilating ocean of whiteness. "Moon," he is piping from the back seat, "moon, moon!"

My Father Always Said

Mimi Schwartz

For years I heard the same line: "In Rindheim,[1] you didn't do such things!" It was repeated whenever the American world of his daughters took my father by surprise. Sometimes it came out softly, in amusement, as when I was a Pilgrim turkey in the P.S. 3 Thanksgiving play. But usually, it was a red-faced, high-blood-pressure shout—especially when my sister, Ruth, became "pinned" to Mel from Brooklyn or I wanted to go with friends whose families he didn't know.

"But they're Jewish," I'd say, since much of our side of Forest Hills was. The eight lanes of Queens Boulevard divided the Jews, Irish, and Italians pushing out of Brooklyn, the Bronx, and Manhattan from the old guard WASPs of Forest Hills Gardens. No Jews or Catholics over there—except for a few blocks near the Forest Hills Tennis Stadium where, from fifth grade on, we kids all went to watch what is now the U.S. Tennis Open, our end-of-summer ritual before school.

"You're not going," my father would announce before all such rituals.

"But everybody's going."

It was the wrong argument to make to a man who fled Hitler's Germany because of everybody. But I couldn't know that because he rarely talked about *that* Germany, only about his idyllic Rindheim where everybody (as opposed to the everybody I knew) did everything right. If my friends didn't have an aunt, grandmother, or great grandfather originally from Rindheim or vicinity, they were suspect. They could be anybody, which is exactly why I liked them—not like the Weil kids whose mother was "a born Tannhauser," as if that were a plus.

"I don't care about everybody!" my father would shout (that was his second favorite line); but it was a losing battle for him. My sister smoked at fifteen, I wore lipstick at twelve; we hung out at Penn Drug after Friday night basketball games

---

[1]I've changed the name, but all else is true.

194

with friends who were third-generation Brooklyn and Rumania—and didn't give a hoot that "In Rindheim, you didn't do such things!"

The irony of those words was inchoate—even to him, I realize now—until we went back to his village to visit the family graves. I was thirteen; it was eight years after World War II ended, and my father wanted to show me where his family had lived for generations, trading cattle. He wanted me, the first American-born in the family, to understand that "Forest Hills, Queens is not the world" (his third favorite line). A hard task to tackle, but my father was tough, a survivor who had led his whole clan, like Moses, out of Nazi Germany and into Queens, New York. He was ready for an American teen-age me.

"So Mimi-a-la, this is Rindheim!" my father boomed as the forest opened upon a cluster of fifty or so red-peaked houses set into the hillside of a tiny, green valley. We had driven for hours through what looked like Hansel and Gretel country, filled with foreboding evergreens that leaned over the narrow, winding roads of the *Schwarzwald*. Even the name, *Schwarzwald*, which meant Black Forest, gave me the creeps after being weaned on Nazi movies at the Midway Theater on 71st Avenue; but I was optimistic. Life here did look prettier than in Queens.

We drove up a rutted main street and stopped before a crumbling stone house with cow dung in the yard. "This was *our* house!" my father announced, as I watched horse flies attacking the dung, not just in *our* yard but in every yard on Eelinger Weg. And there were cows and chickens walking in front of our rented car. What a bust! My mother at least came from a place with sidewalks (we had driven by her old house in Stuttgart, sixty kilometers north, before coming here). My father, I decided at once, was a hick. All his country hero adventures about herding cows with a book hidden in one pocket and his mother's home-baked raspberry *linzertorte* in the other were discounted by two cows chewing away in stalls where I expected a car to be.

A stooped, old man with thick jowls and a feathered leather cap came out of the house with a big smile and a vigorous handshake for my dad who, looking squeezed in his pin-striped suit, nodded now and then and looked polite, but did not smile back.

"*Sind Sie nicht ein Loewengart, vielleicht Julius oder Artur?*" The man jabbered on, and my mother translated. He was Herr Schmidt, the blacksmith, and recognized my dad at once. "Aren't you a Loewengart, maybe Julius or Arthur?" This man had bought the family house in 1935 from Uncle Julius, the last of my family to leave Rindheim, and was remembering how my father and his brothers, Sol and Julius, used to play in his shop—with all his tools. "*Eine nette Familie, sehr nette,*" ("A fine family, very fine") he kept saying.

I understood nothing because I had learned no German in our house in Queens. When my father reached Ellis Island, he announced that our family would not speak the language of those who drove them out of Germany. Which was fine with me. It was embarrassing enough in those days to have parents who, for all my coaching, couldn't stop saying '*fader*' and '*moder*' to my American-born friends.

The man beckoned us towards my dad's old house, but my father shook his head, *"Nein, Danke!"* and backed us quickly away. I wanted to go in and see his old room; but my father did not. It would be forty years before I'd follow Frau Hummel, the blacksmith's daughter, up the narrow, dark stairs to a loft with two windows like cannon holes and search the heavy low beams for my dad's initials—A. L.—carved in the worn, smooth wood.

"And here's my downtown! No Penn Drugstore to hang around here!" my Dad said cheerfully, as we drove past four buildings leaning together like town drunks. "And here's where Grunwald had his kosher butcher shop and Zundorfer, his dry goods. And here's the *Gasthaus Kaiser*! We Jews had wonderful *Purim* and *Shuvuott* dances here—with green branches and ferns and pink flowers, like marbles in the candlelight. . . ." I could picture Mr. Grunwald—he sold sausages in Queens—but I couldn't picture my big-bellied, bald-headed Dad dancing, a kid like me.

We turned into an alley and stopped next to a gray building with stone columns in the doorway and corners decorated with what looked like railroad ties set into stone. I wouldn't have noticed it tucked among the houses.

"Here's where we spent every Friday night," my father said, getting us out of the car to look at the old synagogue. He pointed to a Hebrew inscription carved onto a stone plaque above the doorway: "How great is God's house and the doorway to Heaven," he translated haltingly in his rusty Hebrew. Right below the stone plaque was a wooden beam with another inscription, this one in German. It said the same thing, my father said, but it was new. He'd never seen it before.

I found out later that the German inscription had been added in 1952, the year before we came. That's when the Jewish synagogue was converted into the Protestant Evangelical Church to accommodate Eastern Germans who, fleeing the Russian troops late in World War II, resettled into the empty Jewish houses of this Catholics/Jewish village. Keeping the same words on the doorway inscription was meant as a tribute of respect: that this building was still God's house. But the 250 Rindheim Jews who had fled to America and Israel were never grateful. Their beautiful synagogue was no more; that's what counted.

"Well, at least it didn't become a gymnasium or a horse stable, like in other villages," the mayor's wife told me huffily in 1993 when I returned to Rindheim on my own. Two other villagers nodded vigorously, but a lively woman, who said she used to live next door to my great uncle, said, *"Na Ja*, I wouldn't be so happy if our Catholic church became a mosque—and believe me, we have plenty of Turks here. . . ."

". . . They are our new Jews," someone interjected.

". . . *Na Ja*," the lively woman shrugged and continued, "and I wouldn't feel good just because the Moslems said our church was still God's house."

They pointed out "the Moslems," four men squatting around a table and sipping Turkish coffee in a terraced yard below the synagogue. Many came, according to the lively woman, in the the 1960s as guest workers from Turkey and Afghanistan and now made up twenty percent of Rindheim. These men lived in the old *Gasthaus Kaiser*, where my father danced at *Purim* Festivals and where my Aunt Hilda and family once lived above the restaurant. This village is more like Forest Hills than you thought, Dad, I told myself, wishing he were around to discuss these ironies of migration. (The Forest Hills Gardens of my childhood is now owned by wealthy Asians and our block on 110th Street is now filled with Iranians.)

My father loosened his tie and wiped beads of sweat from his forehead with a checkered handkerchief. "And if you weren't in your synagogue by sundown on Friday, and not a minute later, *and* all day on Saturday, you were fined, a disgrace to your family. Three stars had to shine in the evening sky before *Shabbat* (the Sabbath) was over and you could go home."

I thought of his fury whenever I wanted to go bowling on Saturday at Foxy's Alley where all the boys hung out. Not that my father went to synagogue in Queens. The most religious he got, as far as I could see, was to play his record of Jan Pierce singing the *Kol Nidre* on *Yom Kippur*, the day of repentance. And he fasted—which I tried once or twice but got hungry when my mother ate a bagel. She never fasted.

The sun was high, the car seat sticky on my thighs, so I happily sat in the shade of four tall, arched windows which someone had been fixing. But my mother was heading for the car, saying she didn't like standing in the open where everyone could see us. We should go. In fact, she would have skipped Germany altogether and stayed in Belgium with my sister who had married a Belgian Jew (instead of Mel from Brooklyn); but my father insisted that we make this pilgrimage.

"Aren't we going inside?" I asked when my father started to follow my mother. He was usually the leader on everything, the man who, in 1933, as soon as Hitler came to power, convinced his brothers, sister, cousins, and parents-in-law, forty people in all, to leave Germany as quickly as possible; the man who figured out schemes for smuggling money taped to toilets on night trains to Switzerland—it took two years—so that they'd have enough cash for America to let them in. (Jews without a bank account or sponsor had no country willing to take them from Hitler's Germany.)

"No reason to go in. The building is just a shell. Everything was gutted by fire during *Kristallnacht*."

"What's that?"

I imagined some Jewish festival with candles out of control. In 1953 there was no *Schindler's List*, no Holocaust Museum, so I never heard about one night in 1938, when the Nazis systematically burned all the synagogues in Germany to destroy the Jewish life. All I knew was good Americans, who looked like Jimmy Stewart and Gregory Peck, fighting mean-looking men in black uniforms who clicked their heels a lot and shouted, "Heil Hitler." And we won.

"*Kristallnacht* was when the Jews finally realized they had to leave—and fast—even from Rindheim where it wasn't so bad. Jews felt safe here, too safe—until the synagogue was torched, everything in flames."

He stopped talking. "Go on!" I urged, but he held back, tentative. Not at all like him.

"My cousin Fritz. . . . Do you remember him?" I shook my head, no. "He lived over there once," my father pointed down the alley, "and when he smelled smoke, he raced over. He was part of the Fire Brigade and began shouting to others in the Brigade, 'Why don't we do something? Get the hoses!' Men he knew all his life were standing around, silent. 'Against orders!' snapped a Nazi brown-shirt, a stranger. 'Except if Christian houses start to burn!' He pointed his rifle at Fritz. So everything inside was lost—the Torah, the Ark. . . ."

I thought about the old blacksmith who lived in our house. Was he there? Was he one of those firemen? Why was he so friendly if he hated the Jews?

"But these people weren't from Rindheim," my father said quickly. "They were thugs from outside, brought in trucks by the Nazis to do their dirty work."

My father, already in America by then, had heard this from many Rindheim Jews who, like Fritz, left as soon after *Kristallnacht* as they could get exit visas. "The Rindheimers we grew up with didn't take part. They wouldn't do such a thing!" my father had been assured by those who resettled in America.

He opened the car door. "In fact many Non-Jews helped the Jews fix the store and house windows that were also smashed that night. But for that the Non-Jews got in trouble. Everyone who helped was sent to the Front as cannon fodder."

"What's that?" I asked.

"It's what you feed into big guns so they will shoot."

I imagined a young man being stuffed into a cannon, like at the circus, and aimed at American guns, his mother in the red doorway of the house we just passed, getting a telegram, crying like in the movies. But I wasn't going to feel sorry, not when they let the synagogue burn.

Later I would hear this term, cannon fodder, used again and again by Rindheim Jews—and always with the same "broken window" story. It was as if they had decided collectively on this tale and how it illustrated that their Non-Jewish neighbors meant well. "It wasn't their fault. They were afraid, too," they'd say with more sympathy than anger. But, like my parents, the Jews who returned to Rindheim to visit the family graves did so quickly, never wanting to stand and talk in the open or re-enter old rooms of memory.

I was hungry, but my father stopped again, this time in front of a shabby building with three tiers of windows. This was his school, he said, and it looked like mine, but P.S. 3 had a paved playground and good swings. This just had dirt.

"We Jews had the first floor and one teacher, Herr Spatz, who taught every-body, in all eight grades, everything. The Christians had the other two floors."

"How come?" I asked, for I'd never heard of dividing kids by anything but age.

My father looked surprised. "That's how it was done. We learned Torah and they didn't. They went to school on Saturdays and we didn't. But to high school, we went together, six kilometers to Horb, those who went."

"And did you talk to each other—and play games?" I thought of Tommy Molloy in the schoolyard, saying that I killed Christ, but then he asked me to play stickball on his team, and I said okay.

"Of course. We all got along. Rindheim was not so big."

I wouldn't argue about that! The schoolyard was deserted and, looking for movement in a meadow on the far hill, I saw a giant white cross ringed by menacing forest that kept its distance, like dark green bodyguards. The cross was also new, my father said. It wasn't even there when he was a child or even when he came home for a *Shabbat*, after moving to the city of Frankfurt in 1921 to work and later to marry.

"Remember how we had to park the car two kilometers away and walk to my father's?" He nudged my mother. "No Jew dared to drive here on *Shabbat*! Am I right?"

"Absolutely not. You'd be run out of town." My mother laughed for the first time all day and turned to tell me about how she, a big city girl from Stuttgart, first came to this village for her cousin Max's wedding. She wore a red, lace dress. "Very shocking!" she said with delight. "Everyone was whispering but your father. He came up and asked for every dance!" Her shoulders eased with nostalgia, wisps of black hair loosened from her chignon, and I leaned forward, close to her neck that always smelled of almond soap, to hear more about my parents having fun.

My father made a sharp left turn up a dirt road that zigzagged up a hill and stopped in front of a run-down stone farmhouse with half a roof. We needed a key for the Jewish cemetery and it was hanging on the peg "where it has always been," my father said. This was the Brenner family house; they were the gravediggers, who had been burying the Rindheim Jews for generations. Before Hitler, of course. A quarter of a mile farther, a giant stone portal emerged from nowhere—the kind that led to castles—and the fat key opened the heavy gate that led us deep into woods.

I still remember the sunlight on that day, how it streamed on the gravestones, a thousand of them tipped but all standing, in an enchanted forest light. It was a place to whisper and walk on tiptoe, even if you were an American thirteen. I remember the softness of the ground, a carpet of moss and leaves, and the stillness, as if the trees were holding their breath until we found everyone: my grandmother, Anna, born Tannhauser (1872–1915), and my grandfather, Rubin (1866–1925), both marked by sleek, dark marble gravestones that looked new despite the underbrush. And Rubin's father, Raphael (1821–1889), and his father, Rubin Feit (1787–1861), their pale sandstone gravestones carved with elaborate vines and scrolls eroded by time.

I tried to imagine faces: a grandfather who enforced strict rules about work, manners, and Torah; a grandmother who, in the faded photo over my parents' bed, laughed with my father's twinkle, when life pleased him. She had died when my father was not much older than I was, of infection, not Hitler, my father said. So had his dad, who refused to go to the hospital two hours away.

But all I could picture were the grandparents I knew: the *Omi* and *Opa* who lived three blocks away in Queens and "babysat," against my loudest objections that I was too old for that. This grandfather walked my dog so I didn't have to and wove yards of intricately patterned shawls and slipcovers on his loom in our attic. This grandmother made delicious, heart-shaped butter cookies and told stories of how they escaped in a little boat from Denmark to Sweden, and then to a chicken farm on Long Island where she, a city woman from Stuttgart, sang to her hens every morning—until my grandfather's heart attack made them move three blocks from us.

"Do you want to put down stones?" my father asked, placing small ones on his father's grave, his lips moving as in prayer, and then on his mother's grave—and on the others. He had found the stones under the wet leaves, and my mother, wobbling in high heels, was searching for more, enough for both of us.

"What for?" I asked, not wanting to take what she was offering. I would find my own.

"It's how you pay tribute to the dead," my father said, looking strangely gaunt despite his bulk. "The dead souls need the weight of remembrance, and then they rise up to God more easily. . . . If we lived nearby, there'd be many stones," he said softly to his father's grave.

In later years, there would be more stones, as more Rindheim Jews came to visit the graves of their ancestors, but eight years after the war there were no others. I placed a smooth, speckled white with mica on Anna's grave and rougher grey ones on the men's. My father nodded. Some connection had been made, he knew, the one he had run from and returned to, the one I resisted even as I lay stones.

There were Loewengarts all over the place, mixed in with Pressburgers and Froehlichs and Grunwalds and Landauers, the same names again and again for they all married each other—or someone Jewish from a nearby village. There were four or five with Jews. My father said he had been daring to marry a woman from so far away—sixty kilometers! But when my mother found a gravestone that might be her second cousin on her mother's side, I thought: not *so* daring!

We were next to a wire fence in the far end of the cemetery where the weeds were high. My mother had disappeared, so it was just my father and I among rows of tiny graves no higher than my kneecaps, their writing almost rubbed off.

We were among the children's graves, my father said, slipping on wet leaves, but catching himself as I reached for his hand. I wanted him standing, especially with my mother gone. Above me, I heard the warble of a single bird and shivered. My father pointed out a headstone carved like a tree trunk but with its limbs cut off. It meant the person died young, in the prime of life, he said, and I thought of my sister Hannah who died soon after they arrived in America—before I was born. I didn't know the details then—how their doctor, also a German refugee, didn't know about the new antibiotics on the market—only that the sweet face with green eyes who hung over my parents' bed was buried in New Jersey somewhere.

I was glad to move back among the larger stones, worn and substantial like adults. I saw one dated 1703. You could tell the older stones, my father said, because all the writing—what little was left—was in Hebrew. The newer gravestones were mostly in German because by 1900, Jews no longer had to pay extra taxes as Jews, so they had started to feel very German, as if they really belonged.

"Did all the Rindheim Jews move to New York?" I was thinking about how many came to our house in Queens and pinched my cheeks over the years.

"Many, yes," he lectured, "but some moved to Palestine as a group. Others went to Chicago, Paris, even Buenos Aires. . . ." We were now before a headstone carved with a broken flower, its stem snapped in two. He touched it. "And some stayed," he said quietly. "There were many, especially old people, who were like my *Tante* Rosa and thought no one would bother her. 'I'll be fine,' she kept saying. Later . . . we tried to send her money, but then. . . ." His voice trailed off.

"Is she buried here?"

He shook his head. "She was deported." I asked no more, for I knew what deported meant, had seen the pictures of Auschwitz in *Life* magazine. I'd always been relieved that my Dad was smart and had gotten the whole family out in time—except for this *Tante* Rosa. I imagined a handful of old people getting into a wagon, but no one I knew, so it didn't seem so bad.

The sun rays had faded, the forest turned gray and dank, and we were near the entrance again, standing before a large monument in black stone, with the inscription, "Erected to honor the victims of the persecution of the Jews—1933–1945." No individual names were listed, so I kept imagining only a handful of old people and walked on, stopping at a memorial that had a face: Joseph Zundorfer, his features carved in bronze above his name. He had been a Jewish fighter pilot in World War I with many medals. "Shot down," my father said, placing a stone on the grave, and I pictured a hero like Gregory Peck.

Eighty-seven Jews, not a handful, were deported from my father's village during 1941 and 1942, I found out forty years later. They died in the concentration camps of Lublin, Riga, Theresienstadt; but with no names engraved in stone and no faces to admire, they remained anonymous to me that day. What registered to an American teenager who lost no one she really knew was the sunlight on my family's graves, and how a thousand Jews, related to me, were buried, safe and secure for centuries in these high woods.

"In Rindheim, we didn't do such things!" suddenly carried more weight, giving me a history and legitimacy that would have made me not mind, as much, if my father continued to say that line. But he didn't. When we came home from that trip, he took up golf and played every weekend with American friends who never heard of Rindheim. Their world of congeniality became ours and I was expected to enter its promise. "Smile, smile! You are a lucky girl to be here!" is what I remember after that as my father's favorite line. His magical village of memory had disappeared among the graves that weren't there and the weightless souls with no stones of remembrance.

An E-Book Is Not a Book, In Which I Launch the Slow Book Movement

Tracy Seeley

So everyone's all a-twitter about e-books. And why not? As a species, we're like magpies, squawkily flocking from one over-hyped shiny new thing to the next. Gunpowder? Railroads? Lightbulb? Telegraph? Telephone? Airplanes? E-mail? Shiny! Marry the age of consumerism with the age of gadgets and the pace e-quickens. Every six months now, someone tosses a new shiny thing out there into the public square, and we're all over it like pigeons on popcorn. Ooh, ooh ipod, ilike, iphone, iwant, ipad, ineed, gimme that shiny new thing.

I'm not a saboteur, much. I Twitter, I FB, I LMAO at times. In fact, I was watching a video just the other day touting all the great things that an e-reader can do. Can't find the link, sorry. But its promises were great: a little red dot would follow my reading progress, and when I hit the word "bird," say, up would pop a little picture of the bird in the margin. Wow! Or if I might want to know what a word meant, I could just click a doo-hickey and up would pop the definition. Or a voice would tell me how to pronounce a word! I have to confess that for a moment I was nearly taken in.

But what if I wanted to just stare at the little bird picture for awhile before I even started to read the page? What if I wanted to flip through the pages to look at all the little pictures before I even started to read the book? And why should everything be so E-Z?

Ah, the pleasures to be found in looking up words in a, you know, "physical" dictionary. Sure, I can click on the little button, but if I look up, say, "relevant" in my Random House Webster's College, I get to not only look at the picture on the page anytime I like (which is a drawing of "relief"), but I get to visit the neighbors: "relentless," "reliable" and "relic." All of which seem relevant to this here blog post.

(On the very same page of my dictionary, I also find the word "relaxin," which I learn is a "polypeptide hormone" but which I also hope describes my afternoon plans.)

Which leads me to the pleasures of browsing. Say I walk in to a library looking for a book about water buffalo. Then say all that thinking about water buffalo makes me thirsty, so I start wandering around (under my own non-EZ steam), looking for water, and I take a short cut down a physical aisle filled with books, and what do you know, there's Balzac! Not having ever read Balzac, I take him home and fall in love with Eugenie Grandet. Who knew? Well, that's really the point, eh. The pleasures of serendipity.

The "pleasure" argument proffered in defense of old-fashioned books is often pooh-poohed. You may think, this woman is clearly over 50. You may roll your eyes. But here's what I'm thinking this morning. We live in our bodies and the sensory world is rich, why not revel in it? Why not celebrate the sensory pleasure of the book? Why not flock to the book as object, as something we take in not only with our eyes, but our hands and our noses—because who doesn't love the smell of paper and mustiness and bindings and glue? It's hard to get high on e-words.

Sure, the soul of a book is a bunch of words, so who cares what the "text delivery system" looks like? I do. I don't want just the soul of a book, I want its body. I want its body to rub up against other bodies on the shelf. I want to caress the spine and hold it in my hand while I'm reading at the beach. And ten years from now, or fifty, when fifty generations of e-readers are not decomposing in the landfill, I want to take that book down from my library shelf, and when the sand falls out from between the pages, that whole day will come rushing back. I will feel the sand on my wrinkled old skin, and I will smell the sea. And the sun and the sand and the memory of being young will all be tangled up with those papery pages, the story that they tell and the way that they feel in my hands.

So, I hereby launch the Slow Book Movement, to be rolled out in parts, since that is in keeping with slowness. It is not shiny, it is not new, it is decidedly old-ladyish. But it tastes better than e-books, it's more nutritious, and I got time.

Source: Seeley, Tracy. "An E-Book Is Not a Book, In Which I Launch the Slow Book Movement." *Tracy Seeley's Blog*, April 2, 2010. http://tracyseeley.wordpress.com/2010/04/02/an-e-book-is-not-a-book-in-which-i-launch-the-slow-book-movement/

Natural History, or What Happens When We're Not Looking

Sherry Simpson

It wasn't easy, clambering forty feet up this stony bluff of greenstone and slate for a better look across the water. Otter biologists call this kind of high, protected place an "altar." I feel something like a supplicant as I kneel in the moss to study the oddments strewn beneath a twisted young hemlock. A half-dozen sea urchins lie cracked into green and lavender hollows. The shells of blue bay mussels scatter in pearly constellations, and chalky steamer clams rest in the moss like weathered bones. A few drops of rainwater pool in lustrous curves that once cupped briny, living flesh. The water spills across my hands as I turn the shells over, fingering their coolness.

Once it would have puzzled me to find these shells washed up at the foot of trees, so high above the tideline. Now I recognize the leavings of otters, who scampered up the bluff more effortlessly than I. They search out high reaches to eat what they've gathered along the shore: chitons, mussels, octopi, herring, urchins, fish, crabs. Despite the meal's marine character, these are not the sea otters of Southeast Alaska's outer, wilder coast, but river otters. Sometimes people call them land otters, the ambiguity of the name reflecting the way they forage at sea and along rivers, lakes, and coastlines, but den, sleep and give birth in the forest. Few animals are so fluent in the ways of both water and earth.

I struggle out of my daypack and lean against a rock to see what I can see. Bridget Cove puckers the coast forty miles north of Juneau in a rumple of rocky beaches and shoals. Mab Island floats a few hundred yards away, a forested buoy that shields the cove from northerly winds funneled through Lynn Canal. The water gathers rare July sunlight and tosses it about frivolously, like small change. High tide brims against the shoreline. Maybe I'll get lucky. Maybe an otter will come along.

It pleases me how easily I can name what I see. I learned something about otters from Richard Carstensen, a naturalist who observes the world with the devotion of a monk and the acuity of a scientist. Richard is the kind of person who each March writes down the exact date that varied thrushes return to his part of the forest. He can fit together Lilliputian bones of a meadow vole teased from an owl casting, or draw in fine, stippled detail the sassiness of a red squirrel or the wingstroke of a Canada goose in flight. Every scrap of information, every act of attention, weights his ideas about forest succession, glacial uplift, ecosystems.

"We're not just tracking otters, or voles, or bears," Richard likes to say. "We're tracking something larger." He calls it natural history, but I'd call it what happens when we're not looking, the way the world shapes and scars and rearranges itself, leaving behind the spoor of glaciers, rain forests, otters.

No tracks brand this high point, but the duff doesn't lend itself to the footprints of otters. I'd know them if I saw them. One misty spring morning, Richard led me and other tracking novices along the banks of Eagle River, thirty miles northwest of Juneau. We knelt to study five-toed otter tracks pressed into glacial silt so clearly we could distinguish claw points and even webbing between the hind toes. Three inches or so across the tread, an otter's prints spread large enough to be mistaken for a dog's. A dog has four toes, though, and usually lacks the sense of purpose revealed in the direct course of an otter.

By learning to read tracks, to name what I see, I understood for the first time the way every living thing somehow inscribes its passage through the world. All we need do is look for the markings, decipher the signs. Now when I tramp through the tidal meadows near Eagle River, whose glacial waters spill into a delta thirty miles northwest of Juneau, I search along salt marshes and riverbanks for clues. Sometimes the grass reveals where otters have wrestled beach rye into secret beds to mark their territories. Along a grassy dike, rain dissipates otter scat dense with thready fish bones and the rosy splinters of tiny shells, and I crouch to sniff the pungent odor so I will recognize the territory of otters. I peer into shadows eddying below spruce trees, looking for dens hollowed among the roots. Beside sloughs I inspect mud for skidmarks that show where otters slip into the water.

Once, near Eagle River, a friend spied on a family of five otters frisking on a slide. She described the way they skidded down the muddy chute, splashed into the slough and then romped back up the bank, over and over. It was as if a magician had parted the curtains for a few moments to reveal backstage sorcery usually unwitnessed. My friend's account of the otters' unselfconscious play fills me with envy and longing. I have walked and walked along those banks, hoping my steps would somehow pay the price of admission to such a sight. The search leaves me kneeling in the rain poking at bones, or stooping low to the ground as I follow tracks, hoping to look up and see the animal pausing to look back at me.

I suppose that by looking for otters, learning to name otters, I am trying to name the world, to organize what I see into a sensual glossary of the life that surrounds us. Porcupine, beaver, marten, and bear: I recognize the eccentricities of their prints. I can distinguish a hermit thrush from a varied thrush by sight and by sound. From afar I know the difference between a sea lion and a harbor seal by the shape of their heads, their motion through waves. Paging through pictures and descriptions in field guides to birds and flowers, mushrooms and mammals, I try to divine a deeper meaning from names both English and Latin, echoes of my forgotten Catholicism. *Corvus corax*, I murmur at the derisive croak of a raven. *Strongylocentrotus droebachiensis*, I sound out, wondering how the name of a green sea urchin can stretch longer than its spines. I intone scientific nomenclature as if reciting fragments of lost poems: *Nereocystis luetkeana*. Bull kelp. *Ursus arctos horribilis*. Brown bear. *Lutra canadensis*. River otter. Say it again, like an incantation: *Lutra canadensis*.

Names are the tracks people leave, autographing the world as we go along, practicing Adam's original trade. We name and name, believing that once we name something, we know it, we own it. It is a comforting act. Early explorers to Alaska often called strange marine creatures they encountered by the common names of animals already known to them. Perhaps they craved some familiar hold on a landscape that must have overwhelmed them. So the sea otter was known to Vitus Bering's 1741 expedition to Alaska as "sea beaver." Sailors knew the fur seal as a "sea cat" by its long, feline whiskers. Russian hunters called the gentle northern manatee a "sea cow" and ate them into extinction within a quarter century. Georg Steller himself, the first Western naturalist on these shores, lent his name to the sea cow, the sea lion, and the brilliant blue jay that stays the winter. A mysterious creature he glimpsed in the Gulf of Alaska he called a "sea ape." Each creature was likened to some unrelated animal rather than being named for its own remarkable self.

I am no different. I take refuge against the heave and tangle of life by classifying, ordering, sorting out the world and its belongings. Not content to simply admire the pink blush of a certain flower that grows in the shade of a giant Sitka spruce, I hunt through a wildflower guide, comparing photographs, reading descriptions, finally discovering what I believe to be its "true" name: *Calypso bulbosa*. Calypso orchid. And yet, when I look from the picture back to the flower, the bloom trembles slightly in the breeze, not any truer than it was a moment before, nor any pinker, nor any lovelier.

Name all you want, and see where it gets you. What can names reveal of the world? They say nothing of the raven's glottal stops, the urchin's slow creep through life, the supple way bull kelp travels with the tide, the bend of rye grass before a southeasterly. Naming is a way to assemble the realm before you, the way Richard Carstensen can reconstruct the splintered scaffolding of a vole.

Still the name is not the thing, just as a five-toed track etched in wet sand is not an otter. A name, though useful, cannot draw the world any closer, nor make it any dearer. A name, in fact, can veil the purity of sight so delicately that you never notice that you do not see. A sea lion is no lion at all. A brown bear is not horrible. And Georg Steller walked but a single day on an island drifting off this continent before sailing back across the cold Bering Sea, leaving only his name behind.

So I look for otters. I walk along the sloughs, climb altars, wait by the shore for the world to reveal itself. It happens suddenly, like this:

On a sunny morning, as I sat on a damp rock just above the high tide line, an otter slid ashore a hundred feet away, a small flounder clamped in its mouth. I stilled myself. The otter gulped the fish in a few swallows, using clever paws to cram in the white flesh. Somehow the act of eating, the most ordinary and necessary event of life, became something miraculous because I was witnessing a creature completely at ease in its world, a world perceptible only for a moment. The otter slipped back into the bay, and I leapt up and scrabbled across seaweed-covered rocks to the water's edge. It glided past me just below the surface, a shadow that did not even dimple the membrane separating this world from that. So smoothly, so elegantly, did the animal swim that it seemed an idea given shape and purpose by the sea itself.

Decades ago, the Tlingits left a dead shaman in a gravehouse not far from where I saw the otter. George Thornton Emmons, a nineteenth-century friend of Tlingits, wrote that they considered the river otter most powerful of all animal spirits, and essential to the shaman's strength. A man who would become a shaman entered the forest and fasted for days or weeks, chewing only the bitter bark of devil's club. When an otter appeared to the novice, he killed the animal by shouting a certain sound four times, in four different notes. Then he cut out the otter's tongue, wrapped the sliver of flesh in a bundle of twigs, and wore the amulet around his neck so that it dangled over his breast.

I cannot expect to know the true names of animals, or how to call them to me, or the proper way to carry their tongues near my heart. What I really want—others confess this longing, too—is for the land to possess me, to name me. Thus the compulsion to recite all the names inscribed in all the books, even though the world does not require me to unscroll the register of names, to labor at Adam's task, to trace the handwriting scrawled across the universe. But I try to remember something related by Richard Carstensen, a man who can name, a man who knows much more than names. He once paraphrased an observation by Northrop Frye: "People spend a lot of time trying to figure out who they are. The real question is not who am I, but where is here?" And so I answer:

Here is a summer day on an uninhabited cove washed by an ocean perpetually arriving from somewhere else. Forty feet above the beach, on a stone shelf rimmed by rainforest, a woman touches the cracked shells of creatures that once lived within the clock of tides. Some sleek, dark animal carried them up this plateau, far above the pull of water, and pried them open to gulp the cool, living flesh. You can call this place an altar. You can name the shells. It does not matter to the woman. She lies against the green mat of living moss and closes her eyes. The sun circumnavigates the sky and the ocean sucks mildly at the shore and a gleaming black bird swoops low over the promontory, taking a better look at the world naming itself.

Chin Music

Michael Steinberg

I was wrapping up a discussion of *Huck Finn*, and as I began to recite the assignments, my students were already shuffling their feet, packing up books, and grabbing for their coats—the usual cues that it's time for the teacher to quit talking. In the past, I'd often take the hint and end the hour quickly. But lately, I noticed, I'd become less and less patient.

I paused for a second to look at my notes. That's when I spotted Drew—a student I'd already targeted as a trouble maker—moving toward the door. Just as he was about to open it, I said in a tone that was sharper than intended. "Excuse me, but class isn't over yet."

"I thought you were done," he said. Then he murmured under his breath, "You've been lecturing at us for over an hour." Whether it was deliberate or not, he said it loud enough for everyone to hear.

I knew I should let it go, or make light of it somehow. But before I could catch myself, it slipped out. "Drew, you're a fucking piss ant," I said. "Sit your god damned ass down 'til I dismiss the class."

Everyone, including me, was stunned. His eyes blazing, Drew shuffled back to his seat, deliberately kicking the trash can on his way. "Keep it up, pal," I whispered to myself. His coat buttoned to the throat, Drew sat down very slowly and turned his head toward the window.

This wasn't the first time we'd done this little dance. In the first week of the semester, Drew had written an exercise that I liked so much I read it to the class. When I praised the authenticity of the writing, he intervened. "None of that crap was true," he said. "I made the whole thing up."

Students had challenged me before, but never quite this aggressively, and certainly not without some provocation. So, I approached this kid a little more cautiously than I normally do.

"Why did you make it up?" I asked, making certain to keep my tone as neutral as possible.

"Because it was such a Mickey Mouse assignment," he said. So much for being tactful, I thought.

There were some "oohs," followed by a round of nervous giggles. I wanted to lash back, say something nasty or sarcastic. But instead, I took the high ground again. "Fiction or nonfiction," I said, "it's still a good piece of writing." And I left it at that.

Not so tonight, though. Visibly flustered, I stumbled through the litany of assignments. And when the class had filed out, I called Drew up to my desk.

"Look, Drew," I began. "I think you should know why I said wha . . .".

He cut me off in mid-sentence. "You showed me up in front of the whole class," he said. "You owe me an apology."

Then he waited a few seconds while I searched for a reply. Did this kid really believe that he'd done nothing wrong? Just as I was about to respond, he pivoted and headed for the door.

By the time I got home, I was furious—at him, of course—and at myself, for taking the bait. I took a walk around the block to try and calm down. But all I could think about was the anger and resentment that had been building inside me for such a long time.

Even before the eye surgeries, my patience with freshmen was wearing thin. When students said goofy things like "This sucks. Why can't we read happier books?" my comments were becoming more defensive. I even tossed a few guys out of class when they showed up unprepared or without books. Also a first for me.

The eye surgeries had given me a chance to step back from teaching for almost two years. Sometimes an enforced absence is just what you need to reinvigorate yourself. But when I got back in the classroom, I could see right away that things had changed.

Or maybe it was me who'd changed. By mid-semester, I felt like a space invader in my own classroom. Some of my freshmen glided mindlessly into class on skateboards or roller blades. Some wore headphones and others ate snacks and drank soda while I talked. A few even had the chutzpah to take calls on their cell phones.

Conditions outside of class had also changed. For one, I was receiving frequent reports from the counseling center, bureaucratic memos informing me about students who were in alcohol or drug rehab, or who had eating disorders and histories of family abuse. And then there was the student who sent me an email apologizing for not doing her essay on time. She said, without a trace of irony, that she missed the deadline because she'd attempted suicide that weekend. She hoped I'd understand and that I'd give her an extension. Coupled with the effects of over two decades of student papers, mind-numbing faculty meetings, and obligatory committee work, this latest confrontation left me wondering if maybe it wasn't time to move on.

The next day, I was having lunch with a colleague from the Physiology department—someone who I meet with regularly to talk about teaching. She was telling me about two of her colleagues, one of whom she referred to as "an educator," and the other whom she called "a coach."

The word "coach" hit a nerve, and for a moment I drifted away from the conversation. In a sudden flashback, I saw myself at fifteen, standing next to Tom Sullivan, my old V.F.W. baseball coach. My God, I hadn't thought about this guy in almost forty years. Why now?

Just before I fell asleep that night, it all came rushing back. In my second year on Sullivan's team, I'd had a run-in with him, a skirmish that made me think seriously about quitting the game. A game I loved more than anything else in my adolescent world.

The episode came about on a bone-chilling Saturday morning in early March. It was the last day of tryouts and we were down to the final cut. I was on the mound and my best friend, Mike Rubin, was at bat. Last year we'd both made it to the final tryouts. But for some reason, Sullivan cut Rubin and kept me.

I only got to pitch in a few games that summer, so I was apprehensive when right before this year's tryouts began, Sullivan called me into his office. The room was a steam-heated cubbyhole above the St. Francis De Sales gym. Amidst the banging and hissing of the old pipes he told me in no uncertain terms that if I wanted to pitch this season I'd have to convince him that a Belle Harbor "sugar baby" had what it took to play ball for him.

And now, here I was on the mound of the church field staring down at Mike Rubin, who stood sixty feet six inches away nervously taking his practice cuts. Last year's team almost made it to the state finals at Cooperstown. We got eliminated in Westchester County—the final game of the regionals. I'd been thinking about it all winter, and I didn't want to blow my shot at playing summer league ball. But what about Mike? Since we were eight years old, we'd played on every team from Little League through P.A.L. This was his last chance to make the V.F.W. team. Next year we'd move up to American Legion, a tougher, more competitive league.

I knew Rubin couldn't hit the curve ball. If I threw him low breaking balls, my stock-in-trade, he was finished. Kaput. But if I pitched him too fat, Big Tom would know it. Then I'd be history too. While I was trying to figure out what to throw, Sullivan yelled, "Game situation," and ordered Andy Ortiz to be the runner at third. This was not a good sign. Ortiz was a football player from the Arverne projects. And he could hurt you. That's when Sullivan called for a suicide squeeze. It's a risky play, and it's meant to work like this: as soon as I go into my wind-up, Ortiz will head for home and Rubin will square around to bunt. My job is to make certain he doesn't bunt the ball in fair territory.

Instead of tossing me the ball, Sullivan swaggered out to the mound. As he slapped the grass-stained baseball into my glove, he deliberately sprayed black, bitter tobacco juice across the bridge of my nose. Then he motioned Danny Whalen, another football goon, to the mound.

Sullivan and I were inches apart. I could feel his breath on my right cheek. His nose was red and swollen, and slanted to the right. Broken three times in his college football days. Just as Whalen arrived, Coach rasped, "Steinberg, when Ortiz breaks from third, throw it at his head."

He meant the batter, Rubin. Why would I want to throw a baseball at my best friend's head? It wasn't the right strategy. It was another one of Big Tom's stupid tests of courage. I knew that sooner or later he'd be testing me. I just hadn't expected it to happen now.

"At his head, Coach?" I said, stalling for time.

Sullivan gave me his "that's-the-way-it's-done-around-here" look. It wasn't like I didn't know what he was doing. Everyone on the team understood that if you wanted to play ball for Big Tom you did what you were told and you kept your mouth shut. Why was I being such a smart-ass? It wasn't like me. Why was I so willing to risk it all here?

I tried to calm myself down, remind myself what the costs were. I kept telling myself to cool it. Just try and think it through. Pretend to go along with Big Tom's program. The whole time, though, I could feel the knot in my stomach twist and tighten.

Sullivan glared at the third base bleachers where the final eight guys fidgeted nervously, waiting for their chance to bat. Then he looked back at me. With his cap pulled low, the coach's steel-blue pig eyes seemed all the more penetrating. He smiled, but because part of his mouth was distorted from taking too many football hits without a face mask, it came off looking like a mocking leer. The gesture unnerved me even more. I could feel my palms getting clammy and my armpits were drenched with perspiration.

He said loudly for everyone to hear, "Steinberg, you've been with me for two years; let's show this wet-nosed bunch of rookies how we play this game."

Then he grabbed his crotch with his left hand. It was the old comrade routine. He was giving his second-year pitcher a chance to look like a leader by pretending we were buddies. But we weren't. Big Tom and I didn't operate in the same universe. He was a bull-yock Irishman from Hell's Kitchen, a high school stud who learned to fight in the streets. His platoon had fought in the Pacific, and the pride still showed in his eyes. To him, guys like Rubin and me were too privileged. And he resented us for it.

I turned to glance at Rubin. He looked like a Thanksgiving turkey on the block. I was embarrassed for him. Maybe the wind was just blowing at his sweatpants, the stiff ocean breeze we get on the Long Island south shore in early spring. Then again, maybe his knees really were shaking.

"Let's get the god-damned show on the road," Sullivan muttered. I thought about quitting, but our team was good. I had visions of Linda Foreman, our head cheerleader, walking around school wearing my V.F.W. jacket. And there was another incentive. We all knew that our high school coach, Jack Kerchman, scouted his players in the summer—looking to see who was getting better and who was dogging it.

Whalen trotted back behind the plate and Sullivan turned to leave. To him this kind of stuff was routine. I wanted to refuse, but this was my only chance to make it to Cooperstown, to see my dad sitting in the stands watching me pitch at Doubleday Field. I was red-in-the-face pissed, hoping it looked like windburn.

I tried to buy some time, hoping I could reason with Sullivan. Convince him there was another way to do this.

"You want me to stop the bunt, right?" I said meekly.

He turned. What the hell was I saying? Nobody second-guesses the Coach. Sullivan walked back to the mound and spat another wad of chew on the ground, making sure to splatter some on my new spikes. He looked at Whalen, then at Ortiz. Then he turned to me and shook his head from side to side.

"That's right, Steinberg. You stop the bunt. Now, let's please execute the fucking play, shall we?" He muttered to himself through clenched teeth as he trotted back toward the dugout.

It was out of my mouth before I knew it. "Suppose I hit him in the head?" Sullivan's own head swung around like a tetherball making the last tight twist at the top of the pole.

"Don't worry, it's not a vital organ. Pitch."

I think Big Tom knew that he was undermining his credibility by arguing with a piss-ant kid. So he turned and silenced everyone's murmurs with a long glare. As if rehearsed, the eight guys behind me started to grumble, distancing themselves from me and Sullivan's wrath.

"Pitch the fuckin' ball," yelled Whalen from behind the plate.

"Do what Coach tell you, man," spat Ortiz from third.

To those guys, Sullivan was George God. If he told them to take a dump at home plate, they'd get diarrhea. But me? I'm Gary Cooper in *High Noon*. Everyone's watching, no one's volunteering to help.

Then I noticed Mike Rubin, still frozen in his batter's crouch. He looked like a mannequin with bulging eyes. Poor Mike didn't have a prayer. But before I could think, the words slipped out.

"It's the wrong play, Coach."

It was my voice, all right, but it couldn't have been me who said it. I'd never have the guts to say anything like that to Sullivan's face.

Dead silence. You could hear the breeze whistling through the wire mesh of the backstop. At first, Sullivan was too surprised to even curse me out. But after a long moment, he turned and strode up to Rubin, who was still frozen in the box.

It was a considered ploy. I'd seen it before, in the streets. Coach was going to punish me by humiliating my best friend. Like all of us, Rubin was jack-rabbit scared of Sullivan. And just like a rabbit about to be prey, he stood riveted to the ground.

"God damn it," Sullivan ripped off his cap, exposing a jet black crewcut and sunburned forehead. He spoke like rolling thunder, enunciating every word.

"WHAT DID HE SAY, RUBIN?"

My stomach turned over watching Sullivan humiliate my best friend just for the amusement of the guys in the bleachers. And Big Tom knew it. Knew it oh so well.

Rubin managed weakly; "Uh, wrong—wrong play, Coach?"

Louder then, like a Marine D.I.: "NOBODY IN THE STANDS CAN HEAR YOU, RUBIN."

"WRONG PLAY, COACH."

Still advancing, Sullivan took it to the grandstand.

"ALL YOU LADIES, SAY IT!"

The accusing chorus rained down.

"WRONG PLAY, COACH."

"AGAIN."

"WRONG PLAY, COACH."

Then he ran out to the mound yelling, "YOU TOO, STEINBERG, YOU SAY IT."

He was hopping up and down like someone had pranked him with a hot foot. Adrenaline overcame me then, and before Sullivan could order another round, I let the words tumble out in a single breath. "If I throw a pitch-out chest high in the left hand batter's box all Danny has to do is take two steps to his right and he has a clear shot at Ortiz." I was parroting what Joe Bleutrich, my P.A.L. coach, had taught me two years ago.

By now, my stomach was in knots, Rubin's eyes looked like marbles, and the whole team was hungry to see what would happen next. Sullivan squared himself and casually put his cap back on. He was trying to regain his composure. He'd let a snot-nosed high school kid get to him and now he had to regain control.

Softly now: "That's enough, Steinberg."

Then to Rubin: "Get back in the box. Let's do the play."

And to be sure there was no misunderstanding, he took it right back to me: "My play," he said deliberately. "My play, my way."

He was giving me a second chance. Why didn't I just fake it? I had good control. I'd brushed off plenty of hitters before. Maybe deep down I believed that Sullivan was right about me. Maybe I didn't have what it took to play for him.

I wanted to give in, get it over with. So I said, "I can't do it."

Sullivan slammed his cap to the ground, and in one honest, reckless moment, it came out:

"You Belle Harbor Jews are all alike. No god-damn guts. You're a disgrace to your own people."

Nobody moved. The wind whipped a funnel of dust through the hard clay infield.

So that's what this was all about. Some of the guys, I'm sure, had thought the same thing. But we were teammates and they'd never say it to my face. We all knew that Big Tom didn't favor Jews. But even in my worst moments I believed that this stuff was for the anti-Semites from the sticks, the ones who say "Jew York."

There was no chance Sullivan would apologize. He'd used tactics like this before—to get us mad, to fire us up. If I wanted to be a real putz, I could report him to the league's advisory board. My dad knew most of the officers. But I knew I wouldn't do it. Because if I turned him in, it would confirm what he already thought of me. And I didn't want to give him the satisfaction. Besides, I needed him. And in some odd way, I must have sensed that he needed me. Why else would he be testing me like this? For the moment we were yoked to each other, like Sidney Poitier and Tony Curtis in that movie *The Defiant Ones*.

I think Sullivan believed that somehow I had made him say what he said. He was angry at me for making him look bad. So to cover himself he had to make it seem like it was my fault.

"Get out of my sight, Steinberg," he snapped. "You make me wanna puke."

He motioned toward the bullpen. "Levy, get your butt in here and pitch."

Why Levy? Bert was also a Belle Harbor Jew. And to my mind, he was more timid than anyone else in the neighborhood. On second thought, maybe that was part of Big Tom's design.

Sullivan grunted, the cords of his muscular neck wound tight. He reached to take the ball. Just as he grabbed for it, something snapped inside me; I snatched the baseball back. Then an eerie calm began to wash over me. My stomach stopped churning, my chest didn't feel as if it was about to burst, and my neck wasn't burning. I could tell that Sullivan sensed something was going on, but he wasn't sure what it was. Neither was I. Not yet, anyway.

"I'm not leaving, Coach," I said.

Yeah, he sensed it all right. But he misread it. He waved Levy away. Maybe this was Sullivan's obtuse way of atoning for the Jew remark, by allowing me to stay on *his* pitcher's mound.

"Get back in the box, Rubin," he snapped.

"No, Coach," I said.

"What?"

"You grab a bat, Coach."

A frozen moment. Was I really doing this? I recalled the day at football practice when Stuie Scheneider had knocked Coach Kerchman right on his ass. Kerchman goaded him into it, and Stuie took the bait. Is this what was happening here?

Sullivan looked at me, then he looked at the guys in the bleachers and laughed out loud. We all knew he was going to do it. He ripped off his windbreaker and took a couple of practice cuts, biceps rippling. Sullivan didn't seem to mind when muffled cheers rose up from the third base side. He was wearing that crooked-ass grin of his. The players in the bleachers spilled into foul territory, inching closer to the backstop.

"Okay, Coach," I'm thinking. "You're gonna get just what you asked for."

I was ready to play me some chin music. Chin music, where the ball whistles as it passes under the batter's throat. Before I went into my windup, Whalen took two steps up the first base line. He was sure I was going to throw the pitch-out.

Can't blame him. It's what he would have done. It's what anyone in his right mind would have done. Sullivan must have thought so too, that's why he was grinning.

It was the smirk that did it. "Screw chin music, I'll take his goddamn head off."

Then I saw Ortiz streaking from third toward home. In that split second I realized, maybe for the first time, that this really was happening. As Big Tom squared to bunt, I zeroed in on the black line that runs along the inside corner of the plate. "Calm down," I told myself. "Brush him back. Just let him know you're here."

That's what my head was saying, but when I started my motion I lifted my eyes away from the plate and locked them on the bill of Sullivan's cap. Then I pushed hard off the rubber and cut loose. I watched the ball tailing in, in, in, right toward Sullivan's head. But he didn't back off, not even an inch. That shit-eating grin was still on his face. I yelled, "HEADS UP," tucked my chin into my chest and shut my eyes. Then I heard a dull thud. I opened my eyes and watched his cap fly off his head. And as I saw him crumble, feet splayed in the dirt, I felt nauseous.

Stunned players surrounded the fallen Sullivan, not knowing what to do. With leaden strides, I joined them, growing a little more lucid. Rubin shot me a "Man, you are dead meat" look, and I thought about suspension from school. Jail even. But the coach sat up. Jesus, was he lucky. Was I lucky. I must have clipped him right on the bill of the cap. Why was I so surprised? It was the target I was aiming at.

Sighs escaped as one breath. Legs and arms unraveled. Players backed away. Slowly, Big Tom lifted himself up and brushed the dirt off the seat of his pants. He shook his head like a wet cocker spaniel who'd just taken a dip in the ocean. Then he wobbled to the bleachers, looking like a young girl testing out her mother's high-heeled shoes.

Before I could collect my thoughts, Sullivan's voice boomed out: "All right, here we go again. Ortiz, hustle back to third, Rubin, up to bat, Steinberg, get your butt back on the hill. Suicide squeeze, same play as before. This time I know we will get it right, won't we, ladies?"

He'd caught me by surprise again. I should have known that he'd have the last word. But this time I couldn't—wouldn't—jump through his hoops again. So, I took a deep breath, bowed my head, and slowly walked toward the mound—all the time knowing exactly where I was headed. When I got to the rubber, I kept going. At second base, I pushed off the bag with my right foot and began to sprint. I began unbuttoning my shirt, and as I passed our center fielder, Ducky Warshauer, I tossed my cap and uniform jersey right at him. Ducky stared at me like I'd just gone Section Eight. When I stepped onto the walkway outside the locker room, I heard the metallic clack, clack, clack of my spikes on the concrete floor. I opened the door and inhaled the familiar perfume of chlorine, Oil of Wintergreen, and stale sweat socks. For a moment I thought about going back out there; instead I headed straight for the shower and pushed the lever as far to the right as it would go. As the needle spray bit into my shoulders, I watched the steam rise up to surround me.

On the bus ride home, I was thinking about what I'd just done. I did it, I told myself, because he provoked me. It wasn't a conscious decision; it was a knee-jerk response.

All weekend, I thought about the incident. Should I take what was left of my uniform to his office right before the next practice? Nope, all that would do is let him know he'd won. Ok, I'll wait for him to ask for it. But what if he doesn't? Will I lose my nerve and give in?

Sunday night, seven-thirty, he called me at home. Ten minutes later I was back in that stifling office, the steam pipes hissing and banging away. Sullivan was sitting at his desk, head down, shuffling papers. He made me wait for about two minutes. Didn't even look up. When he knew I couldn't take the tension any longer, he said matter-of-factly—as if nothing had ever happened—"I'll see you at practice on Saturday."

Without taking his eyes off his papers, he handed me my cap and jersey and said, "Get your butt out of here, kid. I got work to do."

Of course I went back. That's what you do when you're fifteen and your identity is wrapped up in playing baseball. I had a pretty good season too. And though we didn't win the state title, we did make it to Cooperstown.

While I was on the mound that summer I'd hear Sullivan razzing us from the bench. I always listened closely, curious to see how far he'd push me. But whatever else he yelled, I never heard him shout "sugar baby." And I later found out that Sullivan did indeed invite Coach Kerchman to scout me. He just never took the trouble to tell me about it.

The "incident" happened over four decades ago, and I still couldn't decide whether I won or lost that confrontation. Sometimes I think I got the best of him, and sometimes I think I misread him—that he deliberately goaded me into throwing the ball at his head.

But wondering who won or lost, I told myself, is really to miss the point. Like me, Sullivan was in his early fifties when this happened. Could it be that now in my fifties, I was turning into a version of my old coach?

In the past few years, I noticed that many of my colleagues had turned cynical in the latter stages of their careers. But they stayed on anyway—out of a kind of inertia or fear, perhaps. Or because they needed to put more time in before they could take their benefits or pensions. It was certainly not the way I wanted to end my teaching career.

When I first began to teach, I promised myself I'd never use fear or intimidation to motivate or punish my students. And for the most part, I'd kept that promise. But in the past decade, I'd noticed that there were more and more students like Drew, who, for one reason or another, could push my hot buttons. They could provoke me in the same way that Sullivan had done four decades ago. And the impulsive severity of my retaliation surprised me as much now as it did then. Having crossed that line with Drew, I wanted to make sure it didn't happen again.

The first order of business was to talk privately with him. Yes, he was a mean-spirited kid. But he was also one of the best writers in the class. And despite our run-in, or maybe even because of it, I knew he would expect a high grade—probably a 4.0. I also knew that if he didn't get it, it was within his rights to file a grievance against me.

You walk a fine line with students like that. You don't want to let their insolence pass. Nor do you want to reward them for it. I thought again about the incident with Sullivan. As bigoted as Big Tom was, and as much as I hold him responsible for the Jew remark, I was still the one that hit him in the head with a baseball. And he was the one that put me back on the team. In his own misguided way then, Sullivan had allowed us both to save face and move on. It wasn't pretty, but it was precisely the outcome I wanted to affect with my belligerent student.

Three days later, I called Drew into my office and calmly explained my side of the story—including the earlier scenario that had triggered my outburst. I waited for him to respond, and when it was clear that he was going to hold his ground, I simply apologized.

Naturally, I was disappointed. But, there were two more issues left to resolve. The next night, I apologized to the class for what I'd said to Drew. But I made it clear that I didn't condone or approve of what either of us had done.

For the final month of the semester, Drew and I did not bait one another again. Nor did I single his work out for praise or censure. As if nothing had ever happened, he continued to write with the same insight and imagination—and defiance—as he had before. And when it came time to give the final grade, it was a 3.5, not the 4.0 I knew he was expecting.

Two weeks after the spring semester ended, I applied for early retirement.

Everything But Your Wits

Joni Tevis

"And I followed her to the station / with a suitcase in my hand."

"Love in Vain," Robert Johnson, 1938

Station

The pump brays as someone works the enameled handle, a grip heavy and cool, marked with duller places from the oils of many palms. Then water stutters from the iron spout, and travelers step forward, canteens in hand. Children squeal as the cold water splashes them. Water puddles on the concrete.

Imagine a place filled with waiting people. They stitch patches to frayed pant legs, swap stories, smear lard on cracked sandals. Every now and then, a latecomer steps onstage and attaches to a group. Over there is someone stretched full length on the sand (or bench, or low-pile patterned carpet), catching a few winks. Gather your strength while you can.

So: the singing pump, the low hum of conversation, light snoring, dripping water. And a clicking, as from shuffling a stiff deck of cards, emanating from a large ebony *Departures* sign. It hangs in a conspicuous place, and the travelers glance up at it before turning back to their different tasks. Occasionally, after such a glance, a group jumps to its feet, collecting its knapsacks and bedrolls, and rushes off to some platform or trailhead. The purring click of the sign fires the travelers' blood. Bikers bound for the mountains pass around a tire pump, a roll of red grip tape. The travelers jig with excitement. Then a whistle blows, and they hurry to their respective gates.

Gate/Platform I: Matamoros, Mexico

I dropped my quarter in the slot, and the turnstile gears clicked. A man launched himself toward me, saying *what is it you want, I help you*. I kept my eyes down. Under a warped ramada, a man played an upright bass with dark strings worn down, in places, to nylon white as a finger bone. Behind a plate glass window, meat roasted over glowing charcoal, the animal splayed on a rod, legs spread wide, muscles dry and purple red, revealing the twin ditches of its rib cage.

Then she appeared, a natural on high heels, pulled through the crowd by her father. It was her *quinceanera*, and the hem of her lavender gown flounced around her nylon-covered ankles. Dark curls, shiny with pomade, clung stiffly to her smooth temples. If that's what it was to be queen for a day, it wasn't anything she hadn't practiced, nothing she was scared of. So what if she was late for the party? They couldn't start without her.

Border-town girl, fifteen that long-ago day in July, I remember your poise, the flame your eyes held. Let men hurry; time is not your master. You vanished around the corner, past the taxi stand, but when I close my eyes I see you.

Gate/Platform 2: Tucson

The car seemed to come out of nowhere, a black Nova, glass packs so loud we suddenly had to shout. Once it roared past, four things in quick succession: I felt a sudden, sharp pain; the boys in the Nova shouted something out the window; an egg, stone hard, bounced off my side; it smashed on the sidewalk. Then the Nova was gone, blasting off into the night, taillights streaming red. Yolk smeared the concrete yellow. I thought: at least it wasn't a rock, at least it wasn't a bullet. The purple bruise below my rib cage faded to green, then yellow, and after ten days was gone.

Gate/Platform 3: Murrell's Inlet, South Carolina

She might have been thirteen, the girl on the bicycle, pedaling up and down Schooner Court all day long. Heavy, her hair in a lank ponytail, she kept her head down over the handlebars, and her blue shorts were dark with sweat. In mid-July, a mile from the beach—where those looking to economize stay— there's not much of a breeze. The early morning air is like a damp towel, and by noon, people who aren't used to the heat have a hard time catching their breath. In the evening the mosquitoes whine, the air smells like gunpowder from the fireworks, and little frogs make regular, taut calls, like car alarms. All that long day, the tires of her red bike hissed on the asphalt. No breeze rattled the palmetto fronds; the marsh air was thick enough to spoon, like custard. What did she think about, the girl on the bicycle? Once I think she saw me, sitting on the porch with a sweating drink in my hand, watching her. She just kept going, and as the sky got dark and the streetlights flickered on, I caught a snatch of the song she whistled: "Embraceable You."

Gate/Platform 4: Siracusa, Sicily

Their aim was very bad; the slanting rain got in their way, and the chain-link fence. But they were determined and resourceful, focused as children can be. One found a stone; the others slung mud. The women, tending braziers of coals that smoked in the rain, ignored them. I had passed their camp on my way to a fountain in Siracusa where, according to legend, you can drop a flower and later it'll surface in Greece. But when I found the fountain I'd forgotten to buy a flower; my heart wasn't in it. I leaned over the pool's edge and looked at the rain-dimpled water. Everything was gray, the stones lining the well, the streets, the old palazzi turned into storefronts selling gloves and copper cookware. I took a different way back to the train station; someone in the street showed me how. I'm sure those children—adults by now—forgot me by the time the sun set. What did I look like to them, a dripping girl with a backpack and a broken umbrella? They hated me; their eyes burned with it.

Gate/Platform 5: Main Street

Savor the melancholy that comes from driving through a strange town after dark. It doesn't even have to be late; once the stores have shut down for the day, their display windows burn like stage sets under fluorescent lights. Notice the hardware store with cans of paint in its window, an assortment of beveled mirrors, canning jars. Signs read *We Sharpen Everything But Your Wits: Carbide Blades, Skates. Glass Cut. Custom Framing Available*. Pause there until the traffic light changes, then touch the gas. You don't belong here. By the time the workday starts again, you'll be long gone.

Gate/Platform 6: Terlingua, Texas

No shade nor scrap of green as far as the eye could see, and the sun bore down like a hammerhead. Rusty barbed wire edged the old graveyard. I walked slowly down the rows, sweating and reading the faded names, thinking of the well-watered city cemetery where I worked once, its green grounds studded with granite monuments polished to glass and gracefully lettered. Nothing like that here. The mourners' own hands had painted the names on the wooden monuments, piled stones at head and foot, smeared mortar between bricks. They filled the altars they had built with silk flowers, bottles of beer, and votives, spent now, tufts of blackened wicks at their bottoms. They must have dug the very graves, and what would that take in country like this? A whole day of swinging a pick-axe, stony chips flying, denting ground hard enough to twist metal. They did it themselves, those mourners; they paid no one, laying their lost ones away instead watered with their own labors' sweat, heralded with their own bodies' hurt. That work had hallowed the red dust under my feet. A wooden tablet ringed with stones (violet, chalk blue, paprika) read, "In the arms of my beloved desert, know I am at rest."

Gate/Platform 7: Pumpville

Seemed like the wind always blew in west Texas, rubbing paint from the boarded-up storefronts, making the faded signs creak and bang. In a plate glass window, a menu yellowed, and an empty trailer hulked by the dry riverbed. I turned the car radio to "scan," and it riffed through empty air, picking up static. I listened for hours. There was no shade; there were no churches, and the only shadows were those cast by cinder-block buildings built by men who had left long ago. An old sign read "Hang Your Hat in Sanderson." When I drove through the next year, the sign was gone.

Gate/Platform 8: Easley, South Carolina

The passenger train used to run through Easley at 10:42 every night. I worked at the movie theater then, and by that point in the evening I'd be sweeping up out-side, emptying the urn of cigarette butts, beating dust from doormats. From the theaters came the muffled sounds of scripted mayhem—tanker explosions, percus-sive laughter. I brushed grit off the sidewalk under the humming sodium flood-light. It was a pensive time. And then the Klaxon of the passenger train. I leaned on my broom and watched the train approach, its headlight burning brighter as it rounded the curve. The train's wheels clicked, one-two, one-two, and across Highway 123 I saw passenger car windows, some lit, flash by. I wondered about the people on the train, where they were going, if they felt the excitement I did, whether any of them looked out their windows at the town, my town, that must have looked nondescript, to them. They would not know the story of the boarded-up textile mill, would not have gone to a funeral at the cemetery by the tracks (pale headstones sliding by in the dark), would not have stopped at the ice cream parlor for supper every Sunday after evening service, would not have tilted high above the tired crowd in the rickety Ferris wheel, set up by the tracks every Fourth of July, looking toward the dark place in the west where invisible mountains bunched.

Gate/Platform 9: Iowa

On the Fourth of July, I dreamed a soldier. Walking a highway shoulder, his back to me, he wore a green uniform and carried a duffel. The material of his jacket stretched taut between his shoulder blades. This was corn country, and I saw waves of green plants, tall on the ridges, stunted and yellow in the low places where rainwater had stood. *Knee high by the Fourth*, we used to say. Every now and then, he bent to pick up a stone. He'd carry it a little while, then drop it, pick up another. One at a time. He looked solid, corporeal, his dark shadow moving over the gravel, but he was dead, I knew. He walked inexorably towards home.

Spreading the Word

Judith Thurman

The 2008 Big Apple Scrabble Tournament took place on a weekend in early October. Meg Wolitzer, the novelist, had signed up for the three-day event with her son, Charlie Panek, a thirteen-year-old eighth grader who was competing in Division 4, the lowest tier, but was holding his own against adult rivals. His mother, in Division 3, invited me to watch them play their final games, and we arrived at the venue, a loft on lower Fifth Avenue, a little before nine o'clock on Sunday morning. A light rain was falling, and the Avenue had been closed to traffic for the Pulaski Day parade. A high-school marching band from New Jersey, wearing Polish folk costumes, was disembarking from a tour bus with a clatter of drums and cymbals. "Uh-oh," Wolitzer said anxiously. "Oompah music—just what we needed."

Players were drifting in from a hearty breakfast at the Comfort Diner, on West Twenty-third Street, armed with leftover carbohydrates. The diner's owner, Ira Freehof, runs the tournament. His assistant director, Joel Sherman, a wiry bachelor from the Bronx known as G. I. Joel, is a legendary player and a former world champion who figures prominently in "Word Freak," a pungently written best-seller by Stefan Fatsis about the competitive Scrabble subculture. (Sherman's nickname refers to the soundtrack of gastrointestinal disturbances that often punctuate his games.) When Wolitzer introduced us, Sherman covered his ears with both hands and huddled near a wall. "I have sinusitis," he said. "You're distracting me. Go away." Later in the afternoon, we had a cordial chat about his role as the "official adjudicator," but he was hard to draw out. "Socializing is a challenge for a lot of us in the Scrabble community," John Chew, the tournament's Webmaster, noted tactfully. At that moment, we heard a scream, followed by a thud, and a young woman fell to the floor, apparently having a convulsion. A few people rushed over to help, but she turned out to be convulsed, for obscure reasons, with hilarity.

The room was a bright rectangle crowded with tables arranged hierarchically. Wolitzer and her son found their places in "steerage," as she put it. Once the games began, a hush fell, and players hunched over their boards. The tension and the brainpower were palpable. Tiles rustled in cloth bags, and I watched as a top-seeded player laid "pealike," using all seven letters—a "bingo"—which his opponent countered with another bingo, "cr[e]olise." Chew and his colleague Sherrie Saint John—anchors of a live Webcast—took the time to point out a few celebrities. Saint John whispered, "The guy with the red hair, taking notes and shaking his head at careless moves, is Adam Logan, a world champion. Like Joel, Adam doesn't talk much, but he went to Princeton at sixteen. Over there is Sal Piro, the president of the "Rocky Horror Picture Show" fan club, playing with Frank Tangredi, who wrote an Off Broadway play. The handsome Latino guy to his right is Winter." Winter, a software engineer, just goes by one name. He is the subject of a documentary about his quest to visit every Starbucks on the planet. He told me, "I plot my itineraries to dovetail with Scrabble tournaments. So far, I've been to about eighty-nine hundred branches."

Wonkish misfits with awesome powers of recall, most of them male, seemed to dominate Division 1, and, during a break, I met John O'Laughlin, the baby-faced genius who designed Quackle—a Scrabble computer program that, Saint John said, "thinks almost like a human, which can't be said of everyone here." But Robin Pollock Daniel did not fit the mold. She is a chic blond Gestalt therapist from Toronto, and the highest-ranked female player in North America. While I was watching, she "bingoed out" (emptying her rack to win with a seven-letter coup de grace, "bli[n]dgut"), and whooped for joy. A little crowd gathered to congratulate her. A few feet away, however, the great Joe Edley didn't look up or even twitch. He is a three-time national champion, and one of the few players to have memorized the entire dictionary of official Scrabble terms (which, if you were wondering, accepts "blind gut" as one word). Some thirty years ago, he became enamored of The Seth Material, a New Age text in eleven volumes that was supposedly dictated by Seth, an enlightened being, to Jane Roberts, a medium and psychic, who received the teachings while in a trance. Edley was inspired by Seth to realize his full human potential, and he chose to express it through Scrabble. Meditation and breathing exercises are part of his mental-fitness program. I hovered behind his chair (he has the posture of a yogi and the sang-froid of a Vulcan) while he replenished his rack. "Aneurin," "dentil," "wab," and "pavid" were already on the board, and he instantly played an arcane bingo: "residua." Most top players have day jobs—many in computer science and mathematics—but Edley is a full-time pro, who earns a living by consulting on and writing about the game and teaching workshops for beginners. "There is no point to playing Scrabble unless I make it a spiritual practice," he told me. "The secret is emotional control."

Charlie Panek is a third-generation Scrabble fiend. His mother still plays with her mother, the novelist Hilma Wolitzer, who is seventy-eight. If novel-writing runs in families, so does Scrabble addiction, and I was hooked at a tender age by my own mother, an English teacher who always hated to sacrifice a lovely word like "glaive" or "deodar" for a more prosaic play with a higher score. She was initiated by my uncle Roy. In 1949, the second year that Scrabble was on the market, 2,413 sets were sold, and Roy bought one of them. He sailed a schooner on Chesapeake Bay, and a friend at the marina had previously introduced him to Scrabble's precursor, Criss-Cross Words, which helped the old salts to while away their becalmed hours. After Roy died, I found the set in his den, with all the tiles—ninety-eight letters and two blanks—still accounted for. (He had kept it with his boating trophies and Army relics, including a Luger that he'd captured at El Alamein.) It has since helped me to while away many of my own becalmed hours. One summer, on a torrid afternoon in Carl Schurz Park, the worn tiles, like a saint's femur, wrought a miracle: I trounced my opponent with the bingo of a lifetime: "bar[o]ques," worth three hundred and eleven points. (It spanned two triple-word squares, with the "q" on a double letter.)

Scrabble is enjoying a second hey-day. The first was in the early nineteen-fifties, when demand for sets outstripped production. (In 1954, an advertisement in this magazine showed a wedding party stampeding from a church; the bride explains to the baffled clergyman that the toy shop next door has a new shipment.) Between one and two million sets are sold yearly; one in every three American households is reported to own one; and thirty thousand new games are said to begin, somewhere in the world, every hour. Players of note are a heterogeneous confraternity that includes Barack Obama, the Queen of England, Madonna, Igor Stravinsky, Rosie O'Donnell, Duke Ellington, Nora Ephron, Meadow Soprano, Dustin Hoffman, Justin Timberlake, Chris Martin, Maya Angelou, Carol Burnett, Richard Nixon, and Ludacris, who plays "hip-hop" Scrabble, using words like "crunk," "hizw," and "pajawa"—a version of the "dirty" Scrabble that was popular with Hollywood swingers fifty years ago. (I heard one of their ancient jokes at the tournament: "'Cervix' is my favorite opening.")

Scrabble is both mindless and cerebral, which may account for its appeal to writers—it gives you a chance to push words around without having to make them mean something. As a symbolic battleground of family life, it has often come in handy as a plot device. Graham Greene, Anne Tyler, Jonathan Franzen, Margaret Atwood, Sylvia Plath, Rick Moody, and Patricia Highsmith are among those who have savored the game, injected it into their fiction, or done both. In Ira Levin's *Rosemary's Baby*, the tiles spell out a Devil worshipper's name. Nabokov's Ada is an elegant player, probably in the image of her creator, who also designed crossword puzzles. In Spike Lee's "She's Gotta Have It," the heroine's suitors squabble over their board. And Scrabble, one imagines, would have appealed to Shakespeare and Moliere—it lends itself to the comic comeuppances that occur at class intersections, where gullible plebeians affect courtly language, and pretentious know-it-alls are cornered by their bluffs. (In a famous episode of "The Simpsons," Homer, Springfield's Bottom, draws "oxidize" but plays "do," while Bart tries to sucker him with "kwyjibo"—a species of ape, he explains, dumb and balding, that's native to North America.)

The game of Scrabble is native to America, though none of its charm has been lost in translation. The Senegalese, who mostly speak Wolof but play in French, celebrate their Scrabble champions as national heroes. Sets are available in twenty-eight other foreign languages, including Hebrew, Malay, and Welsh (which has seven "Y"s, three more than the English version; one "LL"; and two "FF"s), and in Braille. With the publication of a CD-ROM, in 1996, one could test one's mettle against Quackle's prototype, the formidable computer anagramming and crossword program known as Maven—Scrabble's Deep Blue. But Maven, like all of us, is subject to the democratizing luck of the draw, and every so often even I have outplayed him.

The Scrabble board has fifteen rows, each with fifteen squares, sixty-one of them worth extra points. In chess or checkers, the only occult element is a player's strategy: checkers is won or lost primarily on concentration; chess on skill, brainpower, and aggression. These factors count in Scrabble, too, though not, perhaps, to the degree that chance does. Brian Sheppard, the computer scientist who created Maven, described Scrabble, in the journal *Artificial Intelligence*, as "a game of imperfect information with a large branching factor," which means that no one can precisely control or anticipate the changing shape of the word tree.

Sheppard, John O'Laughlin, and their peers have modelled Scrabble mathematically in an ongoing effort to create an invincible program, and most champions are likelier to have played on their high-school chess team than to have written for the newspaper. The National Scrabble Championship is an annual event that was held last year in Orlando. The winner, Nigel Richards, a forty-one-year-old New Zealander, took home a purse of twenty-five thousand dollars. He also won the biennial World Championship, which was last held in Mumbai, and is more prestigious, though less lucrative (first prize was fifteen grand), and in 2007 he won the Thailand International, the largest of the major contests, with eight thousand entrants. (The Thai government promotes Scrabble as a tool for learning English, although some Thai masters are famous for competing at the highest echelons without speaking or understanding much, if any, of the language, relying on eidetic memory and spatial intelligence. English is just a quarry for the playing chips.)

Top competitors, whatever country they represent, subject themselves, like Olympic athletes, to gruelling training regimens—mostly with speed anagramming and memory exercises that employ flash cards. No one rises through the ranks of his local and national Scrabble associations without doing "alphagram" drills (mastering a long list of commonly occurring letter combinations that contain multiple bingos); memorizing the "vowel dumps" ("aalii," "aerate," "aioli," et al.) that help to clear out an unpropitious rack; and learning the hundred and one two-letter words ("aa" to "za"), along with their common "hooks" ("ex," for example, has seven front hooks: "dex," "hex," "kex," etc., while "ta" has sixteen back hooks—"tab," "taj," etc.). Also essential is a knowledge of scientific terminology; variant spellings ("wangun"/"wanigan"); high-scoring slang words ("zin," "tranq," "mojo"); exclamations ("jeez," "huic," "yucch"); eccentric plurals (one "pirog," but two "piroghi"/"pirogen"); archaic past tenses ("throve," "thriven"); units of weight or currency—a fertile category ("jiao," "qursh," "vatu," and "zloty," among dozens); and admissible letters of a foreign alphabet ("kaph," "peh," and "fe," all Hebrew, but I could go on). *"Mens sana in corpore sano"* may not be Scrabble's motto, but there are many odd deities on Olympus, and any virtuoso who can unscramble a fifteen-letter anagram in a minute or two, mentally, as Sherman, Edley, and Logan can, deserves a niche there. (You can try one of the words that humbled, but also hooked, Stefan Fatsis, who started his research as an embedded reporter and became a combatant: "megachiropteran." Your time is up—it's "cinematographer.")

Crazes behave like epidemics, but in Scrabble's case the bug has never died out, and the Internet has revived its potency. Toward the end of 2000, games.com, a site then owned by Atari, which was owned by Hasbro, which controls the rights to Scrabble in North America (Mattel owns the trademark for the rest of the world), offered one of the first interactive, multiplayer versions of the game, and it was suddenly possible, at whatever hour, to find a partner, or to make a foursome, and to join a community of besotted logophiles from every continent. (A number of Scrabble clubs also hosted games, and still do, including The Pixie Pit, a British site, and ISC.ro, which is frequented by Joel Sherman and many other cognoscenti.) I have probably met more interesting strangers playing online Scrabble than I have in a lifetime of travel to exotic places. A Ghanaian taxi-driver from Brooklyn invited me to Prospect Park, where his Scrabble club held weekend tournaments. A tattoo artist in Alberta surprised me, between plays, with her knowledge of Gerard Manley Hopkins. An Oxford don beat me soundly, but so did a used-car salesman. I have played Aussies and New Zealanders (Scrabble is popular in the antipodes), an impertinent prodigy who confessed to being eleven, a cardsharp in Las Vegas, a lawyer in Bangalore who traded places with his wife for the endgame ("She's the family closer," he said), a corgi breeder, and a Jane Austen fan ("elizabennet"), who added a few words that Jane never used— "feeb," "ottar," "vas," and "zineb"—to my vocabulary.

A virtual board is identical to the horizontal model. The computer randomly assigns the tiles, and you can swap or shuffle them electronically. Once you register, your point rating (a kind of batting average) is posted next to your screen name. It is calculated by the system used to seed competitors in club and tournament play, where games are weighted, so that you forfeit more points for losing to a weaker player, and win more for beating someone who outranks you. The urge to improve one's status in the pecking order easily becomes a fixation that sometimes inspires unsportsmanlike behavior: downloading an anagramming program, or disconnecting from the server to avert a loss. And here I should like to alert those parents and educators who promote Scrabble as a wholesome exercise for young minds that the online version, like amphetamines or video games, seems to induce a state of fiendish hyperfocus in susceptible subjects. ScrabbleBlitz (high-speed

Scrabble), on games.com, transformed Nora Ephron, she wrote, into a "teenage boy." The *Times* columnist Deborah Solomon told me, "I used to be a productive individual who read serious fiction in the hours before I went to sleep. But that was in the innocent, un-Scrabbled past." She plays every night on ISC under the screen name Duchamp—a nod to the French Dadaist, who claimed to have renounced art for chess, and who, Solomon says, "in that sense, deserves to be seen as a pioneer of the ruined-by-games online present." My own ruination became apparent to me one morning, as dawn was breaking, after an all-night marathon with a regular partner who called himself qatmandu ("qat" is one of eleven admissible "q" words without a "u"). Careless with exhaustion, I failed to block a triple-letter score that permitted him to exit with a game-cinching, fifty-point play: "xi" and "xu." ("Xi" is a Greek letter; "xu" is a monetary unit of Vietnam.)

In 2004, a new gaming site, quadplex.com, began offering free Scrabble, and among its habitués were two plump, bookish brothers in Calcutta—Rajat and Jayant Agarwalla—who were twenty-three and eighteen, respectively. They grew up in an extended Marwari family (the Marwaris are famous traders), and, in 2000, Rajat, who has a business degree from the University of Bradford, in England, started a software company that Jayant, who is an avid tournament player (India is a Scrabble hotbed), joined as a partner when he finished college. They originally employed three engineers, and now have a staff of twenty-five.

The Agarwallas became "distraught," Jayant told the Calcutta *Telegraph*, when Quadplex started charging a fee—like many of their peers in the Napster generation, the brothers ardently believe that "the contents on the Internet should be free as far as possible so people across the world benefit from them." In 2005, they decided to implement a word game identical to Scrabble in most respects, which they originally called Bingo-Binge. Too many bugs, and too much volume, crashed the Web site, and an improved version of the program, renamed Scrabulous, was released later that year. At the suggestion of an American user, Jayant said, the brothers "checked out" Facebook, and, in 2007, they launched a Scrabulous application that quickly became Facebook's most popular game. It is widely rumored that Hasbro offered to pay ten million dollars for it, although the company denies having done so, and, in July, it sued for copyright infringement. Facebook was pressured to disable the application in North America, infuriating some of the half million users who were logging on every day. (A number of them argued that Hasbro should have been grateful to the Agarwallas for recruiting a new generation of customers for the travel sets, custom editions, tile jewelry, and other Scrabble merchandise and paraphernalia on the market.) Mattel, meanwhile, had pursued legal action in India. In late September, the Delhi High Court ruled in the brothers' favor: it was legitimate to clone the Scrabble board for online play, so long as its name didn't capitalize on the trademark. Scrabulous has since become Lexulous. It is played with eight tiles, and the bonus squares have been rearranged. As of this writing, the Web site and the Facebook application are up and running, in competition with an authorized Scrabble application designed by Electronic Arts. Jayant told me via e-mail that his lawyers had advised him to make no comment while Mattel's appeal is pending. (Hasbro dropped its suit in December.) He and Rajat continue to collect ad revenues from their site. They have, however, professed innocence of any intent to trespass on intellectual property, casting their enterprise as a public service.

Before Lexulous, Scrabulous, Scrabble, and Criss-Cross Words, there was a game called Lexiko. It was invented during the Depression by Alfred Mosher Butts, a young architect from New York. (If there were a Nobel Prize for relieving the ennui of adolescence, family life, unhappy marriages, happy marriages, and the Friday after Thanksgiving, he would deserve it.) Butts lost twenty dollars on Lexiko the first year he was in business. He eventually earned about a million dollars in royalties from Scrabble, and kept track of every penny, Fatsis writes, using some of it to buy back an ancestral farmhouse near Poughkeepsie, but he was never resentful of the vastly greater profits that accrued to others. (One has the feeling that he wouldn't have bothered to sue the Agarwallas.)

When Butts's architectural firm downsized, in 1931, and he was laid off, he took stock of his mental assets, and decided to invent a game. The idea for Lexiko came to him while reading "The Gold Bug," a story by Edgar Allan Poe, in which the hero decodes a cipher that protects the hiding place of a pirate treasure by correlating its symbols with the alphabet. Butts realized that the key to Lexiko would be a formula for distributing the vowels and consonants, and assigning them point values, that represented their relative frequency in educated English usage. In the course of his research, he hand-computed every letter in every word on the pages of several newspapers, primarily the *Times*. The Scrabble letter count is a tribute both to his genius and to his doggedness. A more generous allotment of "S"s or blanks, for example, would have made the game too easy, and a stingier allotment of "E"s, "A"s, and "R"s would have made it too discouraging. With only four "U"s, the "Q" is a potential albatross but also, with a value of ten points, a potential bonanza. If you try to play English Scrabble with a French set, you begin to appreciate how much finesse and calculation Butts's feat required.

Butts, by his own admission, wasn't a good speller, and he was always happy when his Scrabble score reached the humble benchmark of three hundred points. (The highest individual score on record is eight hundred and thirty.) His wife, Nina, a former schoolteacher—she had, in fact, been Alfred's teacher—is said to have out-played him. But the couple's matches helped Butts to tinker with the game's design. He added the board, the blanks, and the colored premium squares that doubled or tripled words and letters, and he changed the name to Criss-Cross Words, in 1938. The big game companies, however, rebuffed his overtures, and the U.S. Patent Office twice rejected his applications.

By word of mouth, Criss-Cross Words began to acquire a small fan base, and Washington, D.C., where my uncle Roy spent his shore life, was one of its epicenters. Butts made the sets in his living room, and sold them by mail order—at two dollars each, plus a quarter for shipping. Friends did the product testing, and gave him their critiques. He also organized Criss-Cross socials at his parish church, in Jackson Heights, Queens. One of the testers, a social worker, gave a copy of the game to James Brunot, who had served under President Roosevelt, as the executive director of the War Relief Control Board. Brunot was ready for a new career, and, in 1947, he approached Butts with a business plan: he would assume responsibility for the manufacturing and the marketing of the game and pay Butts a royalty. Alfred accepted—he was tired of his unprofitable cottage industry, and his firm had rehired him.

Brunot made some minor changes to the board and to the rules, notably adding a fifty-point bonus for using all seven letters. He and his wife also came up with a catchier name. But Scrabble was a sleeper until 1952, when Jack Straus, the chairman of Macy's, who had discovered the game while on vacation, placed a big order, which triggered an avalanche. Brunot, his wife, and a small staff of workers had been making the sets in a converted schoolhouse in Connecticut, but they couldn't keep up with the demand. He licensed Scrabble to Selchow & Righter, the company that owned Parcheesi (which was later sold to Coleco Industries, which went bankrupt and was acquired by Hasbro in 1989). By 1954, Fatsis writes, "an astounding 3,798,555 units of Scrabble were sold." (Total sales are now estimated to be more than a hundred million sets, in twenty-one countries.) David Riley, the director of the NPD Group, a market-research company that tracks the toy and game industry, described Scrabble to me as "one of the greatest success stories in the business." He added, "New dolls, stuffed animals, action figures, and lawn games are fads that come and go, but Scrabble, like Monopoly, is an evergreen."

Until last spring, when I fell off the wagon and registered my old nom de guerre on scrabulous.com, I hadn't played Scrabble for a year, except once, at a ski lodge, with an old friend, on my uncle's set—I'd sworn off the Net. The new site took some getting used to. Some of its features were appealing—you could, for example, set your dictionary preference. At a hundred and seventy-eight thousand six hundred and ninety-one words, the Tournament Word List (TWL), used in the United States, Canada, Israel, and Thailand, is considerably shorter than SOWPODS, the combined American and British tournament word list (two hundred and sixty-seven thousand seven hundred and fifty-one words), which is used everywhere else that Scrabble is played in English. Games.com automatically censored slurs, curses, and profanities. Not every player was happy to be deprived of versatile little score-enhancers like "wog," "spic," "jew" (the verb), "lez," "goy," "honky," "cunt," "darkie," and "fuck." Even the chat box blocked bad language, and some of the best players were super-friendly evangelicals whom I met late at night, perhaps resisting more carnal temptations. Temptation takes many forms, however, and loitering in a "lobby"—an entrance foyer where one waits for a "table"—before leaving it to pair off with a perfect stranger isn't unlike cruising a mixer. You size up potential partners by their ratings and their screen names—a mask tells something about the face behind it.

At games.com, the matches were untimed, and sometimes one got stuck with a dawdler. My favorite partners, however, shared my traditional view that fifty minutes, the length of a tournament game, was just brisk enough and just leisurely enough to make the most of one's tiles. (I doubt that I could have found some of my proudest bingos—"ki[n]gpins," "reovir[u]s," and "tequila"—had I been rushed.) At lexulous.com, you can choose a practice game against the computer, although, compared with Maven or Quackle, the Agarwallas' digital mastermind is a nitwit who leaves the triple-word scores undefended, offers lame hints, misses bingos, and squanders the blanks, and whom I beat at least half the time. Most people, however, seem to prefer a ten-minute quickie, and it took me a while to realize that some of my perkiest opponents were actually "coffeehousing"—trying to rattle my concentration by keeping up a steady stream of banter while the clock was ticking.

Facebook is a place for more desultory encounters, live or delayed, single or several at a time, some lasting all day, some for a month, with players making a word whenever the spirit moves them. (A monthlong game of Scrabble, in my opinion, is about as appealing as a monthlong sex act.) The young have always mocked their elders by throwing time away, and Scrabulous became notorious among employers as a waster of man-hours. Last year, a YouTube takeoff by Kreole Parody, set to the tune of Fergie's "Glamorous," captured the anarchic thrill. The song spawned parodies of the parody, including a video that featured a coy, scantily clad Fergie imitator furtively playing Scrabulous in her office cubicle; hiding her board from a prissy supervisor with a handlebar mustache; and, supine on a bed, receiving a shower of tiles, like a hip-hop Danae. Another video nicely sums up the phenomenon: "Used to do all kinds of shit, all I do is type and sit." But, as Jayant Agarwalla pointed out, some players can't do much more than type and sit: they are the housebound, the elderly, or the disabled, for whom, as he put it, the game is "their only window to the world."

My own obsession has often made me a willing recluse. Until the CD-ROM went on sale, powered by Maven, I used to keep in form between matches by playing Scrabble solitaire at the kitchen table. The greatest drawback was that I couldn't bluff myself by laying a "phony" (a plausible but nonexistent word like "pukha" or "burlock"), or by deliberately misspelling a common noun ("fetter") to lure an opponent into making it plural, then challenging it off the board—a legitimate if churlish ploy. In some games, I assigned the racks different strategic functions or personalities—the tortoise and the hare, logic and intuition—one hand playing fast and free, and the other with cool deliberation. When my son was little, this spectacle troubled him. "You're a schizo," he once told me, proud of his fancy insult, and shaking his head sadly at the score pad, which had page after page of columns marked "J1" and "J2." One day, he may appreciate that "schizo" is worth eight points more than "cervix" if you can open with it.

How I Became a Bed-Maker

Kate Torgovnick

I realized a very scary thing this morning: I've become the kind of person who makes her bed every day. I woke up to the evil buzzing of my alarm clock, like always. And as I came out of that two minutes of post-sleep daze, I found myself at the end of my bed, wrestling to get the lines of my comforter parallel to the edge of my mattress.

I, Kate Torgovnick, make my bed every morning. *Every* morning. Not just days when friends might be coming over or days when I've done the laundry and need to change my sheets—we're talking every weekday, weekend, and holiday. It doesn't matter if I'm running late for work or if I have a hangover from too many gin and tonics the night before. No matter what, I make my bed.

And I'm not just talking about the throwing of covers over everything and thinking, *The bed is done, man, the bed is done*, like that kid with the long hair in *Don't Tell Mom the Babysitter's Dead* would say. I make my bed in a way that would please any drill sergeant. First, I fluff each sham (I don't even know where I picked up this term) and prop it up against my headboard, making sure no edges are flopping over. Then I shake out both of my pillows. I tuck three sides of the top sheet—yes, there's a *top sheet*—between the mattress and box spring and pull the loose end over my pillows. Next, I attack the comforter. I pull it over the whole kit and caboodle and take at least a minute to straighten it out (this was the point I was at when I came to this awful, dizzying realization this morning). Oh, but we're not done yet. Next, at the head of the bed, I fold the top sheet and comforter down about four inches, the way maids in hotels are taught to do. Finally, from the right side of the bed where I've neatly stacked my toss pillows, I grab each one individually and arrange them big ones in the back, small ones in the front. I've developed a meticulous process that takes approximately four minutes to complete—yet until today, I never even realized that I do any of it at all.

How could this have happened? Trust me, I am *not* a bed-maker. Or, at least, I wasn't a bed-maker? I like to think of myself as laid back, cool, smart, funny, and not nearly compulsive enough to attend to the details listed above. I'm hardly someone you would call organized—I've barely touched the day planner I bought years ago and instead jot my appointments down on paper scraps that become a jumbled mess at the bottom of my purse. I pay my bills late and they're often stained with jelly. As a teenager, my room was messy with the requisite piles of clothing, mix tapes, and the occasional abandoned cupcake. I actually remember making fun of my parents for their always-made bed. My freshman dorm room was a respectable pigsty—the floor a sea of crumpled jeans, half-written papers, and trash I couldn't be bothered to bring to a trashcan. Nowhere in my life has bed-making ever entered into the equation. So when did this happen?

First step, I must figure out how long this bed-making has been going on. It's 8:30 a.m., but I panic and call my boyfriend, Chuck. After three long rings, he finally picks up.

"Hey," he says, his voice betraying that I'm calling well before his alarm clock. "Everything okay?"

I try to think of the best way to phrase this. "Have you noticed that I make my bed?" I ask.

I hear a relieved sigh on the other end of the line. He seems thankful that the serious note in my voice is not anything bad. "Um . . . yeah."

"How long have I been doing this?" I delve. "Do you remember when it started?"

He pauses for a minute. "You've always made your bed. At least since we've been together."

Wow. That's three years. How can someone make their bed every day for three years and not even notice? I snap back into the conversation. "Did you ever think that's a little strange?"

"Not really," he says. "I mean, that's pretty normal. Lots of people do it."

"Well, have there been any days when I haven't made my bed?" I ask in a last-ditch effort.

He thinks. "Not that I can remember. You even make my bed when you're over here." Crap. My bed-making's practically turning me into a fifties housewife.

I say goodbye and do the math in my head. It must have been sometime pre-2004 when the bed-making began. That narrows it down, but doesn't answer the question. I guess I'm going to have to dig back further.

I try calling Christina, my post-college roommate who I lived with for three years before moving into my own studio, but she's not picking up her phone. So I instant message Dana, my college roommate. Maybe she saw the first symptoms. "Hey there," I say. "Do you ever remember me making my bed?"

"No way," she messages back. "I don't think so."

"So I was a slob? On a scale of 1 to 10, how messy was my side of the room?"

"If 1 is a monk's cell and 10 is Britney Spears' career, it was an 8.5. But by senior year, maybe a 6," she offers. Bless her for her bluntness. "But it still looked like you had artfully planned to make sure no horizontal surface was exposed, be it floor, chair, bed, or desk." Maybe she is exaggerating (this is someone who would get annoyed if the toilet paper roll was placed on the holder with the end coming out underneath instead of over the top). But she's narrowed down the time frame considerably. Somewhere between graduating from college in 2002 and getting together with Chuck in 2004, the bed-making began.

Christina is the missing link. Thankfully, she calls back a few hours later. "Do you remember when I started making my bed?" I ask, completely forgetting the normal pleasantries.

She laughs. "Not really."

"Did I ever mention making my bed or anything like that?"

"Hmm . . . not that I can remember," she says.

"Sorry, I realized today that I make my bed every day, and I'm trying to figure out when that started," I say, suddenly aware that I'm sounding like a psycho.

"That's funny," she says. "I've started making my bed, too. In our old apartment I didn't care about it. But in my new apartment, my bed's in the middle of the room. If I don't make it in the morning, I come home and feel like my life is a mess."

This is inconceivable. Christina's now a bed-maker, too? Her room was always twice as messy as mine—mountains of clothes on the floor, books strewn every which way, the works. Is what I'm going though completely normal?

"Really?" I say, feeling calmed that she's going through this, too. "Well, do you ever remember me going on any cleaning spurts or anything like that?"

"When we were both looking for jobs, you'd go on cleaning kicks or resolve to organize the closet or something. Maybe it was then?" she offers.

And all of a sudden, I remember. I started making my bed in the fall of 2002. It makes sense now that I think about it—I was unemployed for months and probably would have slept all day had I not forced myself out of bed. Christina was in the unemployed trenches with me, but our third roommate, Susannah, was two years older than us and had a steady job. In the morning, she would always make her bed before leaving the apartment for work. In the evening, she'd casually tell us about the things she did at the office, and I'd feel embarrassed that the only thing I had to report on was whether Joey and Dawson hooked up in the day's episode of *Dawson's Creek*. So maybe I was copying Susannah, imitating what productive members of society do.

Or maybe I was trying to establish some sort of routine. I remember giving myself a schedule so I didn't fall too out of practice with having things to do. 10 a.m.: the aforementioned *Creek*. 11 a.m.: take a shower and get dressed. Noon: look for a job for an hour. 1 p.m.: Go to the grocery store and make lunch. 2 p.m.: five hours of *Law and Order* reruns. 7 p.m.: Call friends and come up with a plan for the night that didn't involve spending money. I remember one day during this period when the building across the street caught on fire. I noticed the smoke through our bay window just as the fire trucks came into view. I stood there for hours, watching as flames engulfed the building and it burned down to the ground. It never even crossed my mind to go see if anyone needed my help. No one was injured, so it's not as creepy as it sounds—but still, I consider this a low point. The fire seemed metaphorical for how powerless I was feeling at the time. Four years at a highly ranked liberal arts college making Phi Beta Kappa and Summa Cum Laude, and I felt completely ineffectual in shaping my life. Just like the firefighters' hoses did nothing to calm the flames. Looking back, I think maybe my bed-making was my way of taking control of something. I couldn't find a job, not to mention a boyfriend, and my savings account had dwindled to nothing. But if I made my bed, I was the master of my universe, right?

But why do I continue this obscene behavior now that life has settled down— I've found my dream job, I'm halfway through writing my first book, and all and all I'm very pleased with my life? I can think of all sorts of logical reasons. I could say that it helps me wake up, explicitly defining that the night is over and that, as much as I might want to, I can't go back to bed. I could say that coming home to a neat bed after work makes me feel mentally in order. I could say, "Cleanliness is godliness," or some such quote that doesn't really make much sense. And while there might be an ounce of truth in these things, I think that there is more to it than that: I think that my unconscious bed-making means I'm truly an adult.

I've heard friends and coworkers utter the phrase, "pretending to be an adult," and until now I've completely understood the sentiment. This state of perpetual responsibility feels foreign to all of us. We all feel like we're acting out a part—playing dress-up and doing things we're supposed to do, like going to work and setting up 40lKs, but that these things never seem completely natural. In this way of thinking, being an adult is measured in firsts you never quite imagined you'd get to—your first apartment, your first job, the first time someone calls you "Ma'am," the first paycheck that reflects a salary and not an hourly rate, the first time you say "I'll pencil you in," the first property you own, the first birthday cake with number candles rather than individual ones, the first time you think about getting married and having children and it doesn't seem completely far-fetched. But I've been through every one of these milestones, and, while they sound big on paper, the truth is that I felt no different on the day before any of these things happened than I did on the day after.

But today, the day I realized that I am a bed-maker, I feel very, very different. See, I've come to realize that adulthood is a diffuse thing. It creeps up in the subtlest ways possible. It's making to-do lists on a regular basis instead of just doing things. It's getting annoyed at shows when people bump into you when you use to think that was big fun. It's no longer telling your friends to just come on over, but giving them a specific time to arrive so that you can clean up and make a cheese plate (preferably with grapes). Adultness seeps into the tiniest crevices of your everyday life, to the point where you don't even recognize it. It seems so natural that you can't pin it down. It's when stability and routine become the things you really want. When having the wildest-night-ever pales in comparison to the simple pleasure of untucking the comforter, crawling inside, pulling the sheet all the way up to your neck, and drifting off to sleep.

I know I have friends who'd be willing to stage an intervention to try to shake me free from making my bed. Maybe there's even a twelve-step program. But the truth is, I don't want to stop. I like the way this ritual feels—easy, small, and comforting. Sure, I don't ever want to be grown up to the point where the phrase "bed-maker" seems like a fitting way to describe myself. But I can accept this. I can accept that I make my bed every day, that I'm an adult, that my priorities are shifting, that there is no Never, Never Land.

I have to go now. Toss pillows to rearrange.

Bathing

Kathryn Winograd

In 45 years, since I was a young child bathed by my mother, I have taken, I think, exactly five baths. Most have been this past year, in a claw-foot tub my husband and I hauled up Rainbow Pass to this cabin in the shadow of Nipple Mountain, where longhorns still linger at the brink of old prospecting glory holes. It's not that I don't understand the need to purify the body: the dark stain of consciousness still flowering out of the old garden, out of the old wounds—Eve the rib fleshed and wanting. I have stood at the mouth of ancient baths in underground ruins, know of the ritual mikvah baths of my husband's Judaic heritage: lover, bride, menstruating wife, all the grieving who have placed their hands on the newly dead—equally impure and so immersed in the living waters of springs and deep groundwater wells. It's simply that I did not bathe.

In Ohio, when I was 13, we lived on a farm behind a cemetery where the metal hulls of parked cars glinted beneath the moon, where high school lovers swam into each other above the soft and dented graves, mornings the damp grass I wept over littered with their beer bottles and spent balloons. Here, the Catholic milk farmers raised their sons and daughters in long barrack rooms, ate meals on heavy wood tables longer than caskets, swam naked to cleanse themselves in summer cow ponds. I remember the daughters of the cemetery caretaker who bathed in metal horse troughs with the well water they heated on the kitchen stove, carried steaming into loafing sheds sagging beneath the weight of their long winters. In our house of brick and stone behind farm fences and locked gates, half built in the years of the Civil War above vanished pig yards, and filled with ghosts my mother sometimes heard—voices of those dead farmers passing idly beneath our bay windows—I took my daily showers like a confessional in bathrooms of tile and indoor plumbing.

I sit now in water pumped from an aquifer some 465 feet below me, where I imagine the calcified bones of thirsty dinosaurs must rest. Outside the window, jets cruise over me, weave the sky with their white contrails above this mountain plain where once miners washed in the phantom springs I've named. Before the well, before this cabin, we had no real water, bringing the little we could in small coolers when we camped out dirty and ashy, the wild din of coyotes crowding us from the far valley, the summer stars above our small fires blurred.

I will tell you I did not bathe because I am almost 5'10", because I don't have the body for it—my knees awkwardly splayed above the water since I was an adolescent. I will tell you I did not bathe because I've never had the predilection for it—the words of my mother, a "shower" pragmatist, filling me with disdain for the lingering dirt of my own body. I will tell you I did not bathe because I grew up guilty as this "landed gentry"—my father, a successful doctor in a wealthy suburb of Cincinnati, moving us to those cow ponds and horse troughs, to those dirt roads named for the grog once brewed in Prohibition stills rusting now in fields and creek beds and bounded by such resentful poverty. What I won't tell you is that I never loved my body enough.

Once I read that young victims of rape will sometimes go through a stage of promiscuity. I think of the lonely, vulnerable, adolescent girl I was, listening beneath the kitchen window to her parents discussing their concern that she wasn't "over it yet," this girl the one ghost my mother could not hear. In Ohio, I sometimes swam naked with the Catholic girls. They didn't like me, but they came anyway to swim in our spring-fed pond, to shed their suits at our sand shores, half hidden by the weeping willows. I remember covering myself with shamed hands while a birthmark like the whole of a virginal country I had left long ago stained unembarrassed the pelvis of the prettiest girl I wished to be. It seems you live your whole life beneath a bruise, and though you push it down, anything can bring it back—an unexpected glimpse at a science study you are too afraid to follow up on, the words of a girl you hear who asks, "Why would anyone want to rape her?" When the Catholic girls stepped into the water, I watched their backs skim the surface like new pennies—this a baptism I could not receive.

I crack the window open—the moon a thumbnail now, and the earth gone flat beneath the night snow. My own breathing rocks me. I imagine the motion of my mother walking, her belly full with the weight of me rising and falling, the sound of her voice through the placental waters. Even in this tiny amount of bath water, my hands want to lift into the air, swell out of the water like the pale fish at dusk that swam with me those summer nights I was so alone, insects cratering the small moon of my sinking body. Into my 20s, I could count the men in my life on two hands, their bodies slipping finally and always just past me below the stilled waters. For a while, I forgot, that 13th year disappearing unnoticed, until I saw the weak, frail sex of my premature daughters, my mother holding them beneath

the kitchen tap to cleanse them because I could not, afraid to touch their nakedness, afraid to touch their fragile skin still flushed with those thimblefuls of my
own blood. I think of them now at 17, of the stranger who stared at them on the
light rail, finally mouthing the word "beautiful" to them before he stepped off—
how long they waited for this, the moment when a girl suddenly realizes her own
beauty, comes into the whole body of it, and the world awakens to her. I sat next
to them, beaten in that florescent light, remembering too, though I never realized
that moment, never.

The dog pushes his long, delicate snout through the cracked door. He cries and
whimpers. I pull the plug and step out of the water, bath bubbles clinging to me.
In the dim mirror, my body is a study of shadow and light. I think it was made to
be seen against the warmth of cabin wood, the knots and linear waves of Douglas
fir, the brown tones of it melding into the long grain the air darkens, all the voices
finally gone. Tonight I will sleep on the couch in front of the woodstove, where
the aspen stump I dug out of the drifts cracks and burns. The wind sings through
the window like a siren, and the steam floats from my skin like thin milk.

Part 2

Talking About Creative Nonfiction

One exciting aspect of the fourth genre is the role of writers and teachers of creative nonfiction in defining the terms of the conversation. Because we ourselves have benefited from that conversation, we're certain that writers entering the genre can gain from hearing these nonfictionists talk about the making of their own work. After all, in the long tradition of the genre, essayist/critics from Montaigne through Addison, Steele, Lamb, and Hazlitt to E. B. White have not only written the most enduring examples of the essay but also provided the most valuable commentary on the form.

Therefore, in Part 2, Talking About Creative Nonfiction, we've chosen pieces—several of them written by authors in Part 1—that reflect these writers' thoughts, opinions, speculations, theories, and critiques of creative nonfiction. They provide a multivoiced discussion of the genre on a wide range of topics related to writing creative nonfiction—definitions of the form, personal accounts of writing, hints about strategies and practices. Some offer us insight into the particular forms of creative nonfiction in which they work: Steven Harvey and Carl Klaus offer their approaches to the personal essay; Mary Clearman Blew and Patricia Hampl give us different perspectives on the memoir, especially the ways imagination transforms and transposes memory; Tracy Kidder discusses his views and his experiences in literary journalism; Marianna Torgovnick discusses the reasons she practices and promotes experimental critical writing with its use of personal voice in academic discourse; and Laura Miller offers an online example of personal criticism in a review/essay centered on a new book about Montaigne. In addition, Robert Root explains and illustrates how and why he writes disjunctive or segmented essays; Jocelyn Bartkevicius attempts to define and identify creative nonfiction; and Michael Steinberg shares his writerly approach to the essay and the memoir.

As the fourth genre expands its horizons, new forms gain greater prominence and need to be added to the conversation: Roger Ebert talks about the effects of blogging on his writing; John Bresland discusses the origins of the video essay, a form he demonstrates in Part 1; Sonya Huber sends us to the Internet to view her composition of a digital essay, with all its bells and whistles; Judith Kitchen and Brenda Miller give us their insights into the lyric essay, as does Kathryn Winograd, who provides one of the examples in Part 1; Peggy Shumaker makes us think about several varieties of nonfiction prose.

Taken together, these essays gaze at the fourth genre as if it were a prism, each facet offering new perspectives and different possibilities. By examining its traditions at the same time that it explores its options, simultaneously connecting to the power of its history and the potential that new avenues of communication offer, creative nonfiction has multiplied the prospects writers have for understanding their own experiences, reflecting on their worlds, and communicating more widely.

Although some of these selections involve critical analysis, they do not present a detached theoretical approach. All of these essays are designed to offer a writerly perspective on the evolving dialogue about creative nonfiction. As a result, the works selected for Part 2 ground creative nonfiction in the behaviors and motives of working writers and teachers, reflect back on the examples of the form in Part 1, and project ahead to essays on composing the fourth genre in Part 3.

Note: Sources for online versions of the writing by John Bresland, Roger Ebert, Sonya Huber, Laura Miller, and Kathryn Winograd are found at the end of their pieces.

The Landscape
of Creative Nonfiction

Jocelyn Bartkevicius

[I]naccuracy is very often a superior form of truth.

Virginia Woolf, "Incongruous Memories"

1. The Stranger

I was standing in a garden, tomato plants ripening, chickens dashing about, when I first learned I was a stranger. I was quite young, maybe six or seven, watching my grandmother pick tomatoes and tell stories about her life as a farm girl in Eastern Europe. She had just gotten to the part about hiding in the forest from waves of invading armies—Russians then Prussians then Russians again—when she stopped, stood up, looked me in the eye, and said: "But you are an American; you don't understand."

How can I convey the force of these words? Of course, as a school girl I was familiar with the idea of "being an American." I said the pledge of allegiance, hand on heart like all the other kids. I sang the "Star Spangled Banner" (except for those unreachable glaring red high notes). But this identity had never been pinned upon me so specifically, so singularly, or as an impediment. "Being an American" had never made me an outsider. Standing in my grandmother's garden, among plants and animals raised the old ways, I was the other.

In memory, when she speaks these words, my grandmother is looking me right in the eye. She was a small woman, possibly reaching five feet at her healthiest, before the osteoporosis formed a permanent stoop. And I was a gangly girl who got all her height early. But now that I look at the memory, examine it instead of experiencing it, I must admit that a five-foot-tall six year old is an unlikely creature. Something is wrong with the memory. It is incongruous.

And then there are holes in the memory: I can't remember whether my grandmother continued her story after she stood up and spoke to me. Or whether she returned to her gardening. Or why she began the story at all. It was hard to get her to talk about Lithuania, especially about the years when, as a very young woman, she had to bury food in the forest to survive, had to prepare constantly to flee soldiers and their various hungers, had to watch city people (who could not grow their own food) sicken and die. Perhaps my father stood off to the side prompting her. But he is not in the memory. Maybe I—normally a very shy child and fearful of misunderstanding her difficult Lithuanian accent—had a rare fit of boldness and asked her a question about Europe.

The scene is one that I return to often, for her words fixed the moment as indelibly as a brand. I used to think that the memory drew me in spite of its incongruities and holes. But I am beginning to realize that this memory compels me *because* of the incongruities and holes. The pitted, nearly invisible landscape of the past is a mysterious, inviting place. Each exploration reveals a different topography.

Looking back, I find that my grandmother bequeathed layers of strangeness that day. Her words taught me that I was a stranger in her world. And they taught that, while there had been some unevenness in my life—near poverty, my parents' divorce, and so on—I was nevertheless a stranger to profound suffering and struggle. And now, looking not just at the moment but at the memory itself, at the moment as incongruous memory, I find that my grandmother's words taught me that there is a stranger within. That is, certain moments will not survive unravaged, that going back in time and memory I will discover losses, unreachable territories. Some of the territories remain, buried beneath the surface of daily life and ordinary reminiscence, inaccessible but for accident or imaginative self-interrogation.

In the case of my grandmother's garden, incongruities and obvious gaps drew me back to the memory, signaled its importance. Other moments may disappear without a trace, leaving no path, and the act of writing may be the only way to unearth them.

A few years after I stood with my grandmother in her garden, my father bought a farm—or what I called a farm before I moved from Connecticut to Iowa and saw working farms, counted among my friends actual farmers, and learned that in relation to Iowa farms, my father's place had been not a farm at all but an acreage. There on his land I built a miniature version of my grand-mother's garden using compost from the manure pile, sprinkling lime from a stocking to discourage bugs. I followed my father around, riding barely trained horses, acting the cowboy, zipping through forests, sleeping under the stars. And this is how I remember those years, as a little grandma, a little immigrant, a peasant girl in a store-bought peasant blouse (it was the sixties), bringing home-grown organic carrots to high school for lunch. I remember a peaceful Eden punctuated by moments of playing the stereo in my father's hand-built log cabin, Joni Mitchell singing about getting back to the garden, Neil Young loving his country girl.

But recently, I found buried in an old trunk a black and white snapshot of my father and me, pitchfork and all like the pair in Grant Wood's *American Gothic*. Our pitchfork, though, is angled; we both stare at it, and impaled upon one of the tongs is a small bat. In my memory, I am a Romantic peasant girl, gardening as it has been handed down by my Eastern European ancestors, embracing Woodstock, barefoot to Joni and Neil. In the photograph I am a party to the slaughter of a benign and beneficial mammal. Writing about the photograph awakened darker memories from the farm: another child's pointing a loaded pistol at me, my aiming a loaded BB gun at a sleeping bat as it hung from the shed door, and leaving the cabin after an argument to disappear alone into the dark country night.

The self—at least *my* self—is composed of misremembered and unremem-bered scenes. The path back to that uneven landscape is the path of the mind. Students in my creative nonfiction workshops frequently ask me to define for them, concisely and with directions for construction, "the personal essay." Usually I try to do so by offering a variety of creative nonfiction pieces along with several writers' working definitions of the form. But at times I ask them to define for me, concisely (but without directions for construction), "a person." The definition of "personal essay" is as complicated and various as that of "person," and the personal essay is just one possible manifestation of creative nonfiction.

In writing creative nonfiction, in order to tell the truth, I must let the in-congruities be. I was standing in the garden with my grandmother and we were eye to eye although we could not be the same height. I was six while also being ten—perhaps six with shyness and the language barrier and ten chronologically. Or ten in my boldness and six chronologically. Or I was somehow taller for being a stranger and my grandmother was somehow shorter for changing my world. And in order to tell the truth in creative nonfiction I must explore the gaps. I was an earth child on my father's farm and yet I was shooting bats. I focus on the unremembered photograph and dig for more. Memory, the mind's path, enacts wonders, and the creative nonfiction writer's work is not to reason those wonders away with mathematical formulae, but to embrace them, to recreate layer after layer of incongruity.

2. The Terms

The first time I heard the term "nonfiction," I was sitting with twenty other third graders at a veneered table in a grammar school library. I watched the librarian walk from wall to wall tapping books and signs with her pointer. Each book had a hand-typed Dewey decimal system number taped to its spine. Each section had a hand-printed sign fixed above it. She paused at the section labeled "fiction," tapped a row of spines, tapped the sign above, and said: "These books are fiction. They're made up; they aren't true." She stepped to the left, swung her pointer at the next section, labeled "nonfiction," tapped the sign, and said: "These books are not fiction. They aren't made up; they are fact." While the librarian went on with her presentation, my mind went elsewhere. Fiction was not true and nonfiction was not fiction; therefore nonfiction was *not* not true. She was using the forbidden double negative. I sat at the table wondering what made fiction, the not-true, so central that the term "nonfiction" was formed from it.

I probably would have forgotten that moment in the library if similar moments had not recurred throughout my life. The string of assumptions goes like this: Fiction is "made up," and thus crafted, invented, "made." Fiction is art because its creator draws upon imagination. Nonfiction is "not made up," and thus recorded, reported, "unmade." Nonfiction makes itself, the writer is a mere tape recorder or camera. Or, in cases where the material of nonfiction needs some shaping, the writer draws upon reason and logic alone.

Such assumptions are in part an issue of terminology. "Fiction," the root word, comes from "fingere," to form, mold, devise. "Non" simply means "not." Thus we get the implication that nonfiction is not formed, molded, or devised. Although this "non" negates the term "fiction," it is not the strongest available negative prefix. "Dis," which implies expulsion, as in "disfrock" or "disbar," would give us disfiction, a genre deprived of fiction, even, perhaps, expelled from it. "Un," which means "against" or "anti," would give us unfiction, a genre opposed to fiction. Nonfiction, looked at in this context, is not deprived of fiction or opposed to fiction, but simply, like the librarian said, not fiction.

There remains, however, an unsettling nuance to "non." While calling someone non-American does not brand them an enemy (as calling that person un-American would), it still suggests that they are other. A non-American is a foreigner, or, as my grandmother was sometimes called, an alien. Nonfiction is to fiction as non-American is to American. Thus, nonfiction is the stranger, the foreigner (or alien) in the land of fiction. What's more, in both cases, the root word is the point of reference. Many writers and editors add "creative" to "nonfiction" to mollify this sense of being strange and other, and to remind readers that creative nonfiction writers are more than recorders or appliers of reason and objectivity. Certainly many readers and writers of creative nonfiction recognize that the genre can share some elements of fiction; dialogue, place, characters, and plot, for example, might occur in both. When a piece of creative nonfiction resembles fiction, the "non" might suggest not so much "not," as something like "kicking off from." Why else insist that it is not fiction unless it is in danger of being mistaken for fiction?

If "nonfiction" might mean a work that is related to but different from fiction, perhaps works in the genre that are more akin to poetry—sharing with it lyric and image or a structure built on association and repetition rather than on narrative—would benefit from another name. I read some of Virginia Woolf's nonfiction (her lyrical, personal pieces like "Evening Over Sussex," and "The Death of the Moth," for example) for its poetry. Other writers come to mind: Terry Tempest Williams's *Desert Quartet*, for example, a lyrical, concentrated work with gaps and craters, a book written not only from reason, but also from imagination, dreams, and the body. Such works, while not poems per se, use poetry as their inspiration, their model, their "kicking off point." For them, I suggest the term "nonpoetry."

To play with terms and search for definitions can be more than an academic exercise. I'm interested in the genre's possibility, a possibility not just theoretical but practical—that is, involving practice. Rather than map out territory (and thus limit it) I mean to expand it. Rather than build fences, knock them down.

3. The Stars

A few months ago, a formerly estranged cousin gave me a copy of an old home movie. Over antipasto made the old way, we watched ourselves together, children moving in and out of a series of silent, disjointed scenes in black and white. My cousin and I sat together as his father's last birthday party unfolded before us; we watched ourselves celebrate just a few yards from the spot where an accident would later kill his father, shattering our family for decades. But on that night preserved on film, we all sit together on the pool deck of the hotel and nightclub his father and my stepfather ran together, happy beneath the stars. We sit at a long table, laughing and talking silently. Suddenly, my stepfather rises up, grabs a torch-like candle, and begins dancing around our table. While he circles the rest of us, we watch my uncle cut his Italian rum cake from Romano's.

My cousin broke the silence of that old flickering movie. "There must have been bugs," he said, "that's got to be a bug torch and he's spreading the fog around our table." But that's not what I saw. Though I didn't at first remember the scene, I knew my stepfather. He was dancing out his joy, his exuberance, the energy that pored from each cell of his body. "I'd rip the stars out of the sky for you," he used to tell my half sister, the child of his middle age, and there he was, ripping the stars out of the sky, lighting the night for one of our last happy moments together.

The camera recorded the scene for perpetuity. And yet my cousin and I, with similar family experiences, with memories of that moment, and with objective evidence before us, saw it differently. If put alone in separate rooms and interrogated or given blank sheets of paper and told to write that scene, we would come up with different stories. We both sat at the family table that night, and so the party is in our memories, embedded in the very matter of our brains.

And we both watched the tape, separately and together, several times in recent months. Nevertheless we tell different stories. Which one is true? Which one imagined? His story and mine, I believe, contain elements of fact and imagination. Both are true, for they are true to how we remember, how we see, they recreate the topographies of our minds. We can return to the film and we can return to our memories. Either way, each of us returns to a different place.

Recently, I attended another birthday party, for a friend who is a writer. After he blew out the candles, and everyone made the requisite jokes about aging, our conversation turned to writing and memory. "You could never write this scene as nonfiction," one friend, a fiction writer, said. "You couldn't remember the dialogue verbatim; you'd end up remembering words wrong and so you'd have to change them. You'd forget things and leave them out. That would make it fiction." Several others at the table agreed, assuming that without a tape recorder you'd be left with fallible memory and therefore be incapable of creating nonfiction. There were only two ways to write the scene with dialogue, they believed, to write it as fiction (and freely invent and recreate words), or to write it as nonfiction (and record, transcribe, and then report the words exactly as spoken).

One of the guests, a lawyer, objected. "You should read briefs," he said. "Recorded dialogue doesn't make any sense."

"You need the background," another friend, a nonfiction writer, added, "the color of the walls, the smell of the food. How can you understand the dialogue without the scene?"

"What if someone's words trigger a memory?" I asked. "Let's say that as you're speaking, I'm reminded of a scene from my past, like standing in my grandmother's garden. Even if we filmed and taped this party, that wouldn't show up, and yet it changes my experience of the party."

"I was wondering," the literary theorist said, "what I'd do with that moment when I became obsessed with the pattern on this plate, or when I concentrated on the taste of the red beans and rice."

If my birthday party companions read this dialogue, they would no doubt revise it according to their own memories and perceptions. In fact, that same night we suggested—as a joke or perhaps as a challenge—that each of us, two fiction writers, a poet, two creative nonfiction writers, a theorist, a lawyer, and a decorator—should go off immediately and write the scene. By the time we were well into the cake and coffee, we more or less agreed that if we were true to the events as we'd each experienced them, if we didn't write, for example, that the lawyer had stood up, reached across the table, and punched the guest of honor as he blew out his candles (since he had done nothing of the kind), we would be writing creative nonfiction.

We reached common ground in the end, I think, because we shifted both our working notion of genre and our view of "the person." When my friends claimed that nonfiction could work only with the aid of a tape recorder, their concept of the person was external, the person as captured by a machine. They had shared the assumption, arrived at by habit, that nonfiction was restricted to objectivity and reporting, that incongruity must be reasoned away. Fact, as Virginia Woolf points out, is not necessarily the same as truth, and as we talked that night, we explored what it means to be at a birthday party, what it means to participate in a conversation, how much more it is than the sounds we make, the words we speak. What we say and how we move—what machines can pick up—is only the surface of the scene. "Nonfiction" is not a synonym for "recorded surface." It has the range to sweep inward, follow the path of the mind, add layers of contemporaneous imagination, memory, and dream to the observable events of the present moment.

Patricia Hampl, who has said that memory is a place, has also said that the nonfiction writer is homeless.

One such occasion was an informal talk after her reading in the third floor lounge of a certain university's humanities' building. Graduate students used to joke about the symbolism of the building's design: Fiction and poetry were on the top floor. Freshman composition was in the basement. In the middle (just above philosophy) was nonfiction, tucked away in a corner of the literature department. Although Hampl's reading drew a large audience, only a small group of die-hard nonfictionists showed up for the talk.

In our small quarters, nearly invisible in a wing of the literature department, her discussion of the nonfiction writer's homelessness rang true. The department had just changed the name of our program from "expository writing" to "nonfiction writing" and would soon rename it "creative nonfiction." We could see that we were the new kids on the block, that to many, our genre was ill defined and invisible. But there we sat listening to a writer who had made a career of creative nonfiction, who had written two memoirs and many personal essays, and who spoke optimistically about the genre's range and possibility. Many of us felt at home for the first time—not in our lounge, but in her words.

The prospect of literary homelessness drives and limits certain writers to formulae, say, memoir in five parts (action scene followed by predictable summation followed by continuation of the action and so on, like a sitcom or a mini series). They find a "home" and hole up in the corner. And they pass along a favored formula to groups of beginner or intermediate writers, regardless of any particular student writer's emphasis, place of origin, gender, culture, aesthetic, or concept of the self. Handing over a prepackaged piece of creative nonfiction is, in essence, putting the writer into a cell. The bolder explorers, happy not to be enclosed, take advantage of the unsettled terrain of nonfiction, wandering and exploring, allowing themselves to be vulnerable, following the path of the mind even when they enter shadows, pressing on into the territory of the unknown, the mysterious, the incongruous.

Creative nonfiction is at once flourishing and invisible, set and contested. The genre that embraces the often paradoxical nature of the self is itself often paradoxical (in its position in the world of writing and letters). Patricia Hampl provides the metaphor of the creative nonfiction writer as homeless. And she also turns it around. We're lucky, she says, we get to be out under the stars.

The Art of Memoir

Mary Clearman Blew

One of the oldest and loveliest of quilt patterns is the Double Wedding Ring, in which bands of colors lock and interlock in endless circles. If you want to make a Double Wedding Ring quilt, be a saver of fabric. Treasure the smallest scraps, from the maternity dress you have just sewn for your oldest daughter or the Halloween costume you cobbled together for your youngest, from the unfaded inside hems of worn-out clothing or the cotton left over from other quilts. Keep a pair of sharp scissors on hand, and also a pattern, which I like to cut from fine sandpaper, and which will be about an inch wide by two inches long and slightly flared, like a flower petal that has been rounded off at both ends. Whenever you have a scrap of fabric, lay out your pattern on it and snip out a few more blocks.

Save your blocks in a three-pound coffee can. When the can is full, empty the blocks out on the floor and arrange them in the shape of rainbow arcs with a juxtaposition of colors and textures that pleases you. Seven pieces to an arc, seventy-two arcs to a quilt. You can sew the blocks together on a sewing machine, but I like the spell cast by hand sewing. I use a #11 needle, which is an inch-long sliver of steel with an eye so fine that it will barely take the quilter's thread, which measures time by growing infinitesimally shorter with each dip and draw of the needle, and I wear the hundred-year-old thimble of a woman named Amelia Bunn on my finger.

When you have pieced your seventy-two arcs, you must choose a fabric to join your arcs, in a process that is called "setting up" the quilt. Traditionally a Double Wedding Ring quilt is set up on white, but remember that you have all colors to choose from; and while choosing one color means forgoing others, remind yourself that your coffee can of pieces will fill again. There will be another quilt at the back of your mind while you are piecing, quilting, and binding this one, which perhaps you will give to one of your daughters, to trace her childhood through the pieces. Or perhaps you will give it to a friend, to speak the words the pattern spoke to you.

For years I thought of myself as a fiction writer, even during the years in northern Montana when I virtually stopped writing. But in 1987 I came to a divide. My father had died, and my husband was suffering a mental breakdown along with the progressive lung disease that eventually killed him. I was estranged from my older children. Then I lost my job. It was the job that mattered the most. I had a small child to support. And so I looked for another job and found one, teaching in a small college in Idaho, with the northern Rockies between me and the first half of my life.

Far from home and teaching again after years in higher-ed administration, I felt a hollowness that writing fiction seemed to do nothing to fill. And so I started all over again, writing essays to retrieve the past—in my case, the Montana homestead frontier with its harsh ideals for men and women, its tests and its limitations. The conventions of fiction, its masks and metaphors, came to seem more and more boring to me, like an unnecessary barricade between me and the material I was writing about. But because fiction was what I knew about, I used the techniques of fiction in these essays: plot, characterization, dialogue. What I began to discover was a form that worked for my purpose.

I would select an event out of family legend and retell it in a voice that grew out of my own experience and perceptions. Often the events that beckoned to me the most urgently were the ones that had been preserved in the "secret stories" my grandmothers and my great-aunts told around their Sunday tables after the dishes had been washed, elliptical and pointless and mystifying, in hushed voices that dropped or stopped altogether at the approach of one of the men or an unwise question from an eavesdropping child. Eventually I was trusted with a few of the secret stories, myself. I remember how my aunt's voice fell and her sentences became sparing when she told me a story about her mother, my grandmother. The story was about a time when my grandmother had lived alone on the homestead north of Denton, Montana, for eighteen months without seeing another woman. She had two small children and another baby on the way—her husband was away for weeks on end, trying to sell life insurance to make ends meet—and she had to carry her water in a bucket from a spring a quarter of a mile from the homestead shack, which she did at twilight, when the heat of the sun was not so oppressive. She began to hallucinate. She saw the shapes of women on the other side of the spring, shapes that looked like her dead mother and her dead sister, beckoning to her. She decided she was going crazy. She had her little children to think about. They might not be found for weeks if she broke down. And so she began to go for her water in the heat of the day, when the sun scorched her trail and bleached the color out of the grass and rocks. She never saw the beckoning shapes again.

Unlike my grandmother, I have chosen to follow the beckoning shapes. I don't understand the significance of that story for my grandmother, or why she kept it a secret except for the one time she whispered it to her younger sister in, I presume, those same stark sentences in which her sister whispered it to her niece, my aunt, the same sentences in which my aunt whispered the story just one time to me. But then, I don't fully understand why I continue to wear Amelia Bunn's thimble—it is sterling silver and engraved AB in a fine script—any more than I know what my great-grandmother looked like in life or as she appeared in the dying heat waves of that long-ago Montana twilight.

But sometimes I think I can see the turning points in the lives of dead men and women. For example, my grandmother's decision to return to schoolteaching in 1922, even though it meant breaking up her family, boarding out her oldest daughter, taking the younger children to live with her in a teacherage, leaving her husband alone on the homestead. What did that decision mean to her? I know what it means to me. Or my aunt's mowing machine accident in June of 1942, when a runaway team of sorrel horses spilled her in the path of a sickle bar that nearly cut off her foot. The disaster forced her out of the path of teaching in rural schools that she had been following and into a new life on the Olympic Peninsula. Did she understand the opportunity in the teeth of the sickle bar?

I feel an uneasy balance between writing about my grandmother and my aunt as their lives "really" were and writing about them as a projection of my own experiences. I keep reminding myself that the times when they lived are not my times. Nor do the nuances of their stories necessarily reflect my assumptions about language. And yet I am who I am because of these women and the stories they told; and, as I write about them, they live and breathe again through the umbilical tangle between character and writer.

I've been fortunate in my family's being one of storytellers and private writers who have "documented" their past. Tales, diaries, notebooks, and letters— they saved every scrap. Of course their stories were fictions as much as mine are, told over and over again and given shape and significance. Their connection to literal truth is suspect.

For my part, I struggled for a long time with the conflicting claims of the exact truth of the story and its emotional truth as I perceived it. I restrict myself to what I "know" happened: the concrete details, the objects, the history. When I speculate, I say so.

But any story depends upon its shape. In arranging the scraps that have been passed down to me, which are to be selected, which discarded? The boundaries of creative nonfiction will always be as fluid as water.

Students often ask, what can you decently write about other people? Whose permission do you have to ask? What can you decently reveal about yourself?

I can only speak for myself. I own my past and my present. Only I can decide whether or how to write about it. Also, I know that once I write about the past, I will have changed the past, in a sense set it in concrete, and I will never remember it in quite the same way. The experience itself is lost; like the old Sunday storytellers who told and retold their stories until what they remembered was the tale itself, what I will remember is what I have written.

Certainly, something personal is being sacrificed, for when I write about myself, I transform myself just as I do the past. A side-effect is that while the writing process itself can be painful, I experience a detachment from the finished essay, because I have come to exist in it as a character as separate from myself as any fictional character. I find that I can read my essays to audiences with very little emotion, although once, reading Annick Smith's essay "Homestead" to a creative writing class, I began to cry and thought I would not be able to go on. Her nonfiction character moved me in a way my own could not.

Lately I have been reading my aunt's diaries, which she kept without fail for fifty years. I feel haunted by the parallels between her life and mine. She chose, perhaps with greater self-discipline, perhaps from being closer to the source of the old punishing pressures, to stay all her life on a straight and narrow path I had been perilously near to embarking on. Her diaries reveal her unhappiness, her gradual, unwilling resignation to her lot, and finally, in her old age, her reconciliation with the lone woman she had set out to be. Which has left me with an enormous determination to resist those pressures and to try a new direction: having written my past, I will write the present and transform myself, as she did, in the interstices between fragment and pattern, through the endless interlocking connections between storyteller and story.

We'll see, we'll see. Opportunity lies in the teeth of the sickle bar.

On the Origin
of the Video Essay

John Bresland

Beginning with this Spring 2010 edition, *Blackbird* is featuring a new form of creative nonfiction we've chosen to call the video essay. In its intent the video essay is no different from its print counterpart, which for thousands of years has been a means for writers to confront hard questions on the page. The essayist pushes toward some insight or some truth. That insight, that truth, tends to be hard won, if at all, for the essay tends to ask more than it answers. That asking—whether inscribed in ancient mud, printed on paper, or streamed thirty frames per second—is central to the essay, is the essay.

So it's been, since shortly after Christ, when a Delphic priest named Plutarch wondered which came first, the chicken or the egg. A thousand years later in Japan, Sei Shōnagon compiled a list in her *Pillow Book* of "Hateful Things" and "Things That Give a Hot Feeling." These early works of nonfiction were meditations, lists, biographies, diary entries, advice. But it took an amateur in the time of Shakespeare—a French civil servant in midlife crisis who quit his job to become a writer—to attach a name to the act of exploring the limits of what we know. He called these works *Essais*. Attempts. Trials.

Michel de Montaigne drew thematic inspiration from Plutarch, but his meditations could be associative, rambling, prickly, polyvalent. Like Shōnagon's. Which isn't to say a personal assistant to the Japanese empress during the Heian dynasty shaped the work of Montaigne. She didn't, so far as we know. But Shōnagon's essay, "Things That Quicken the Heart," is the central, soulful motif of Chris Marker's *Sans Soleil* (1982), one of the first great film essays of our time. In *Sans Soleil* Marker channels his meditation on truth and memory through Sandor Krasna, an offscreen personage whose letters (in the English-language version) are voiced by Canadian actress Alexandra Stewart. Despite the fictional scrim, *Sans Soleil* remains solidly an essay, a work of nonfiction that casts multiple lines of inquiry—among them, how images rewrite memory—and renders them as poetic evocations of lived experience. Watching *Sans Soleil*, you can almost hear Chris Marker whisper, "Here is the problem of being alive right now."

I suspect the heart-quickening now of sound and image is what drew the otherwise reclusive Marker to film. And by reclusive I don't mean he was a poet and novelist with a promising literary career ahead of him—though he was, too, that kind of recluse, a writer, before he was anything else. Today, on the eve of his 90th birthday, Marker is still making films, yet less than a dozen photographs of the man exist. He avoids media, rarely gives interviews. When Marker appears in Agnes Varda's video essay *The Beaches of Agnes* (2008), he does so in the guise of a talking cat. Filmmakers who let their work speak for itself, who hold their audience in high esteem, do exist. But they're rare. And how like an essayist to refuse to explain his work. How like a poet to grant his audience a lasting measure of imaginative space.

Chris Marker grew up in Neuilly, on the posh rim of the Bois de Bologne outside Paris. Probably he read Montaigne as a boy—not from any precocity we know of, but rather because French kids read their Montaigne, just as they memorize the poems of Hugo and La Fontaine. After World War II, in which he fought for the resistance, he published a collection of poetry and, in 1949, his first novel. Then, like so many other writers and critics seduced by the French New Wave—Godard, Rohmer, Truffaut—Marker turned to celluloid, and so, for that matter, did the rest of the world.

Alongside Jean Cayrol, Marker wrote uncredited for Alain Resnais's *Night and Fog* (1955), a film essay about the Holocaust, a work that welds haunting visuals (and a color scheme Spielberg later cribbed for *Schindler's List)* to a refreshingly human voiceover. In a brilliant essay he wrote for *Threepenny Review*, Phillip Lopate describes that voiceover as "worldly, tired, weighted down with the need to make fresh those horrors that had so quickly turned stale. It was a self-interrogatory voice, like a true essayist's, dubious, ironical, wheeling and searching for the heart of its subject matter." That voice, I suspect, is Marker's. And it's the lone voice, decidedly unobjective, that resides at the heart of the visual essay. Or film essay. Or video essay.

What do we name it, anyway—this thing, this half-essay, half-film?

Lopate calls this hybrid literary form a centaur. "I have an urge to see these two interests combined," he writes, "through the works of filmmakers who commit essays on celluloid." The essay-film, as he terms it, barely exists as a cinematic genre. And this confounds Lopate. He puzzles over the rarity of personal films that track a person's thoughts as she works through some mental knot. Why, he asks, aren't there more of these things?

Lopate cites "promiscuity of the image" as one reason for the rarity of essay-films—the tendency of the motion picture, owing to its density of information, to defy clear expression of a filmmaker's thoughts. And he gestures toward the belief, widely held in commercial film circles, that the screen resists language in higher densities. Even if an artist were to beat the odds, the thinking goes, even if she were to combine powerful visuals with an artful text and weave it all together with economy and grace, who'd pay twelve bucks at the cinema to see an essay?

That the image resists the precision of language is indeed a complication for the essayist. Much in the way, I would argue, that pianos complicate singing. That is to say another skill is called for but the payoff can be sublime. Images and sound are visceral stimuli that even animal sensoria can tap into. When my mother's Italian Greyhound sees another dog on TV, he lunges for it, tries to maul the Samsung. And when a fish takes its last dying gasp on a sunlit pier in Ross McElwee's *Time Indefinite* (1993), I'm consumed with sadness over our capacity for cruelty. Looking that creature in the eye while a young boy stomps on it, I find myself wanting to save the fish and stomp the boy. A canny essayist, McElwee knows that a literary text—the lone voice confronting hard questions—is only the beginning. Images and sound, those engines of emotion, have their own story to tell. Promiscuity of the image isn't a weakness of the essay-film. It's a feature. A volatile one, sure. And it's changing the way we write, changing our conception of what writing means.

Film is visual; the essay is not. Film is collaborative; the essay is not. Film requires big money; the essay costs little and makes less. Essays and film, Lopate notes, are two different animals, and I agree with him on one condition: that it's 1991. That's when Lopate wrote "In Search of the Centaur" for *Threepenny*. The Internet was just a baby then, nursed by dweebs. Then, financial considerations reigned. If you wanted your film made, you first needed grants, financing, distributors. Today, to make a small-scale personal film, you can shoot the thing on an inexpensive digital camera and upload it to any number of free video sharing sites. In '91 you had to hustle for eyeballs. Now, of course, the artist still hustles (post a video in the middle of a digital forest, there's no guarantee it'll make a sound) but those once formidable barriers to entry—obtaining the gear to shoot your film, and getting it in position to be seen—have been leveled by digital technology. As more literary magazines migrate online, editors are discovering that the old genre categories—fiction, nonfiction, poetry—which made perfect sense on the page, no longer do. The Internet is a conveyance for images and sound as well as text, and print media is scrambling to catch up.

Today artists have access to video editing tools that ship free on computers. A generation ago, such capability didn't exist at any price. Now all it takes for a young artist to produce a documentary is an out-of-the-box Mac, a camera, and the will to see an idea through to its resolution. The act of writing has always been a personal pursuit, a concentrated form of thought. And now filmmaking, too, shares that meditative space. The tools are handheld, affordable, no less accessible than a Smith-Corona. You can shoot and edit video, compelling video, on a cell phone.

Brave new world, right? But what do we call it?

We're calling it the video essay. Because most of us experience the motion picture as video, not film. Film is analog. Film requires a shutter to convey motion. That shutter, Chris Marker told *Libération* in 2003, is what distinguishes film from video: "Out of the two hours you spend in a movie theater, you spend one of them in the dark. It's this nocturnal portion that stays with us, that fixes our memory of a film in a different way than the same film seen on television or on a monitor." Video, on the other hand, from the way it's acquired (on small, light digital cameras with startling image quality) to the way it's consumed (on mobile devices, on planes, as shared links crossing the ether) is now being carried everywhere, the way books and magazines once were. And there's a certain texture to video, a telltale combination of compression artifacts, blown-out whites and noisy blacks that isn't pretty. But it's not ugly, either. It's real. (It may also be, as Don DeLillo once described it, realer than real.) The video essay. *Video* in the Greek sense, from the verb *vidēre*—to see. *Essay* in the Greek sense, meaning to ask. In the Japanese sense, to quicken the heart. In the French sense, to try. I can think of no better way to take on the problems of being alive right now than to write this way, with a pen in one hand and a lens in the other.

Source: Bresland, John. "On the Origins of the Video Essay," *Blackbird: An Online Journal of Literature and the Arts*. 9:1 (Spring 2010) http://www.blackbird.vcu.edu/v9n1/gallery/vebresland_i/ve-origin_page.shtml

I Think I'm Musing My Mind

Roger Ebert

Blind people develop a more acute sense of hearing. Deaf people can better notice events on the periphery, and comprehend the quick movements of lips and sign language. What about people who lose the ability to speak? We expand other ways of communicating.

There are three ways I can "speak." I can print notes. I can type on my laptop, and a built-in voice says them aloud. I can use my own pidgin sign language, combining waving, pointing, shrugging, slapping my forehead, tracing letters on my palm, mime, charades, and more uses of "thumbs up" and "thumbs down" than I ever dreamed of.

Another path is open to me in the age of the Internet. I can talk with new friends all over the world. Writing has always been second nature to me, as satisfying in a different way as speaking. Maybe because I was an only child with lots of solitary time, I always felt the *need* to write, and read. I was editor of my grade school, high school and college newspapers. I published the "Washington Street News" with a primitive Hectograph system when I was 9 or 10. I was a full-time newspaper sports writer and reporter (not an intern) when I was 16. I am a quick writer. It flows conversationally.

I know I could become fluent in American Sign Language, but the problem is, I need another person who speaks ASL. Selfishly, at this stage in life, I would rather learn to read a new language than speak one.

There is one thing I can do as well as ever. I can write. When I am writing my problems become invisible and I am the same person I always was. All is well. I am as I should be.

After my first stretch in the Rehabilitation Institute of Chicago, I began to write again, a little. After my second, I returned to a nearly normal schedule. This spring during my third rehab, I was able to log onto a wi-fi network and begin writing much more. This year, which has included two major surgeries, I have so far written 170 reviews, 22 Answer Man columns, 28 Great Movie essays (not all yet published), and 37 blog entries.

In May, I began to sense a change going on. At first it was subjective. This autumn it has become undeniable. My writing has improved.

By that I don't mean it's objectively better from the reader's point of view. I mean it has expanded within my mind, reaches deeper, emerges more clearly, is more satisfactory. Sometimes I glory in it—not the quality of the prose, but the quality of the experience. I find myself writing more, because I will return to that zone longer.

I take dictation from that place within my mind that knows what to say. I think most good writers do. There is no such thing as waiting for inspiration. The idea of "diagramming" an essay in advance, as we are taught in school, may be useful to students but is foolishness for any practicing writer. The Muse visits *during* the process of creation, not before.

At first when I could not speak, I could not read easily, because sedation had undermined my attention span. I was depressed. I could turn on the TV, but why? My wife brought a wonderful DVD player to my hospital room, but I could not make myself watch movies. My life was stale and profitless. I would spend hours in a murky stupor. Knowing I had always been reading a book, my concerned wife began reading to me: Jane Austen, Charles Dickens.

Curiously, my love of reading finally returned after I picked up Cormac McCarthy's *Suttree*, a book I had already read not long before my first surgery. Now I read it two more times. I was not "reading the same book." I was reentering the same experience, the same occult and visionary prose, the life of Suttree so urgently evoked. As rarely before, a book became tactile to me. When Suttree on his houseboat pulled a cord and brought up a bottle of orange soda pop from the cool river, I savored it. I could no longer taste. I tasted it more sharply than any soda I've ever really had. When Suttree stopped at the bus station for a grilled cheese, I ate it, and the pickle, and drank the black coffee. I began to live through this desperate man's sad life.

Then movies came back, and then writing. Then contentment. I may have things to be depressed about, but I am not depressed. My remaining abilities have expanded to fill the empty spaces left. My life seems full again, almost. I am busy. I am useful. I am happy.

Cyrus Freidheim, the CEO and publisher of the *Sun-Times*, said he'd like me to try writing a blog. Didn't I already have enough to do? Apparently not. I started writing the blog in April. I looked at the comments. I became involved. I wrote, people wrote back. I started adding remarks of my own after some of the comments. I was in conversation.

Some readers are amazed that I read all the comments. Of course I do. There is no one else to vet them; Jim Emerson is too busy, and besides, after all, they are my comments. See my blog entry "Confessions of a blogger," written in a rush of pleasure about the whole process.

But this entry is not about blogs. It is about my mind and about writing. It is true I still "take dictation." But over the summer and autumn, my mind has started dictating before I am at a keyboard. Ideas and words present themselves at any time. My wife noticed me motionless, and asked if I would like to take lessons in meditation. I replied, "Actually, I'm very happy with my thoughts."

Of course I don't think only about writing. I spend time with my wife, family and friends. I read a lot, watch a lot of politics on TV. But prose is beavering along beneath, writing itself. When it comes time to type it is an expression, not a process. My mind has improved so much at this that it's become clearly apparent to me. The words, as e. e. cummings wrote, come out like a ribbon and lie flat on the brush. He wasn't writing about toothpaste. In my fancy, I like to think he could have been writing about prose.

Yes, I had that cummings line in mind before I began. I knew I was heading for it. By losing the ability to speak, I have increased my ability to communicate. I am content.

Source: Ebert, Roger. "I Think I'm Musing My Mind." Roger Ebert's Journal, *Chicago Sun-Times*. October 24, 2008. http://blogs.suntimes.com/ebert/2008/10/i_think_im_musing_my_mind.html

A Narrator Leaps Past Journalism

Vivian Gornick

I began my working life in the 1970's as a writer of what was then called personal journalism, a hybrid term meaning part personal essay, part social criticism. On the barricades for radical feminism, it had seemed natural to me from the minute I approached the typewriter to use myself—to use my own response to a circumstance or an event—as a means of making some larger sense of things.

At the time, of course, that was a shared instinct. Many other writers felt similarly compelled. The personal had become political, and the headlines metaphoric. Immediate experience signified. But from the beginning, I saw the dangers of this kind of writing—people rushing into print with no clear idea of the relation between narrator and subject, falling quickly into confessionalism or therapy on the page or naked self-absorption—and I resolved to work hard at avoiding its pitfalls. The reliable reporter, I vowed, would keep the narrator trustworthy.

One day a book editor approached me with an idea that struck a note of response. I had confided to her the tale of an intimate friendship I'd made with an Egyptian whose childhood in Cairo had strongly resembled my own in the Bronx, and now I was being invited to go to Egypt to write about middle-class Cairenes. I said yes with easy pleasure, assuming that I would do in Cairo what I had been doing in New York. That is, I'd put myself down in the middle of the city, meet the people, use my own fears and prejudices to let them become themselves, and then I'd write as I always wrote.

But Cairo was not New York, and personal journalism turned out not exactly the right job description. The city—dark, nervous, tender; intelligent, ignorant, fearful—invaded me, and I saw myself swamped by thoughts and feelings I couldn't bring into line. When I had been a working journalist, politics had provided me with a situation, and polemics had given me my story.

261

Now, in Egypt, I found myself confused by a writing impulse whose requirements I could not penetrate but whose power I felt jerked around by.

What, exactly, was the situation here? And where was the story? Above all, where was my familiar, polemical narrator? I seemed to have lost her without having found a suitable replacement. At the time I didn't understand that it wasn't personal journalism I was trying to write; it was personal narrative. It would be years before I sat down at the desk with sufficient command of the distinction to control the material, to serve the situation and tell the kind of story I now wanted to tell.

A dozen years after Egypt I set out to write a memoir about my mother, myself, and a woman who lived next door to us when I was a child. Here, for the first time, I struggled to isolate the story (the thing I had come to say) from the situation (the plot, the context, the circumstance) and to puzzle out a narrator who would serve.

I soon discovered that if I wanted to speak truthfully in this memoir—that is, without cynicism or sentiment—I had to find a tone of voice normally not mine. The one I habitually lived with wouldn't do at all: it whined, it grated, it accused; above all, it accused. Then there was the matter of syntax: my own ordinary, everyday sentence—fragmented, interjecting, overriding—also wouldn't do; it had to be altered, modified, brought under control.

And then I could see, as soon as I began writing, that I needed to pull back—way back—from these people and these events to find the place where the story could draw a deep breath and take its own measure. In short, a useful point of view, one that would permit greater freedom of association—for that of course is what I have been describing—had to be brought along. What I didn't see, and for a long while, was that this point of view could only emerge from a narrator who was me and at the same time not me.

I began to correct for myself. The process was slow, painful and riddled with self-doubt. But one day I had her. I had a narrator on the page who was telling the story that I alone, in my everyday person, would not have been able to tell. Devotion to this narrator—this persona—became, while I was writing the book, an absorption that in time went unequaled. I longed each day to meet again with her. It was not only that I admired her style, her generosity, her detachment (such a respite from the me that was me); she had become the instrument of my illumination. She could tell the truth as I alone could not.

I reread the greats in the personal essay, the ones we think of as open, honest, confiding—Montaigne, Hazlitt, Orwell, Didion—and now I saw that it wasn't their confessing voices I was responding to, it was their brilliantly created personae, their persuasive truth speakers: Orwell's obsessed democrat, Hazlitt's irascible neurotic, Didion's anxiety-ridden Californian.

Each delivers that wholeness of being in a narrator that the reader experiences as reliable; the one we can trust will take us on a journey, make the piece arrive, bring us out into a clearing where the sense of things is larger than it was before.

Living as I now did with the idea of the nonfiction persona, I began to think better than I had before about the commonplace need, alive in all of us, to make large sense of things in the very moment, even as experience is overtaking us. Everywhere I turned in those days, I found an excuse for the observation that we pull from ourselves the narrator who will shape better than we alone can the inchoate flow of events into which we are continually being plunged.

I remember I once went on a rafting trip down the Rio Grande with the man who was then my husband and a friend of ours. The river was hot and wild; sad, brilliant, remote; closed in by canyon walls, desert banks, snakes and flash floods; on one side Texas, the other Mexico. A week after we'd been there, snipers on the Mexico side killed two people also floating on a raft.

Later we each wrote about the trip. My husband focused brightly on the "river rats" who were our guides, our friend soberly on the misery of illegal immigrants, I morbidly on what strangers my husband and I had become. Reading these pieces side by side was in itself an experience. We had all used the river, the heat, the remoteness to frame our stories. Beyond that, how alone each of us had been, sitting there together on that raft, carving out of our separating anxieties the narrator who, in the midst of all that beauty and oppressiveness, would keep us company and tell us what we were living through.

It mimics one of the earliest of narrative impulses, this kind of writing: to pull from one's own boring, agitated self the one who will make large sense of things; the persona—possessed of a tone, a syntax, a perspective not wholly one's own—who will find the story riding the tide that we, in our unmediated state, otherwise drown in.

That is what it means to become interested in one's own existence as a means of transforming event into writing experience.

Memory and Imagination

Patricia Hampl

When I was seven, my father, who played the violin on Sundays with a nicely tortured flair which we considered artistic, led me by the hand down a long, unlit corridor in St. Luke's School basement, a sort of tunnel that ended in a room full of pianos. There many little girls and a single sad boy were playing truly tortured scales and arpeggios in a mash of troubled sound. My father gave me over to Sister Olive Marie, who did look remarkably like an olive.

Her oily face gleamed as if it had just been rolled out of a can and laid on the white plate of her broad, spotless wimple. She was a small, plump woman; her body and the small window of her face seemed to interpret the entire alphabet of olive: her face was a sallow green olive placed upon the jumbo ripe olive of her black habit. I trusted her instantly and smiled, glad to have my hand placed in the hand of a woman who made sense, who provided the satisfaction of being what she was: an Olive who looked like an olive.

My father left me to discover the piano with Sister Olive Marie so that one day I would join him in mutually tortured piano-violin duets for the edification of my mother and brother who sat at the table meditatively spooning in the last of their pineapple sherbet until their part was called for: they put down their spoons and clapped while we bowed, while the sweet ice in their bowls melted, while the music melted, and we all melted a little into each other for a moment.

But first Sister Olive must do her work. I was shown middle C, which Sister seemed to think terribly important. I stared at middle C and then glanced away for a second. When my eye returned, middle C was gone, its slim finger lost in the complicated grasp of the keyboard. Sister Olive struck it again, finding it with laughable ease. She emphasized the importance of middle C, its central position, a sort of North Star of sound. I remember thinking, "Middle C is the belly button of the piano," an insight whose originality and accuracy stunned me with pride. For the first time in my life I was astonished by metaphor. I hesitated to tell the kindly Olive for some reason; apparently I understood a true metaphor is a risky business, revealing of the self. In fact, I have never, until this moment of writing it down, told my first metaphor to anyone.

Sunlight flooded the room; the pianos, all black, gleamed. Sister Olive, dressed in the colors of the keyboard, gleamed; middle C shimmered with meaning and I resolved never—never—to forget its location: it was the center of the world.

Then Sister Olive, who had had to show me middle C twice but who seemed to have drawn no bad conclusions about me anyway, got up and went to the windows on the opposite wall. She pulled the shades down, one after the other. The sun was too bright, she said. She sneezed as she stood at the windows with the sun shedding its glare over her. She sneezed and sneezed, crazy little convulsive sneezes, one after another, as helpless as if she had the hiccups.

"The sun makes me sneeze," she said when the fit was over and she was back at the piano. This was odd, too odd to grasp in the mind. I associated sneezing with colds, and colds with rain, fog, snow and bad weather. The sun, however, had caused Sister Olive to sneeze in this wild way, Sister Olive who gleamed benignly and who was so certain of the location of the center of the world. The universe wobbled a bit and became unreliable. Things were not, after all, necessarily what they seemed. Appearance deceived: here was the sun acting totally out of character, hurling this woman into sneezes, a woman so mild that she was named, so it seemed, for a bland object on a relish tray.

I was given a red book, the first Thompson book, and told to play the first piece over and over at one of the black pianos where the other children were crashing away. This, I was told, was called practicing. It sounded alluringly adult, practicing. The piece itself consisted mainly of middle C, and I excelled, thrilled by my savvy at being able to locate that central note amidst the cunning camouflage of all the other white keys before me. Thrilled too by the shiny red book that gleamed, as the pianos did, as Sister Olive did, as my eager eyes probably did. I sat at the formidable machine of the piano and got to know middle C intimately, preparing to be as tortured as I could manage one day soon with my father's violin at my side.

But at the moment Mary Katherine Reilly was at my side, playing something at least two or three lessons more sophisticated than my piece. I believe she even struck a chord. I glanced at her from the peasantry of single notes, shy, ready to pay homage. She turned toward me, stopped playing, and sized me up.

Sized me up and found a person ready to be dominated. Without introduction she said, "My grandfather invented the collapsible opera hat."

I nodded, I acquiesced, I was hers. With that little stroke it was decided between us—that she should be the leader, and I the sidekick. My job was admiration. Even when she added, "But he didn't make a penny from it. He didn't have a patent"—even then, I knew and she knew that this was not an admission of powerlessness, but the easy candor of a master, of one who can afford a weakness or two.

With the clairvoyance of all fated relationships based on dominance and submission, it was decided in advance: that when the time came for us to play duets, I should always play second piano, that I should spend my allowance to buy her the Twinkies she craved but was not allowed to have, that finally, I should let her copy from my test paper, and when confronted by our teacher, confess with convincing hysteria that it was I, I who had cheated, who had reached above myself to steal what clearly belonged to the rightful heir of the inventor of the collapsible opera hat. . . .

There must be a reason I remember that little story about my first piano lesson. In fact, it isn't a story, just a moment, the beginning of what could perhaps become a story. For the memoirist, more than for the fiction writer, the story seems already *there,* already accomplished and fully achieved in history ("in reality," as we naively say). For the memoirist, the writing of the story is a matter of transcription.

That, anyway, is the myth. But no memoirist writes for long without experiencing an unsettling disbelief about the reliability of memory, a hunch that memory is not, after all, *just* memory. I don't know why I remembered this fragment about my first piano lesson. I don't, for instance, have a single recollection of my first arithmetic lesson, the first time I studied Latin, the first time my grandmother tried to teach me to knit. Yet these things occurred too, and must have their stories.

It is the piano lesson that has trudged forward, clearing the haze of forgetfulness, showing itself bright with detail more than thirty years after the event. I did not choose to remember the piano lesson. It was simply there, like a book that has always been on the shelf, whether I ever read it or not, the binding and title showing as I skim across the contents of my life. On the day I wrote this fragment I happened to take that memory, not some other, from the shelf and paged through it. I found more detail, more event, perhaps a little more entertainment than I had expected, but the memory itself was there from the start. Waiting for me.

Or was it? When I reread what I had written just after I finished it, I realized that I had told a number of lies. I *think* it was my father who took me the first time for my piano lesson—but maybe he only took me to meet my teacher and there was no actual lesson that day. And did I even know then that he played the violin—didn't he take up his violin again much later, as a result of my piano playing, and not the reverse? And is it even remotely accurate to describe as "tortured" the musicianship of a man who began every day by belting out "Oh What a Beautiful Morning" as he shaved?

More: Sister Olive Marie did sneeze in the sun, but was her name Olive? As for her skin tone—I would have sworn it was olive-like; I would have been willing to spend the better part of an afternoon trying to write the exact description of imported Italian or Greek olive her face suggested: I wanted to get it right. But now, were I to write that passage over, it is her intense black eyebrows I would see, for suddenly they seem the central fact of that face, some indicative mark of her serious and patient nature. But the truth is, I don't remember the woman at all. She's a sneeze in the sun and a finger touching middle C. That, at least, is steady and clear.

Worse: I didn't have the Thompson book as my piano text. I'm sure of that because I remember envying children who did have this wonderful book with its pictures of children and animals printed on the pages of music.

As for Mary Katherine Reilly. She didn't even go to grade school with me (and her name isn't Mary Katherine Reilly—but I made that change on purpose). I met her in Girl Scouts and only went to school with her later, in high school. Our relationship was not really one of leader and follower; I played first piano most of the time in duets. She certainly never copied anything from a test paper of mine: she was a better student, and cheating just wasn't a possibility with her. Though her grandfather (or someone in her family) did invent the collapsible opera hat and I remember that she was proud of that fact, she didn't tell me this news as a deft move in a childish power play.

So, what was I doing in this brief memoir? Is it simply an example of the curious relation a fiction writer has to the material of her own life? Maybe. That may have some value in itself. But to tell the truth (if anyone still believes me capable of telling the truth), I wasn't writing fiction. I was writing memoir—or was trying to. My desire was to be accurate. I wished to embody the myth of memoir: to write as an act of dutiful transcription.

Yet clearly the work of writing narrative caused me to do something very different from transcription. I am forced to admit that memoir is not a matter of transcription, that memory itself is not a warehouse of finished stories, not a static gallery of framed pictures. I must admit that I invented. But why?

Two whys: why did I invent, and then, if a memoirist must inevitably invent rather than transcribe, why do I—why should anybody—write memoir at all?

I must respond to these impertinent questions because they, like the bumper sticker I saw the other day commanding all who read it to QUESTION AUTHORITY, challenge my authority as a memoirist and as a witness.

It still comes as a shock to realize that I don't write about what I know: I≈write in order to find out what I know. Is it possible to convey to a reader the enormous degree of blankness, confusion, hunch and uncertainty lurking in the act of writing? When I am the reader, not the writer, I too fall into the lovely illusion that the words before me (in a story by Mavis Gallant, an essay by Carol Bly, a memoir by M. F. K. Fisher), which *read* so inevitably, must also have been *written* exactly as they appear, rhythm and cadence, language and syntax, the powerful waves of the sentences laying themselves on the smooth beach of the page one after another faultlessly.

But here I sit before a yellow legal pad, and the long page of the preceding two paragraphs is a jumble of crossed-out lines, false starts, confused order. A mess. The mess of my mind trying to find out what it wants to say. This is a writer's frantic, grabby mind, not the poised mind of a reader ready to be edified or entertained.

I sometimes think of the reader as a cat, endlessly fastidious, capable, by turns, of mordant indifference and riveted attention, luxurious, recumbent, and ever poised. Whereas the writer is absolutely a dog, panting and moping, too eager for an affectionate scratch behind the ears, lunging frantically after any old stick thrown in the distance.

The blankness of a new page never fails to intrigue and terrify me. Sometimes, in fact, I think my habit of writing on long yellow sheets comes from an atavistic fear of the writer's stereotypic "blank white page." At least when I begin writing, my page isn't utterly blank; at least it has a wash of color on it, even if the absence of words must finally be faced on a yellow sheet as truly as on a blank white one. Well, we all have our ways of whistling in the dark.

If I approach writing from memory with the assumption that I know what I wish to say, I assume that intentionality is running the show. Things are not that simple. Or perhaps writing is even more profoundly simple, more telegraphic and immediate in its choices than the grating wheels and chugging engine of logic and rational intention. The heart, the guardian of intuition with its secret, often fearful intentions, is the boss, its commands are what a writer obeys—often without knowing it. Or, I do.

That's why I'm a strong adherent of the first draft. And why it's worth pausing for a moment to consider what a first draft really is. By my lights, the piano lesson memoir is a first draft. That doesn't mean it exists here exactly as I first wrote it. I like to think I've cleaned it up from the first time I put it down on paper. I've cut some adjectives here, toned down the hyperbole there, smoothed a transition, cut a repetition—that sort of housekeeperly tidying-up. But the piece remains a first draft because I haven't yet gotten to know it, haven't given it a chance to tell me anything. For me, writing a first draft is a little like meeting someone for the first time. I come away with a wary acquaintanceship, but the real friendship (if any) and genuine intimacy—that's all down the road. Intimacy with a piece of writing, as with a person, comes from paying attention to the revelations it is capable of giving, not by imposing my own preconceived notions, no matter how well-intentioned they might be.

I try to let pretty much anything happen in a first draft. A careful first draft is a failed first draft. That may be why there are so many inaccuracies in the piano lesson memoir: I didn't censor, I didn't judge. I kept moving. But I would not publish this piece as a memoir on its own in its present state. It isn't the "lies" in the piece that give me pause, though a reader has a right to expect a memoir to be as accurate as the writer's memory can make it. No, it isn't the lies themselves that makes the piano lesson memoir a first draft and therefore "unpublishable."

The real trouble: the piece hasn't yet found its subject; it isn't yet about what it wants to be about. Note: what *it* wants, not what I want. The difference has to do with the relation a memoirist—any writer, in fact—has to unconscious or half-known intentions and impulses in composition.

Now that I have the fragment down on paper, I can read this little piece as a mystery which drops clues to the riddle of my feelings, like a culprit who wishes to be apprehended. My narrative self (the culprit who has invented) wishes to be discovered by my reflective self, the self who wants to understand and make sense of a half-remembered story about a nun sneezing in the sun. . . .

We only store in memory images of value. The value may be lost over the passage of time (I was baffled about why I remembered that sneezing nun, for example), but that's the implacable judgment of feeling: *this,* we say somewhere deep within us, is something I'm hanging on to. And of course, often we cleave to things because they possess heavy negative charges. Pain likes to be vivid.

Over time, the value (the feeling) and the stored memory (the image) may become estranged. Memoir seeks a permanent home for feeling and image, a habitation where they can live together in harmony. Naturally, I've had a lot of experiences since I packed away that one from the basement of St. Luke's School; that piano lesson has been effaced by waves of feeling for other moments and episodes. I persist in believing the event has value—after all, I remember it—but in writing the memoir I did not simply relive the experience. Rather, I explored the mysterious relationship between all the images I could round up and the even more impacted feelings that caused me to store the images safely away in memory. Stalking the relationship, seeking the congruence between stored image and hidden emotion—that's the real job of memoir.

By writing about that first piano lesson, I've come to know things I could not know otherwise. But I only know these things as a result of reading this first draft. While I was writing, I was following the images, letting the details fill the room of the page and use the furniture as they wished. I was their dutiful servant—or thought I was. In fact, I was the faithful retainer of my hidden feelings which were giving the commands.

I really did feel, for instance, that Mary Katherine Reilly was far superior to me. She was smarter, funnier, more wonderful in every way—that's how I saw it. Our friendship (or she herself) did not require that I become her vassal, yet perhaps in my heart that was something I wanted; I wanted a way to express my feeling of admiration. I suppose I waited until this memoir to begin to find the way.

Just as, in the memoir, I finally possess that red Thompson book with the barking dogs and bleating lambs and winsome children. I couldn't (and still can't) remember what my own music book was, so I grabbed the name and image of the one book I could remember. It was only in reviewing the piece after writing it that I saw my inaccuracy. In pondering this "lie," I came to see what I was up to: I was getting what I wanted. At last.

The truth of many circumstances and episodes in the past emerges for the memoirist through details (the red music book, the fascination with a nun's name and gleaming face), but these details are not merely information, not flat facts. Such details are not allowed to lounge. They must work. Their work is the creation of symbol. But it's more accurate to call it the *recognition* of symbol. For meaning is not "attached" to the detail by the memoirist; meaning is revealed. That's why a first draft is important. Just as the first meeting (good or bad) with someone who later becomes the beloved is important and is often reviewed for signals, meanings, omens, and indications.

Now I can look at that music book and see it not only as "a detail," but for what it is, how it *acts.* See it as the small red door leading straight into the dark room of my childhood longing and disappointment. That red book *becomes* the palpable evidence of that longing. In other words, it becomes symbol. There is no symbol, no life-of-the-spirit in the general or the abstract. Yet a writer wishes—indeed all of us wish—to speak about profound matters that are, like it or not, general and abstract. We wish to talk to each other about life and death, about love, despair, loss, and innocence. We sense that in order to live together we must learn to speak of peace, of history, of meaning and values. Those are a few.

We seek a means of exchange, a language which will renew these ancient concerns and make them wholly and pulsingly ours. Instinctively, we go to our store of private images and associations for our authority to speak of these weighty issues. We find, in our details and broken and obscured images, the language of symbol. Here memory impulsively reaches out its arms and embraces imagination. That is the resort to invention. It isn't a lie, but an act of necessity, as the innate urge to locate personal truth always is.

All right. Invention is inevitable. But why write memoir? Why not call it fiction and be done with all the hashing about, wondering where memory stops and imagination begins? And if memoir seeks to talk about "the big issues," about history and peace, death and love—why not leave these reflections to those with expert and scholarly knowledge? Why let the common or garden variety memoirist into the club? I'm thinking again of that bumper sticker: why Question Authority?

My answer, of course, is a memoirist's answer. Memoir must be written because each of us must have a created version of the past. Created: that is, real, tangible, made of the stuff of a life lived in place and in history. And the down side of any created thing as well: we must live with a version that attaches us to our limitations, to the inevitable subjectivity, of our points of view. We must acquiesce to our experience and our gift to transform experience into meaning and value. You tell me your story, I'll tell you my story.

If we refuse to do the work of creating this personal version of the past, someone else will do it for us. That is a scary political fact. "The struggle of man against power," a character in Milan Kundera's novel *The Book of Laughter and Forgetting* says, "is the struggle of memory against forgetting." He refers to willful political forgetting, the habit of nations and those in power (Question Authority!) to deny the truth of memory in order to disarm moral and ethical power. It's an efficient way of controlling masses of people. It doesn't even require much bloodshed, as long as people are entirely willing to give over their personal memories. Whole histories can be rewritten. As Czeslaw Milosz said in his 1980 Nobel Prize lecture, the number of books published that seek to deny the existence of the Nazi death camps now exceeds one hundred.

What is remembered is what *becomes* reality. If we "forget" Auschwitz, if we "forget" My Lai, what then do we remember? And what is the purpose of our remembering? If we think of memory naively, as a simple story, logged like a documentary in the archive of the mind, we miss its beauty but also its function. The beauty of memory rests in its talent for rendering detail, for paying homage to the senses, its capacity to love the particles of life, the richness and idiosyncrasy of our existence. The function of memory, on the other hand, is intensely personal and surprisingly political.

Our capacity to move forward as developing beings rests on a healthy relation with the past. Psychotherapy, that widespread method of mental health, relies heavily on memory and on the ability to retrieve and organize images and events from the personal past. We carry our wounds and perhaps even worse, our capacity to wound, forward with us. If we learn not only to tell our stories but to listen to what our stories tell us—to write the first draft and then return for the second draft—we are doing the work of memoir.

Memoir is the intersection of narration and reflection, of story-telling and essay-writing. It can present its story *and* reflect and consider the meaning of the story. It is a peculiarly open form, inviting broken and incomplete images, half-recollected fragments, all the mass (and mess) of detail. It offers to shape this confusion—and in shaping, of course it necessarily creates a work of art, not a legal document. But then, even legal documents are only valiant attempts to consign the truth, the whole truth and nothing but the truth to paper. Even they remain versions.

Locating touchstones—the red music book, the olive Olive, my father's violin playing—is deeply satisfying. Who knows why? Perhaps we all sense that we can't grasp the whole truth and nothing but the truth of our experience. Just can't be done. What can be achieved, however, is a version of its swirling, changing wholeness. A memoirist must acquiesce to selectivity, like any artist. The version we dare to write is the only truth, the only relationship we can have with the past. Refuse to write your life and you have no life. At least, that is the stern view of the memoirist.

Personal history, logged in memory, is a sort of slide projector flashing images on the wall of the mind. And there's precious little order to the slides in the rotating carousel. Beyond that confusion, who knows who is running the projector? A memoirist steps into this darkened room of flashing, unorganized images and stands blinking for a while. Maybe for a long while. But eventually, as with any attempt to tell a story, it is necessary to put something first, then something else. And so on, to the end. That's a first draft. Not necessarily the truth, not even *a* truth sometimes, but the first attempt to create a shape.

The first thing I usually notice at this stage of composition is the appalling inaccuracy of the piece. Witness my first piano lesson draft. Invention is screamingly evident in what I intended to be transcription. But here's the further truth: I feel no shame. In fact, it's only now that my interest in the piece truly quickens. For I can see what isn't there, what is shyly hugging the walls, hoping not to be seen. I see the filmy shape of the next draft. I see a more acute version of the episode or—this is more likely—an entirely new piece rising from the ashes of the first attempt.

The next draft of the piece would have to be a true re-vision, a new seeing of the materials of the first draft. Nothing merely cosmetic will do—no rouge buffing up the opening sentence, no glossy adjective to lift a sagging line, nothing to attempt covering a patch of gray writing. None of that. I can't say for sure, but my hunch is the revision would lead me to more writing about my father (why was I so impressed by that ancestral inventor of the collapsible opera hat? Did I feel I had nothing as remarkable in my own background? Did this make me feel inadequate?). I begin to think perhaps Sister Olive is less central to this business than she is in this draft. She is meant to be a moment, not a character.

· And so I might proceed, if I were to undertake a new draft of the memoir. I begin to feel a relationship developing between a former self and me.

And, even more compelling, a relationship between an old world and me. Some people think of autobiographical writing as the precious occupation of a particularly self-absorbed person. Maybe, but I don't buy that. True memoir is written in an attempt to find not only a self but a world.

The self-absorption that seems to be the impetus and embarrassment of autobiography turns into (or perhaps always was) a hunger for the world. Actually, it begins as hunger for *a* world, one gone or lost, effaced by time or a more sudden brutality. But in the act of remembering, the personal environment expands, resonates beyond itself, beyond its "subject," into the endless and tragic recollection that is history.

We look at old family photographs in which we stand next to black, boxy Fords and are wearing period costumes, and we do not gaze fascinated because there we are young again, or there we are standing, as we never will again in life, next to our mother. We stare and drift because there we are . . . historical. It is the dress, the black car that dazzle us now and draw us beyond our mother's bright arms which once caught us. We reach into the attractive impersonality of something more significant than ourselves. We write memoir, in other words. We accept the humble position of writing a version rather than "the whole truth."

I suppose I write memoir because of the radiance of the past—it draws me back and back to it. Not that the past is beautiful. In our communal memoir, in history, the death camps *are* back there. In intimate life too, the record is usually pretty mixed. "I could tell you stories . . ." people say and drift off, meaning terrible things have happened to them.

But the past is radiant. It has the light of lived life. A memoirist wishes to touch it. No one owns the past, though typically the first act of new political regimes, whether of the left or the right, is to attempt to re-write history, to grab the past and make it over so the end comes out right. So their power looks inevitable.

No one owns the past, but it is a grave error (another age would have said a grave sin) not to inhabit memory. Sometimes I think it is all we really have. But that may be a trifle melodramatic. At any rate, memory possesses authority for the fearful self in a world where it is necessary to have authority in order to Question Authority.

There may be no more pressing intellectual need in our culture than for people to become sophisticated about the function of memory. The political implications of the loss of memory are obvious. The authority of memory is a personal confirmation of selfhood. To write one's life is to live it twice, and the second living is both spiritual and historical, for a memoir reaches deep within the personality as it seeks its narrative form and also grasps the life-of-the-times as no political treatise can.

Our most ancient metaphor says life is a journey. Memoir is travel writing, then, notes taken along the way, telling how things looked and what thoughts occurred. But I cannot think of the memoirist as a tourist. This is the traveller who goes on foot, living the journey, taking on mountains, enduring deserts, marveling at the lush green places. Moving through it all faithfully, not so much a survivor with a harrowing tale to tell as a pilgrim, seeking, wondering.

The Art of Self

Steven Harvey

On a flight recently I met a fiction writer. Both of us were on our way to a writer's conference in Portland, Oregon, and when I told her that I wrote personal essays she laughed. "Oh, I love the form," she said. "It's so easy." I heard the ice in our drinks rattle in the silence that ensued. I had plenty of time, before we landed, to think about what she had said.

Confusion about the essay begins with a misconception: that art must be invented. To be creative—the argument goes—literature must be made up. Since the personal essay begins with a real life, it is less creative, less artistic, than fiction. Such a view, I think, is mistaken, based not only on confusions about writing, but on confusions about art as well. What makes writing—writing of any kind—an art is not invention, but shape. Shapeliness. The facts, the events, the invented flights of fancy do not make up a work of art. The shapeliness of the author's composition takes us to that level.

The urge to shape begins in loss. All of us are losers, of course, because we are human, but artists console themselves, redeem losses, with their creations. John Logan has written that the baby, weaned from its mother's breast, begins moving its mouth as if to shape words, language beginning with the first loss. For the writer, these mouthings never stop. Understood this way, art does not begin with ego, but with feelings of self-annihilation, the artist creating a surrogate self. So, the potter shapes a pot. The painter catches a scene. The musician holds a note.

And the essayist fashions a text. "My advice to memoir writers," Annie Dillard writes, "is to embark upon a memoir for the same reason you would embark on any book: to fashion a text." The result is that the text—even if taken from the writer's life—has a life of its own, separate from the author. "After I've written about my experience," Dillard adds, "my memories are gone; they've been replaced by the work. The work is a sort of changeling on the doorstep." Only the text, shed of ourselves and hammered into shape, can redeem us. The enemy of the text, then, is what happened, and this is true whether the work is fictional or not. What happened may matter to us, but it is lost on us if we do not transform it into art.

Writers fashion a text, giving shape to our joys and fears, but making choices on the page. Choice—not invention or reportage—gives direction and purpose to a work of literature and there are certainly many choices to be made: When to begin? When to end? Do I fess up or lie? Should I use a pencil or a computer, yellow legal pad or typing paper? To drink or not to drink—and when! In the course of sifting through these and a thousand other choices, writers make a series of essential decisions that give singular shape to the work.

First, they must, at some point, settle on beginnings and endings. Life has none. It goes on and on. My dog lives in a constant blur, a stream-of-consciousness from Purina to Purina. Only humans can choose beginnings and endings. Meaning starts the moment we say "in the beginning" and "here endeth." These are crucial shaping choices.

The essayist also must make choices involving proportion and pace. There is much art in what is relegated to background information, the essential but dull material in an essay. Any editor will tell you there is art, as well, in what is left out entirely. By the same token, the writer must decide what counts and when to bear down. In a memoir, this may be the penultimate moment—that brink when an event can go either way. Sometimes, for the essayist, the moment is given over to an idea as nuances and ambiguities are exploited and explored. Here the writer chooses to savor an event by giving it its due.

Most crucial of all in shaping a text are the choices an author makes about language. A memoir writer comes to terms with an experience, and the terms that the writer settles on tell all. Each of us has many voices—the voice for a friend, a colleague, a student, a lover—and each voice is different. Personal essayists do not need to have enormous vocabularies or—spare us—a gift for grandiloquence, but they must constantly adjudicate the voices in their heads and choose the right language.

These, then, are the essential shaping devices, the tools of the essayist's craft: beginnings and endings, proportion and pace, and language. They do not involve invention, but they are the way to art—and they are rarely easy.

Recognizing that art is in the shaping of language, not in inventing or being true to life, can be liberating for students. They do not need to have exciting lives in order to write about themselves, nor do they need to resort to fanciful creativity. Instead they can find that any event, when fashioned in words, can have meaning. But all of us, whether we be students, teachers, writers, or—bless their souls!—readers, reap benefits from carefully shaped composition. "All that you love you lose," Yeats wrote. Our life slips through greedy fingers even as we live it. Works of art may not give us our lives back, but they are money in the spiritual bank. With these hard-earned things of beauty we redeem a lifetime of losses.

The Digital Essay:
An Introduction

Sonya Huber

I make text and teach the creation of text. I use computers constantly, and I hardly ever write with pen and paper anymore. But beyond word processing and email, I was skeptical about any boost of meaning that might come from the addition of new-fangled hypertext-flash-online-multimodal foolishness. Then I got the chance to attend a two-week Digital Media and Composition Institute at the Ohio State University. I learned to think about composition (creative writing in all genres) in new ways. I thought about and re-examined my own composition process as part of my initial assumption that writing was only "text."

Most importantly, as a creative writer, I got to *play*. Dr. Cynthia Selfe and her crew put cameras in our hands, taught us Flash and Dream Weaver, and I found myself back at square one, understanding composition as a process that teaches through *doing* and *making*, a connection that was intuitive based on my background in creative writing workshops. I roamed around outside, very unplugged. I took pictures of parking meters and shoes, trophics and stuffed fish. I squatted in the center of the road to take a close-up of a cracked and layered stripe of yellow paint. These images meant something to me because I had a place to put them; I took a break from writing to capture writing through image, and I made a strange little photo essay about the writing process that I am quite fond of.

This attention to learning through making projects relevant to student's lives—projects that are therefore rhetorically, personally, and socially important, using modes the students have a background in to capture the rhetorics that interest with their experiences—prompted me to examine my writing process as a way to see the ways in which digital modes might inform and expand creative writing and composition pedagogy. The simple version: I made things in new ways and thought about new connections. Then those new connections linked with what I already know about teaching and writing.

Where I'm at, and what the institute stresses, is that technology itself is neither inherently a problem or a solution. The medium is the message, but the message can also transcend this container, with all due respect to Marshall McLuhan. Content is still the brains. I love gadgets: audio, video, etc., but the medium can't make up for a message.

Source: Huber, Sonya. "The Digital Essay: An Introduction"; "How Do I Write? An Exploration of the Writing Process." <http://www.sonyahuber.com/project/Huber/fourmenu.html>; "What Is Multimodal Composition and Does It Mean We Have to Give Up the Alphabet?" <http://www.sonyahuber.com/project/Huber/front.html>

Courting the Approval of the Dead

Tracy Kidder

I have never written much about myself, but, like most writers I know, I am interested in the subject. We live in an era surfeited with memoirs. This is my contribution to the excess.

My writing career began at Harvard College about thirty-two years ago, shortly after I enrolled as an undergraduate. I planned to fix the world by becoming a diplomat. I began by studying political science. Thinking I should have a hobby, I also took a course in creative writing. I didn't invest a lot of ego in the enterprise and maybe for that reason the first short stories that I wrote were rather sprightly. I think they contained some dialogue that human beings might have uttered. Anyway, the teacher liked them and, more important, so did some of the young women in the class. My first strong impulse to become a writer sprang from this realization: that writing could be a means of meeting and impressing girls.

The next year I got into a class taught by the poet and great translator Robert Fitzgerald. He admitted only about a dozen students from among dozens of applicants, and I seem to remember that I was the youngest of the anointed group. This mattered to me. In high school I had been addicted to competitive sports, and I conceived of writing in sporting terms. I figured I had won part of the competition already, by being the youngest student admitted to the class. The yearning for distinction is common among writers, and in that sense I had begun to become a writer.

I want to try to summon Mr. Fitzgerald back from the dead. I remember him as a small, elegant man, then in his sixties, I believe. Occasionally during office hours he smoked a cigarette, and did so with great deliberation, making every puff count—I think he'd been warned off tobacco, and had put himself on short rations. He would enter the classroom with a green bookbag slung over his shoulder, and would greet us with a smile and a sigh as he heaved the bag onto the long seminar table. Mr. Fitzgerald's green bag contained our work, *my* work, with his comments upon it. I could not have been more interested in that object if Mr. Fitzgerald had been our adult provider, returning with food he'd found out in the world. But the way he sighed, as he heaved that sack onto the table, insinuated that what lay inside wasn't as valuable as food. Certainly it looked like a heavy load for one professor to carry.

I have always talked too much and listened too little. What is it about certain people that has made me pay attention to everything they say? Their confidence and wit, I guess, but most of all their interest in *me.* Mr. Fitzgerald paid his students the great compliment of taking us seriously. He flattered us, dauntingly. I remember the first day of that class. From his place at the head of the table Mr. Fitzgerald eyed us all. He had a pair of reading glasses, half-glasses, which he often used to great effect. He lowered them and looking at us over the top of them, said something like, "The only reason for writing is to produce something *classic.* And I expect that you will produce *classic* work during this term."

I recall thinking, "You do?"

Of course, none of us did, with the possible exception of one young woman who wrote a poem entitled "The Splendor and the Terror of the Universe as Revealed to Me on Brattle Street." I don't recall the poem, but I still like the title.

Having told us of his expectations, Mr. Fitzgerald offered his first advice for meeting them. He jabbed an index finger at the wastebasket beside him and said, "The greatest repository I know of for writers. And I do hope that it will *precede* me."

After a few weeks of Mr. Fitzgerald, I gave up on political science. I quit right in the middle of a lecture by the then-not-very-famous professor Henry Kissinger. The lecture bored me. Professor Kissinger was only partly to blame. I now described myself as a writer, and I thought a writer shouldn't be interested in politics. I had not yet realized that a writer ought to know about something besides writing, so as to have something to write about. When I left that lecture I went right to the English department office and signed up. I'd already begun to do a lot of reading on my own, mostly fiction, which I was consuming at a rate I've never equaled since. At the same time, I had suddenly acquired an assigned-reading disability and a sleep disorder. I had trouble reading books that appeared on formal course lists, and I often worked all night on stories for Mr. Fitzgerald, then went to sleep around the time when my other classes began.

During the first part of Mr. Fitzgerald's class, he would talk about writing and read aloud to us, very occasionally stuff that a student had written, and more often works by wonderful, famous writers he had known, such as his old friend Flannery O'Connor. He read us one of her stories, and when he finished, he said, "That story unwinds like a Rolex watch." Listening to him read such estimable work made me want to try my hand. I think he aimed for that effect, because in the second half of every class he had us write. He warmed us up, and then made us exercise. It is a testament to those warmups of his that I can't recall ever being unable to write *something* in that room for him. In his presence, even poetry seemed possible. Mr. Fitzgerald insisted I try my hand at a poem now and then. I struggled but complied. Finally, I got one off that he seemed to like. It came back from him with this comment at the bottom: "This is very like a poem."

I prefer other memories, especially this one: I had written a short story, which an undergraduate, literary friend of mine had read and disliked. This was the first and at the time the only literary friend I'd acquired, and I thought him very wise and perspicacious, because he had encouraged me. I guessed that my friend must be right about my story. Once he'd pointed out its flaws, I saw them clearly, too. But I decided to show the thing to Mr. Fitzgerald, just so he'd know that I was working. He opened the next class by saying that he was going to read a student's story, a story that he particularly liked, and I remember sitting there wishing that he would some day single out a story of mine in that way and I recall vividly the moment when I realized that it was my story he was reading. The mellifluous voice that had read to us from the likes of James Agee and Wallace Stevens and Flannery O'Connor was reading something of mine! I felt frightened. Then I felt confused. I don't think it had ever occurred to me that intelligent people could disagree about the quality of a piece of writing. If my literary friend thought the story was lousy, Mr. Fitzgerald surely would, too. I see myself sitting at that table with my mouth hanging open—and closing it fast when I remembered the young women in the room. At first I wanted to ask Mr. Fitzgerald to stop, and then I hoped he never would.

I hoped, indeed expected, to have that experience again. I remember that I had given Mr. Fitzgerald a story I knew to be marvelous, a story I knew he'd want to single out in class. When I came into his office for the private visit all of us periodically received, I said to him, in a voice already exulting at his answer, "How'd you like that story, Mr. Fitzgerald?"

He performed his ritual of the reading glasses, pulling them an inch down his nose and looking at me over the top of them. "Not much," he said.

And then, of course, he told me what was wrong with the story, and I saw at once that he was right. I still have this problem. My judgment of my own work sometimes seems so malleable as not to rate as judgment at all. Any critic, no matter how stupid in praise or transparently spiteful in blame, convinces me—at least for awhile. Generally, harsh criticism tends to make me fear that the critic has an intelligence far superior to mine, and has found out things about my writing that I've been too blind to see myself. A person as easily confused by criticism as I am might well have quit writing after a few rejection slips came in for stories that my girlfriend and my mother thought were really good. Perhaps inadvertently, Mr. Fitzgerald taught me the value of trusting the judgment of just one person above all others—and of getting that judgment as the work is in progress, and a lot of help besides. Which is the role I've inflicted on a single editor, Richard Todd, for more than two decades.

I took Mr. Fitzgerald's course again and again, right up until I graduated. After my first semester with him, I didn't perform very well. It wasn't for lack of trying or, God knows, desire. I had become self-conscious about writing. At one point I started a novel. I wrote twenty pages or so, but the most interesting parts were the comments and little drawings I made in the margins—and created with greater care than anything in the actual text—imagining, as I created these notes in the margins, my biographer's delight in finding them. During this period, almost all of the stories I wrote in my room late at night, and the pastiches I committed in class, came back with such brief comments as "O.K., but no flash," all written in an elegantly penned script, which I can still see in my mind's eye, my heart sinking all over again. Mr. Fitzgerald used to talk about something he called "the luck of the conception," an idea I still believe in, but no longer dream about. I used to have a dream in which I had come upon the perfect story. The dream did not contain the story itself, just the fact that I possessed it. It was a dream suffused with joy, and I'd awake from it with a kind of sorrow that I haven't felt since adolescence. As a reader I felt then as I feel now, that any number of faults in a piece of writing are forgivable if there is life on the page. And there was no life in anything I wrote. Oddly, as the small natural talent I'd had for making up stories began to wane, my ambitions grew immense. Or maybe it was the other way around, and ambition stood in my way.

I can't blame Mr. Fitzgerald. He had only suggested that writing could be a high calling. I alone invented my desire to write for posterity. I am embarrassed to admit to this, but what I really had in mind was immortality. Once as a very young boy at a lecture at the Hayden Planetarium in New York, I learned that the earth would be destroyed in some two and a half billion years, and in spite of all my mother said, I was inconsolable for weeks. Maybe I was born especially susceptible to the fears that attend the fact of human mortality. Maybe I was influenced by certain of the English poets, those whose poems declare that their poems will make them immortal. Or it may be, as my wife suggests, that once a young man has solved the problem of how to meet and impress girls, it just naturally occurs to him that his next job is to figure out how to become immortal.

After college I went to Vietnam as a soldier—not the most likely way of gaining immortality, though I was never in much danger there. I came home with my body and my vaunting literary ambitions still intact and wrote a whole novel about experiences I didn't have in Vietnam. I designed that book for immortality. I borrowed heavily from Conrad, Melville, and Dostoyevsky. About thirty-five editors refused to publish it, thank God. I went to the Iowa Writers Workshop, where it began to seem to me that the well from which I drew for fiction had gone completely dry. (I have written fiction since then, all of it published, but the sum total is three short stories.) I decided to try my hand at nonfiction. That term covers a lot of territory, of course, from weighty treatises on the great problems of the world to diet books—some diet books qualify as nonfiction don't they? I dove into something then labeled The New Journalism. As many people have pointed out, only the term was new. I believe that the form already had a distinguished lineage, which included work by George Orwell and Joseph Mitchell and Mark Twain and Lillian Ross and Edmund Wilson and, my particular favorite, A. J. Liebling. This kind of nonfiction writing, whatever it's called, relies on narrative. Some people describe it by saying that it borrows techniques of fiction, but the fact is that it employs techniques of storytelling that never did belong exclusively to fiction. It is an honorable literary form, not always honorably used, but one can certainly say the same about fiction.

When I first started trying to write in this genre, there was an idea in the air, which for me had the force of a revelation: that all journalism is inevitably subjective. I was in my mid-twenties then, and although my behavior was somewhat worse than it has been recently, I was quite a moralist. I decided that writers of nonfiction had a moral obligation to write in the first person—really write in the first person, making themselves characters on the page. In this way, I would disclose my biases. I would not hide the truth from the reader. I would proclaim that what I wrote was just my own subjective version of events. In retrospect, it seems clear that this prescription for honesty often served instead as a license for self-absorption on the page. But I was still very young, too young and self-absorbed to realize what now seems obvious—that I was less likely to write honestly about myself than about anyone else on earth.

I wrote a book about a murder case, in a swashbuckling first person. It *was* published, I'm sorry to say. On the other hand, it disappeared without a trace; that is, it never got reviewed in the *New York Times.* And I began writing nonfiction articles for the *Atlantic Monthly*, under the tutelage of Richard Todd, then a young editor there. For about five years, during which I didn't dare attempt another book, I worked on creating what many writer friends of mine call "voice." I didn't do this consciously. If I had, I probably wouldn't have gotten anywhere. But gradually, I think, I cultivated a writing voice, the voice of a person who was well-informed, fair-minded, and temperate—the voice, not of the person I was, but of a person I sometimes wanted to be. Then I went back to writing books, and discovered other points of view besides the first person.

Choosing a point of view is a matter of finding the best place to stand from which to tell a story. It shouldn't be determined by theory, but by immersion in the material itself. The choice of point of view, I've come to think, has nothing to do with morality. It's a choice among tools. I think it's true, however, that the wrong choice can lead to dishonesty. Point of view is primary; it affects everything else, including voice. Writing my last four books, I made my choices by instinct sometimes and sometimes by experiment. Most of my memories of time spent writing have merged together in a blur, but I remember vividly my first attempts to find a way to write *Among Schoolchildren*, a book about an inner-city schoolteacher. I had spent a year inside her classroom. I intended, vaguely, to fold into my account of events I'd witnessed in that little place a great deal about the lives of particular schoolchildren and about the problems of education in America. I tried out every point of view that I'd used in previous books, and every page I wrote felt lifeless. Finally, I hit on a restricted third-person narration.

The approach seemed to work. The world of that classroom seemed to come alive when the view of it was restricted mainly to observations of the teacher and to accounts of what the teacher saw and heard and smelled and felt. This choice narrowed my options. I ended up writing something less comprehensive than I'd planned. The book became essentially an account of a year in the emotional life of a schoolteacher. My choice of the restricted third person also obliged me to write parts of the book as if from within the teacher's mind. I felt entitled to describe her thoughts and feelings because she had described them to me, both during class and afterward, and because her descriptions rarely seemed self-serving. Believing in them myself, I thought that I could make them believable on the page.

Belief is an offering that a reader makes to an author, what Coleridge famously called "That willing suspension of disbelief for the moment, which constitutes poetic faith." It is up to the writer to entertain and inform without disappointing the reader into a loss of that faith. In fiction or poetry, of course, believability may have nothing to do with realism or even plausibility. It has everything to do with those things in nonfiction, in my opinion. I think that the nonfiction writer's fundamental job is to make what is true believable. I'm not sure that everyone agrees. Lately the job seems to have been defined differently. Here are some of the ways that some people now seem to define the nonfiction writer's job: to make believable what the writer thinks is true, if the writer wants to be scrupulous; to make believable what the writer wishes were true, if the writer isn't interested in scrupulosity; or to make believable what the writer thinks might be true, if the writer couldn't get the story and had to make it up.

I figure that if I call a piece of my own writing nonfiction it ought to be about real people, with their real names attached whenever possible, who say and do in print nothing that they didn't actually say and do. On the cover page of my last book I put a note that reads, "This is a work of nonfiction," and listed the several names that I was obliged to change in the text. I thought a longer note would be intrusive. I was afraid that it would stand between the reader and the spell that I wanted to create, inviting the reader into the world of a nursing home. But the definition of "nonfiction" has become so slippery that I wonder if I shouldn't have written more. So now I'll take this opportunity to explain that for my last book I spent a year doing research, that the name of the place I wrote about is its real name, that I didn't change the names of any of the major characters, and that I didn't invent dialogue or put any thoughts in characters' minds that the characters themselves didn't confess to.

I no longer care what rules other writers set for themselves. If I don't like what someone has written, I can stop reading, which is, after all, the worst punishment a writer can suffer. (It ought to be the worst punishment. Some critics seem to feel that the creation of a book that displeases them amounts to a felony.) But the expanded definitions of nonfiction have created problems for those writers who define the term narrowly. Many readers now view with suspicion every narrative that claims to be nonfiction, and yet scores of very good nonfiction writers do not make up their stories or the details in them—writers such as John McPhee, Jane Kramer, J. Anthony Lucas. There are also special cases that confound categories and all attempts to lay down rules for writers of narrative. I have in mind Norman Mailer and in particular his *Executioner's Song,* a hybrid of fact and fiction, carefully labeled as such—a book I admire.

Most writers lack Mailer's powers of invention. Some nonfiction writers do not lack his willingness to invent, but the candor to admit it. Some writers proceed by trying to discover the truth about a situation, and then invent or distort the facts as necessary. Even in these suspicious times, writers can get away with this. Often no one will know, and the subjects of the story may not care. They may not notice. But the writer always knows. I believe in immersion in the events of a story. I take it on faith that the truth lies in the events somewhere, and that immersion in those real events will yield glimpses of that truth. I try to hew to what has begun to seem like a narrow definition of nonfiction partly in that faith, and partly out of fear. I'm afraid that if I started making up things in a story that purported to be about real events and people, I'd stop believing it myself. And I imagine that such a loss of conviction would infect every sentence and make each one unbelievable.

I don't mean to imply that all a person has to do to write good narrative nonfiction is to take accurate notes and reproduce them. The kind of nonfiction I like to read is at bottom storytelling, as gracefully accomplished as good fiction. I don't think any technique should be ruled out to achieve it well. For myself, I rule out only invention. But I don't think that honesty and artifice are contradictory. They work together in good writing of every sort. Artfulness and an author's justified belief in a story often combine to produce the most believable nonfiction.

If you write a nonfiction story in the third person and show your face in public afterward, someone is bound to ask, "How did your presence in the scenes you relate affect the people you were observing?" Some readers seem to feel that third-person narration, all by itself, makes a narrative incomplete. The other day I came upon a book about the writing of ethnography. It interested me initially because its bibliography cited a couple of my books and one of its footnotes mentioned me. The author spelled my first name wrong and gave one of my books a slightly different title from the one I chose. I swear I don't hold a grudge on account of that. My first name is a little weird, and the title in question is a long one. But those little mistakes did make me vigilant as I read the following passage:

> Writers of literary tales seldom remark on the significance of their presence on the scenes they represent, and this is in some instances a bothersome problem to field workers in addition to the common concerns for reactivity in any situation. It is, for example, very difficult to imagine that as famous and dandy a writer as Tom Wolfe was merely a fashionable but unobtrusive fly on the wall in the classic uptown parlor scene of *Radical Chic* (1970), or that Tracey [sic] Kidder did not in any way influence the raising of the Souweines' roofbeams in *House* (1985). Since writers of ethnographic tales have begun to break their silence on these matters, it is seemingly time for writers of literary tales to do so too—especially when their accounts so clearly rest on intimacy.

I believe it's possible to learn something from anyone, including ethnographers who have begun to break their silence. But I can't work out the mechanics for calculating the *reactivity* that occurs during *field work.* As I imagine it, field work that is mindful of reactivity would have to proceed in this way: I'd open my notebook in front of a person I planned to write about, and I'd ask, "How did you feel when I opened my notebook just now?" Then I would probably be bound to ask, "How did you feel when I asked you that question about opening my notebook?"

I don't know for sure how my presence has influenced the behavior of any of the people I've written about. I don't believe that I can know, because I wasn't there when I wasn't there. To do the research for a book, I usually hang around with my subjects for a year or more. After a while, most seem to take my presence for granted. Not all do. It worked the other way with one of the carpenters I wrote about in *House.* I remember his saying at one point that he and the other builders ought to put a bell around my neck, so they'd know where I was at all times.

Obviously some readers expect to hear about the story behind the story. But all writing is selective. I think that a narrative should be judged mainly on its own terms, not according to a reader's preexisting expectations. As a reader, I know that I won't always sit still for the story behind the story. As a writer, I have often decided that it isn't worth telling.

I wrote my most recent book, *Old Friends,* which is about some of the residents of a nursing home, in the third person. I hope that I put my own voice in it, but I chose not to write about how I did my research and how I was affected by what I encountered inside the nursing home—never mind how my presence might, arguably, possibly, have affected the inmates' behavior—mainly because what I did—asking questions, listening, taking notes—was much less interesting than what I observed. It is true, however, that my solution to the problem that the book presented did have something to do with my own experience of life inside that place. After writing for a while, I realized that I wanted to reproduce, in a limited sense, the most important part of my experience there.

I entered the nursing home in the late fall of 1990. The place, which is situated in western Massachusetts, is called the Linda Manor Extended Care Facility. I went there with a notebook—I filled ninety notebooks eventually—and prowled around inside almost every day, and many nights, for about a year. And then for another year or so I spent about three days a week there. I chose a decent nursing home, not one of the very best but a clean, well-lighted place where residents weren't tied up and were allowed some of the trappings of their former lives.

I had visited a nursing home only once before in my life, and since then had averted both my eyes and thoughts as I passed by. That was part of the attraction; nursing homes seemed to me like secret places in the landscape. I went to Linda Manor tentatively, though. I was afraid that I might find it dull. I thought I might find myself in a kind of waiting room, a vestibule to eternity, where everything had been resolved or set aside and residents simply lay waiting to die. But waiting was the least of what went on in many of those clean, motel-like rooms. Nearly everyone, it seemed, was working on a project. Some were absurd—one resident kept hounding the office of a U.S. senator to complain about his breakfast eggs. Some were poignant—many of the demented residents roamed the halls searching for exits, asking everyone for directions home. A lot of projects were Quixotic. There was, for instance, one indomitable, wheelchair-bound woman who had set herself the task of raising about $30,000 to buy the nursing home its own chairlift van. She intended to do so through raffles and teacup auctions and by getting other residents to remember the van in their wills. There was also an elderly actress who kept herself and the place somewhat invigorated by putting on plays. Staging those productions took great determination, because Linda Manor had no stage and most of the actors and actresses were confined to wheelchairs and walkers. In between plays, when things got dull, the old actress livened things up by starting fights. There were many residents working doggedly to come to terms with the remorse they felt for past mistakes and offenses. There was also a man in his nineties named Lou Freed who summoned up memories with what seemed like the force of necessity, re-inhabiting his former life with something that resembled joy. And there were, of course, a number who knew their deaths were imminent and struggled to find ways to live in the face of that knowledge.

Even in a decent nursing home, the old often get treated like children. And yet many of the residents refused to become like children. The roommates Lou and Joe, for instance. Let me try to prove this point with a short passage from my book.

> Joe and Lou could not control most of the substance of their life in here, but they had imposed a style on it. The way for instance that Joe and Lou had come, in the past months, to deal with matters of the bathroom. Joe had to go there what seemed to him like a ridiculous number of times each day and night. He and Lou referred to the bathroom as "the library." The mock-daintiness of the term amused Joe. The point was to make a joke out of anything you could around here. Up in the room after breakfast, Joe would say to Lou, "I gotta go to the library. I have to do my, uh, uh, prune evacuation."
>
> This room was now their home. As in any household, people entering were expected to follow local rules. The nursing staff was overwhelmingly female. Lou and Joe referred to all of them as girls, and indeed, next to them, even the middleaged did look like girls. The staff had all, of course, been quite willing to talk frankly about matters of Lou and Joe's biology. Too frankly for Lou. Too frankly for Joe, once Lou had made the point. The aides, "the girls," used to come to the doorway, cradling opened in their arms the large, ledger-like Forest View "BM Book," and they'd call loudly in, "Did either of you gentlemen have a bowel movement today?" It was Lou, some months ago now, who responded to this question by inviting in the girls who asked it, and then telling them gently, "All you have to say is, 'Did you or didn't you.'" The way Lou did that job impressed Joe, Lou did it so diplomatically, so much more diplomatically than Joe would have. Lou, as he liked to say, had trained all the girls by now. Joe took care of reinforcement.
>
> It was a morning in December. Joe had the television news on. He and Lou were listening to the dispatches from the Middle East. Joe wasn't waiting

for the aide with the BM Book, but he had a question ready for her. When the aide came to the door, she asked, "For my book. Did you?"

"Yes." Joe tilted his head toward Lou. "And so did he." Then, a little smile blossoming, Joe looked at the aide and asked, "And what about you?"

"None of your business!" The aide looked embarrassed. She laughed.

"Well, you ask me," Joe said.

"But I get paid for it."

"*Goodbye*," Joe said pleasantly, and went back to watching the news.

Many residents insisted on preserving their dignity, in spite of the indignities imposed by failing health and institutional confinement. Many people in there were attempting in one way or another to invent new lives for themselves. In the context of that place and of debilitating illnesses, their quests seemed important.

So when I began to write *Old Friends*, I didn't lack for interesting characters or stories. I felt I had an overabundance. I told myself before I started writing that I couldn't fit in everything, and then for about a year I tried to do just that. In the end I had to jettison a lot of portraits and stories that I had written many times and polished up. Among other things, I wrote four or five times and finally discarded what in all modesty I believe to have been the most riveting account of a session of Bingo ever composed. But the plain fact was that about half of what I wrote and rewrote got in the way of the main story that I wanted to tell.

Hundreds of articles and books deal with the big issues that surround aging in late-twentieth-century America. I read some of them. But I didn't want to approach this subject in a general way. It is useful, maybe even necessary, to imagine that a definable group called "the elderly" exists. But all such conceptions inevitably fail. It is accurate only to say that there are many individuals who have lived longer than most of the rest of the population, and that they differ widely among themselves. For various reasons, some can no longer manage what are called the activities of daily living at home, and, for lack of a better solution, some of those people end up living in nursing homes. I chose to write about a few of those people partly because so much well-meaning commentary on old age depicts white-haired folks in tennis clothes—a tendency, it seems to me, that inadvertently denigrates the lives of the many people who haven't been as lucky.

About five percent of Americans over sixty-five—about 1.5 million people—live in nursing homes and, according to one estimate, nearly half of all the people who live past sixty-five will spend some time inside a nursing home. Obviously, they are important places, but nursing homes weren't really the subject I wanted to address. There were already plenty of published exposés of bad nursing homes. I decided to do my research inside a good nursing home on the theory that a good one would be bad enough, inevitably a house of grief and pain, and also because I didn't want to write about the kinds of policy and management issues that would have assumed primary importance in a story set in an evil place. I wanted to write from the inside about the experience of being old and sick and confined to an institution. I wanted to come at the subject of aging, not through statistics, but through elderly people themselves. I wanted to write an interesting, engaging book. The residents of even a decent nursing home are people in a difficult situation, and I think that stories about people in difficult situations are almost always interesting, and often dramatic.

In some ways, research in that place was easy work. In the course of every story I'd done before, I had run into people who hadn't wanted to talk to me. But people in a nursing home never have enough willing listeners. A nursing home like Linda Manor may be the only place on earth where a person with a notebook can hope to receive a universal welcome.

Various sights, smells, and sounds distressed me at first. But gradually, I got used to the externals of the place and people. Almost everyone who has spent some time inside a nursing home begins to look beyond the bodies of the residents. It just happens. But around the time when that happened to me, another problem arose. I remember leaving the room of a dying, despondent resident and stopping in my tracks in a Linda Manor corridor, and hearing myself say to myself, "This is amazing! *Everybody* dies." And, of course, my next thought was, "Including me." I know that sounds silly. One is supposed to have figured that out before pushing fifty. But I hadn't believed it, I think.

I arranged some other troubling moments for myself, during my research. At one point, I decided that I ought to check into Linda Manor for a couple of days and nights, as if I were myself a resident. I hate the kind of story in which a perfectly healthy person decides to ride around in a wheelchair for a day and then proclaims himself an expert in what being wheelchair-bound is like. But I believe in the possibility of imaginatively experiencing what others experience, and I thought I might learn something. With vast amusement, a nurse ushered me into a little room. My roommate, an ancient man who couldn't speak much, terrified me as soon as I climbed into bed. He kept clicking his light on and off. At one point I saw his hand through the filmy, so-called "privacy curtain." His hand reached toward the curtain, grasping at it. He was trying to pull the curtain back, so that he could get a better look at me, and I had to stifle the impulse to yell at him to stop. Then, a little later, I heard a couple of the nurses in the hall outside, saying loudly, speaking of me, "Shall we give him an enema?" An old source of amusement among nurses, the enema.

I didn't learn much that I could use in my book, from my two-night stand at Linda Manor. Except for the fact that a few minutes can seem like eternity in a nursing-home bed and the fact that, from such a perspective, cheerful, attractive, average-sized nurses and nurse's aides can look huge and menacing. Those two nights I kept getting up and looking out the window, to make sure my car was still in the parking lot. I had planned to stay longer, but went home early the third morning in order to get some sleep.

At Linda Manor I got to know a nurse's aide who, when one of her residents had died, insisted on opening up the windows of the room. Asked why she did this, she said she felt she had to let the spirit out. All but a few of the staff were religious, at least in the sense that most believed in an afterlife. I think belief was a great comfort to them. At least I imagined it would be for me. But I possessed only a vague agnosticism. And I couldn't simply manufacture something stronger for the situation.

What troubled me most during my time at Linda Manor wasn't unpleasant sights or smells or even the reawakening of my fears about mortality. It was the problem of apparent meaninglessness. I watched people dying long before life had lost its savor for them or they their usefulness to others. I couldn't imagine any purpose behind the torments that many residents suffered in their last days. Sometimes I'd leave a resident's room feeling that everything, really everything in every life, was pointless. I remember thinking that we all just live awhile and end up dying painfully, or, even worse, bored and inert. What meaning could life have, I'd find myself wondering, if the best of the last things people get to do on earth is to play Bingo? At such times, I'd usually find my way upstairs to the room of the two old men named Lou and Joe. Gradually, I began to notice that a number of the staff did the same thing, even giving up their coffee breaks to go and chat with Lou and Joe. I didn't usually plan to go to their room at these moments of vicarious despair. I'd just find myself wanting to go there. After about ten minutes in their room, I usually felt much better. Lou and Joe had been placed together in one of Linda Manor's little rooms, in what for both would likely be their last place on earth, and they had become great friends. Other residents had formed friendships inside Linda Manor, but none was durable or seemed to run very deep. Out in the wider, youthful world, this accomplishment of Lou and Joe's would have seemed unremarkable but in that place it was profound.

The main thing I wanted to portray was that friendship, surrounded by the nursing home and all its varying forms of claustrophobia. I wanted to infuse the story of that friendship with sentiment, but not in a sentimental way. The difference, as I see it, is the difference between portraying emotion and merely asserting its existence, between capturing the reflection of something real on the page and merely providing handy cues designed to elicit an emotional response. It is, I realize, harder to depict manifestations of human goodness than manifestations of venality and evil. I don't know why that is. I do know that some people think that kindness, for example, is always superficial. That view is the logical equivalent of sentimentality. It's an easy way to feel and it gives some people a lot of pleasure. It has nothing to do with a tragic vision of life. It has about as much to do with an accurate vision of life as a Hallmark card. Anyway, that's how it seems to me. The world seems various to me, and depicting some of the virtue in it seems like a project worth attempting. I do not say that I pulled it off, but that's part of what I had in mind.

After my book was published, I continued to visit Linda Manor about once a week. I went partly because doing so made me feel like a good guy. But I had other reasons. Growing old with dignity calls for many acts of routine heroism, and some of the people I knew at Linda Manor were inspiring, admirable characters. All of them have died now, except for Lou, who has achieved the ripe old age of ninety-six. Joe died last winter. I visit only Lou now, but I used to go mainly in order to visit the two men. I *liked* visiting them. Their room was one place where I knew I was always welcome. They gave me good advice, on such subjects as child-rearing. They were funny, both intentionally and otherwise. Most important, their room was one place in the world where I could count on finding that amity prevailed. That was unusual, in my experience of the world. The crucial thing about Lou and Joe was that they remained *very good* friends, better friends every time I visited. They presented an antidote to despair, which is connectedness, and for me, I learned, it is only the connectedness of the human tribe that can hold despair at bay. Connectedness can, of course, take many different forms. One can find it in religion, or in family, or, as in the case of Lou and Joe, in friendship. Or perhaps in work, maybe even in the act of writing.

Harold Brodkey, who recently died of AIDS, wrote in an essay a couple of years ago, "I think anyone who spends his life working to become eligible for literary immortality is a fool." I agree. But I also think that only a fool would write merely for money or contemporary fame. I imagine that most writers—good, bad and mediocre—write partly for the sake of the private act of writing and partly in order to throw themselves out into the world. Most, I imagine, *endeavor* for connectedness, to create the kind of work that touches other lives and, in that sense at least, leaves something behind. I don't dream of immortality or plant marginalia for my biographers anymore. But I do wonder what Mr. Fitzgerald would think of what I've written and, especially, of what I'm going to write.

A few days after I got back from Vietnam, in June 1969, I traveled to Cambridge and called Mr. Fitzgerald from a pay phone. He invited me to lunch at his house the next afternoon. Of course, I didn't tell him this, but I wanted something from him, something ineffable, like hope. He had prepared sandwiches. I'm not sure that he made them himself, but I like to think that he did, and that he was responsible for cutting the crusts off the bread. I'm not sure why I remember that. It seemed a sweet gesture, a way of making me feel that I was important to him. It also made him seem old, older than I'd remembered him.

I saw Mr. Fitzgerald a few times more over the next year or two, and then he moved away and I moved out west for a while. I fell under other influences. My dreams of writing something classic gave way to my little dreams of writing something publishable, of making a living as a writer, which seemed hard enough. But those early dreams were dormant, not dead. When, almost ten years later, a book of mine, *The Soul of a New Machine*, was awarded the Pulitzer Prize and the American Book Award, my megalomaniacal dreams of literary glory came out of storage. I could tell myself at moments that I'd achieved them all. But I hesitated for a while before sending my book to Mr. Fitzgerald. I was afraid. When I finally worked up the nerve, I wrote an inscription to the effect that I hoped this piece of writing began to approach his expectations. I soon received a letter from him, in which he thanked me, remarked upon the "modesty" of my inscription—no doubt he saw right through that—and apologized for his inability to read the book just now. I wrote right back, proposing that I visit him. He did not reply. I never heard from him again. I don't remember exactly when he died. I think it was a few years later.

His silence has bothered me for a long time, not immoderately but in the way of those embarrassing memories that suddenly appear when you're checking the oil in your car or putting a key in a door. Two summers ago I met one of Mr. Fitzgerald's sons and told him the story. He insisted that his father would never have failed to answer my last letter, if he'd been able to read and write by then. I believed him. And I believe that if Mr. Fitzgerald had been able to read my book, he would have told me what he really thought. It's probably just as well that he never did. I've written other and, I think, better books since then. I'd rather know what he thought of *them*. I've been courting his approval ever since my first day in his class, and I continue to court his approval now, when he's certain to withhold it. That makes me sad sometimes, but not in my better moments. I'll never know if he'd approve of what I've written and am going to write. But I'll never know if he'd disapprove either. He's left me room to go on trying.

Mending Wall

Judith Kitchen

My father sat with his feet on the desk, a cup of coffee still steaming in front of him. I had just walked in the door of his workplace—an old storefront in Corning, NY, where the physicists at Corning Glass Works had temporarily located themselves while a new lab was being built. So, for the first time in my young life, I could see where my father "worked." I put quotations around the word even then because it didn't look like work, sitting with his feet propped up, his chair tilted back, just thinking.

When I asked about his work, he tried to define it for me, but eventually he settled for something like "sometimes an idea just comes, and then you have to try to prove that what you think is true is actually true." My father's conversation was peppered with words like "hypothesis" and "theorem" and "proof" and "therefore," and so I did kind of understand what he was getting at. Later, after I had a degree in literature and talked about writing and books and movies, he vociferously resisted the phrase "metaphorical truth" as something impossibly silly. Stonewall: trochaic verb, something to obfuscate and override. Stone wall: the spondee of what we built between us, so we agreed to agree that we did not speak each other's language.

Here's what I remember about those days with scientists: my Uncle Willy, a mathematician, insisting that Robert Frost really meant "good fences make good neighbors."

"He said so, didn't he?"

"No," I replied, "he let someone else say so, so he could question it."

I was in seventh grade, and my Uncle Willy just turned away in disgust. I grew more insistent: "Don't you see what he called his neighbor—an 'old-stone savage'? You're a scientist. You ought to know what *that* means."

Uncle Willy did not back down, and suddenly it felt as though his ability to read was compromised by his science. "It's right there, on the page." Yes, it was, but so was tone, and nuance. If Frost circled back to reconsider that idea, it was not for want of trying on other ways of thinking—and he does not give away whether he eventually agreed to agree with his neighbor.

"Too bad," said my wonderful professor, "that you have so many good ideas, and no vehicle with which to express them." Well, I had a vehicle, but it just wasn't the one he recognized—the language of the scholarly article. It just didn't dot the i's or cross the t's or proceed logically on its way to its point. It circled and spiraled; it doubled back; it digressed and prodded; it spoke in tongues. And yet I knew I knew what I knew—knew it in ways that, if I thought to remember, sounded a bit like my father's way of knowing something that he then had to prove. But since there is no such thing as "proof" in literature, it seemed to me that all I had to do was find a way to show the direction of my thoughts. Demonstrate them. Point the reader toward my inconclusive conclusions.

That was 1962. It took more than a quarter of a century for me to discover that, yes, you could simply put your feet on the desk and think on the page. You could let your thoughts float out—in their incomplete sentences, their sinuous meanderings—and maybe, sometimes, they would find a way to coalesce and become a larger thought, a meaning. So that's what I'm doing here: thinking my way toward what I suspect a lyric essay is, or should be, can, or should do. Thinking my way into the lyric part of the definition, because the essay part is easier, more down-to-earth. Why the qualifier? Well, because there are Uncle Willies out there, waiting to pounce: *It doesn't say so, so how do you know? It doesn't flat-out say so.* No, it doesn't; however, like a poem, the lyric essay must not only mean, but be. It is a way of seeing the world. A hybrid—a cross between poetry and nonfiction—it must, as Rene Char said of the poet, "leave traces of [its] passage, not proof," letting mystery into the knowing. Or the knowing to incorporate its mystery. And part of that knowing is through sound—the whisper of soft consonants, the repetition of an elongated vowel that squeaks its way across the page, the chipping away of k-k-k-k, the assonance and consonance of thought attuned to language. The internal rhyme of the mind. Which is something my father would have resisted also.

How do I know that? How can I say that with such certainty? Because his method of reading was that of a scientist. There were too many books to read in one lifetime, he said, so he would wait until the critics concluded which was the best book by an author, then he'd read that book. Save himself the trouble of reading all the others.

Maybe, I thought even then, but look at what he would miss if, in reading *The Great Gatsby*, he would never see Dick and Nicole on the beach in France, would never have to watch the war itself become a character, something lit from within. If, in reading *Grapes of Wrath*, he might never see the soft underbelly of empathy for Lenny. And what of Hemingway, because at that time—as now—there was no consensus as to which was best? What, for heaven's sake, of Faulkner, whose whole county unfolded from book to book? At the time, I did not ask myself the question of poetry, but thinking about it now I wonder if reading a poet's "best" poem is any way to know the poet at all. Isn't poetry, in the end, a way of experiencing the world? Another way not of meaning, but being?

So that is what I hunger for in the lyric essay—the author's way of inhabiting his or her own mind. Of responding, in language, to my Uncle Willy. To my beloved professor. To the world at large.

This past year, I attended a reading of "lyric essays," and nothing I heard was, to my mind, lyric. My ears did not quicken. My heart did not skip. What I heard was philosophical meditation, truncated memoir, slipshod research, and just-plain-discursive opinion. A wall of words. But not a lyric essay among them. The term had been minted (brilliantly, it seems to me) by Deborah Tall, then almost immediately undermined. Not all essays are lyric. Repeat. Not all essays are lyric. Not even all short essays are lyric. Some are merely short. Or plainly truncated. Or purely meditative. Or simply speculative. Or. Or. Or. But not lyric. Because, to be lyric, there must be a lyre.

That said, I believe there must also be some allegiance to the nonfiction aspect of the essay. The run-of-the-mill, workaday nature of reality. Of fact. The job of the lyric essayist is to find the prosody of fact, finger the emotional instrument, play the intuitive and the intrinsic, but all in service to the music of the real. Even if it's an imagined actuality. The aim is to make *of*, not *up*. The lyre, not the liar.

First, let's deal with the difference between a lyrical essay and a lyric essay. Any essay may be lyrical, as long as it pays attention to the sound of its language, or the sweep of its cadences. But a lyrical essay is often using its lyrics to serve a different end. A lyric essay, however, functions as *a lyric*. Can be held in the mind—must, in fact, be held in the mind—intact. It means as an entity. It swallows you, the way a poem swallows you, until you reside inside it. Try to take it apart and you spin out of control. It is held together by the glue of absence, the mortar of melody, the threnody of unspent inspiration. Like a Latin declension: inspire, inspirit, inspiration. Inspire: breathe in, (formerly) breathe life into. Something there is that animates the lyric essay. Something that doesn't love a wall.

The music of the lyric essay?

Maybe it's a music of language: "And so I reached out and there was the great, wet fruit of his nose, the velvet bone of his enormous face"—Stephen Kuusisto, *Eavesdropping*.

Maybe it's a music of structure: "Brown made Americans mindful of tunnels inside their bodies, about which they did not speak; about their ties to nature, about which they did not speak; about their ties to one another, about which they did not speak"—Richard Rodriguez, *Brown*.

Maybe it's a music of silence, of what is not, or cannot be, said: "It can't be found outside, this green—not exactly, though it wants to be, in a way that haunts the edges of almost knowing. It is not the green of pear-tree leaves nor the green of rhododendron; not even the green-gray of certain aromatic sages that can make you weep for a smell lost from childhood; not even the triple-dark green of a trout stream under cloud cover"—Marjorie Sandor, *The Night Gardener*.

Maybe it's not melodious, but at least it knows its own temperament, its timbre: "When the kids had gone to school and her husband to work, she would sometimes sit in the living room holding tightly to the arms of the chair feeling afraid and think, Maybe it is the woodwork getting me down"—Abigail Thomas, *Safekeeping*.

Maybe it's the grace note of white space—a gap, or a suspension bridge.

Maybe it's the music of the spheres—the sense that even though we don't know everything down to the last quark, there is some scientifically magical design in the way things keep spinning and work together to make up our explosive, expanding universe. The knowledge that light from some dead star will reach our eyes sometime ten years from now. As Albert Goldbarth says, "Go know."

So, does any of this say anything about the lyric essay? Probably not, or not in any way that has a vehicle with which to say it. A rocketship. A cable car. A handcart. On the other hand, I want to read the words of those authors I've quoted. H. D. said she would like to dance with Ezra Pound just for what he might say—I'd read them not for what they might say, but for the way they would dance. The way their hand might rest confidently at my waist, and their words brush my ear, just a tickle of thought. The way they would hold me lightly and, with one sure touch, send me twirling out, then, just as lightly, draw me back in.

I'd read for that lyric moment when I could inhale their very way of occupying mindspace, for that time when, somewhere before words, science and art speak the same language and I can catch them both with their feet on the desk and the coffee offering up its distinct aroma of anticipation.

QED.

Days into Essays:
A Self for All Seasons

Carl H. Klaus

Even now, fifteen years later, I can still see the soap suds in the wine glass, still behold my reflection in the kitchen window that mid-December evening, when out of nowhere, it seemed, I was visited by something like the muse. How else to account for the writing project that suddenly came to mind while doing the dishes? As it first occurred to me that night in the waning days of 1994, the task was relentlessly simple—I would write a brief weather report every day during the coming year, from January first to December thirty-first of 1995. Just a paragraph or two, but enough to produce a detailed record of the year's weather, taking stock of the temperature, wind speed, rainfall, snowfall, and other measurable phenomena, and describing what it looked like and felt like each day on my hillside lot in Iowa City—a place where I'd spent twenty-five years witnessing the flow (and sometimes the clash) of arctic- and gulf-born weather systems. What better to do, I thought, than make something of that experience and the tempestuous weather that often blows my way? What I didn't think of just then is how I could produce a book about the weather without any knowledge of it, except from the perspective of a fanatic vegetable gardener. Nor did it occur to me that anyone might be put off by the prospect of reading incessantly about the weather. For the minute that bizarre project came to mind, it took hold of me like an obsession, so that even Kate, my resident skeptic and wife, came to think I'd go through with it.

Strange as it now seems, the more I thought about the project, the more alluring it became, for it appealed to an intense hunger I was feeling back then to do something completely different from the personal essays and memoirs I'd been reading and teaching and writing about over the previous thirty years. The weather would give me the opportunity to see if I could produce a substantial work of literary nonfiction about something outside of myself, beyond my inner life, something that didn't rely on long-term memory but on a firsthand observation of things that I could put into words like "north wind," "snowfall," "hailstorm," and "hoarfrost"—words that seemed to correspond to the things themselves. The writer's inescapable delusion, but a necessary one, especially for a weather book or any other kind of nature writing. And that's what I fancied myself doing, as if I had the scientific knowledge to be an authentic nature writer.

Given such an irrational presumption, it should come as no surprise that I was also driven by a high and mighty ambition. For by New Year's Day, I thought of my work-to-be as the embodiment of a new literary hybrid—an essayistic journal. Not just a series of brief weather reports as I'd originally planned. But a sustained record of daily observations and reflections, each entry both a free-standing essay in its own right and an episode in the overarching story of the year's weather. A five-hundred-word essay each day, so I wouldn't ever lapse into mere jottings or notations of data. The same average length each day, so that every day and every entry would have equivalent weight in my story of the year's weather. In other words, my work-to-be would ultimately constitute a daybook/essaybook/yearbook all wrapped in one. Or as my best friend called it, "a monstrous personal project." Or, as I told myself in a soothing reverie, "my journal will be something like a Renaissance sonnet sequence, but in this case a contemporary essay sequence, the likes of which has never been tried before." So, it's no wonder that I scoffed at the suggestion of a colleague who advised me early in January not to worry about missing a day now or then. "It's the kind of liberty," he said, "that contemporary writers feel free to take now and then." But as I saw it, one could no more skip a day than drop a day from the calendar—or from life itself.

Having settled upon the topic, form, and length of my daily essays, it seemed as if my persona was a foregone conclusion—how else to report things but in a plainly-worded style that would let the weather speak for itself? I would be its friendly, reportorial mouthpiece. A simple enough matter, one might suppose, except that it required me to shed the academic style I'd learned in graduate school and replace it with an unpretentious voice that I found in the no-nonsense guidelines of Strunk and White. In other words, straightforward, declarative sentences in an Anglo-Saxon rather than Latinate vocabulary. And just to be sure that my entries had the ring of a spontaneous diarist, I also decided to enliven my prose with colloquial expressions, sentence fragments, and other conversational usage. How strange it now seems to have made such deliberate decisions about a style that came to feel as if it was second nature. But as with any such change, it required a self-conscious effort to avoid my academic predilections and to develop the style of an observant, straight-talking, spontaneous self. A self that would be suitable for all seasons. With a persona like that, one needn't worry, I thought, about Woolf's cautionary remark in "The Modern Essay"—that "to write daily, to write shortly," one must forsake "the natural richness of the speaking voice." Besides, the weather and its manifold variations would surely endow my prose with the richness of a spoken voice. When New Year's arrived with the first snowfall of winter, it seemed like the heavens had smiled upon my project, especially given the depth and sweep of the snow, which I highlighted in the opening of my first day's essay, like this:

> New Year's Day and a newly fallen snow. Four inches of it, covering the ground with a blanket so vividly white in the morning sun that it makes me wonder why no one ever sings of a white new year. A fresh start. Last year's leavings so well hidden, it's hard for me to believe how green things were just a week ago.

Having launched myself so easily with three sentence fragments and a flurry of one-syllable words, I spent the next few hours taking note of everything I could see, from the rabbit tracks and deer tracks in the early morning snow to the shadows of tree trunks crisscrossing the snow-covered yard at midday. Later that day, I concluded the piece with a report of my impressions during a hike that Kate and I took in mid-afternoon. In other words, I wrote each part shortly after my first-hand observations had taken place, for I wanted the piece to reflect my immediate impressions and reactions—distorted as little as possible by the passage of time and the refraction of memory.

The next few days, the weather turned out to be so striking, so cooperative one might say, that I had plenty to write about—a sub-zero temperature drop and a corresponding increase at the bird feeders, a midnight snow-walk with Kate, a sudden January thaw. With each set of conditions, the cityscape, the landscape, and the skyscape were variously transformed. And with each set of changes, I adapted the mood of my entries to the weather at hand. Sometimes playful, sometimes solemn, sometimes matter-of-fact—I made my way from day to day, as briskly and changeably as the weather. Glibly taking stock of things even in a dense morning fog:

Wednesday, January 11

> In a great fog, as I discovered this morning, there's no ground at all. No there there. Only here. A fog so dense that even looking out the attic window, I couldn't see any farther than a block away. The familiar background of trees and houses had virtually disappeared, leaving only the foreground of our immediate neighborhood. But that was enough to consume my attention, for yesterday's warm-up to the mid-thirties followed by last night's freezing temperatures had produced a heavy coating of rime on all the shrubs and trees. A patina of hoarfrost backed by a veil of dense fog. White on white. Winter art. A monochromatic landscape.

Rereading that passage now some fifteen years later, I remember how pleasing it was to describe the fog and the rime and the hoarfrost in fragments so crisp as those last four details. The self I had chosen was clearly facile enough—and shallow enough—to get me from day to day without raising any serious questions about the instability and uncertainty inherent in the weather. And with each passing day, I was not only learning how to track the weather and describe it but also how to write about it accurately and evocatively within the five-hundred-word limit that I'd set for myself. Just to make sure that I didn't exceed the limit by more than twenty-five words, I set my word-processing program to produce a page of that approximate length. So whenever the page break appeared, I knew that I had encountered my word limit and would have to pare down what I'd written if I wanted to include additional material. Writing tight, I called it, trimming and trimming again, whenever I had more to say than words to spare. Pacing myself so differently from the leisurely rhythm of a piece like this one that it sometimes seemed as if I was doing a hundred-yard dash rather than a long-distance run. The tempo of one's prose and the tenor of one's voice, I discovered, are subtly but powerfully influenced by the length of one's discourse. In my case, it provoked such an irrepressible impulse to wrap up each entry in one or two pithy sentences that a colleague said I was beginning to sound like a newspaper columnist rather than a journal writer. A telling observation which led me to realize that the elliptical style engendered by my self-imposed word limit was also pushing me toward Baconian epigrams—a mannerism that unconsciously bespeaks a will to dominate things through the power of language.

But it soon became clear that tightening my prose was nothing compared to dealing with the constraints of my topic, especially when the skies were overcast for nine straight days, and those unchanging weather conditions made me wonder what I'd do with the long stretches of hot, sunny, rainless days that usually come in July and August. How would I avoid repetitiousness in midsummer, if I was already having trouble with redundant weather conditions in early winter? To remedy the problem, I decided to expand my horizon a bit and take into account not only our local situation but also conditions around the country and then around the world, given the worldwide influence of the El Nino phenomenon, which was then making its presence felt in Iowa. Actual weather, fictional weather, present, past, and future weather—every aspect of that mysterious phenomenon would be grist for my reports, thanks to a handful of guidebooks and websites that provided me with a treasure-trove of meteorological lore. Given my expanded weather perspective, I also decided to make myself a more expansive and entertaining weatherman, especially after watching a movie version of *Little Women*, so fraught with vivid snow-scenes and other seasonal displays that I devoted a whole entry to its cinematic—and contrived—evocation of the weather. So my reconceived project was well underway, until something happened the evening of January 17 that challenged my complacent role, as I explained the next day:

Wednesday, January 18

The sky was so clear last night and the moon so bright I could easily see the dark-shaded craters on its surface, when I went out to the compost pile. The air had finally dried out, and the wind died down, leaving a comfortable chill in the high twenties—a perfect winter night for a walk with Pip. But my thoughts were heavily overcast by reports of the catastrophic earthquake in Japan.

Almost two-thousand dead, more than six-thousand injured, and the city of Kobe, a city of almost one and one-half million, burning out of control. In the face of such colossal suffering and loss, my weather-watch suddenly seemed unspeakably trivial and beside the point. And I suddenly felt even more stung by the recollection of Kate's remarks at dinner—"You can't just go on twittering about the sun and the moon. You have to make something more of it." I instinctively wanted to defend myself, to say that I'm not just twittering— that in writing about the sun and the moon and the clouds and the snow, I'm really paying reverence to the things in this world that matter most deeply to me. But the words didn't come readily to my lips, especially when I was savoring the crab-stuffed flounder, steamed artichoke, and chilled sauvignon blanc we were having for dinner. And it wasn't any better this morning, not even during the rare spectacle of watching the sun rise in the east just after I'd seen the full moon set in the west, for I knew that when I went downstairs to get the morning newspaper, the front page would be covered with stories of Kobe. The front page, in fact, offered me a distinctly different kind of sunrise from the one I'd just seen—a full-width color picture, dominated by the reddish-orange sweep of fire raging through the city of Kobe. And above the picture, the haunting remark of Minoru Takasu, a survivor of the quake, just a couple of years older than me—"I thought it was the end of the world."

Again my weather project seemed trivial, especially compared to his remark. But then it occurred to me that I make these reports because, like Minoru Takasu, I cherish the world. I do not want to see the end of it any more than he. I want it to continue, sunrise and sunset, moonrise and moonset, world without end. And I want to take note of its continuance, if for no other reason than to make a record of my reverence for it. Pious sentiments, I realize. But those are the only pieties I know.

In the process of writing that piece, I started to shake and sweat, for I felt more intense about what I was saying there, more emotionally involved, than in any of the preceding entries, thanks to the earthquake, Kate, and Minoru Takasu. Such disturbing provocations that the next day I wrote another essay on Kobe and envisioned myself doing other pieces in that vein, with a more intensely personal slant on things. But two days later, back in the mode of an entertaining weatherman, I did a breezy piece about the north wind, decked out with literary allusions, verbal puns, verse-like echoes, and a snappy conclusion, but strangely aloof from its menacing implications. No wonder one of my graduate students who'd been reading the entries said, "You're keeping people at a distance, allowing them to come this close and no closer."

But I also remember how empowering it felt to produce a carefully wrought, five-hundred-word essay every day—an unprecedented feat, I thought, especially for someone in his sixties. As if age had given me the ability and tenacity to do something I could never have done before. So it seemed all the more urgent to stay in the groove, especially because my daily pieces also made me feel as if I were controlling the weather, as if one could harness such a complex and powerful thing through the magic of language. Talk about an intoxicating venture! I was imbibing it every day, like an addict, from the minute I got up to the moment I went to bed, and often in the middle of the night as well, when I would gaze out the attic windows to check on the moon or the nighttime sky for signs of the next day's weather. How strange that writing, or a misguided conception of it, turned me into a monomaniacal version of myself without realizing it. And only something painfully close to home brought me back to my senses, as I discovered from an experience that took place on Valentine's Day:

Tuesday, February 14

Thirteen above this morning—a balmy start by comparison with the last several days. A good omen for St. Valentine's. But when I put Pip out on his leash, the air must've hit me the wrong way because it suddenly felt intolerable. So cold, so harsh, I didn't even want to look at the sky or eyeball the back yard or anything else outside. I just wanted to get back in as fast as I could. And when I got back inside, something inside me almost screamed out what I was feeling just then in every part of my being. "I've had it. Had it with the cold, the wind, the ice, the ice-covered driveway, the ice-pack over the backyard, the iced-over sidewalks, the iced-up car, my ice-nipped ears and toes and fingertips. And the heavy clothing. And the dry air. And the overheated rooms. Everything." Or words to that effect. But Kate was still asleep. I didn't want to wake her up. And besides, the feeling passed so quickly I was left musing upon the suddenness of its appearance as if out of nowhere. Like the dream I'd had just a few hours earlier about the end of the semester. It was the last week of classes, or perhaps exam week, or the week after graduation. No one around. And I was wandering the hallways, looking for someone to talk to, to have coffee with. But all the offices were shut. And no signs of light or life were visible in the gaps between the office doors and the floor. I was standing alone in an empty hallway, in an empty building. Not an uncommon experience when school is out. And sometimes, in fact, a pleasurable image to contemplate, especially in the midst of a semester when the press of students and committees becomes unbearable. But in my dream last night, I felt desolate beyond belief and a great heaving in my chest. An anguish so intense I was suddenly on the verge of tears. And then I awoke, shaking. And then it gradually came to me that I must have been grieving the prospect of my retirement. A strange twist, given the pleasure I've had this semester, on "phased-in retirement," teaching only one course with just a dozen students and a few auditors, who leave me almost completely free to write my daily reports and to contemplate the time when I will be completely free to write, travel, and garden as I wish. I thought I'd adjusted to the chilly side of retirement, just as I thought I'd adjusted to the harshness of winter. But when all is said and done, it must be that I'm troubled by a long run of bitterly cold weather, no matter where it occurs—wide awake or in a dream, in an empty hallway or right outside the back door.

After finishing that piece in mid-morning, I had almost a whole day to mull it over, which enabled me to see that what I had written about there, and perhaps should have been writing about in other entries, was not just the weather outside but the weather inside. Especially given the surprising discovery of my anguish at the prospect of retirement. But the thought of writing about such personal matters day in and day out made me uneasy, for it seemed like a self-regarding activity that I didn't want to indulge just because of a bad dream, though two years later, in February 1997, I started such a journal when the bad dream suddenly turned into a waking nightmare three months before my impending retirement. In February 1995, though, I was still committed to producing emotionally restrained pieces about tangible things in the world of my daily experience—pieces in the spirit of E. B. White, my onetime literary idol, whose personal essays are so carefully buttoned-down that more often than not they only hint at the depth of his emotions. Yet White would never have been content with so confining a subject as the weather. Even during World War II, when he withdrew to his saltwater farm in Maine, he wrote not only about life on his farm and in the nearby town of Brooklin, but also about events taking place around the country and the world. So it seemed reasonable to shift my primary focus from the weather to my vegetable garden as well as the entire world of my daily experience, including Kate, our dog Pip, our cat Phoebe, as well as the gardens, trees, and shrubs on our three-quarter-acre lot. Also the wild animals that lived on our land or that passed through it. Groundhogs, moles, possums, rabbits, deer, raccoons, and squirrels—all the vermin that trouble the heart of an ardent vegetable gardener. Also our neighbors, our neighborhood, the university where I taught, as well as other places and people I encountered or thought about on my walks in the city of Iowa City where I live. In other words, I would write about virtually everything in my life, but without dwelling on the internal weather of my life—or at least not so overtly or extensively as to become too personal. I'd be personal without being personal.

What I didn't realize was that in opening the journal to the full scope of my life, I would inevitably be compelled to write about the inner storms as well as the outer ones. It was only a few weeks, in fact, before my feelings were engaged, when Phoebe, our twenty-year-old cat, came up with a cancerous tumor, and I was deeply anguished over the prospect of her demise. Then a few weeks later, an unpleasant episode at the university drew the full force of my anger, and shortly after that, in mid-May, the recurrence of Kate's breast cancer drew the full force of my panic. So, as May gave way to June, I felt compelled to track the diagnosis of her condition as closely as I had been observing the weather, my vegetable garden, the university, and Phoebe. Especially given the fact that one doctor considered Kate's tumor to be merely a local recurrence at the point of the previous surgery, whereas another specialist, whom my brother referred to as "the doctor from hell," considered it to be the mark of a systemic, and therefore incurable, condition. Torn between two such radically different views of her condition and her fate, my essays of that period were as emotionally varied and unstable as spring weather. By early June, I'd become so preoccupied with the uncertainty and instability all around me—including my neighbor Jim's attempt to identify the sex of a groundhog which was then threatening my garden—that I ended one of my pieces with the following reflection:

The more I've thought about it, everything seems to be on the move—from the sex of the groundhog to the status of El Nino to the diagnosis of Kate. As if everything were playing possum. Dead one minute, alive the next. Female one day, male the next. So, I'm beginning to feel uncertain about everything. I mean, if I can't trust my own eyes, or Jim's animal know-how, or the weather service's prediction, or a doctor's opinion, what can I rely on? My colleagues worry about problematic literary texts. But right now the whole world looks problematic to me.

Two days later, still vexed by the problematic nature of things, I wrote the following piece, so completely interiorized, so given over to self-flagellation that it seems like the work of a completely different person from the self-confident one who just a few months before had been writing dispassionate weather reports:

Saturday, June 10

My son, Marshall, called this morning, and I'd just finished telling him about the disagreement between Kate's cancer surgeon and the Doctor from Hell, when Marshall said, "It must be really difficult to be faced with two such different interpretations." Initially, it was difficult to understand how one doctor could treat her recent cancer as just a local recurrence while the other believed it to be systemic. Far worse was the hopeless future that seemed in store for Kate, according to the Doctor from Hell, who repeatedly asserted that her cancer was systemic and therefore certain to recur. "Maybe, it won't come back for four or five years. Or it could suddenly show up everywhere in the system six months from now." But once my brother explained how unlikely it would be for a cell to travel throughout Kate's entire system and return exactly to the site of her last breast cancer, I've not had any trouble weighing the merits of the doctors' radically different interpretations. Now, instead, I'm troubled by how quickly I was willing to accept the extreme diagnosis of the Doctor from Hell. Oh yes, I was initially puzzled, so I asked him how all the tests could be negative, yet the cancer be systemic. But once he began talking about the crudity of the tests and then told me to think about a dandelion gone to seed and the difficulty of finding its seed in the grass, my skepticism was readily dispelled.

   As I look back on that afternoon, I wonder why I was so quick to accept the opinion of someone I'd never met before, even though it contradicted the view of the distinguished cancer surgeon who's been taking excellent care of Kate for the past six and a half years. Partly, I think it was the unusual frankness with which the Doctor from Hell announced his dire view of things. Partly his highly articulate manner, so different from the uncomfortable behavior of the surgeon, who usually says little and explains much less. But ultimately, I think the dandelion metaphor took me in, for it spoke to me in terms I know from firsthand observation. Kate, as usual, took a more hard-nosed view of things. "Didn't you notice how I was trying to lead him on, to see how far he'd go? I've always known that it can recur, but the way he was talking just didn't make sense to me, not in terms of the evidence from the tests. And besides, he didn't have any research studies to back up what he was saying. Even he admitted that."

So, I can't help wondering why I too didn't notice the weakness of his case. I've been chiding students for years whenever they don't provide evidence for their assertions. And why didn't I tell him that his dandelion analogy was badly chosen, for the body is not like a lawn any more than a cancer cell is like a dandelion seed. Maybe, it's because the dandelion analogy did embody a germ of common sense—that some things are so small they cannot be detected even by the most sophisticated technology. But a germ of sense doesn't necessarily lead to an epidemic of truth.

Looking back on those reflections, I'm fascinated to see how much my voice had changed—altered, it would seem, as a result of being distressed by Kate's situation, by the differing diagnoses of her condition, and by my failure to assess them with a properly critical eye. In other words, my voice had changed under the press of circumstances, rather than the force of a consciously willed choice such as I had made to begin with. And I didn't immediately notice the difference, partly because I was so distressed, but also because I mistakenly thought that I was still writing in the plain and simple style of my early weather reports, whereas my diction in that entry had become more polysyllabic and my syntax more complex, more intricately balanced, more rhetorically heightened. How strange, to think of my persona as having changed without being aware of it, as if I'd undergone a drastic facial transformation without taking note of it in the mirror. How often, I wonder, do we hear ourselves on paper? How often do we listen to the changes taking place in our voice; how often do we take stock of our morphing selves? Montaigne listened to himself incessantly, and the more he listened the more voices he heard. But my ear was so attuned to the changes all around me that by contrast I came to feel almost Gibraltar-like in my stability. For whatever strange turns the world might take, and whatever might happen to Phoebe and Kate, I arose each morning devoted to producing a five-hundred-word essay, and each day without fail I completed a piece before going to bed. Pieces about everything from the progress of my tomatoes to the breakdown of our air-conditioner on the hottest night of the summer. So, in a sense, my daily essays enabled me to transcend the vicissitudes of the weather, of experience, and all that flesh is heir to.

Yet my voice was not only changing, but the changes were taking place more often than I might have imagined, for just a couple of weeks after the stylistic complexities of that interiorized piece about the differing diagnoses, I was back in something like my earlier voice, almost as plain in style as before, in this entry about our Welsh terrier, Pip.

Saturday, June 24

Kate and I were kneeling on the ground, looking at Pip, his eyes glazed, his body limp. We were trying to figure out what had caused him to vomit and then go into something like shock, when just a few minutes before he'd been prancing around a tree while Kate worked in her flower bed. So I went to get our neighbor Jim, who knows more about animals than anyone around, but after a few minutes without much improvement, we all agreed that a trip to the vet was in order. And it was. Pip had evidently eaten something that caused him so much pain and panic he'd almost gone into a severe shock. So today, tomorrow, and Monday, he's on stomach relaxants, fluids, and light food. And he's been acting the part whenever he sees me. Head down, tail between his legs, moping over the absence of his usual rations and treats, especially the rawhide chips that probably caused some of the trouble.

But the real trouble that's got me feeling a bit hangdog too is that Pip's clearly aging, as Kate's been trying to tell me whenever we have an episode like this. "I keep telling you I've been running a geriatric ward around here the past year." But I guess I've been ignoring her, because Pip has generally had such a good constitution, so few illnesses, such a handsome, well-marked coat—full black saddle, reddish brown legs and head—that he often seems to be just a few years old. And often he still behaves that way, wanting to get ahead of us on a walk, even when he doesn't have any idea of where we're going, sometimes taking the leash in his mouth and jumping around with it, like a young puppy. But he's ten years old—old for his breed, according to the vet. His eyes are beginning to cloud up a bit, his stomach is evidently beginning to act up a bit, he doesn't wake up early anymore, and he doesn't try to run away much anymore, as he did just a year or two ago. It used to be that instead of calling Jim to diagnose an ailment, I'd be imploring him to help me track Pip down, usually at ten or eleven in the evening. Probably that's why Jim was so surprised by his behavior last night.

But I don't mean to be writing an obituary here. I'm just taking stock of things, noting the seasonal changes. Besides, Jim's help last night gave me a good excuse to give him and Carol one of the five heads of cauliflower I harvested this morning. One good head deserves another. And it was especially good at lunch today, when Kate served one steamed and cooled, dressed with a Creole vinaigrette.

I can still remember making that entry, for the words came so readily to mind that it seemed as if I was transcribing them rather than composing them, taking dictation rather than writing a piece of literary nonfiction. The ultimate payoff, I thought, for the straightforward style I'd been honing the previous six months. What I didn't realize just then was that the words came quickly not just because I was in a stylistic groove and the groove of a five-hundred-word essay, but because I was in possession of an outlook, a way of thinking about things—an intense consciousness of time, change, and mortality—that had begun to take shape with the discovery of Phoebe's tumor and the recurrence of Kate's breast cancer, and that colored many of my pieces the rest of that year, particularly given an exceptionally severe mid-summer drought and heat-wave that ravaged crops, livestock, and people throughout the Midwest. Thus in looking now at that entry about Pip, I'm struck not only by its prose style but also by its air of sadness, by its retrospective turn of mind, as if the persona inhabiting the piece were quite a bit older and more hangdog than the self-assured fellow who was making weather reports six months back. Same style but drastically different voices—so different they ultimately led me to question my longtime supposition that style is the overriding determinant of voice. In the backward abysm of time, that supposition so beguiled me that I created a course called "Style and Voice," in which

I required students to write up the same memory in four or five distinctly different styles. A sequence of assignments intended to show how different stylistic choices inevitably alter both the depiction of an experience and the projection of one's self. But I've come to believe in recent years that the self inhabiting a piece of prose is the product of so many things in addition to style—the length of a piece, as well as its form, its mode, its mood, its gist, its pacing, its point of view, its state of mind—that "gestalt" is the only word I can think of to suggest the multiplicity and complexity of its determinants. Change anyone of them, and you alter most of the others—and by extension the whole gestalt.

Why so long, one might ask, to arrive at such a self-evident truth—as if it were news that the whole is greater than the sum of its parts? I'm tempted to answer that question by taking refuge in the obvious—in the memory of my former attachment to a notion of voice so closely linked to the sound of the words, to the structure and rhythm of a sentence, that it seemed to be engendered more by style than by anything else. And why such a fierce attachment to so reductive an idea? What else, but the inescapable hunger for control—in one's thinking, one's teaching, and one's writing. Control the words and you control everything—a comfortable and convenient idea, especially for a teacher of writing. But how to account for those moments when the words come quickly as if from nowhere, in a rush that seems like nothing so much as the welling up of things from deep within? Such moments, of course, are neither teachable nor explicable, but their occurrence is indisputable. By late August, for example, when Phoebe was gone and the walnut leaves began to yellow and fall, I was having so many such moments that my journal often seemed to be writing itself. And not just in elegiac essays but also in zestful and hedonistic pieces. In the face of mortality, what else to do but seize the day? All of which led me to feel that I finally had a glimmering of what people mean when they speak of finding one's voice—an expression that had often troubled me before, because it suggested a mystical and static idea of self. And yet for the rest of that journal, I had found a voice and found it not just in a style but in a state of mind—in an awareness and acceptance of time and change that moved me to write about my daily experience without the self-conscious deliberation of my earlier entries. So, I came to think of that journal as having saved my life, and not just because it helped me through a difficult time in my life, or because I turned it into two published daybooks about my life, *Weathering Winter* and *My Vegetable Love*, but because it led me to see how a voice can give rise to life, invoke life, embody life, particularly when it is animated by one's deepest convictions.

That said, I should also acknowledge that the day after I stopped keeping the journal, I felt a great sense of relief at not having to write anything that day, though I made a brief entry just in case I might need something for a postscript. And the day after that another brief entry, as well as a great sense of exhaustion and bone-racking pain—a message from my body, according to Kate, of the stress I'd been putting on myself (and her). And the next five days another batch of shorter and shorter entries, evidently the sign of an inner momentum running down, an inner need pouring itself out. And then at last the feeling that I had finally put that voice to rest—only to discover a year or so later during the angst of impending retirement that it was still seemingly there, suddenly roused to vent itself in another book-length journal, followed by a promise to Kate that I would never undertake another such project—a promise I kept until she was suddenly swept away by a cerebral hemorrhage. And then my voice returned yet again, having its say once again in a year of letters to Kate. A life after death in language. So, I've sometimes been tempted to think that the voice I found when Kate was still alive is a voice for all seasons. Still with me, though she's long gone. And yet when I recently gave a reading from *Letters to Kate*, I heard such a different person from the days of that gardening journal fifteen years ago—a person so burdened by loss and grief—that I wonder how I could possibly have thought they were akin. Especially given the difference between journal entries and love letters. How often do we listen to ourselves on paper? How often do we hear our morphing selves? How often do we heed the weather reports? Change, after all, is in the air—it touches us, touches our words, touches our personae, as it touches all things. So, a voice for all seasons could only exist in a world without change, a life without death. The "I" is mutable, whether we will it or not.

"Brenda Miller Has a Cold," or: How the Lyric Essay Happens

Brenda Miller

It happens like this:

I have a cold. It's what might be termed "a perfect cold," for while my head is stuffed up and my throat tickles (making me cough exactly every six minutes), I'm actually in good spirits, the cotton batting in my head a fine insulation between me and those pesky thoughts that normally bat about in my brain. I can't walk for long without losing my breath, and my muscles ache just enough to make me gravitate toward whatever couch or chair or bed is handy. I can't think very clearly, and when I speak my words come out in a voice hoarse and disguised, echoing in my plugged ears. I may be speaking too loudly or too softly—I can't really know, and this person who speaks seems a separate self, one who is a simpleton, focused only on what is right in front of her: the cup of tea, the box of tissues, a blanket wrapped around her feet. She can see only what happens to flit across her mucoused line of vision.

It's a perfect cold, because it just so happens that for this particular week I don't have to do anything but watch the ailment make its way through my body, stopping to gather a bit of snot here, to drain a bit there. I'm on an island, and I'm with a friend who ferociously writes poetry for ten hours at a time in a room near the water. I can't do much else but sit with a cup of tea in hand, staring at the fake fire or out the window, where I see a mess of deer fence caging saplings already so nibbled by said deer it's difficult to tell what they're trying to become.

I have a cold, and this means I wake up at odd hours, the night wholly black, and snatches of language float through my brain and stick there, fluttering like any caught prey. In my ordinary body—my clear, un-mucoused, narrative life—such fragments glide through continually, but rarely do they sit down and stay, even for a few moments, and lately I bustle right past them even if they do. Instead, my omnipresent, stalwart "to-do" list pulses like one of those massive black magnets you'd see in a sci-fi flick, bent on destroying the world.

What I'm trying to say is: *The lyric essay happens when I'm sticky.*

Or it happens like this:

My friend wakes a few minutes after I do, and we say few words to one another, as the day is still dark, and there's coffee to be drunk, and porridge to be shuttled into the mouth, and we're barely aware of one another until I hear her in the shower, and she emerges, fresh and clean and smelling of roses, her briefcase packed, and she wishes me *adieu* as she swings down the path to her studio. Me—I've barely moved from the couch, into which I keep sinking deeper and deeper, my pajamas warm like a second skin, my eyelids ratcheting back down by increments to the sleep position.

But all this time, the pen stays in my hand, the notebook on my knee, and something is happening; words I can't explain—can't direct, not yet—dump onto the page. I write something like: ". . . saplings already so nibbled by said deer it's difficult to tell what they're trying to become. . . ."

What I'm trying to say is: *The lyric essay happens when I've forgotten to get dressed. When I'm disheveled. When I'm not wearing any shoes.*

Or maybe it happens like this:

I've just returned from Michigan, where I probably caught this cold from shaking so many hands in friendly and earnest greeting. And there, the women's NCAA basketball tournament was underway; many, *many* tall young women wandered the hallways of my hotel, crowding the elevators—stunning in their gray T-shirts and shorts, everything about them declaring *athlete:* their radiant good health, the muscles sleek and toned with practice. They seemed eerily calm in the face of the competition ahead, but then I had no idea who these teams were, or what place they held, or how confident they deserved to be. I couldn't ask, because their beauty made me mute. I pushed the elevator button and nodded at them, got off at my floor without a word.

And what skids through my brain at the sight of these beautiful women is the way I've always loved basketball—to watch it, mind you, not to play—ever since I was a kid and my brothers played on the backyard court. I love the way action— beautiful, controlled—darts out of what appears to be a chaos of frenzied motion on the court. Bodies seem to sprout limbs more muscled, more gleaming, just all around more flesh, and then from the morass comes the arc of a steady three-point shot (the shooter can feel it in his hands when he knows it's clean, he turns and trots nonchalantly back to the other side of the court, arms spread wide, palms up, shoulders raised in the barest shrug, as if to say: what else did you expect?) . . .

. . . Or the inside layup—the point guard ferreting out traces of a path through all those bodies that jostle for position under the net, slinking through for the soundless score.

. . . Or the clean block, all ball, the hand arriving in position at exactly the right moment, the force of it, the surprise . . . .

I knew even then—as a little girl in the LA Forum, or shyly watching my brothers from the sidelines in our own backyard—I knew even before I knew the words I'm going to use now: the aesthetic power of instinct coupled with improvisation, of training hitched to transience, the clarity of a plan of action amid a sea of flesh doing its darnedest to make you fail. Of course, I know now that teams have carefully choreographed plays; they know the strengths and weaknesses of every player on the court. That point guard who just made the impossible layup? She knows the exact moves to make, the quick head-fake, the dribble between the legs, the two-and-one-half steps it would take to lay it up and in. The fall-away reverse jump shot? Practiced dozens of times. Piece of cake.

But even so: you never know. If all we saw were the practiced drills, the results completely predictable every time—the crowds gathered in the bleachers with their giant "We're Number One" foam fingers and huge plastic tumblers filled with beer—we'd soon grow restless, long before the beer became warm, unappetizing dreg at the bottom of the cup. For much as we love to watch the athletes perform, we don't really want the practiced drill with the predictable outcome. We want the thrill of the unknown, the possibility of utter failure, the exultation of the barest victory, the high-fives in the stands . . . the sense that the crowd (the ones who watch) are a part of it all, making it happen with their steadfast attention.

So. Look there, down below, illuminated: The court is a given. The ball, a given. The referees with their shrill whistles, their heavy-footed lumber from one end of the court to another to make sure there is *some* comportment after all—they, too, are a given, and we hardly note their presence as we shuffle in sideways to our seats. But when those athletes trot onto the floor, that's when it all begins. Expectations rise (literally lift us out of our seats, cheering) and the game begins. From the initial tip of the ball, that first whistle—who knows what will happen next?

What I'm trying to say? *The lyric essay is a three-point shot. It's a desperation thirty footer. It's a technical foul in the last two seconds of the game.*

*

I have a cold, which means that at first I get up frequently to fetch the things that surround me—the box of tissues ("specially soft," according to the soothing voice on the box, "made in a special way with soft fibers on the outside and strong fibers on the inside. This gives you the softness you want and the strength you need."). A cup of Breathe Easy tea. A glass of grape juice. A few Advil to stave off the sinus headache lurking in the wings. But in all these forays off the couch, I've never, not even once, looked at myself in the mirror. For someone who usually checks her reflection at any opportunity, this avoidance of my reflection seems peculiar, an aberration. It feels as though—because I have a cold, and because I'm writing so hard, with all I've got—I've become diaphanous. Transparent. There's nothing really left of me to see.

What this essay is trying to say (ignore for a moment, its author, sitting on the couch, blowing her nose—pay no attention to her, she's getting a little carried away): The lyric essay doesn't look too long at itself in the mirror. It is not "self-reflective," in that it does not really reflect the self who scribbles it down. Rather, it is the mirror, the silver film reflecting whatever passes its way. Brenda does not think to look at herself this morning—this morning of the perfect cold—not because she'd rather spare herself the sight of her ugly mug, but because for these few hours she really has no self to speak of. That self—it's battened away for the moment, put away for safekeeping. And that's how the lyric essay happens: When there's no bothersome self to get in the way. When the writing finds its own core. When it finds the language it needs on its own. The lyric essay is *made in a special way with soft fibers on the outside and strong fibers on the inside. This gives you the softness you want and the strength you need.*

*

So I tell my friend Lee (and I'm lying to her, I'm making it up as I go along): "It's kind of an homage to Gay Talese. To that essay 'Frank Sinatra Has a Cold.'" And she glances at me with that startled, wide-eyed look she gets when she's delighted. I know that "Frank Sinatra Has a Cold" is one of her favorite essays of all time, and that's another reason I've made up this half-truth, to give some plea- sure, to have this fleeting connection.

"Really?" she says. "Do *you* at least show up?"

In the Gay Talese profile, made famous on its publication in *Esquire* in 1966, Frank Sinatra has a cold. Which changes everything. The narrative shifts. Expectations shuffle and scuttle and get out of the way. The interview Talese was after? Gone. Sinatra never even looks at him. Sinatra's in a bad mood. The songs now will be difficult to sing. Not as polished. Not as rehearsed. Sinatra can't stand it. It feels as though the cold will last forever, that his voice will never be the same.

Talese hangs around anyway. Takes notes on all the things surrounding Sinatra, his ostensible subject. The notebook from his research is a thing of beauty itself, a piece of art, with doodles and arrows and words spilling across the margins. Nothing stays in place, but even through the scribble we see a structure emerge, a sense of direction: SCENE TWO, he writes in big block letters, surrounded by asterisks. ACT ONE. He watches Sinatra's character emerge, gain complex- ity, through his interactions with others. Sees him blow up over a pair of boots that Harlan Ellison wears at a club. Sees him smile at a woman in the crosswalk, disarming her completely, and then disappear. Sinatra's at the center, but we can't access him directly. He shows up, but only in flashes, only in transit. We have to sit on a bar stool a few feet away, just watching to see what might be revealed.

Do I show up? Sometimes I do, and sometimes I don't.

You try to tell a simple story, walk a simple path. But you keep losing sight of your destination. The destination is no longer as interesting as the diversions. You hear a wren sing so loudly inside the deer fence, and she startles you, and then you see her, how easily she slips through that cage around *saplings so nibbled by said deer, you can't tell what they're trying to become*. You are just trying to become. No, not trying. Trying is too trying. You're just becoming.

Anyway, you have a cold, so you're not going to walk too far. You'll sit down for frequent rest stops, just to catch your breath. Your breath will fascinate you, become something you can no longer take for granted, the rhythm of it: in . . . pause . . . out, and then, without even trying, the body's insistence on keeping you alive.

What I'm trying to say is: *The lyric essay happens in the gaps. In the pause before the next breath demands to be taken.*

So here's the deal:

You have a cold, and then you don't. Gradually you get better. Or you get worse, and then you get better. Rarely does anyone die of a head cold.

Sometimes you notice you're getting better, and sometimes you don't. Sometimes you just wake up one day and realize you didn't cough all night, that you have not one crumpled, sticky tissue lying next to your bed. Your body has been returned, intact and clear.

And your self? You can, if you so desire, now go to Point B from Point A with a brisk, direct stride, hardly pausing, undistracted by the scenery. You can go to work, and be your workaday self; you can be productive as all get-out. When people ask how you are, you can say "I'm fine" without lying. You can tell the truth, the unvarnished truth, no half-truths, no need to make anything up just for the heck of it. Well, that's *good*, people will say, I'm glad you're feeling *better*, and you'll nod in agreement, but some part of you, some part that's not fit for civilized company, wonders if this self—this clear, narrative, undeterred self—really is *good*, really is *better*. Some part of you longs to be sick again—not *sick* sick, just enough so that you can be buffered a little while longer, not quite so direct and so clear.

The poet, Mark Doty, says it happens like this: "Grace might descend in its odd, circuitous routes. We are visited by joy, seem to be given a poem or a song, something we encounter fills us to the rim of the self. Those things point the way, but who lives in that heightened state of awareness?"

In Michigan—amid the basketball players and the spring rains—protestors clog the streets with signs, commemorating the fourth anniversary of the Iraq war. They only want us to notice. Just notice. And to remember, even before that, the bombing of Afghanistan.

So I oblige. I'm an obliging person. I remember a large hall, with red-planked floors. Candlelight. A scattering of people sitting on *zafus* and *zabutons*, waiting for a bell, a bell that sits in front of me, waiting to be struck. Then someone hands me a slip of paper, and I nod, like a judge when she's just been apprised of the verdict. I deliberately set the piece of paper aside on my cushion, all eyes now on me, expectant, and I know, fleetingly, what it means to age: to have a snippet of knowledge a split second before someone else, to have the power to impart this knowledge or not, and the passing of this knowledge through you, leaving its trace.

I don't know what voice to use, how to convey the information that the world we live in—this noisy, familiar, workaday world—has now changed. That piece of paper changes everything.

I nod and set the paper aside. In a low voice, neutral, I whisper this bit of information to the people gathered here in a circle, these people who had come to the hall on a Wednesday evening with no particular agenda in mind but to practice breathing in and breathing out, to observe how predictably the mind will wander from that simple task to more complicated things. "They have started dropping bombs in Afghanistan," I say, and a dozen heads nod, as if we know what is meant by *they*, as if we know what is meant by *bombs*, as if we know *Afghanistan*. As if we know what to do with such knowledge now that it has become ours.

But they are only words on a piece of paper. I set it aside. I ring a little bell. We sit and breathe in and out—some of us, I'm sure, thinking (trying not to think) of children, of what happens to a body when it's dismembered. We know something has happened. But we don't really know. All we can do is imagine. All we can do is try to put the pieces together again.

What I'm trying to say is: In the lyric essay, it all shows up. The good and the bad—they jostle one another, rub shoulders, emit sparks. The stuff we try to remember, and the stuff that remembers itself.

The lyric essay . . . *it's happening.*

That's all I'm trying to say. It's *a* happening, like those hippie gatherings I dreamt of as a teenager, as I walked to Patrick Henry Junior High, the suburban streets so calm, so predictable. Somewhere to the north of us, students burned the star-spangled banner, singing anthems that bore no resemblance to the patriotic hymn we belted out on the playground. In the streets of San Francisco, young men and women danced in circles, smiling at one another, *loving the one you're with.* They dropped acid and smoked pot and heard the *doors of perception* clatter open in their brains.

But we—my classmates and I—we lived in the suburbs of Los Angeles where life proceeded in routines so smooth we barely noticed them. Our parents did not get divorced, our houses did not fall apart, even in the occasional earthquake that rocked the town.

And then I read *The Electric Kool-Aid Acid Test* three times in a row, and I wanted nothing more than to attend a *happening*. A *happening* would change me forever. I imagined a large warehouse filled with beautiful people dancing their hearts out, breathing hard, doing strange and wondrous things to one another. The great thing about *happenings* was the way they just happened. No one planned them. No one knew what to expect.

You bring together a few elements as givens: A big empty space, some musicians prone to improvisation, a few substances geared to short-circuit one's capacity to make logical, streamlined narratives. But that's it. The rest is up to you. Well, not *you*, exactly, because there is no longer a solid concept of you, a you that has any true agency or control.

And who knows what might be alchemized in this mix? Maybe someone will make balloon animals, his breath huffing to bring them to life, squeaking them into the shapes of deer and foxes and wrens that really take flight. Maybe two someones will make love in the dark; one of them might have a cold, and the kisses will make her wheeze, but this will not diminish the force of her desire. A basketball game might erupt on the floor, or a hula hoop contest, or Frisbees might float weightless, suspended in the air. Maybe Sinatra will show up, crooning love songs, beaming his bright blue eyes to make us swoon. Maybe two giant puppets will lurch toward the stage, cradling the war dead in their arms.

The poet Paisley Rekdal says: *I suppose it is an accident anything is beautiful.*

But whatever happens, certainly we'll dance. Heads bopping, arms swinging, sweat glazing our backs. A feral, impulsive dance—one that makes itself up as it goes along. That's the only thing we can know for sure.

How to Live: Grandfather of the Writing We Love to Hate

Laura Miller

Although it's a bit embarrassing to admit it, who among us doesn't come to great works of literature looking for some hints on improving our own lot? That was the double joke behind Alain de Botton's bestselling *How Proust Can Change Your Life*—both the absurdity that anyone would turn to one of history's most neurotic, hypochondriacal closet cases for lessons on how to live and the irony that you can actually pick up a few good tips from *In Search of Lost Time*.

Michel de Montaigne would not look down on you for seeking a little self-help in the pages of his revolutionary opus, *Essays*. As described by Sarah Bakewell in her suavely enlightening *How to Live, or A Life of Montaigne in One Question and Twenty Attempts at an Answer*, Montaigne is, with Walt Whitman, among the most congenial of literary giants, inclined to shrug over the inevitability of human failings and the last man to accuse anyone of self-absorption. His great subject, after all, was himself.

Bakewell, a British writer and librarian, begins with the observation that every generation of readers see themselves in Montaigne, even if they've often had to gloss over certain facts to do it. "To read Montaigne," she writes, "is to experience a series of shocks of familiarity." For a French aristocrat (albeit a country one) he puts on no airs. He confesses that he is lazy and dilatory, the very opposite of self-disciplined: "What I do easily and naturally I can no longer do if I order myself to do it by strict command." He laments the shortness of his stature (and his penis). He notes that he thinks better on his feet ("My mind will not budge unless my legs move it"). He describes stopping his work to play with his cat and thinking, "who knows if I am not a pastime to her more than she is to me?"

Most Renaissance authors seem to be speaking to us across a vast historical and cultural divide; we may find shared experiences there, but we have to work at it. Not so with Montaigne. The Austrian writer Stefan Zweig found a copy of *Essays* while exiled in Latin America during World War II and felt, when reading them, "four hundred years disappear like smoke." This sensation is so powerful that many readers in the centuries after Montaigne's death were compelled to either battle his "seductive" charm or make him over in their own image. Blaise Pascal, an impassioned idealist, deplored Montaigne's pragmatism, his credo of "convenience and calm"; Enlightenment thinkers embraced him as a champion of reason; the Romantics swooned over his devotion to his best friend, Étienne de La Boétie, but then turned around and accused him of insufficient political zeal.

The word Bakewell uses most often to describe her subject's outlook is "nonchalance." Inspired by classical philosophers of the Epicurean, Stoic and Skeptical schools, Montaigne adopted a Zen-like attitude in which everything is subject to doubt and nothing should be taken too seriously. As Bakewell puts it, "He went with the flow." Since he lived his adult life in a France shredded by civil wars and religious extremism, this position was both understandable and rather dangerous. Somehow, Montaigne, whose book became a fashionable bestseller during his own lifetime, managed to survive a fairly successful political career—he served as the mayor of Bordeaux and ran diplomatic errands for Catherine de Medici and the king—although he much preferred to hole up at home and write. (Among the many delightful illustrations in *How to Live* is a photograph of Montaigne's restored study, now a museum.)

Above all, Montaigne invented the personal essay, that unpredictable and strangely addictive literary form devoted, as Bakewell puts it, to "re-creating a sequence of sensations as they felt from the inside, following them from instant to instant." Montaigne constantly revised and expanded *Essays* throughout his life; it was never really finished. "I do not portray being," he wrote, "I portray passing. Not the passing from one age to another ... but from day to day, from minute to minute." Bakewell, who dances from philosophy to history to biography with enviable ease, also has a gift for literary criticism, describing his style thus: "He seems constantly to turn back on himself, thickening and deepening, fold upon fold. The result is a sort of baroque drapery, all billowing and turbulence."

Montaigne's essays can be meandering, yes, and often only tangentially related to their supposed themes. He filled them with anecdotes and examples collected from classical literature but also stories he got from friends and the peasants on his estate. In this and other qualities, he probably had more influence on the free-form English essay than on the lofty, abstraction-prone style of Académie française-sanctioned French. And even back in the day, people complained that he shared too much trivial detail, such as his preference for white wine over red; "Who the hell wants to know what he liked?" one crabby scholar retorted. In the 19th century, Montaigne's candid discussion of carnal matters led concerned editors to produce a bowdlerized version of his works, more suitable for the tender minds of young ladies.

In short, Montaigne was accused of every sin attributed to today's memoirists and bloggers, whose literary great-grandfather he is. Nevertheless, you will find *Essays* in every one of those collections of great books you used to be able to buy by the set, bound in "full genuine leather," with gold lettering. This suggests that the line between trash and literature may be less firmly drawn than some would have us believe, a notion that would probably please Montaigne himself. Or perhaps the real lesson here is that it doesn't really matter what you write about, provided that you do it well.

Source: Miller, Laura. "*How to Live*: Grandfather of the Writing We Love to Hate." *Salon.* October 10, 2010. http://www.salon.com/books/memoirs/index.html?story=/books/laura_miller/2010/10/10/montaigne

Collage, Montage, Mosaic, Vignette, Episode, Segment

Robert L. Root, Jr.

It's a common problem among student writers, starting too far back in the narrative or trying to encompass too much time or too much activity in a single chronology. A paper about high school begins at the moment the writer entered the building for the first time in ninth grade and moves inexorably toward the moment of graduation, growing more perfunctory year by year; a paper about making the team or the cheerleading squad presents a minute by minute account of decision, preparation, and competition that loses more and more energy the longer it goes on.

But it isn't just a novice writer's problem alone. Any writer runs up against the insidious demands of linear presentation of material whenever he or she selects chronology—from the beginning to the end, from the first step through each individual step to the final step, from the inception through the planning and execution to the result—as the organizing principle of an essay or article. Linear schemes of organization come easily to us. We all tell stories and chronology is the simplest system of organization ("We began by . . ., then we . . ., and finally . . ."); process is the most accessible scheme of exposition ("First you . . ., next you . . ., and you conclude by . . ."); linear movement structures description the most directly ("Her hair was the color . . . her feet spilling out of tattered sandals"; "On the east side of the building . . . in the middle was . . . on the west side we saw"). But linear schemes don't automatically help with issues of compression and focus, particularly in an age of increasingly shorter attention spans and little patience for leisurely development of plot and character and theme.

The more complex the story is, the more interwoven with other subjects, ideas, incidents, experiences, the harder it is to make it all connect in a linear way that doesn't extend the narrative or the development beyond the patience of writer and reader alike. Moreover, the connections and associations that come so readily in the memory and in the imagination often defy simple linearity, easy transition from one subtopic to the next, when the writer has to force them into words on a page.

Mike, now past fifty, has been cleaning his mental attic for the past several years, rummaging through his souvenirs and writing essays about a lifetime playing sports—the high school pitching, the conflicts with coaches, the visits to historic ballparks. Now he begins an essay about how he came to give up his annual summer stint as manager and player for a fastpitch softball team.

He starts an early draft with a brief scene set in the present which serves as the trigger for a flashback that gives him the opportunity to review his long career with the team. "It's a lazy summer evening and I'm driving home from campus," he begins, and then tells how his weariness momentarily vanishes when he notices a game in progress at the ball park where he used to play: "for a moment I want to jump out of the car, climb into my softball uniform, and trot out to my old position in left field." He describes gazing at the field and continuing home. After these two brief paragraphs of introduction, he introduces the past in the third paragraph: "That night while reading my mind wanders, and for a suspended moment it is 1969 again. That summer, I was. . . ." From here he relies on the act of composing itself to help him rediscover the subject matter. Chronology decides the order. He traces the arc of his involvement from the moment he decided to join the team, and one memory provokes another until he reaches his last game and the end of the draft.

By then he has covered a lot of ground. His draft surfaces deep-seated feelings about playing ball, about giving it up, about the satisfactions of moving on to new places in his life and expending his energies elsewhere. But it takes a long time to get to the place where these important and powerful feelings get voiced, because so much detail has emerged in his review of the chronology—early days on the team, the change from player to manager, road trips, destinations, the interaction with players, the near-misses for spots in regional and state tournaments, the interests that distracted him from the game, the aging processes that slowed him down. In the associative links of memory every detail makes sense, makes connections, but on the page the slow linear march of the chronology dissipates all the emphatic force of the narrative—there's a reason no one is proposing to cash in on the natural disaster film genre ("Twister," "Volcano") with a movie called "Glacier!" These narrative elements establish not only theme but also tone and voice, and many of them need to stay in the next draft, but he knows that he needs to lift scenes out of this linear history and highlight them as well as give more emphasis to the final summer.

His revision starts almost at the end of the previous draft, placing him on the road to the final tournament. "It's three A.M. Friday Labor Day weekend 1985. I left Sutton's Bay at ten P.M. headed for Houghton, which is about as far as driving to Nashville. I'm wearing my softball uniform and my wife Carole is asleep in the back seat, cotton balls stuffed in each ear while the tape deck blasts out a medley of Beach Boys and Beatles tunes—my favorite road music." But the present-tense narrative of that summer experience has barely begun before Mike inserts a paragraph break, white space on the page signaling a shift of scene or time, and in the past tense recounts his initial involvement with the softball team years before. A page later he inserts another break and shifts back to the present tense and the immediate circumstance to establish that he and his wife have plane tickets for Paris that conflict with the tournament dates (a point of information barely mentioned in the earlier draft's conclusion) and that they have put off foreign travel in the past to be available for championships that never materialized. The dramatic tension in this conflict makes the reader wonder from the beginning which option they will take in the end. Telling this part of the essay in present tense heightens that tension and establishes a sense of immediacy about the experience, as if the outcome had not been decided long ago.

Throughout the remainder of the essay past tense vignettes of a softball life alternate with present tense scenes from the decisive summer. Paragraph breaks allow Mike to crosscut between the past and the present and to ignore connections and transitions in either chronology. When he has finished his revisions, he has avoided the linear chronology that bogged down his earlier draft and achieved a tight, dense essay with more dramatic and pointed individual segments. The overall effect of the essay is the same he had hoped to achieve in the earlier draft, but it is more focused and consequently more powerful.

The white spaces on the page—the page breaks or paragraph breaks—are part of the composition. They serve as fade outs/fade ins do in films, as visual cues that we have ended one sequence and gone on to another. Often, somewhere in the early part of each segment, a word or phrase serves as a marker indicating the change of time or place, very much as a superimposed title on a movie scene might inform the viewer: "Twelve years later. Northern Michigan," to suggest that a lot has happened since the screen went dark and a new image began to emerge.

In almost any contemporary collection of creative nonfiction, many selections are segmented, sectioned off by white spaces or rows of asterisks or subheadings in italics or boldface. A thematic issue of the travel narrative journal *Grand Tour* has no unsegmented essays. In a recent essay issue of *Ploughshares*, fourteen of the twenty-three essays are segmented by paragraph breaks or, occasionally, some more pronounced method of subdividing. In a similar issue of *American Literary Review*, fifteen out of nineteen essays are segmented, their segments separated by rows of diamonds or white spaces, divided by subheadings, or numbered; only four essays are completely unsegmented.

In some of the *ALR* essays the segmenting in the fifteen is barely noticeable, almost a printer's convention rather than an actual break in the flow of thought or language; in most, however, the segmenting is emphatic, crucial. William Holtz numbers his thirteen segments in "Brother's Keeper: An Elegy" and begins eleven of them with the same sentence, "My brother now is dead," usually as the main clause in sentences with varying subordinate or coordinate elements. The repetitions give the segments the power of incantation or prayer. Lynne Sharon Schwartz, writing about translating the book *Smoke Over Birkenau*, begins her essay with a series of English words she listed in an Italian edition of the book—the opening line reads: "Strenuous. Grim. Resolute. Blithe. Alluring. Cringe. Recoil. Admonish." Occasional excerpts from the list interrupt the essay from time to time in place of asterisks or numbers or subheadings between segments ("Haggard. Cantankerous. Imploring. Dreary. Plucky. Banter. Superb. Vivacious. Snarling. Prattled.") Frederick Smock's "Anonymous: A Brief Memoir" opens with a section of Gwendolyn Brooks's poem, "Jane Addams," and is divided into segments subtitled by locations in his anonymous subject's home: "The Great-Room," "The Landing," "The Dining Room," "The Grotto," and so on. Paul Gruchow's "Eight Variations on the Idea of Failure" has eight numbered sections with self-contained vignettes of varying length that thematically explore the subject of failure. These are essays that call attention to their segmentation; they announce very early on to the reader that progress through them will not be linear, although it may be sequential, and that the force of the segments will come from their juxtaposition with one another and the effect of their accumulation by the end.

These are not traditional essays, the kind that composition textbooks usually teach you to write, the kind that begin with some sort of thesis statement, then march through a linked, linear series of supporting, illustrative paragraphs to a predictable, forceful conclusion. Textbooks tend to teach either the unattainable and ideal or the undesirable but teachable. The segmented essay has been with us for quite some time and may well be the dominant mode of the contemporary essay, but we are only just beginning to recognize it and try to teach it.

Shaken by her son's death in the crash of his Air Force jet, Carol sets out to retrace the path of his life. She and her husband drive from Michigan across the country to California, and then come back by way of the southeastern United States, all the while trying to connect to the life he led in scattered places. Throughout the trip she keeps a journal of her travels and eventually decides to write an essay about the journey.

As she begins writing, she finds herself hampered by the amount of detail she has accumulated about the trip, about her son's life, about her reactions to each location. So much information seems relevant and interrelated that it is difficult for her to be inclusive and yet get to the end of both the essay and the trip, where the real significance of her pilgrimage comes home to her. It is a trip of several weeks and thousands of miles and, unless she is to make it booklength, which she doesn't want to do, she needs to find another way to come at this mass of strongly felt material.

Eventually she discovers the key to the composing in the materials on which she bases the essay: the narrative of the trip, the reflections in her private journal, the references to her son's life. Alternating among episodes of narration, reflection, and reference, she uses the separate strands of her materials to comment on one another and to justify her breaking off one segment to move to another. The essay begins with a passage of narration and description about the onset of the journey ("We need this trip like the desert needs rain. For months the dining area has looked like a war games planning room with maps everywhere."); it is followed by an excerpt from her journal remarking on how she feels a few days later, set in italics to identify it immediately as separate from the narrative ("*June 7. Badlands. Last night when we walked back to our campsite in true dark, stars in the sky notwithstanding, we became disoriented.*"); this is followed by description of another location, further down the road ("In Wyoming, as we drive north toward Sheridan, we watch antelope standing far off . . ."); then another excerpt from the journal; then a section reflecting her son's experiences ("Kirk loved Wyoming. In 1976 his father and I took him and his brother and sister to Yellowstone . . ."), and so on throughout the essay. Paragraph breaks between segments and changes in font make it easy for the reader to follow the shifts and jumpcuts. It becomes a travel montage with "voiceover" commentary and an alternating strand of personal history. The juxtaposition of landscape, biography, and commentary move us more quickly through the essay than full linear chronology could do, and yet the chronology is there, a beginning, a middle, and an end, given an almost cinematic force by the accumulation of a series of concentrated segments.

The recognition of the segmented form, if not the form itself, is so new that we have not yet settled on a name for it. At present it is most often called a "collage" essay, a term coined by Peter Elbow, referring to the technique in visual art of assembling disparate images into an integrated whole which expresses a specific theme (like the "American Dream" collage) through the interrelationships of the parts. Some use the filmmaking term "montage," the editing technique that arranges a series of shots and images into an expressive sequence. Carl Klaus, who has mulled over the terminology and objected to both collage and montage, has suggested "disjunctive" (as opposed to the more unified and "conjunctive" linear form), which he admits may have negative connotations, or "paratactic" (a grammatical term for "segments of discourse" arranged without connections or transitions), which may be too obscure. Rebecca Blevins Faery has described the form as "fragmented" and "polyphonic." At times all these terms seem applicable to some essays and not to others, perhaps because segmented essays tend to invent their own forms, not merely imitate established forms.

Take, for example, "The Ideal Particle and the Great Unconformity" by Reg Saner. In this complex essay, Saner connects two terms from geology which identify two different concepts of scale. The ideal particle is the term for a grain of sand one tenth of a millimeter, "the size most easily airborne in wind, thus the likeliest to begin a surface effect known as saltation," where one grain strikes other grains with enough force to make them capable of becoming airborne (163); the Great Unconformity is a gigantic gap in the geological record, a place where, following the Grand Canyon walls down the deposits of millennia, you encounter a layer so much older than the layer above it that 1,200 million years of deposits must have been erased before the layers you have been following were laid down. The Great Unconformity was created by the erosive power of the ideal particle and the enormity of the span of time in the life of the planet.

But Saner is not simply explaining these two concepts as a geology textbook might readily do in a paragraph or two. Rather, he is attempting to give the reader some sense of the scale involved here as well as what it is like to experience the scale. Thus, while the essay discusses the history of geological studies and major markers for dating the planet, it also has a personal narrative running through it. Saner recounts a hike into the Grand Canyon, alternating speculations and observations about geological theory and evidence with vignettes of encounters with other hikers. In order to understand the subject of the essay as Saner understands it, the reader has to experience it with him, not simply have it explained to him.

> Slowly we accepted the curve of the earth. It dawned on us like a great change of mind, after which, earth's size came easy. Not its age. Evidence was everywhere underfoot, unmistakable. We chose not to see it. (154)

This opening segment is a brief verbal fanfare that sounds the theme of the essay. The segments that follow alternate exposition and argument with narration and description, taking the reader deeper and deeper into both the subject matter and the experience. We dig down through the segments, like layers of sedimentary deposits, the white spaces between segments marking them like layers of geologic time. Perhaps this is a geologic essay, then, or a tectonic essay, where the segments are like plates moving and colliding and rearranging themselves on the crust of the essay.

The ability to arrange and rearrange segments frees writers to generate unique forms. Mark Rudman has created a series of essays he refers to as "mosaics," such as his "Mosaic on Walking." The mosaic metaphor suggests an essay composed of little sections, like mosaic tiles, which create a larger picture by the way they are cumulatively arranged. For example, the opening tiles are these segments separated from one another by the grouting of white space:

> In this season I am often sulky, sullen, restless, withdrawn. I feel transparent, as if inhabited by the weather.
>
> Only while walking am I relieved from distress, only then, released from the burden of self, am I free to think. I wanted to say walking brings relief from tension without sadness and then I think it is not so—these walks bring their own form of *tristesse*. There is discomfort when movement stops.
>
> Though not exceptionally tall (a shade under six feet), I am a rangy, rambly walker. I take up a lot of space! (138)

In "Mosaic on Walking" the sequentiality of the arrangement is difficult to perceive; it might well have been written simply by composing a random number of segments which in some way relate to the theme of walking and then either haphazardly or systematically arranging them in a disjunctive or non-sequential order on the page—the way you might copy a list of sentences about walking in the order you discovered them in *Bartlett's Familiar Quotations*. The mosaic, at least as Rudman uses it, seems lacking in design, capable of being read in any order, virtually devoid of transition or sequence; it uses an accumulation of associative segments to create mood or attitude. Maybe we should use the term "cumulative essays" or "associative essays."

But Nancy Willard, in "The Friendship Tarot," begins with the image of a tarot card arrangement on the page ("I lay out the cards of our friendship"). Each section of the essay which follows is named for a specific tarot card in that arrangement—The Child, The Journey, The Garden, The Book—and opens with a description of the picture on the card ("The card shows a child with chocolate on his face wandering through an art gallery in downtown Poughkeepsie devoted—for two weeks—to illustrations from children's books."). The segments lead us through the sequence of the tarot reading to get at issues of change and growth in a particular friendship. Perhaps it is a "tarot essay" but I don't know if the term applies to all segmented essays or, in all the history of essays, to her essay alone.

It isn't that collaging or segmenting abandons structure—it's that it builds essay structure in ways that may be organic with the subject, ways that may not be immediately recognizable but which incrementally explain themselves as the reader progresses through the essay. In the models of structure that composition textbooks traditionally provide, the ancient and venerable rhetorical topic of arrangement is handled by providing molds into which to pour the molten thought and language of the essay: comparison/contrast, thesis/support, process—all prefabricated shapes to be selected off the rack to fit the body of the topic—or the five-paragraph theme, the one-size-fits-all product of the rhetorical department store. The segmented essay, on the other hand, attempts a tailor-made design, a structure that may be appropriate only to itself.

I am at a writer's workshop in Montana, happy to be among a talented group of writers who have brought manuscripts on the outdoors and thrilled by my first experience in the Western mountains. In the mornings we workshop one another's manuscripts under Gretel Ehrlich's directions; in the afternoon we hike the foothills of the Bitterroot Range or raft the Bitterroot River or ramble the valley floor. Late at night or early in the morning I write in my journal about the workshop sessions and the hiking, particularly where I have gone and what I have seen. In the end I have records of three hiking expeditions, one that takes me only a little way up Blodgett Canyon, one that takes me to a falls a few miles up the Mill Creek Trail, and a third that brings me to the awesome Bear Creek overlook on the shoulder of a mountain. When I try to analyze my frustrations and satisfactions about those hikes, I begin to see the possibility of an essay coming out of the experience.

Back in Michigan after the workshop, tinkering sullenly with the critiqued manuscript, I drop everything and instead begin writing about my Montana hiking. I give the essay the working title "Bitterroot" but eventually call it "Knowing Where You've Been," a title inspired by a Normal Maclean story about Blodgett Canyon which had helped me set a hiking destination in the first place. Perhaps because the other essays in the workshop have so often been segmented, divided into brief episodes or scenes or vignettes, I don't consider for a moment constructing an argumentative essay built around conclusions reached and made up of rationales for reaching them. At once I understand that I have come to the conclusions I have by taking three separate hikes, each of which went successively further into the wilderness, all of which culminated at the end of the final hike with a blissful moment of triumph and contentment, with a sense of arrival I hadn't had in the earlier hikes. I wonder if I can come at this by taking my reader through the three hikes with me, taking her deeper on each hike, leading her to the same moment and the same site of discovery that I reached. In brief, I wonder if I can somehow get the reader to reach my conclusions for herself by experiencing through my prose the same things I experienced.

This is risky, I know. Gretel Ehrlich's off-hand crack about the "plodding mid-western prose" of my workshop manuscript still chafes my ego like a fresh wound I can't stop picking at long enough to let heal. If I am to make my readers hike, the hiking better be brisk, lively, and limited, and each hike better be distinctive, so that it becomes clear why they've had to do three of them. I write the hikes in present tense, to make them feel more immediate, and I start them off the same way: I chip away at narrative that fills in the gaps of time between the hikes and tighten the prose for strength and speed. I also insert reflective interludes between the hikes, past tense segments responding to the hike just completed and pointing towards the next hike.

In the end the essay has five tight segments: hike ("The first afternoon. We walk the Blodgett Creek Trail"); interlude ("'When you look back at where you've been,' Norman Maclean writes, 'it often seems as if you have never been there or even as if there were no such place.'"); hike ("The second afternoon. We mill around after the morning workshop, plans shifting, destinations uncertain, finally resolving to go back into the mountains, to another trail."); interlude ("When I asked my friend from Montana about places to hike in the Bitterroot Valley, he looked thoughtful for a moment, shook his head, and said, 'Well, as early as you're going, there'll be too much snow to bag a peak.'"); hike ("The final afternoon. The morning workshop over, the group disperses for various tours and activities."). Each hike takes the narrator (and the reader) deeper into wilderness; each interlude raises issues that only an additional hike can resolve; the physical experiences of moving deeper and higher are echoed by intellectual and spiritual experiences, so that the physical moment of final achievement coincides with the spiritual moment of arrival. The successive drafts make me better understand exactly what it is I was feeling at the end of that hiking and push me to prepare the reader for that epiphany on the mountain ("It isn't how far at all but how deep. I need to go as deeply into wilderness as it takes before the wilderness comes into me.") in a way that makes it unnecessary for me to explain it afterward or add an epilogue of explication that breaks the reader down both physically and emotionally. The essay has to end on the mountain and the segmented format invites me to end it there.

The segmented essay makes demands not only on the writer but on the reader as well. Carl Klaus has noted how segments can be read both as isolated units and as reverberating links to other segments; it is "a strange reading experience, unlike that produced by any other kind of prose" which produces in him "an irresolvable tension between two different ways of reading and responding." From reading each segment "as a discrete entity as well as . . . in connection with its immediate neighbor," he finds that his "accumulating sense of recurrent or contrastive words, phrases, images, metaphors, ideas, topics, or themes" forces him to "intuitively mak[e] connections or distinctions between and among the segments, almost as if I were experiencing some of the very same associative leaps that might have provoked the essayist to write a piece in disjunctive form" (48). These "associative leaps" may replicate the fragmentary nature of "recollection and reflection" but they also suggest a willingness to accept unresolved or undefined associations.

Such writing demands that the reader learn to read the structure of the essay as well as its thought. That is a task for which the twentieth century reader is well prepared, because the episodic or segmented or disjunctive sequence is a familiar design in many other genres:

- the interrelated collection of short stories, for example, a concept suggested by Hemingway with the interludes between stories in *In Our Time* or carried out in Ray Bradbury's *The Martian Chronicles*;
- the playing with chronology and the episodic structure of novels like Milan Kundera's *The Unbearable Lightness of Being* and Kurt Vonnegut's *Slaughterhouse-Five*;
- cycles of thematically linked poems, each poem separate and independent but enriched by juxtaposition with poems on similar subjects or with similar perspectives;
- the "concept" album of interlinked songs—the Beatles' *Sgt. Pepper's Lonely Hearts Club Band* or the "suite" on half of *Abbey Road*, Pink Floyd's *The Wall*, or the more loosely thematic *Nebraska* and *Born In the USA* albums of Bruce Springsteen;
- sequences of brief scenes in motion pictures—Quentin Tarantino's *Pulp Fiction*, Gus Van Sant's *To Die For*, the recent critical favorites *The English Patient* and *Shine* all present their stories out of chronological sequence. In none of these is it hard to reconstruct the chronology, but telling the story in strict chronological order would have changed the emphases of these films. But even in strictly chronological films, the film progresses by sequences of shots or scenes, each separated from one another by visual cues as definite as chapter headings or theatrical intermissions.

Examples abound. It might be argued that the modern reader/viewer is more accustomed to disjunctiveness than to strict continuity.

I write this essay in segments. How can I explain what the segmented essay is like, or how it comes about, in an unsegmented essay?

I get up early in the morning to write, a common writer's habit. I am following a vague outline in my head of alternating segments—a more or less narrative example of someone composing a segmented essay alternating with a more or less expository section discussing the form. Practice alternates with theory. I have a lot of examples in mind that I think I might be able to use, and sometimes I type a section break or white space and insert a line of reference to spur my memory when I get to that segment ("Sandra's essay is giving her lots of trouble"; "I write this essay in segments"). Sometimes, by the time I reach that line, I have decided not to use it or have already used the example and I delete the line.

Some days I complete the draft of a segment in a single session, partly because I know I will have to revise it—go back to Mike's drafts to compare them again and to dig out more material for illustration, reread Carol's essay to refresh my memory about specific references, ask somebody about tarot readings, work on the concreteness of the language and clarity of the explanations. At first I am interested chiefly in having a structure to work in, and I have already cut and pasted segments in this draft to juxtapose them in different sequences.

Other days I only get through a portion of a segment. Some are harder than others to write, some have more detail, more development, quotes to look up and copy. I don't mind leaving them undone, because I think that when I return to them the next day my subconscious will have worked on them a little bit and it will be easier to launch into the drafting again. Even in an essay that isn't segmented we still work from section to section; it really isn't much different here.

And finally one morning when I feel I've said enough and need to worry less about finding something more to say than about finding ways to say what I've said better, I run off the full draft and try to work with what I have. Sometimes whole segments disappear or merge with others, sometimes new segments announce their necessity and have to be drafted and revised, sometimes the order of the segments changes again and again. I work harder on the language now, when I'm certain the ideas will stay. I am always reassured by a quote whose source may or may not have been Oscar Wilde: "I always revise everything eleven times, ten times to get the words right, and the eleventh time to put in that touch of spontaneity that everyone likes about my writing."

I teach creative nonfiction and composition classes, talk to friends about their essays, work on essays of my own. Sometimes I bring work in progress to my students, like a draft on men's rooms I photocopied, cut up, and distributed in pieces to see how different people would reassemble them and why. Often I advise other writers stuck in linearity and chronology, "Why don't you try collaging this?" I like making a verb of the noun, outraging any grammarians who overhear me.

I insist that my nonfiction students write at least one segmented essay during the term and provide such ways into the segmented essay as these:

- *definitions:* Simply explaining the segmented essay form calls up a range of alternatives: collage, montage, mosaic, vignette, episode, segment—all ways of approaching the form that suggest alternatives at that same time that they define distinctive forms.
- *models:* Readers respond to a handful of segmented essays with immediate understanding—Nancy Willard's "The Friendship Tarot," Annie Dillard's "Living Like Weasels," Susan Allen Toth's "Going to Movies," William Holtz's "Brother's Keeper," Naomi Shihab Nye's "Three Pokes of a Thistle," Reg Saner's "The Ideal Particle and the Great Unconformity."
- *strategies:* Segmented essays tend to go together in several different ways—

  - by juxtaposition, arranging one item alongside another item so that they comment back and forth on one another (Toth's "Going to Movies" is four vignettes, three dates with different men, the fourth a solitary trip to the theater);
  - by parallelism, alternating or intertwining one continuous strand with another (a present tense strand with a past tense strand, a domestic strand with a foreign strand, the alternate strands of a piece like "The Ideal Particle and the Great Unconformity");
  - by patterning, choosing an extra-literary design and arranging literary segments accordingly (as Willard does with tarot cards in "The Friendship Tarot" or Frederick Smock does with rooms in "Anonymous: A Brief Memoir");
  - by accumulation, arranging a series of segments or scenes or episodes so that they add or enrich or alter meaning with each addition, perhaps reinterpreting earlier segments in later ones, up to a final segment (as Holtz does in "Brother's Keeper");
  - by journaling, actually writing in episodes or reconstructing the journal experience in drafts (Sydney Lea asks students to write lyrical essays trying to connect disparate items in their journals; Gretel Ehrlich uses the journal form as a narrative device in many of her works, such as the recent "Cold Comfort").

In the classroom I make students cluster and list and map ideas, all of which encourage segmentation, separate items to work from. They produce partial or full rough drafts in whatever format they choose and then they help each other find ways of collaging or segmenting appropriate to the pieces they're working on. Once they're open to the possibility of the segmented essay, there's virtually no limit to the variations a roomful of imaginative young writers can bring to the form.

Collage, montage, mosaic, vignette, episode, segment—I've never found a descriptive term for anything that, if I pressed on it, wasn't somehow incapable of bearing the weight of definitive definition. I don't worry about the most accurate term for this kind of essay, because when one writer suggests to another, "Why don't you collage this?" the result may as much define the form as conform to it.

Works Cited

Best American Essays 1991. Ed. Joyce Carol Oates. Series Editor: Robert Atwan. Boston: Ticknor and Fields, 1991.

Dillard, Annie. "Living Like Weasels." *Teaching a Stone to Talk: Expeditions and Encounters*. New York: Harper, 1982. 29–34.

Ehrlich, Gretel. "Cold Comfort." *Harper's* 294:1762 (March 1997): 34–44.

Elbow, Peter. *Writing With Power*. New York: Oxford University Press, 1981.

Faery, Rebecca Blevins. "Text and Context: The Essay and the Politics of Disjunctive Form." *What Do I Know? Reading, Writing, and Teaching the Essay*. Ed. Janis Forman. Portsmouth, NH: Boynton/Cook, 1996. 55–68.

Grand Tour, "Virtues & Vices" 1:4 (Fall 1996).

Gruchow, Paul. "Eight Variations on the Idea of Failure." *Old Friends, New Neighbors: A Celebration of the American Essay, American Literary Review*. Ed. W. Scott Olsen. 5:2 (Fall 1994): 31–38.

Holtz, William. "Brother's Keeper: an Elegy." *Old Friends, New Neighbors: A Celebration of the American Essay, American Literary Review*. Ed. W. Scott Olsen. 5:2 (Fall 1994): 147–63.

Klaus, Carl H. "Excursions of the Mind: Toward a Poetics of Uncertainty in the Disjunctive Essay." *What Do I Know? Reading, Writing, and Teaching the Essay*. Ed. Janis Forman. Portsmouth, NH: Boynton/Cook, 1996. 39–53.

Nye, Naomi Shihab. "Three Pokes of a Thistle." *Never in a Hurry: Essay on People and Places*. Columbia: University of South Carolina Press, 1996. 26–31.

Old Friends, New Neighbors: A Celebration of the American Essay, American Literary Review. Ed. W. Scott Olsen. 5:2 (Fall 1994).

Ploughshares. Ed. Rosellen Brown. 20: 2–3 (Fall 1994).

Rudman, Mark. "Mosaic on Walking." *The Best American Essays 1991*. Ed. Joyce Carol Oates. Boston: Ticknor and Fields, 1991: 138–153.

Sanford, Carol. Unpublished essay ["Always Looking"].

Schwartz, Lynne Sharon. "Time Off to Translate." *Old Friends, New Neighbors: A Celebration of the American Essay, American Literary Review*. Ed. W. Scott Olsen. 5:2 (Fall 1994): 15–30.

Smock, Frederick. "Anonymous: A Brief Memoir." *Old Friends, New Neighbors: A Celebration of the American Essay, American Literary Review*. Ed. W. Scott Olsen. 5:2 (Fall 1994): 68–72.

Steinberg, Michael. Unpublished essay ["'I've Got It, No, You 'Take It': An Aging Ballplayer's Dilemma" and "On the Road Again: A Softball Gypsy's Last Go-Round"].

Toth, Susan Allen. "Going to the Movies." *How to Prepare for Your High-School Reunion and Other Midlife Musings*. New York: Ballantine Books, 1990. 108–112.

Willard, Nancy. "The Friendship Tarot." *Between Friends*. Ed. Mickey Pearlman. Boston: Houghton Mifflin, 1994. 195–203.

Prose Poems, Paragraphs, Brief Lyric Nonfiction

Peggy Shumaker

Brief pieces of prose, meant to stand on their own, capture our attention via compression. In *Short Takes,* the entries range from a couple of hundred words to a couple of thousand—leaving little space for grand exposition or lengthy character development. And yet the pieces in this volume compel us with their intensity, sustain us with their impact.

Mark Spragg, a novelist and memoirist accustomed to the expanse of three hundred pages, becomes a lyric poet for the two and a half pages of "In Wyoming." His gritty prose becomes an ode to the unforgiving land and weather of this mostly wild place. "This place is violent, and it is raw," Spragg writes. "Wyoming is not a land that lends itself to nakedness, or leniency. There is an edge here, living is accomplished on that edge."

This hymn to harshness sings. Spragg says, "There are precious few songbirds. Raptors ride the updrafts. The hares, voles, mice, skunks, squirrels, rats, shrews, and rabbits exist squinting into sun and wind, their eyes water, their hearts spike in terror when swept by the inevitable shadow of predators. The meadowlark is the state's bird, but I think of them as hors d' oeuvres, their song a dinner bell."

An ode in prose, Spragg's piece ends like this, ". . . I remain alert. In Wyoming, the price of innocence is high. There is a big wind out there, on its way home to our high plains."

Spragg's few words scour us, our faces tight against the wind. We know we'll end up like the bison whose bones have fallen to earth, bleached rose then white, then fallen finally to dust. This brief piece takes on how it's possible to live in extremity, how it's possible to live, period. What's come before us, what will endure, and the certainty of mortality—all these ideas whip through this piece, cutting as stiff winds.

Naomi Shihab Nye takes on big questions by focusing in on matters of daily life—the only kind we live. In *Mint Snowball,* her book of paragraphs, Nye's author's note reads as follows: "I think of these pieces as simple paragraphs rather than 'prose poems,' though a few might sneak into the prose poem category, were they traveling on their own. The paragraph, standing by itself, has a lovely pocket-sized quality. It garnishes the page as mint might garnish a plate. Many people say (foolishly of course) that they 'don't like poetry' but I've never heard anyone say they don't like paragraphs. It would be like disliking five minute increments on the clock."

Her selection in *Short Takes,* "Someone I Love," begins as she gets up at dawn, jetlagged after a long trip, and goes out to water her garden, to feel rooted again to the earth. She's stunned to discover that someone has destroyed her carefully- cultivated patch of primroses, has marched through it with the handmower, slicing down all the buds about to open. "He must have pushed really hard to get it to go," Nye tells us. She's distraught, too stricken to speak of her loss. ". . . I will not mention this, I am too sad to mention it, this is the pain this year deserves." That quiet mention of the year, a year of war and upheaval and dehumanizing, throws the whole piece into context. Suddenly we're not talking about a son failing to notice what matters to a mother. Instead we're talking about what gets taken away, how we live with loss, how we live with those who hurt us or our loved ones. In the piece, Nye cannot contain her fury, and goes "a little strange." She confronts her bewildered son. He responds by saying, "I don't notice flower things like that."

Her piece ends this way: "And it was the season of blooming and understanding. It was the season of pulling weeds in other corners, hiding from the headlines, wondering what it would do if the whole house had been erased or just the books and paintings and what about the whole reckless garden or (and then it gets unthinkable but we make ourselves think it now and then to stay human) the child's arms and legs, what would I do? If I did not love him, who would I become?"

Nye, whose relatives have lived in a war zone all their lives, makes peacemaking a matter of personal responsibility, a matter of conscience. Her piece asks us, how do we live with those who have taken possessions, land, languages, loved ones from us? Until we learn this, we will not know peace.

My own contribution to the *Short Takes* anthology mixes the lyrical language of poetry with the urgency of a narrative scene. All the poets in this volume give up line breaks. Without that tool so intricate for pacing and emphasis and wordplay and rhythms, sentences swell. Watch how varied sentences work—fragments, bits of dialogue, quick exposition, complex rhythms, and the great gush of language flash flooding.

Moving Water, Tucson

Thunderclouds gathered every afternoon during the monsoons. Warm rain felt good on faces lifted to lick water from the sky. We played outside, having sense enough to go out and revel in the rain. We savored the first cool hours since summer hit.

The arroyo behind our house trickled with moving water. Kids gathered to see what it might bring. Tumbleweed, spears of ocotillo, creosote, a doll's arm, some kid's fort. Broken bottles, a red sweater. Whatever was nailed down, torn loose.

We stood on edges of sand, waiting for brown walls of water. We could hear it, massive water, not far off. The whole desert might come apart at once, might send horny toads and Gila monsters swirling, wet nightmares clawing both banks of the worst they could imagine and then some.

Under sheet lightning cracking the sky, somebody's teenaged brother decided to ride the flash flood. He stood on wood in the bottom of the ditch, straddling the puny stream. "Get out, it's coming," kids yelled. "GET OUT," we yelled. The kid bent his knees, held out his arms.

Land turned liquid that fast, water yanked our feet, stole our thongs, pulled in the edges of the arroyo, dragged whole trees root wads and all along, battering rams thrust downstream, anything you left there gone, anything you meant to go back and get, history, water so high you couldn't touch bottom, water so fast you couldn't get out of it, water so huge the earth couldn't take it, water. We couldn't step back. We had to be there, to see for ourselves. Water in a place where water's always holy. Water remaking the world.

That kid on plywood, that kid waiting for the flood. He stood and the water lifted him. He stood, his eyes not seeing us. For a moment, we all wanted to be him, to be part of something so wet, so fast, so powerful, so much bigger than ourselves. That kid rode the flash flood inside us, the flash flood outside us. Artist unglued on a scrap of glued wood. For a few drenched seconds, he rode. The water took him, faster than you can believe. He kept his head up. Water you couldn't see through, water half dirt, water whirling hard. Heavy rain weighed down our clothes. We stepped closer to the crumbling shore, saw him downstream smash against the footbridge at the end of the block. Water held him there, rushing on.

Every time I read this piece, someone in the audience asks, "Did he live?" That tells me that 400 words are enough to create a character people can care about, and to tell a story convincing enough so that they want the next piece. The language has drawn them in, as surely as kids standing on the bank of an arroyo spellbound by dangerous floods.

The compression of the brief form, completely familiar to poets and to those who read poetry, gains a fine elasticity in nonfiction. Tone can range from somber to whimsical, lament to praise. Anything writers can do with long forms has parallels in brief forms.

Finding the Inner Story in Memoirs and Personal Essays

Michael Steinberg

The comment I find myself making most frequently to my students and to many of the writers who submit personal narratives to *Fourth Genre* is, "The main thing that's missing in this piece is *your story*." You're probably thinking, here comes another endorsement of those confessional narratives—the ones that give creative nonfiction a bad name. Actually, one of the reasons why I think we're seeing too many of those pieces is because a lot of nonfiction writers are narrating *only* the literal story of their experience, and leaving out the "inner story"; that is, the story of their thinking.

Let me give you a personal example. A while ago, I wrote a memoir called "Trading Off." It was about a four-year struggle I had with a high school coach who might or might not have been anti-Semitic. While I was writing it, I was trying to recall the shame I felt and the humiliation I allowed myself to put up with—both of which, I discovered, were the price I paid for wanting to play baseball for this punitive coach. At readings, whenever I introduce the piece as a baseball memoir, I watch the expressions on the faces of several of the women in the audience. Some roll their eyes, some cross their arms, some even grimace. To them, it's another baseball story, about some poor kid's bad experience with a mean-spirited coach—the kind of jock story their boyfriends or husbands may have told them over and over again.

It doesn't always happen that way, but often enough by the time I've finished reading the piece, the audience's body language has changed. Some people, men and women alike, have figured out that the memoir isn't really about baseball. Baseball is the setting, the stage for the conflict between the young boy and the coach. The coach is the gatekeeper and the narrator wants more than anything

333

else at 13 to pitch for the high school baseball team. But the more interesting and important story is what goes on in the mind of the narrator as he agonizes over how badly he wants this, at the same time as he's questioning his decision to put up with this coach's tactics.

What he repeatedly asks himself throughout the memoir is "Why am I doing this?" Indeed, why *is* he doing it? What makes him so determined, and so desperate? And how much humiliation is he willing to put up with in order to make the team? Quite a bit, it seems. That's why I titled the memoir "Trading Off."

Often, during the question-and-answer period, or after the reading, some of the same people who initially resisted the piece will tell me their own stories about humiliating experiences they've had with similar kinds of gatekeepers: punitive teachers, abusive parents, cruel childhood friends, and so on. A woman once volunteered that the memoir reminded her of her own teenage struggle with a harsh and demanding ballet teacher.

That's exactly the kind of response I hope for. I don't want the reader to come away from the memoir thinking that it's another "poor, poor, pitiful me" story. I want the reader to feel the humiliation and shame that I did, as well as to understand that I willingly chose to make this tradeoff in order to prove myself to this hard-nosed coach.

But, I doubt that readers—especially the skeptical ones—would have been able to make those personal connections had I written only the literal "here's what happened to me" story.

In her book *The Situation and the Story: The Art of Personal Narrative*, Vivian Gornick makes this same point when she writes, "Every work [of literature] has both a situation and a story. The situation is the context or circumstance, sometimes the plot; the story is the emotional experience that preoccupies the writer: the insight, the wisdom, the thing one has come to say" (13).

When I teach workshops in personal narrative, most students bring memoirs. At *Fourth Genre*, over 75 percent of our submissions are memoirs. There are as many different reasons or impulses for writing a memoir as there are memoirists; some write to tell their story; some write to preserve a family history; some simply want to reminisce.

When I teach the form, I'm always urging my students to go beyond or probe beneath the literal story. My own editor for the memoir I'm currently writing is always challenging me to "dig deeper," to write, as she describes it, "more vertically."

I nudge my students, as well as myself, to examine why they're telling this particular story, and why it matters enough to write about it. How, I ask them, did this experience shape you? How did it change you? What were the costs? What was at stake? What, in other words, is compelling you to write the piece? Hopefully, these will all be discovered in the process of writing.

I also advise writers to think about memoir as having two stories: the story of the actual experience—the surface subject, the facts, the sequence of remembered events (what Gornick calls "the situation"), and the story of their thinking—that is, what do those facts and events mean? What are you thinking and feeling as you write the specific scenes? What I'm really asking the writer is: How do *you* interpret the story of your own experience?

A memoir, then, can have more than one voice. Sometimes it must. There's the voice that tells the surface story, and another, more reflective voice that comments, digresses, analyzes, and speculates about the story's events—in other words, a voice or narrative persona that looks to find a human connection or larger meaning in his/her personal experience.

Everything I've said about finding the inner story in memoir comes from reading, writing, and reading about personal essays. Since one of the hallmarks of the personal essay is its intimacy, most personal essays are inner explorations that open a window to the writer's inner life.

Scott Russell Sanders says that the "essay is the closest thing we have, on paper, to a record of the individual mind at work and play . . . the spectacle of a single consciousness making sense of part of the chaos' of experience" (189–90). The essay works by "following the zigzag motions of the inquisitive mind. . . . The writing of an essay is like finding one's way through a forest, without being quite sure what game you are chasing, what landmark you are seeking."

Working in the essay form, according to Phillip Lopate, "allows you to ramble in a way that reflects the mind at work . . . [I]n an essay, the track of a person's thoughts struggling to achieve some kind of understanding of a problem is the plot, the adventure. The essayist must be willing to contradict himself . . . to digress, and even to end up in an opposite place from where he started. . . . The essay offers the chance to wrestle with one's own intellectual confusion" (qtd. in Heilker 93).

The late critic and memoirist Alfred Kazin says, "The genuine essayist . . . [i]s the writer who thinks his way through the essay—and so comes out where perhaps he did not wish to. . . . He uses the essay as an open form—as a way of thinking things out for himself, as a way of discovering what he thinks. . . . [A]n essay is not meant to be the 'whole truth'. . . . [I]t is an expression of the self thinking" (qtd. in Heilker 90). In an essay, it is not the thought that counts but the experience we get of the writer's thought; not the self, but the self thinking."

In "The End," an essay by Judith Kitchen, she suggests that Kazin's point is the purpose of writing creative nonfiction. "The building of a process of thought," Kitchen says, "is what interests the reader. In essays, we participate by paying attention to the attention that is paid. The intimacy of the essay is a sharing of thought. We look as much for how an author approaches a subject as for the subject itself" (228). Kitchen closes the essay with some useful teaching advice. She writes,

> Here are five things my students deny themselves as their stories draw to a close:
>
> 1. Retrospection—a looking back, an assessment
> 2. Intrusion—a stepping in, a commentary
> 3. Meditation—a thinking through and around, finding a perspective
> 4. Introspection—a self-examination, honest appraisal and discovery
> 5. Imagination (as distinct from invention)—which allows for alternatives, projections, juxtapositions, whatever could provide a larger frame (228)

I agree with Kitchen when she says that these are things her students "deny themselves." It's a generous and, I think, accurate way to phrase it. I'll add these others:

- reflection: thinking things out, searching for meaning
- speculation: playing "what if"
- self-interrogation: asking the hard questions, the ones you don't always want to know the answers to
- digression: allowing the mind to wander away from the subject
- projection: trying to predict what might happen

There are many other touchstones we could all add. But the point is that in any human situation or encounter, we can't get through 30 seconds without utilizing most or all of these things. We're *always* reacting internally.

The mind never stops searching for connections and asking questions. And that's the thinking/feeling self I'd like to see more of in the personal narratives I read, both as a teacher and as an editor.

Works Cited

Gornick, Vivian. *The Situation and the Story: The Art of Personal Narrative.* New York: Farrar, Straus and Giroux, 2001.

Heilker, Paul. *The Essay: Theory and Pedagogy for an Active Form.* Urbana: NCTE, 1996: 90.

Kitchen, Judith. "The End." *Fourth Genre.* 3:2 (Fall 2001): 228–234.

Sanders, Scott Russell. "The Singular First Person,"*Secrets of the Universe: Scenes from the Journey Home.* Boston: Beacon, 1991. 187–204.

Experimental Critical Writing

Marianna Torgovnick

At the 1988 MLA Convention I gave a paper called "Malinowski's Body." Since I was afraid to give this paper, I had announced it in the program by the deliberately neutral title "Looking at Anthropologists" so that I could change my mind up to the last minute and substitute something else instead. I was afraid because "Malinowski's Body" does not resemble the usual MLA paper in style or content. I knew that the audience would listen to it and respond to it, and I knew that some members of the audience would not like it and might even walk out—and not because there was another talk they wanted to hear at the same hour.

"Malinowski's Body" did not begin its life in any of the ways I have been taught to consider legitimate. In fact, I wrote it, almost as a dare, after my writing group found the first material I wrote on Malinowski dull. To prove I could do better I went home and wrote several pages that begin this way:

> Malinowski's body looks like Lord Jim's. It's cased rigidly in white or beige trousers and shirt that sometimes becomes stained a muddy brown. When this happens, Malinowski summons his servants and has the clothes washed, immediately. For his clothes somehow seem to him an important part of his body, not just a covering for it.
>
> It's a small body, well fed but not kindly disposed enough toward itself to put on flesh. It has a narrow chest—pale, with just a few hairs and no nipples to speak of. It has thin legs yearning for massive thighs; in fact, if this man does put on weight in later life (and he may) it will show in his thighs first. The buttocks lie flat, unwelcoming, with maybe a stray pimple. The penis is a center of anxiety for him but is in fact no smaller—and no bigger—than anyone else's. It's one of the few points of identification he can settle on between his body and theirs.
>
> Their bodies—almost naked—unnerve him. His body needs its clothes; his head, its hat. He rarely looks at his body—except when washing it. But he has to look at theirs. The dislike he sometimes feels for the natives comes over

him especially when in the presence of their bodies. "Come in and bathe," the natives say from their ponds and rivers. "No, thanks," says Malinowski, retrieving the pith helmet and camera he momentarily laid aside on the grass. He looks at their bodies and takes notes about size, ornamentation, haircuts, and other ethnographic data. He takes photographs. He talks to them about customs, trade, housing, sex. He feels okay about the customs, trade, and housing, but the sex makes him uneasy.

The pages are based on an intuition and a hunch about what Malinowski looked like that were formed before I had found any pictures of him. They begin with an image rather than with the kind of concise generalization that had been my customary opening. And they were designed to loosen my prose by giving my imagination free play. Inevitably, I used what I had read by and about Malinowski—but in an almost unrecognizable way. My premise was that I would undress the ethnographer for study as Malinowski himself undresses subjects in his ethnographies and undresses, in his diary, the women he meets in daily life. When I wrote "Malinowski's Body" I did not intend to use it in the book I was writing. My goals were simply to limber up my style and to get in touch with what I wanted to say. But "Malinowski's Body" makes so many points about the ethnographer's scripting of himself according to conventional ideas of what is moral and manly that I decided to include it in my book. It is a creative piece, risky for the MLA. And yet my audience, or at least most of its members, seemed delighted. They asked questions about my "intentions" and "effects" that made me feel like a writer, not just a critic—a heady moment for me and a reception that gave David Laurence reason to invite me to present my thoughts on experimental critical writing. And it was a moment that had not come easily.

When I began to write my newest book—called *Gone Primitive* and published in the spring of 1990—I knew that I wanted to write something significantly different in tone and style from my first two books. I had recently been tenured and then promoted to full professor, and I felt that I was no longer writing for any committees—I was writing for myself. It was not that I would rewrite the books I had written; I am in fact proud of them. What I wanted was to reach a larger audience and to go somewhere new. What I discovered was that at first I did not know how.

The turning point came when I showed an early chapter to the members of my newly formed writing group. I was writing on an untraditional, uncanonical topic—Edgar Rice Burroughs' Tarzan novels—but my approach was conventional and scholarly. I began by surveying the critical literature on Tarzan and protesting (a little uneasily) that earlier critics either had overidentified with Burroughs or had not taken Tarzan seriously with regard to race and gender relations. I tried to pack lots of statistics and facts in the opening paragraphs to prove that Tarzan was important. In my eagerness to meet accepted standards of academic seriousness, I had succeeded (to borrow a phrase Wayne Booth once used to describe the freshman essay) in being "boring from within."

The members of my group, from whom I had asked no mercy that day, showed none. The chapter was sluggish, they said; the prose was lifeless and cold. It had no momentum, no narrative. Instinctively, I defended myself; I talked about all the interesting things that happened as I was researching and writing the chapter, telling them how I often found articles on the rebirth of the Tarzan phenomenon in issues of magazines that report the assassination of President Kennedy and reproduce those astonishing pictures we all remember of Jackie and little John-John and of Oswald. I had tried in the chapter to place the Tarzan series in the contexts of the twenties (the decade of its first great popularity) and the sixties (the decade of its rebirth). But I had used a style that censored my own experiences and visceral responses and that hid my writing's source of energy. One member of the group said, cannily, "You know, none of what you've just said comes out in this chapter. And there's a huge difference between the things you say and the things you write. You never write anything funny. You often say funny things." She was right. The other members of the group asked me to say more about La, a barbarian priestess in the Tarzan novels whom I had mentioned in passing. As I warmed to my description of La's importance and La's wrongs, my friend said, "When you start to get dull, pretend you are La—because you *are* La." And she was also right.

For me, "writing like La" became a metaphor for getting to a place where I was not afraid to write in a voice that had passion as well as information—a voice that wanted to be heard. "Writing like La" meant letting myself out of the protective cage of the style I had mastered—a style I now call the thus-and-therefore style because it naturally tends to include distancing words like those. Before I could change my thus-and-therefore style, I had to defamiliarize it; I had to know my cage so that I could open it at will. A fifteen-minute exercise I did with my writing group was a significant breakthrough. In this exercise, I parodied my own dullest style in a description of grocery stores in Durham, North Carolina. I began the description with just the kind of generalization that was one of my primary tics as a writer: "In Durham, one can shop at Food Lion for bargains, or Kroger's for selection. The most interesting shopping of all, however, is done at Harris Teeter." This exercise made me laugh at my own habits and made it impossible for me afterward to write unknowingly in my usual way. But there were still many low points, when I found myself unable to do anything *but* write in my dullest style. In fact, I wrote my excruciatingly bad beginning on Malinowski— the material I replaced with "Malinowski's Body"—roughly eighteen months after I vowed to leave my old style behind.

In preparing this presentation, I discovered in my files my first draft on Malinowski. I would like to share part of its beginning with you as an example of one sort of standard academic prose:

> Implicitly, I have been suggesting that "objectivity" is a delusory principle undergirding both important strands of social scientific and ethnographic thought and aesthetic and artistic-literary theories and methods. Rereading Malinowski, I think I've found a direct and interesting analogy.
>
> Malinowski founded what is called functionalism in anthropology, the theory (and derived method) that explains all elements of a culture in terms

of interlocking functions: the ethnographer explicitly "constructs" a model in which all the parts are presumed to contribute to a whole that is organic and unified (though quirkier than a machine). To make his construction, the ethnographer lives inside the culture, inhabits it as a text. He tries to replicate the native's point of view, which is the ground and touchstone of meaning and "accuracy." Functionalism leads, in anthropology, to what is called structural functionalism and then, later, to structuralism.

A point-by-point analogy with New Criticism and other formal approaches exists. Here too the "student" (critic) inhabits the text, assuming the unity of the parts as a whole and constructing an account of that whole in terms of the interlocking functions of its parts. The original ground of meaning is the author's intentions.

What I was doing in these paragraphs was the writerly equivalent of scratching at a scab. I had to say what was closest to the surface of my mind in order to get rid of that content, in order to discover whether it was useful or not, interesting or not. Sometimes, what I write first as a throwaway turns out to contain the intellectual core of my argument; sometimes, as in this real throwaway, it does not. The difference is usually whether I begin with material that I really care about or with material that I think I should care about. In this instance, I began with critical categories and genealogies of influence that I knew, by training, were considered important—and I trotted them out dutifully. Other critics had scratched these scabs; now it was my turn. The paragraphs include a lot of qualifications and distinctions, often inserted in parenthetical remarks, that would be unlikely to interest anyone but me. Sticky academic language coats the whole—"implicitly," "explicitly," "strand of thought." And I explain things in more detail than most people would want to read.

I would be too embarrassed to reproduce this rejected passage if I did not realize that it's representative of the prose that I—and I suspect many of you—habitually write. For this style typifies a great deal of academic writing. How did it come to be a norm? Largely, I think by establishing itself in an era when less criticism was published and the circle of critics was small enough to allow its members to believe they were contributing to the building of a common edifice. In this construction project all the names could and should be named, like those of contributors on a memorial plaque; Professor Z would build on what Professors X and Y had said in their essays; years later, Professors A and B would come along and add some decorative touches or do major renovations.

All of us who write criticism today wrote dissertations yesterday. And our teachers often tried, and succeeded in handing on what they perceived as the correct—that is, the careful, the judicious, the fair—way to write. But the styles we were taught can't work now in the same way as they worked fifty or even fifteen years ago. No one who gets around to writing a book, or even an essay, ever reads everything that has been written about its subject. Yet we cling to the fiction of completeness and coverage that the academic style preserves. This style protects us, we fondly believe, from being careless or subjective or unfair. It prescribes certain moves to ensure that the writer will stay within the boundaries that the academy has drawn.

Like many people who choose an academic life, I have a fundamental need for approval. I needed approval from my graduate advisers, tenure and promotion committees, and reviewers; I need it from my students and colleagues. It has been crucial for me in the last few years to have a writing group that approved of my new writing style: the group provided a different audience from the one I once imagined as my academic superiors, who judged the material I wrote according to more traditional standards. But I have also become aware that I am now not just someone in need of approval but also someone (like many of you) who gives or withholds approval. When we pass on the academic style to our graduate students or newest colleague, we train them to stay within the boundaries, both stylistically and conceptually. When we encourage experimental critical writing, we do not always know what we will get, but we stimulate the profession to grow and to change. We don't control the future of the profession only when we give grades or make hiring or tenure decisions; we control it at the level of the sentence.

At this point I need to back up a bit. It seems pretty clear to me that if all we want to do is to write for professional advancement, to write for a fairly narrow circle of critics who exist within the same disciplinary boundaries as we do, there is nothing really wrong with the traditional academic style. In fact, it's the right style, the inevitable style, because it says, in every superfluous detail and in every familiar move, You don't need to read me except to write your own project; I am the kind of writing that does not want to be heard.

But when critics want to be read, and especially when they want to be read by a large audience, they have to court their readers. And the courtship begins when the critic begins to think of himself or herself as a writer as well, a process that for me, as for some other critics of my generation, means writing as a person with feelings, histories, and desires—as well as information and knowledge. When writers want to be read they have to be more flexible and take more chances than the standard scholarly style allows: often, they have to be more direct and more personal. In a very real way (although my writing includes precious few autobiographical revelations), I could not think of myself as a writer until I risked exposing myself in my writing.

I am not talking here, necessarily, about full-scale autobiographical writing— though I am not ruling it out either. But I am saying that writerly writing is personal writing, whether or not it is autobiographical. Even if it offers no facts from the writer's life, or offers just a hint of them here and there, it makes the reader know some things about the writer—a fundamental condition, it seems to me, of any real act of communication. And real communication is exciting. For me, at any rate, the experience of this new kind of writing—which not only recognizes the pitfalls of the standard academic style but goes out of its way to avoid them—has been exhilarating.

(Note to Self): The Lyric Essay

Kathryn Winograd

I must confess that what I first want to tell you is a lie. That what propelled me to creative nonfiction was the owl my husband and I stalked in a ragged stretch of woods along the South Platte River some long winters ago, that symbolic air, I'll want to tell you, thick with the crash and grind of a cement factory that halted only on Sundays in deference to a holiness I couldn't name. What I won't want to tell you is that it was really the words of a humble Southern essayist—he laughs in the yellow shade of his straw hat even now—who said, "I'm a failed poet," words I have grappled with myself since my first book and that river of Poesies, that pushed me toward such compression, dammed.

What is creative nonfiction? Or more specifically, what I yearn toward—the lyric essay? Even as I write down these questions, I see in my head the first disconnected threads of my answer weaving themselves together—that owl in dead winter draping its nest with the carcasses of rabbit. And the dry buzz of the electric wires overhead, something like rain falling down over us in those cold woods. (Note to Self: What is it about a suspended, hot electrical wire that makes the air weep? Look it up.) And that student in my first creative nonfiction class—the round-faced, middle-aged mother from India I broke the heart of—dead now.

Already I run my fingers over the weft and woof of my words—ahh, the terms of weaving again, and, better yet, the word *baana*, from India, derived, Wikipedia tells me, "from another Hindi word, *bun na* or *bunai*, which means making with threads or strings." (Note to Self: image of my Indian mother unwittingly weaving her essays with the long golden threads of her Indian childhood, what she never realized the beauty of—those pungent, spiced boxes from her own mother arriving overseas to her forlorn, American kitchen. Do something with this.) And now I think of Penelope, three years weaving and unweaving her shroud against the din and banter of her unwanted suitors who would marry her mourning for her lost Odysseus—

Is this the siren call of the lyric essay? Its utter plasticity—(Note to Self: stick with weaving)—its intricate tapestry, its finger-worn threads guided into the freed forms the creative nonfiction writer calls *braided, collage, hermit crab*? The whole spectrum of writing—poetry, essay, fiction, drama, the personal "I" reflective, objective, ruminating—possible as opposed to the linearity and stifling objectivity of the journalist's prose? Or the rack and ruin of the purist's freshman student composition?

But how is this prose-making different from poetry? I think of the crystalline globe of the lyric poem, of that Keatsian nightingale, "light-winged Dryad," singing forever in the frozen moment as if truth or beauty,—as if our postmodernist truth or beauty, multi-voiced, suspect—could be held to such a singular note.

Floyd Skloot, poet, novelist, memoirist, author of *In the Shadow of Memory*, his account of the viral attack that left him brain-damaged, who left me dazzled one summer seminar, describes his writing process in creative nonfiction as a matter of folders, each day's fragmented writing filed into subject-coded folders until finally amassed on his work desk, his fragments begin their weaving—he, himself, still novitiate to the silent loom of the soul.

My owl, harbinger of death, it seems, beats like a moth at the long flame of my student. She sits, like Penelope, alone in the television's blue blare, far from those she loves—mother, children, husband. I told her once that she could write creative nonfiction, and when, much later, she came to me in despair and said that someone had told her there was no such thing as this, what she could love now, I laughed and dismissed her. And then nothing. And then her death. And then this essay she wrote that some friend forwarded to me long after her burial in which she laments how I (Note to Self: unnamed poet failed poet) had deceived her, this creative nonfiction nothing she could hold onto.

I look up the names of Eastern spices, what I imagine her mother sent her, like Tulsi and Gulab Jal, Holy Basil and Rose Water, and give them to her in this world, and the other, so that she can taste them on her tongue, as I can taste them now.

Source: Winograd, Kathryn. "(Note to Self): The Lyric Essay." *Colorado Poets Center E-Words* #9 http://www.coloradopoetscenter.org/eWords/issue9/winograd.html

Part 3

Composing Creative Nonfiction

Elsewhere in this book you've been able to read what some people write when they write creative nonfiction (in Part 1) and then read what those same people talk about when they talk about creative nonfiction (in Part 2). In Part 3 we pair the writing of five writers with their comments on composing those particular pieces of writing.

When writers describe the processes they went through to complete an essay or an article, they explain strategies other writers can adapt for their own writing. When experienced writers find themselves stymied by a project they've been working on, they usually have strategies to fall back on to get the writing going again. Often their strategies arise from the example of another writer. For example, writers in all genres subscribe to Horace's advice, "Never a day without a line," and try to write every day, even if only for a limited time, because it adds new ideas and new dimensions to the work-in-progress that a long delay would make evaporate. Writers often have to rummage among various sound principles and practices in the creative life for the ones that work for them and be prepared to discard those that don't, even if they were useful for a previous project. They have to be flexible and adaptable in order to be productive, and often the best place to find useful strategies and techniques is among those that other writers use themselves.

Even when writers have been successful in the past and would appear to know a number of moves they might make in their writing, they sometimes need to be reminded of the things they already know about writing. Sometimes the press of a work-in-progress makes it difficult to step back from it and apply alternative approaches, until the writer stumbles on something someone else did and remembers that he or she knew about that approach before. Some writers collect quotes about writing and, to help them remember, tape them to the wall or the word processor—some writers have *a lot* of stuff sticking to their wall, because there's *a lot* of relevant advice out there.

Consider this section, then, as a way to see what other writers have done as they wrote the kind of writing you've been reading in this book. We've arranged five pairs of essays alphabetically by author. The first piece in each pair is the work that serves as the focus of the second piece, which explains the writer's composing processes on that particular work. Reading all ten pieces together is like sitting in on a writing group where each member reads something she's written and then explains what she went through to get the final draft. The writing is different enough that the responses of the writers and the shifting demands of purpose and form offer a range of strategies and creative decisions. Abigail Moore Allerding's essay "Home" reflects on the challenges of a decision she and her husband must make; "Unwrapping Surprises in the Personal Essay" details what she discovered in the process of writing that essay. In "Warping Time with Montaigne" Emily Chase links the practices of Montaigne, the original essayist, with those of contemporary writer Richard Rodriguez in his essay "Late Victorians"; in her "Notes from a Journey Toward 'Warping Time'" she explains how this piece of what Marianna Torgovnick calls "experimental critical writing" came about. Valerie Due writes about her first experience assisting the birth of a lamb in "Lambing Midwife," and then details her efforts to get in touch with the past in "Gestating Memory: Capturing Narrative Details in 'Lambing Midwife'." Mary Elizabeth Pope's "Teacher Training" follows two parallel strands about her first teaching experience and about her fifth-grade teacher; "Composing 'Teacher Training'" follows the essay's development from inception to publication, including changes after the piece was accepted. Maureen Stanton writes a very personal memoir of her fiancé's illness in "Zion" and recounts how she composed the essay in "On Writing 'Zion'." Very different essays, very different composing processes.

The selections here also connect to pieces in other parts of the book, as our alternative table of contents suggests, but we hope they also connect to your writing. The process pieces here don't prescribe failsafe procedures to which you should conform—quite the contrary. As these examples show, writers don't follow a rigid set of universal rules for composing; instead, they rely on general approaches and alternative strategies that they can alter to fit the shape of their individual works-in-progress. The experiences of these writers suggest strategies that you might be able to adapt to your own projects. They would be valuable to consult when you find yourself beginning or developing similar writing projects.

Finally, as you compose your own essays and assignments, you might consider keeping a journal on your own composing processes, to get a handle on what you generally do when you write and what you've done especially for certain projects. Think of Composing Creative Nonfiction as sitting in on a writing group in session, and feel free to enter the conversation with your own writing about your own composing.

Home

Abigail Moore Allerding

I see him going west on Interstate 71, just before entering Morrow County—a single crow floating above our car in the frigid winds. The landscape speeds by but the image of the circling crow stays with me, and I envy him. His practiced nonchalance, his ability to float, almost literally, above the passing cars beneath, creates a sense of longing that swells in my chest. I covet his freedom, the certainty with which his wings stay extended as he glides effortlessly back and forth. I wish I could fly, beat my wings against the invisible air. It's on my list of things to do before I die—right up there beside a several week stint to Ireland and Scotland. I guess some things are more feasible than others. I wonder where he'll land, where he might nestle in to fight the bitter cold.

I am headed south with my husband, Brian, towards home. Or at least what we call home for the time. I still call my parents' house home, in North Canton, Ohio. It's the place where I grew up—where I got picked up before my high school prom, where I slept the night before I was married, where I threw up the first and last time I got puke-my-guts-out drunk. I call my in-laws' house home, in Loudonville, Ohio, where my husband grew up, and where I set up camp on the hide-a-bed on visits when we dated. And I am beginning to call our tiny apartment in Sunbury home, where we are headed now, after a long weekend visiting family.

We argue—Brian and I—endlessly about where home will be when he finishes veterinary school:

"I'll have a good customer base if we start out in Loudonville," he says. "A better opportunity to make a start in the large animal business."

"I know people, too," I argue back. "Besides, isn't there more money in the small animals?"

"It's not about the money," he reminds me—something I already know, but which plays in my favor.

"Yes, but there's opportunity to do *both* large and small animals in Canton," I say, hoping for a breakthrough.

It is the endless back and forth banter—the type of ridiculous argument one might watch on *Saturday Night Live*. This argument is certainly well rehearsed, but instead of laughter it frequently ends in tears.

The road takes us along, down I-71, and a billboard flashes by, asking us to "Discover Amish Cooking" if we would only take the next exit. But we don't. The wheels keep turning and the yellow strips of paint flash by like pictures on an old movie reel. I see a red barn nestled back off the highway with a tall green silo. I look over at Brian as he continues to drive. The familiar argument races to mind: Will we live on a farm? Will we live in "the city"?

American crows can be found throughout the continental United States. In particular, the food source and openness agricultural areas provide can make these places a potential habitat. The American crow can also be found along the coast, in suburban areas, as well as city parks and many other areas, making them a bird one might encounter across the United States.

I wonder where this crow, floating above our car, is going—where home is or was. Is he really all alone or are there others anticipating his return?

It seems no matter where I've traveled, whether in the United States or beyond its borders, I can always find a native Ohioan vacationing along with me, whether sitting next to me at the bar sipping a margarita or on the chair lift, skiing the same slopes. I remember vacations as a little girl to Hilton Head Island in the summer. We would venture to the part of the island with the lighthouse and sit under an old tree while a locally famous musician played songs for the children. I can still recall my favorite song: "There's a Booger in Your Sugar." Inevitably, every year, he would ask how many visitors made the trek from Ohio, and inevitably, nearly half the crowd would raise their hands. At first, I assumed it was because Ohioans wanted to get away—from the cold, from the hustle and bustle, from the ordinariness of it all. But as I grew older, I recognized not the going away, but the coming back—the feeling of returning home, where I belonged.

I love so many aspects of Ohio: the changing of all four seasons, particularly the fall. The way the leaves turn to gold and the way the smell of the damp morning permeates my body when I take a deep breath during early October. The sense of identity and pride Ohioans feel towards their sports teams. The way I could waltz into the local Kroger for groceries and yell "O-H" and be certain to hear back, whether from the old man in line at the checkout or the new mother shushing her baby, "I-O." Ohio, though, in all its beauty, is made up of many different parts—it offers the full buffet—bustling cities and open countryside.

When I first met Brian, he kept referring to my home as "the city." Our childhood homes are but sixty miles apart, only an hour's drive, and yet so drastically different. It was strange to me, almost a bit insulting with the tone in which he let "the city" roll off his tongue, as if it were some dirty, shameful place where the disconnected, withdrawn people of the world reside. I constantly corrected him, explaining that we too play Mellencamp's "Small Town" to commemorate our high school years. It's all in the eye of the beholder. Yes, I lived in a city, but one with a small town feel. It is this, more than anything, which I desire for my children. We can both agree on this—a town where the people in the checkout line at the grocery store are friendly neighbors and the tellers at the bank don't require an ID. It's the small town culture we both love. It's the shared part of the dream that plays behind our eyelids when we lie down every night.

We both love our families; I can't fault him for that. It's partly why I married him. We come from parents hopelessly devoted to the American dream—work hard, love your family, do what you love and love what you do. Both families are rooted in the soils of northeast Ohio.

Brian is of the fourth generation of the rolling hills of Loudonville—people whose hands have worked the soil for centuries. People who know and appreciate the contour of the landscape and look forward to a quiet night on the deck where the only lights are the flicker of the fireflies and one lamp in the old farmer's upstairs window several acres away.

He grew up working the land of his uncle's farm, molding his muscular physique with physical labor under a hot summer sun. Three times each summer he baled hay in the fields, riding the wagon on the back of the old red tractor and baler, like a participant on a float in the county parade. I imagine he'd watch the tractor's tires rolling with ease over the soft soil, gripping the earth and kicking up its remnants with each turn. The small, square bailer swung out to the side so the monstrous tires would not mat down the hay. He sat patiently, waiting for the bales to march from the chute, with the rhythm of the plunger firing every few seconds, creating a song in the fields with which even their bodies rocked back and forth. A sort of game this became, like the strategic tic tac toe, calculating with each bale where the next would lay in order to produce a sturdy, stable stack.

If he was not baling hay, the animals needed tending. Even then, he loved the farm creatures—cows, sheep, pigs, the latter of which needed much attention in the summer months. His job was to collect the week-old piglets, not much bigger than two child-size hands, for vaccination and castration, to trim their needle teeth and dock their tiny tails. With all four legs together, awaiting its destiny, the piglet would send up a high-pitched squeal that would set the barn off in a tizzy. Its mother, from inside the farrowing crate, would grunt with indignation.

And this is how he spent his summer months, when the rain stopped pounding and the vegetation along the back roads was covered in dust from the trucks kicking up dirt. I know this is what he sees in his mind when he closes his eyes at night to dream of our future together: a farm of our own built in the rolling hills of his sacred Loudonville, with a son and a daughter following behind, catching the bales of hay.

My family is of the third generation of Canton residents, who were brought here long ago by the Pennsylvania railroad—people who go downtown for an evening out, walk into the old Bender's restaurant, and know half the customers.

The summer months of my childhood years were spent in a neighborhood within the city limits. The closest sound to the squealing pigs we could hear was the howling of Mr. Harter's dog. My best friend, Brooke, lived next door in a gray brick house with a red door, and we'd scurry down the mulch-filled incline that separated our yards as we chased our little brothers from one yard to the next. In her backyard, beside an old, circular fountain grown over with ivy, we'd set up our tent to camp out at night. We'd tell ghost stories until the heat lightning and scary thoughts chased us indoors to the safety of our mothers' arms.

The cars buzzed by on nearby Fulton Road, while we played within the protection of the great oaks that canopied the neighborhood. We loved the trees—they were our imaginary friends. Even before I knew the realm of Tolkien's Middle Earth, I believed in such fantasies. We lived within our own world there, yet we were close enough to the busy roads to hear the smack of crushing metal when my father pulled out in front of a car one street over. "Somebody just got hit!" I imagine we all said, perhaps pausing for a solitary moment before returning to our games and giggles, never contemplating the potential fate of any accident. We were still children, then, and our hearts still bled with a purity now long gone.

Brooke Eaton, the second Brooke in the neighborhood, used to make us eat clovers—they tasted like mint—and we'd watch as she climbed to the top of an old pine, jumping from one branch to the next, getting smaller and smaller as she climbed higher. It would sway slightly with her weight to the left and then the right, like the trees in cartoons bowing like rainbows under the weight of human intrusion. I always wondered what her mother would think. Mine would have killed me (if the climb didn't), so I never ventured such a risk.

Kick-the-can with the neighborhood gang started soon after dark before our mothers forced us in, sweaty and breathing hard, for baths and bedtime stories. We made do with the resources we had—playing house in the small wooded area behind Brooke's house. Pinecone and mud stew we had for supper when we played house in the backyard and berry cobbler for dessert.

We cemented our first basketball hoop on Darlington Avenue. The driveway became a multi-purpose sports facility—a basketball court and a hockey rink, the place where my brother chipped his front tooth. And from that driveway, I witnessed the majesty of a storm whose edge fell like a curtain, the rain beating on my neighbor's lawn but not my own.

We were in close proximity to one another; each house we felt was our own. But my arms did not ripple with the muscles toned from hours on a hay wagon, and my hands did not reek of the piglets' smooth skin. My backyard was not a wheat field, and my closest neighbor was not down the street, but in my own backyard.

Young crows require much attention. After they hatch, they are considered virtually helpless creatures, relying on parents and other birds or helpers to feed and help care for them. Even after leaving the confines and safety of a nest, young may need protection and resources from family. For these social birds, caring for and raising young can be a process involving the entire family.

Brian is a wonderful husband—the kind who cooks dinner so I can keep working, brings home flowers just because, and tells me how beautiful I am on days when I don't feel it. He is selfless and patient, a product of being the fourth child of five and the brother to three demanding sisters. We don't argue often, and when we do it is usually about where we will live when he finishes vet school. It usually begins casually enough, but in the end I am unwilling to budge: I want to be near my family. He wants to be near his.

I can picture the familiar argument, me facing the window as the silent tears drip from my cheeks onto the gray leather windowsill. I love this man I'm arguing with. I am stubborn, and I don't want to give in, but I don't want to hurt him either. Silence swallows the car, making the already close proximity of driving seem even more suffocating. Thoughts, the things I've already said and those I want to say now, flash through my reeling mind.

On these long car rides back to our apartment after a long weekend with the family, the wheels rolling beneath us remind us just how mobile our lifestyle currently is. It's easy to balance trips to our hometowns on the weekends—spontaneously decide to make a surprise trip home on some random Saturday. We have no children, no pet to keep us tied down. The only second thought we have is for our blossoming lily, which can recover even after two weeks of water deprivation. But with the hope of a family of our own in a few years, we understand the necessity for a permanent residence—consistency for children. We realize sooner or later we will be forced to choose—that we will grow tired of constantly packing up our lives on the weekends. That eventually our lives and our children's won't allow for such spontaneity. While an hour may seem like a short skip and a hop to some people, we covet the opportunity to see family on a regular basis, to be able to "just stop in" unannounced.

While some crows are known to migrate, others are considered cooperative breeders, meaning they stay near their place of birth to aid in the upbringing of other young crows and to help protect the territory from predators.

"What about Wooster?" Brian looks over at me as he's driving. "It's in the middle. Between both parents."

I think about this—a solution we've discussed before. "But then it's like we're with neither. We still don't have anyone to help in an emergency, and instead of only having to travel to see one, we have to travel to see both."

"Besides," he agrees, "a business stands a better chance where we already have somewhat of a customer base—we're guaranteed of that in one of our hometowns."

The middle is a solution that makes neither one of us happy.

When I was a young girl, these car ride sessions—intense discussions with the man behind the wheel—were with my father. After a basketball game, he'd critique my performance—encourage when I lacked confidence, scold when I broached arrogance. *Abbey,* he'd say, *you can't let her do that to you. You gotta go at her. Use your spin move—stay low.* Did I have the desire to out will my opponent, to wear her down?

At the time, I always thought he was only referring to the game of basketball, but now I recognize there was so much more behind his words. These were some of the most valuable lessons in my life—my father was like the therapist, my shot-gun seat the couch. He talked to me about basketball on those car rides, but he also taught me about life. I learned success requires sacrifice and taking risks. He reminded me that the hours we spent on the driveway shooting hoops was my ticket to being a leader—that I couldn't ask people to follow me if I didn't out work every one of them.

He helped me make decisions on those car rides, as well. I remember choosing a college. It was between Ashland University in Ohio and Indiana University of Pennsylvania. "What do you think, Dad?" I remember asking, wanting him to make the decision for me.

"I don't know, Abs." He looked at me, a look of understanding. "What do *you* think?"

"Well, I liked Ashland. But IUP seemed like a better fit. I liked the coach, the academics, and it's a full ride. . . ."

He supported me when I chose to go to Pennsylvania and then later supported my decision to transfer back closer to home. I guess we don't always get it right on the first try.

"That's part of growing up," he would say.

As I got older, out of high school, and no longer playing basketball, the car ride sessions transitioned to my next car ride discussion partner, my husband. This time it wasn't about basketball—it was about our future—where we would live, what kind of car we would purchase, in what religion we would raise our children. Some topics I was more willing to compromise on than others. On some issues, however, I was less willing to bend. Perhaps this is because I've always imagined my marriage would be similar to my parents'. Growing up I knew I wanted with my husband the same love and relationship I saw between my own mother and father. High school sweethearts, they've been married over thirty years. Our stories are very similar. Both my husband and father used basketball scholarships to help earn their way through college before moving on to graduate school. My mother, like me, supported her husband's dream, while also pursuing her own. I wonder sometimes if I want to move back to Canton because it's what my parents did after my father graduated from law school. We would be like them, one step closer to happily ever after as I imagined it as a child.

Crows, which can migrate in flocks, are known to forage in agricultural areas. Despite their sometimes negative reputation, the same crows that can negatively impact crops can also have a positive impact by eating pesky insects.

I recognize all of the things my husband loved about his childhood—some I even appreciate, can picture in my mind's future dreams—the golden wheat fields that ripple in the wind like waves on a silent ocean and the animals grazing nearby, but although I admire them, I do not see the rolling hills in my dream. We love two different parts of Ohio. I appreciate close proximity to the city limits, require it almost for its obvious conveniences and easy access to the shopping mall. Most importantly, when I close my eyes and dream, I selfishly see my mother and father nearby, playing with the grandchildren. I see my father a stone's throw away, teaching my daughter the jump shot he once taught me on the same beat-up old rim, and I see my mother taking her shopping for clothes.

When we lie down in our bed together at night, Brian and I hold each other and pray. It is a practice that binds us together—to come before God as one being. We pray for guidance and help in making decisions. But faith is not like magic. We cannot click our fingers and bring the answer instantly before us. Faith is difficult in all its ways because it requires just that: faith in what we cannot see. So for now, we continue our heated discussions, believing a breakthrough is around the corner or on the next drive home, that if we continue to discuss our future, together we will find a solution.

We stare out the great glass windshield and discuss our dreams, recognizing our differences. And it is in these conversations that I utilize the tools my father taught me only a little while ago, when I sat in the same seat, albeit a much different person—a girl then, now a woman. And although he talked of offense and defense, those lessons still ring true. I am a well-seasoned attacker, not with the ball in my hand any longer, but rather with my words. He was a lawyer, after all, and I not only attempted to learn the techniques of his jump shot but also his ability to formulate and articulate a strong argument. I use these techniques on my husband, both knowingly and because they have become second nature.

I look over at Brian, who is now silent, and wonder what he is thinking too. Is he shouting in his head like I am in mine: *I want this! Why can't you understand? I love you, and I want you to be happy. But I want to be happy, too! Don't you know this decision could change our lives forever?* I turn my head away, so he won't see. The tears well up and drip down my cheek.

And this, more than anything, is why the tears flow. Not out of sadness, but rather out of a somber recognition of the magnitude of the decision we are making—the attachment we both feel to the places that hold our former selves and the guilt at the possibility of winning the battle. The tears flow for the weight this decision places on our dreams, so suddenly and unusually separate, and because ultimately, I see his side too and recognize almost subconsciously that if I truly wanted my way—in my most selfish moment—he would give in.

Perhaps I am taken with the crow because I feel within me a certain connection to this wandering creature—wonder if I will always feel like a wandering creature myself, uncertain where home will be. I do my best thinking in the car, watching as the landscape speeds by, wondering about life.

I look again towards the sky and wonder what the floating bird feels as he soars above the busy world below. Does he do his best thinking in the cold, winter air, free and alone? Free. Perhaps that is the key. No decision being permanent, when you have wings to take you away, tires to push you farther from reality. Perhaps it's the idea of not being grounded at the moment, the road flying by beneath the car that inspires me so. We could go whichever way we want—we don't have to go anywhere in particular.

And still I can't shake the bird. I see him, in my mind's eye, circling above. Where will he end up? Where will the road take us?

Unwrapping Surprises in the Personal Essay

Abigail Moore Allerding

The first essay I ever loved I read in *The Brief Arlington Reader*, a book of "Canons and Contexts" I bought at the Malone College Bookstore. I can still see its soft yellow cover and the "used" sticker slapped on the binding. It was for an expository writing class—one I signed up for without a complete understanding of the class description. I simply knew it was required for my major. When I stumbled upon "In Search of Our Mothers' Gardens" by Alice Walker, I remember feeling like I wanted more. This thing my professor called the personal essay was, for the first time, piquing my interest in a way only Tolkien had before. But it was different— it was raw, it was honest, it was *true*.

For me, the essay was a new and exciting challenge in the world of both reading and writing—one that asked a great deal of the author beyond the mere craft. Suddenly, I was being asked not only to write, but to put my name on a perceived truth, to invest in my writing not only ideas and characters, but my very own, vulnerable being.

It wasn't until years later, when I read Steven Harvey's "The Art of Translation," that I began to better understand (or at least better articulate) the magic that sprang to life on the page when I first discovered the personal essay— the significant leap in form my young writer's mind was attempting to grasp. Harvey suggests that the phrase "personal essay" is more appropriate than "creative nonfiction" or other pretentious labels, in part because "the reader, expecting some dull tract, can be surprised" (Harvey 364). Looking back, and now as an avid reader of the personal essay, I've begun to understand that it is this very "surprise" that keeps me coming back for more.

Harvey also suggests something further—that the writer of a personal essay is "drawn to the mundane rather than the sensational" (365). It seems our world today is full of the sensational—in the grocery line, on the television, on billboards, even in the daily newspaper. We are inundated with sensation. So for me, who has led a rather mundane life, this is the value of the essay. That beneath the ordinary there lurks a surprise—not necessarily a "sensational" one—in its truest, unexpected form. That writing about the family dinner table or baking cookies with my husband may lead to a moving essay is evidence that the seemingly mundane can serve as a promising vehicle for discovery and entertainment. The draw is in these simple surprises, waiting to be revealed like the click, click, click of a tricky combination lock. We simply need to discover the right amount of clicks, in the right order, for the lock to open.

In his essay "The Singular First Person," Scott Russell Sanders contemplates the subject of the personal essay:

> Whatever its more visible subject, an essay is also about the way a mind moves, the links and leaps and jigs of thought . . . each doggy sentence, as it noses forward into the underbrush of thought, scatters a bunch of rabbits that go bounding off in all directions. The essayist can afford to chase more of those rabbits than the fiction writer can, but fewer than the poet. If you refuse to chase any of them, and keep plodding along in a straight line, you and your reader will have a dull outing. If you choose too many, you will soon wind up lost in a thicket of confusion with your tongue hanging out. (418)

Since reading these two essays on craft—both Harvey and Sanders—discovering the surprise within material that is expected to be mundane has become more evident both in my reading and my writing. It has become quite clear that to find these treasures, one must reach into a repertoire of tools, use them carefully—always sincerely—and dig them out of the recesses of one's mind.

Thinking about this digging, the uncovering of something so ordinary yet so special, came at a convenient time. I was in the process of writing an essay that's beginnings started off much in the same rabbit-chasing fashion I've referred to above. The essay began on a car ride home with my husband after a long weekend visiting family. When I saw a crow flying above our moving car, I was immediately taken with his grace, his freedom, and began to wonder about the creature's life and its relationship to my own. As I stared out the window, a pattern of thinking unfolded, and of course, being a writer, I grabbed a pen and paper and began to jot down notes. As the crow—this ordinary bird I see almost daily on my commute to and from school—got me thinking, I realized I had the beginnings of an essay. Here's what I began with:

> I saw him going west on Interstate 71, just before entering Morrow County—a single crow floating above my car in the frigid winds. And I wondered where he'd land, where he might nestle in to fight the bitter cold. I was headed south with my husband towards home. Or at least what we called home for the time.
>
> We argue—my husband and I—endlessly about where home will be when he finishes veterinary school. It is the endless back and forth

brigade—the type of ridiculous argument you watch on *Saturday Night Live* with well rehearsed back and forth banter. This argument is certainly well rehearsed, but instead of laughter it frequently ends in tears.

I call my parents' house home. It's the place where I grew up—where I got picked up before my high school prom, where I slept the night before I was married, where I threw up the first time I got drunk. I call my in-laws' house home—where my husband grew up. And I am beginning to call our tiny apartment in Sunbury home, although I know for certain that is not where I want home to be in several years. It seems I'm far better at knowing what I don't want versus what I do.

Looking back on that drive home, I realize now that I was not taken with the bird because I wondered about where home might someday come to be but rather because I felt within me a certain connection to this wandering creature.

I watched as the landscape sped by and wondered about life. I've felt heavy lately, as though something is literally weighing on my chest. Like an ankle bracelet that keeps its prisoner homebound, I've felt bound to worry. And while lifting my worries in prayer always works, it's the waiting period I despise. We pass a sign reading "Right lane must use shoulder." And I wonder, What the hell does that mean? Was that my sign from God? No, it's only something to do with the semi trucks. Another mangled orange barrel rests on the side of the road, probably the product of an overzealous SUV. On my right I see a sign—fresh Amish Cooking: next exit.

It's short and simple—a developing idea really, rather than any concrete form of writing. The rest of the page has notes and other ideas jotted down. I then began getting at the root of the crow, allowing my "doggy" nose to investigate the terrain lurking beneath the animal I've used to frame my developing essay. What unfolded was an essay about my young marriage and our decisions regarding where we will live in the future after my husband graduates from vet school.

Originally, the essay ran in many directions—perhaps *too* many, Sanders might say. I included a rather lengthy section about my father and our ventures in basketball. I began to realize that, throughout the course of my life, two men had played influential roles: first my father, then my husband. The revelations about my father, however, went far beyond the immediate impact this essay needed. It drew the reader away from the crow, from the issues of new marriage and discovering home, to a different time in my life and the impact my father's influence had on the current state of affairs. In many ways, it was another essay altogether. I soon realized it was one rabbit that simply went too far in a direction I could not sustain with the other, more relevant threads.

Expanding an essay, I began to realize, is like remodeling a home. The bare bones are there, but one must find the little treasures lying around the house and convert them to relevant material. One must also search the recesses—the attic and the forgotten boxes—as well as shop for the new, completely fresh and innovative additions. While there may be items that are hard to let go, sometimes it's in the best interest of the final result to leave them out. They simply don't match.

In terms of my own essay, it was time to go rabbit hunting. What was at the core of the crow? Why did he catch my attention that day? And where was this essay supposed to be going? Answering these questions, I believe, is very much the art of essay. The job before me, then, was to uncover the meaning of this crow, as well as to honestly search out the details of my relationship and internal struggle. I discovered uncovering the right details and events requires a kind of honest introspection that can be life altering.

As the crow essay developed and the details and events that surfaced were primarily about discovering a home with my husband, I pieced together scenes and background that exposed complicated feelings I didn't even fully understand. The essay went through many early revisions and incrementally found its form. Soon I felt it was ready for other writers to see. During a workshop, a classmate responded to the following scene:

> And so I constantly wonder, will we live on a farm near his family? Take over a vet clinic that already exists? Make long drives to my parents' house so they can visit with the grandkids? Or will we live on the outskirts of the city where I grew up, with the cornfields and barns only a few miles from tall buildings and the shopping mall? Or will we live in the middle, not totally his way, not totally mine? Which area offers the prime market for a large and small animal practice? I know not to worry, that God will answer our prayers, and yet I almost covet these arguments in the car, enjoy them despite the heated emotions. They allow us to dream and recognize the differences in our dreams as we stare out the glass windshield, the great mediator who will long know the secrets of our hearts.

What he wrote was this: "You're losing me as a reader and I suspect you're backing away from something. You mentioned before you shed tears. I am not inclined to accept this peaceful image here. I want to know more about what is behind the tears. I think that's where the truth will be."

I don't think it was until this review that the parts of the essay fell into place and, in fact, the above paragraph is not in the final draft at all. I found that the surprises that hide within the personal essay aren't so much in the essay itself but rather the laying out on the page of one's most intimate moments with the self—the actual writing process. What I find provocative about the personal essay, perhaps more than anything else, is the honesty, and thereby intimacy, the reader experiences *with* the author. The writer's obligation lies not in telling it as it first reveals itself on the page but in molding and remolding the soul's secrets. I realized the readers weren't getting all of me. It wasn't until my classmate challenged me to go deeper that the essay found its true sincerity.

As readers, we crave relationship and to know that we are not alone in our struggles—to know that we are not the only one who thinks the sometimes twisted ways we do. Self-deprecation can go a long way with readers. However, recognizing our pitfalls can be a challenging aspect of the writing process, albeit a required step to developing an honest voice and establishing trust with the reader. If it isn't sincere, it will be obvious and probably a failure. What I discovered in my own essay was that there was more lurking beneath the surface than even I first realized. As a result, I searched deeper, discovering something about myself even I didn't want to admit. What I was forced to face were some of the ugliest qualities about myself, particularly the selfishness with which I handle the topic of finding a home with my husband. What resulted, however, was a paragraph of reflection that reveals the deepest complications and struggles of our decision:

> And this, more than anything, is why the tears flow. Not out of sadness, but rather out of a somber recognition of the magnitude of the decision we are making—the attachment we both feel to the places that hold our former selves and the guilt at the possibility of winning the battle. The tears flow for the weight this decision places on our dreams, so suddenly and unusually separate, and because ultimately, I see his side too and recognize almost subconsciously that if I truly wanted my way—in my most selfish moment—he would give in.

Comparing the essay to the novel, Steven Harvey says, "Novelists put ideas on the lips of characters they don't trust and say to the reader, in essence, 'You decide, I can't.' That is why essayists turn the ideas over and over, considering possibilities, allowing for contradictions, aware that the blame will, eventually, fall their way. . . . There is out there in the world of readers, a longing for a reality behind words" (368). The essay provides for this reality that readers long for when it creates a level of intimacy and trust in the writing. Part of the success, I believe, is allowing complications and contradictions and exploring them without a pointed explanation. Reality can't explain away our faults, our struggles, so why should our writing?

I experienced this struggle with "Home" during a writing workshop session. An important part of the decision I talk about in the essay is based on our faith that God will help lead my husband and me to a decision. Here is what I wrote in the earlier drafts:

> I know not to worry, that God will answer our prayers, and yet I almost cherish these arguments in the car, enjoy them despite the heated emotions. They allow us to dream and recognize the differences in our dreams as we stare out the glass windshield, the great mediator who will long know the thoughts in our hearts.

In response, my professor challenged me with these remarks: "Does this seem to contradict the tension/momentum of the essay—the urgency of a decision that we readers have been ASKED to care about?" When I considered her remarks, I was immediately defensive and disagreed—*No*, I thought (and eventually said in a discussion within the workshop), *that is part of having faith—this contradiction. It's part of the difficult struggle—to have faith and yet to grapple with the humanity in us—that we want to know what will happen, that we are prone to worry. . . .* When I relayed to the group the more complicated thoughts I was grappling with, they responded by reminding me that what I just said (not what was currently in the essay) was more honest and, therefore, a much more effective way to talk about faith in the essay.

At one point, I also wondered if it would be better to remove the paragraph altogether—after all, it was a short paragraph and the flow of the essay probably would not be disrupted if it was gone. Ultimately, it came down to what Harvey suggests is the draw of the personal essay—the "reality behind the words" and the honesty of the voice. I needed to be true to myself in order to be true to my readers—the faith part was far too important to remove. It was a very real and close aspect of the struggle. Regardless of the difficulties it might present in regards to craft, it was far more imperative that it be there to maintain the integrity of the essay. The following, albeit not perfect and perhaps still waiting to be revised once again, is what found its way onto the page:

> When we lie down in our bed together at night, Brian and I hold each other and pray. It is a practice that binds us together—to come before God as one being. We pray for guidance and help in making decisions. But faith is not like magic. We cannot click our fingers and bring the answer instantly before us. Faith is difficult in all its ways because it requires just that: faith in what we cannot see. So for now, we continue our heated discussions, believing a breakthrough is around the corner or on the next drive home, that if we continue to discuss our future, together and with God, we will find a solution.

The difference, I believe, between the first and second versions is an honesty both with myself and with the reader, which required an act of discovery that came as a result of the writing.

Ultimately, the discussion of faith was what made my writing about finding home unique to me versus other authors who might be writing about similar endeavors. Another way to separate myself, I found, was to find a unique form. While arranging an essay or memoir may seem a simple feat, I find it to be one of the most challenging parts of writing. The organization of the writing on the page plays an important role in the way readers perceive the writing. It makes a difference when and how they are introduced to key "characters," for example, or how the chronology of events is presented—whether in flashback or a simpler, more straightforward chronological order of the events.

How, then, do I handle the use of time to help organize my essay? This is not an easy answer. The essay begins in the present tense, at the moment when I am driving with my husband. The crow, the vehicle by which I frame the essay, is first mentioned here. The essay then goes back and forth between the past and the present. I felt it was important to show both the elements of our childhoods (since they play such a significant role in the decision we are making) as well as the current relationship (especially the discussions about where home will be) with my husband in the present. Because I chose to frame the essay with the image of the circling crow, the essay ends in the present tense with me wondering about the crow and our future.

The choice to frame the essay with the crow is a calculated part of the organization of the essay—one that in workshops people seemed to like. It provided a sense of being grounded, an image to hold onto. However, in the early drafts of the essay, the crow seemed to be out of the essay for too long, so that in the end, readers almost forgot about him from the beginning of the essay. In other words, the essay was lacking something in terms of its arrangement on the page. There wasn't a great use of white space, any type of real segmenting, and it seemed to simply go on for too long without solid transitions.

The image of the crow, what it seemed to symbolize or represent in my writing, and the overall purpose, was part of the discussions my group had during writing workshop that ultimately helped realize the final structure for the finished product. What resulted was the idea of a segmented essay—one that would incorporate some research about the habits of crows relating to the subject of my essay—family and home. In doing so, the hope was that the essay would also start to become more fluid, moving back and forth between the crow and the decisions about settling on a place to live.

This was one of my goals as I considered incorporating the research on crows into my own essay—I wanted to make sure whatever voice resulted in the segments on crows flowed with the rest of the essay. What I realized as I began my research, that I don't think I could have understood without actually doing it myself, is that in researching something that relates to the topic at hand (family and finding a home), one is forced to think more deeply about those topics in order to draw real and not contrived connections.

What I discovered was that the simple, ordinary crow I saw on my way home that winter day was actually connected to me in ways I never dreamed. As Harvey so aptly suggested, I was drawn to the mundane and pleasantly surprised by the results.

The voice in these segments is certainly more scientific, a bit like a reporter, but it also contrasts with the more intimate tone in the rest of the essay. Each segment, whether about where crows are prone to live, the raising of the young and the organization of the family unit, their tendencies to migrate, and the impact they have on society, all serve to highlight the issues my husband and I struggle with on a daily basis regarding where we will live and raise a family.

Ultimately, the crow becomes a unifying factor for the essay. In my last revision, it became all about structure and organization. I printed the essay on paper and cut each paragraph out separately. I then took each paragraph and laid them out on the floor, deleting unnecessary paragraphs and adding transitions where they were needed. The process was long, and probably still in progress, yet seeing where it started and looking at it now, I feel the process of writing is such a rewarding endeavor.

Harvey says that personal essays "supply information, entertain, and provide flawless and therefore irksome models for millions of college students learning how to write decent prose, but their main business is the expression of the solitary soul in a changing world, a clear and valuable mission" (365). Considering I've been that college student, reading Alice Walker and for the first time awakening to the genius that can stem from the personal essay, I appreciate this notion perhaps more than others. Yes, an essay can provide information, teaching me about subjects I never knew, and of course, they can certainly entertain—I nearly always draw pleasure from reading a beautifully crafted piece of writing. Yet this idea of expressing the soul is what gets me every time I read an essay. It's why I write, no matter how painstaking the process may be.

For this also is what makes writing the personal essay an exciting and rewarding endeavor. That amidst the ordinary and mundane there springs to life a sense of meaning from something as simple as a crow. That chasing rabbits is not a futile occupation but rather, if done carefully and taken seriously, the writer, in his/her attempt to dig for treasure, can be the single voice that changes the world.

Works Cited

Harvey, Steven. "The Art of Translation." *The Fourth Genre: Contemporary Writers of/on Creative Nonfiction.* Ed. Robert L. Root, Jr. and Michael Steinberg. 4th ed. New York: Longman, 2007. 364–69.

Sanders, Scott Russell. "The Singular First Person." *The Fourth Genre: Contemporary Writers of/on Creative Nonfiction.* Ed. Robert L. Root, Jr. and Michael Steinberg. 4th ed. New York: Longman, 2007. 416–24.

Warping Time with Montaigne

Emily D. Chase

I sit bent over the breast beam of my 38 inch LeClerc floor loom pulling individual threads of brilliant, durable yarn through the metal heddles of its six harnesses. The heddles that have already been threaded hang in orderly lines waiting for the command to raise and lower those threads of yarn in the process of creating fabric; the unthreaded heddles hang in unorganized clusters patiently waiting for their turn to take part. This threading process is called "warping the loom" because the yarn that is being threaded onto the loom will become the "warp"—or lengthwise threads—in the fabric that will be woven. This process of reaching through the heddle with the threading hook, catching a strand of yarn, and pulling it back through the heddle does not require a lot of thought, other than that required to make sure the right piece of yarn gets threaded through the right heddle. My mind is free to wander as it will while I prepare my loom. "My style and my mind alike go roaming," Montaigne said (761). Of course I think of Montaigne; I have just spent two weeks reading essays by Montaigne, about Montaigne, and about essayists who have written essays on Montaigne. I have Montaigne on the brain: What sort of essays would Montaigne write if he were still alive? What would he say about the essays being written today? In particular, what would he say about Richard Rodriguez's essay "Late Victorians"? I pull a strand of yarn through a heddle and think of Montaigne and Rodriguez.

Rodriguez's essay uses many of the elements of the genre that Montaigne created. If Montaigne had not spun the first ideas of the essay into a new genre of literature, Rodriguez would not have been able to write "Late Victorians" without first spinning the thread of the genre on his own. I see that Montaigne's thoughts and ideas have been pulled through time to be used as the warp of essays since Montaigne's book *Essais* was first published in 1580. Now I am the one sitting at the loom of time, pulling the thoughts and ideas of Montaigne through the heddles. The full body of Montaigne's essays lies rolled up upon itself on the warp beam of the loom, waiting to be used by anyone with the knowledge and patience to thread it through time and secure it to this side of the past.

I reach through the eyelet of a heddle for a piece of Montaigne and imagine Rodriguez doing the same thing as he created "Late Victorians." For, certainly, he pulled Montaigne's motto through time—"Que scais-je?" (What do I know?). Rodriguez explores this question in "Late Victorians" as he asks himself how he should live his life and how he should *have lived* his life. These are the central questions and themes of his essay. He asks himself if he should have pursued "an earthly paradise charming," like the gay men he has known who have since died of AIDS (131). He considers the possibility of having pursued a career in office buildings which "were hives where money was made, and damn all" (128). At the end of "Late Victorians," he questions his future: Should he remain shifting his "tailbone upon the cold, hard pew," or should he rise to join the volunteers of the local AIDS Support Group (134)?

The genre of the essay offers Rodriguez an opportunity to explore these issues by using Montaigne's question, "What do I know?" Montaigne says:

> This . . . happens to me: that I do not find myself in the place where I look; and I find myself more by chance encounter than by searching my judgment. I will have tossed off some subtle remark as I write. Later I have lost the point so thoroughly that I do not know what I meant; and sometimes a stranger has discovered it before I do. If I erased every passage where this happens to me, there would be nothing left of myself. (26–27)

The form of the essay as Montaigne conceived it allows Rodriguez the freedom to seek answers, or to appear to seek answers, *while* he writes rather than exclusively *before* he writes. For Montaigne, writing was an *essai*, a trial or attempt. The presence of self and the absence of conclusion create a sense of freedom within Montaigne's essays. As he says: "The surest thing, in my opinion, would be to trace our actions to the neighboring circumstances, without getting into any further research and without drawing from them any other conclusions" (241). Like Montaigne, Rodriguez comes to no irrefutable conclusions in "Late Victorians." Instead, his thoughts wander through memories and observations as he seeks an understanding of the world by examining the things which touch his life directly.

As I consider the themes of "Late Victorians," I think of the title of one of Montaigne's essays, "By diverse means we arrive at the same end" (3). It occurs to me that this title describes the realm in which Rodriguez's thoughts wander. For what is Rodriguez writing about but diverse lifestyles and inevitable death? Running across his essay are the threads of gay life and death from AIDS. The texture of the weave is enhanced by Rodriguez's use of details from his own experience; these details form the weft of his essay, the crosswise threads. This weft is beaten into the fabric of "Late Victorians," as the "beater" on a loom locks the warp and weft tightly together by pushing each strand of weft snugly against the preceding strand, creating a cohesive, durable piece of fabric. Rodriguez weaves the fourteen sections of "Late Victorians" in this way, choosing different yarns for the weft of each section to create different textures and density of prose.

The first section is brief and is composed of two conflicting quotes. The first, by St. Augustine, hints at our discontent on earth in our mortal form due to our intuition that we are destined for a better life after death. Life is something to be restlessly passed through. The second quote, by Elizabeth Taylor, speaks of "cerulean" days in this life being undermined by sadness in the knowledge that these days and this life must end. These quotes show that, like Proteus, we are able to change our shape (the shape of our thoughts) as we try to avoid being bound by life. We are free to choose which way we will view life, whether we will suffer life and rejoice the end or embrace life and mourn the end. In "Late Victorians," Rodriguez tries to decide which view is the better view. He weaves these two quotes into his text to prepare us for the creation which is to follow. What is life? What is death? Which one wears the mask covering reality?

Throughout the essay, Rodriguez portrays the paradox of homosexual life in San Francisco. He uses the image of the Victorian house to help him accomplish this. By noting that the "three- or four-story Victorian house, like the Victorian novel, was built to contain several generations and several classes under one roof, behind a single oaken door" (123), he reveals the irony of the housing market whereby "gay men found themselves living with the architectural metaphor for family" (122). From this image, Rodriguez goes exploring through the homosexual landscape of his life and discovers multiple conflicting images. Rodriguez says, "The age-old description of homosexuality is of a sin against nature," yet he observes that as the peaceful, domestic, homosexual community of the Castro district thrived, the perverted "assortment of leather bars . . . outlaw sexuality . . . eroticism of the dark" on heterosexual Folsom street also thrived (124–25). In the Castro district, thanks to gays, "where recently there had been loudmouthed kids, hole-in-the-wall bars, [and] pimps," there were now "tweeds and perambulators, matrons and nannies" (125). The gay men, who have chosen to embrace "the complacencies of the barren house," have made the streets safe once again for the family (127).

This depiction of peaceful homosexual life is strikingly linked to another paradox of gay life as Rodriguez describes two parades in which gay men with AIDS march for gay rights. Rodriguez depicts gay men in one Gay Freedom Day parade as "the blessed in Renaissance paintings," martyrs who cherish "the apparatus of [their] martyrdom" (119). This passage is followed immediately by a description of a parade five years later, which includes "plum-spotted young men." The juxtaposition of the two passages creates the disturbing impression that these people are fighting to choose the way they wish to die rather than the way they wish to live.

How is Rodriguez going to reconcile all of these conflicting images? I pull another strand of Montaigne through time and see that the essay, as a form, allows Rodriguez to go exploring without *having* to reconcile these images. Montaigne says in his essay "Of repentance":

> This is a record of various and changeable occurrences, and of irresolute and, when it so befalls, contradictory ideas: whether I am different myself, or whether I take hold of my subjects in different circumstances and aspects. So, all in all, I may indeed contradict myself now and then; but truth, as Demades said, I do not contradict. If my mind could gain a firm footing, I would not make essays; I would make decisions; but it is always in apprenticeship and on trial. (611)

Montaigne is speaking of his contradictory thoughts and ideas, and yet the passage is equally applicable to Rodriguez's treatment of the paradox of gay life.

Montaigne's passage makes me wonder, as I slowly and steadily thread my way across the loom, if ALL of Montaigne is present in the warp of Rodriguez's essay. Would all of Montaigne's writings have to be threaded through time as an inseparable skein of thought, in order to remain true as a body of writing? Or could a person be selective when choosing which parts she pulled through time? I think of the warp on my loom, and I know that it is not possible to thread just part of a warp through the heddles. ALL of the strands of warp must be threaded, or the warp becomes tangled and knotted on the loom. For this reason, I have to think that all of Montaigne's thoughts are present in the warp of an essay, even when an essay presents an opposing view of that held by Montaigne.

I ponder this question because of the way I have linked Montaigne's quote from his essay "Of repentance" to the image of the AIDS victims in the Gay Freedom Day parades. The quote is pertinent as it applies to the issue of contradictions and paradox, yet Montaigne and Rodriguez do not agree completely on the actual subject of repentance. Both Montaigne and Rodriguez recognize the value of youth and of what is often deemed youth's foolishness. Rodriguez says:

> Though I am alive now, I do not believe that an old man's pessimism is truer than a young man's optimism simply because it comes after. There are things a young man knows that are true and are not yet in the old man's power to recollect. (120)

This is similar to a passage of Montaigne's, in his essay "Of repentance" in which he says:

> I should be ashamed and resentful if the misery and misfortune of my decrepitude were to be thought better than my good, healthy, lively, vigorous years, and if people were to esteem me not for what I have been, but for ceasing to be that. (619)

On the issue of repentance itself, however, Montaigne and Rodriguez differ. While Montaigne declares, "If I had to live over again, I would live as I have lived" (620), Rodriguez says, "It was then I saw that the greater sin against heaven was my unwillingness to embrace life" (132). There is an edge of repentance in Rodriguez's text, which does not exist in Montaigne's writings.

We are never sure, however, of what it is that Rodriguez feels the need to repent. In boldly talking about the gay community in San Francisco, Rodriguez appears to be revealing himself as a gay man, yet Phillip Lopate says, "Richard Rodriguez, for instance, is a master of the confessional tone, yet he tells us that his family calls him 'Mr. Secrets,' and he plays a hide-and-seek game of revealing himself" (xxvii). This is the case in "Late Victorians." Rodriguez describes the gay community of San Francisco from the perspective of a person who has been a part of that community. He has marched in a Gay Freedom Day parade; he has many male friends who are gay; he lives in a Victorian house which has been reclaimed and redecorated by gay men and now contains "four apartments; four single men"; he says, "To grow up homosexual is to live with secrets and within secrets" (122). And yet, on his deathbed, a friend of Rodriguez's, Cesar, says with irony that Rodriguez "would be the only one spared," that he was "too circumspect" (131). Rodriguez never actually says that he is gay. What are we to think?

I continue the process of pulling strands of yarn and thought through the loom: Does it matter if Rodriguez is gay? Does it matter if he tells us he is or isn't gay? What do I, as a reader, think of the authority of voice in the piece if this information appears to be purposefully concealed? Essayist E. B. White declared, "There is one thing the essayist cannot do—he cannot indulge himself in deceit or in concealment, for he will be found out in no time" (xxvi). And yet Alexander Smith wrote of Montaigne, "If you wish to preserve your secret, wrap it up in frankness" (Lopate xxvii). Montaigne said, "We must remove the mask," but he also said that he has "painted [his] inward self with colors clearer than [his] original ones" (504). Clearly, the act of making one's private thoughts public is not as simple as just recording the observations of one's life or even of simply attempting to capture one's mind in the act of thinking, as Montaigne set out to do.

I look back across the loom at the threads I have pulled through the heddles and am reminded that essays consist of explorations, questions, and contradictions. In his essay "Late Victorians," Rodriguez questions his life and lifestyle. Should he embrace life and mourn death, as his gay friends do, or should he withhold himself from life and look forward to death, as he does in his role as a skeptic? "Skepticism became my demeanor toward them—I was the dinner-party skeptic, a firm believer in Original Sin and in the limits of possibility" (Rodriguez 131). Rodriguez does not find the answer to his question in "Late Victorians." In the essay, he remains shifting his "tailbone on the cold, hard pew" while he tries to decide which role to play—which mask to put on or, perhaps, which mask to take off.

It is the *quest* for answers rather than the answers themselves that distinguishes the Montaignian essay. In this respect, "Late Victorians" is a good example of a contemporary essay that has been woven on a warp of Montaigne. In other respects, such as the inclusion of quotations, the essay differs from those of Montaigne. (Montaigne's essays include numerous quotations, Rodriguez's few.) However, when I gaze across the warp threaded through my loom, I am reminded that even this difference is a tribute to Montaigne, for I see Montaigne's strand of thought that advocates rebellion against accepted forms of discourse, including his own.

It is likely that Montaigne's thoughts go warping through most literary nonfiction essays. This is very different from what Montaigne envisioned when he wrote the preface, "To the Reader," for his book *Essais:*

> I have had no thought of serving either you or my own glory. My powers are inadequate for such a purpose. I have dedicated it to the private convenience of my relatives and friends, so that when they have lost me (as soon they must), they may recover here some features of my habits and temperament, and by this means keep the knowledge they have had of me more complete and alive. (2)

I think of this quote as I pull the last strand of warp through its heddle and secure it to the cloth beam on my side of the loom. My loom is now ready to be used to create a piece of individuality. I wonder what I will create. Shall I weave in some of the texture of Rodriguez or of Reg Saner? Emerson or Ehrlich? The possibilities are endless. I step on a treddle to open the warp, throw my shuttle of weft across the threads, and allow "my style and my mind alike" to go roaming. I have warped my loom with Montaigne.

Works Cited

Lopate, Phillip, ed. *The Art of the Personal Essay.* New York: Anchor Books, 1994.

Montaigne, Michel de. *The Complete Works of Montaigne.* Trans. Donald M. Frame. Stanford: Stanford UP, 1957.

Rodriguez, Richard. "Late Victorians." *The Best American Essays 1991.* Ed. Joyce Carol Oates. New York: Ticknor & Fields, 1991. 119–34.

White, E.B. *Essays of E.B. White.* New York: HarperCollins, 1977.

Notes from a Journey Toward "Warping Time"

Emily D. Chase

The path that I took to create the essay "Warping Time with Montaigne" was not a direct path through the writing process. I meandered through personal experiences and through unfamiliar research before I found a thread to connect the two and to help me reach some sort of meaningful understanding of Montaigne and of myself. Since writing that essay, I have noticed that my path through the writing process is almost always indirect and that quite often the meandering path is the most direct way for me to get to insight and understanding. What follows here is essentially a travelogue of my journey toward "Warping Time with Montaigne."

The first time that I heard of Michel de Montaigne was in a course in Graduate Composition. Before that time, the term "essay," to me, was a generic term used by English teachers to refer to short pieces of nonfiction writing. I had no sense of the history of the term or the genre; however, I immediately became interested in Montaigne's writings and therefore decided to write about him for the required research paper in the class. The research paper was written immediately prior to "Warping Time with Montaigne" (the essay included here) and provided me with enough background information to pique my interest and to make me want to have some fun with the information in another piece of writing.

As part of the in-class prewriting for the research paper, I did a cluster/web off of the central term "literary nonfiction." The freewriting that followed the cluster exercise reveals the general direction in which I was drawn:

> Having to research an area of, or a figure in, literary nonfiction, I might like to compare and contrast the original essays everyone quotes—Montaigne, Newman, Emerson, Thoreau—with the modern essayists (especially the nature writers)—Dillard, Ehrlich, Selzer, White—to see if the originals have

> affected the moderns. I'd like to find the ties, if any, between personal inter-
> action with nature, religion . . . and the desire to write LNF essays. Part of
> this study would be taking a look at how each essayist recorded his thoughts
> (i.e., Thoreau and his journals). Is each day a personal scrutiny of life? an
> appreciation of being alive? Part of LNF is taking a real daily event and per-
> sonalizing it by recording your interaction w/it.
>
> But where is this going in terms of research?—Study the masters,
> study the moderns, draw conclusions. What are people already saying about
> this link? Has anyone already taken this tack? Is this productive? Is this
> worthwhile?

I see in this freewrite the idea of not just the original research paper I did on
Montaigne but perhaps also the germ of the idea behind "Warping." I never let
go of this interest in the correlation between the early essayists and the current
essayists.

In just ten days, I discovered a topic and pulled together a reasonable essay
about Montaigne and his influence; I used the metaphor of building construction
as I discussed the construction of the genre of literary nonfiction upon the foundation of Montaigne's writings. I think better and have more fun writing when I
use metaphors to organize and present my thoughts. This fact, no doubt, played a
major role in the process that I went through to create the "Warping" essay.

As I was finishing the research paper on Montaigne and just before I began the "Warping" essay, I read Gerald Early's essay "Life with Daughters:
Watching the Miss America Pageant" and Jane Tompkins' essay "At the Buffalo
Bill Museum." I was overwhelmed by the power of Early's piece, and my original
reaction to this essay in my journal reflects this:

> Wow! What an essay! . . . Like a freight train, the fully loaded essay started
> slowly, exerting effort to overcome inertia, then slowly accumulated speed
> until it rushed, unstoppably, toward its destination. With Early's final sen-
> tence, "My knees had begun to hurt and I realized, painfully, that I was
> much too old, much too at peace with stiffness and inflexibility, for children's
> games," the train rushed off the end of the track into the great unknown void
> of the future. Wow!

By contrast, I did not like Tompkins' essay—or rather I did not understand her
essay. My journal reaction to her essay is one long attempt to understand her
point; I never do reach that understanding but come to the conclusion that "this
is a disturbing piece because I can't see where the author is coming from. I'm not
sure a rereading would help." It may seem irrelevant that I read these two essays
between writing my two Montaigne essays, yet I think it was crucial that I read as
powerful a creative commentary essay as Early's and that I read (and struggled
with) Tompkins' essay just as I was directed to write an analysis paper of current literary nonfiction in which I would "explore an individual essay, a series of
essays, or a particular author or authors." Both Early and Tompkins use objects

and events that they see in their surroundings to launch themselves into realms of contemplation. I must have subconsciously hung onto this technique such that it resurfaced later as I tried to figure out what to do with the analysis assignment.

My initial plans for the analysis paper returned to my interest in the link between Montaigne and the essayists that are writing today. I was still too interested in Montaigne and too convinced of his importance as a crucial element in the genre of literary nonfiction to let go of him. However, we were instructed to comment upon (interpret/analyze) a more current essay. I began to play with possible ways to link Montaigne with current essayists.

On the day that we began working on the analysis paper, I wrote the following prewrite in class:

> Having the chance to write on one element or author in nonfiction, I think I'd like to pursue the elements of Montaigne's essays which can be found in the works of other essayists. Perhaps I could tackle Emerson's essay, "Montaigne," and show how that essay uses Montaignian practices in the process of praising Montaigne. This is a possibility. However, I'd also like to look at Montaigne versus Bacon in terms of voice in the essay and then apply that comparison to critical articles today—(i.e., tackle the 4-woman writers' group who are trying to write "readable" literary criticism [Tompkins, Kaplan, Torgovnik, Davidson]). I'd need to find out if there is much out there in terms of articles/essays on this debate. If *College English* is including these articles now but labeling them as opinion, is anyone reacting to this practice? Is Tompkins? Is Sommers? I think that this could be a much more interesting topic/issue than the piece on Emerson. It would also get me involved in a current intellectual discussion. Having had "Critical Theory" I feel that I have a fairly good base to stand on. Where would Dillard's book, *Living by Fiction,* fit in? or would it? Robert Coles? Who is arguing for Baconian essays in academia? Does Montaigne ever get mentioned in support of personal criticism?—Probably not. But a discussion of Montaigne vs Bacon could be fairly enlightening. I have lots of articles discussing this. I have the background material. I'd just have to dig into the contemporary information. Back to the MLA Bibliography. . . .

I find it interesting as I reread this entry and as I dig through various drafts of the "Warping" essay that one comment I received during a peer editing session of the paper says, "Personally, I think this is better than a lot of the jargon-filled stuff I've read in academic journals." Again, I must have internalized the idea of "readable" criticism such that it resurfaced on its own later in the process.

On the same day that I wrote the above journal entry, as I was beginning work on this final paper, I kept trying to find a way to bring Montaigne into a criticism of a current essay. Because I have watched innumerable episodes of "Star Trek," it did not seem inconceivable to me that one of those hypothetical warps in the space-time continuum could allow Montaigne to suddenly appear in person to comment on the essays being written today. In the preceding research paper, I had already looked at how essayists since Montaigne had used his ideas and examples to help them create their own essays, so it seemed only fair that Montaigne should now have his say about the current essays that are being written. The word "warp" turned out to be the necessary spark that ignited an inspirational firestorm.

I remember the excitement that I felt when it struck me that the word warp carries a number of different meanings. I had been thinking of the term with a Star Trekian mentality of traveling through time and dimensions of reality, but I am also a weaver, and so as I thought of "warping time," I automatically thought of "warping a loom"—threading a warp onto a loom. After writing the journal entry about Montaigne and Bacon, I jotted down the following notes to myself:

                                                               exciting
        Some^ thoughts-   "Warping Time: Montaigne on _____"
        & ideas   sitting at loom, threading warp, thinking about
                                     assignments/readings
                               critique article in my head by remembering
                                     what Montaigne & critics of M.
        this   have said.
        could   get up to pursue details for more specifics
        be   tie in with images of: thread
        really   warp/weaving
        fun!   distorted/warped time
                               structure & patterns & variations of woven cloth
                                     lay warp on loom, like laying _____ on M.
                                     or like laying M on _____.

In one moment of inspiration, I made the connection between the elements and process of threading a loom and the elements and process of writing an essay. I couldn't wait to start writing; all I needed was a modern essay to interpret in order to fulfill the requirements of the paper assignment.

It is probably important to note here that I had only one week in which to select and interpret a current essay. The title of Richard Rodriguez's "Late Victorians" drew me to his essay, and then his mix of dry humor and deadly seriousness fascinated me. As I read his essay with the warping idea in mind, I began to see Rodriguez as a weaver of essays and the fourteen sections of "Late Victorians" as variations of weft on the same warp. His essay seemed to be the perfect one for me to work with, and I could barely contain myself as I told my editing group about the ideas for my paper. I can still picture my teacher leaning forward on his chair with keen interest as I explained what I envisioned for my paper.

The writing of both my Montaigne papers was aided in large part by exercises and peer editing that were conducted as part of coursework in the Graduate

Composition class. The drafting of each paper was preceded by a number of prewriting exercises to generate and organize ideas, and then once the drafting had begun, several different drafts of each paper were shared with a group of fellow students. I was a part of a four person editing group that provided valuable feedback and suggestions for revisions at every step of the drafting and revising process. The interaction of the editing group also tended to nurture creativity and spontaneity that proved to be crucial in the creation of "Warping Time with Montaigne."

Once I had shared my ideas for the paper with my group and with just two days left before my paper was due in class, I wrote the following journal entries as a way of organizing my thoughts and figuring out what I wanted to do with them in my paper:

"Warping time" has the potential to be a really interesting essay. I need to list everything I want to be sure to say about Rodriguez's essay, those quotes of Montaigne's which directly apply to the points I want to make, and, then, the precise affiliations I want to assign to each metaphor of time and the loom. I wish I had more time to work on this.

What are the parts to my metaphor? If the loom = time, the warp = Montaigne, and the weft = Rodriguez, then what is the process of "warping the loom"? Is the threading of Montaigne through the hettles of time, the same as Montaigne's transcendence of time? His thoughts have to be durable enough to stand the strain put on the warp by the tension of the loom as well as the wear of the opening and closing of the shed and the friction of the beater as it swings along Montaigne and locks the weft of Rodriguez's ideas into the grasp of Montaigne's warp, while at the same time the interlocking of Rodriguez into Montaigne creates a brand new unique object formed by the interaction of the inter-working parts of time with the materials of Montaigne and Rodriguez.

The ideas of original thinkers get spun into yarn for warp. Rodriguez's end product is a piece of cloth which is available to the reader to use to make other things such as clothing, blankets, or _____?

If Montaigne is the warp, what do the 2 ends signify? The first end is the full body of Montaigne wound around itself in its full potential. The end I am threading is his ideas being taken through time to be used in the creation of new essays. 2 steps to trip through time—hettles and dent. What are they? hettles = individual thoughts and quotes (arranged to create potential of a pattern). dent = combining and spacing of ideas to assure a solid, even weave of the new fabric—literature vs nonliterature? Final step is to tie off Montaigne in the present on the cloth beam in order to hang onto his thoughts in the present to enable the creation of new essays.

My thoughts as I thread the loom consider the process Rodriguez went through in the creation of "Late Victorians." As I tie off the warp on my loom, I have secured Montaigne for use in my own creation and I have examined the creation of an accomplished weaver to glean ideas and techniques. I am ready to write—conceivably the result is essay in the reader's hands. How to do that?

Ending—my thoughts pull Montaigne into the present, now I am ready to weave my thoughts into an essay, I step on the treadles to raise the shed,

throw the first pass of the shuttle and create, "I sit bent over the breast beam of
my 38 inch LeClerc floor loom. . . ."

This last journal entry was written after I had begun drafting my paper but before
I had figured out how to conclude the essay. I have quoted the first line of the
paper, yet my ideas are still just beginning to take form. I had originally planned
to create a circular essay in which the ending leads back to the beginning in a
never-ending retelling of this process; however, that idea got too confusing to be
adequately developed in the limited amount of time that I had and therefore was
changed in favor of the current ending.

I had a number of issues that needed to be sorted out as I tried to create
a complete draft of the paper; therefore, as a way of figuring out what ideas I
wanted to weave into the paper, I entered in my journal the following lists of
what I believed were critical points to be dealt with in my paper:

Individual thoughts of Montaigne:

- Que scais-je?
- I want to be seen in simple, natural . . . it is myself I portray
- essai = trial or attempt
- self-portrait vs autobiography
- to be known not remembered
- to follow wanderings of his mind in process of thinking
- my mind & my thoughts . . .
- find self through writing
- loose disconnected structure—mirrors spontaneous thought
- portrait as friendly gesture
- familiar tone
- rebellion against rigid styles, formal language
- absence of dispositio
- sense of honesty

Points from Rodriguez:

- we choose our lifestyles
- sometimes we choose our deaths
- we all die
- wisdom in youth's foolishness
- R. focused on tragedy Cesar—you cannot forbid tragedy
- R. full-time skeptic (131)(121)
- jealousy of responsible of irresponsible
- Victorian house as symbol of family—gay reclaim neighborhood
- new residents, new vision of family (Yuppies—birth control)
- masks (123)(131)

- caustic language (124–5) shock value, coarse cloth
- flipping of normal perspectives
- gays vs feminists
- nakedness (129)
- self-questioning in text (129)
- flowing thoughts (131)
- regret, repentance? (132)(134)

I spent successive late nights in the final week of the class working on this paper, as well as on revisions of other papers from that class. On the day before the final draft of the warping essay was due, my eyes felt unnaturally wide open from too much coffee and too little sleep, and yet still every time I thought about my paper, I felt excited about its possibilities. Not only did I not want to sleep, I knew that I couldn't sleep as long as I had the potentials of the warping metaphor at play in my head. It was with enthusiasm and playfulness, not with fatigue or despair, that I wrote the following journal entry:

> I am making progress on my "Warping" essay, but I have so far to go in the 24 hours I have left before I have to hand in the paper. I realize that I cannot get it into a polished state of existence in that time, but I would like to at least have the skeleton of the complete essay put together with some of the shaping musculature before I hand it in to be graded. I can drape it with the appropriate clothing after that. At this point I have 8 1/2 pages written and I feel as if I am 3/4 of the way through the essay. The essay still seems extremely muddy to me, so I am unable to see clearly the points I am trying to make. I need to sort out *exactly* what I want to say about Rodriguez's essay in order to clarify my essay. From there I need to weave my metaphor of the loom more thoroughly and securely into the piece. The entire piece has the substance of gauze, when I want the density of linsey-woolsey. It is also patched together with scraps of yarn, when I want high quality materials. And so I work on it. It is still fun and exciting to play with this essay. The metaphor of the loom and the warp has *many* possibilities. Time. I need a bigger loom for this project.

The final push through those twenty-four hours produced the tenth draft of the essay "Warping Time with Montaigne."

As with the first Montaigne paper, the beginning of this paper appeared in the first draft and remained largely unchanged throughout the remaining drafts. The rest of the essay changed drastically from draft to draft, and it was not until the eighth draft that I found the conclusion to the paper. The middle of the essay continued to grow and take shape, but the ending remained loose and unfinished. I had a loose collection of quotes and comments at the end of the early drafts that I knew I wanted to fit into the paper somewhere. I tend to do this when I write: I cultivate a garden patch of interesting and related thoughts at the end of whatever I am working on as a way of feeding life into my essay (and as a way of keeping me from forgetting insights I may have along the way). There are wonderful passages in that collection that never made it to the final draft. If I were to revise this paper again, I might try harder to fit them into the essay. At the time I was drafting this paper, though, I didn't have time to fit them in, and so after the essay became complete in the eighth draft, I used the ninth and tenth drafts to polish the language and the metaphor. I was forced to be done polishing when the due date arrived and I needed to submit the paper for a grade.

Looking back upon the process I went through to create "Warping Time with Montaigne" makes me realize that I almost always contain a heightened sense of excitement when I am in the process of learning something new or when I am playing with language. I love every stage of the writing process because I am at play throughout all of it. Even when I am struggling with a concept or with an adequate way to present a concept, I am excited by the infinite possibilities that present themselves to me. I may procrastinate before I start to write, but once I sit down to write, the rest of the world disappears, or becomes a resource at my beck and call. In this sense, the process I went through when I wrote "Warping Time with Montaigne" is not unlike my normal writing process. It was simply heightened by a metaphor that possessed particularly great potential. As part of my response to a journal prompt that was given at the end of the class asking me to "compare the Research and Analysis papers with the earlier papers in the course (my experience)," I wrote the following passage:

> It was very difficult to make the transition from personal essay to academic paper. I felt like I had just gotten the hang of the personal essay and was enjoying the freedom of the collage essay, when suddenly, I had to juggle references, documentation, and other people's arguments. It was not that the research paper was particularly difficult, as the *switch* was difficult. However, having made the switch, I then felt like I was on excellent footing for writing the analysis paper. I had felt the freedom of the personal essay and had plumbed my depths to discover the wealth of details I have within me to use for my writing; I had then felt the rigid demands of the research paper with all of its formality and tradition. Having gone through these two exercises, I was better able to appreciate what literary nonfiction essayists are trying to accomplish. I was able to appreciate Tompkins' "Buffalo Bill" essay in a way that I was incapable of at the beginning of the course. As a result, I felt tremendous excitement about writing the analysis paper. I understood the requirements expected of me in terms of scholasticism, yet I felt the freedom to assert my own voice and technique. What fun!

THIS is the process that led me to "Warping Time with Montaigne." It was a journey of discovery: first of myself and my knowledge, then of different forms of writing available for my use, and finally of the power of freedom, innovation, and inspiration. Fortunately for me, I am now able to start from here as I prepare future journeys through the writing process.

Lambing Midwife

Valerie Due

"Listen to that. You hear that chuckle?" Dad's breath floated gray in the halo from his flashlight and I shivered deeper into my coveralls, my eyes gritty with interrupted sleep.

"Who is it, mama?" His voice flowed low and warm, and he began to murmur to the sheep as he pushed among their woolly rumps and wide middles. His arms hung loose, and his knees wormed among the tightly packed sheep without force or speed as he slid the light over noses and tails in search of the noisemaker. I swung my own flashlight beam toward the deep beller of our ram, Earl, trapped in the lean-to while the girls got the warmer insides of the barn. Earl pawed at the gate between him and us, his hoof knocking the wood jam.

"Yeah, well, it's not feeding time yet," I grumbled at him, but he pawed again and I moved against the wall to reach over and scratch his cheeks. He grumbled back at me and his eyes half-closed. Earl was dangerous if you got in a pen with him, especially if there were girls in that pen, too, but we'd spoiled him as a yearling and he craved scratching. Problem was, you'd be scratching and suddenly he'd decide to kill you. A ram his size—about 250 pounds—could snap your femur or crack open your skull with one blow.

I heard the chuckle the second time and swung my light in the same direction as Dad's. Old Marybelle stood with her head low, silver teardrop nose nearly touching the ground, and I saw her sides clench and ripple through the six-inch-thick wool. Her eyes squinted and bulged and her nose stretched forward, then she whooshed a deep groaning sigh and chuckled again. She was in hard labor, and we needed to move her into a lambing pen so that we could help her if needed, and so that none of the other old ewes killed her babies when they came out. Ewes could be like that; the smell of a lamb that wasn't their own brought out an instinct to butt it into the ground with the same force that old ram might use to kill you. Dad warned us, and within a year we'd all know this truth firsthand.

For a week now we'd been watching closely each evening for half an hour after we'd fed the ewes; it was one of the few farm jobs at which I was equal to my big brother. "Maybe better," Dad had said as he grinned over the worn green *Animal Husbandry* manual filled with photos, advice, and diagrams related to caring for livestock. I knew what he meant. I was good at working stock—better than my brother, but not so good as Dad—and I had small hands. "Good for pulling," he'd said as he showed me the section I should read on birthing complications in ewes. So while my brother slept, I spent more time shivering in the barn each night with Dad, watching and listening for the signs, the ewe that didn't push in to eat like usual, the one that hung back, the one that seemed uncomfortable, shifting around on her hooves, raising and lowering her head. The one that chuckled was the one you really had to watch for; once they began talking to their babies, they're well on their way.

"Open the pen." Dad's voice was soft, and his tone never changed from the same smooth song he'd kept up since we'd come into the barn after the alarm woke us for the 2:00 a.m. check, except I could make out words now. Usually I couldn't understand much of what he said to the sheep; his vowels slid together like Danish poetry, soft and guttural and indistinct. He'd start these slow words before we'd reach the pool of light fed by our windmill's lamp outside the barn door, and by the time we'd open the door the old girls were awake and standing or lying comfortably against their favorite walls, confident that it was only us, no bother, nothing to get excited about. They shuffled and snuffled the last grains in the feed trough but didn't move off. If you didn't talk before you opened the door they wouldn't hear you coming, and when you opened the door they were likely to panic, scrambling out the rear door or crowding against the wall, jumping the feeder and risking a cut leg, or worse, losing their lambs, stillborn due to injury.

But our sheep never scrambled to escape the sudden appearance of humans the way some of our neighbors' stock did. Dad always talked to the sheep as he approached the barn, and I'd learned to do it, too. "No sense in spooking an animal," Dad said. "Scarin' 'em doesn't help them or you."

I sat my flashlight down and unwired the slat door on the solid walls of the lambing pen against one wall of the barn. During chores the sheep had seemed jumpy and two of them didn't push for grain, so I'd spread half a bale of straw in one pen and wired a two-gallon bucket and a heat lamp in the corner. Now I opened the gate between the main pen and the alleyway to the two lambing pens. My toes were already cold, despite thick wool socks snug in my cowboy boots. No wind scraped the icy plain that glittered an eternity in the dark, but the sky was clear and the cold so dry and deep that it seemed the air itself might crack like glass. The wire on the lambing pen's gate caught in my thick deerskin gloves and I tugged them off with my teeth to try again. The wires were cold; they seared bare skin, and my fingers jerked back as soon as the scrap of baling wire gave. I spat the taste of mud and manure and lanolin, then tugged the gloves back on.

Dad's singsong lowed over the ewes behind me, and I slipped into the flock and began to imitate his movements, hands low and close to my body, torso erect, relaxed, leaning back as I moved, eyes sliding over each animal but not staring at any ewe's face. Dad stood near Marybelle, but she seemed too immersed in her own suffering to care. He motioned me to circle behind her. I slipped sideways around the edge of the shifting flock, boots sinking in straw and warm manure. Marybelle heaved forward as Dad slid behind her and the flock shifted, the collective air now alert, the shuffling and sniffling louder. A ewe sneezed and farted simultaneously, breaking through Dad's talk. He laughed, and the sheep lifted their ears to him. A few of the tamest pushed against him for pets; Snowflake nearly knocked me down from behind in her trademark back-end sideswipe-and-lean, her "itch me here" maneuver. Marybelle trundled away from us, seeking privacy, and I moved alongside, body back, arms loose, just outside her comfort zone. Dad did the same on his side and the sheep flowed around him, away from the aisle and the lambing pen.

Marybelle tried to follow her flock, turning just before the open gate, and if I had been on Dad's side I'd have jumped forward to block her, causing her to leap back and sideways, so that the person on the other side would also have had to react with rapid blocking movements, and we'd have had to grab her and force her through the gate, her sides heaving with contractions. I'd tried that maneuver while sorting and catching for shearing; I could separate and catch any sheep of any size, even though I was barely 115 pounds myself and the big rams were over 200, but sometimes I couldn't read sheep the way Dad could, and I didn't always know how to back off before they panicked or how to head them off without driving them back. In that instant of movement and decision, damp wool and acrid manure, I knew that if I'd been on his side I'd have leaped to block her, and we'd have had to manhandle her into the pen, stressing her when she least needed it, and it would have been my fault, not the ewe's.

But Dad didn't leap to head off Marybelle. He just leaned forward and raised one hand slightly, fingers splayed, and kept talking.

"C'mon now girl, c'mon," he said, and she hesitated, turned slightly my way, then stepped into the alleyway toward Earl's pen and the lambing pens. Dad stepped behind her. He touched her woolly rump and she trotted into the open stall gate and the light of the heat lamp as he followed. I closed the alley gate and joined him outside her pen. He inspected her carefully; her thick wool had been "crutched" by us weeks earlier, so that her hind end looked bald and bare and there was no thick wool caked in sheep manure to risk contaminating the birth canal if we had to pull the lamb. He showed me how the trickle of fluid indicated the stage of labor, how if she'd eat and lie down we might gain another hour of sleep before we should check again, but since she wasn't a first-time mama, she might go quick, and one of us should sit with her.

Marybelle had narrow hips despite her broad loin, and Dad was worried. She'd had problems last year, and Dad expected a repeat; it was why we were able to buy her, with her pedigree and show-winning physique, from a breeder with a nationwide reputation. This was my first midwife job, the first time Dad said I could pull if the lamb needed pulling, and I knew I wouldn't sleep again, so

I stayed in the barn with her, waiting, shivering, wiring another heat lamp in the alley for my toes and fingers.

When the straining and grunting stretched long and deep and the fluid ran thick, I knew it was time to get Dad. No tiny hooves appeared, but the ewe strained, and the blood and fluid meant one was close, in the birth canal. Before I could run to the house, though, I heard Dad's voice, and the sheep and I all relaxed. The wood door scraped open and he called to me in the same low tone he used for the ewes.

For the next hour things happened fast but slow. I ran for the bucket of warm water from the house, lugging it up the long dirt driveway that cuts through our farm buildings, grumbling as I did during morning chores about the distance from our barn to the house, so far that you couldn't hear a scream from one to the other. I brought the pile of rags and the soap and the little loop of soft nylon on the end of a slim PVC pole, a lamb puller, but Dad hated to use it. He said you could kill the lamb or rip out a uterus if you didn't get it right, and the old sheepmen at the state fair and stock shows said the same. Better to have narrow hands and pull them yourself. That was going to be my job, and tonight would be my first. I could taste fear and anticipation on the back of my tongue as I hovered in the pen, the ewe long since ignoring me in her solo struggle. Dad talked as I watched him scrub his naked arm, his coat and denim shirt half off, long-johns sleeve pulled up to the armpit.

"She's tired. Been trying too long and nothin's coming out." He rinsed his arm in the white bucket, then dried it with a clean towel. "I'm going to feel if the lamb is breech, or just caught."

The ewe was down, head stretched flat out, eyes half closed as she strained again. Dad kneeled behind her, pattering, reassuring as she raised her head, concerned but too tired to stand. Dad slid his hand inside the blood, prodding for a tiny hoof or nose. He told me what he felt as his arm slid deeper, to mid-forearm, then elbow.

"Got a nose here. It's soft. Hooves are soft, too, but they have edges. You should get hooves first, not a nose first. The legs are back." The old ewe strained. Dad's arm muscles bulged; he gritted his teeth and stopped talking while she pushed against him. Then she relaxed and he started again, murmuring to her, describing to me.

"I'm trying to get my fingers behind the elbow, pull the leg forward," he said. "First you have to hook the leg with your fingers." Another contraction wrung grunts from them both. "Then when you have the leg, you push the chest back with your thumb and pull the leg forward." He swore; the leg slipped. Blood stained his long johns, and I grabbed the loose denim sleeve and pulled it behind him. He caught the leg again. After several long minutes broken by straining and grunting, he had pulled one leg forward but couldn't get the other. The lamb moved further into the canal now that one leg was forward in the proper position, but there wasn't enough room to maneuver his hand. He looked at me.

"Think you can do it?"

My own arms were thinner, my hands broad and long for a girl but smaller than a man's. I nodded and unzipped the warmth of my coveralls. My stomach flipped and tongue swelled; I wanted to do this well, to save the lamb and the ewe, to do something even Dad couldn't do. But I was also afraid.

After a scrub in the now-cool water, I knelt and slid my fingers inside the ewe, apologizing for the cold. She grunted and strained, and viselike pressure ground the bones in my palm and wrist against one another. It passed, and I felt the lamb's first hoof, tiny and soft with little edges, and now much closer to birth. Then my thumb found its little nose and face, slimy and slick as I worked under it, searching for the base of the neck, the chest, the other leg. After a while I began to think this lamb was missing a leg, a defect, but Dad told me it was further back, stretched behind whereas the other was stretched forward. A lamb doing the splits. The ewe was straining, and Dad told me we didn't have a lot of time; if we couldn't pull it soon we would need to use the puller or call the vet, and by the time he'd arrive we might need to abort the lamb to save the ewe. I didn't waste time slipping my finger in the lamb's mouth to check for a suck reflex, proof that the lamb was okay. I just kept pushing and feeling for a leg, straining against each contraction.

My fingers felt a bony protrusion—the lamb's shoulder—and I worked my way down, thinking of last year's lambs and how thin and scruffy they seemed for the first weeks, all bone and skin and nappy tight wool like Berber carpet. Then they fattened up and ventured beyond mama, bouncing off one another and the adult ewes, exploding in four-legged hops that we called "popcorning" around the yard, long tails wriggling as they tasted everything in the pen and charged up on the backs of the sleeping ewes. My fingers worked down and up the shoulder twice before I got far enough back to find the rubbery little elbow and circle it with my thumb and forefinger. Catching my breath, I waited for a contraction to end and then pushed as hard as I could, the heel of my hand against the lamb's chest. The lamb slid back, just as Dad said it would, and I pulled up on the leg, sliding my fingers down the foreleg like I was milking one of Lee's dairy goats. The upper leg came forward, knee bent, foreleg still back. A new contraction forced me to pause and fight the ewe, who by now didn't seem to care much whether the lamb was born or not. I fought to keep the lamb from sliding toward me again with the leg still half-bent under, and it didn't feel like my arm would break, the way the books described, but like my arm was being flattened, bones squished in a pressure roller. Then it passed and I pushed back again and pulled up, and the little leg slid forward so fast and easy that my eyes widened and I yelped to Dad. "Got it! I got it!"

"Shhhh . . . gooood old girl," he soothed, stopping the ewe from struggling at my yipping, and I felt ashamed. I'd broken a cardinal rule. From under the brim of my itchy blue stocking hat I peeked up to see my fate. Dad looked right at me, but he wasn't angry. He was grinning, his stubbled face red with cold under the brim and earflaps of his winter seed hat, and I forgot the cold and the lamb. He looked like I'd just won an award, his eyes wrinkled around the edges and his smile off-center.

"Now pull that baby out," he said, like it was the easiest thing in the world, and I grabbed the slippery hooves and pulled. Marybelle strained, and with a whoosh of blood and slime and yellow fluid, a black lamb poured three-quarters of the way out onto the straw between my knees, then oozed the last bit of gangly leg and tail. Marybelle revived and scrambled to her feet, chuckling in that low, soft, mama-ewe grunt. The lamb struggled to raise his wet head, and I knew he'd be okay. I didn't care at all that this lamb was a ram and might be castrated and sent to slaughter next fall. It was alive, and I helped it come out that way. It wasn't even a big lamb. It was just twisted the wrong way.

Dad tossed me a towel. "Wipe him off and come on out. We'll give them some time alone." He grinned and leaned against one of the barn's thick dark support beams, waiting for me. I dragged the towel down the lamb's wet limbs, and felt as though the sky itself could not contain my skin.

Gestating Memory: Capturing Narrative Details in "Lambing Midwife"

Valerie Due

> *We are lonesome animals. We spend all our life trying to be less lonesome. One of our ancient methods is to tell a story begging the listener to say—and to feel—"Yes, that's the way it is, or at least that's the way I feel it. You're not as alone as you thought."*
>
> John Steinbeck

The beauty and beast of narrative nonfiction is the specificity of human experience: The narrator is relating a specific event that happened only to him or her, but the telling of that experience must leave the reader feeling less alone in the world, feeling as though he or she has lived the same event under the same circumstances. I've often heard this called the *universal experience*, but that's inaccurate. For me, it's about universal emotion. Experiences are almost never universal; people live infinite experiences, each unique. It's emotions that we share; they are limited in both type and degree, and they allow us to identify with those whose lives we cannot otherwise fathom. I have never lost a husband to a heart attack while my daughter clung to life in intensive care, yet Joan Didion's *The Year of Magical Thinking* left me feeling as though I understood intimately the narrator's unique pain, anger, and confusion.

For me, a successful narrative requires transporting the reader into the author's physical world, so that the reader, too, lives the unique events that created the emotion, which in turn closes the gap between author and reader, between disparate lives. These narratives bring to life the colors and scents of someone else's experience; they animate the precise physical manifestations of emotions, ring with the sounds and unmet expectations alive on the lips of the storyteller. They dance with details rather than exposition. This is what I enjoy reading in nonfiction narratives; it's what I try to accomplish when I write.

"Lambing Midwife" is a single-scene narrative, born of a memory, and it's an example of three common experiences for nonfiction writers: It required me to recall minute details from long ago, it was not what I'd intended to write, and when it first appeared in my writing, I wasn't certain what significance this memory held for me or my readers.

This essay came about in my thesis semester. In stumbling into "Lambing Midwife", I started by trying to drill into the connection I have with animals raised for slaughter, seeking the origin of my beliefs about our responsibility as stewards to care for livestock humanely, even as we know they are heading for slaughter. My father taught me the language of animals, some by talking, but more by doing, and my brain's storage banks are crammed with scenes that form this whole. The essay I wanted to write when I started this piece wasn't an essay; it was a scene in a book-length narrative that I hoped would allow the reader to connect emotionally with some of what one child had lost—what all farmers and rural towns had lost—during the transition from self-sufficient family farming to large corporatized agriculture. The scenes that I'd hoped would resonate for the reader had proven elusive at the time that I wrote this essay draft.

Knowing that I wanted to illustrate my father's role in shaping my beliefs, I jotted a short list of related memories and began free-writing. Several of these had potential; all would eventually find their way out of my pen and onto paper. The scene in "Lambing Midwife" was not on this list, yet it was delivered from memory first.

Details cool and dull with the distance that memories naturally acquire over time. Even writers who kept notes and diaries will find themselves struggling to recover the brilliance of an event from long ago (this is doubly true if, like me, you burned 10 years' worth of childhood diaries in a fit of 18-year-old despair). Traditional journalistic research techniques work well for discovering details that can be used to write scenes and places, and much has been written about using research as part of the nonfiction craft, both before writing and to fact-check after. But when writing personal memories that are difficult to verify—a barn long-ago splintered by a tornado, a father who, like any of us, has changed in 30 years such that he both is and is not the man in my memory—many of these details must be found within the memory itself, then verified after. This process lies opposite the one that I learned as a young reporter.

This is the writing-from-memory process that works for me and that created "Lambing Midwife": I start with physical details from the memory's unique place. Place, to me, is the core of a memory. Often, a memory's physical place burns brightly in memory, while words blur to become general intent or meaning.

A single physical detail inevitably opens up memory for me, and I find myself reliving that moment from my senses at that time: Sights, sounds, smells, emotions, tastes.

I should note here that, like many people, I remember things visually and emotionally, rather than in the abstract. My mind captures images of memories, short movie clips and snapshots that are filed along with my feelings. As a writer, I find it odd that I don't often store spoken words unless they adhere themselves to a snapshot or film clip in memory (either the memory of the speaker speaking, or a visual somehow related). Likewise, written words become memory only when the words trigger an image or become one, such as an entire page of text from a college history textbook that captured my interest, a memory not of the content in the abstract but a visual snapshot of the page, which I can read now as easily as today's newspaper. This type of memory makes recalled dialogue both rare and distinct for me: If I remember actual words rather than distilled meaning or intent, then the words are as precise and crisp as the colors of the speaker's skin and clothing. This way of remembering no doubt shaped my writing process. It certainly helps me ease into difficult memories through first capturing physical descriptions, which tend to be non-threatening and thus a good starting point. The details are also exactly what I as a reader need to help me imagine an author's experience, imagine it richly enough that I, too, feel what the author felt.

Because I write from a visual memory, I focus on bringing back the physical and emotional details of the place in which the memory took place. I sit with my notebook or laptop, and shut out the world, focusing on one physical detail that I know to be true of the place where the event took place. This lets my mind relive the memory, sliding from my writing chair back to that barn, from age 40 to 11, losing knowledge and distance along the way, so that each detail sharpens and focuses long enough for capture by pen.

Smells are strongest; if I can recall a scent, images and sounds flood around it, emotions within. But the detail that opened this memory's floodgates was the taste of my work glove as I tugged it off to un-twist the rusty metal baling wire holding the gate closed. That taste remains as vivid and sharp today as it was then, and my tongue is now recoiling in response.

Ultimately, my writing process for "Lambing Midwife" was one I've unconsciously used for years, but only recently learned to trust: Sit, focus on one physical detail as a gateway, begin reliving the memory, write everything down as it comes, set it aside before seeking structure. For me, this process is fail-safe: If I follow it, something good will come, though not always what I'd intended.

Sometimes the memory I'm calling refuses to come back to life, and another wakes to take its place. "Lambing Midwife" is one of those serendipitous found narratives. The scene I'd intended to capture seeped with unresolved emotion, a bloody lambing with a very different long-term outcome. Settling in to write that memory, I found that I couldn't find a way into those details; the best I could manage was a logical, distant overview of what happened, how I'd reacted and felt at the time, and how it changed my perceptions.

That's one risk with writing from memory: Memories are intense full-senses experiences, rich with details of place, emotion, relationship, expectations, actions, sounds. But our gray matter turns them into flat, lifeless postcards, vignettes casually relayed as cocktail chatter, as a way of insulating ourselves from difficult emotions and their effects. It's not that we've forgotten each memory's particular intensity of joy or pain, it's that we can't successfully navigate life if our emotions crash from the exhilaration of a first kiss to the crush of a father's death in the instant, as those memories rouse to names, places, sounds, or scents.

What *happened* in a memory is usually the only thing I recall easily and can jot without effort. My first attempt at the story I'd intended to write stalled at this point; the logical side of my brain refused to step into that magic screening room where my memories still live as cinematic outtakes and Super-8 clips. Instead, it recalled another lambing in that same lambing pen, with a different ewe, in an earlier year. It sidestepped my intentions and seized a different memory.

When this happens, I've learned to let my brain go: This unexpected memory needs to come out. Sometimes it's the precursor to the memory I'm seeking. Sometimes it's not. Almost always, it becomes an entity of its own, and often it becomes the seed of an essay. What it ultimately becomes is irrelevant. What is important is the process of fully remembering and capturing a scene that affected me such that it remains in my mind's cinematic storage. The only way for me to understand the effect this event has had on me is to analyze it not just with the logic of acquired wisdom, but also with the shock of physical details and visceral emotions of a present-tense experience. That's the connection between my unique experience and my reader's unique experience.

When writing from memory, I write everything down. *Everything*. Only after the memory has been exhausted of details do I attempt to layer reflection or create a structure. I used to approach structure early, often before committing anything to paper, and this created mental blocks. I've learned that the physical details of a place are a starting point more effective than any plan or outline; this is how my memory works, how my brain connects. The rough draft from a concentrated memory-writing session is usually enough to tell me where a piece is heading and what structure it requires, though often not until it's been set aside for months— one disadvantage of the way I write is that I need to regain emotional distance after reliving the event in my mind.

The first draft of "Lambing Midwife" was thus an attempt to capture the moving pictures in my head, simply to put details on paper, whether they would be used or not. Editing can remove information that serves no purpose; but adding detail where there is none is impossible, in the same way that it is impossible to bring a blurry photograph into sharp focus, regardless of which high-priced photo-editing software you use. Also, remembering takes effort; it is exhausting, particularly when dealing with painful or highly emotional memories. When I've tapped into one, I stay with it as long as I can and write everything I see, hear, smell, touch, taste, and feel. When I'm finished, I know that I don't have to return to the memory again in search of details; if they existed, I've written them down.

If not, I will need to use other techniques and research to uncover and add them during revision.

While I write the memory, my mind often interrupts itself with background information or related memories. For instance, as I wrote "Lambing Midwife", my mind took a detour from the visual action to remember how hard I concentrated on remembering the diagrams in the green hardbound *Animal Husbandry* textbook Dad had given me, and I wrote this down because I remembered thinking of it while standing in the barn. During revision, I fleshed out the memory of sitting at our kitchen table together over the book's worn linen cover and thin, crackling pages.

I only write what comes to me in those memories; if there are holes or fuzzy details, I add or correct them while checking facts during revision, and this essay was no different. Fact-checking this memory was problematic, because the barn had long ago splintered, sheep pens moved, windmill light shattered. My few photographs of the barn and these ewes and lambs that year helped; as a born pack rat, I still had them. Likewise, essays and letters from elementary through high school confirmed occasional details, and a few volumes survived the diary-burning incident. My father remembers some of this night; he found nothing amiss.

Readers deserve to know about gaps in time or knowledge, or that details are in question, and in this essay language sets apart anything that I could not know at that time or that was not verifiable. However, while fact-checking, I stayed true to the memory that shaped me; details that differed in others' memories did not change the fact that my memory affected me. For this childhood memory, my family was a good starting point, though not a definitive source: My mother once insisted that my childhood dog had never had puppies, only to recall weeks later not only the birth, but traumatic details surrounding the deaths of those formerly nonexistent pups. Research uncovered facts reported elsewhere, such as the weather report in a local newspaper, but details for which no record existed remained problematic. My treatment of these was simple: If a family or community member corroborated, it remained. Had someone disagreed, it would have been noted in reflection. Any information that could not be known during the memory or is not part of my memory is indicated clearly:

> *Ewes could be like that; the smell of a lamb that wasn't their own brought out an instinct to butt it into the ground with the same force that old ram might use to kill you. Dad warned us, and within a year we'd all know this truth firsthand.*

This reflection and the background paragraph following were written as I wrote the memory, in the rough draft. In my memory of that night, my brain recalled the later experience with ewes hurting lambs, at the same time that it replayed standing in that cold pen, ewes blinking in the yellow light of the bare overhead bulb Dad had snapped on, and thinking I ought to open the pen. I wrote this knowledge as it came to me, in future tense, and when I revised the essay to shape it, I left it as such to signal that it was not firsthand knowledge at that time. During revision, that bit of exposition prompted the background on our nightly lambing vigils, which I added to help the reader understand my world as a child then, on that farm.

This first draft looked much as the finished essay does, and I suppose I should apologize for that. But I find this is often the case. The memories that slide nearly whole from my mind are those that require little additional work to become fully formed essays. This, I believe, is part of the unconscious act of writing. Because I'd been thinking about this topic for a long time—nearly 18 months at the time of writing—my mind had made connections that would otherwise have been done on paper during the editing process. This particular piece was revised only twice, once to fact-check and add background and exposition before submission to *River Teeth*, and once after, for grammar. Neither revision changed the content of the memory itself.

At first draft, I disliked "Lambing Midwife." I wasn't sure why this memory had stayed with me, or why it fought to come out. But after setting it aside for a month, I re-read it to see if I could find a meaning in the memory. That month helped me regain distance, and I recognized that the memory's significance to the child-me narrator and to me now—and, I hoped, to my readers—was already in the essay, in two short sentences near the end: *"I didn't care at all that this lamb was a ram and might be castrated and sent to slaughter next fall. It was alive, and I helped it come out that way."*

Because this essay's emotional significance turned out to be complete in the original draft—if only this happened more often!—that first revision added only bits of background and exposition about lambing and our flock at that time, and removed details that I felt added nothing to the reader's experience of this memory, such as the precise L-shape of the barn's alleyway and exact location of each gate. The final revision also added the essay's final sentence as it appeared in publication in *River Teeth*: *"We'd saved this one together, and it felt better than rain on a July-scorched hide."* I remembered this elation; thinking that nothing I'd done before felt so right, so connected with our farm and the earth itself. The closest emotional memory I had was of rain during a drought several years earlier, an event we celebrated by dancing over our cracked-dirt driveway, fat raindrops cooling sunburned skin. That final sentence always bothered me, though. It didn't fit the imagery of that night, the sense that the cold, still air itself gestated possibilities. For this publication, I revised the end; proof that I never quite feel that I've finished a piece.

During revision, I fact-checked everything possible, using those photographs and my brother's and father's memories. I checked our flock record books to verify my age at the time, though unstated, and the ewe and lamb in question. I used the lambing dates on record to further confirm some of those physical details that help readers bridge that gap between their experiences and mine. The weather that night was exactly as I remembered: Cold, clear, and sharp; dry and still; expectant.

Teacher Training

Mary Elizabeth Pope

I stand at the drinking fountain in the hallway outside my classroom. It is the first day of classes, and it is my first day as a graduate teaching assistant. I have no teaching certification to prepare me for this position, and as my qualifications are limited to the grades I earned as an undergraduate in English, I have no idea how I will meet the challenge of teaching Freshman Composition. Earlier, as I passed the classroom, I glanced in to see a number of students sitting in their desks, waiting. I think of all those students now, and wonder about all their different needs—how can I address them collectively, and still address them as individuals? How can I know what they need from me when I have no training or experience with teaching? My watch reads 7:59 am, so I move reluctantly toward the door behind which my students sit. My hands are shaking, and the knot in my stomach is threatening to snap me in half. My heels click on the tiled floor as I enter the classroom and make my way to the podium.

I sat in the new desk on the first day of fifth grade, watching my new teacher pass out textbooks. It was all I could do to sit still for so long; I had been waiting for this day all summer. The new pencils and paper and folders I'd saved my fifty cent allowance for were already arranged in my tray, and I placed each new textbook that Mrs. Crane handed out beside them, feeling very mature. The first day of school was like a clean slate for me; all of the mistakes from fourth grade left safely behind me in Mr. Smith's room and in Mr. Smith's mind. I watched my new teacher as she handed out books; she was a woman of about fifty, and very pretty in a hard sort of pancake makeup way. She walked more purposefully than any woman I had ever known, her posture perfect as she slowly, deliberately put one high-heeled shoe out and placed it carefully in front of her before shifting her weight directly onto it. Her careful, composed walk would be something I would never forget—the way her shoulders moved as she walked, the way her hair didn't, the angle at which she held her chin. I knew instantly that I wanted her to like me, that I wanted to do well in her class, to please this woman whose authority radiated from her every gesture, rang clear in her every word. I rode the bus home that afternoon, bursting with excitement, anxious to tell my mother all about my new teacher.

My students stare at me the first day. Some of them look at me directly; others avert their gaze in case my eyes meet theirs. They are sizing me up. That's okay; I am sizing them up, too. I pass out the syllabus, and discuss classroom policy and course requirements with them. I tell them they must have a C in order to pass my class. They say nothing until I ask them to introduce themselves to the class and say where they are from. After much shifting in their seats, and mumbling out their introduction sentence, they gratefully return their eyes to me. I try hard not to smile too much on the first day, although it is hard. I try to encourage them to understand how my class will help them with all of their classes; I try hard to make them understand that they all have something important to say, that they are all unique and no single other person has the perspective they do. They look at me. I look back at them. I don't know if they believe me or not when it is time to dismiss them, but I watch them file out, and feel hopeful.

I stood in the dime store for maybe thirty minutes, wondering what Mrs. Crane's favorite color was. The folders were there on the shelf—pink, yellow, green, blue, red. On another shelf sat the folders I wished for: clear, plastic binders with front picture slots on the cover. I could just see a collage of Abraham Lincoln underneath those picture slots—Mrs. Crane would like that for sure. But I had only fifty cents, and the clear plastic binders were ninety-nine cents, while the colored cardboard folders were thirty-nine cents. Mrs. Crane wore a lot of blue—navy blue—but since the dime store only carried a cornflower color of blue—and because it seemed the only color suitable for Abraham Lincoln of the colors available, I took one blue folder to the counter, and watched the lady ring it up. I was sad. What could I do with a plain blue folder that would make Mrs. Crane notice it? I wanted her to know how hard I'd worked on my report, and how much I wanted to do everything right for her. I wanted her to like me.

Holly comes to my office at least once a week. She worries all the time; so much so, that she is terrified to commit anything to paper. She is careful to meet all of the requirements in an assignment, yet she is so careful that it stifles all of the creativity in her expression. She always asks me what I want her to write. Today, her curly brown hair is pulled back in a bun, and above her ruddy cheeks, her eyes are tired and bloodshot, no doubt from staying up all night working, or worrying that she should be working. She is a perfectionist to the point of self-destruction, and although I am pleased with her work, I know she could be more expressive if she were not so afraid of making mistakes.

The assignment I give today is to freewrite about what they want to say in their coming papers. I tell them I won't be grading these and that the only thing that matters is what they discover about their topic. I give them thirty minutes, and I watch Holly hunch over her desk and begin writing. After class, I ask her to stay behind a moment so I can look at her writing. It is thoughtful and original, and much better than what she has been turning in to me on a regular basis. I tell her I want to see her this week, knowing I will anyway. I am hopeful that we can make some progress.

Mrs. Crane stood regally before the class, holding a stack of reports in her hand. I could hardly wait to get mine back and read what she had written. I had worked so hard, and had so carefully and creatively constructed the cover, that I was sure that she would love it. "Class," she began, "why don't we take a look at some of the reports you handed in to me?" I was even more excited—I just knew she would pick mine as a good example for a creative cover, and I could hardly wait to see what she said about it when she held it up. "This is James' report—see how he pasted a mapped picture of Michigan on the cover of his folder for his Michigan report? Very nice. . . ." Next, she held up a crumpled sheet of paper which was half written on in pencil. "This . . ." she paused and her voice fell, as she extended the paper away from her body and pinched it between two fingers, as if it were dirty, or smelled bad, ". . . is Kevin's report." She quickly put Kevin's report on the bottom of the pile, and picked up the next one, commenting favorably on the reports she liked, and giving the same disdainful look and treatment as Kevin's report got to those she did not appreciate. I waited excitedly. I could see the blue edge of my folder sticking out of the pile . . . closer and closer it came to the top . . . and then it was in her hand. "This is Mary Beth's report," she said quickly, and made no comment on it at all, quickly replacing it on the bottom of the pile. I was crushed. My blue folder, with the pennies glued on to form the letters A and L, looked pitiful in the light of Mrs. Crane's disinterest in it. I had been so proud of it, had so carefully selected the shiniest pennies in my father's penny jar to use for the lettering, had handed it in with such confidence; now it seemed a pathetic idea, and I felt embarrassed as my cheeks glowed hotly, wondering how many students were looking at my flushed face, my burning ears.

Jonathan demands a lot of attention. He sits in the front row of my 9:00 class, and has assumed the role and voice of ringleader for the class. He is very entertaining, and I enjoy having him in class most of the time. His constant need to prove that he is the "best" or the most intelligent student in my class, however, is frustrating, because when the class gets into a debate over a particular issue, he cannot let a subject go until he feels he has won. I try to remain a neutral facilitator, although I have at times had to interrupt when Jonathan gets out of hand. I can tell this frustrates him, and I struggle to understand this unfulfilled need he has to be in the spotlight at all times.

Today, I hand back all of the papers except for one that I have saved to read to the class. It is well written, funny, and it meets the assignment's requirements. I choose it because it is a good example, but I have another motive. "I have a paper I'd like to read to you," I tell them. "I enjoyed it and I think all of you will, too." As I read, the class laughs appreciatively, and I do, too. When I am finished, I launch into a description of the next assignment. The students bend over their notes and begin writing, and I casually set Jonathan's paper on his desk. He is smiling, and beads of sweat have formed on his forehead. He is happy, and I am glad. For the rest of the period, things go well.

When Mrs. Crane handed back the folders, I had a second flash of hope: maybe she had only disliked the cover—maybe she had liked the report itself. I watched the other students read her comments, and when my folder was finally in my hands, I flipped through the pages, anxiously looking for her scrawling red script. I couldn't find anything, except for a check mark to signify that she had read it. I looked again, more frantically, and then realized that she had written nothing at all.

Nicole sits in the fifth row, hidden behind Drew, who is tall, and Thomas, who is large. I can just see the top of her blonde head peering at me occasionally as I teach; she is tentative, curious, nervous. Sometimes when class is over and she is on her way out the door, she will glance at me shyly and smile, a blush travelling from her ears to her nose. Nicole works very hard at my assignments; all of her in-class writing is printed, perfectly neat and straight. She is always the last to finish writing. Her papers are very well done, and she is meticulous about meeting every requirement I ask for in each paper. Her writing also reflects the deep thought she puts into the ideas we discuss in class. In Freshman Composition, I could not ask for a better student. .

I like to watch her when I hand back papers. On this particular day, what little of her face I can see is lit up, and I am glad for what I have written on the bottom of her paper. "Nicole—this is excellent. Again, I commend you. You meet all of the requirements for this paper, and express your depth of thought on these issues very well. This is the highest grade I have given on this paper, so you should feel proud." I can see all the way from the front of the room that she does.

My name was on the blackboard. Mrs. Crane posted the names of students who had misspelled words in their weekly assignments there until those students could find the correct spelling for the words they had missed. On Monday, my name stood out among the other names simply because it was my name and it had never been on that list before. Then, as the names were gradually erased, those spelling ex-convicts were allowed to join the ranks of the anonymous students who had spelled perfectly that week. Slowly, the list dwindled, and by Thursday, my name was the only one left. I was frustrated. The word was "no one" and it was not one word, as I later learned, but two. I had written "noone," and Mrs. Crane had circled it. I had stared at it for a long time, and then fetched a dictionary from the back shelf of the room. I knew that "someone" and "anyone" and "somebody" and "anybody" and "nobody" were all words. Where was "noone"? I tried "noon," thinking it could be used two ways. Still, it came back marked wrong. I tried "nowan," and again it was marked wrong. On Thursday, I showed Mrs. Crane that it was not in the dictionary. "Well," she had replied frostily, "I can't do anything about that, Mary Beth. The ways you have tried are all wrong." She then dismissed me. I walked back to my desk with heavy heart and burning cheeks, staring at my name on the board. All of the other names were gone, and now everyone knew that I was the stupid girl who couldn't spell. For two long weeks, I stared at my name on the board, the chalky white letters seeming to jump off the blackboard and proclaim to the class my ignorance. Every night, I would hope that some diligent custodian would erase my name by accident. Every morning, my mark of shame would still be there. And every day, Mrs. Crane told me, "It's still wrong."

Darrin sits in the second row of my 9:00 class. I have just returned his paper, and I can see the disappointment that registers on his face. Most mornings, Darrin hides beneath a baseball cap, watching me furtively from beneath it, retreating turtle-like under the visor if my gaze lands momentarily on him. He is a hard worker, and shows up regularly to my office hours to ask for help. I am sorry when I receive his work to have to give it a C+ because of his errors. Darrin has difficulty with spelling and commas, but his work in general is often entertaining and interesting. On the bottom of this particular paper, I have written, "Darrin— this is very funny—I enjoyed reading it. I can see that you are improving the organization and maintenance of focus in your writing. Keep it up (smiley face)! I am still concerned about your use of commas and number of spelling errors that have appeared here. Come see me and we'll talk about it. Good work overall." I know that Darrin will come to my office hours after class. I know what I will say to him. I know how he will respond. And regardless of whether or not he uses the dictionary or spellcheck, regardless of whether the exercises with commas that I will cover with him improve his writing, I know that he will leave my office feeling that he is a good writer who needs a little brushing up, rather than feeling he is a bad writer who is hopeless. He will leave knowing he is capable of doing better, and hopefully this will drive him to improve on his next paper.

On the day before Christmas vacation, we'd made ornaments in Mrs. Crane's class. My ornaments did not look like everyone else's. I had taken the pastry dough and twisted strips together to form candy canes, like the cookies my mother sometimes made at home. I loved art lessons, and I was happy with my ornaments. Mrs. Crane strolled up and down the aisle and paused to compliment those ornaments that she liked. She paused at my desk, and I waited, hopeful that she liked mine. She looked confused for a moment, and then walked quickly up to the front of the room and said, "Now class, let me show you again how to use the cookie cutters. Remember, these ornaments are going to hang on the tree in the big hallway, so we want them to look nice and neat." She searched for a particular cutter. "See," she said with false brightness, as she showed us how to cut the starchy dough, leaving a row of perfectly straight Gingerbread Men in her wake, "they all come out exactly the same if you use a cookie cutter."

Eric is angry. Ever since the first day he walked into my class, it has radiated from him, the aura of anger that surrounds him reminding me of the cloud of dust that follows the *Peanuts* character Pigpen everywhere he goes. With his long, red ponytail and goatee, he sits, withdrawn from the rest of the class, in the back corner, hiding behind his black leather jacket. Eric is brilliant; his forcefully written, anti-establishment, rebellious papers are testimony to this. He is by far the most openly creative student I have, and I handle him carefully because I know he is volatile. However, when he misses several classes in a row, I decide to take action. I stop him on his way out the door and ask him if he will make an appointment with me. He says yes, and we agree on a time. I don't know what I will say to him yet, or whether he will even show up. I only know that I do not want to lose this incredibly bright student, to let him slip through the cracks and disappear, never to return to my class. I am hoping that all he needs is some encouragement.

On the last day of fifth grade, we were allowed to take our brown bag lunches outside and sit on the lawn in front of the school. I sat with my class and watched Mrs. Crane talk to the students who sat around her. I sat far on the outside of the circle with another girl, and we traded Lifesavers and halves of our sandwiches. When the buses pulled up to take us home that day, Mrs. Crane stood by the door, and hugged each of us. I waited, dreading the hug, but knowing I couldn't get past her. She made a big show out of it, telling the students how much she would miss all of them. When my turn came, she put her mushy arms around me and my cheek burned where it touched her neck. When she finished hugging me, she put her hands on my shoulders and shook me a little. "I'm expecting big things from you, Mary Beth." My eyes filled up with tears. I managed good-bye and followed the other students on to the bus. I hated her even more for lying like that in front of all of my friends. As I stood behind the other students in line for my bus, I wondered why she would say such a thing. The way she had treated me all year told me everything I ever wanted to know about what she expected from me.

Mark sits in the back row of my classroom with Walter and Jonathan. All three are football players, and while Walter and Jonathan often doze or talk disruptively, Mark tries to listen closely to what I have to say. He asks questions in class and comes to my office regularly. He is creative and earnest, and usually manages to separate himself, if only in attention span, from his teammates.

I hand his paper back without a grade. While his writing is nearly error free, and might have been an "A" for another assignment, he has not met any of the requirements for this paper. Were I to grade it, it would have failed. I know he is a good writer and I do not want to discourage him, so I write on the bottom of his paper, "Mark—your writing, in terms of mechanics and style, is excellent. As a creative piece, this would have received an "A." However, for this assignment, you haven't met the requirements I needed to see. I know you are busy, but I'd like to meet with you and discuss what you need to change here. This is very good writing, Mark, but it doesn't meet the criteria I spelled out in class. You can take your time with it. See me first and we'll talk." Mark reads my comments and looks confused for a moment, but he nods slowly, and I know he understands. I know I haven't crushed him, and I know he will come see me and do better the next time.

Composing "Teacher Training"

Mary Elizabeth Pope

The idea for the "Teacher Training" piece came out of a journal activity assigned in a graduate nonfiction class asking each of us to make a list of all of the topics we would never write about and why. I wrote down "Mrs. Crane" [not her real name] among other things, because even though I was in fifth grade when I had her for a teacher, she was still affecting me in a negative way as a graduate student. The reason, though, that she had made it on the list of things I would never write about was because several months after I'd had her for a teacher, she'd been killed in a car accident. Although I'd never admitted it to anyone but my mother, I had gone home every day in fifth grade praying she would die somehow. I was still harboring a lot of guilt over that, because for years after she was killed, I had nightmares about her; I was convinced that God had answered my prayers and that I was responsible for her death. I still won't ever write about that aspect of my relationship with her, but the exercise got me thinking.

The third paper was to be a personal, non-fiction essay and we were all encouraged to experiment with a format we hadn't used very often. I wasn't sure what to write about, so I went back to my list of things I would never write about, took her name, put it in the middle of a blank page and did some clustering, just to see what would happen. As I clustered, I realized that I had a lot to say about this woman; from the clustering page, I started to freewrite and couldn't believe how angry I was getting just thinking about the things she used to do to me in class. She was the kind of teacher who used humiliation tactics to teach her students, and she really disliked me, even though I tried hard to be a good, hard-working, well-behaved student. I wasn't sure of what aspect of her teaching I wanted to focus on, or if I really wanted to focus more on my reaction to her techniques, but I knew I had a lot to say because I couldn't stop writing.

Another circumstance enters into this topic and my choosing to write about it—at the time I began to write this piece, I was in my second semester teaching freshman composition as a graduate assistant. The whole time I was scribbling about the things she used to do to me in class, I was thinking about myself as a teacher and couldn't imagine ever treating my students the way she treated me. My own teaching position had given me a new perspective on the whole Mrs. Crane issue, and it was one I could never have had before then, because I'd never taught. So as I "freewrote," I kept thinking about that aspect of it, although it didn't enter into any of my initial writing.

It actually took me a long time to determine what I wanted to do with this piece, because I knew I had a lot to say about it, and it felt really good getting it on paper. I'd been carrying it around for about thirteen years and had never really discussed it in detail with anyone, except for my mother at the time Mrs. Crane was killed. She had had a profound effect on my confidence as a student. Before I had her for a teacher, my other teachers always made me feel like I was really bright and put me in advanced reading groups and had given me higher level workbooks; I'd always assumed that I was one of the "smart kids," I guess. Before I had her as a teacher, I'd never questioned my abilities or my intelligence; after I had her, I always questioned it, even into graduate school. Getting it out on paper gave me a sense of relief, but at the same time, there was this urgency to do something with it because I needed to make sense of it.

I started with a segmented essay. Although I knew I wanted to use specific episodes from my year in her classroom—I had most of those written—I wasn't sure what to juxtapose with them. I thought of, and actually played around with, a speech I'd been forced to give about her at a tree dedication ceremony. The circumstances were odd—no other student was available to give the speech, and so my sixth grade teacher asked me to do it and gave me about two weeks to prepare. So I had to think about what I could say. No matter what I said about her, if it was nice, it would be a lie. My mother and I worked out a way where I could give the speech without actually saying that I had liked her or that I missed her. And so I played around with juxtaposing the day I gave that speech and the episodes in her classroom. One of the segments went like this:

> "My name is Mary Beth Pope," I began hesitantly, and swallowed out of fear involuntarily. "I was a student in Mrs. Crane's class last year." I paused, thinking of the things I was about to say, and looked at my first notecard. "Mrs. Crane taught us to sing The Grand Old Flag," I said, thinking that all she really taught us was to doubt ourselves, to be afraid, to never put yourself into anything you did lest it be rejected utterly and completely. "She . . . she, uh, liked us to push our . . . uh, chairs in. . . ." She also liked to push us until we cried. I looked out at the crowd, and the principal, and at her husband and sisters who sat directly below me. I did not belong here, giving this speech. The wind blew my dress and made me shiver. My voice broke and I began, "She also. . . ." I stopped.

It worked okay, but it wasn't really saying what I needed it to say.

After I had done that first freewriting, I prepared for this piece further by visiting the school and classroom where I'd had her for a teacher. The building wasn't being used as an elementary school at the time; it was part of an adult education site, and so there were big desks and bulletin boards with announcements instead of seasonal decorations. But the green shag carpet was still there, and the low chalkboards, and the same heaters where we used to dry our mittens under the window ledges. And the smell was exactly the same. I just stood there and looked. I couldn't breathe very well and the whole thing felt very claustrophobic. I couldn't believe how nothing had changed in terms of my reaction to the room; I instantly felt stupid and ashamed and on guard just by walking through that door at the age of 23, as intensely as I had felt it every morning when I would get off the bus and head for the room when I was ten. It was wild—it really triggered a lot of memories that helped me to remember more specific details in the segments from fifth grade.

After I made that visit to the classroom I talked to my mom about it. We talked about different days that I had come home crying because of something she'd done to me, and Mom even remembered things I had forgotten. The combination of the visit to the classroom and the discussion with Mom helped me to gel some of the ideas that had been brewing or seemed disconnected, and really got me going on the Mrs. Crane segments, although I still was playing around with the "speech" contrast idea and not feeling like it was going in the right direction.

What ultimately happened was that in a peer workshop session, I brought up my concerns about it, and a fellow graduate assistant and I talked about how awful some of our teachers were, and how, now that we were teachers, we couldn't imagine treating our students the way we'd been treated. This was very much an issue for me as I'd been working on the piece, and my friend suggested that maybe I should focus on that aspect of it and drop the whole "speech" thing. Everything fell into place when she said that, and I went home that night after class and just wrote it all out, using different students to compare my teaching style with Mrs. Crane's. I started with a clustering exercise using a few students who struggled with things similar to the issues I struggled with in Mrs. Crane's class, and tried to line up my fifth grade issues with their issues in my class. Then I did a journal entry on how to put it together in the essay, which went like this:

> What I need to do with this paper is show how having been through Mrs. Crane's class, I am much more sensitive to their feelings—I see the defenses, I see the fear, I see the need for approval in them. What I need to do is match one incident from fifth grade with one I've had with my students. For instance, match Darrin with my spelling, Nicole with my need for Mrs. Crane to like me, Mark with the math problems, Jonathan with my need to be admired, Brian with my frustration level, Eric with my need to be understood and accepted, Jason with my need for freedom and creativity within an assignment.
>
> I need to show the little fight I have every day trying to build their confidence while improving their writing skills.
>
> A final paragraph might be me, hunched over a stack of papers late at night. My comments are long—I write at the very least a half a page per student. I am tired. It would be easier to pick out the wrong things and scribble all over their pages, but I cannot.

I still wasn't sure about the exact structure the paper would take—like what student or incident in Mrs. Crane's class to use first, second, etc., but I knew what direction I wanted to go with it, and started writing and rearranging.

Once I had that figured out, the major problem I ran into was how to introduce the piece and how to conclude. I wasn't even sure what exactly I was trying to say, except that having a teacher who made me feel badly about myself helped me to be more sensitive to my own students—I remembered how it felt when she would ignore me or downplay my efforts or tell me I was stupid or wrong. I figured that a logical way to begin would be with the beginning of my first semester teaching, or at the end, looking back on how I had felt at the beginning. I had worried a lot about having had no training in teaching, only in English, and it had bothered me that whole first semester. Over the course of the semester I realized that I had plenty of experience with teaching because I'd been a student my whole life, watching teachers teach. I would think about my favorite English teachers (which was easy because all of my favorite teachers in high school and college taught English) and how they did things, and I'd try and be like them. It never occurred to me that I might have learned the most about how to teach from the worst teacher I'd ever had.

Also, I wanted to conclude by saying that having Mrs. Crane for a teacher made *me* a better teacher—that I had a better understanding of student needs because I'd had experience with my own needs not being met. The problem was how to get it across without making it sound like, "Mrs. Crane was a terrible teacher and I'm a great teacher because I don't do things the way she did," as that wasn't the point. The point was to show that I was able to turn that negative experience into something positive for both my students and myself. I also was hoping that it would be the kind of thing that other teachers could read which would make them think about teachers *they'd* had who'd hurt *them,* and get in touch with their own perspectives as former students. It's kind of a universal experience—I mean, we've all had bad teachers—and I was banking on that so I wouldn't have to do so much explaining.

Actually, I did a lot of explaining anyway in the first draft of the paper—the first paragraph began at the end of the semester of teaching, looking back, and sort of telling what I had learned. This is what it looked like:

> For weeks before my first semester of teaching began, I suffered from severe nausea. My main concern was that I had no experience with teaching—no classes, no training, no nothing. I walked into class on the first day, opened my mouth to speak, and before I knew it the semester was over. I wondered where I had learned to teach, and it was only after that first semester was over, and I had time to think about it, that I realized that I had been a student my whole life. I realized that my real training began in the fifth grade with Mrs. Crane. I have come to believe that only so much of teaching is curriculum; the rest is instinct. For most of my life I have hated this woman who destroyed my self-esteem and all the confidence I'd ever had in myself as a student at the age of eleven. Now, I thank her. Perhaps because of her—or maybe in spite

of her—I am too sensitive to my students' needs, and at times I worry that I am too gentle with them. But I am not sorry; in fact, I prefer to be that way, because I know now that my experiences in her classroom that year have made me a better teacher.

It's awful, when I look at it now, because I manage to sound exactly the way I didn't want to. I concluded the same way, with the teaching evaluations the students wrote at the end of the semester, and I used examples of what they said about me to confirm what I "said" in the body of the paper, comparing my experience with Mrs. Crane to my experience as a teacher. The truth is that when I got back the evaluation sheets that the students had written at the end of that first semester, I sat on the floor of my kitchen and was terrified to open them. When I finally did, and I read the nice things that the students had said about my teaching, I realized that maybe I was a good teacher and that I hadn't done the horrible job that I thought I had. I cried for about two hours that day because the whole semester I'd been afraid I wasn't a good teacher and that my inexperience showed. A lot of them said that they felt like I really cared about them, and that made me think about Mrs. Crane, and how she hadn't cared at all. So when I wrote the conclusion, all that went into it because it was exactly what I was experiencing at the time.

I didn't recognize immediately that both the introduction and conclusion were too self-conscious, and told more than they showed. I didn't really need either—I'd made my point by virtue of the contrast—but I felt obligated to set up some kind of a chronology and demonstrate what I'd learned about my teaching. When my composition instructor handed back the first draft, he said that he liked all of it except the introduction paragraph, which he felt "covered too much ground," and so I took that out and changed it to a scene of me waiting outside my classroom on the first day of class, worried about how I would manage to teach fifty students when I had no experience with teaching at all. Once I did that, I was really happy with it—it gave it the feeling that the reader was going to be there with me, walking into the classroom, scared to death like I was, and it removed that filter of my self-consciousness. I also did some major revisions on what my students said to me in the evaluations—because although I'd taken the quotes right off the evaluations, they were so unbelievably positive and sweet that it made me sound like I was bragging which, again, wasn't the point. What I was trying to do with the evaluations was to give the reader the same sense of "wow" and relief that I'd felt when I read them myself on the floor of the kitchen that day.

That was the point the paper was at when I handed it in for a final grade at the end of the semester, and that was close to the form it was in when I submitted it to the *Language Arts Journal of Michigan*. I did feel at one point that the sections on Mrs. Crane were too wordy, too self-pitying, and that the segments about my teaching were too self-righteous; however, when I was writing it, it felt good to discover something positive had come from that terrible year, and I got really excited about it. Before I submitted it to *LAJM*, I tried to tone it down a little, although after I went back and read it again, I realized I didn't need to make as many changes as I thought.

The draft I sent out ended with the following segments (I had chosen to distinguish past and present by putting the experiences with Mrs. Crane in past tense and italics and my experiences as a teaching assistant in present tense and plain text):

The tears in my eyes blurred the long division problems together until I couldn't see anymore. This was the best day of the month—free morning—and all of the other kids were down in the gym playing games and having fun. Three times I had redone the missed problems, eight of the forty she had given us, and run excitedly down the three flights of stairs to the gym, anxious to join my friends. Three times I had trudged back up the stairs, and been made to sit and rework the problems. I was so frustrated that I couldn't even see the paper, which had been erased so many times that I could see the pattern on my desk through what was left of the paper. Added to this were the tears that now made the page not only wet, but the answers I had gotten right, blurry. I couldn't bring myself to face her again, and I just knew that I could never do it right for her. I hated long division. Mrs. Crane hated me. And I had no idea what to do about it. I couldn't understand why she had singled me out to rework my missed problems—after all, I had worked as hard as all of the other students. And how was it that they all had answered their questions right? Was I the only one who couldn't get the problems right? Maybe it had nothing to do with the work, I thought. Maybe I wasn't pretty enough. She liked Erin and Laurie, who were both pretty. That had to be it—I worked as hard as both of them, but she still didn't like me. Or maybe it really was that I was the only one who didn't know how to do long division exactly right every time. I gave up wondering, and forgot about the gym. It hurt too much to hope that she would let me be like everyone else, so I abandoned my problems and went to look out the window instead.

Mark sits in the back row of my classroom with Walter and Jonathan. All three are football players, and while Walter and Jonathan often doze or talk disruptively, Mark tries to listen closely to what I have to say. He asks questions in class and comes to my office regularly. He is creative and earnest, and usually manages to separate himself, if only in attention span, from his teammates.

I hand his paper back without a grade. While his writing is nearly error free, and might have been an "A" for another assignment, he has not met any of the requirements for this paper. Were I to grade it, it would have failed. I know he is a good writer and I do not want to discourage him, so I write on the bottom of his paper, "Mark—your writing, in terms of mechanics and style, is excellent. As a creative piece, this would have received an "A". However, for this assignment, you haven't met the requirements I needed to see. I know you are busy, but I'd like to meet with you and discuss what you need to change here. This is very good writing, Mark, but it doesn't meet the criteria I spelled out in class. You can take your time with it. See me first and we'll talk." Mark reads my comments and looks confused for a moment, but he nods slowly, and I know he understands. I know I haven't crushed him, and I know he will come see me and do better the next time.

On the last day of fifth grade, we were allowed to take our brown bag lunches outside and sit on the lawn in front of the school. I sat with my class and watched Mrs. Crane talk to the students who sat around her. I sat far on the outside of the circle with another girl, and we traded Lifesavers and halves of our sandwiches. When the buses pulled up to take us home that day, Mrs. Crane stood by the door, and hugged each of us. I waited, dreading the hug, but knowing I couldn't get past her. She made a big show out of it, telling the students how much she would miss all of them. When my turn came, she put her mushy arms around me and my cheek burned where it touched her neck. When she finished hugging me, she put her hands on my shoulders and shook me a little. "I'm expecting big things from you, Mary Beth." My eyes filled up with tears. I managed good-bye and followed the other students on to the bus. I hated her even more for lying like that in front of all of my friends. As I stood behind the other students in line for my bus, I wondered why she would say such a thing. The way she had treated me all year told me everything I ever wanted to know about what she expected from me.

I sit on the floor of the living room on the day I receive my student evaluations back. I have no idea what they have said, and I wonder if after reading them I will feel better or worse about my performance this past semester. I open them slowly, afraid of what they could say. I can remember really giving it to some of my teachers; I wonder if anyone has done that to me. I pick up the first one and read what it says: "I really liked this class and teacher. She was always so chipper in the morning." I smile, wondering who wrote it. I pick up the next one: "Miss Pope was a very good teacher. This was a great class, even though it was at 8:00 in the morning. The journals were fun—maybe you could do more of those in your next class." The next one reads: "This is the only class I didn't drop." I laugh, flattered by this student who chose to stick with me, and read another one. "Miss Pope really cares about her students and always has something positive to say about our work, even when we get a low grade." I pick up the next one, and the next. I smile until I come to the one that reads: "Miss Pope's class was my favorite class of all—and the only reason I got up for any of my classes." I don't recognize the writing, but I don't care. It is then that I realize my face is wet from my tears. I think about Mrs. Crane. And I thank her.

When the editors at *LAJM* wrote to me and told me they wanted to publish it, they asked that I make a few changes—essentially, take out two segments: one about the math exercise Mrs. Crane had made me rework instead of letting me play with the other kids in the gym, and the conclusion. I felt kind of funny chopping out the math segment part because I was so angry at her for that—and I think it showed, too, because it was long (probably why they wanted it out). Taking out the conclusion was fine with me, though, because once I realized that it was going to be published and other people besides my composition instructor and classmates would read it, it occurred to me that the conclusion could seem exaggerated or too slanted toward glorifying my teaching success that semester.

The editors also asked me to make the last day of school the final segment for fifth grade, and finish with a segment about my student, Mark. In the passage above, then, I was dropping the first and last segments and reversing the order of the middle two. I was actually really happy with that revision because it gave the piece a nice feeling of continuity, instead of closure, which made it seem as if there had been an end to what I'd learned. And for the purposes of the journal, I could see why they wanted it that way.

When the journal came out, and I saw it in print, and read it again, I realized that I was really happy with the way that it was written. The whole experience of writing it and revising it and then seeing it in print was important for me for a couple of reasons. The first was that I felt like it was okay for me to have really disliked Mrs. Crane as much as I had—I'd never wanted to admit that after she died because it seemed like such an awful thing to say about someone who was dead (especially since I'd wished her that way so often before it happened). Also, it helped me to see that I had left that year in her class with something important—that she really did teach me something significant by not giving me the things that I needed, and that though it was difficult to endure at the ages of ten and eleven, it had become a really significant learning experience for me.

There has been some carryover from writing this piece into the writing I am doing now indirectly. I learned that when I am writing, I need to watch myself think, and not try so hard to make everything go in a particular direction right away. For instance, if I had paid attention to the fact that I kept thinking "I would never treat a student that way" as I was writing the segments about Mrs. Crane, maybe it wouldn't have taken me so long to recognize that *that* was the direction the writing really wanted to go. A lot of times, I will sit down with what seems like a great idea, but then I can't figure out where to go with it. If I just pay attention to what I am thinking, and trust it, and not dismiss it as just an external observation about the work I'm doing, I can get a better perspective on how I really feel about what I am writing. It's hard to do, but I've been trying.

Zion

Maureen Stanton

Sometimes I wake up in the middle of the night and I don't know where I am. My bed is a flying carpet. Flat on my back, I am looking up at the stars, whizzing around in blackness. Then I slow down, the carpet lands. I figure out which direction I am facing and get a map of the room in my head. I recognize the window and the streetlight. The bed, the door, the lamp. I remember where I am, the longitude and latitude of my life. Fixed to locale, nailed to a place, I can begin to make order.

I am dozing in the hospital bed with Steve when he pulls me.

"Mo, something is happening to me. My head is shrinking."

"What do you mean? What does it feel like?"

"It feels like it's the size of a grapefruit." He starts to cry, the first time since all this started. I run to the nurses' station. "Help. Something weird is happening to Steve." Fay and Dora come and give Steve a shot, but this causes his tongue to swell and his eyes to roll back in their sockets. Fay holds his mouth open, while Dora gets a doctor who injects something into Steve's bicep, and after a few seconds he breathes normally.

"It was just a reaction to the new pain medicine," Fay tells us, like it was nothing more than a bee sting. I stand near Steve's head and try not to touch him too much. The feeling that his head is small stays with him the whole night.

We are at the hospital of last resort, a small brick building in Zion, Illinois, an hour north of Chicago. It's a hospital where the bedspreads are worn thin and have holes. A hospital that serves carrot and celery juice, and offers alternative treatments for cancer. One week a month we come here. Steve gets his poison. I bleed.

The doctors here are different than at the hospital Steve checked out of back in Michigan. For one thing, most of them are Filipino. It unnerves Steve's parents who discourage our decision (false hopes, grasping at straws). But here the doctors don't give up as easily. Steve's first oncologist wrote a note on his chart which we read during our flight to Chicago. *It is very sad to see that the patient cannot accept the poor prognosis.* Two months, she predicted for a twenty-nine-year-old man with three small children, then patted his hand and walked out of the room, dry as a desert, tearless, leaving us in the starkness of Steve's future.

Dr. Sanchez and Dr. Melijor give us information, allow us to see Steve's nuclear scans. Married to gray film, Steve's skeleton glows. Small black dots are sprayed from his skull to his kneecaps as if someone plugged him with bird shot. Cranium, sternum, ribs, vertebrae, pelvis, femur. It is a frightening lesson in anatomy. I try not to act shocked, but the black dots are more numerous than I had envisioned when the previous doctors spoke of "widespread metastases" and "multiple tumors." "Multiple" meant six or seven, a six-pack, a touchdown, a number we could beat. I count more than two dozen specks on the little x-ray man that is Steve—malignancies humming inside his flesh. Not to mention his liver, marbleized like a high priced cut of beef, with cancer cells. Now it is real.

I arrive at the hospital at nine in the morning and climb in bed with Steve as if I am joining him in his body, unzipping his skin like it's a space suit, and snuggling in. His roommates, Greg and Chuck, don't seem to mind. Greg is an insect exterminator from South Carolina with testicular cancer. He sleeps most of the time, or reads his Bible. The only noises he makes are vomiting, or buzzing for the nurses. Hand him his urine jug, fix his pillow, bring him a drink. He thinks he is at a resort.

Chuck is in the other bed. He has a clear tube taped inside his nose that pumps oxygen from tanks on the side of his bed into his drowning, malignant lungs. He is an earthbound scuba diver. Chuck breathes loud and heavy, and coughs wet, phlegmy coughs which temporarily paralyze his wife's kinetic fingers as she sits in a chair by his bed and knits violently, like she is weaving Chuck a new set of lungs.

Days pass by slowly. Flowers arrive for Steve from his parents. *When God closes a door, he opens a window.* I put the card on the nightstand, open the curtains and watch activity below, cars and people. Fat, slow winter flies buzz against the sealed glass. They appear out of nowhere, it seems, these retarded creatures, and now they are desperate to get out, as if they know they are trapped, as if they have some power of cognition. That's what I learn when I accompany Steve to the hospital. Empty hours. Time to think.

We walk around the hallways, Steve holding onto his pole like a staff. Bottles are suspended from the pole, clear liquids that feed the catheter in Steve's chest and flow into the big subclavian vein direct to his heart, like a fast underground train. Nitrogen mustard, 5-FU, methotrexate. The names remind me of the defoliants that were dropped on Vietnamese jungles. They cause hair to fall out of Steve's head, off his chest. His underarms and legs are bare. His eyebrows are missing. His pubic hair is gone. He looks like a fetus, a tall, skinny fetus. Still, he is handsome with his heavy eyelashes and soupy blue eyes, purple hollows be-low them, like watercolor. His eyes look bigger with his face so thin and his skin wrapped so tightly over his bones. Delicate bones.

Visitation ends at eight, but the nurses understand that hours matter and allow me to stay until midnight. Then I walk to the room I have rented from a notice I saw posted in the hospital cafeteria. Three blocks away and ten dollars a night. The couple who own the house are up when I arrive.

"Wipe down the shower before you get out. Don't use too much toilet paper. And use the towel more than once." Noma scolds me before I have transgressed. She is a tiny woman with messy gray hair and one sharp, pointy tooth, like an egg tooth a baby bird uses to peck its way out of a shell.

"Who've ya got in the hospital?" she asks.

"My boyfriend."

"Isn't that a shame." She asks me where I am from, and then says, "Emil's got a cousin in Detroit."

Emil has filmy blue eyes and hair that is sugar white with bangs cut straight across his forehead. He looks like an old angel.

"They come from all over to go to that hospital. We've had people from Florida, Kentucky . . . New Zealand! Staying right in your room," he says, as if I am privileged.

"We're blessed with good health, thank the Lord," Noma cuts in. "Emil broke his ankle forty years ago. It was healed by a miracle at our church and it never bothered him since, right, Em?"

"Still march with the Brothers of Zion band sixty years now. I'm the oldest clarinet player." Emil opens a closet and pulls out a red, wooly coat and matching pants with gold braiding up the seams.

"It's no coincidence you're in Zion," he says. "This is a holy town. Miracles take place all the time."

"That's very nice," I say, and manage to excuse myself. Behind the bed-room door, I flop onto the lumpy single bed and cry. I do every night. It's part of my sleep.

Later I am poked awake by noises in the kitchen: a spoon clinking against a dish, footsteps, cupboards opening and shutting, a toilet flushing. Then the sequence repeats. I can hear snoring from Noma and Emil's room. They would have had to pass me to get to the kitchen, but I didn't hear anyone in the hall. I become convinced there is a ghost just outside my door, making that last meal over and over again, unable to let go. I pull my blankets up around my chin. My heart is pounding, pushing my tired blood, echoing in the small room. I pray. *Please, God, don't let it come in here.* I lie in stiff fear until gray light when spirits are banished, then wake up at eleven, groggy. Emil's white toupee is on a styrofoam head on the kitchen table and his teeth in a jar of water on the bathroom sink. I ask Noma if she heard noises in the night.

"Just me eating my cereal," she says. "I get up about three every morning and have some cereal."

"What about the flushing?"

"Oh, that's the pump clearing water out of the basement."

In the daytime, I can get along. There are objects, events, people to hold on to, give texture to time, divide up space. But at night, I lose my way, lose my mind. It's easy.

The next month I find a room for $75 a week at the Harbor Hotel. The office is the living room of a small house that smells like curry. A boy is playing on the rug in the fuzzy penumbra of the television. A woman with a red dot on her forehead gives me a key and says there are no refunds, then directs me to their other hotel down the street.

The rooms are in the basement of a small, brick apartment building. There is no front desk, only a broken pay phone, and leaves blowing around the hallway. A disheveled man is loitering near the telephone. As far as I can tell, I am the only guest.

Ramona and Sue and Estherine and Georgia are on the same chemotherapy schedule as Steve, so we see them every month. Steve flirts with them, bald and in their bathrobes. They laugh when he tells them he is going to wear his camouflage hunting shirt and fatigues for his upper G. I. test. He likes the audience, but I don't care to share him much. Of what little he has left, I want it all. I am with him most of the time, in the bathroom even, keeping him company. He sits on the toilet and rests his head on the back of a fold-up chair. I sit on the chair and touch his back lightly. His skin is hot all the time now and I like to put my cold hands on it. We sit there in silence waiting for him to pee.

Steve naps and I read. Mysteries. Cheap little stories that completely absorb me, simple words I can eat, pages I can bend and fold. Perry Mason novels are the main staple of my diet. Perry always finds the killer, always wins his cases. I like the surety of that. There isn't anything in the stories to disturb me, or throw me off balance. They ask nothing of me.

At night I read to Steve, poems, clips about U.F.O.'s from *Omni* magazine, and stories from supermarket tabloids. GIANT FLYING CATS TERRIFY TOWN. WOMAN ABDUCTED BY ALIENS CAN NOW TALK TO ANIMALS. CANCER MAN'S LAST REQUEST: A JAGUAR CAR PARTS CATALOGUE. I envision a man in a leotard and cape with a big "C" on his chest, an action hero defying death. Cancer Man.

This month Cancer Man is undergoing an experimental treatment—whole body hyperthermia. His body temperature will be raised to 108 degrees Fahrenheit. The theory is that abnormal, mutant cancer cells slough off at 107 degrees, while healthy cells, skin, organs, muscle, brain tissue, begin to die at temperatures just above 108. It is a precarious balancing act to reach the right temperature, sustain it long enough to do specific damage, then lower it again. Steve has signed a liability waiver, a disclaimer of some kind that contains the words "result in possible death."

Dr. Kim, the anesthesiologist, brings me into the treatment room to see Steve. He has been stripped naked and wrapped head to toe in gauze like a mummy. To raise his temperature, he is wrapped in a heated plastic blanket filled with water and alcohol. A thermometer in his mouth, one in his rectum, and two others will monitor his fever for the next eight hours.

I spend the day wandering along Lake Michigan, the Illinois side which is not as sandy and beautiful as the Michigan side. Blame it on the wind, I think, noticing this habit I have of searching for culprits. I go to the library and draft a letter to Steve's insurance company pleading with them to pay for the hyperthermia. In the park, a large bird boldly garbed in a blood red hood and black and white tuxedo clings to the bark of a tree, a red-headed woodpecker. It stands out among the muted browns and greens and feels like a gift, blatant beauty. When I return Steve is knocked out, in intensive care, sleeping it off. He wakes later delirious, mumbling like a drunk, lashing out with his hands, yanking at the tubes and bandages. Wild. For two days Steve sleeps fitfully. Finally, he recognizes me. I say, "Tell yourself each day you are going to get better and better." He says, "I'm going to get better and better. I'll be the best."

These treatments—chemicals, radiation, hyperthermia—attempt to murder Steve each time; push him to the brink, lull him back, give him time to fortify then zonk him again. It's a tease, an oxymoron, Orwellian doublespeak. We must kill you to cure you, make you sick to make you better. It's a lie, a trick with fun house mirrors. We don't trust anyone.

The Harbor Hotel is quiet all week. Then late Friday night I hear people yelling and kicking the doors to the rooms, moving towards mine. I click off my lamp so they won't see a sliver of light leaching under my door into the hallway. I'm afraid that if they find me they will kill me. It is my nighttime logic. I practice saying "Who's there?" in a deep, male voice. After a while, they manage to break into a room a couple of doors down and party all night. I make myself small and quiet like the tiny baby cockroaches that scatter whenever I turn on the fluorescent light in the bathroom. I plan my escape out the small casement window above the television, level with the ground. Finally I sleep hard and wake up to the sounds of Big Wheels on pavement.

Outside, I blink at the sunlight. Mothers sit on the brick steps smoking cigarettes. They stare at me like I am an alien, out of my country, away from my land. Timeless, placeless, bodiless.

When I get to the hospital Chuck's bed is empty. He died during the night after a long coughing fit. His wife, Carol, is gone without a trace, not one thread left behind. Steve has gotten scorched from the hyperthermia. Bad wrapping job. The soles of his feet and his scrotum are tender. He's pissed off about this, but when Jane, a volunteer, comes around he forgets for a while. Steve and I stare at her round and bouncy firm flesh encased in stretchy nylon like she is wearing beach balls, at her unruly white hair and huge blurry eyes behind thick glasses. She hands out newspapers and carnations, and speaks in a flat, nasally voice, yogic, like a Sufi chant. "I have five dogs, two cats, a mallard (now in my freezer waiting for the Guinness Book of World Records to verify it as the oldest albino duck—seventeen years, as old as my niece), and a pet starling that barks like a dog and shouts 'thief' every time a stranger comes in my house."

Jane invites me to eat with her in the hospital cafeteria. She talks while she chews, projecting bullets of deviled ham and masticated bread bits. One lands on my cheek and it is all I can focus on, don't know what words she is saying. I avoid her after that. I give Steve enemas, put my fingers in his rectum, mop up his vomit, swab the raw, pink flesh around his catheter site, but none of that fazes me the way having to eat with Jane seems an insurmountable task. Everything seems odd. Off.

This life develops a rhythm: three weeks home, one in Zion. Months go by this way. I dial a number pinned to the hospital bulletin board and a woman named Martha says she has an extra room in her apartment. When I get there Martha is gone and her son, Jeff, is playing chess on a small hand-held computer, smoking a cigarette with a puddle of gray cat on his lap. He explains that Martha was called to take care of someone for the week. She is a home-care aide.

"Bummer," he says, after he asks why I am there. He is in his early twenties with long hair parted in the middle and scruffy sideburns zigging down his jaw line.

"I'm trying to quit drinking," he says. "I haven't had a drink in over two weeks."

"Good." I feel my head bobbing up and down like one of those spring-necked ceramic cats you see on dashboards. I've noticed this: when you tell people your boyfriend has cancer they feel they must ante up their own pain and lay it on the table. At first, I thought it was nice, a kind of offering, but now it just makes me mad. Nobody's pain is equal to ours. I feel self-righteous and chosen. Anointed and doomed at the same time.

When I get up the next day, Jeff is mixing a glass of lemonade, smoking a cigarette and playing chess.

"I guess you like to play chess." I feel obliged to address this man in whose living room I am a stranger.

"Keeps me out of trouble," he replies. "I'm on probation for dealing drugs."

"Good luck," I say. Fucking wingnut, I think. Who cares? It feels good to be mean.

Put your troubles in the hands of the Lord and he will help you. Steve flings this month's card from his parents across the room. I pick it up and set it on the nightstand. I can't stomach the tension of a thing being where it doesn't belong, throwing off order, tempting chaos. I fill a plastic urine jug with water for the flowers and arrange them. I check selections on Steve's menu card, cut his toenails, get ice from the machine down the hall for his pitcher, try to keep busy before succumbing, inevitably, to watching television. Nothing airs in the morning except for talk shows, game shows, and odd sports, like curling, a bizarre contest involving a puck and a broom, a tight little silly game. Lunch arrives. Steve looks at it and puts the metal lid back on. I walk across the street and pick up some Kentucky Fried Chicken.

Later Steve unhooks himself from the tubes and we escape from the hospital. Outside it is cold and gray. We walk around holding hands. I like Steve's hands, his long, slender fingers, nails brittle and yellowed, his palms still rough and callused though he has not worked in over a year. He has two warts on his left hand, stubborn, rubbery bumps that I like to bite. They're large, these hands, but deft as he glues a part on a model car with his son, or takes an eyelash out of my eye. Steve used to stand behind me and press my nipples between his fingers while I stirred spaghetti sauce, and when we slept, his leg draped over mine, clinging like sweaty children, he cupped my breast in his palm like it was a dove. Now touching hurts him, so the only kisses I give are little brush strokes.

Steve makes it one block to a park near the hospital before he tires. We sit on a bench and watch a mother absentmindedly hand bread to her daughter. The little girl stuffs fistfuls of the bread into her mouth, every now and then flinging a crust at the ducks. Steve laughs, and I kiss his knuckles as the girl fills her cheeks and her mother stares at something else across the pond.

Friday night Jeff is playing chess with the television shouting in the background. I crawl into bed and stare at squares of light on the wall. Street lights, window panes, simple inanimate objects make me feel sad.

Hours later I am awakened by a cat screeching, then Jeff laughing loudly. The sound is distorted, like in a tunnel. Too loud for laughing alone, I think. My eyes are wide open, sucking in the dim light. I hear Jeff's maniacal laugh again and the cat yelps painfully. I envision Jeff screwed up on hallucinogens, torturing the cat. Greenish street light burnishes the door knob, which I expect to rotate at any moment, Jeff entering my room to rape me and carve me up with a knife, laughing that wild, enormous laugh the whole time. I stuff the corner of the pillow in my mouth to muffle sobs.

Nights can be like this—scenes from frightening horror films. Disaster is no longer an abstract concept. Anything is possible and danger is everywhere. I have a hard time differentiating the real from the imagined. Steve used to scare me, curling his index finger and growling, "redrum redrum redrum" like the little boy in *The Shining*, amused by how I had to skulk from light switch to light switch to pee in the middle of the night. I have asked him not to come back and haunt me, even if it is just a joke. He has asked me not to write about him, wants to disappear. I am terrified of his leaving, waking up next to a stiff corpse. I think about it every night when I lie down beside him, of being left alone, abandoned.

I wake up at seven stiff-necked, and for a second surprised to be alive and okay. Lines pressed into my face from the wrinkled sheets make a map, look like a place. I gather my stuff, don't stop to wash. Downstairs, Jeff is gone. I leave the key on the table and walk to the hospital. The nurses break the rules and let me sleep in Chuck's old bed for one night. In the morning, the long black hospital limousine delivers Steve and me to the airport. People in cars pass us on the highway and stare into our opaque windows like we are celebrities. We can see them, but they can't see us, as if we are ghosts. We exist in a parallel life: we can see our peers (getting married, having babies, buying houses), but we can't touch them anymore. We are headed somewhere else.

On Writing "Zion"

Maureen Stanton

"Zion" began as journal entries made in 1986 when the events in the essay were taking place. I wasn't thinking then that in the future this might be a story or an essay, but was writing for the same reason I record anything in my journal—to understand what is happening in my life. (This isn't always the case. There are other experiences that I know I will want to turn into an essay, so I keep specific notes, though they are mostly facts, ideas, and observations rather than the "talking to myself" of journal writing.)

I didn't look at the journal until probably two years after the experience. Grief over the death of Steve, the subject of this essay, consumed me, and I was busy trying to figure out how to fill up my life, which had revolved around Steve's cancer for eighteen months. Also, Steve had asked me not to write about him and I was struggling with this issue. When I started to write Zion as a "piece," I talked with a counselor who had helped me through this period about whether I could write about Steve. She was blunt and logical. Steve was dead, and this was my story too so I had a right to tell it.

After the fogginess of grief started to lift I began to remember interesting details of the experience, interactions and events I couldn't seem to recall when I was engulfed by emotions. The lifting of the veil of grief brought a flurry of raw material forward and I jotted notes everywhere, often waking up at night to write down a sentence that would later trigger a whole episode.

This has become my modus operandi for writing. I get very excited about an idea and become preoccupied with it. My mind is constantly tugged back to that subject whenever it is not engaged (usually when I am trying to sleep, but I will always sacrifice sleep for inspiration, even when it means arriving at work the next day a bit exhausted).

These scribbled thoughts, observations, words, and memories are stashed in a file because they seem somehow related. The file thickens and at some point reaches a critical mass. Visually, I think of it as a bunch of free-floating atoms and molecules ranging around in their own individual orbits, then something like the Big Bang happens, a tiny pop perhaps, and these particles react to one another and begin to attract and repel, combine and multiply to create a cluster of raw material. This is accompanied by an almost physical restlessness to write the piece, and suddenly (it often seems) I begin to work on it in earnest (leaving other pieces I am working on half-finished).

For this piece, which at various times was titled, "Cancer Man," "The Rooms I Stayed In" (thankfully that one didn't last long), then "Dreaming in Zion," the critical mass occurred about three years after Steve died. I pulled the piece together and brought it to a fiction workshop at the Iowa Summer Writing Program. I had been writing short stories exclusively, largely because that is what I focused on in creative writing classes in college. No one ever mentioned anything about essays. In fact, in four undergraduate and one graduate creative writing classes, I never heard the word essay mentioned, nor was it offered as a course on its own. Even in the writing groups I joined everyone seemed to be writing fiction.

The version of "Zion" I took to the workshop was only slightly different than this final version, yet I was naively trying to pass it off as a short story. That version was straight narrative, factual recitation with detailed description but little reflection. The workshop attendants wanted to see more of "me" in the piece, and they thought that, although it was moving, it was not complete and was not a successful short story. As with nearly all of my writing at that time, I didn't know what it was or what to do with it. I wasn't really writing short stories but I kept trying to squash my pieces into that mold.

I tried to put more "me" into the story but what came out, I see now, was not poignant reflection but raw emotion, untempered anger and resentment mostly. The piece took on a maudlin and self-pitying tone. I did not know what to do with Zion at this point, so I did nothing. It sat for a while before I decided to bring it to a living room writing group I participated in (after removing the added "me"). Two of the members of the writing group were professors of English and accomplished writers, and the others were professionals of all ages, all good writers and critics. This group felt the piece was flat, and although the writing was good, it lacked something. I still did not know what to do with the piece, so it landed back in hibernation, this time for about three years. But it was in that living room group that I first heard the term creative nonfiction from Mike Steinberg. I didn't grasp immediately what he was talking about, but as I slowly began to open up to this genre, I felt like I was finding my way home. This was the type of writing I naturally tended to and I was excited about it, but I still didn't know what made good creative nonfiction.

Having been somewhat liberated from my fixation with short stories and the constraints of trying to fit my personal experiences into that format (and feeling like a liar and a fraud doing so), I began to write about whatever stirred me without trying to set up dialogue, point of view and develop characters. (Although I think what I learned in fiction workshops helped me with pacing, tone, freshness of language, and precision.) I wrote two more essays, both about Steve, who managed to work himself into nearly everything I was writing regardless of how remotely related he seemed to be to the subject at hand. Both of these essays were published, but I felt that it was dumb luck, that I had stumbled into something that I couldn't sustain or duplicate as I was unaware of how I did it or why people liked the essays.

At this time, I began to get increasingly frustrated with my demanding job, which was eclipsing my free time and energy to write. (Writing had always been my umbilical cord to a meaningful existence.) I saved money for over a year, quit my job, and moved to the homes of friends and family members where I could live inexpensively. (Although this was frightening financially, as soon as I did this part-time and consulting opportunities began to fall into my lap. It was uncanny.) This is significant because if I had not done this, I feel strongly that "Zion" and many other pieces would never have been resurrected at all. (More importantly, continuing to live an artless, passionless existence and working a thankless, dull job would have caused my soul to wither on the vine, the marrow in my bones to dry up.) With the luxury of time I could put my heart and soul into creating more finished works that gave me a greater sense of satisfaction.

Having bought myself time to write (I envisioned a big parking meter into which I deposited my hard-won savings that now registered one year of time, ticking, ticking . . .), I began to work on my essays and to read other essayists in literary journals, collections, and magazines. It was this reading that helped to bring me along. Who knows how long it would have taken for me to discover truths about writing creative nonfiction on my own? Although I did not retrieve "Zion" to work on right away, in this incubation period I was beginning to get a sense of what makes a good essay, and why people bother to write essays after all. (I do think that it was good, though, to write creative nonfiction without formally studying it at first. There was a terrific freedom about not knowing what I was trying to do, to let the writing range freely. I think it allowed my voice to emerge.)

I attended a creative nonfiction workshop at the Stonecoast Writers' Conference in 1996, encouraged by Mike Steinberg, the man who had first introduced me to the term "creative nonfiction." This was the first time I had ever taken a workshop in this genre. The workshop was excellent. It reminded me of a trip I took to Brazil where I was immersed in the Portuguese language, yet could only pick up a word or two from each exchange. Then, after three weeks there, something happened, some leap of understanding, where I began to be able to interpret whole sentences and chunks of conversation. I liken that experience to Stonecoast because afterwards, instead of moving towards the writing blindfolded, occasionally glimpsing into some secret chamber of knowledge, I began to comprehend holistically the concept of creative nonfiction so that I could now purposefully sculpt the subconscious or "blind" part of my writing.

After the workshop, I pulled "Zion" from its entombment. It had been one of my favorite subjects, the surrealness of the experience, and I wanted to perfect it as much as I could. I didn't want it to sit in my file drawer forever. I wanted people to read it, like most anything I write. I wanted to create a thing of beauty, a story that intrigued and moved people. A decade had passed since the actual experiences in Zion, but writing it in the present tense returned me to the scene, placed me squarely back in the hospital and those seedy rooms where I slept. I cried every time I read each revision. It was biologically ordained, this weeping, from a deep, forgotten place inside me.

My process is to work on a computer draft, then to rearrange paragraphs, edit, and mark up the text by hand, then back to the computer, only to repeat the process. I revised the manuscript probably two dozen times over the course of a month or so, sometimes setting the piece aside for a day or two and working on something else, or gardening, which is my form of meditation. I originally intended to change the piece from present to past tense after getting it all down. I was only using the present to make the experience come alive for me again, to sharpen details, but as the writing progressed, I began to grow attached to the piece the way it was. I liked the immediacy of the story, the sense of being transported into the hospital or hotel room. And I had a strong desire to preserve the authenticity of that section of my life, to keep it intact, like a clipping from a film reel. I wanted to keep the memory pure, not to muddy the events with thoughts that represent how I feel now rather than how I felt then.

I can become obsessed with a piece, and lately I am fortunate enough to have time for obsessions. With Zion, the prose seemed sparse, pared down (compared to all that happened in real life and compared to earlier drafts). Every word mattered so I often spent a half-hour on one word, going back and forth, changing my mind then changing it back to the way it was originally. I realized I needed to be exact about Steve's chemotherapy instead of relying on my memory. Staring at the names of cancer drugs in the library released waves of memories about this experience. Sometimes I would go in search of metaphors, once sitting in the library all afternoon reading the Biblical references to Zion (which I didn't import into the essay after all since they felt forced). Sometimes I think I was trying too hard to create a "thing" instead of letting the "thing" create itself, but I usually recognized the artificial passages after a few days time and removed them (no matter how fond I was of the phrase or image I wanted to push into the piece).

I dug back into my original journals of a decade before, reread my old letters from Steve and listened to a tape of his voice. In the end, I added little to the factual bulk of the piece. I reviewed earlier drafts with comments made by my peers at the Iowa Workshop and in my writers' group. My typed out questions to the living room group at the bottom of the essay demonstrate my confusion about what I was attempting. These "questions for the group" were: what tense should the story be told in? Should this be a short story or an essay? Is there such a thing as true fiction? It seems I was still leaning towards writing fiction.

I found the copy of the manuscript from Mike Steinberg. His comments, thoughtfully offered four years prior to this rewrite, were exactly what the piece needed. He liked a lot of the external description, but said, "I'd like to see you get more reflective about the experience . . . and yes, we'll talk about your questions regarding autobiographical essay/fiction." He pointed out places where the piece could be "opened up." It appears I wasn't ready for his comments when he gave them to me years ago, but after the Stonecoast workshop, I finally understood what he was getting at. (I have saved all the manuscripts from workshop reviewers over the years because I value their comments, but interestingly, Mike Steinberg was the only one who referred to Zion as an "essay" and treated it as such when critiquing it.)

When it was obvious that I was doing nothing more than fiddling with prepositions and articles, the tiniest bits of text, I decided the piece was done. In any event, I simply didn't know where else to go with it and called it done. I may someday rewrite this piece in past tense, as I have been encouraged to do, and maybe this will strengthen the story and give it more weight and relevance. But more time will have to pass. When I work on something as intensely as I did this, I get weary of it. I start to feel ridiculous about the amount of time I am spending on it (which feels disproportionate to things taking place in the larger world around me). This happens often with my writing. I tire of pieces (they wear me out), so I put them away, which usually turns out to be a good thing. When I return to them later, what is missing, what is false or contrived, what is sloppy or sophomoric becomes more obvious. And I, for the distance passed (often years), am wiser in my approach to the piece. Unfortunately, this does not make me a prolific writer, only a careful one.

Overall "Zion" has not changed dramatically since its original incarnation nearly a decade ago and many, many hours of labor later. The format turned out to be the same, and the opening and ending paragraphs are similar. Some passages are verbatim from the original draft. But the difference lies in telling phrases, observations, and reflections, which give the narrative facts a luminescence that only distance and learning can yield. It seems that finally, after a decade, I could look with relative detachment at this experience and see it for what it really was, and in subtle ways, infuse these small epiphanies into the essay.

In looking back, I see four stages that this, and most of my other essays, passed through. The first is the molecular stage, that early collection of bits of information, what I find fascinating, unusual, funny or poignant at the time it occurs, whether I retain it in memory or in a physical form on pieces of paper. The critical mass stage is next. The particles are vibrating on their own in proximity to one another until they reach a critical mass and a reaction occurs. The writing begins in a fury, raw data, raw memory, stream of consciousness writing.

Incubation happens throughout the writing when I walk away from the piece and it sits inside me, silently arranging itself, so that when I next visit it, I have made important connections. Then I edit and rewrite. The placement of events and observations creates irony, mood, pathos, humor. Events are taken out of the chronological or random order and purposefully placed, refined, commented on. With Zion, incubation occurred over ten years as I intermittently resuscitated the piece, but also during the active writing periods, each night when I turned off my computer and went to bed with the essay on my mind. This seems important, that the essay was written only partially at the desk. Much of it was written while I gardened or walked or lay in bed mulling it over.

Insight is the last thing to come, what the story is really about. I often don't know until very late in the process, and the story is frequently about something other than I intended, if I let the piece take the path it wants (which I did not do when I was forcing it to be a short story). The sensation I get when taking a train from Grand Central station, sitting in a seat facing where you just came from (not being able to see where you are headed) is the same one I feel when I read "Zion." Distance. Perspective. It took me ten years to learn how that experience sculpted me, to tell the story, to locate its pulsing heart.

Notes on Authors

Abigail Moore Allerding teaches seventh-grade reading and language arts at Mount Vernon Middle School, Ohio, and has an MFA in Nonfiction from Ashland University.

Jocelyn Bartkevicius is the editor of *The Florida Review* and winner of the Annie Dillard and *Missouri Review* awards for the essay.

Jo Ann Beard is the author of the essay collection *The Boys of My Youth*.

Eula Biss is the author of *Notes from No Man's Land,* an essay collection, and teaches nonfiction at Northwestern University.

Robin Black's personal essays and fiction appear in such literary journals as *Colorado Review, Alaska Quarterly Review, Bellevue Literary Review*, and *Indiana Review*.

Mary Clearman Blew, University of Idaho, wrote *All But the Waltz, Balsamroot: A Memoir,* and *Bone Deep in Landscape.*

Michelle Bliss is the news director of WHQR Radio in Wilmington, North Carolina, and a student in the MFA program at the University of North Carolina Wilmington.

Lisa Groen Braner is the author of *The Mother's Book of Well-Being.*

John Bresland is an artist-in-residence at Northwestern University, an essayist, and a documentary filmmaker. His video essays can be found at http://bresland.com.

Shari Caudron, a freelance writer and teacher, is the author of *What Really Happened: Unexpected Insights from Life's Uncomfortable Moments* and *Who Are You People?*

Emily Chase is a ferrier in Michigan.

Steven Church, California State University at Fresno, is the author of *The Guinness Book of Me: A Memoir of Record* and editor of *The Normal School: A Literary Magazine.*

Judith Ortiz Cofer is the author of *Silent Dancing: A Partial Remembrance of a Puerto Rican Childhood* and *Woman in Front of the Sun: On Becoming a Writer.*

Edwidge Danticat, the recipient of a MacArthur genius grant, is the author of *Create Dangerously: The Immigrant Artist at Work* and several novels about Haiti.

Meghan Daum is the author of the essay collection, *My Misspent Youth,* and *Life Would Be Perfect If I Lived in That House.*

Valerie Due, a writing coach and founder of eLegacy, an online legacy coaching and storage company, has an MFA in Nonfiction from Ashland University.

Roger Ebert is the movie critic of the *Chicago Sun-Times,* author of several books about movies, and blogger at rogerebert.com.

Matt Farwell is a sergeant in the United States Army, 10th Mountain Division.

David Gessner, University of North Carolina Wilmington, is the author of *Return of the Osprey* and blogs at billanddavescocktailhour.com.

Dagoberto Gilb is the author of the essay collection *Gritos.*

Vivian Gornick is the author of *Fierce Attachments, Approaching Eye Level*, and *The Situation and the Story: The Art of the Personal Narrative*.

Patricia Hampl is the author of *A Romantic Education, Spillville, Virgin Time, I Could Tell You Stories: Sojourns in the Land of Memory, Blue Arabesque*, and *The Florist's Daughter*.

Steven Harvey's essays are collected in *A Geometry of Lilies, Lost in Translation*, and *Bound for Glory*; he teaches at Young-Harris College.

Sonya Huber, the author of *Opa Nobody* and *Cover Me*, teaches at Georgia Southern University and the MFA in Creative Writing Program at Ashland University.

Jennifer Kahn is a contributing editor for *Wired Magazine*.

Tracy Kidder is the author of *The Soul of a New Machine, House, Among Schoolchildren, Old Friends, Hometown, Mountains Beyond Mountains*, and *My Detachment*.

Judith Kitchen, Rainier Writing Workshop, is the editor of *In Short, In Brief*, and *Short Takes*, and the author of two essay collections, *Only the Dance* and *Distance and Directions*.

Carl H. Klaus is the author of *My Vegetable Love, Taking Retirement, Letters to Kate*, and *The Made-Up Self: Impersonation in the Personal Essay*, and co-editor of *Essayists on the Essay*.

Jonathan Lethem is the author of a collection of essays, *The Disappointment Artist*, and several novels.

Phillip Lopate is the author of *Bachelorhood, Against Joie de Vivre, Portrait of My Body, Waterfront*, and *Getting Personal* and editor of *The Art of the Personal Essay*.

Nancy Lord's books of creative nonfiction include *Fishcamp: Life on an Alaskan Shore, Green Alaska: Dreams from the Far Coast*, and *Rock, Water, Wild*.

Debra Marquart, Iowa State University, is the author of *The Horizontal World: Growing Up Wild in the Middle of Nowhere*, a memoir.

Maggie McKnight is an illustrator and graphic memoirist.

John McPhee has published 26 books, including the Pulitzer Prize-winning *Annals of the Former World*.

Brenda Miller, Western Washington University, is the author of *Seasons of the Body* and editor-in-chief of *The Bellingham Review*.

Laura Miller is a co-founder of, and a senior writer at, *Salon.com* and author of *The Magician's Book: A Skeptic's Adventures in Narnia*.

Ander Monson, University of Arizona, is the author of *Neck Deep and Other Predicaments* and *Vanishing Point: Not a Memoir*.

Tom Montgomery-Fate, College of DuPage, is the author of *Steady & Trembling: Art, Faith, and Family in an Uncertain World*.

Michele Morano, DePaul University, is the author of the essay collection *Grammar Lessons: Translating a Life in Spain*.

Mary Elizabeth Pope, Emmanuel College, writes nonfiction and fiction.

Lia Purpura, writer-in-residence at Loyola University Maryland, is the author of the essay collections *Increase, On Looking*, and *Rough Likeness* and three books of poems.

Chet Raymo's nonfiction includes *Honey From Stone: A Naturalist's Search for God, The Soul of Night, Natural Prayers*, and *The Path: A One-Mile Walk Through the Universe*.

Robert L. Root, Jr., Ashland University MFA Program, is the author of *The Nonfictionist's Guide* and the essay collection *Postscripts*, and editor of *Landscapes with Figures*.

Shelley Salamensky teaches in the UCLA School of Theater, Film and Television and has written plays, fiction, and nonfiction.

Scott Russell Sanders's books include *Writing From the Center*, *Hunting for Hope*, *The Country of Language*, and *The Force of Spirit*.

Mimi Schwartz, is the author of *Good Neighbors, Bad Times: Echoes of My Father's German Village* and *Thoughts from a Queen-Sized Bed*, and the co-editor of *Writing True*.

Tracy Seeley, University of San Francisco, is the author of *My Ruby Slippers: The Road Back to Kansas*.

Peggy Shumaker, Rainier Writing Workshop, wrote *Blaze*, a collaboration with the painter Kesler Woodward, and *Just Breathe Normally*, a lyrical memoir.

Sherry Simpson, University of Alaska Anchorage, is the author of the essay collections *The Way Winter Comes* and *The Accidental Explorer*.

Maureen Stanton, University of Missouri at Columbia, is an award-winning essayist and associate editor of the journal *Fourth Genre: Explorations in Nonfiction*.

Michael Steinberg, author of *Still Pitching*, is the founding editor of *Fourth Genre: Explorations in Nonfiction*.

Joni Tevis, Furman University, is the author of *The Wet Collection*, a book of essays.

Judith Thurman, *New Yorker* staff writer, is the author of biographies of Isak Dinesen and Colette and the essay collection, *Cleopatra's Nose: 39 Varieties of Desire*.

Kate Torgovnick is the author of *Cheer! Three Teams on a Quest for College Cheerleading's Ultimate Prize*.

Marianna Torgovnick's essays are in *Crossing Ocean Parkway: Readings by an Italian-American Daughter*; she also edited *Eloquent Obsessions: Writing Cultural Criticism*.

Kathryn Winograd, Arapahoe Community College, is the author of *Air Into Breath*, a book of poems, and *Stepping Sideways into Poetry Writing*.

Credits

Text and Photo Credits

Index